D0208604

CRITICAL COMPANION TO

George Orwell

CRITICAL COMPANION TO

George Orwell

A Literary Reference to His Life and Work

EDWARD QUINN

Facts On File
An imprint of Infobase Publishing

Critical Companion to George Orwell

Facts On File, Inc.
An imprint of Infobase Publishing
132 West 31st Street
New York NY 10001

Library of Congress Cataloging-in-Publication Data
Quinn, Edward, 1932–
Critical companion to George Orwell : a literary reference to his life and work / Edward Quinn.
p. cm.
Includes bibliographical references and index.
ISBN 978-0-8160-7091-6 (hc : alk. paper) 1. Orwell, George, 1903–1950—Handbooks, manuals, etc. I. Title.
PR6029.R8Z765 2009
828'.912—dc22 2008026727

Facts On File books are available at special discounts when purchased in bulk quantities for businesses, associations, institutions, or sales promotions. Please call our Special Sales Department in New York at (212) 967-8800 or (800) 322-8755.

You can find Facts On File on the World Wide Web at http://www.factsonfile.com

Text design by Erika K. Arroyo
Cover design by Cathy Rincon

Printed in the United States of America

MV Hermitage 10 9 8 7 6 5 4 3 2 1

This book is printed on acid-free paper and contains 30 percent postconsumer recycled content.

Contents

Acknowledgments

In recent years, anyone who sets out to write about Orwell must acknowledge a massive debt to Peter Davison, the editor of the *The Complete Works of George Orwell,* a 20 volume editorial masterpiece (a 21st, follow-up volume, *The Lost Orwell,* was published in 2006). In the first nine volumes, each of the full-length books written by Orwell is reprinted with scrupulous concern for accuracy and the author's probable intentions. The remaining 11 volumes contain the letters; essays; poems; BBC war commentaries; "As I Please" columns; book, theater, and movie reviews; journal and diary entries; and selected letters written by others, such as Orwell's wife, Eileen. Furthermore, these pieces, not simply reprinted, are annotated with clarifying notes identifying people, places, and events. Orwell has only a simple stone above his grave, but now, thanks to Peter Davison, he has a much more significant monument,

My thanks to Philip Bader, who first began work on this volume but had to leave it because of other commitments. Specific acknowledgments are indicated by his name following his contributions. Among the many other people to whom thanks are due, I wish to single out Larry Fleischer, a tireless Internet researcher, who put in my grateful arms mounds of Orwell-related material, and Karl Malkoff, who played a comparable role. I am also pleased to mention my key keyboarders, Liam Kirby, Caitlin Quinn, and Adam Kirby, and also the support I received from heroic David Quinn and Renaissance man Richard Louria during critical computer crises. Bill Herman contributed two excellent photos of contemporary Paris. I also benefited from the advice and comments of Arthur Waldhorn, Leonard Kriegel, Earl Rovit, Paul Dolan, Pat Forrestal, Deirdre Quinn, Joseph Jordan, and Bill and Pat Driscoll. I am indebted to Stephen Wright of the Orwell Archive at the University College London (UCL) for his help in securing most of the photographs in the book. Jeff Soloway at Facts On File has consistently and patiently advised and usually consented with his usual calm efficiency. Thanks also to Jeff's assistant, Miranda Ganzer, and to the library of the City University of New York and the grand old Main Reading Room of the New York Public. And deepest gratitude to Barbara Gleason, who with her usual tact and patience, kept the show going.

INTRODUCTION

There is no objective evidence to support the view that when Eric Blair opted for the pen name George Orwell he was consciously choosing a new identity or hoping to erase his past. In fact, he never completely repudiated his birth name. Even on the brink of death, he specified that his gravestone should read "Eric Arthur Blair," without so much as an allusion to his, at the time, mildly famous nom de plume. He may have felt that the sudden popularity he experienced in the last five years of his life would soon pass and that calling attention to that name would seem pretentious, an ironic example of the fragility and transience of fame. His own toughest critic, he would have found it difficult to believe that well into the next century, the noun *Orwell* and its adjectival form *Orwellian,* would, in a substantial part of the world, have acquired a life of its own.

It was an article of critical faith with him that the final test of a writer's value was survival. In his wonderful essay "Charles Dickens," he cites Dickens's continued popularity, as much as his critical reputation, as evidence of the greatness of his achievement. Orwell wrote this essay in 1938, 68 years after the death of Dickens. It seems appropriate to note that, 58 years after his own death in 1950, Orwell's presence, among readers and critics, is more vital and pervasive than it was the day he died, with no indication of a significant slackening of interest. All of which is not to claim an equivalence of the two literary figures. Dickens is one of the masters of English literature. Orwell was not a great novelist—by his own overly critical account, he was not a novelist at all—but he has survived to emerge as, not the finest, but the most influential, English writer of the 20th century and of the opening decade of the 21st.

As to the nature of that influence, it is nothing if not various and complex. Orwell spelled out loud and clear who he thought he was, but his readers, because there have been so many, spread around the globe and living in radically different societies, have naturally enough picked and chosen their own version. Although the one characterization Orwell and most of his readers agree on is that he was a political writer, he was not interested in politics qua politics. It was the ethical implications of politics that constituted his real subject. He was a moralist writing at a time when the great moral questions were contained and expressed in political terms: the twin evils of fascism and Soviet communism, the lesser evil of capitalism, and the qualified good of democratic socialism, being four of the major ones. He envisioned the possible rise of superstates that would contain elements of all four, in which individual freedom might be ruthlessly suppressed, but that strong possibility did not, as is frequently asserted, result in despair on his part. Instead, he chose to fight back, employing a literary weapon he had absorbed through a lifelong reading and rereading of *Gullliver's Travels*—satire. He had learned from Jonathan Swift that satire, when keyed to a general tendency in human nature, could maintain its vitality long after its immediate targets had passed into oblivion. His immediate target both in *Animal Farm* and *Nineteen Eighty-Four* was the Soviet Union, but he knew that Joseph Stalin would not live forever and even entertained the remote possibility that a new generation of Russians might arise "eager for more freedom." His permanent target, of which, after the defeat of Nazi Germany, Stalinism was the current example, was the totalitarian impulse. He believed that modern technology, weaponry (nuclear and otherwise), and the decay of the Judeo-Christian ethical and religious order had unleashed on a global scale the chimera of absolute power. He set out to combat the lure of that power, using the satirist's weapons, exposure and ridicule, while tacitly affirming freedom and justice.

He was particularly keen to recognize the importance to the totalitarian mind of the control of language. In his two great satires, he placed language center stage. In *Animal Farm* he employed the simple device of adding qualifiers to each of the seven commandments in order to advance the interests of the pigs, while pretending to adhere to the original text. This gradual accretion eventually leads to the linguistically absurd "more equal" proposition, the final corruption of the ideals of "animalism." *Nineteen Eighty-Four* makes a quantum leap from here, with its tongue-in-cheek description of a language that makes a dissenting thought impossible. Orwell would doubtless enjoy the irony that some NEWSPEAK words are now entries in standard English dictionaries.

His attention to language grew out of his search for his own authorial voice. At first, he found it in his essay writing. As early as 1931, he had written "A Hanging," an essay that reads like a modern short story, with its agonizing epiphany, the prisoner avoiding a puddle as he stumbles toward the gallows. But the formal excellence of "A Hanging" should not blind us to the fact that Orwell had a social, even moral, purpose in writing it. This purpose always took first place but never to the neglect of the language he chose, always adhering to the principle of letting the meaning choose the words. As a result, Orwell developed a variety of styles, all of which, however, were marked by a clarity and vitality that was recognizably his. Although he makes no specific reference to it, he may have been guided by a line from a play he wrote about memorably, *King Lear*, "Speak what we feel, not what we ought to say."

It is this sense of authenticity that has created a personal presence we do not want to lose. Combine that with a willingness to face "unpleasant facts," and you have the hint of an explanation for Orwell's extraordinary influence. Some examples of that influence: In *Lenin's Tomb*, his compelling account of the collapse of the Soviet Union, David Remnick records a conversation with the Russian philosopher Grigori Pomerants, in which Pomerants remarks that Russians, reading outlawed copies of *Nineteen Eighteen-Four*, realized that Orwell ". . . discovered the soul or soullessness of our society better that anyone else." In *Finding George Orwell in Burma*, Emma Larkin's description of her recent travels in Burma (Myammar), she writes of encountering a very old man, living the last decades of his life in the police state that is present-day Myanmar. When asked if he recognizes the name George Orwell, after a few moments, the man answers, "Ah! The prophet." One need hardly add that Orwell's works are banned in Myanmar, with the single exception of *Burmese Days*, viewed by the government as an anti-imperialist novel.

Closer to home, we have seen the more than 50 years of Orwell's roller-coaster reputation in Britain and America. Like Stephen Sondheim's ex-Follies star, he's "been through" the CIA/ MI 6 cold warriors, the Angry Young Men of the '50s, the student radicals of the '60s, the neo-con "body snatchers," of the '70s, the pop media celebrity of the year 1984, the academic Marxist "de-mythifiers" of the 80s, the theorists of the 90s—and he's "still here," alternately praised and pilloried but very much a presence. The year 2003 marked the centenary of Eric Blair's birth, an occasion celebrated, not alone by literary and political people, but by a wide range of specialists. It seems that a fair number of philosophers, theologians, social psychologists, economists, technologists, and historians still have Orwell on their radar screens. Among recent social and moral issues in which his authority has been invoked are animal rights (now seen as a major theme of *Animal Farm* and of "Some Thoughts on the Spotted Toad," an essay revealing Orwell as his light-hearted best), the conservation of nature (in

Coming Up for Air and the essay "A Good Word for the Vicar of Bray"), and the threat to individual privacy by technological advances (of which *Nineteen Eighty-Four*'s telescreen was an early and ominous portent).

Perhaps the most compelling appearance of Orwell on the current scene relates to the issue of torture. Writing in the 1980s, long before Abu Ghraib and related tactical innovations in Anglo-American foreign policy, the philosopher Richard Rorty identified torture as a critical theme in *Nineteen Eighty-Four*. He argued that the entire third section of the novel is not, as one might expect, about being tortured but about torturing, not about Winston Smith but about O'Brien. Rorty suggests that O'Brien represents the logical fate of the humanist intellectual in a totalitarian state, the kind of figure who in earlier times might have adopted an "art for the sake of art" posture. In a totalitarian world, there would seem to be no obvious place for such a person. His/her only viable function would be to identify, torture, and crush people of a comparable temperament, thereby removing potentially dangerous dissidents from the scene. The torturer's particular satisfaction might be described as "torture for the sake of torture." This may seem to some a far-fetched interpretation, but it stands as an example of Orwell's ongoing engagement, through his interpreters, with the life of the mind.

About This Book

This volume aims to serve as a guide to students and readers wishing to know more of Orwell, learning about the man, being introduced to many of his lesser known works, or deepening their knowledge of his best-known ones. Part I provides a mini-biography, both of his life and his reputation. Part II gives detailed accounts of his nine full-length books, his major essays, his wartime writing for the BBC, and his other journalism. Part III provides brief accounts of family members, of friends, an enemy or two, and fellow writers (those who influenced him as well as those whom he influenced) and brief sketches of his relation to schools of thought, the various *-isms* he contended with in his career. Part IV contains a chronology and a bibliography of Orwell's writings and the many books and articles about the man and his writings. References to other entries are given in SMALL CAPITAL LETTERS the first time that they appear in an entry.

PART I

Biography

Orwell, George (Eric Arthur Blair)

(1903–1950)

From Ida Blair's diary for February 1905:

> Sunday, 6 February: Baby not at all well, so I sent for the doctor, who said he had bronchitis . . . Saturday, 11 February: Baby much better. Calling things "beastly"!!

It is rare that a person's life can be encapsulated as early as 19 months, the age of Eric Blair at the time of these diary entries. Rarer still that the evidence should touch upon two of his most determinate features: his physical frailty and his distinctive employment of language. The bronchial condition of baby Eric would plague him throughout his life, oscillating, like his mother's entries ("Saturday, 4 November: Baby worse so sent for the doctor"), between better and worse until 45 years later, when worse moved to worst as Eric, on the brink of universal fame under his pen name, George Orwell, died from a hemorrhaged lung on January 21, 1950.

Beastly would come to be enshrined as one of the signature Orwellian words. In Orwell's first novel, *Burmese Days,* a "memsahib-in-the-making," Elizabeth Lackersteen, is seen as one who divides all experience into two categories, "lovely" and "beastly." The novelist and critic Margaret Drabble suggests, quite plausibly, that Orwell learned the word from his mother, herself a former memsahib, overhearing her conversations with women friends on a favorite topic: the beastliness of men. As for his beastly health, that continuing problem had led, as it did for so many writers, to a more-than-usual time at home reading. In Orwell's case, the most important of the books he read in his childhood was *Gulliver's Travels,* a book that turns the beast/man contrast on its head. Thus the beastliness of poor lungs and of men may have been hidden sources, funneled through the creative mind of the writer of the finest beast fable of the 20th century, the Swiftian masterpiece *Animal Farm.*

Baptismal photo of Eric Blair with his mother on October 30, 1903 *(Orwell Archive, UCL Library Services, Special Collections)*

THE LIFE

Eric Arthur Blair was born on June 25, 1903, in what was then the Bengal Province of northeastern British India. His father, Richard Blair, was a sub-deputy agent in the Opium Department of the Indian Civil Service. In this period, the opium trade provided a lucrative source of revenue for the British government. Richard was the product of a family whose fortune had steadily declined in the 19th century. The son of a clergyman, he had joined the service in 1875 and, by 1903, had enjoyed very little advancement from his initial rank. In 1896, at the age of 39, he married Ida Limouzin, the 21-year-old daughter of a French father and an English mother. Her father, Frank, an émigré from France, ran a successful timber business in the Burmese city of Moulmein. The newlyweds set up house in the Bengal District in India, where Richard was posted. Their first child, Marjorie, was born in 1898. By the time of Eric's birth in 1903, India had been ravaged

Eric as a chubby three-year-old, in standard sailor suit *(Orwell Archive, UCL Library Services, Special Collections)*

by a plague that would last throughout the first decade of the 20th century. In 1904 alone, more than 1 million people died, probably prompting the decision that Ida and the children would move back to England. Richard took a sabbatical leave to accompany them, and they settled in the village of Henley-on-Thames, in Oxfordshire. Although the fear of plague may have been the primary reason for the move, Orwell's biographers have generally agreed on another motive. IDA BLAIR was a lively, sophisticated, sociable young woman in her twenties, probably bored and unhappy with life in a remote, hot, isolated Indian village. (Orwell would provide a painfully graphic description of such a life in *Burmese Days.*) Moreover, her husband appeared to be a rather stuffy, humorless exemplar of the British colonial civil servant. Ida, on the other hand, was a supporter of, although not an active participant in (as were her sisters, Nellie and Nora), the women's suffrage movement. In 1908, she gave birth to her third child, Avril, after a three-month home leave by Richard the previous year. Either despite or because of his fragile health, Eric was his mother's favorite, dictating his first poem to her, composed before he could write, at the age of four. She also gave him his introduction to the British class system when she told him not to play with certain children, whose father was a plumber.

Young Eric's formal education began in a convent school, which was run, according to biographer Gordon Bowker, not, as previously had been thought, by Anglican nuns, but by French Catholic nuns. The nuns, members of the Ursiline Order, had opened their school as exiles after religious education in France had been temporarily outlawed in 1903 (Bowker, 21). Whether this early introduction played a role in Orwell's intense but somewhat ambivalent feelings about CATHOLICISM—fierce hatred of its politically reactionary, quasi-totalitarian orientation, very slightly offset by grudging admiration for its historical endurance and theological sophistication—is a moot question.

At the age of eight, Eric was eligible for admission to a prep school. The preparatory feature of such schools was paramount in that its goal was to prepare students to move on at the age of 13 or 14 to a good, and in unusual cases, a great, public school, such as ETON or Harrow. The preparatory schools lived or died on their reputations as schol-

Eric and his sister Avril with their mother and father, late 1917 *(Orwell Archive, UCL Library Services, Special Collections)*

Left to right: Prosper Buddicom, Guinever Buddicom, Eric Blair (George Orwell), September 1917 *(Orwell Archive, UCL Library Services, Special Collections)*

arship factories, that is, by the number of honors their students would win. To enhance their reputations, the schools would admit talented prospects at reduced rates. This was the possibility Ida Blair was hoping for when she visited St Cyprian's School in Eastbourne. Instead of 180 pounds a year—a crippling fee for a family living on a civil servant's pension—tuition for Eric would be 90 pounds. This half-scholarship was not revealed to the boy until he had already been at the school for a few years, long enough to have endured the humiliation of seeing himself as one of the poor students at a rich boys' school. The revelation of his status by the headmistress and headmaster, CECILY and LEWIS VAUGHAN WILKES, (who accused him of ingratitude), cemented the hatred he felt for the school where he, as a child of eight, had been publicly caned on a number of occasions for chronic bedwetting. And worse than the pain and humiliation of the caning was the sense that his oppressors were right. He did wet the bed, and he had no control over it. In one part of his mind, he was guilty and got what he deserved. Therefore, he saw himself as a victim, but not an innocent one. He would go on to have two poems published in a local newspaper (with one of them being read aloud to the entire school), win scholarships to Eton and Westminster, and yet come away from St Cyprian's convinced that, on some fundamental moral level, he was a failure.

Thirty years later, near the end of his life, George Orwell would exact revenge for eight-year-old Eric Blair in his essay "SUCH, SUCH WERE THE JOYS," an indictment of his English boarding school as searing as the one he was bringing against the totalitarian world of *NINETEEN EIGHTY-FOUR*. Indeed, the two are closely related in time. Orwell took time out from writing the novel in order to finish the essay. In the words of Orwell's friend George Woodcock, "Just as Orwell earlier saw the resemblance between the condition of animals and that of oppressed people, so now he saw the resemblance between the child facing the arbitrary rules of an adult world and the bewildered individual locked in the equally arbitrary system of a totalitarian society (164)." As with almost all of Orwell's autobiographical writings, doubt has been cast on the literal truth of "Such, Such Were the Joys." Others who were at the school at about the same time as he felt that his descriptions were exaggerated. It may have been that he altered his account to add to its polemical impact, but the suggestion of one critic that the essay is in effect the expression of a "hidden wound," which would later find expression in the deep pessimism of *Nineteen Eighty-Four,* is an interesting but sweeping overstatement of the case (See ANTHONY WEST).

Fortunately, the misery and gloom, real or imagined, of life at St Cyprian's were alleviated by holidays at home and with the Buddicoms, a neighboring family with three children, named Jacintha, Prosper, and Guinever. Their relationship with Eric began in the summer of 1914, when the children, while playing in their garden, noticed a boy on the neighboring property, standing on his head. Walking over to him, they asked why he was doing such a thing. Eric's reply: "You are noticed more if you stand on your head than if you are right way up," an insight he would later put to good use in shaping a prose style that frequently employed attention-getting, memorable opening sentences, as in the beginning of "SHOOTING AN ELEPHANT:" "In Moulmein, in Lower Burma, I was hated by large numbers of people—the only time in my life I was important enough for this to happen to me." It was a brilliant verbal equivalent of standing on your head.

At the time of this first meeting with the Buddicoms, Eric was 11, Jacintha, 13, the boy Prosper, 10, and Guinever, 7. They were to become close friends for the next eight years. One of Eric's great passions in this period, which he indulged in both at school and at home, was reading. He and JACINTHA BUDDICOM, another avid reader, traded books and the ideas they generated throughout his prep school and college years. Their relationship is described in detail in Jacintha's memoir, *Eric and Us* (1974), in which she describes the happy vacations he spent with the Buddicoms, including long country walks taken by the two of them. Among the other activities Eric relished on vacation was fishing, a sport that he invests with a kind of spiritual power in his novel *Coming Up for Air.*

Eric Blair (George Orwell) at Eton *(Orwell Archive, UCL Library Services, Special Collections)*

Moving on to Eton was liberating, perhaps too much so. The fierce regimen of intense study for the scholarship he had won to the most prestigious public school in England left Eric drained of any further effort or at least reluctant to participate in what he was coming to see as a rat race up the social ladder. He spent his four years there just getting by, never really applying himself academically, though he did a fair share of writing for student publications. Although he depicted himself at Eton as an "odious young snob," Eric enjoyed the friendship and respect of fellow students CYRIL CONNOLLY, whom he had known at St Cyprian's, DENNIS KING-FARLOW and STEVEN RUNCIMAN. He also seems to have participated in what appears to be a rite of passage in English public schools: having a romantic crush on a fellow student, as indicated in a letter he wrote to Cyril Connolly, asking him not to interfere. Connolly, quoting the letter, in another letter, concludes that there is little chance of Eric's succeeding since the object of his affection "hates Blair" (*CW,* 10, 79–80). He also participated in some athletics and generally absorbed one of the qualities that graduation from England's greatest public school conferred on a young man: "a certain authority and assurance of manner, as later in the authority and assurance of his prose" (Stansky and Abraham, 143). At one point, he credited Eton with something deeper: When a woman friend complimented him on "his passion for justice, his dislike of prejudiced remarks about anyone, and his sense of fairness in the minutest dealing," Eric replied that these qualities "were the most important part of the education I received at Eton. That and the capacity to think for myself" (Shelden, 101).

The logical next step for Eric would have been to move on to Oxford or Cambridge. Of the 16 King's scholars in his class, he was one of only three who did *not* pass on to Oxbridge. But having compiled a mediocre record, he would not have been eligible for a scholarship, and his parents—or, according to Jacintha Buddicom, his father—was not prepared to pay his tuition. In any case, Eric appeared to be deeply ambivalent about continuing his formal education, perhaps sensing the need for new experiences if he was going to pursue his ultimate goal—with him since early childhood—of becoming a writer.

In the meantime, his relationship with Jacintha had taken on a romantic tone, at least on his end. As early as 1918, he was composing love poems to her ("Our minds are married, but we are too young. For wedlock by the customs of this age . . ."), but by the summer of 1921, he was lamenting in the last line of a poem titled "Friendship and Love" that "My love can't reach your heedless heart at all." Jacintha replied to that poem with one of her own:

By light
Too bright
Are dazzled eyes betrayed
It's best
To rest
Content in tranquil shade.

Something had gone wrong. The answer was not forthcoming until 2006, with the publication of a new edition of Jacintha's memoir, *Eric and Us,* which contains a postscript written by Dione Venables, a relative of the Buddicoms. It reveals that Jacintha wrote—but probably did not send—a letter to Eric, alluding to his attempted rape of her while they were walking in the woods. Apparently, he pounced on her, trying to overwhelm her by sheer force, finally giving up when faced with her continued resistance. The fact that Jacintha was a diminutive, tiny woman only adds to the sordidness of the event. Ironically, *Eric and Us* contains a chapter titled "Sex," which describes Eric as basically uninterested not only in the act itself but also even in talking about it. But adding to the credibility of the charge is the description of two near-rapes of Dorothy Hare by the roué Mr. Warburton in *A* C*LERGYMAN'S* D*AUGHTER* and Orwell's reputation among the women he knew in 1940s London (sophisticated women, not afraid to kiss and tell) as a "pouncer." It is not to extenuate his behavior but to put it in historical context that it is probable that he saw "pouncing" as a kind of seduction, something that you did not persist in if the woman continued to resist. It is quite right to suggest that it is a distinction without a difference, but in his day, he would not have been alone in sharing that view, as opposed to, say, his friend ARTHUR KOESTLER, who apparently did rape at least one woman (and possibly others) in the course of his life.

The following Christmas, in 1921, Eric joined the family at their new home in SOUTHWOLD, a resort town on the coast of Suffolk. Now 18 years old, having decided not to go to university, he needed to find suitable work. Not surprisingly, his father recommended colonial service, specifically the Indian Imperial Police, which had the advantage of comparatively good pay and retirement after 20 years. Doubtless those practical reasons were less convincing than the appeal of an exotic foreign place, radically different from the hothouse atmosphere of Eton and the dull and dreary, at least in winter, social life in Southwold. He spent the winter cramming for the eight-day competitive entrance exam. Having successfully passed the exams, he chose to serve in Burma, where he still had relatives, including his maternal grandmother, THÉRÈSE LIMOUZIN, living in Moulmein, the town alluded to in the memorable opening lines of Kipling's "The Road to Mandalay" ("From the old Moulmein pagoda. . . .") and in Orwell's "Shooting an Elephant."

He was not prepared for the hostility that greeted him as a member of the Imperial Police. In the 1920s, the anger he encountered was not personal but the product of a nationalist spirit that had begun to surface across a broad spectrum of the Burmese people. The reform movement led by Gandhi had won concessions in the Government of India Act (1921), but at first, no such accommodations applied to Burma. (Under British rule, Burma was treated as an administrative province of India.) The result was a marked Burmese increase in activist resistance to the colonial government, often led by Buddhist monks. Ambivalent at first and later fiercely anti-imperialist, Eric confessed to an early feeling that the greatest joy in the world would be to "drive a bayonet into a Buddhist priest's guts." But doing "the dirty work of empire" and expected to restrict his socializing to the whites-only club in whatever town he was stationed in (*Burmese Days* contains a remorseless account of such a club), he eventually came to see British colonialism as hypocritical—"the white

Police training school in Mandalay, Burma, 1922. Orwell is in the rear row, third from the left. *(Orwell Archive, UCL Library Services, Special Collections)*

man's burden" lie—and mutually corrupting for both colonizers and colonized.

In addition to its role in *Burmese Days,* Burma is the setting for the memorable Orwell essays "A Hanging" and "Shooting an Elephant." As with "Such, Such Were the Joys," some have raised questions about the truthfulness of these two essays, wondering whether Orwell actually witnessed an execution or did in fact shoot an elephant; in short, do the two essays constitute fact or fiction of some mixture of both? Although the preponderance of evidence testifies to their historical and biographical truth, one school of thought argues for the overriding importance of the two essays, not as journalism but as literature, a sphere in which the fact/fiction question becomes irrelevant. In both essays (or stories), we are being forced to participate in, not just witness, an event we would prefer not to be caught up in. In "Shooting an Elephant," we are uncomfortably aware that the killing of the animal is a face-saving act. Not to kill would be interpreted by the large local population as a sign of weakness and would undermine British control at a time when that control was coming increasingly into question. In "A Hanging," we see the death penalty, another form of governmental control, exposed as an act that sullies and paradoxically imprisons its perpetrators as well as its victims. Both are powerful examples of the dirty work of empire and are beautifully written truths that transcend facts.

As for *Burmese Days,* which is clearly identified as fiction, there are, as in all of Orwell's novels, direct biographical connections. One example is the incident in which a member of the British colony viciously attacks a young native student, precipitating a Burmese uprising. Apparently, before boarding a train, Eric was once jostled by a Burmese university student fooling around with his friends and fell downstairs. "Blair was furious and raised the heavy cane which he was carrying to hit the boy on the back on the head, checked himself and struck him on the back instead" (Aung). An angry discussion ensued between Blair and the students on the train ride but was resolved without further incident.

Another biographical question that *Burmese Days* gives rise to concerns Blair's sexual life during his five years in Burma. Did he, like John Flory, the novel's protagonist, keep a Burmese mistress? Anecdotal evidence suggests the strong probability that, at the least, he frequented Burmese brothels. Witness his poems "The Lesser Evil" and "My Epitaph by John Flory" from an early draft of the novel, which includes the couplet "He has spent sweat enough to swim in / Making love to stupid women." The "stupid women" phrase is an early example of the sexism, not to say misogyny, that Orwell exhibited periodically in his writing. If he were looking for examples of miscegenation, he could have found precedents in his own family. His maternal great-uncle William, brother of his grandfather Frank, had fathered a Eurasian child, and Frank's son, also called Frank, had married a Burmese woman, who had given birth to his cousin Kathleen.

In her highly interesting *Finding George Orwell in Burma,* Emma Larkin reports meeting a Eurasian man whose father had known Orwell during his tour of duty in Moulmein. He maintained that Orwell fraternized widely with members of the Anglo-Burmese community. Harold Acton, an Eton colleague, recalls Orwell's rhapsodizing about the physical allure of Burmese women. On the other hand, Roger Beadon, a fellow Imperial Police officer, observed, ". . . as for female company, I don't honestly think I ever saw him with a woman." (Coppard and Crick, 62). In any case, the one indisputable autobiographical element in the novel is not sexual passion but John Flory's passionate denunciations of British imperialism. Whatever grievances the author harbored against Burmese college students and Buddhist monks, he never lost sight of the fact that colonialism was a radically unjust system that victimized both the oppressor and the oppressed, even when its form was relatively benevolent. The fact that English colonizers were probably the best of a bad lot did not ameliorate the situation; it only supported the hypocrisy that served to justify the system.

In 1927, having served five years with the Imperial Police, Orwell returned to England on home leave. A year earlier, England had endured a general strike, which had paralyzed the nation for a week. The strike was symptomatic of the economic crisis Europe was experiencing in the 1920s, the prelude to the worldwide depression that would be ignited by the stock market crash on Wall Street in October 1929. Much to the distress of his mother and the shocked incredulity of his father, he announced his decision to resign from the Burmese police force in order to pursue a career as a writer. As if that announcement alone were not bad enough for a respectable "lower-upper-middle-class" family (Orwell's own characterization), it was followed by his determination to explore "tramping" in order to experience the lives of those on the bottom rung of society. In late 1927 he spent some time in "spikes" (sleeping wards where tramps were allowed to stay one night before moving on the next day). While he was home, he visited the Buddicom family, but Jacintha was not there. Dione Venables's postscript to *Eric and Us* supplies the surprising reason for her absence. Shortly before his return, she gave birth to a child out of wedlock, which she eventually gave up for adoption. Not knowing this, Orwell doubtless took her absence as a sign of a continuing rejection.

In the spring of 1928, he moved to Paris to join the small army of young writers and artists who had converged on the city in the aftermath of World War I. That was a late date to qualify as a member of the lost generation (Ernest Hemingway however, was still living there, only a few blocks from Orwell's rooming house in the rue du Pot de Fer). Orwell lived there for 18 months, working continually, producing one or possibly two novels, which

The Closerie des Lilas café in Paris. The Closerie may have been the model for the Chestnut Tree Café in *Nineteen Eighty-Four*. *(Photo by William Herman)*

were rejected by publishers and later destroyed by the discouraged author. A few short stories met a similar fate. He did achieve some success publishing his short articles in French and English journals. His first article in an English publication was "A Farthing Newspaper" in G. K.'s *Weekly*, published by G. K. CHESTERTON. When he was not writing, he explored the city, visiting local cafés such as the Deux Magots, where he thought he saw JAMES JOYCE, and restaurants, like the Closerie des Lilas, a favorite haunt of writers and revolutionaries. Lenin and Trotsky frequented it at one time, playing chess at one of the tables. Peter Davison suggests that the Closerie was the model for the Chestnut Tree Café in *Nineteen Eighty-Four*, where the old revolutionaries Jones, Aaronson, and Rutherford sit before a chess board, awaiting their final arrest (Davison, *Literary*, 26). He was also a regular visitor at the home of his mother's sister HELENE "NELLIE" LIMOUZIN and her husband, Eugene Adam, one of the founders of the Esperanto movement. Adam had fought on the Bolshevik side during the 1917 Russian Revolution but was completely disillusioned with the Soviet system, even under Lenin. At this time Orwell appears to have been somewhat sympathetic toward the Soviets, thus prompting some loud arguments between nephew and uncle.

In March 1929, Orwell spent two weeks in a public hospital in Paris recovering from the flu, an experience he recounted later in his essay "HOW THE POOR DIE." After his release, he found work as a dishwasher in a posh Paris hotel, an experience he memorably described in *DOWN AND OUT IN PARIS AND LONDON*. Shortly before Christmas 1929, he returned to his parents' home in Southwold, where he lived off and on while writing three drafts of *Down and Out* and submitting them to publishers with no success. Finally, through the intercession of a friend, MABEL FIERZ, he acquired an agent, LEONARD MOORE, who placed the work with the publisher VICTOR GOLLANCZ.

Down and Out was published in January 1933 under the pseudonym George Orwell. Blair had decided not to use his own name partly to save his family any embarrassment they might feel over some of the personal details of the book and partly because of Orwell's own sense of its unworthiness. He had never liked his first name, in any case. Apparently, he believed, as he wrote to his friend RAYNER HEPPENSTALL in 1940, that "[p]eople always grow up like their names. It took me nearly thirty years to work off the effects of being called Eric" (*CEJL*, 2, 22.). Orwell is the name of a river in East Anglia and a small rural parish in Cambridgeshire; George is the name of the patron saint of England. Orwell felt certain that his first book would be a failure, but *Down and Out*, while not a commercial success, was seen by critics as a promising debut. Although most of his reviewers had serious qualms about the book's structural weaknesses, many of them recognized that a fresh and interesting new voice had arrived, dealing with a subject to which too little attention had been paid. In America, which had plunged into the Depression, the book was reviewed by the novelist James T. Farrell as driving home a very clear point: "Poverty is an unnecessary and disgusting waste of human life" (Meyers, *Critical*, 46). In general, the critics recognized that the name George Orwell was one that they would be hearing more of, suggesting new possibilities of growth and achievement. The positive critical response may have contributed to Orwell's decision to continue to use the pen name. Some have detected in the choice of a pseudonym the expression of a deeper impulse, hinted at in the comment to Heppenstall, to escape from his past, and with it the self-image of a failure, acquired at St Cyprian's. If so, it seems odd that in his private life he never repudiated his real name, even when it would have been to his advantage to be known as George Orwell. Up until the very end, when he gave explicit instructions that his tombstone display the name Eric Arthur Blair and no other, he acknowledged his past.

Critical esteem was one thing, but it didn't pay the rent. In April 1932, he took a position teaching at Hawthorns, a boys' prep school at Hayes, in Middlesex, where he wrote and directed a play, *KING CHARLES II*. He was also charged with making the costumes, an experience that created "untold agonies" for him. He was later to describe the experience in detail in *A Clergyman's Daughter*, in which the heroine, Dorothy, struggles with the costumes for a play called *Charles I*. It may be worth noting that *King Charles II,* set in 1651, takes a distinctly pro-royalist stance, treating Cromwell as a cruel usurper. Meanwhile, working on his first novel, *Burmese Days,* during this period, he was interested in two women, Eleanor Jaques, a Southwold neighbor, with whom he had a sexual relationship but who married a friend, DENNIS COLLINGS, and BRENDA SALKELD, to whom he proposed marriage. Brenda, however, was intent on keeping their relationship on a platonic level and apparently succeeded. Orwell always regarded her as the one who got away. In the fall of 1933, he took another teaching position but soon was hospitalized with pneumonia and had to give up teaching. While convalescing, he finished *A Clergyman's Daughter,* his second novel. In October 1934, he moved to London to take a job as a part-time clerk in the Booklovers' Corner, a bookshop near Hampstead Heath, in North London.

In the same month, Harper's published *Burmese Days* in New York, where it sold modestly well, prompting Gollancz to bring out an English edition the following year. Gollancz had originally rejected the book on the grounds that he might be sued for libel. Having relented, following the modest success of the American edition, he still insisted on a number of minor changes in the names of some characters and locations. The English edition, in Orwell's view botched because of the changes, was published in June 1935 to mixed reviews. Most reviewers felt that the negative picture of the Raj was overdone. In a later look at the novel, written shortly after Orwell's death in 1950, MALCOLM MUGGERIDGE, his conservative friend, thought he detected an ambivalence toward rather than a total rejection of British imperialism. Muggeridge went on to compare Orwell to RUDYARD KIPLING, the two sharing the same inner conflict, with Kipling coming down on one side and Orwell on the other. Muggeridge's comment seems less relevant to the mature Orwell, who was a consistently committed anti-imperialist, even in his presocialist phase, when he described himself as a "Tory radical."

In the same year, 1935, Gollancz published *A Clergyman's Daughter,* which received fewer favorable responses than *Down and Out* and *Burmese Days.* By this time Orwell had developed a very low opinion of the book himself, and would later stipulate that it and *Keep the Aspidistra Flying* should never be reprinted. But, in fact, these two early efforts, while far from perfect, mark important steps in Orwell's formation as a novelist and thinker. The crisis of the loss of faith that he explores in *Clergyman* was not so much a part of his personal experience as it was his view of modern Western society. Although by no means a conventional Christian, he was acutely aware of the value of religion as a center that had kept the social fabric together until the 20th century, when the center, in W. B. Yeats's terms, could no longer hold. It is interesting to note that, while Orwell was writing the book, he befriended an Anglican clergyman and posed as a devout believer in order to absorb the experience he wanted to describe, much as he did posing as a tramp for *Down and Out.* In this case, though, he had qualms about deceiving others.

Another lesson he derived in writing *Clergyman* was that he was not JAMES JOYCE. However much he admired the author of *Ulysses,* he learned that his talents lay not in the mode of symbolic, modernist prose but in the traditional style of realistic storytelling. His flirtation with the former style is evident in the novel's Trafalgar Square scene, which owes much to the Nighttown episode in *Ulysses.* Although a failure, this foray into expressionist surrealism reveals a writer willing to test his limits and one willing to take pains to do it well in representing the unnerved, near-delusional state of Dorothy Hare, the novel's protagonist (Fowler, 109–118). In a more traditional mode in another section of the novel, he successfully brings to life a Dickensian character, Mrs. Creevy, the headmistress from hell. Unfortunately, he fails to breathe life into his main character. Peter Quennell's review sums up the other reviewers' reactions: "Dorothy, alas! remains a cipher. She is a literary abstraction to whom things happen. . . . We have no feeling that her flight from home and her return to the rectory have any valid connection with the young woman herself." (Meyers, *Critical,* 61).

While working at the bookstore, he used his experiences as the background of a new novel, *Keep the Aspidistra Flying.* At this time, he was struggling financially, though he was developing a reputation as much for his reviews and essays as for his novels. He renewed his prep-school friendship with Cyril Connolly, editor of the literary magazine *Horizon.* He spent his mornings writing *Aspidistra,* some book reviews, such as his important critique of HENRY MILLER's *Tropic of Cancer,* and even the occasional poem, such as "St Andrew's Day," which appears in *Aspidistra* as an example of the protagonist's work. He also developed a fairly active social life with Mabel Fierz, KAY EKEVAL (a girlfriend), and RICHARD REES, editor and publisher of *Adelphi,* a socialist journal to which he became a frequent contributor. In the spring of 1935, at a party he cohosted, he saw "a stranger across a crowded room," EILEEN MAUD O'SHAUGHNESSY, a graduate student in psychology at University College, London. By the end of the evening, he had confided to his cohost and landlady, Rosalind Obermeyer, "That's the sort of girl I'd like to marry." This he would do in June of the following year. Meanwhile, he moved into a three-room flat in Kentish Town, which he shared with two young writers, Rayner Heppenstall and MICHAEL SAYERS. The arrangement lasted only a short while, ending in a brawl between Orwell and an inebriated Heppenstall.

The next eighteen months proved to be decisive ones in Orwell's life. In January 1936, he completed the manuscript of *Aspidistra* and then submitted himself to a list of changes required to avoid libel suits. The book was published in April to disappointing reviews. As with his two earlier novels, he seemed to be having trouble with his main character. Gordon Comstock, a would-be poet, has set out on a crusade against the money god who rules modern life. But what begins as a young writer's admirable rebellion—throwing over a well-paid position as an advertising copywriter in order to pursue his writing career—soon degenerates into a whiny, adolescent wallowing in the sense of failure, demonstrating that money assumes much greater significance to one who tries to do without it than to the average person. What seems to be the inevitable conclusion is that the novel is satirizing its protagonist, a notion supported by its jaunty title. However, this interpretation flies in the face of the alternative view that it was written in the somber, realistic mode of GEORGE GISSING, depicting with utter solemnity the degradation of an honest man. What is clear, in any case, is the presence of autobiographical elements in the book, suggesting that Orwell is reflecting an earlier phase of his life, when he was having no success in finding a publisher. Perhaps the "happy ending," so distasteful to readers determined to take the novel at face value, is a reflection of the presence in his life of Eileen, a partial model for the character of Rosemary Waterlow, who breathes fresh air into Gordon's solipsistic misery. It is Rosemary who, taking matters into her own hands, rescues Gordon from himself. She also rescues her creator from the not unreasonable feminist allegation that Orwell was incapable of creating a credible, well-rounded female character.

A few months before the publication of *Aspidistra,* at the end of January, Orwell had set forth on a journey, commissioned by Gollancz to write a book on unemployment in the industrial north of England. He spent the next two months traveling to the cities of Liverpool, Birmingham, and Manchester, with his longest stay being in the coal town of Wigan. In the 1920s, most of the mines in Wigan had shut down and, along with them, the town's semi-mythical pier, the one appealing aspect of a place that had become a dreary industrial slum. The often reported statement that Orwell received a 500-pound advance from his publisher has been effectively refuted (Davison, *Literary* 67–69). That he was on a strict budget (possibly self-imposed) is clear from his "Wigan Pier Diary," a collection of his notes and comments that illuminate the background of the book. He spent two months in the North visiting the factories, homes, and, on three occasions, coal mines.

In June, Eileen completed her coursework at the university and was ready to take on the formidable task of becoming George Orwell's wife. The wedding took place on June 9, 1936. Eileen was a warm, attractive, intelligent, and sympathetic person, and she really loved George. The 300-year-old cottage in Wallington, a village in Hertsfordshire, into which they moved after the wedding, doubled as a sort of local general store. In the latter capacity, as a source of additional income, it was a dismal failure. The minute profit it yielded derived mostly from the penny candy sold to local children. But what the cottage lacked as an income producer, it more than made up for in satisfying Orwell's perverse taste for ascetic living. There was no electricity, hot water, or indoor plumbing. The roof leaked in a dozen places, and the outdoor privy was located some distance from the house. Orwell was not the easiest or most thoughtful of husbands in the best of times, and when he inevitably fell ill, the burden of keeping the place going, including at one point cleaning out the backed-up privy, fell to Eileen.

Until recently, Eileen's reaction to these less-than-ideal conditions was unknown, but a newly discovered cache of letters she wrote to a close friend, Norah Myles (1906–94), sheds a sobering light on the situation. In a letter dated November 1936, Eileen apologizes for not having written sooner. She offers her friend a sardonic explanation:

> I lost my habit of punctual correspondence during the first few weeks of marriage because we quarreled so continuously and really bitterly that I thought I'd save time & just write one letter to everyone when the murder or separation had been accomplished. . . . I forgot to mention that he had his "bronchitis" for three weeks in July & that it rained for six weeks during the whole of which the kitchen was flooded & all the food went mouldy in a few hours. (Davison, *Lost*, 64).

Adding to this grim situation is the news that the newlyweds had a visitor for two months, Orwell's bohemian aunt Nellie fresh from Paris. From this letter alone, it is clear that those admirers who referred to Orwell as a "saint" after his death were canonizing the wrong member of the family.

Nevertheless, the two appeared to be happy. Orwell's friend GEOFFREY GORER visited the couple—his training as an anthropologist doubtless stood him in good stead in adjusting to the cottage—and later recalled that he had never seen Orwell happier than he was in the first year of his marriage (Bowker, 190). One feature of the couple's relationship, a war of words, triggered by an outlandish generalization on Orwell's part—for example, "All tailors are fascists"—is replicated in the exchanges between Gordon and Rosemary in *Keep the Aspidistra Flying*: "There was a merry war between them. Even as they disputed arm in arm, they pressed their bodies delightedly together. They were very happy. . . . Each was to the other a standing joke and an object infinitely precious."

During this period in Wallington, Orwell completed the manuscript of *The Road to Wigan Pier*, which he delivered to Gollancz on December 15. For his ironically employed title, he drew on the famous Kipling poem "The Road to Mandalay," in order to contrast the dreary, mining town of Wigan and its nonexistent pier with the imperial splendor that Kipling's poem evoked for the English public: "Mandalay," yesterday's myth; "Wigan," today's reality. The book opens with a celebrated description of the boarding house/tripe shop in which he stayed for two weeks. This account received the highest praise in a letter from an unlikely reader, the aristocratic, modernist poet Edith Sitwell: "The horror of the beginning is unsurpassable. He seems to be doing for the modern world what Engels did for the world of 1840–50. But with this difference. That Orwell is a born writer" (Quoted in Meyers, 137). Equally impressive is the suffocatingly powerful account of his trip through an underground coal mine from the lift to the coal face, a distance of a mile, from which it took him days to recover. The notion that someone with his medical history (and six-foot-two-inch frame) would find himself anywhere near a coal mine is part of the mystery of the man, but as a writer, at least he could justify it in the light of the artistic result.

Wigan Pier is divided into two sections, the first being somewhat like the descriptive documentary that Gollancz had in mind. The second, however, turned into a problem that had the publisher tearing out what little hair he had left. What had occurred between the time Orwell left for the North and his return was Gollancz's inauguration of the LEFT BOOK CLUB, a book-of-the-month club appealing largely to socialist and communist readers. Knowing that he was jeopardizing his chances of having the book chosen as a selection, Orwell used the second half of it to focus on two subjects, the English class system and a critique of English socialism. On the first topic, he offers a brief autobiography of his own class consciousness, from his early years, when he was warned against playing with the plumber's children, to his teenage time at Eton as "an odious little snob," to his last years at the college, when he joined with his classmates in being "both a snob and a revolutionary." In effect, everything about him, even his sense of good and evil, is the product of his "lower-upper-middle-class" background. His own history—the most shocking example of which is the imbued view that the lower classes smell—would suggest that class consciousness seems to him to be an ineradicable feature of the English character, not to say of human nature in general.

These comments, however provocative, were not what raised the red flag for Gollancz. That occurred in the final section of the book, when Orwell confronts the question of why, in the midst of the depression, when capitalism gives every indication of being in its death throes, socialism has failed to develop a significant following in England. Orwell's answer to the question is first to examine the problem not of socialism but of socialists. Typical socialists, largely comfortable, middle-class types, are so busy talking to one another that they have never reached out effectively to the working classes. This is due to the fact that, at heart, they have no intention of giving up their privileges. Many of them, "cranks" addicted to drinking fruit juice, wearing sandals, and advocating birth control, are hopelessly out of touch with "real people." As for socialism itself, it projects an image of a soulless, dehumanized, mechanized future of which decent people want no part. Also, it needs to rid itself of an association with Russian communism if it expects to withstand the growing threat of fascism. With Orwell refusing to accept an abbreviated text as a Left Book selection, Gollancz finally agreed to publish the book both in a regular trade version and as a selection for the club. He reserved the right however, to write a preface to the book club version, expressing his disagreement with Orwell's arguments.

But by the time the book was published, in March 1937, Gollancz's uncontrollable author had other things on his mind. Stationed on the Aragon front as a Loyalist soldier in the SPANISH CIVIL WAR, he was busy combating the lice invading his trousers. The previous Christmas, he had left England, ostensibly to serve as a correspondent for the INDEPENDENT LABOUR PARTY (ILP). On his way to Spain, he stopped off in Paris, paying a visit to Henry Miller, whose *Tropic of Cancer* he had so much admired. He was startled when Miller told him he was a fool to join the fight against fascism out of a sense of duty. A few years later, Orwell would consider Miller's position at considerable length in his *INSIDE THE WHALE.*

Arriving in Barcelona, while the city was still basking in its initial victory over Franco's forces, he was immediately caught up in the general euphoria. At last he was seeing a genuine socialist society in action: "It was the first time I had ever been in a town where the working class was in the saddle. . . . I recognized it immediately as a state of affairs worth fighting for." He encountered the English socialist JENNIE LEE on his first day and asked her how he could join. The next day, he enlisted in the POUM (*PARTIDO OBRERO DE UNIFICACION MARXISTA*), an independent group affiliated with the British ILP. At this point, Orwell was completely innocent of the infighting taking place on the Loyalist side. As the supply of arms from the Soviet Union increased, so, too, did the influence of the communists in the conduct of the war. However, Orwell's principal concern as he took up his duties on the Aragon front was that he was missing the real action, which was then taking place in the Madrid area. He intended at the first opportunity to transfer to the International Brigades fighting there. In the meantime, Eileen arrived in Barcelona to take a secretarial job at the ILP headquarters as an assistant to JOHN MCNAIR. On the verge of leaving England, she wrote to Norah Myles, illustrating her ironic wit. She speaks of John McNair as being very kind but "having an unfortunate telephone voice and a quite calamitous prose style." She indicates that George was currently on the Aragon Front, where the Loyalists "ought to be attacking," and hoping "that that is a sufficient safeguard against their doing so" (Davison, *Lost,* 68). She soon won over everyone who came in contact with her, particularly GEORGES KOPP, a Belgian soldier of fortune who was Orwell's battalion commander. At one point, she convinced Kopp to drive her to the front to visit her husband. During the visit, there

Eileen O'Shaughnessy Blair's visit to the Aragon front, March 1937. Orwell is standing slightly behind and to her left. The kneeling rifleman wearing a beret is American Harry Milton. *(Orwell Archive, UCL Library Services, Special Collections)*

was a slight skirmish, which she described in a letter to Orwell's agent, Leonard Moore: "The Fascists threw in a small bombardment and quite a lot of machine gun fire . . . so it was quite an interesting visit—indeed I never enjoyed anything more." At one point, Eileen's relationship with Kopp took an amorous turn, which she confessed to in another letter to Myles, written on New Year's Day 1938, but she makes it clear that her husband is the love of her life.

Eileen's high spirits following her visit to the front did not last long. When SIR RICHARD REES visited her in Barcelona a month later he noticed that "she seemed absentminded, preoccupied and dazed. . . . When she began talking about the risk, for me, of being seen in the street with her . . . I realized afterwards, she was the first person in whom I had witnessed the effects of living under a political terror" (Rees, 139). The Moscow-dictated suppression of the POUM had begun.

When, after four months on the line, Orwell's company was granted leave back to Barcelona, they found themselves enmeshed in street fighting with the newly reconstituted national police. As a result, Orwell abandoned his attempt to transfer to the International Brigades and, not surprisingly, opted to remain with the underdogs: "When I see an actual flesh and blood worker in conflict with his natural enemy, the policeman, I do not have to ask which side I am on." The skirmishing in the streets of Barcelona in May was represented in the European left-wing press as an uprising by irresponsible POUMists and others. The truth, later confirmed by documents from Soviet archives, show that the fighting was part of a carefully calculated effort on the part of Moscow to eliminate the POUM and other dissidents. Shortly after his return to the front, while talking to an American comrade, HARRY MILTON, Orwell was shot in the throat by a sniper, the bullet miraculously passing through, perilously close to the carotid artery, without causing permanent damage, although partially paralyzing his vocal chords and his right arm. Eventually, both the voice and the arm regained their near-normal functions.

Meanwhile, in Barcelona, the anti-POUM activity had intensified. A communist spy, DAVID CROOK, a young Englishman, had infiltrated the ILP office, carefully compiling dossiers on McNair, Kopp, and "Eric and Eileen Blair," which were dutifully transmitted to the KGB archives in Moscow. After a brief recuperation in a local sanitorium, Orwell, having been discharged from the army, returned to Barcelona, where Eileen met him in the lobby of her hotel and whispered in his ear, "Get out." They were in imminent danger. Earlier that day, the police had invaded her room while she was still in bed and confiscated all their papers and personal items. Fortunately, they did not find their passports and checkbooks, which were hidden under the mattress she was lying on. He spent the next few days hiding out while they waited for travel documents from the British consulate. Meanwhile, Kopp had been arrested, and BOB SMILLIE, a particularly admirable young comrade, had died while in police custody. After a heroic attempt to aid the imprisoned Kopp, the couple crossed the border into France. Shortly thereafter, they were indicted for treason *in absentia* by the communist-controlled Spanish authorities.

Once Orwell was back in England, his anger at the misrepresentation of events in the English press intensified when his article "Eye-Witness in Barcelona" was rejected by Kingsley Martin, editor of the highly regarded left-wing journal *New Statesman and Nation*, on the grounds that its revelations of communist perfidy would undermine the antifascist cause. Orwell met the same fate with Gollancz after proposing a book on the subject. He was later able to place the book, memorably titled HOMAGE TO CATALONIA, with the firm of Secker & Warburg, who published it in April 1938. Sales were disappointing. In the words of the publisher, FREDRIC WARBURG, *Homage* "caused barely a ripple on the political pond. It was ignored or hectored into failure." There were some positive reviews, but many of the major reviewers ignored, or, as in the case of the anonymous TLS critic, misrepresented it: "Mr. Orwell . . . concludes by recording his hope that all the foreigners will be driven out of Spain" (Meyers, *Critical*, 119). Orwell was convinced that the poor sales and scanty reviews were part of a plot by Gollancz and his communist friends to suppress its message. If so, the plot was successful: The book sold only 500 copies. The proper homage to *Homage* would have to wait for the first American edition (1952), in which the introductory essay by LIONEL TRILLING not only paid respect to a work now regarded as among Orwell's finest but also established an image of the author as "a virtuous man," contributing significantly to the "Orwell Myth" in the years to come (Rodden, *Politics*, 73–82).

One month before the publication of *Homage*, Orwell was hospitalized with a tubercular lesion (later confirmed as an early stage of tuberculosis) in his lungs and spent the next six months recuperating in a sanitorium in Kent, his progress monitored

George Orwell's identity card photo, September 1938 *(Orwell Archive, UCL Library Services, Special Collections)*

by Eileen's brother, Dr. Laurence O'Shaughnessy. (That Eileen was the sister of a prominent chest surgeon was another of the many reasons to consider their marriage the best thing that ever happened to him.) Convalescing under orders not to work, he nevertheless began outlining a new novel. While in the hospital, he also joined the ILP, the first and only time he joined a political party, adopting for a while the party's position that a war with Germany would be, like World War I, just another "imperialist war."

In September 1938, in the mistaken belief that the climate would be good for his lungs, he and Eileen sailed to Marrakech in French Morocco, arriving on the eve of the signing of the Munich Pact. The trip was financed by an anonymous gift of 300 pounds. The donor proved to be the novelist L. H. MYERS, an admirer of Orwell's work who had visited him in the hospital. In Morocco, he kept a wary eye on the movement toward war in Europe and on the fate of his friends in Spain, where the war had drawn to an end with Franco's forces victorious. He also kept his eye on the local female population. According to the memoir of his friend Tosco Fyvel, "He said that he found himself increasingly attracted by young Arab girls and the moment came when he told Eileen he had to have one of these girls, on just one occasion. Eileen agreed and he had his Arab girl." Fyvel adds, "True or false. It does not matter" (Fyvel, 109). Of course, there is a possibility that he was merely teasing Fyvel, an ardent Zionist.

He began work on his new novel *Coming Up for Air,* which he had completed by the time of their return to England, in April 1939. Two months later, the book was published by Gollancz. Shortly after, his father, Richard Blair, died at the age of 82. Though the two were never close, their relationship had improved as Orwell's reputation grew. In a letter to Leonard Moore, Orwell described his end: ". . . his last moment of consciousness was hearing that [favorable] review in the *Sunday Times* [of *Coming Up for Air*] . . . my sister took it in and read it to him, and a little later he lost consciousness for the last time" (CW, II, 365).

Coming Up for Air had a brief flurry of popular as well as critical success, the importance of which was soon overwhelmed by the outbreak of war on September 1. Later critics (not to mention Orwell himself) have looked at *Coming Up for Air* as the completion of an important phase of Orwell's career, representing his efforts to produce a first-rate traditional, realist novel. Of the four novels he produced in this period, most critics see the first and last, *Burmese Days* and *Coming Up,* as the most successful, largely because of the relative depth or appeal of the main characters, John Flory and George Bowling. Interestingly enough, the two figures are generic opposites: Flory is tragic, and Bowling, comic. But they share with their author a vision of a rotten society, the one inherently so, resting as it does on the profound injustice of colonialism; the other acquiring rottenness, having fallen from the Eden that was pre-1914 England. The myth of the Edwardian past invoked in *Coming Up* was to assume a significant role in Orwell's attempted synthesis of idyllic past and revolutionary present.

These four novels have enjoyed little popular or critical success, although many feel that they are better than Orwell thought they were, referring to himself as "not a novelist at all, but a kind of pamphleteer." It is true that he lacked the storyteller's gift of one of his favorite authors, W. SOMERSET MAUGHAM, or the ability to get inside the skin of an average man, as James Joyce did in creating Leopold Bloom, or the depth and power of D. H. LAWRENCE, but his four 1930s novels represent a kind of collective work in progress. He is clearly learning as he goes, experimenting, as the critic Lynette Hunter argues, with narrative techniques that might enable him and his readers to expand the limited confines of the naturalist novel (Hunter, *Search*). The critic and novelist David Lodge puts it another way, maintaining that buried within *Coming Up for Air* is a "mythopoeic, metaphorical level," hinted at, if not fully realized, in the chapter devoted to a mysterious, hidden pond. (Lodge, 192).

As for the three nonfiction books of the 1930s, *Down and Out, The Road to Wigan Pier,* and *Homage to Catalonia,* they represent a progression in Orwell's political thought. *Down and Out* is the preparatory work, identifying poverty as an injustice that seems an inevitable consequence of the capitalist system but never zeroing in on a possible political solution. With *The Road to Wigan Pier,* socialism is clearly on his radar screen, but before he can commit to it, he feels duty bound not to shoot it down but to fire a few warning shots to bring socialists to their senses. His case against the "sandal-wearing vegetarians" is that they were essentially middle class with the no real understanding of the working class. But his doubts about a socialist society dissolved in the first few days in Barcelona, where he saw the working class in the driver's seat for a brief period. Orwell's dream had become a reality, only to be destroyed by the force that was to become the major target of his work for the rest of his life: Soviet Communism. *Homage to Catalonia,* his nonfiction masterpiece, is the eloquent, powerful portrait of that betrayal.

With the world on the brink of war, the Hitler-Stalin Pact in August 1939 caused Orwell to abandon his ILP pacifist stance. In what seems like an overreaction on his part, he became a particularly severe critic of PACIFISM, even falling into the Marxist jargon he despised, calling it "objectively fascist." He tried to enlist in the army but was rejected on health grounds. Eventually, he became a sergeant in "Dad's Army," the HOME GUARD, whose duties he regarded with the utmost seriousness, viewing the guard as the possible precursor of a People's Army. In May 1940, he moved into London, subordinating his preference for country life not in spite of but because of the Blitz. As Cyril Connolly put it, "He felt enormously at home in the Blitz, among the bombs, the bravery, the rubble, the shortages, the homeless, the signs of rising revolutionary temper" (283). Here, once again, Eileen matched, if not outdid, him. At their first London address, they rented a flat on the top, the most dangerous, floor. Her friend LYDIA JACKSON recalled that when the sirens went off, "Eileen would put out the lights . . . open the windows and watch the happenings in the street. I don't think she ever used the air raid shelter herself." However, Eileen's high spirits were permanently shattered by the news that her brilliant, much-beloved brother Laurence had been killed on the beach at Dunkirk while attending the wounded.

The year 1940 saw the publication of *INSIDE THE WHALE,* Orwell's first collection of essays, highlighted by the title piece, dealing with the work of Henry Miller, whom Orwell compared to the biblical Jonah. Like Jonah, Miller had chosen to stay inside the whale—that is, he sealed himself off from active involvement in world affairs. Given his own social and political commitments, we might expect Orwell to condemn Miller's position, but in fact he expresses a deep sympathy with its honesty and lack of pretense. He recognized that there is a type of writer who can be true to his work only by remaining inside the whale. However, in a later (1946) look at Miller's work after *Tropic of Cancer,* Orwell criticizes Miller's "remaining passive in the face of war, revolution, fascism or anything else" while taking care "to stay inside bourgeois democratic society, making use of its protection while disclaiming any responsibility for it."

The collection also included his essay on CHARLES DICKENS, his most extended foray into literary criticism, and "BOYS' WEEKLIES," a path-breaking essay in what became the field of cultural studies. He also began writing THEATER REVIEWS and FILM REVIEWS for *Time & Tide* magazine, assignments that he essentially "mailed in."

February 1941 saw the publication of an attempt to define the English national character and tie it to the future of socialism. Written when the Battle of Britain and the Blitz were in full force, *THE LION AND THE UNICORN, SOCIALISM AND THE ENGLISH GENIUS* (1941) is an impressionistic pamphlet divided into two sections. The first part, "England Your England," celebrates the distinctive features of English life. Orwell's opening line ("As I write highly civilized human beings are flying overhead, trying to kill me") typified the wry humor mixed with fear with which Londoners responded to the bombings. His central proposition—the war could not be won unless a socialist government came to power—he would later acknowledge to be mistaken, while applauding the wartime leadership of WINSTON CHURCHILL. This faulty prediction may have been the reason Orwell later included *The Lion and the Unicorn* among those of his works that he did not want reprinted. One of Eileen's recently discovered letters contains an ironic summary of the pamphlet's message: "Explaining how to be socialist though Tory" (Davison, *Lost,* 80). As Cyril Connolly would put in a 1945 review of *Animal Farm,* "Mr. Orwell is a revolutionary in love with 1910."

In March, he published the first of fifteen "Letters from London" in PARTISAN REVIEW, the respected literary and political journal, published by the group that came to be known as the New York Intellectuals. The letters brought him to the attention of a new audience that would serve him well in the years ahead. Among the *Partisan Review* circle were three people who would play crucial roles in the reception of Orwell's work in America: IRVING HOWE, DWIGHT MACDONALD and Lionel Trilling.

A few months later, he began working in the Indian Section of the BBC's Eastern Service. Over the next two years he would do an astonishing amount of work, writing, producing, and often reading reports and commentaries on the war for audiences in India and other areas of Southeast Asia. He also produced a number of cultural programs, drawing on the talents of figures such as T. S. Eliot, and writing the first chapter of a story for the radio completed by four other authors. Although the commentaries and reports were subject to wartime censorship and designed to present the Allies in the best light they were a version of propaganda that Orwell accepted with relative good grace. (See BBC WRITINGS.) This writing was his contribution to a war effort in which his innate patriotism blossomed. Orwell had always been an Anglo-centric writer, but in the war years he became a patriot. The sheer volume of work he produced for the BBC is impressive but even more so is the quality of most of that work, which included commissioning, editing, revising, and maneuvering through the thickets of wartime censorship a battalion of fighters in the propaganda war against the Nazi and Japanese misinformation machines. Never descending to their levels of lying, he would put the case in clear windowpane prose, whether the news was bad or good. Here for example are excerpts from two of his commentaries—the first for February 14, 1942, on the imminent fall of Singapore:

> . . . We must face the fact that it is unlikely that Singapore can be kept out of Japanese hands much longer. This is a very serious piece of news, and even more serious for Asia than for the West. One American expert has already estimated that the loss of Singapore will lengthen the war by about a year.
>
> . . . This is not an encouraging picture, and we have deliberately put it at its worst, in order to get a realistic and unvarnished view of the situation. . . . With the loss of Singapore, India becomes for the time being the centre of the war, one might say, the centre of the world.

The second is from November 28, 1942, shortly after the Soviet army had successfully surrounded the German Sixth Army at Stalingrad, thereby all but guaranteeing a Soviet victory and marking a turning point in the war:

> Well, now that almost certainly the Germans will be forced to retreat from Stalingrad even that claim can't be made any longer. The German propagandists, therefore, will be in the unenviable position of having to admit that their military commanders have poured out lives and material on an enormous scale for an objective which finally wasn't achieved. The effects even on German morale must be bad, and on Germany's so called allies they may be disastrous. The war has already lost most of its meaning from the Italian point of view, and it will not make the Italians any happier to know that tens of thousands of their sons are being frozen in Russia for absolutely nothing, at the same time as their African empire is slipping away from them and their cities are being bombed to pieces.

He confined his griping to his private diary: "But even when one manages to get something fairly good on the air, one is weighed down by the knowledge that hardly anybody is listening." Nevertheless, he took pleasure in the literary programs he developed, particularly "Voice," in which a group of poets would each read a poem, followed by a panel discussion of one of the poems. The series ran for six episodes, each one with its own theme.

Eliot participated in one of the episodes, the two men enjoying an amiable but guarded (at least on Eliot's part) relationship. Despite the political and social chasm between them, they respected each other. Orwell was an admirer of Eliot's earlier work, "The Love Song of J. Alfred Prufrock" and *The Waste Land,* but less enthusiastic about the later religious work, such as *The Four Quartets.* Even Eliot's famous rejection of *Animal Farm* was qualified by his description of it as "a distinguished piece of writing."

In March of 1943, Orwell's mother, Ida, died of a heart attack, but the death certificate also listed two secondary causes, suggesting a hereditary element in Orwell's condition—acute bronchitis and emphysema. (Shelden, 362). In November, Orwell left the BBC to become literary editor and regular columnist at *Tribune,* an independent leftist journal edited by ANEURIN BEVAN, the future minister of health in the first postwar Labour government. Orwell's weekly column was titled "As I Please," short, informal essays on any subject that caught his fancy. Unerringly, he would bring an original point of view to his topic, couched in a relaxed, informal style. More often than not, the point of view he adopted would be provocative, inviting a large number of indignant replies from readers. Here is a sample from his column for February 11, 1944: "There are two journalistic activities that will always bring you a come-back. One is to attack the Catholics and the other is to defend the Jews" (CW, 16, 91). In addition to his *Tribune* duties and his letters to *Partisan Review,* he also signed on as a regular book reviewer for the *Manchester Evening News.*

As if this were not enough, between November 1943 and February 1944 he also completed a little "fairy story" he called ANIMAL FARM. In composing it, he abandoned his lone-wolf approach to writing and began sharing the work in progress with Eileen. At the end of each day, he would read a portion of it to her for her reaction, often taking her responses as clues to revising or expanding the work. Having completed the manuscript, he was to spend the better part of a year trying to find a publisher on either side of the Atlantic. At the same time, he produced an essay on an important contemporary, ARTHUR KOESTLER, in which he identified Koestler's basic position as "revolutions always go wrong," a point he had illustrated in his not-yet-published *Animal Farm.*

In this period, his roving eye had fixed on Sally McEwen, his secretary at *Tribune.* Eileen became aware of their affair and was extremely upset. Prior to that time, he had assumed that they had an open marriage as far as sexual affairs were concerned. In any case, in May 1944, perhaps in an effort to strengthen a marriage that was threatened, he and Eileen adopted a newborn child, christened Richard Horatio Blair. The following month, while they were absent, their apartment was flattened by a "buzz bomb." Prematurely, as it turned out, he had published a poem in *Tribune* earlier that year, titled "Memories of the Blitz." The couple and their new baby settled down in a flat in Canonbury Square in London's Islington district, Eileen leaving her job at the food ministry to take care of Richard full-time. The baby brought her back from the prolonged depression she had suffered with her brother's death. In the same month, October, Orwell published "RAFFLES AND MISS BLANDISH" in *Horizon.* The essay contrasted two works of popular crime fiction, the earlier presenting a turn-of-the-century sophisticated burglar and the later, an American-influenced best seller that featured violence and sadistic behavior. This essay, along with two earlier *Horizon* essays, "THE ART OF DONALD MCGILL" and "BOYS WEEKLIES," represented Orwell's incursion into—some say "discovery of"—the field of POPULAR CULTURE, a combined sociological/literary analysis of various forms of popular entertainment. Unlike later studies in this field, however, his analyses tended to disparage contemporary versions in favor of his "golden age" of popular culture, the years of his childhood. For example, "Raffles and Miss Blandish" looks at the gratuitous violence in the 1940s shocker *No Orchids for Miss Blandish* as a disturbing development in English popular culture. In addition to this work, as PETER DAVISON points out, in the thirteen months from November 1943 to December 1944 Orwell reviewed 86 books (CW 16, xvi).

Early in 1945, with the war in Europe moving toward its end, he was able to go abroad as a war correspondent for the *Manchester Evening News* and *The Observer*. While he was there, he received notice of Eileen's death on March 29, 1945. She was to undergo surgery (a hysterectomy) but had suffered heart failure when the anesthesia was applied. Characteristically, she had held off telling him about the operation until a few days beforehand. Her last letters reveal her lovely, self-sacrificing character:

> I rather wish I'd talked it over with you before you went. I knew I had a "growth." But I wanted you to go away peacefully anyway, and I did *not* want to see Harvey Evers [her physician] before the adoption was through in case it was cancer. I thought it just possible that the judge might make some enquiry about our health as we're old for parenthood and anyway it would have been an uneasy sort of thing to be producing oneself as an ideal parent a fortnight after being told that one couldn't live more than six months or something (*CW* XVII, 97).

And her unfailing high spirits:

> Dearest I'm just going to have the operation, already enema'd, injected (with morphia in the *right* arm which is a nuisance), cleaned & packed up like a precious image in cotton wool & bandages. When it's over I'll add a note to this & it can get off quickly. Judging by my fellow patients it will be a *short* note. They've all had their operations. Annoying-I shall never have a chance to feel superior (*CW* 17, 112).

He came home for the funeral, returning to Europe two weeks later, in an effort to shake off the depression that had set in. No doubt a part of that depression was a sense of guilt. Like many people who are hard on themselves, he was hard on those close to him as well. He loved Eileen, but he had not been the best husband. One expression of that guilt, according to the psychoanalytic critic Laurence Porter, may be Winston's "guilt and exaggerated sense of responsibility" in *Nineteen Eighty-Four*:

> "He ignored his wife's symptoms of uterine cancer . . . and seems to have opposed her having a hysterectomy. Adding insult to injury, because these very symptoms made having sex very difficult, Orwell had several affairs during the last years of the war. The paperweight that Winston treasures . . . in which a small piece of pink crimpled coral is embedded, may well memorialize Orwell's feelings about this disaster. . . . The prefix of O'Brien's name as a vehicle of guilt links it with Orwell's wife O'Shaughnessy . . ." (Porter, 70).

Porter overstates the case in asserting that Orwell "ignored" his wife's symptoms. If anything, the evidence indicates that she concealed her condition from him. As for the paperweight and O'Brien's name, Porter's conjectures join a long line of ingenious interpretations of those two features of the novel.

Orwell traveled through France, Germany, and Austria until after the German surrender. What he saw, particularly the postwar divisions of Berlin and Vienna into four "watertight" zones, left him with the conviction that a cold war was inevitable. (It is not certain that he was the first to use the phrase, but he was certainly among the first.) Back in England, he was astonished, as he confessed in a *Partisan Review* letter (Summer 1945) to find that "we could have gone through nearly six years of war without arriving at either socialism or fascism and with our civil liberties almost intact." (This was written a few weeks before the 1945 election of the Labour Party government.)

Two days after the Japanese surrender on August 15, Secker & Warburg published *Animal Farm*. The book had been rejected by five English publishers, notably T. S. Eliot's firm, Faber and Faber, and some 15 in the USA. (The most memorable refusal came from Dial in America, asserting that "it was impossible to sell animal stories in the USA.") The initial run was 4,500 copies, soon to be dwarfed by the Book of the Month Club selection's 540,000. Within five years, the book would be translated into 18 languages, the most significant of which from Orwell's point of view was Ukrainian, in an edition intended to be smuggled into that Soviet province. As a result, he wrote a special introduction to that edition. (See ANIMAL FARM: PREFACES.) Earlier in the year,

Orwell had met Ernest Hemingway in Paris and asked to borrow a pistol for protection against Soviet agents, for whom he suspected he was a target (Meyers, 234). It is not at all certain that he was still a Soviet target, but had they known about *Animal Farm,* they doubtless would have had him in their sights. A work that did incalculable damage to the Soviet image worldwide, *Animal Farm* was soon enlisted as a powerful weapon in the cold war. One striking example: In 1955, the CIA provided the financial backing for an animated film production of the book, with the ending altered to include a successful counterrevolution against Napoleon's regime (Shaw, 159). For Orwell, the success was dimmed by the fact that while the critics applauded it, nobody said that the writing was beautiful. Actually that was not true. Cyril Connolly called it "deliciously written, with something of the feeling, the penetration and the verbal economy of Orwell's master, Swift" (Meyers, *Crtical,* 201); Edmund Wilson described it as being "written in a prose so plain and spare, so admirably proportioned to its purpose, that *Animal Farm* seems very creditable if we compare it to Voltaire and Swift" (205); even T. S. Eliot, in his famous rejection of the manuscript, allowed ". . . that it is a distinguished piece of writing, that the fable is very skillfully handled and that the narrative keeps one's interest on its own plane—and that is something very few authors have achieved since *Gulliver*" (Crick, 315). (It is stunning to realize that Eliot could write such a sentence in a letter of rejection.) Another distinguished critic, his BBC colleague WILLIAM EMPSON described its "beautifully limpid prose style," but he also issued a warning that "you must expect to be 'misunderstood' on a large scale about this book" (Bowker, 335–336). Empson seems to be referring to the interpretation of the book not merely as anti-Stalinist but antirevolutionary in general. As Jeffrey Meyers puts it, "Once in power, the revolutionary becomes as tyrannical as his oppressor" (Meyers, *Guide,* 145).

Barnhill, Orwell's home on the island of Jura in the Hebrides, located off the coast of northern Scotland *(Orwell Archive, UCL Library Services, Special Collections)*

Animal Farm would turn out to be the purest example of his ultimate goal as a writer, as he expressed it in "WHY I WRITE,": "to make political writing into an art." In 1946, he published "Why I Write," in which he outlines his writing efforts from the age of four, citing as the most significant event the Spanish civil war. "Every line of serious work I have written since 1936 has been written *against* totalitarianism and for democratic socialism, as I understand it."

The end of 1945 saw him writing one of his most influential essays, "POLITICS AND THE ENGLISH LANGUAGE," published in *Horizon* (April 1946), in which he lays down a fundamental principle: "If thought corrupts language, language can also corrupt thought." As for 1946, the title of volume 18 in Peter Davison's *Complete Works* tells it all: "Smothered by Journalism." In the course of the year he produced a number of major essays, in addition to "Why I Write" and "Politics and the English Language;" his study of his master, JONATHAN SWIFT; "The Decline of the English Murder," another foray into popular culture; the pamphlet *James Burnham and the Managerial Revolution,* a detailed critique of a fashionable postwar theory (see BURNHAM, JAMES); two delightful short pieces, "A Nice Cup of Tea" and "THE MOON UNDER WATER"; two BBC radio plays, "The Voyage of the Beagle" and a version of "Red Riding Hood," the latter for a children's program; and a *Partisan Review* "letter" that required extensive subsequent correspondence. By the summer of that year, he had had enough of journalism.

Delighted by the sales of *Animal Farm* but appalled by the fact that he was becoming a celebrity, he looked for a retreat where he could continue work on a new book he had in mind and provide Richard a taste of country life. To that end, he moved to the remote island of Jura, in the Hebrides, off the coast of northern Scotland. If the island was remote, Orwell's home, Barnhill, was even more so. Once having arrived on Jura, no small feat in itself, a visitor would have to hire a car and drive to the village of Ardlussa. The final seven miles of the trip would be on foot, carrying whatever luggage he or she had, on a broken path. The house itself was large, but it had no hot water, electricity, or telephone. For three months of summer, it was bearable, but after that, the wind, rain, and cold made it the last place someone with Orwell's lungs should be living. In her fierce, mean-spirited, but perceptive analysis of Orwell, Mary McCarthy cast a cold eye on his asceticism, suggesting some life-denying pathology at its core. One answer to McCarthy's charge lies in the fact that he was not a hermit. He encouraged visitors. The hardships of travel (and of living there, once you had arrived) did not prevent a goodly number of people from making the trip. And it suited him perfectly. He was joined there by his sister Avril, who became housekeeper and guardian of Richard after successfully routing Susan Watson, who had played that role in London. After three months on the island, the family—Orwell, Avril, and Richard—returned to London.

Ever since Eileen's death, he had had to come to grips with a dual problem—his own mortality and the welfare of his son. He figured he would be lucky to have 10 more years, given the state of his lungs, his addiction to the particularly foul tobacco in his roll-your-own cigarettes, and his affinity for damp, cold, leaky places in which to live. He began looking for a young, preferably attractive, intelligent woman who might serve as a suitable companion for him and as a stepmother for Richard. To that end, he proposed to several different women. One was CELIA KIRWAN, a beautiful, accomplished woman whose twin sister was married to ARTHUR KOESTLER. Koestler revered Orwell and begged his sister-in-law to accept the proposal, but she was not in love with or even physically attracted to Orwell. Another prospect was his downstairs neighbor at Canonbury Square, Anne Popham, to whom he wrote an extraordinary proposal letter: "What I am really asking you is whether you would like to be a widow of a literary man. If things remain more or less as they are there is a certain amount of fun in this, as you would probably get royalties coming in and you might find it interesting to edit unpublished stuff. . . ." (*CW,* 18, 248–249).

The years 1947 and 1948 were devoted to the composition of a book tentatively titled "The Last Man in Europe," which would eventually evolve into *Nineteen Eighty-Four.* Unfortunately, a good deal of this period would find Orwell in an ongoing, steadily losing battle against ill health. After spending winter 1946 in London, he returned to Barnhill the following April. The winter had been one of the worst in years, resulting in a serious shortage of coal. The lack of heat took an additional toll on his lungs. Once at Barnhill, he settled into work on the new book, finishing the first draft by the end of 1947. The summer had been sunny and dry. He had a number of visitors, including at one point his nephew, HENRY DAKIN and two nieces, Jane and Lucy, the children of his sister Marjorie. Along with Avril and Richard, they sailed in Orwell's boat around the northern tip of the island. On their return, Orwell misread the tide schedule and, as a consequence, their boat was caught up in currents from one of the whirlpools in the area. They managed to get ashore onto a little island, "just rocks covered with sea birds," from which they were rescued a few hours later by a fishing boat. He, his son, two nieces, and a nephew had come very close to being drowned. In a letter to Brenda Salkeld, Orwell concludes his description of the adventure with a typically stiff-upper-lip, Etonian understatement: "Our boat luckily wasn't damaged, apart from the loss of the engine, but I'm trying to get hold of a bigger one as these trips are really a bit too unsafe in a little rowing boat" (*CW*, 19, 196).

Happily ensconced on Jura, Orwell intended to stay through the winter, but in November, he began spitting up blood, requiring his removal to the Scottish mainland, at Hairmyres Hospital, near Glasgow. There he was diagnosed for the first time with a disease, long hinted at in his case, tuberculosis. One promising possibility was a new drug from the United States, streptomycin. The problem was that the drug had yet to be approved by British authorities. At this point Orwell's friend DAVID ASTOR stepped in to help, using his wealth to pay for the expensive new drug and his influence to bring the case to the attention of the new Labor Minister of Health, Aneurin Bevan, who had been Orwell's boss at *Tribune*. The drug seemed to work, its powerful side effects nothwithstanding, including hair loss and skin rashes, but his lungs improved. While still in the hospital, he completed the passionate autobiographical essay "Such, Such Were the Joys." Orwell had begun a version of this essay, probably as early as 1938, the year of the publication of Cyril Connolly's *Enemies of Promise*, which contained a bittersweet memoir of St Cyprian's, too sweet for Orwell's taste. However, he realized that his account of the school could never be printed as long as the principal figures, Lewis and Cecily Vaughan Wilkes, were alive. The essay was not published until 1952; even then it appeared in the American *Partisan Review*, presumably still too hot to handle for a British publisher, given the prevailing libel laws.

In July, he returned to Barnhill, where he began working again, revising the first draft of his novel. It was November by the time the revision was completed but by then the manuscript had to be completely retyped. Having no success in securing a typist who would come to Barnhill, he set about retyping it himself, a task that left him exhausted. His publisher, Warburg, later confessed, "This failure on my part still haunts me." Well, it might, considering the stakes. Warburg should have made a greater effort to send a typist to Barnhill. In December, having completed the typing, Orwell suffered a relapse, again spitting up blood. This time he was removed to a sanatorium in the Cotswolds, where doctors experimented with new drugs, including streptomycin, but without positive results. Strict bed rest was ordered; anything that resembled work, proscribed.

June saw the publication of the new novel, Orwell having agreed upon *Nineteen Eighty-Four* as the title. The book was published in the United States by Harcourt, Brace, but for a special edition of their own, the Book of the Month Club wanted permission to delete two sections: Emmanuel Goldstein's "Theory and Practice of Oligarchical Collectivism" and the appendix on Newspeak. Orwell held his ground, refusing to agree to the cuts. Eventually the club gave in, resulting in the sale of more than 190,000 copies of the book club edition in the first year alone. As usual his own worst critic, he wrote to JULIAN SYMONS, "My new book is a Utopia in the form of a novel. I ballsed it up rather, partly owing to being so ill when I was writing it. . . ." The reviewers did not agree. The praise came from critics of the most discriminating literary temperament: V. S.

Pritchett in the *New Statesman and Nation*, who ranked the author with Swift; Lionel Trilling in the *New Yorker*, who characterized it as a "momentous book," dealing with the "mystique of power."

One feature of the novel that raised—and continues to raise—a serious question about the author's intention relates to his identification of the ruling party in Oceania as Ingsoc. When Fredric Warburg first read the novel, he wrote a detailed internal memorandum to this staff. He included among his observations the opinion that the choice of Ingsoc constituted "an attack on socialism and socialists generally . . ." and that the book is "worth a cool million votes for the Conservative party." Thus Orwell's publisher was the first of many readers to see political possibilities inherent in the novel that deviated widely from his intention. As soon as Orwell heard of this reading, he issued a disclaimer, and then did so more than once. In a letter to a United Auto Workers official, he made his intention clear:

> My recent novel is NOT intended as an attack on Socialism or on the British Labour Party (of which I am a supporter) but a show up of the perversions to which a centralized economy is liable and which have already been partly realized in Communism and Fascism (Crick, 398).

But as it happened, in 1946, two New Critics, William Wimsatt and Monroe Beardsley, had introduced the idea of the "intentional fallacy," in which an author's conscious intention was relegated to second place behind the text itself as the most reliable guide to its meaning. It was one of those pronouncements that gained immediate attention and prestige in academic circles, at least in the United States. Of course, those who insisted on reading Orwell's novel as an attack on English socialism might well have been guilty of the obverse of the "intentional fallacy," what the same authors dubbed the "affective fallacy," determining the meaning of a text from "its results in the minds of its audience." Thus a New Critic might pronounce a pox on both approaches in favor of a formalist reading. William Empson had warned Orwell of this possibility in connection with *Animal Farm*, when he suggested that certain literary forms, the fable being one of them, invite interpretations beyond the author's intention. But the academic world was only a small, if important, part of the book's phenomenally wide readership. The point was that Orwell had probably made the mistake of assuming that he was addressing an inside-the-family group, such as the readers of his *Tribune* column. These socialist readers would understand that as V. S. Pritchett's obituary put it, ". . . in politics [Orwell] was more likely to chasten his own side than the enemy." But in fact he did see the threat of totalitarianism, latent as much in a socialist government as in a fascist one. How could he not, looking at the example of the Soviet Union? As it turned out, of course, it was the countries behind the iron curtain that came closest to the world of *Nineteen Eighty-Four*, all of which ultimately added to the novel's appeal to partisans on the right. That being said, on Orwell's part, the Ingsoc name was, as Bernard Crick put it, "at best incautious, at worst, foolish" (397).

Meanwhile, as his health worsened, a letter arrived that momentarily revived his spirits. It came from Jacintha Buddicom, breaking a nearly 30-year silence. Orwell responded with two letters, expressing the hope of renewing their friendship. Jacintha never responded, possibly because she may have feared his asking her to become the mother of Richard. At one point, after describing the boy, he asks, "Are you fond of children? I think you must be."

While he was at the sanatorium, he had a steady stream of visitors. One of these was Celia Kirwan, whose earlier rejection of his marriage proposal had not interfered with their friendship. During one of her visits, she wondered whether he would be interested in writing something for the agency where she was working, the Information Research Department of the British Foreign Office. He replied that he was too ill to tackle any new writing assignments, but he offered to suggest names of some anticommunist writers. A short while later he wrote to her saying that he had a list of names of people he considered "crypto-communists, fellow travelers or inclined that way & should not be trusted as propagandists." The list, which he subsequently submitted, had been compiled with Sir Richard Rees as a kind of game in which they tried to guess which public figures would turn out to be traitors or collaborators. (See Part III: ORWELL'S LIST.)

Meanwhile another candidate for a marriage proposal appeared on the scene, SONIA BROWNELL, Cyril Connolly's assistant at *Horizon.* In addition to being extremely attractive, she was a very efficient if somewhat imperious editor. Raised in an exclusive convent school, she lost no time throwing over the traces upon graduating.

Early in her career, she moved in the circle surrounding the Euston School of Art, living with the artist William Coldstream. Orwell and she met at Connolly's home in 1940, but it was not until 1946 that they renewed their acquaintance, eventually having an affair, in which Orwell acted like the not-so "young man carbuncular" in Eliot's *The Waste Land,* "making a welcome of indifference" on her part. He proposed to her at that time but was rejected. Shortly after, Sonia left for Paris, where she encountered the "love of her life," the French existentialist philosopher Maurice Merleau-Ponty. The two had an intense, extended affair that ended when Merleau- Ponty made it clear he would never leave his wife and children. Orwell did not meet Sonia again until 1949, when she began to visit him in the sanatorium, bringing life into a room where death was pervasive. When EVELYN WAUGH visited Orwell there, he saw the emaciated figure lying in bed as "very near to God." Sonia's visits raised the possibility that the inevitable end might be postponed if he had something to live for. When proposed to again, she consulted her friend and his publisher Fredric Warburg. Perhaps operating out of mixed motives—genuine feeling that the marriage would give Orwell added incentive to live and to keep producing books for Warburg—he urged her to accept. As for Orwell himself, he too felt that marriage to a young and vibrant woman would help to keep him alive. Insofar as he was looking for a future widow who would be protective of his work—Sonia was an experienced operator in the publishing world—he made the right choice, but as a potential mother of his son or as a companion at Barnhill, he could not have chosen worse. Sonia was a woman at home in the smart social circles of London and Paris. It was agreed that Richard would be raised by his sister Avril, an arrangement that Eileen would not have been happy with. In any case, by the fall of 1949, Orwell, now removed to University College Hospital, in London, where Sonia could visit him every day, decided to go ahead with the marriage. With Sonia by his side, he planned to move to a Swiss sanatorium in a last-ditch effort at recuperation. The wedding took place at the hospital on October 13, 1949. Three months later, on January 21, 1950, shortly before he was to fly to Switzerland, he passed away.

Sonia Brownell, Orwell's second wife and controversial keeper of his flame *(Orwell Archive, UCL Library Services, Special Collections)*

Two days earlier, he had made an addition to his will, indicating his desire "to be buried (not cremated) according to the rights of the Church of England . . . ," an acknowledgement of his profoundly rooted identity as an Englishman and his respect for the liturgy of the Anglican church. Perhaps he was motivated by the feeling he attributed to his protagonist, Dorothy Hare, in *A Clergyman's Daughter:*

> For she perceived that in all that happens in a church, however absurd and cowardly its supposed purpose may be, there is something—it is hard to define, but something of decency, of spiritual comeliness—that is not easily found in the world outside. It seemed to her that even though you no longer believe, it is better to go to church than not; better to follow in the ancient ways, than to drift in rootless freedom.

The funeral took place at Christ Church in London, followed by interment in All Saints' Churchyard in the village of Sutton Courtney, Berkshire. David Astor had used his influence with the rector of All Saints to permit the burial of an outsider in the parish graveyard, prompting Malcolm Muggeridge to record in his diary, "Orwell was born on Lenin's birthday and buried by the Astors." Substantially more heartfelt was Fredric Warburg's reaction in a letter to Orwell's American editor Robert Giroux, describing the funeral as "one of the most melancholy occasions in my life" (*CW,* 20, 187).

The "death-bed wedding" raised eyebrows that remain elevated into the 21st century. In her exculpatory biography of Sonia, Hilary Spurling describes the vicious reaction that pictured Sonia "as a cold, calculating gold digger who shortchanged her husband by marrying him for money, squandering his fortune, exploiting his name and copyrights" (Spurling, 176). Instead, Spurling depicts a warm, attractive, spirited human being, a caring and sympathetic friend who married Orwell because she genuinely thought she could prolong his life. She tried to respect his wishes not to have a biography written. Her greatest weakness was that she put absolute trust in anyone she regarded as a friend, including the accountant who controlled the income of Orwell's estate.

Sonia made three important contributions to Orwell's reputation. The first was the publication of the four-volume *Collected Essays, Journalism and Letters,* which she edited with Ian Angus in 1968. It was the basic source of information about him and his work until the massive 20-volume *Complete Works* (1998), edited by Peter Davison. The second was the establishment of the Orwell Archive at the University of London. The third was the commissioning of a biography by Bernard Crick, which she disliked when she read it, but which has been much admired by Orwellians. Her last years were spent in an alcoholic haze, and she died penniless in 1980, 30 (largely unhappy) years after her husband. She left, belatedly in the eyes of her critics, a reduced estate to Orwell's son, Richard, who had been raised by Avril and her husband, Bill Dunn.

In 1936, Orwell wrote to a fellow Etonian, Dennis King-Farlow, summarizing his life since leaving Eton: "I have had a bloody life a good deal of the time but in some ways an interesting one." At that time, those words constituted a more or less accurate description, allowing for a certain degree of understatement. Not a hint there that he would go on to become the most important English writer of the 20th century. Nor is there a vision of the bloodiness that would lie ahead: the visits to the infernal regions known as coal mines; the bullet in the neck; the narrow escape from Stalinist perfidy in Spain; the leperlike treatment of him when he tried to "spill the Spanish beans"; the Blitz and the wartime privations that may have contributed to his wife's death; the steady rejection by publishers of *Animal Farm,* the one book he knew he had written as well as it could be written; the misreading, partly his fault, of his most famous book; and always the beastly lungs and the final, fatal hemorrhage, bloody indeed.

Yet despite all that—or is it because of all that—he towers over his contemporaries. Not as the best, not necessarily for the ages, but as the most important writer of his time. As one of his staunchest American admirers, Irving Howe, put it, some writers "redeem their time by forcing it to accept the truth about itself and therefore, perhaps, saving it from the truth about itself. Such writers, it is possible, will not survive their time, for what makes them so valuable and so endearing to their contemporaries . . . is not likely to be a quality conducive to the greatest art."

It may be true that his importance can be attributed not to the innate quality of his work but to an accident of history. His work "just happened" to appear at the beginning of the cold war, and his last two books became weapons in that war, but two decades after its end, he is still read, alluded to, and studied. He has also continued to serve as a creative source for others. Thus the Academy Award for Best Foreign Film of 2006 went to *The Lives of Others,* a film set in East Berlin in 1984. It is impossible to view that film and not be aware of the degree to which the science-fiction of 1949 became the historical reality of 1984 for the people of Eastern Europe. Nearly 60 years after his death, it is clear that *Nineteen Eighty-Four* did not "just happen"; it was the product of Orwell's powerful, sensitive, politically acute and morally appalled imagination, and his vision continues to alarm and inform the contemporary world.

THE AFTERLIFE

The simple tombstone inscription "E. A. Blair" is undoubtedly a reflection of the author's aversion to the spotlight, but lurking beyond it may have been a glimmer or recognition that, although Eric Blair was dead and buried, George Orwell was alive and well.

That second life began with the obituary notices, written by such prominent figures as Arthur Koestler, Bertrand Russell, STEPHEN SPENDER, and V. S. Pritchett. Koestler placed Orwell as a rebel and "the only writer of genius among the *literateures* of social revolt between the two wars. Russell saw in him "a love of humanity and an incapacity for comfortable illusion" and adds ". . . but he lost hope," presumably thinking of *Nineteen Eighty-Four,* regarded by many, then and now, as a cry of despair.

However, Pritchett's beautifully written tribute was the most influential of these eulogies. Published originally in *New Statesman and Nation,* a journal with which Orwell had had a longstanding feud, it was reprinted, with slight variation in *The New York Times Book Review.* Pritchett's moving piece included four memorable epithets. The first of these characterized Orwell as "the wintry conscience of his generation," the word *wintry* having a piercingly accurate impact. The second vivid metaphor described Orwell as a scout who "always woke up one miserable hour earlier than anyone else . . . broke camp and advanced alone to some tougher position in a bleaker place," beautifully invoking his lonely integrity. The third depicted Orwell as "a rebel gone native in his own country," capturing perfectly the Orwell of *Down and Out* and *Wigan Pier.* Pritchett's fourth allusion portrays the author of *Nineteen Eighty-Four* as an elusive figure, "the passing traveler who meets one on the station, who points out that one is waiting for the wrong train and vanishes" (Meyers, *Critical,* 294). After reading Pritchett's obituary, Malcolm Muggeridge wrote that it was the stuff from which "the legend of a human being is created" (Coppard and Crick, 271).

The obituaries, appropriately enough, place their emphasis on the man rather than on his works. Later, *Animal Farm* and *Nineteen Eighty-Four* went on to become not simply best sellers but forces in shaping the social and political consciousness of the West and in the undergrounds of Eastern Europe. But in the years immediately following Orwell's death, there also developed a series of images or myths about Orwell the man. These were so complex, contradictory, and interwoven, that his afterlife biographer John Rodden identified

George Orwell's gravestone in All Saints' Churchyard in the village of Sutton Courtney, Berkshire, England *(Orwell Archive, UCL Library Services, Special Collections)*

four distinct images of Orwell that emerged posthumously: the rebel, the common man, the prophet, and the saint. Rodden then proceeded to detail the process by which these images came into being and the social, political, cultural, and even religious consequences that ensued. In the end, the four categories converged so that Orwell became "a human kaleidoscope whose variegated imagery has represented nearly all things to all people, or at least all political writers—the Zelig of modern intellectuals" (Rodden, *Politics,* 400).

The reference to Zelig may be somewhat misleading: The Woody Allen character is essentially passive, and passivity was never an Orwellian trait. In fact, the diversity that Rodden so carefully delineated demonstrates that Orwell was too active to sit still for any one portrait. In that respect, he may resemble another English writer, William Shakespeare, whose literal "portraits"—pictures of him by various artists—continue to raise questions about which of them gives an authentic likeness.

Rodden's study focuses on Orwell's reputation as it appears in politics and literary circles, and as reflected in psychoanalytical and Marxist studies, in his "plain style" and his early death, and, most important, in the title of his last work, a specific year. The anticipation of 1984 kept a good part of the public and the media aware of the novel and the man behind it as the calendar moved toward the year.

While he lived, Orwell had, by 1945, developed a distinct reputation in intellectual leftist circles as a maverick, whose independence and straight talk ruffled many feathers and bruised a number of prominent egos. His name was particularly anathema to members of the British Communist Party. His reputation as an independent thinker grew as a result of his "As I Please" columns in *Tribune* and, on the other side of the Atlantic, in his "Letters from London" for *Partisan Review,* but at most he was regarded as a pesty gadfly who could be safely ignored. That perception changed with the publication of *Animal Farm* and its selection in America as a Book of the Month Club choice. The process was repeated and intensified when *Nineteen Eighty-Four* was chosen by the Book of the Month Club. The relatively unknown journalist and essayist had become the best-selling author of his generation and one of the world's best known anticommunists.

His death, only seven months after the publication of *Nineteen Eighty-Four,* intensified the already keen interest in the man and his work. Orwell's obituaries represented the first step in the process of creating a legend. Written by intellectuals for intellectuals, these tributes established his reputation as someone who had lived his life marching to a different drummer, a model of a free man, not tied to any of what he called "the smelly little orthodoxies." And it was precisely that image that made him a valuable commodity in the cold war. He was seen as a free spirit with no ideological axe to grind, a view which added power to his critique of communism. To his left-wing critics, however, his independence was characterized as a failure of nerve, an example of the easy liberal unwillingness to take a risk or make a commitment. However, the more positive image survived both appropriation from the right and denunciation from the far left. In England in the 1950s, he was adopted as a model by the Movement, a group of young poets, who exhibited in verse characteristics they saw in Orwell's prose, the plain style dealing with ordinary life, a repudiation of the romanticism of Dylan Thomas or the abstract intellectualism of T. S. Eliot. One of the group, Robert Conquest, who would later produce powerful prose indictments of the Soviet era, saluted him in a line from his poem "George Orwell": "Because he taught us what the actual meant." At first, the Movement was scrupulously apolitical, determined to stay "inside the whale." The Suez crisis, however, which blackened the eye of the British government so severely that the Americans joined with the Soviets in condemning their invasion of Egyptian territory, led to an awakening of the political instincts of young English writers, particularly those who became known as the Angry Young Men. Orwell proved to be relevant here as well, since Gordon Comstock, the protagonist of *Keep the Aspidistra Flying,* could easily be seen as a prototype of the Angry Young Men.

In America, the increasing esteem in which Orwell was held was enhanced in 1952 with the first American publication of *Homage to Catalonia,* where it was acclaimed for both the purity of its prose and the authenticity of its message. Adding to the impact of the book itself was the eloquent introduction by Lionel Trilling, extolling Orwell personally as "a virtuous man." Trilling's admiration was echoed in the writings of Irving Howe, who viewed Orwell as a great moral figure.

But the reception of Orwell in the narrow realm of literary and political intellectuals was only one facet in establishing him as an iconic figure in the postwar world. He was about to emerge on a broader stage. The critical event in that process occurred in December 1954, when the BBC aired a televised adaptation of *Nineteen Eighty-Four.* Generally regarded by reviewers as a faithful and impressive translation of the book to the new medium, the production raised a storm of protests from viewers, many of them appalled by the graphic violence of the torture scenes. The protests grew louder when the BBC showed the drama again four days later, to what was, at the time, the largest audience in its television history. Some of the viewers, unaware of Orwell or of the commentary on the book, even took O'Brien to be the author's spokesman. Others spoke of it as though it were a BBC documentary depicting real life behind the iron curtain (Shaw, 156). The controversy was taken up in parliamentary debates, centering on the suitability of such material for viewing at home. The fact that television viewing had become a family experience, shared by children and adults, emerged as an important social phenomenon. Moreover, the name *George Orwell* began to take on a broader and more complex connotation.

In the same month, December 1954, a full-length animated film version of *Animal Farm* premiered in London and New York. A seemingly depoliticized version of the book, this CIA-backed film introduced English and American youth to Orwell, a figure they would encounter in the curricula of higher grades. While superficially nonpolitical, the film minimized the negative depiction of human beings (allegorically, capitalists), and in the final scene, in which the pigs and humans first raise a toast to and later quarrel with each other, the humans are cut out, leaving only pigs celebrating. Another popularization of Orwell appeared in 1956 with the film *1984,* but this mediocre effort did little to enhance the author's reputation.

In the 1960s, the most significant event in Orwell's afterlife was the publication of the four-volume *Collected Essays, Journalism, and Letters of George Orwell,* edited by his widow, Sonia Orwell, and Ian Angus, providing the opportunity to see the chronological Orwell, from his 1920 letter to fellow Classmate STEVEN RUNCIMAN, describing an inadvertent tramping experience to a 1949 letter to his friend Tosco Fyvel, thanking him and his wife for a gift. For most readers and reviewers, the four volumes confirmed a view of the author that echoed Lionel Trilling's "a virtuous man," honest, straightforward, and committed to a basic standard of "decency," a favorite Orwellian word. Among the few dissenters was Mary McCarthy, who was skeptical about the absence of any personally revealing letters in the collection. As for the man, she saw him as a hater of fashion—he wanted out of whatever was in—with a deep emotional commitment to socialism that was, however, intellectually incomplete. "It is a question whether Orwell's socialism, savagely felt as it was, was not an unexamined idea off the top of his head: sheer rant" (McCarthy, 5). Offsetting McCarthy's criticism, George Steiner's review of *Collected Essays, Journalism, and Letters of George Orwell,* in the *New Yorker* (March 29, 1969), declared, "These four volumes are a place of renewal for the moral imagination" (Steiner, 139).

McCarthy's criticism expressed a developing idea in the late 1960s about Orwell. The book appeared in 1968, the year of massive student revolts in the United States and Europe (both in Paris and in Prague), along with the controversy over the Vietnam War. The activist spirit of that time tended to see Orwell as a hindrance, a rhetorical do-nothing, who talked a good game but offered no program for action. Some student radicals took the case against him even further, as illustrated in Saul Bellow's novel *Mr. Sammlers's Planet* (1976), in which a student interrupts Sammler's speech quoting Orwell by shouting that Orwell was "a sick counterrevolutionary. It's good that he died when he did" (Bellow, 35). McCarthy had written: "As for the student revolt, he might well have been out of sympathy . . . But would he have sympathized with the administrators? If he had lived he might have been happiest on a desert island, and it was a blessing for him probably that he died" (McCarthy, 6).

Orwell's rejection by the "new, new left" was cemented by one of its most respected fathers, RAYMOND WILLIAMS. Williams's complicated relationship with Orwell demonstrates an almost oedipal conflict on Williams's part. He went from seeing Orwell as a sort of intellectual father to completely rejecting him. "I found him unreadable" was Williams's judgment, conveyed in an interview with a radical journal's editorial board.

The 1980s became the "Orwell decade," as the "countdown" to 1984, the year itself, and the aftermath offered a media orgy that featured soaring book sales of the novel, televised documentaries, countless tedious magazine ads playing off terms such as *Big Brother, Orwellian,* or *newspeak,* and a seemingly numberless series of rock songs invoking Orwell or Big Brother. Academic conferences at universities cropped up all over with participants from a wide range of disciplines (Orwell was one writer who was never the exclusive property of the English department); the proceedings more often than not were reprinted by university presses.

Two notable television productions were shown during the year. One was a presentation of *Nineteen Eighty-Four* by the BBC. This production, directed by Michael Radford, starred John Hurt as Winston and Richard Burton as O'Brien. Although it was an intelligent and realistic treatment of the novel, it did not create anything like the storm that followed the first televised version 30 years earlier (Rodden, *Politics,* 286). The other TV production (an ironic but revealing tribute to the author of *Nineteen Eighty-Four*) was a one-time, enormously expensive Super Bowl ad for Apple computers, subtly associating its rival IBM, known as Big Blue, with Big Brother. The ad, directed by action-film director Ridley Scott, went on to win a number of prizes, including a grand prix at the Cannes Film Festival (Rodden, *Scenes* 9–10). As he demonstrated at length, Orwell deplored the presence of advertising in its modern forms. In a *Tribune* column, he roundly criticized an ad featuring a young man and his personal manservant as helping to perpetuate and idealize the privileges of the upper class (*CW,* 16, 286). He was always quick to recognize the political implications of popular culture fashions, but this Apple ad was strictly business.

The year 1984 also witnessed the appearance of the most sustained attack from the left on the Orwell reputation, *Inside the Myth: Orwell, Views from the Left,* a collection of essays edited by Christopher Norris. In his introduction, Norris divides the essays in this volume into two groups, those, one of which is his own, that are rooted in "theory," the poststructuralist critique of Orwell's and everybody else's "common sense," and more traditional approaches. Norris focused on Orwell's alleged prejudices, "half-truths and predisposed pessimist conclusions. . . ." (Norris, 11). Norris's essay looks on Orwell's "naive" view of language as the vehicle through which we communicate the truth. Orwell maintained that it was the task of the autonomous individual to speak the truth, despite the powerful conditioning that tries to undermine individual autonomy. Norris answers that, from the perspective of theory, individual autonomy is a myth, the illusion of which enables the powers-that-be to retain their power. He suggests that while Orwell never perceived this distinction consciously, his defense of common sense had a back-to-the-wall desperation about it. Malcolm Evans's essay takes us deeply into the contradictions in Orwell's writings on literature and politics, which he sees as shifting back and forth "from aesthetic idealism to the material production within ideology of a body of texts *deemed* aesthetic and valuable." (Norris, 21). Orwell, in Evans's reading, never resolved the contradiction, with the result that on A-level examinations, in questions about *Nineteen Eighty-Four,* the "political message" is invariably seen as a flaw that weakens the novel.

Non-theory-oriented contributions include two essays on Orwell's treatment of women in his writing, and two critiques of his naïveté or dishonesty in his account of the Spanish civil war. The most balanced essay in the collection is Lynette Hunter's description of Orwell's developing skill in the early novels in creating a complex narrative voice (Norris, 163–184). Another important anti-Orwell publication in 1984 was Daphne Patai's detailed look at Orwell's pervasive "androcentrism," Patai's preferred term for Orwell's particular form of sexism.

The significant Orwellian event of the 1990s was the 1998 publication of Peter Davison's 20-volume edition of *The Complete Works of George Orwell.* A monument of serious scholarship, it made an implicit statement as to Orwell's importance: Nine of the volumes are reprints of Orwell's book-length work, including six novels and three works of nonfiction. The remaining eleven volumes contain everything else he wrote: letters, essays, columns, BBC broadcasts, diary and notebook entries, as well as relevant writing by others, such as letters by his wife Eileen, rebuttals from people he had attacked, and publisher's responses, such as T. S. Eliot's famous rejection of *Animal Farm.* In his review of the edition, Timothy Garton Ash lists the names of better 20th-century writers who have yet to receive such a sumptuous "complete works" treatment. Ash's answer to why this should be so is to cite "the unique fascination and lasting importance of [Orwell's] work." The fascination lies in the comment of Cyril Connolly: "Anything about Orwell is interesting." The importance for Ash lies in the fact that ". . . Orwell is the most influential political writer of the 20th century."

One of the distinguishing features of the complete works is that it included the most complete and accurate description of Orwell's List, the term used to describe the list of thirty-eight names that he had submitted to the Information Research Department, a government bureau engaged in promoting anticommunist propaganda. Orwell's list consisted of names of people he advised the department *not* to hire. When this information became public, some papers had a field day, labeling Orwell a government informer. Peter Davison's scrupulous account of the affair helped to quiet these hyped-up press accounts.

Two examples of the Orwell controversy that have carried over into the 21st century are Christopher Hitchens's *Why Orwell Matters* (British title: *Orwell's Victory*) and Louis Menand's "Honest, Decent, Wrong: The Innovation of George Orwell" (*New Yorker,* January 27, 2003). Hitchens's basic

George Orwell at Canonbury Square, 1946 *(Orwell Archive, UCL Library Services, Special Collections)*

thesis asserts that on "[the] three great subjects of the 20th century: imperialism, fascism, and Stalinism," Orwell got them right. Among the important issues, unmentioned by Hitchens, that Orwell got wrong, however, was capitalism, which Orwell assumed was in its death throes.

Menand picks up on Hitchens's thesis by asserting that many people were against imperialism, fascism, and Stalinism: "The important question now was what to do about them and how to understand the implications for the future. On this level, Orwell was almost always wrong" (Menand, 66). On imperialism, he was against self-determination for small nations such as Burma. He questioned the idea of war against fascism as late as August 1939. At this point, Menand skips over Orwell's anticommunism to discuss various other predictions of his that did not pan out. Menand concludes with the judgment that "Orwell is admired for being a paragon when he was, self-consciously, a naysayer and a misfit" (91).

Menand's *naysayer* is an updating of the old charge *pessimist,* and *misfit,* the negative version of *independent.*

The Orwell centennial year 2003, validated the epigraph to *Coming Up for Air:* "He's dead but he won't lie down." The year saw the publication of two full-length biographies (D. J. Taylor's *Orwell: The Life* and Gordon Bowker's *Inside George Orwell*); one double-barreled attack from the left (Scott Lucas's *Orwell: Life and Times,* 2003, and *The Betrayal of Dissent,* 2004); numerous academic conferences; and John Rodden's sequel to *The Politics of Reputation: Scenes from an Afterlife: The Legacy of George Orwell.* A major section of Rodden's second book deals with the reaction to Orwell in East Germany during and after the cold war.

WORKS CITED

Aung Maung Htin. "George Orwell and Burma." In *The World of George Orwell,* edited by Miriam Gross, 19–30. New York: Simon and Schuster, 1973.

Bellow, Saul. *Mr. Sammler's Planet.* New York: Viking Press, 1970.

Bowker, Gordon. *Inside George* Orwell. New York: Palgrave Macmillan, 2003.

Buddicom, Jacintha. *Eric & Us* (including a Postscript by Dione Venables). Chichester, U.K.: Finlay, 2006.

Connolly, Cyril. *The Evening Colonnade.* London: David Bruce & Watson, 1973.

Coppard, Audrey, and Bernard Crick. *Orwell Remembered.* New York: Facts On File, 1984.

Crick, Bernard. *George Orwell: A Life* Boston: Little, Brown, 1980.

Davison, Peter. *George Orwell: A Literary Life.* New York: St. Martin's Press, 1996.

———. *The Lost Orwell.* London: Timewell Press, 2006.

———, ed. *The Complete Works of George Orwell.* 20 vols. London: Secker & Warburg, 1998.

Fowler, Roger. *The Language of George Orwell.* New York: St. Martin's Press, 1995.

Fyvel, T. R. *George Orwell: A Personal Memoir.* New York: Macmillan, 1982.

Garton Ash, Timothy. "Orwell in 1998." *New York Review of Books,* 22 October 1998.

Hitchens, Christopher. *Why Orwell Matters.* New York: Basic Books, 2002.

Hunter, Lynette. *George Orwell: the Search for a Voice.* Milton Keynes, England: Open University Press, 1984.

Koestler, Arthur. Orwell obituary in the *Observer,* reprinted in *George Orwell: The Critical Heritage,* edited by Jeffrey Meyers, 296–299. London: Routledge, 1975.

Larkin, Emma. *Finding George Orwell in Burma.* New York: Penguin Press, 2003.

Lodge, David. *The Modes of Modern Writing.* Ithaca, N.Y.: Cornell University Press, 1977.

Lucas, Scott. *Orwell: Life and Times.* London: Haus Publishing, 2003.

McCarthy, Mary. "The Writing on the Wall," *New York Review of Books,* 30 January 1969, 3–6.

Menand, Louis. "Honest, Decent, Wrong: The Invention of George Orwell." *New Yorker,* 16 January 2003, 84–91.

Meyers, Jeffrey. *Orwell: Wintry Conscience of a Generation.* New York: Norton, 2000.

———, ed. *George Orwell: The Critical Heritage.* London: Routledge, 1975.

———. *A Reader's Guide to George Orwell.* Englewood Cliffs, N.J.: Prentice-Hall, 1974.

Norris, Christopher. *Inside the Myth: Orwell, Views from the Left.* London: Lawrence and Wishart, 1984.

Orwell, Sonia, and Ian Angus. *The Collected Essays, Journalism and Letters of George Orwell.* 4 vols. London: Secker & Warburg, 1968.

Patai, Daphne. *The Orwell Mystique: A Study in Male Ideology.* Amherst, Mass.: 1984.

Porter, Laurence. "Psychomachia versus Socialism in *Nineteen Eighty-Four.* In *The Revised Orwell,* edited by Jonathan Rose. East Lansing: Michigan University Press, 1992.

Pritchett, V. S. "The *New Statesman & Nation*'s Obituary." In *Orwell Remembered,* edited by Audrey Coppard and Bernard Crick, 275–277, New York: Facts On File, 1984.

Rees, Sir Richard. *George Orwell: Fugitive from the Camp of Victory.* Carbondale: Southern Illinois University Press, 1961.

Rodden, John. *The Politics of Literary Reputation: The Making and Claiming of George Orwell.* New York and Oxford: Oxford University Press, 1989.

———. *Scenes from an Afterlife: The Legacy of George Orwell.* Wilmington, Del.: ISI Books, 1989.

Shaw, Tony. "Some Writers Are More Equal Than Others: George Orwell, the State and Cold War Privilege." *Cold War History* 4, no. 1 (October 2003): 143–170.

Shelden, Michael. *Orwell. The Authorized Biography.* New York: HarperCollins, 1991.

Spurling, Hillary. *The Girl from the Fiction Department.* London: Hamish Hamilton, 2002.

Stansky, Peter, and William Abrahams. *The Unknown Orwell.* New York: Knopf, 1972.

———. *Orwell: The Transformation.* New York: Knopf, 1979.

Steiner, George. "True to Life," *New Yorker,* 29 March 1969, 139–151.

PART II

Works A–Z

Animal Farm

Satiric fable, published in 1945, generally considered to be Orwell's finest work of fiction. *Animal Farm* transformed Orwell from a respected English journalist and minor novelist into an international best-selling author. It had appeared in 18 foreign translations prior to Orwell's death in 1950 and has since been published in languages as diverse as Afrikaans, Icelandic, Yiddish, and Persian. The success of *Animal Farm* can be attributed primarily to Orwell's masterly combination of lucid prose and trenchant political allegory. Comprising roughly 30,000 words, this tale of an animal revolution betrayed by the avarice and corruption of a small minority within the farm resembles imaginative and moralistic fiction in the tradition of Aesop's *Fables* and the tales of Beatrix Potter, which Orwell read as a child.

HISTORICAL CONTEXT

Orwell began writing *Animal Farm* in November 1943, right after the Teheran Conference, the first meeting of the Big Three, the British prime minister Winston Churchill, the American president Franklin Roosevelt, and Soviet premier Joseph Stalin, to discuss war strategy and postwar plans. Earlier in the war, Churchill and Roosevelt had formed a close relationship, but Teheran (Tehran) represented the first opportunity for the three allies to take the measure of one another. On the surface all was harmonious at the conference, with Stalin basking in the success of the Red Army, which at that point had pushed the Germans back to the border of East Prussia. With an air of genial magnanimity, he promised his two allies that the Soviet army would enter the war against Japan as soon as Germany was defeated. But in fact, simmering beneath the surface was a deep mutual distrust. As Orwell expressed in his preface to the Ukrainian edition, "I wrote it [*Animal Farm*] immediately after the Teheran Conference, which everybody thought had established the best possible relations between the USSR and the West. I personally did not think that such good relations would last long."

Meeting of "the big three" (Joseph Stalin, Franklin D. Roosevelt, and Winston Churchill), November 1943 *(Library of Congress)*

In fact, the "good relations" did not survive the Conference itself. The meeting corresponded consistently with the depiction of it in the final chapter of *Animal Farm.* First, the actual Teheran meetings took place on the grounds of the Soviet Embassy, and Roosevelt was persuaded for security reasons to stay at a villa within the Soviet grounds. Thus, the fact that the human beings are visitors to Animal Farm neatly parallels the arrangement at Teheran. At the meetings, Roosevelt took a more amenable attitude to Stalin's ideas than to those of his close ally, Churchill, which strained the relations between the two friends. The American president hoped he could win over the Russian by the charm of his own personality. Churchill and Stalin tangled directly over the date of D-day, the planned invasion of France, the British prime minister wanting to delay in favor of Allied action in the Mediterranean. Stalin may have seen Churchill's desire to open a new front as an attempt to limit Soviet influence in postwar Eastern Europe. (If he did, he was right.) On November 29, the second night of the conference, the Russians hosted an elaborate dinner party, punctuated, in high Russian style, by a large number of toasts. At one point, Stalin made a remark that Churchill found offensive, and the prime minister stalked out of the room. Stalin had to pursue him to assure him that he was only joking. In the words of the historian William McNeill, "This incident . . . was symptomatic of the state of feeling among the three men who were deciding the fate of a large part of the world . . . (360). As it happened, the next meetings of the Big Three, at Yalta in February 1945 and six months later at Potsdam, ensured Soviet domination of Eastern Europe for the next 45 years. Whether Orwell picked up the tension from gossip by members of the English negotiating party or simply intuited it, he was careful to include the quarrel between Pilkington and Napoleon as a significant, ominous development at the end of the novel.

Animal Farm was published in England on August 17, four months after Germany's surrender and 11 days after the bombing of Hiroshima. As Orwell anticipated, the compliments and flattery between the Russians and their Western allies would soon erupt into the struggle that became known as the cold war. (*The Oxford English Dictionary* credits Orwell with the first use of the term in 1945).

BIOGRAPHICAL CONTEXT

On his return from Spain in 1937, Orwell encountered a formidable wall of opposition to the message he was trying to bring home. Many highly intelligent people did not want to hear the news: that the war in Spain was not a simple case of heroic republicans versus evil fascists but an internal struggle within the republican ranks. When the communists took over the conduct of the war from the loyalists, it became an instrument of Soviet foreign policy. In the service of that goal, Moscow decreed the destruction of the POUM, the anarchic, anti-Stalinist group that had successfully defended Barcelona early in the war. Orwell wrote *Homage to Catalonia,* a book he rightly considered his best up to that time, in an attempt to expose the lies and treachery of the Soviet machine. Once it was published, the book was ignored, leaving Orwell astonished at "how easily totalitarian propaganda can control the opinion of enlightened people." Poor health and the demands of World War II delayed his next attack, now made even more complicated by the alliance of the Soviets as allies, and extraordinarily effective ones at that, in the desperate struggle with Hitler. It was not until 1943, when the tide of the war had turned and an Allied victory seemed inevitable, that he could leave his post at the BBC and begin his career at *Tribune,* which would leave him time to take another shot at his old enemy (Stalin), who was by this time everybody's great friend.

He began writing the book in November 1943, right after the conclusion of the Teheran Conference, the meeting of Churchill, Roosevelt and Stalin that ran from October 28 to November 1. Used to working alone, this time he had help, his wife Eileen. Each night he would read his latest pages of the book and she would respond with questions and suggestions. In his memoir, Orwell's friend, Tosco Fyvel speaks of her contribution:

> It has so often been remarked that unlike Orwell's other works, *Animal Farm* is a supremely well-written little satire. Its autumnal sadness is presented with the lightest touch, with not a word too many in a book not directly meant for children, but read by them avidly . . . And if *Animal Farm* is a tale so perfect in its light touch and restraint (almost 'unOrwellian'), I think some credit is due to the conversational influence of Eileen and the light touch of her bright, humorous intelligence (137–138).

The book was completed in February 1944. The preparation for the allied invasion of France was well under way, but the British and American forces were stalled in the Italian campaign. Only the Soviet army was having continued success against the Germans, increasing the British and American regard for the army and its tough leader, whom the Western forces had taken to calling Uncle Joe. It was an unpropitious time for a strong anti-Soviet satire. Orwell was not surprised when his own publisher, Victor Gollancz, turned it down. Gollancz, a fellow traveler with a history of cooperation with the British Communist Party, had previously rejected *Homage to Catalonia.* The next rejection came from Jonathan Cape, who returned the manuscript after being advised by someone at the Ministry of Information (MOI) that the book would harm British relations with the Soviet Union. The MOI official's identity remained a mystery until 1998, when PETER DAVISON, editor of the 20-volume *Complete Works of George Orwell,* revealed that the official was almost certainly Peter Smollett, a former editor at the *Times* (London) and head of the Russian section at the MOI. After his death in 1980, Smollett was identified by papers in the KGB archives as a longtime Soviet agent, recruited by Kim Philby in the 1930s. Orwell would later include Smollett's name on a list of crypto-communists or fellow travelers. (See ORWELL'S LIST).

Orwell then submitted it to Faber and Faber, specifically addressing it to the firm's famous editor, the poet T. S. ELIOT. Eliot praised the book as "a distinguished piece of writing" but then cited "the political situation at the present time." The archconservative Eliot, however, would presumably not have hesitated to publish a beautifully written attack on the Soviet Union simply because of the political situation. He went on to indicate his personal objection, that the "effect is simply one of negation," that is, the book offers no viable alternative between the oppression of Farmer Jones and that of Napoleon. Eliot's basic objection would be reproduced from different points of view by other critics (see LATER CRITICISM).

In the meantime, Orwell's agent, LEONARD MOORE, was having the same bad luck trying to find an American publisher. No fewer than 12 firms had rejected it. Finally, Orwell turned to Fredric Warburg, the publisher of *Homage to Catalonia* and *The Lion and the Unicorn.* One reading convinced Warburg that he had a masterpiece on his hands. On the other hand, it was a political hot potato, and for Warburg also a personal one—his wife half-seriously threatened to leave him if he published it (Warburg, 49). Nevertheless, he went ahead. Printing was delayed by the shortage of paper and the V1 and V2 rockets, one of which destroyed Warburg's home and another, his office. Finally, on August 17, 1945, the book was published in an edition of 4,500 copies. A year later, an American edition was published by Harcourt, Brace, and it was chosen as a selection of the Book of the Month Club. By 1949, this edition had sold 460,000 copies. The combined paperback and hardcover sales in England and America exceeded a million copies. Adding to this figure were the foreign translations of the book.

In his 2003 biography of Orwell, Gordon Bowker lists some of the possible sources of names in *Animal Farm*:

> Not far from St Cyprian's School was a village called Willingdon with a Red Lion pub and a stone quarry nearby, which he could hardly have avoided on his schoolboy rambles across the Sussex Downs. Callow End had its Manor Farm, its Farmer Jones and Mr. Pilkington, while Wallington had its Farmer John Innes and a Manor Farm, which reared pigs. All of these in their way must have furnished Orwell with the setting and landscape for his novel. . . . there are echoes, too, of H. G. Wells's *The Island of Dr Moreau* in which pig-men walk on their hind legs and where there are rules about walking on four legs (308–309).

PREFACES TO *ANIMAL FARM*

Orwell wrote two prefaces to *Animal Farm.* The first was designed for the original edition, and the second was directed to a special audience, Ukrainian refugees, who at the time were living in displaced-persons camps in Germany.

Preface to the Original Edition

Orwell wrote this preface for the first edition of the book, published by Secker & Warburg, in August 1945. He chose as a title for the preface "The Freedom of the Press." For some unknown reason the preface was not included in the first edition. In 1972, Ian Angus, coeditor of *The Collected Essays, Journalism and Letters of George Orwell* (1968) and assistant to the editor of *The Complete Works of George Orwell* (1998) found the original typescript.

Orwell begins the preface by explaining that this book was rejected by four publishers. One of these planned to accept it but decided to first consult the MOI, which advised that it not be published because it would give offense to our Russian allies. What is disturbing about this decision, Orwell suggests, is not the specter of government censorship but the cowardice of supposedly independent publishers. He suggests that even then, in 1945, the "prevailing orthodoxy is an uncritical admiration of the Soviet regime." This tendency to treat Stalin as sacrosanct and above reproach was not due simply to the fact that they were our allies at the moment. Uncritical adherence to the Marxist line, at least among members of the English liberal intelligentsia, extends back at least as far as the Spanish civil war.

He cites as a recent example of the British press's unquestioned acceptance of Russian propaganda their treatment of Colonel Mihailovich, the Yugoslavian anti-Nazi guerrilla leader. The British government and press went along with the unproven allegations that Mihailovich collaborated with the Germans, thus clearing the way for his rival, the communist Marshall Tito, to seize power in Yugoslavia.

He goes on to state that what is most disturbing about the censorship of criticism of the Soviet Union from the Left is that it is largely self-imposed. A large number of English intellectuals have felt that "to cast any doubt on the wisdom of Stalin was a kind of blasphemy." As for this book, he suggests, it will draw a predictable reaction from the Left, namely, that it should never have been published. The reason they will give is that such a book harms the progressive cause, and if they are true Marxists, they will argue that freedom of speech is, in any case, only a "bourgeois illusion." But they will have failed to realize that every time you suppress dissent, you take a step in the direction of totalitarianism. Here in England, he explains, incarcerating the English fascist Oswald Mosley was entirely justified in 1940 with an imminent German invasion on the horizon, but keeping him in jail, "without trial, in 1943 was an outrage," an example of anti-fascism moving in a fascist direction.

Orwell says that by the time this book is published, opinion may have shifted regarding the Soviets. But if that switch results in another orthodoxy, the problem will remain. The overall problem is the danger to the freedom of expression. "The enemy is the gramophone mind, whether or not one agrees with the record that is being played . . . If liberty means anything at all, it means the right to tell people what they don't want to hear."

Preface to the Ukrainian Edition:

In April 1946 Orwell received a letter from Ihor Szewczenko, a young Ukrainian scholar offering to translate *Animal Farm* into Ukrainian. At this time, Szewczenko was in northern Germany, working on a Polish newspaper for members of a Polish army division stationed there. He had also been reading his own translation of parts of *Animal Farm* to Ukrainian refugee audiences. Their response was so positive that he was asking permission to translate the entire book. Receiving approval from Orwell, he completed the translation. The publishers of the translation were a group of dissident Marxist Ukrainians, who had supported the original revolution but turned against the counterrevolutionary Bonapartism of Stalin. They inquired about the possibility of Orwell's writing a preface. He agreed and sent off the preface, which was then translated by Szewczenko.

Orwell begins this preface by introducing himself to an audience entirely unfamiliar with him and his background. He describes his education, his experiences as a police officer in Burma, in Paris and London with down-and-outers, with the miners in North England, and fighting against Franco in Spain. There he saw the Moscow-directed terror tactics of the Communist Party, hunting down anarchists and other dissidents. He became convinced in the ensuing years that the idea, popular in England, that the Soviet Union represented a true form of socialism is pernicious: It has done more damage to the possibility of forming a true socialism in England than any other single factor. "Ever since my departure from Spain, I had the idea of exposing the 'Soviet myth,' but the idea took shape when I saw a young boy in the country beating a cart horse. It struck me," he explains, "that if only such animals became aware of their strength we should have no power over them, and that men exploit animals in much the same way as the rich exploit the proletariat."

He says that he will not attempt to speak for the work: Either it speaks for itself or it is a failure. He wishes, however, to make two points. One is that, though the incidents in the story are based on Soviet history, the chronology at times has been violated in the interest of the "symmetry of the story." The second point is that, though some readers see the ending as one of reconciliation between the pigs and the humans, this is not the case: "I meant it to end on a loud note of discord." He never thought the seemingly good relations that appeared to exist after Teheran would last. As recent events have shown, Orwell says, "I wasn't far wrong."

SYNOPSIS

Chapter 1

As Mr. Jones, the owner of Manor Farm, who as usual has been drinking too much, reels into his farmhouse to go to bed, all the animals gather in the main barn to hear Old Major, a prize boar, highly respected by the others, recount a strange dream he has had the previous night. Included among those arriving are the dogs, Bluebell, Jessie, and Pincher; the two cart-horses, Boxer and Clover; Muriel, the white goat; and Benjamin, the sullen donkey. Arriving early so as to have room right in front of the podium where Old Major was "ensconced" are the pigs. Arriving late is Mollie, the white mare who draws Mr. Jones's carriage. Last one in is the cat, supremely self-involved, as usual. The only one who does not show up is Moses, the raven.

Old Major begins by announcing as a prelude to his dream that he feels he only has a short time to live, but before he dies, he wants to pass on what he has learned from his life. He has come to see that the "life of an animal is misery and slavery." And if you ask why this should be, the answer is obvious. It is man—man who exploits and enslaves them and, when they're old and no longer useful, slaughters them. It is clear that if they rid themselves of man, they will be happy and free, able to enjoy the fruits of their own labor. In order to achieve this end, they must work with all our strength toward one goal: rebellion. No one knows when this revolution will come, but they all must work for it and pass along this goal to their children. To achieve it, they must keep in mind that all animals—even the rats that they have been taught to hate—are their comrades. Their maxim must be: "Whatever goes upon two legs is an enemy, whatever goes on four legs, or has wings, is a friend . . . we are all brothers."

Then Major tells them of his dream, in which he recalled an old song his mother used to sing to him. The title of the song is "Beasts of England." Now he sings the song, which tells of a golden time in the future when "tyrant man shall be o'er thrown" and all animals shall be free. Gradually, all of the animals learn the song and sing it over and over, until the noise awakens Mr. Jones and he fires his shotgun in the direction of the barn, at which point the animals disperse.

Chapter 2

Three nights later, Old Major dies in his sleep. In the months that follow, the work of organizing and educating the animals falls to the pigs, who are considered the most intelligent creatures. Three of them in particular become prominent: Napoleon, Snowball, and Squealer. From some of the Major's insights, they fashion a whole system of thought they call animalism. In regular meetings at night, the three pigs instruct the others in the new doctrine. Some of the animals are skeptical, raising questions about the revolution. One source of resistance is Moses the raven, who preaches the doctrine that the reward for this life will come in the next, on Sugarcandy Mountain, where all obedient animals go after they die. Another animal wary of the revolution is Mollie, the pretty white mare who draws Mr. Jones's trap. Mollie wants to know if after the revolution she will be able to wear ribbons in her hair as she does now, and Snowball explains that her ribbons "are the badge of slavery." Her freedom is a much greater good than pretty ribbons. The two most ardent followers of animalism are the two cart-horses, Boxer and Clover, who trust everything the pigs tell them and always lead in the singing of "Beasts of England."

Meanwhile, the farm itself deteriorates as Mr. Jones becomes more addicted to alcohol and increasingly fails to maintain order and discipline among the men who work for him. On midsummer's eve, he goes into town, gets drunk, and does not return until the next day, at which time he falls asleep without feeding the animals, who have had nothing to eat for two days. As a result they break into the food shed and feed themselves. At this point, Mr. Jones wakes up and he and four of his men arm themselves with whips to beat the animals. But instead of retreating, the animals attack the men and drive them and Mrs. Jones off the farm. Moses, her pet, flees with her. Stunned by their easy victory, the animals check the farm's boundaries as a security measure, then break into the harness room and promptly dump the whips, harnesses, and butchering knives down the well or burn them. Finally, they all eat a double portion of corn and sing "Beasts of England" seven times before settling down for the night.

First thing the next morning, they survey the property, still finding it difficult to believe it is theirs. As they approach the farmhouse, they hesitate out of fear, but Napoleon and Snowball go to the front door and butt it open. They tentatively enter the house to explore it. At one point they find Mollie primping before a mirror, holding one of Mrs. Jones's ribbons against her shoulder, and they reprimand her sharply. They all agree that the farmhouse is to be regarded as a museum and that no animal should ever live there. Now the pigs declare that they have taught themselves to read and write using an old children's spelling textbook once used by the Jones children. Then they all go down to the main gate, where Snowball paints over the Manor Farm sign and replaces it with the words *Animal Farm.* On returning to the barn, Snowball paints on the wall of the big barn the seven commandments, or the principles on which "All the animals must live forever after." Then the pigs proceed to teach themselves how to milk the cows, and when they finish, the other animals look forward to sharing the milk. But Napoleon steps forward to urge everyone to go to the hayfield and begin the harvest. When they finish the day's work and return, some of the animals notice that the milk is gone.

Chapter 3

The hay harvest is a great success, despite the animals' inability to use the farm equipment designed for human beings. Under the pigs' supervision, the animals work very hard, but no one works harder than Boxer, who wakes up a half hour earlier than everyone else and does the work of three horses. Whenever a problem arises, he has a simple solution: "I will work harder."

Sunday is a day of rest. It begins with a flag-raising ceremony, the flag being an old green tablecloth on which Snowball had painted a hoof and horn. Afterward, there is a general meeting to discuss new resolutions—only the pigs offered resolutions—and to plan the coming week's work. It is noticed that in the debates on resolutions, Napoleon and Snowball never seem to agree. The pigs appropriate the harness room for themselves, where they learn trades like carpentry and blacksmithing. Snowball sets up a variety of committees for the animals, the most successful of which are classes in literacy. In a few months, almost all of the animals have learned to read and write to some degree. Some of the animals, however, are incapable of reading the seven commandments, so Snowball decides to boil them down to one, which he paints on the wall above the original seven: *Four legs good, two legs bad.*

Napoleon, on the other hand, is more interested in the education of the young. When Jessie and Bluebell have puppies, he takes them away from their mothers and secludes them in order to take charge of their education. It turns out that the milk and the apples now falling from the trees are to be reserved solely for the pigs. The other animals mutter when they hear this, but Squealer explains this development, pointing out that it is a scientific fact that milk and apples contain nutrients essential to the health of pigs. Since the whole management of the farm depends upon the pigs, it is their duty to have milk and apples, to guard against the return of Mr. Jones. The specter of the return of Mr. Jones silences the criticism.

Chapter 4

News of the animal rebellion spreads through half the county, as pigeons dispatched by Napoleon and Snowball recount the story and teach other animals the tune and lyrics of "Beasts of England." Mr. Jones, meanwhile, sulks and sops at the local inn, bewailing his fate. His neighboring farmers, Mr. Pilkington and Mr. Frederick, commiserate with him while privately thinking how they might use these events to their own advantage. They are, however, disturbed by this development and spread lies about the farm suggesting all sorts of diabolical and immoral behavior. Nevertheless, the example of Animal Farm begins to influence the animals on other farms. A spirit of rebelliousness on the part of animals everywhere begins to look like a serious threat to the status quo. As a result, Mr. Jones leads a gang of men to the farm in an effort to recapture it. Snowball, who has anticipated the attack by studying Julius Caesar's campaigns in an old book at the farm, concocts a strategy. As the men enter the farm, a group of geese in hiding spring at them, biting their legs, but the men drive them off. Then Snowball leads Muriel, Benjamin, and all the sheep in a second attack. As the men begin to rally, Snowball gives the signal to retreat. As the animals flee, the men rush after them inside the yard. There they are ambushed from the rear while Snowball leads a frontal attack, aiming directly at Mr. Jones, who fires at him, inflicting a flesh wound but not enough to prevent Snowball from smashing him into a dung heap. At the same time, Boxer terrifies the men as he rises up on his hind legs, using his iron horseshoes as a weapon. With one blow, he strikes a stable boy, leaving him apparently dead. The terrified men panic and beat a disorderly retreat. Amid the celebration only Boxer appears depressed over the fact that he has apparently killed someone. Rebuked by Snowball for his "sentimentality," he responds, "I have no wish to take life, not even human life." To commemorate the victory, which the animals decide to call the Battle of the Cowshed, they agree to fire off Mr. Jones's abandoned gun twice a year: once on the anniversary of the Battle of the Cowshed, and once on the anniversary of the rebellion.

Chapter 5

The farm suffers one defection when Mollie disappears and is later seen in town pulling a dog cart and wearing a scarlet ribbon around her forelock.

Another disturbing element is the continuing hostility between Snowball and Napoleon, who seem incapable of agreeing on anything. The friction comes to a head over the windmill. Snowball wishes to build a windmill on a small hill. He acknowledges that it would be a very difficult task, but when completed, it would be a tremendous labor-saving device, so that animals would only have to work a three-day week. Napoleon argues that food production should be the first priority. When the issue comes up for a vote, Snowball is so eloquent that it is obvious he will win. At that moment, Napoleon stands up and emits a weird sound, whereupon nine large, vicious dogs come bounding into the room, heading straight for Snowball. Running for his life, Snowball just barely escapes and then disappears. Surrounded by these strange, menacing dogs, Napoleon ascends the platform and announces a new order: There will be no more Sunday-morning debates. In the future, decisions will be made by a committee of pigs meeting in private.

Squealer later explains to the animals that Napoleon has taken the great burden of leadership on his shoulders in order to prevent the return of Mr. Jones. Left on their own, the animals might have opted for Snowball's moonshine idea of a windmill. Convinced by Squealer's appeal, Boxer expresses the general feeling that Napoleon is always right.

Three weeks later, Napoleon declares that the windmill will be built after all. As Squealer later explains, Napoleon had never really been opposed to the windmill. In fact, it was his idea and had been stolen by Snowball. His apparent opposition was merely a tactic designed to get rid of Snowball. Squealer then repeats a number of times this new word, *tactic.*

Chapter 6

The windmill project proves to be enormously difficult. The animals work a 60-hour week, including Sunday afternoons. The raw material for the building is on the property, but transporting the limestone from the quarry proves to be an almost insuperable obstacle. Only the heroic efforts of Boxer make it possible. Moreover, it is becoming clear that the farm can no longer be self-sufficient. Napoleon issues a new order stating that they will begin trading with other farms. Among the items to be traded will be eggs, a sacrifice on the hens' part that they should view as their contribution to the windmill. So that none of the animals should have to deal with a human, Napoleon himself will operate through Mr. Whymper, to act as a go-between for the farm.

About this time, the pigs move into the farmhouse, a necessity, according to Squealer, because the pigs needed a quiet place to work. When it also turns out that the pigs are sleeping in beds, some of the animals remember the fourth commandment, which forbids this practice, but when they consult the original writing on the wall they are surprised to find that it reads, "No animal shall sleep in a bed *with sheets*." The farm is visited by a wild storm, which results in a major disaster. The windmill, over which the animals have slaved, comes crashing down. Surveying the ruins, Napoleon declares that the cause of the disaster is Snowball. He orders that the rebuilding begin immediately, this time with thicker walls, adding some credence to the human rumor that the windmill collapsed because of structural flaws.

Chapter 7

The task of rebuilding the windmill is made even more difficult by the brutal winter weather and a food shortage. Facing starvation, the animals are told to pretend that food is plentiful whenever Mr. Whymper visits there. Squealer announces that the hens may have to surrender their eggs, to be traded for grain and meal. The hens retaliate by flying up to the barn rafters. Napoleon orders their food supply cut. After five days, during which nine hens die of starvation, the others surrender and return to their nests.

Meanwhile, any problem on the farm is attributed to Snowball, who is said to be sneaking into the farm each night to cause trouble. Squealer introduces a revisionist account of the Battle of the Cowshed, in which Snowball's tactical retreat is said to be really an attempt to surrender, in accord with a plan he had secretly concocted with Mr. Jones. As Squealer renders it, the plan would have succeeded had Napoleon not intervened, turning the retreat into a glorious victory. When Boxer expresses skepticism at this version of the battle, Squealer gives him a steely-eyed glare and replies that this is Napoleon's view of these events. Then Boxer concludes, "If Comrade Napoleon says it, it must be right."

A few days later, Napoleon orders everyone to assemble in the yard. On a signal from him, his dogs seize four pigs from the assembly, dragging them before Napoleon. The pigs confess that they have been conspiring with Snowball, whereupon the dogs pounce on them and tear their throats out. Then the three who had led the hens' strike confess that they had acted after having a dream in which Snowball appeared. These are followed by a goose and three sheep all of them are executed after their confessions. Soon the space in front of Napoleon is taken up by a pile of dead animals.

Clearly disturbed by what they have witnessed, the animals leave the yard. Boxer has only one clear response to this slaughter, a determination "to work harder." Some animals cluster around Clover, looking for an explanation. She thinks to herself that something has gone wrong but can't say what it is. Instead she begins to sing "Beasts of England" and the song is taken up by the group around her. When they had sung it three times, they are approached by Squealer with a new directive: it is now forbidden to sing "Beasts of England." The reason is that "Beasts of England" is a song of rebellion and the rebellion is over; the just society has been achieved. The poet Minimus writes another song, "Animal Farm," and it is sung every Sunday, but somehow it never catches on.

Chapter 8

After the slaying of the confessed traitors, some animals wonder about the apparent violation of the sixth commandment, "No animals shall kill any other animal," but when they consult the wall, they realize that they had forgotten the last two words of the commandment: *without cause*. Napoleon becomes a more remote figure, assuming a sort of mythic status among the animals. All directives and communications are delivered by Squealer or one of the pigs on the executive council. The animals hear disturbing stories about their neighbor Frederick's treatment of the animals in Pinchfield. Not only that, but evidence seems to be building up, suggesting that Frederick is planning to invade Animal Farm. Finally the windmill is completed. The exhausted animals view the finished structure with justifiable pride. Shortly after, Napoleon makes a surprising announcement: He has sold the lumber not, as expected, to Pilkington but to Frederick. He had cunningly appeared to favor Pilkington in order to drive up the price to Frederick. Furthermore, when Frederick promised to pay by check, Napoleon insisted on cash. Napoleon proudly displays the cash for all the animals to see; the money, he says, will be used to buy machinery for the windmill. Three days later comes the shocking revelation: Frederick's banknotes are counterfeit. Furthermore, it is highly likely that Frederick will soon launch an attack on the farm.

The next day, the attack begins. Frederick's men are heavily armed and very soon drive the animals back into the farm buildings. Frederick's men control the rest of the farm, including the windmill, which they proceed to dynamite into smithereens. The destruction of their pride and joy infuriates the animals, and they launch a fierce counterattack. Despite the heavy casualties, they charge the enemy, overwhelming them and forcing them into a desperate retreat. Although the animals now find themselves back at square one, they celebrate what comes to be called the Battle of the Windmill as a great day.

A few days later, the pigs come upon a case of whiskey that had been hidden in the cellar of the farmhouse. Shortly after, Muriel discovers another commandment slightly different from the one she remembered. Instead of asserting "No animals shall drink alcohol," it reads "No animals should drink alcohol to excess."

Chapter 9

Although Boxer is still in pain from the wounds he received in the Battle of the Windmill, he continues to work as hard as ever in the construction of the new windmill. Once winter sets in, rations are reduced, but somehow the pigs seem to be getting fatter. A new rule called spontaneous demonstration is propaganda. Once a week, work stops in order to celebrate the achievements of Animal Farm in general and Napoleon in particular, all of which succeeds in taking the animal's minds off the hunger they constantly feel. Suddenly, Moses the raven reappears, after an absence of many years. He continues to talk of Sugarcandy Mountain, an idea that reassures many of the animals.

Meanwhile, Boxer is approaching his 12th birthday, with its promise of retirement on a decent pension. His indomitable will "to work harder" is beginning to be undermined by his body. A month short of retirement, he overdoes his efforts and collapses. Squealer announces that Napoleon has arranged to have him transferred to a hospital in town, where he will be treated by a veterinarian. When a van arrives to take Boxer away, the animals gather around to wish him good-bye. Then Benjamin furiously reads the words written on the side of the van: *Alfred Simmons' Horse Slaughterer and Glue Boiler*. The others desperately try to urge Boxer to escape. He tries kicking down the doors of the van, an easy task for a young Boxer, but he is too feeble to succeed. A few days later, Squealer announces the death of Boxer in the hospital. He mentions the "foolish and wicked rumor" that Boxer had been sent to the horse slaughterer. In truth, the veterinary surgeon had bought the van but hadn't gotten around to changing the sign. Squealer described his vigil at Boxer's deathbed, quoting his last words, "Long live Comrade Napoleon. Napoleon is always right." On Sunday, Napoleon delivers a eulogy, praising Boxer, and then announces that the pigs intend to hold a memorial banquet in Boxer's honor. Shortly after, a grocer's van delivers a wooden case to the farm. That night the animals hear loud singing and noisy shouting from the house. Apparently, the pigs had acquired enough money to buy a case of whiskey.

Chapter 10

Time slips by; the original rebellion fades into the dim past, recalled by the few remaining old animals, Clover, Benjamin, and Moses. Many others, including Muriel, Bluebell, and Jessie have died, as has Mr. Jones. The farm has become a thriving, expanding enterprise. The completed windmill generates not electricity but "a handsome money profit" in its role as a corn-grinding mill. For the animals, life is pretty much unchanged. They work as hard as ever, for they must support and feed a growing number of pigs, whose work consists in writing things called reports and minutes, all very complicated and beyond the other animals' ability to understand. But they still take pride in their unique status, the only farm in all of England owned and operated by animals. Nor do they ever abandon their belief in the basic principle of the farm that all animals are equal.

Squealer, who has grown very fat over the years but is still an important presence on the farm, separates the sheep in order to teach them a new song. A few days later, the animals hear Clover neighing loudly in the yard. Rushing over to find out why, they see Squealer, followed by a line of pigs, and finally Napoleon himself, all walking on their hind legs. The stunned audience now hears the sheep singing the lyrics of the new song they've learned: "Four legs good, two legs better." Standing at the wall of the main barn, Clover, whose eyes are failing, asks Benjamin to read the commandments, as they appear to be different. Benjamin reads what is now the one and only commandment on the wall:

> ALL ANIMALS ARE EQUAL
> BUT SOME ANIMALS ARE MORE EQUAL
> THAN OTHERS.

A week later, a group of farmers in the neighborhood pay a visit to the farm. They tour the grounds, full of praise for what they see, particularly the windmill. That evening the animals hear the noises of laughter and singing from the farmhouse. Creeping quietly to the window, they peek in at the visitors and the pigs, playing cards and raising toasts. Mr. Pilkington prefaces his toast by stressing the strong similarities between the problems that both farms have: "If you have your lower animals to contend with, we have our lower classes." Then Napoleon rises to announce some new features in the farm, including changing back to its original name, the Manor Farm. Then the pigs and men pick up their cards and carry on with the game, as the animals creep away from the windows. They go a short distance, and then they hear angry cries and threats. It seems "that Napoleon and Mr. Pilkington had each played an ace of spades simultaneously." But from the animal's viewpoint outside, the really strange thing is that it is impossible to distinguish "from pig to man and from man to pig."

HISTORICAL ALLEGORY

For Orwell, the most important of the levels of meaning on which *Animal Farm* might be read was as a satiric allegory on the origins and aftermath of the Russian Revolution and on the history of the Soviet Union from 1917 to 1943. As the collapse of the Soviet system in 1989 recedes into history, this allegorical dimension of the story may appear to be less compelling, offering merely historical interest. People born after, say, 1984, might well be expected to view the Soviet Union with the same lack of interest that their parents view the decline of the Hapsburg Empire. But it is important, and for these readers especially, to be aware that *Animal Farm* not only satirically documented the development of the Soviet system under Joseph Stalin but played a role in its subsequent dissolution. (See section on political influence, below.)

One feature of Orwell's employment of allegory is its flexibility in any specific instance. The references to historical events are not all set in stone. Thus, the connection of Moses the raven to the monk Rasputin is less literally accurate than it is designed to point to the close association of the Orthodox church and the old aristocracy. Similarly, the name Armand Hammer (1898–1990) is included as a specific example of a businessman who dealt with the Soviet Union throughout its long existence and his longer life. Orwell may not have known of him, but Hammer provides a striking example of the go-between type represented by Mr. Whymper.

Correspondences between Soviet Union History and Animal Farm

In the following historical sketch, the corresponding event or figure in *Animal Farm* is given within brackets.

Communist ideology was developed in the late 19th century by KARL MARX and Friedrich Engels (1820–1895). It foretold the future triumph of the industrial working class over bourgeois capitalism by means of revolution. The ultimate result would be a classless society in which the working class (the proletariat) would be in control *[Old Major's speech]*.

In Russia, these ideas were developed at the turn of the century by the left wing of the Russian Social Democratic party, known as the Bolsheviks *[Napoleon, Snowball's principles of animalism]*. In 1905, as a result of popular discontent with the czarist government, a crowd of peaceful workers trying to deliver a petition to the czar was fired upon by government troops. This Bloody Sunday event triggered a series of demonstrations throughout the empire, which were eventually suppressed by the government *[Singing "Beasts of England," Jones's firing shots at the barn]*.

Twelve years later, as a result of heavy losses by Russian armies in World War I, and the mishandling of domestic affairs by the czarina and her too-close advisor, Rasputin, workers in St. Petersburg staged a strike in which they were joined by members of the army and navy, forcing the abdication of the czar *[Flight of Jones, Mrs. Jones and Moses]*. This movement is known as the February Revolution, but the provisional governments that followed it were unable to achieve stability. A second phase of the rebellion, the October Revolution, led by the ruthless and skillful Vladimir Lenin and his associate, Leon Trotsky, vaulted the Bolsheviks into power. Lenin quickly established the *Cheka* (secret police) to secure the new government's power through terror tactics. [*Napoleon's dogs*].

A year later, a counterrevolution was launched against the Bolsheviks on a variety of fronts. Included among the counterrevolutionary forces were elements from the lately victorious allied armies of World War I, the English, the French, and the Americans. Nevertheless, the Bolsheviks prevailed, thanks to widespread peasant support and the military leadership of Trotsky *[Battle of the Cowshed]*. Trouble from within surfaced when sailors at the Kronstadt barracks rebelled *[hens' revolt]*, but the uprising was ruthlessly crushed.

In 1922, Russia was formally renamed the Union of Soviet Socialist Republics (USSR) *[Manor Farm becomes Animal Farm]*. Two years later, Lenin died and the leadership passed not to Trotsky, the heir apparent, but to JOSEPH STALIN, the general secretary of the Communist Party. Stalin and Trotsky clashed over the direction and the future of the Soviet Union, Trotsky argued for emphasis on industrialization at home and the active spread of communism abroad (the Permanent Revolution), and Stalin insisted on a priority of strengthening domestic control (socialism in one nation) and emphasis on agricultural production *[Snowball's promotion of the windmill versus Napoleon's emphasis on the farm]*.

Behind the scenes, Stalin maneuvered the expulsion of Trotsky from the communist party, forcing him into exile in 1929 *[Dogs force Snowball to run away]*. Meanwhile, Stalin instituted his first Five-Year Plan (1928–33), reversing himself while endorsing without acknowledgement Trotsky's emphasis on industrialization, with particular attention to the city named after him, Stalingrad. At the same time, he ruthlessly imposed the collectivization of privately held farms, triggering a nationwide famine and resulting in the deaths of millions of Soviet citizens *[Five-Year Plan]*.

Stalin's ongoing attempt to secure control, as well as his increasing paranoia, set in motion a series of show trials of leading communist figures accused of treason, specifically of conspiring with the exiled Trotsky to overthrow the Stalin regime. The terror soon spread, cancerlike, to include the general staff of the army, intellectuals, writers, and artists *[Pile of corpses before Napoleon]*.

In 1939, Stalin concluded a nonaggression pact with his most formidable enemy, Adolf Hitler [*Frederick*], thereby producing mass defections from communist parties in the West. Accompanying this pact was the Russian German Commercial Agreement, which provided for the shipment of raw material to Germany in exchange for industrial machinery *[sale of timber]*. The Germans did not fulfill their part of the bargain (*Frederick's counterfeit money*). Two years later, Hitler violated the pact by invading the Soviets, which proved to be a critical mistake on his part. After some initial success (*blowing up the windmill*), the German forces were halted and finally defeated at the battle of Stalingrad, one of the turning points of World War II *[Battle of the Windmill]*.

In November 1943, the Big Three (Churchill, Roosevelt, and Stalin) met in Teheran, during which the surface camaraderie disguised a deep distrust and acts of mutual chicanery. The last night of the conference, in the midst of some heavy drinking on everyone's part, Churchill took offense at a remark made by Stalin. Churchill stormed out of the room and returned only after Stalin pursued him and apologized (*Human visitors come to Animal Farm and quarrel over card game*).

Orwell's most notable departure from the historical record is the absence of a figure comparable to that of VLADIMIR LENIN, the leading figure of the revolution and the early years of the USSR. A key contribution of Lenin's to the development of communism was the conviction that the revolution could not succeed if it depended upon the rank and file of the proletariat. Lenin believed that the proletariat must be led by an intellectually elite corps of party members who would direct and secure the revolution. Thus, the assumption of power by the members of the party had to be specifically attributed to Lenin. In chapter 2, the revelation that the pigs have been learning to read prior to the overthrow of Jones suggests that Lenin's ideas play a powerful role in the story, even if he does not.

Chart of Chief Allegorical Elements in Animal Farm

Chapter 1	
Manor Farm	Imperial Russia
Human beings	Capitalists
Animals	Working class
Pigs	Elite Communist Party members
Mr. Jones	Czar Nicholas II (1868–1918)
Mrs. Jones and Moses	Czarina Alexandra (1872–1918) and the monk Rasputin (1869–1916)
Old Major	Karl Marx (1818–1883)
Old Major's speech	Publication of *The Communist Manifesto* (1848) and *Capital* (1867)
"Beasts of England" song	"L'Internationale"
Singing of the animals, put down by Mr. Jones	Russian Revolution of 1905 and Bloody Sunday repression.
Chapter 2	
Napoleon	Joseph Stalin
Snowball	Leon Trotsky
Squealer	Soviet propaganda, *Pravda*
Principles of "Animalism"	Formation of Bolshevik party
Jones's lawsuits	Russian involvement in World War I
Farmhouse uprising over hunger	Revolution of 1917
Ejection of Mr. Jones	Overthrow of Czar Nicholas II
Seven Commandments	Lenin's Ten Bolshevik Commandments
Animals enter the farmhouse	Capture of the Winter Palace (1917)
Chapter 3	
Animal flag: horn and hoof	Soviet flag: hammer and sickle
Chapter 4	
Pigeons spreading the word of rebellion	Soviet propaganda
Foreign enemies: Mr. Pilkington (Foxwood) and Frederick (Pinchfield)	English prime minister Winston Churchill (who opposed the revolution) and German emperor (later Adolf Hitler)
Popularity of "Beasts of England"	Strong appeal of "L'Internationale"
Increased rebelliousness among other farms	social unrest of working classes in post World War I in Western Europe
"Battle of the Cowshed"	Russian Civil War (1918–1921)
Snowball's successful military tactics	Trotsky's leadership of the Red Army during the Civil War
Chapter 5	
Mollie's defection	Russian émigrés to the West
Disagreement between Napoleon and Snowball	Expulsion of Leon Trotsky at the 15th Congress of the Communist Party of the Soviet Union
Veneration of Skull of Old Major	Processions at Lenin's tomb
Minimus the poet	Vladimir Mayakovsky (1893–1930), a Russian poet who celebrated the revolution and the leadership of Lenin; grew disenchanted with the Stalin regime and committed suicide in 1930

Chapter 6	
Mr. Whymper	Type represented by Armand Hammer (1898–1990), an American businessman of Russian descent who brokered business deals for both Lenin and Stalin starting in the early 1920s
Pigs move into the farmhouse	Privileges of elite party members
The destruction of the windmill by gale	Failure of Five-Year Plan
Blaming Snowball	Vilification of Trotsky in Soviet propaganda
Chapter 7	
Rebuilding the windmill	Second Five-Year Plan (1933–1938)
Food shortages	Great Famine of 1932–1933
Disguising the truth of famine to the outside world	False reporting of people like Walter Duranty (1884–1957) in the *New York Times*
Hens' revolt	Kronstadt rebellion
Rumors regarding Squealer's revisionist history of the Battle of Cowshed	Changes in official Soviet accounts of the Bolshevik revolution
Attack of dogs on four pigs and subsequent pile of corpses	Murder of Sergei Kirov (1886–1934) Great Purge trials of Nikolai Bukharin (1888–1938), Lev Kamenev (1883–1936), Grigori Zinoviev (1883–1936)
"Beasts of England" forbidden	Downplaying of "L'Internationale"
Chapter 8	
Sale of lumber to Frederick	German-Soviet Commercial Agreement, USSR agrees to ship raw materials to Germany in exchange for a line of credit to purchase industrial material (part of the Hitler-Stalin pact [1939])
Frederick's attack	German invasion in June 1941
Destruction of the windmill	Initial German success
Battle of the Windmill	Battle of Stalingrad (1942–1943)
Chapter 9	
Pigs' green ribbons	Privileges of party members
Brewing beer	Alcohol consumption of Stalin
Increase in demonstrations, weekly spontaneous demonstration	May Day parade, *et al*
Reappearance of Moses	Reopening of the Orthodox churches
Boxer's fate	Treatment of Stalingrad veterans
Chapter 10	
Two fields bought from Mr. Pilkington	Acquisition of Finland
Increased number of pigs and dogs	Growth of bureaucracy and Secret Police
Visitation from neighboring farmers	Teheran conference of 1943 held on Russian Embassy grounds
Quarrel at card game	Stalin and Churchill attempt to outmaneuver each other at Teheran

COMMENTARY

Despite the intense specificity of references to the history of the Soviet Union, historical allegory is only one level of meaning that emerges in reading *Animal Farm.* Like many, if not all, works of art, *Animal Farm* has taken on additional meanings as different readers living in different times react to it. For example, embedded in the specific historical allegory is the wider political theme, of which Orwell was acutely aware, of the nature of power, particularly dictatorial power, and the employment of terror and propaganda as tools in acquiring and supporting that power. In this respect, *Animal Farm* may be and often is seen as a prelude to *Nineteen Eighty-Four.*

Another level of meaning closely tied to Orwell's thinking is the representation of revolution. In *Animal Farm,* the revolution transforms the animals' view of their own labor. No longer are they alienated from their labor, because now, so they believe, the fruits of that labor belong to them rather than to Mr. Jones. Their entire approach to work has changed, as Old Major predicted. The farm, however, had to be managed. The subsequent battle to preserve the farm from Mr. Jones's counterattack required leadership, and this role fell to the pigs. Therein lie the seeds of corruption: A new superior class is born and one superior figure in that class assumes total control. One question emerges and engages readers: Is Orwell depicting an inevitable process, one that is inherent in the nature of revolution, or is he warning that revolution can be and often has been betrayed?

Still another level of meaning that has become more prominent as the years pass is the animal-rights theme. Orwell himself suggested this possibility when, in the preface to the Ukranian edition, he declared that the inspiration for the book occurred when he saw a young farm lad whipping a horse:

> It struck me that if only such animals became aware of their strength we should have no power over them, and that men exploit animals in much the same way as the rich exploit the proletariat (CW, 19, 88).

Although he had no compunctions about hunting them, Orwell loved animals, with the exception of pigs and rats, two species that play prominent roles in *Animal Farm* and *Nineteen Eighty-Four.* It is unlikely that he would have become an animal rights activist, but he clearly is capable of imagining a powerful case against cruelty to animals.

Finally, there is the literal level of meaning reflected in Orwell's subtitle: *A Fairy Story.* In this respect, as a literal fairy story, *Animal Farm* is well on its way to becoming a children's classic. Here, Orwell may have succeeded in matching, in Cyril Connolly's words, "his master Swift." *Gulliver's Travels* is one of a handful of literary works that coexist as children's literature and as canonical, serious literature, destined to be read in childhood, studied in high school or college, and viewed by all ages in animated-film adaptations, as it straddles the world of popular and high culture.

This mutileveled character of *Animal Farm* is reflected in the variety of terms used to categorize it. It has been variously described by four literary terms: fairy story, beast fable, satire, and allegory. Frequently, all four of them have been employed in a manner suggesting that the four terms are interchangeable, but the fact is that the terms indicate fairly clear and distinct categories.

Fairy story is the first to consider, as it is the term Orwell himself used as the subtitle of the book. J. R. R. Tolkien, whose books *The Hobbit* (1937) and *The Lord of the Rings* (1954–1956) expanded fairy stories to epic proportions, delineates a four-part structure to the fairy tale: fantasy, escape, recovery, and consolation: ". . . fantasy—freedom from the observed fact; escape—or, not an escape from the real world but a breakthrough into another reality; recovery—the return to ordinary life with a renewed spirit; and consolation, the happy ending . . ." (Tolkien, 158) *Animal Farm* exhibits the first two features, while the third—the return to ordinary life—occurs but not in the positive sense implied by Tolkien; in the fourth, the promise of salvation is noticeably absent.

Similarly, the beast fable, the story in which the behavior of animal characters conveys a moral lesson, comes close to describing *Animal Farm* except that the moral lesson is muted in favor of the element of satire, which aims to ridicule its subject, exposing the vice or folly it exhibits, but not delivering an explicit moral. The emphasis on vice or folly determines the type of satire, dark or light, deadly serious or relatively tolerant. Orwell's is clearly of the former type, although its tone is frequently playful. The other element is allegory, one form of which features a surface story to allude to a historical event or to persons. As we have seen, *Animal Farm* most famously allegorizes the history of the Soviet Union, from the revolution of 1917 to the Teheran Conference of 1943.

Clearly, the story integrates and occasionally overlaps these forms in forging its distinctive character. If a modern-day Polonius were available, he might describe it a satirical-allegorical-fairy story, cast in the form of a beast fable. As for the efficacy of this form, the critic Matthew Hodgart has described it well:

> He chose a very ancient *genre,* based on the animal story found in the folk-tales of all primitive and peasant cultures, and reflecting a familiarity and sympathy with animals which Orwell seems to have shared. The central figure is often the trickster, spider in Africa, fox in Europe and pig in Orwell . . . he used the animal-story tradition with great confidence and deftness, and since he wanted to reach the widest possible world public, through translation, he also parodied the style of children's books; but not patronizingly, since Orwell, I think, liked children as much as he liked animals. Although the betrayal of the revolution is a 'sad story' it is told with the straightness that children demand, and with childlike cunning and charm. (138)

However, Orwell himself described the main focus of the book in a letter to his agent Leonard Moore in 1946:

> If they question you again, please say that *Animal Farm* is intended as a satire on dictatorship in general but *of course* the Russian Revolution is the chief target. It is humbug to pretend anything else.

Although in its form and style, *Animal Farm* appears to represent a complete departure from Orwell's early fiction, it adheres to the same thematic arc as *Burmese Days, A Clergyman's Daughter, Keep the Aspidistra Flying,* and *Coming Up for Air.* Like these, it recounts a temporarily successful but ultimately failed attempt to achieve a goal that seems to offer release from a society whose restrictions and limitations poison the possibility of freedom. In *Burmese Days,* the protagonist looks to marriage as the way of ending his loneliness and his resultant dependence on the deadening society of the local European club. In *A Clergyman's Daughter,* young Dorothy Hare searches in vain for an alternative to fill the emotional void left by her loss of religious belief. *Keep the Aspidistra Flying* recounts the jejune crusade of a young poet determined to defy the money god, who rules over modern civilization. George Bowling, the antihero of *Coming Up for Air,* tries to go home again to his Edwardian childhood, only to discover that the past is another country, and one for which he has no passport.

With the exception of Dorothy Hare, the clergyman's daughter, all are propelled by an illusion (with Dorothy, Orwell might say, the loss of an illusion) that they hope will regenerate and liberate their lives. All come to recognize the illusion but from different perspectives: in *Burmese Days,* tragically; in *A Clergyman's Daughter,* stoically; in *Keep the Aspidistra Flying* and *Coming Up for Air,* with comic defiance, in the manner of Parolles, the comic villain in Shakespeare's *All's Well That Ends Well,* who, once unmasked, asserts, "Captain I'll be no more, but simply the thing I am shall make me live."

Animal Farm departs from this scheme slightly in creating, not an individual, but a collective protagonist: the animals at Manor Farm. The action also differs in that the animals seem to secure their goal early on. By the end of the second chapter, their revolt has succeeded, leaving them in the first flush of enthusiasm:

> The animals were happy as they had never conceived it possible to be. Every mouthful of food was an acute positive pleasure, now that it was truly their own food, produced by themselves and for themselves, not doled out to them by a grudging master.

But like Orwell's individual protagonists, the animals lose their way, never quite certain as to how it happened. In chapter 7, after witnessing the wholesale slaughter of dissident pigs and hens, Clover, the maternal carthorse, looks down from the knoll at the farm spread out before her, realizing something has gone wrong:

> These scenes of terror and slaughter were not what they had looked forward to that night when Old Major had first stirred them to rebellion . . . [I]nstead—she did not know why—they had come to a time when no one dared speak his mind, when fierce, growling dogs roamed everywhere, and when you had to watch your comrades torn to pieces after confessing shocking crimes . . . [It] was not for this that she and all the other animals had hoped and toiled. . . .

This persistent motif of shattered illusions in Orwell's fiction has led some critics to stress a deep pessimism lying at the core of his imagination, characterized by one critic as "the politics of despair" (Rai). Others suggest that his so-called pessimism is really a corrective to a danger to which socialists are particularly susceptible: utopianism, the illusion of an earthly paradise. Such utopianism is exemplified in *Animal Farm* in Old Major's dream in chapter 1. There the "golden dream," alluded to in the song "The Beasts of England," is not only dubious by itself, but it also plays into the hands of those who use it to acquire power. He believed that is what happened historically in the religious sphere. It constituted the pattern by which the church had won and maintained power for centuries: the prospect of eternal happiness in heaven.

Later, into the vacuum created by growing disbelief in an afterlife, new creeds such as Marxism had moved, with the promise of retributive justice and equality in a golden future on earth. For Orwell, in this lies the crucial distinction between socialism and communism. In communist ideology, socialism is a temporary phase, characterized by the "dictatorship of the proletariat," a step on the way to the withering of the state and a completely classless society. For a democratic socialist as Orwell conceived it, socialism should have no utopian goals, simply a form of government struggling to implement more justice and equality than existed under capitalism.

Although he felt both Christianity and communism make a similar rhetorical appeal to people, Orwell recognized a significant difference. Despite its flaws, the Hebraic-Christian tradition had inscribed a civilizing and enduring ethical system, an appealing version of which he found in "the poor old C of E" [Church of England]. True believers of that persuasion may find the tribute a bit patronizing, but it was heartfelt on Orwell's part. Witness his deathbed instructions that he be buried according to the rites of the Church of England.

On the other hand, this newer religion, Soviet Communism, had betrayed its principles by using the end to justify the means virtually from day one of its initial appearance in 1917. Nor was Orwell deluded into assuming that it was due exclusively to the figure of Joseph Stalin. Stalinism may have been a particularly egregious symptom, but the essential totalitarianism of his predecessor Vladimir Lenin's rule, as well as in the potential dictatorship that would have emerged if "Snowball" had come to power: "Trotsky, in exile, denounces the Russian dictatorship, but he is probably as much responsible for it as any man now living, and there is no certainty that as a dictator he would be preferable to Stalin, though undoubtedly he has a much more interesting mind."

Within the story, the narrator seems to be exercising a strict neutrality, interested only in reporting its events from the animals' point of view and using their down-to-earth language. This seeming simplicity lends itself to the fairy story/children's literature facet of the book. On the allegorical level, its simplicity strengthens the veracity of the narration, reinforcing the idea that the impersonal, objective narrator is simply recounting what happened, not making judgments. Thus, by underplaying his role, the narrator intensifies the reader's sympathy. The reader is given the task that the narrator has carefully chosen to avoid. The critic Lynette Hunter argues that this strategy is consistent with a developing pattern in Orwell's fictional style.

One of the singular features of the book, in keeping with its fable format, is that the action is presented from the point of view of the animals, not of the narrator. There are occasional minor departures from this focus, but by and large there is no authorial intrusion into the presentation. Thus, as events unfold, we see their impact on the animals, recognizing the growing distinction between the animals and the pigs (Fowler, 162). The novel continually uses the term *animals* to refer to the rank and file, while the pigs constitute an elite class. One outgrowth of this is that it is only the animals whose feelings and reactions are recorded. The feelings of the pigs—and particularly Napoleon—are never shown. In his review of *Animal Farm,* the Canadian critic Northrop Frye faulted the author in this respect: "Mr. Orwell does not bother with motivation: He makes his Napoleon inscrutably ambitious and lets it go at that. . . ." (208) Whether or not he was aware of this particular critique, Orwell may have tried to answer this charge in the character of O'Brien in *Nineteen Eighty-Four,* where the lust for power is attributable less to some psychological motivation than to what Friedrich Nietzche called the "will to power" and Lionel Trilling, in relation to *Nineteen Eighty-Four,* characterized as the "mystique of power," the idea that "power in its pure form has for its true end nothing but itself. . . ." (78)

In his review, Frye introduced another critical point. He suggested that *Animal Farm* was designed to illustrate the theme of the corruption of principle by contingency. But Frye argued that the history of communism demonstrates the opposite development, the corruption of the contingent by principle. The principle, according to Frye, is Marx's 19th century metaphysical materialism, purporting not simply to promote a revolution but to provide a comprehensive account of the world and of human existence. In this all-encompassing explanation of life lay the corrupting seeds of communist doctrine.

Historically the Russian Revolution was, like the animals' initial revolt, a contingent event, brought into being by an incompetent ruler, or "a drunken farmer." This was clearly the case with the so-called February Revolution, the first phase, like the first night of the animals' revolt. But the October Revolution, which brought the Bolsheviks to power, was a carefully planned coup by the party elite. Thus the revolution was corrupted by the principle of Marxism that contended that the end justified the means.

This point would not have been alien to Orwell, who saw Marxist theory as a very useful tool in uncovering the flaws and defects in the existing bourgeois culture and the general consciousness it engendered. However, the contradictions in the overall Marxist scheme were all too apparent. On a philosophical level, it displayed an inherent contradiction between its fundamentally materialist position and its underlying idealist strain, which professed faith in the triumph of the human spirit. This is the element of utopianism that Orwell dismissed as wishful thinking. Thus Old Major's address is most powerful when it describes the conditions under which animals are enslaved. Where he strays is in his depiction of the earthly paradise that will ensue after the revolution, in the concluding words of "Beasts of England": "the golden future time." Orwell saw this utopian future as a serious flaw in the socialist/communist design, a secular twin of Moses the raven's "Sugarcandy Mountain." Orwell maintained that socialism must strive for improvement, not perfection.

The utopian dream seems to be taking on a moment of reality in chapter 2, in the immediate aftermath of the routing of Farmer Jones. The revolution was not planned; it erupted as a result of Jones's failure to feed the animals. It was a truly democratic uprising, capped by casting the harnesses, halters, and whip—the tools of the old regime—into the fire and concluding with the repeated singing of "Beasts of England."

The first hint of inequality emerges in the pigs' revelation that, since Old Major's death, they have secretly taught themselves to read and write. Thus, literacy appears as the initial step in the acquisition of power and in the transition from animal to human. As the third chapter opens, we read, "The pigs did not actually work, but directed and supervised the others. With their superior knowledge it was natural that they should assume the leadership."

Here, another important step in the process is characterized by Alex Zwerdling, as when "equality modulates to privilege" (92). Privilege, in turn, gradually transforms itself into power. A perfect example of the process appears at the end of chapter 3, when the animals learn that fresh milk and ripe apples are to be reserved exclusively for the pigs. This arrangement, so they are told by Squealer, is not a privilege but a necessity. The milk and apples are vital to the production of brain power.

Brain power is embodied most completely in the figure of Snowball, whose clever military tactics result in the animals' victory in the Battle of the Cowshed. Another feature of Snowball's intelligence is reflected in his visionary conception of and outline for a windmill. But in the world of revolutionary politics, brain power is no match for brute force. It might be said that on Animal Farm emerge three classes of creatures: pigs, animals, and brutes, the last being the dogs, taken from their mothers shortly after birth and bred by Napoleon to attack on command. The appearance of this "class" marks another stage in the movement from revolution to totalitarian state, the imposition of state terror to ensure the continued acquisition of power.

Along with terror is the invention of a significant scapegoat. The banished Snowball assumes mythic status as a pervasive evil presence, the root source of anything that goes wrong in the state. The scapegoat is not, however, depicted as a lone figure. His evil is aided and enhanced by "traitors," a term that is easily attached to anyone who offers a dissenting opinion, such as the four pigs who are made to confess their dealing with Snowball, just before their throats are torn out by Napoleon's dogs. Other traitors include any potential rivals of the dictator.

Critical throughout to the process of the totalitarian state is propaganda. In the political-allegory dimension of *Animal Farm,* the character of Squealer represents *Pravda,* the official news organ of the Soviet regime. But in the larger historical sense, a more appropriate model would be Joseph Goebbels (1899–1945), Hitler's propaganda minister. Goebbels created the myth that Hitler, like Napoleon, was "always right." Goebbels's brilliance was particularly evident in the latter part of the war, when his propaganda machine convinced the mass of German people that Hitler would eventually—even miraculously—triumph. Squealer's finest moment occurs in his rendition of the death of Boxer, in which he turns a threat to the regime into a seemingly positive development.

The idea of propaganda engages the problem of the relation of language to truth. In the years immediately preceding the writing of *Animal Farm,* Orwell was intimately involved with propaganda. From 1941 to 1943, he wrote BBC news commentaries, presenting the Allies' case to an Indian audience. Reading those reports today, we can agree that he "kept our little corner of it fairly clean." This was particularly true when contrasted to the atrocious lies of the German and Japanese propagandists, as well as to the egregious falsehoods emerging from the communist press during the oppression of POUM in the Spanish civil war.

The use of language to convey untruths in the service of the state forms a prominent role in *Nineteen Eighty-Four,* but it also occupies a central place in *Animal Farm.* Squealer's distortions, the alteration of the original seven commandments that achieves its ultimate expression in "All animals are equal, but some animals are more equal than others," are not just simple lies. They represent the rewriting of history that makes a mockery of the past.

The final stage of the totalitarian state is the emergence of a vast bureaucracy controlled by apparatchiks, functionaries of the state, the Soviet version of the managerial class envisioned by JAMES BURNHAM. Thus, in the last chapter of *Animal Farm,* Napoleon reveals that the pigs—Animal Farm's managers—hold the title deed to the farm. In the future, the farm will become a collective oligarchy.

CONTEMPORARY REVIEWS

The bulk of the reviews enthusiastically celebrated the book upon its arrival. In the *New Yorker,* Edmund Wilson called it "Absolutely first rate . . . so admirably proportioned to his purpose, that *Animal Farm* even seems creditable if we compare it to Voltaire and Swift (205). Cyril Connolly pronounced it "one of the most enjoyable books since the war," like Wilson, invoking comparison with "Orwell's master Swift" (201). Graham Greene pointed out "[it] is as a sad fable, and it is an indication of Mr. Orwell's fine talent that it is really sad not a mere echo of human feelings at one remove" (196). These were not ordinary good reviews but praise from the best reviewers and writers of the period. Others, like the poet Herbert Read (1893–1968), wrote Orwell, praising the book, in Read's case, not only for its satirical bull's-eye but as a delightful children's story:

> Thank you very much indeed for *Animal Farm*. I read it through at a sitting with enormous enjoyment. My boy of seven and a half then spotted it, and I tried chapter 1 on him. He has insisted on my reading it, chapter by chapter, every evening since, and he enjoys it innocently as much as I enjoy it maliciously. It thus stands the test that only classics of satire like *Gulliver* survive (Crick, 339–40).

There was little controversy about the meaning of the historical allegory, except for the view that it was superficial—the opinion of Isaac Rosenfeld, who compared it unfavorably to Koestler's *Darkness at Noon* (Meyers, 169), or misdirected, the view of Frye, who argued that the Russian Revolution was not, as depicted in *Animal Farm,* an instance of the "corruption of principle by expedience" (207) but the reverse. The revolution, in fact, exemplified the corruption of the expedient, the spontaneous uprising of February 1917, by principle—Marxism's all-embracing "materialist metaphysics," purporting to answer all of life's questions.

Of course, some reviews by communists or fellow travelers also included outright rejections of the allegory. A good example of the latter is Kingsley Martin's review. Martin might be said to be the prototype of Orwell's ideal reader, the left-wing intellectual half in love with Stalin's Russia. It was he who, as editor of the *New Statesman and Nation,* had rejected Orwell's "Eye-Witness in Barcelona" on the grounds that it "could cause trouble." Martin wrote a patronizing review, dismissing the work as an amusing trifle, "historically false and neglectful of the complex truth about Russia" (199).

LATER CRITICISM

Subsequent criticism of *Animal Farm* has focused to a great extent on its social and political meaning, not to the exclusion of its strictly literary merit but with the latter assuming a relatively minor role. The conflict about the meaning of the work primarily turns on the question of whether its theme is revolution betrayed or revolution deplored. That is to ask: Was it Orwell's intent solely to show how the Russian Revolution was corrupted either by an error in Bolshevik theory or by the lust for power of Lenin and Stalin, or was he suggesting that an inherent flaw lies within violent revolution itself? Critics have asserted that "revolution betrayed" (the phrase is the title of Leon Trotsky's own memoir) reflects the corrupting effects of the Leninist/Stalinist strategy of employing an elite core of insiders to "manage" the revolution, with the result that the insiders become a new ruling class. When Stalin, acting out of pragmatic insight or personal paranoia, in the 1930s purged the party and military elite, he tightened control even further, recognizing that any threat to his rule would come from within—in *Animal Farm* terms, from pigs, not from animals. This is the viewpoint of those who accept Orwell's commitment to democratic socialism as unwavering. They see the fable, as Orwell himself saw it, as a warning to the left not to be taken in by the benign image of Stalin prevailing in the West in the waning days of World War II. But his intended audience—left-leaning English intellectuals—turned out to be a minute proportion of the book's actual readers. Once the book was released into the larger world, it took on a variety of shapes that Orwell never really imagined.

Certainly all agreed that the primary target is Stalinism, but Orwell acknowledged on more than one occasion another important theme, most clearly in his letter to DWIGHT MACDONALD:

> I meant the moral to be that revolutions only effect a radical improvement when the masses are alert and know how to chuck out their leaders as soon as the latter have done their job. . . . What I was trying to say was, "You can't have a revolution unless you make it for yourself; there is no such thing as a benevolent dictatorship."

The first warning sign Orwell received about the controversial nature of the book came from his friend, poet and critic WILLIAM EMPSON, in a letter thanking him for sending a copy of the book:

> My dear George,
>
> Thanks very much for giving me "Animal Farm"—it is a most impressive object, with the range of feeling and the economy of method, and the beautiful limpid prose style. I read it with great excitement. And then, thinking it over, and especially on showing it to other people, one realizes that the danger of this kind of perfection is that it means very different things to different readers. Our Mr Julian [his son] the child Tory was delighted with it; he said it was very strong Tory propaganda.
>
> Your point of view of course is that the animals ought to have gone on sharing Animal Farm. . . .
>
> I certainly don't mean that that is a fault in the allegory; it is a form that has to be set down and allowed to grow like a separate creature, and I think you let it do that with honesty and restraint. But I thought it worth warning you (while thanking you very heartily) that you must expect to be "misunderstood" on a large scale about this book; it is a form that inherently means more than the author means, when it is handled sufficiently well (Crick, 340).

Empson was singularly well qualified to make these remarks. As the author of the critical text *Seven Types of Ambiguity*, he had promoted the idea that multiple meanings in a literary work were not only possible but desirable. He defined ambiguity as "any verbal nuance, however slight, which gives room for alternative reactions to the same piece of language." In his book, Empson focused on poetic language, but he did not rule out its application to prose literature, particularly to allegory, which "inherently means more than the author means."

It is interesting that Empson places quotes around the term *misunderstood*. From his perspective, it was not exactly a misunderstanding, so much as inevitable, alternative readings that might contradict the author's intention. When you create a form in which one element stands for something else, and you have made it clear what that something else is, you may feel that there's no room for ambiguity. However, as Empson goes on to say, the more subtle and skillful your creation, the more likely is it to resonate beyond the immediate something else. Successful allegory invites a reader to keep going in that train of thought. If A equals B, does B equal A and something more?

Thus, a reader with a conservative disposition (like Empson's son) could easily read *Animal Farm* as an example of the ultimate futility of all revolutions. In fact, the Empson household constituted a microcosm of the future critical debate: Empson's view, more or less consistent with Orwell's intention, his son's Tory view that the book is antirevolutionary, and Empson's wife, Hetta, a committed communist, who dismissed it out of hand as not worthy of comment. An additional possibility, raised by other critics, is that his larger subject is not revolution but totalitarianism.

Among those supporting Orwell's interpretation is George Woodcock, who calls attention to the fact that our sympathies are disposed on behalf of the animals in their revolt against Farmer Jones. It is not the revolution that is at fault but the betrayal of it by the pigs (158). Averil Gardner suggests that the question arises because of readers' uncertainty as to whether the failure results from the "abuse of power" or because of "ineradicable flaws in human nature—'The darkness of a man's heart. . . .'" (99).

Raymond Williams offers a nuanced negative view. Although "both consciousness of the workers and the possibility of authentic revolution are denied," nevertheless, from this "despairing base," Orwell informs the story with "an actively communicative tone." Williams goes on to say, "A paradoxical confidence, an assured and active and laughing intelligence, is manifested in the very penetration and exposure of the experience of defeat" (74–75). This perception is reflected in the final scene when the animals cannot distinguish between the pigs and the men. The animals realize that "they are the same because they act the same . . . that is a moment of gained consciousness, a potentially liberating discovery" (76). Williams's paradoxical argument offers what appears to be a slim hope, but not one that Orwell would necessarily reject. Orwell may have seen *Animal Farm* as a dark satire, but the darkness offset by the slow, painful birth of awareness among the animals.

The final scene, focused on by Williams, is also considered by Lynette Hunter. Hunter's book-length study *George Orwell: The Search for a Voice* (1989) is a complex theory-oriented, rhetorical approach that looks at the development of the narrative strategies employed by Orwell from *Burmese Days* to *Nineteen Eighty-Four.* Hunter rejects T. S. Eliot's and others' position that *Animal Farm*'s impact is one of "negation." Rather, she opens a different critical path by focusing on Orwell's experiments with the voice of the narrator. In contrast to Orwell's earlier novels, the narrator of *Animal Farm* is detached, stepping back to facilitate the reader's identification with the animals. The narrator creates a vacuum, so to speak, into which the readers step. But the identification of readers/animals breaks down in the final scene, in which the pigs and humans are indistinguishable. The animals don't know what to make of the change, but the readers do. This, according to Hunter, is Orwell's rhetorical goal: to awaken the intellectual left in England and America to their responsibility. Too many of them have been looking at Napoleon/Stalin with the same naïveté as the animals. But they don't have the animals' excuse because they have the communicative skills the animals lack.

This is a critical insight, for it establishes the fact that not negation but the reader's responsibility is the underlying point of the story. Once a reader perceives that the pigs have indeed become "human," which is to say, in the terms of the parable, that the communists have become state-capitalist oppressors, he/she can no longer identify with the animals, because we understand what the animals do not. What occurs at the end is an ironic version of the transformation motif of the Fairy Tale where the beast turns into the handsome prince. Since the reader perceives the irony, that perception carries with it the burden of action.

A position similar to Hunter's is expounded by V. C. Letemendia. He argues that the key to understanding the story is found in Orwell's letter to Dwight Macdonald: "The book itself, Orwell makes clear in his letter, was calling not for the end of revolutionary hopes, but for the beginning of a new kind of personal responsibility on the part of revolutionaries" (Letemendia, 25).

Letemendia goes on to argue that the animals had to take more responsibility for their fate, to recognize that they had more choices than the "false alternatives" Squealer put before them: Obey Napoleon or have Mr. Jones return. Letemendia suggests that just as the animals need to take responsibility for their problem, so, too, do the readers of *Animal Farm.* Orwell is, in effect, challenging the complacency of his readers, "detached from the urgent need for personal involvement in political change" (25). The readers must supply the resolution, just as in reality they must take up the task of rebuilding the revolution. To that end, Letemendia alludes to the final scene, just as Williams had, suggesting that this "grain of hope" is made deliberately difficult for readers to discover. To have made it easy would have undercut its point, that each individual must make an effort for the revolution to succeed.

Adding to the complication surrounding *Animal Farm*'s formal elements is Paul Kirschner's recent wide-ranging, impressive article on "The Dual Purpose of *Animal Farm.*" Kirschner maintains that Orwell was imitating or, more precisely, parodying the style of the "proletarian fairy tale," a species of leftist literature for young children that existed in the 1920s and '30s. He reproduces in his article a typical example of such a story, published in America in 1932, under the title "Battle of the Barnyard," which tells of how one greedy rooster gains control of the water rights on an idyllic farm and thereby suppresses all the other animals by demanding payment for the right to drink water. To protect himself, he hires young roosters to act as guards and sometimes chickens to be preachers, teaching the animals to be submissive so that they will be rewarded in heaven. Eventually, the animals revolt, kill the greedy rooster and his family and drive out the police guard and the preachers. The idyllic farm is restored, and the animals, in the last words of the story, ". . . are all contented as equal."

In 1940, after writing "BOY'S WEEKLIES," Orwell expressed an interest in the possibility of producing children's and young-adult literature with a socialist slant (he had argued in "Boy's Weeklies" that the popular examples he was writing about endorsed the political point of view of their publishers). He was therefore aware of the existence of stories such as

"The Battle of the Barnyard" but not necessarily this particular one. His interest in fairy tales per se is evidenced by his adaptation in 1946 of "Little Red Riding Hood" for the BBC's *Children's Hour.* He was all too conscious and suspicious, however, of the propagandistic character of Marxist-oriented tales such as "The Battle of the Barnyard." Kirschner's point is that Orwell parodies both the form of the "proletarian fairy tale" and its substance, turning the successful revolution, in which the animals end up ". . . completely equal," into the betrayed revolution in which "some animals are more equal than others."

Kirschner concludes that ". . . literary form hindered Orwell's political purpose," which was to denounce in Kirschner's words ". . . *both* private capitalism with its money-based class privilege *and* the shallow self righteousness of the left-wing intelligentsia . . . holding up the train of the USSR's emperor's robes" (171).

POLITICAL INFLUENCE OF *ANIMAL FARM*

In the ideological struggle that was one facet of the cold war, *Animal Farm,* together with its successor *Nineteen Eighty-Four,* played an important role. As a consequence, its author came to achieve an eminence that approached a kind of mythic status. Part of the status derived from his authorship of two books that had a powerful emotional appeal in calling attention to the evils of the Stalinist regime. Of these, it is clear that *Animal Farm* locates that regime as its primary target. *Nineteen Eighty-Four,* on the other hand, while certainly including the Soviet Union as the most obvious example, targets the general threat of the totalitarian state and its looming presence.

The enlistment of *Animal Farm* in the cold war came about initially as a result of the novel's astounding popularity among readers. The American Book of the Month Club offered it as a selection in September 1945, and it proved to be a phenomenal success. In England, also, it became a best-seller, read among others by the Queen mother (the mother of Queen Elizabeth II) and Winston Churchill, certainly not Orwell's target audience. In fact the readership he most immediately had in mind were the left-wing intelligentsia, who had turned a blind eye to the fact that Stalin's Russia represented a total repudiation of socialism and was in fact a murderous, tyrannical dictatorship.

As for its impact beyond the Iron Curtain, its power was made evident after the collapse of the Soviet empire in the testimony of those who had read the book in translations smuggled into Eastern Europe. It turns out that the proliferation of translations was not entirely a natural consequence of the book's appeal. Many of these were financially underwritten by the United States Information Agency (USIA):

> The U.S. government was heavily involved in these translations. At the State Department, Dean Acheson authorized payment for the translation rights to *Nineteen Eighty-Four* in 1951. Beginning with the Korean edition of *Animal Farm* in 1948, the U.S. information Agency sponsored translations and distribution of Orwell's books in more than thirty languages. The voice of America also broadcast *Animal Farm* (1947) and *Nineteen Eighty-Four* (1949) in East Europe (Rodden, *Politics,* 202n).

In the case of one early translation, the Ukrainian, for which Orwell wrote an explanatory preface (see Prefaces), the American authorities intercepted an attempt to smuggle copies to the East. Observing diplomatic protocol, they turned them over to the Russians. But as Allied-Soviet relations deteriorated, the British and the Americans increasingly played hardball, using *Animal Farm* in their pitching repertory. The reason the book proved so effective is that the animals' fate fairly accurately described the lives of people trapped in the communist satrapies of Eastern Europe. In the four decades of the cold war, the book retained its extraordinary popularity in the West. In English and American secondary schools, it was required reading, leaving its young readers with a general, if vague, impression of communism as a malevolent force in the world.

CHARACTERS

Benjamin The only donkey on the farm, Benjamin rarely speaks or laughs and has little to do with the other animals except Boxer, for whom he has an unspoken affection. Whenever the other animals seek his opinion about developments on Animal Farm, he answers cryptically, saying "Donkeys live a long time. None of you has ever seen a dead donkey." While identifying with the plight of his fellow animals, Benjamin remains as indifferent to their revolutionary hopes throughout the story as he does to the encroaching tyranny of the pigs. He views the successes and failures on the farm with equal skepticism. When the animals are divided in their loyalties between Snowball and Napoleon during the debate over the building of the windmill, Benjamin states his unequivocal belief that "life would go on as it had always gone on—that is, badly." He persists in this belief through the course of the novel.

Many critics and readers have seen Benjamin as the author's spokesman, giving voice to the disillusioned skepticism they see as Orwell's final vision both here and in *Nineteen Eighty-Four*. Others might recognize Benjamin as one who is "inside the whale," that is one, like the writer HENRY MILLER, who sees the human condition as hopeless and refuses to do anything about it. The sole exception to that description is Benjamin's reaction to Boxer's being sent to the horse slaughterer. He tries to alert the other animals, but they are too naïve to recognize the truth until it is too late. In the final chapter, Benjamin is depicted as basically unchanged, except for being "a little greyer about the muzzle, and, since Boxer's death, more morose and taciturn than ever."

Among readers who identified Benjamin with Orwell himself were his good friend Arthur Koestler, Koestler's wife, Mamaine, and her twin sister, CELIA KIRWAN, all of whom referred to him jokingly as "Donkey George."

Bluebell, Jessie, and Pincher Three dogs on the farm. Bluebell and the other dogs, Jessie and Pincher, are the first to arrive at the barn for Major's speech. With the pigs, the dogs quickly learn the words to "Beasts of England," and they are considered among the cleverest animals on the farm. Under Snowball's instruction, the dogs learn to read well, though they prefer to read only the Seven Commandments. In chapter 3, Bluebell and Jessie give birth to nine puppies between them (Pincher presumably being the father). Napoleon confiscates the puppies and trains them privately to be his personal guard.

Boxer The devoted and powerful cart horse, whose undying loyalty to the farm—and particularly to Napoleon—is ruthlessly betrayed. From the beginning, Boxer commits himself to the cause of animalism, even though he admits that he doesn't really understand many of the ideas and principles. Boxer is capable of prodigious feats of strength in carrying out his assigned tasks. Nevertheless, the underlying gentleness of his spirit is evident in his reaction to a fallen stable boy, whom he believes he has killed during the Battle of the Cowshed. He asserts tearfully, "I have no wish to take life, not even human life." Later, the boy, who was only stunned, recovers and runs away. Boxer is the bravest and most effective defender of the farm in the battles of the Cowshed and the Windmill. In the latter, he suffers some severe wounds, a split hoof and a dozen pellets in his hind legs, which mark the first signs of a loss of strength on his part. Nevertheless, he continues to adhere to his code, expressed in the phrases "I will work harder" and "Napoleon is always right."

He looks forward to his 12th birthday, when he will retire on a decent pension. One month short of that date, while working overtime on the rebuilding of the windmill, he falls, his lungs having given out temporarily. Squealer announces that Napoleon is arranging to have Boxer sent to a veterinary hospital in town. When a van arrives to take Boxer away, the animals, alerted by Benjamin, gather around the van to wish him good-bye. Benjamin angrily calls their attention to the words on the side of the van, indicating that it belongs to a horse slaughterer, Alfred Simmons. They desperately try to alert Boxer as the van pulls away. Three days later, Squealer announces that Boxer died in the hospital, asserting that Boxer's last words were "Long live Animal Farm, long live Comrade Napoleon. Napoleon is always right."

Allegorically, Boxer represents the working class, the peasantry, and also the veterans of the Battle of Stalingrad, the well-intentioned decent people who were deceived and abused by the rhetoric of the Stalinist regime.

Cat The nameless, supremely self-involved animal, who has a talent for looking after its own interests. The only civic action the cat engages in is to vote against the recognition of rats as legitimate animals.

Clover A female cart horse and a friend of Boxer. Clover takes a motherly interest in the other animals. She warns Mollie, the pretty but frivolous mare, when she sees her fraternizing with a human. She is steadfastly loyal to the principles of the farm, but she becomes increasingly disillusioned when she sees the brutality and injustice that surrounds her. After the bloody slaughter of the animals accused of having conspired with Snowball, she is moved to tears as she looks out over the farm: "These scenes of terror and slaughter were not what they had looked forward to that night when Old Major had stirred them to rebellion."

Dogs In chapter 3, Jessie and Bluebell both give birth, having a litter of nine puppies between them. Napoleon takes possession of them, explaining that he will be responsible for their education. He keeps them in a loft in the harness room, and they are not seen again until chapter 5. At Napoleon's summons, the puppies—now fully grown, vicious, and wearing studded collars—chase Snowball from the farm.

Napoleon's dogs represent in Orwell's allegory the *cheka,* the original Soviet secret police, established by Lenin, right after the October Revolution, to safeguard the Soviet government using terrorist methods. Over the years, they were later known as the GPU and OGPU, and finally, as the NKVD.

Frederick The owner of a neighboring farm, who is regularly involved in disputes with others, "with a name for driving hard bargains." He joins the group of humans who attack the farm in the battle of the Cowshed. Later he negotiates a deal to buy lumber from Napoleon but pays him with counterfeit money. In the Battle of the Windmill, he is defeated by the animals, moved to fury by the destruction of the windmill.

In the historical allegory, Frederick represents Adolf Hitler. The lumber deal parodies the Hitler-Stalin Non-Aggression Pact (August 1939). The Pact included a commercial trade, in which raw material would be sent to Germany in exchange for industrial products. The Germans never lived up to their end of the trade. The Battle of the Windmill stands for the epic Battle of Stalingrad (September 1942–1943), during which the city was destroyed, but which was a great victory for the Soviets and a crushing defeat for Hitler.

Jones, Mr. The owner of Manor Farm prior to the animals' rebellion. Once a capable farmer, Jones let misfortunes and his increasing dependence on alcohol disrupt the management of the farm and make the lives of the animals increasingly intolerable. Jones's neglect of the animals is apparent in the opening lines of the book, where he is too drunk to remember to secure the henhouses. The animals' rebellion in chapter 2 occurs sooner than anticipated because Jones spends a drunken weekend in Willingdon and forgets to feed them.

After his banishment from the farm, Jones spends his time in the village pub where he drinks and complains to the other farmers about his loss of Manor Farm. He tries unsuccessfully to reclaim it in chapter 4. It is mentioned parenthetically in chapter 6 that Jones had given up hope of regaining the farm and moved to a different part of the county. In chapter 10, it is noted that Jones had died in a home for inebriates.

Jones's mismanagement of Manor Farm suggests the reign of Nicholas II, emperor of Russia from 1894 to 1917, whose failure to acknowledge the increasing political unrest of his subjects and whose absence from Russia during World War I contributed to the success of the Russian Revolution of 1917.

Jones, Mrs. Mrs. Jones appears in only two chapters of the book. In the opening paragraph of chapter 1, she is in bed and snoring when her husband goes up to bed. In chapter 2, when Mrs. Jones sees the animals rebel against Jones and his men from her bedroom window, she throws a few possessions in a carpetbag and flees the farm, accompanied by Moses, the raven.

Minimus A pig with a "remarkable gift for composing songs and poems." When Napoleon outlaws the singing of the song "Beasts of England," he replaces it with one composed by Minimus. Later, Minimus is credited with composing the poem "Comrade Napoleon," which subsequently appears on the wall of the big barn, below a painted portrait of Napoleon.

In terms of the historical allegory, Mimimus may be a reference to Vladimir Mayakovsky (1893–1930), the leading Russian poet of the Revolution, who enthusiastically supported the Bolsheviks. Eventually, he ran afoul of Stalin. Disillusioned with the regime and suffering through an unhappy love affair, Mayakovsky committed suicide. He was far from being the talentless toady that Minimus represents, but many members of the Soviet Writers Union did serve that purpose, producing works that conformed to the principles of socialist realism. Much like Minimus, the Writers Union produced works designed to bolster Stalin's image.

Mollie The pretty, vain, and airheaded horse who drew Farmer Jones's cart. Even before the initial revolt, Mollie is dubious about the austere new world summoned up by Snowball. Very early on, she takes the opportunity to defect to the humans. She represents the shallow and self-absorbed people who were against the revolution and defected to the West as soon as the opportunity presented itself. They did the right thing for the wrong reasons.

Moses A raven, the special pet of Mr. and Mrs. Jones. His perch sits on the back porch of the farmhouse and Mr. Jones often treats him to crusts of bread soaked in beer. Moses is the only animal not to attend Major's meeting in the barn. He does no work but spends his time preaching to his fellow animals about a special place above the clouds called Sugarcandy Mountain, where they will go after death. During the rebellion, Moses flees Manor Farm with the Joneses. When he returns in chapter 9, his role on the farm remains much the same.

With his testimony about the existence of Sugarcandy Mountain, Moses represents the Russian Orthodox Church. Communism demonstrated its hostility to the church by destroying or converting religious buildings and oppressing or killing its members. During the final years of World War II, religious persecution in the Soviet Union decreased, and some churches and seminaries reopened their doors. In 1943, Stalin organized a council of church leaders, consisting largely of people released from prison for that purpose, which elected Metropolitan Sergius as patriarch. Church elders were selected by the Soviet regime largely on the basis of their tacit support of the government and its policies.

Orwell portrays none of these details in *Animal Farm,* choosing instead to address the symbolic function of the church as the bearer of tall tales about a mythical heaven. The point is to emphasize that regardless of the particular government, religion's function in the story remains the same: to convince the animals not to resist their present circumstances, no matter how difficult they might be.

Muriel The white goat whom Clover calls on to read the Sixth Commandment when Benjamin refuses to do so. Muriel reads "No animal will kill an animal without cause." Muriel was the name of the goat that Orwell owned at his house in Wallington.

Napoleon The dictatorial pig and principal figure of the farm. Napoleon is introduced to the reader as a "Berkshire boar . . . with a reputation for getting his own way." An example of this occurs when, after the cows have been milked, he diverts the animals' attention from the milk to the work in the field that must be done. By the time the animals return, the milk is gone. As a result of his military skill at the Battle of the Cowshed and his superior intelligence, Snowball seems to be the natural leader of the animals, but Napoleon, working behind the scenes, cultivates the most ignorant members of the farm—the sheep—and, when puppies are born, Napoleon takes them away from their mothers so that he can educate them privately. His rivalry with Snowball reaches a climactic point in the discussion of Snowball's idea of building a windmill. Snowball's eloquence is about to turn the tide in his favor when Napoleon unleashes the former puppies, now trained attack dogs, on Snowball, who barely escapes with his life. Rid of his rival, Napoleon immediately assumes total command of the farm. He is ably assisted by the pig Squealer, whose rhetorical skill can turn black into white.

Thus Squealer announces Napoleon's plan to build a windmill, claiming that the idea for it had been stolen by Snowball. When the poorly constructed windmill is destroyed in a storm, Napoleon accuses the absent Snowball of sabotage. As his power grows, Napoleon is seen less and less in public. His decisions are conveyed through Squealer. It becomes apparent that Napoleon has acquired a new taste, alcohol, despite the commandment specifically forbidding the practice, but Squealer points out what has never been noticed before: The commandment reads "No animal shall drink alcohol *to excess*."

Napoleon surprises the animals when it is revealed that he has concluded a trade deal with the neighboring farmer Frederick, who has a particularly bad reputation as an abuser of animals, but Napoleon boasts that he got a much better deal with Frederick and was shrewd to insist that they be paid in cash. Shortly after, it becomes clear that Frederick used counterfeit money, followed by the warning that Frederick's men were at the gate, invading the farm. At first, the unprepared animals are losing the battle and have to retreat to the barn, but when they see Frederick's men blowing up the windmill they have slaved over, they wage a counterattack that defeats the invaders. Napoleon takes credit for the victory. When the incredibly loyal Boxer falls ill, Squealer announces that Napoleon has arranged for Boxer to be treated by the veterinarian in town. After Boxer's death, Napoleon gives a short speech, stressing Boxer's loyalty. A memorial banquet for Boxer features a case of whiskey delivered to the farmhouse. Years later, the farm is a thriving enterprise, but the animals see little improvement in their lives. They are amazed to see one day the pigs walking on their hind legs. The last one to come out is Napoleon, "majestically upright, casting haughty glances from side to side." A week later, human visitors come to the farm and, in the evening, exchange toasts with the pigs. Napoleon uses the occasion to announce that he is changing the name of the farm back to "Manor Farm," its original name.

The correspondence between Napoleon and Joseph Stalin was clearly Orwell's specific intent, but 50 years after Stalin's death, it could be applied to any number of tyrants that have emerged on the world scene. Napoleon's story is unfortunately still relevant.

Old Major A "prize Middle White boar," a coveted breed of pig popular in Great Britain during the early 1900s. Rather stout and approaching 12 years of age, he is described as being a "majestic-looking pig" with a "wise and benevolent appearance." All the animals of the farm regard him with great respect, and when word travels around the farm that he has had an unusual dream, the animals gather in the big barn to hear him describe it. After inciting them to rebellion, Old Major relates to the animals the details of his dream, in which all animals are free and human beings have been driven from England altogether. He also teaches them "Beasts of England," a song from his youth that captures the spirit of his message of revolution. Old Major provides the philosophical foundation for the animal rebellion, later synthesized by Snowball, Napoleon, and Squealer into the political system called Animalism.

The character of Old Major corresponds, at least in part, to KARL MARX, whose writings, including *The Communist Manifesto* (1848, with Friedrich Engels), provided a sourcebook for socialism and communism worldwide.

Pigeons The pigeons of Animal Farm serve initially as messengers of the revolution by sowing the seeds of dissent among the animals on other farms. Their role becomes increasingly less idealistic (and more political) under Napoleon's totalitarian leadership. They engage in propaganda and disinformation, and their discovery of the whereabouts of Mollie and the injury to Boxer suggest that they may also serve a domestic function on the farm as Napoleon's eyes and ears among the other animals. In Orwell's satirical evaluation of Stalinist Russia, the pigeons represent the Communist Party members who attempted to spread the revolution beyond Russia's borders.

Pigs The most intelligent animals on the farm, the pigs secretly teach themselves to read, thereby establishing the basis for their emergence as a superior class in the supposedly egalitarian society. As a result, the pigs do skilled, not manual, labor on the farm. Eventually, they supervise while the other animals do the actual work. As the farm evolves, the pigs' function becomes increasingly bureaucratic, handling the paperwork. As a result, they are given privileges denied the others, eventually learning to walk on two legs. The pigs stand for the members of the Communist Party leadership, who gradually assumed all the characteristics of a bureaucratic ruling class.

Pilkington, Mr. The owner of Foxwood, one of the farms that adjoined Animal Farm. Foxwood was "a large, neglected, old-fashioned farm, much overgrown by woodland. . . ." Pilkington was an easygoing gentleman farmer who spent much of his time fishing and hunting. Pilkington represents the English Tory ruling class, whom Orwell sees as having become inept and out of touch. However, in the final scene of the book, Pilkington is capable of matching Napoleon when it comes to diplomatic knavery.

Pinkeye In chapter 8, Pinkeye, a young pig, becomes the food taster for Napoleon, as part of the increased security precautions established after three hens confessed to participating in a plot to assassinate Napoleon.

Rats The rats of Animal Farm first appear in chapter 1, when their arrival at the meeting in the barn causes a commotion with the dogs and the cat. Major halts his speech to settle the matter of whether the rats, being wild creatures, should be classified as comrades like the other animals. A vote is taken, and they are named comrades. They appear briefly in chapter 3 as the focus of one the Wild Comrades' Re-education Committee—one of Snowball's numerous social campaigns. They are mentioned only one other time, in chapter 7, when they are said to have been in league with Snowball in sabotaging the farm. Some scholars have suggested that the "wild creatures" represent the unruly and politically unengaged Russian peasantry.

Sheep The sheep of Animal Farm have no individual identities, and they rarely appear in the story except as a group. They serve as unwitting accomplices to the rise of Napoleon's dictatorship. Their cacophonous bleating of slogans disrupts dissent and destroys honest debate. Orwell employs them in the story to represent blind acceptance of authority and power, a vital component to the destruction of liberty. The repetitive and incessant bleating of the sheep suggests the "gramophone mind," which Orwell identified in his unpublished introduction to *Animal Farm* as one of the principal enemies of freedom. The sheep are to Napoleon what the Communist Party loyalists were to Joseph Stalin.

Simmonds, Alfred The local knacker (a person who buys worn-out horses, slaughters them, and sells the meat for dog food). It is not clear that Simmonds is the driver of the van that takes Boxer away. In any case, he says nothing, which does not alter the fact that he plays a key role in the most dramatic and moving scene in the novel. The animals gather around the van to say their good-byes to Boxer, but Benjamin cuts them short by reading the words on the side of the van: "Alfred Simmonds, Horse Slaughterer and Glue Boiler, Willingdon. Dealer in Hides and Bone-Meal. Kennels supplied."

Snowball The most intelligent of the animals on the farm, the hero of the Battle of the Cowshed and the logical candidate to succeed Old Major as the leader of the animals. However, he is no match in ruthlessness for Napoleon, who unleashes his ferocious dogs on Snowball, forcing him to run for his life.

Before being forced into exile, Snowball takes the lead in teaching the animals the principles of Animalism. He paints over an old sign with the new name of Animal Farm, and he paints the commandments on the wall of the big barn.

More than any other pig, Snowball seems to embody the revolutionary spirit of Animalism. He creates the new flag, attempts to set up various committees, succeeds in teaching many of the animals to read and write, and becomes one of the most active and persuasive speakers during the weekly Sunday Meeting debates. He does agree, however, that only the pigs should be allowed the milk and apples, and he rebukes Boxer for being sentimental when he believes he has killed a stable boy during the Battle of the Cowshed.

In succeeding chapters, Snowball becomes the pigs' all-purpose scapegoat. Napoleon blames him for the destruction of the windmill. Every setback attributed to Snowball's sabotage of the farm. He is by turns condemned as an agent of Jones, Frederick, and Pilkington, and is ultimately portrayed as a traitor to Animalism from the beginning of the rebellion.

Snowball's transformation from hero to traitor mirrors the fate of LEON TROTSKY. Trotsky was initially heralded as a hero of the revolution and the subsequent civil war between the Reds and Whites, during which he organized and led the Red Army. He was considered the heir apparent to Lenin, who, before his death in 1924, specifically spoke against Stalin.

Trotsky was banished from the Soviet Union by Stalin in 1929. In exile, Trostky proved to be a powerful critic of Stalin's regime, notably in his study *The Revolution Betrayed* (1937). He was assassinated in Mexico City in 1940. Trotsky also provided the model for Emmanuel Goldstein, a similar scapegoat figure in *Nineteen Eighty-Four.*

Squealer One of the three principal leaders among the pigs in the postrebellion Animal Farm, Squealer is at once one of the most amusing and sinister characters in Orwell's allegory. Squealer's role in the allegory is principally that of a propagandist. He intercedes on behalf of Snowball and Napoleon with the rest of the animals, and he is perfectly suited to this role. "Do you know what would happen if we pigs failed in our duty? Jones would come back!" Much of Squealer's propaganda is directed at undermining Snowball's character, making him the scapegoat for every tragedy that befalls the farm. Squealer's greatest task, however, is justifying actions by Napoleon which appear to contravene the principles of Animalism. In the allegory, Squealer is thought to represent *Pravda,* the official Soviet newspaper, although the singular success he enjoys suggests that he might be modeled on Joseph Goebbels, Hitler's sinister but highly effective minister of propaganda.

Whymper, Mr. A "sly-looking little man with side whiskers," a minor solicitor in town, but one sharp enough to see the financial advantages of the revolution. When Napoleon announces his decision to engage in trade with humans, Whymper becomes a regular visitor to the farm. The animals on the farm view Napoleon's compromise with the humans with suspicion, as they seem to recall that such interactions are forbidden by one of the commandments; however, they come to feel a measure of pride in the spectacle of Napoleon issuing orders to a human.

In Chapter 8, Whymper successfully concludes negotiations over the sale of the timber to Frederick, who grudgingly pays cash for the lot and begins hauling it away. Whymper makes arrangements to use the money to purchase machinery for the windmill, but three days after the sale, he learns that the bills are counterfeit.

It is likely that Orwell intended to parody the controversial Treaty of Rapallo, signed by Walter Rathenau of Germany and G. V. Chicherin of the Soviet Union in Rapallo, Italy, in 1922. The agreement included Germany's recognition of the Soviet government, a mutual cancellation of debt incurred prior to World War I, and a mutual renunciation of all postwar claims. Germany also benefited from a clause that allowed extensive trade between the two countries, which is Orwell's principal focus in the character of Whymper. But there was an existing model for the Whymper character, although it is doubtful that Orwell knew of him. He was Armand Hammer (1898–1990), an American businessman and the son of a Russian immigrant who, despite being a very successful capitalist (he later became an oil tycoon) never let ideology interfere with business. He was a lifelong Republican and a major contributor to Richard Nixon's campaign, but he never did overcome the suspicion that he might be a Soviet agent. His initial contact was with Lenin, but he managed to get along beautifully with Stalin as well. His long association with Soviet governments, through wars hot and cold, suggests that his wheeling and dealing was a deeply ingrained characteristic that trumped his ideology.

FILM AND TELEVISION ADAPTATIONS

Animal Farm (1955) Animated film directed by John Halas and Joy Bachelor, produced by Louis DeRochement. This BBC production has a complex history and has received a curiously mixed reception. The news that this production was subsidized by the CIA was revealed in the memoirs of E. Howard Hunt, former CIA agent and honcho of the Watergate break-in. The State Department and CIA were already aware of the propaganda potential of Orwell's last two works. But they took the propaganda a step further by requesting that the film have a happy ending with the animals' launching a successful counterrevolution. However, what emerged was a film without the effect intended by the CIA sponsors. It seemed devoid of any significant references to the Soviet Union.

Animator Eddie Radage sketching pigs on a farm in Hertfordshire, England, in preparation for animating *Animal Farm,* the film, 1953 *(Getty Images)*

Animal Farm (1999) A partly animated Hallmark television production, directed by John Steppenson, screenplay by Alan Jaynos and Martyn Burke, and produced by Robert Halmi. With the voices of Patrick Stewart (Napoleon), Kelsey Grammer (Snowball), Ian Holm (Squealer), Peter Ustinov (Old Major), Julia Louis-Dreyfus (Mollie), Paul Scofield (Boxer), Peter Postlethwaite (Benjamin, also appearing in the film as Mr. Jones). The technical effects include computer graphics, as well as animatronic and robotic elements. The film presents the human characters, including Jones, Pilkington, and Frederick (the last of whom makes a faint allusion to the historical allegory by sporting a Hitler-like mustache).

The film is narrated by Jessie, the sheepdog, who substitutes for the novel's Clover. As it opens, Jessie, Benjamin, and other animals who had escaped are returning to the now-abandoned farm after years of exile. They had finally fled the farm after the final abomination, the spectacle of Napoleon standing on two legs and wearing clothing. Jessie recounts the story in a flashback, and we see alternating scenes of the human beings and the animals as the latter listen to Old Major's speech. We are told that Jones's drinking and mismanagement of the farm have put him deeply into debt with Pilkington (Alan Stafford), a piglike figure who will assume the function of Mr. Whymper, the commercial middleman for Napoleon. Jones also is given more to do: His shotgunning of the barn results in the death of Old Major; later, he dynamites the windmill and has an amusing but irrelevant sexual adventure with Pilkington's wife. Near the end, the allegorical note takes on a definite anti-Nazi character with the glorification of Napoleon as animals march along to powerful music, and we see geese appropriately goose-stepping to martial music and flying birds assuming the shape of bombers. Then comes what the narrator refers to as "the storm of judgment," which destroys the farm, enabling the exiled animals to return. In the final scene, they watch as the new owners, a blond couple with two blond children, drive up in their convertible while the car radio plays Fats Domino's "Blueberry Hill" and Jessie tells us, "We will not allow them to make the same mistakes."

BBC radio aired at least two adaptations of *Animal Farm,* the first made by Orwell himself in 1947. (The text is reprinted in an appendix to volume VIII of *The Complete Works,* ed. Peter Davison.) A second version, produced as was the first by Orwell's friend RAYNER HEPPENSTALL, was broadcast in 1952.

WORKS CITED

Bowker, Gordon. *Inside George Orwell.* New York: Palgrave, 2003.

Connolly, Cyril. Review of *Animal Farm.* In *George Orwell: The Critical Heritage,* edited by Jeffrey Meyers, 199–200. London: Routledge, 1975.

Cooper, Lettice. "Eileen Blair." In *Orwell Remembered,* edited by Audrey Coppard and Bernard Crick, 161–166. New York: Facts On File, 1984.

Crick, Bernard. *George Orwell: A Life.* Boston: Little, Brown. 1980.

Fowler, Roger. *The Language of George Orwell.* New York: St. Martin's Press, 1995.

Frye, Northrop. Review. In *George Orwell: The Critical Heritage,* edited by Jeffrey Meyers, 206–208. London: Routledge, 1975.

Fyvel, T. R. *George Orwell: A Personal Memoir.* New York: Macmillan, 1982.

Gardner, Averil. *George Orwell.* Boston: Twayne, 1987.

Greene, Graham. Review. In *George Orwell: The Critical Heritage,* edited by Jeffrey Meyers, 195–196. London: Routledge, 1975.

Hodgart, Matthew. "From *Animal Farm* to *Nineteen Eighty-Four*" In *The World of George Orwell,* edited by Miriam Gross, 135–142. New York: Simon and Schuster. 1971.

Hollis, Christopher. *A Study of George Orwell.* Chicago: Regnery, 1956.

Hunter, Lynette. *George Orwell: The Search for a Voice.* Milton Keynes, UK: Open University Press, 1984.

Kirschner, Paul. "The Dual Purpose of *Animal Farm.*" In *Bloom's Modern Critical Views: George Orwell. Updated Edition,* edited by Harold Bloom, 145–179. New York: Chelsea House. 2007.

Lee, Robert. *Orwell's Fiction.* South Bend, Ind.: Notre Dame University Press, 1969.

Letermendia, V. C. "Revolution on *Animal Farm:* Orwell's Neglected Commentary." In *George Orwell,* edited by Graham Holderness, et al., 15–30. New York: St. Martin's Press, 1998.

Mc Neil, William. *America, Britain and Russia: Their Cooperation and Conflict, 1941–1946.* New York: Oxford University Press, 1952.

Martin, Kingsley. Review. In *George Orwell: The Critical Heritage,* edited by Jeffrey Meyers, 197–199. London: Routledge, 1975.

Meyers, Jeffrey. *George Orwell: The Critical Heritage.* London: Routledge, 1975.

Rai, Alok. *Orwell and the Politics of Despair.* Cambridge: Cambridge University Press, 1988.

Rees, Richard. *George Orwell: Fugitive from the Camp of Victory.* Carbondale: Southern Illinois University Press, 1961.

Rodden, John. *The Politics of Literary Reputation.* New York: Oxford University Press, 1989.

Small, Christopher. *The Road to Miniluv.* Pittsburg: Pittsburg University Press, 1975.

Smyer, Richard. Animal Farm: *Pastoralism and Politics.* Boston: Twayne, 1988.

Tolkien, J. R. R. "On Fairy Stories." *Tree and Leaf.* London: Unwin Books, 1964.

Warburg, Fredric. *All Authors Are Equal.* New York: St. Martin's Press, 1973.

Williams, Raymond. *George Orwell.* New York: Viking, 1971.

Wilson, Edmund. Review. In *George Orwell: The Critical Heritage,* edited by Jeffrey Meyers, 204–205. London: Routledge, 1975.

Woodcock, George. *The Crystal Spirit.* Boston: Little, Brown, 1966.

Zwerdling, Alex. *Orwell and the Left.* New Haven, Conn.: Yale University Press, 1974.

Anti-Semitism in Britain

Contemporary Jewish Record, (April, 1945).

SYNOPSIS

Written in February 1945, before the first liberation of the Nazi death camps, the essay begins with a few simple facts: The British Jewish population consists of 400,000 people, plus thousands of Jewish refugees who have fled to Britain since 1934, the first year of the Nazi regime in Germany. Commercially, British Jews have tended to operate in the food, clothing, and furniture industries so that they are neither powerful nor influential enough to stir up resentment, although they are very prominent in intellectual circles. Nevertheless, there had been a recent noticeable increase in anti-Semitism, not of a violent type but one that could have future political ramifications. Orwell quotes a variety of anti-Semitic comments from a cross section of people, revealing two facts. The first is that people above a certain level of education deny that they are anti-Semitic and draw a distinction between being anti-Semitic and disliking Jews. The second, of which the first is a prime example, is the fact that anti-Semitism is irrational, which is to say that it is rooted in the emotions, not in the mind. Nevertheless, anti-Semites are seldom at a loss for assigning reasons for their attitude.

The war is one of the main reasons for the growth of anti-Semitism. Many see this as a Jewish war because Jews stand to benefit the most from an Allied victory. Another is the belief that many Jews, although having the most to gain from the defeat of fascism, are said to be "exceptionally clever at dodging military service." But the fact is that the government deliberately downplays the significant presence and contributions of Jewish soldiers for fear of alienating allies in South Africa and Arab nations. Still another reason is the rumor that Jews act particularly cowardly during air raids, ignoring the fact that the Jewish quarter in London was "one of the first areas to be heavily blitzed," and as a result, many of its residents fled to shelters in other areas of the city.

Nevertheless, Orwell argues that many people are ashamed of being anti-Semitic, and that we need not fear that it will become "respectable." As a result of Hitler's persecution, there has developed a politically correct attitude toward certain traditional expressions of anti-Jewish feeling. One example is the suppression of the "Jew joke," popular in the music halls of the 1920s and early '30s. Another is the protest against the government policy of internment of refugees, many of them Jews, in 1940. Hitler's persecution has also caused many people to accept the Jewish position on Palestine instead of looking carefully at the merits of the case.

British anti-Semitism cuts across class barriers, as prevalent among boys at an exclusive public school as in the slums of the East End in London. Even in literary circles, Orwell cites, among others, the anti-Semitic remarks of a writer he otherwise admires, G. K. CHESTERTON. Orwell goes on to list some of the rationalizations for anti-Semitism, although he holds to his position that it is, in essence, a neurosis. Among these rationalizations, one refers to the fact that Jewish intellectuals have been supporters of international socialism and strongly opposed to the sense of British patriotism that has been reawakened during the war. But Orwell confesses that he has no convincing theory about the root cause of anti-Semitism except to see it as "a part of the larger problem of 'nationalism,'" in which Jews have been forced into the role of scapegoat.

Summarizing his points, he lists the following: Anti-Semitism is more prevalent in Britain than appearances suggest; however, it is not likely to lead to overt persecution; it is at heart an irrational sentiment that is immune to reason; the Nazi persecutions have not eliminated anti-Semitism but suppressed the outward expression of it; and finally, the subject deserves serious study. It seems that no one is exempt from certain types of group prejudices, leaving all of us subject to "the lunacy of believing that whole races are mysteriously good or mysteriously evil." Therefore, anyone attempting to investigate the subject should first ask himself the question *Why does anti-Semitism appeal to me?* But in any case, it is linked in its root cause to nationalism.

COMMENTARY

Orwell's attitude toward Jews appears to be one of increasing awareness and sensitivity, partly the result of his acquisition of Jewish friends and colleagues in the course of his career, but largely as a result of Hitler's persecution. His early writings up until 1936 are sprinkled with disparaging allusions to "the Jew." The use of the term itself in place of an individual name in literature is at least as old as *The Merchant of Venice,* in which Shylock is referred to as "the Jew" many more times than he is called Shylock. In that respect, the casual references in *Burmese Days, Down and Out, A Clergyman's Daughter,* and *Aspidistra* to some otherwise nameless person as a "Jew," is commonly found in other literature of the period. But no doubt, Orwell was conscious of an unexamined attitude behind those when he was writing this essay. He avoids an explicit mea culpa in the essay, but those words are hovering over its conclusion, with the recommendation that anyone wishing to study the subject should engage in a rigorous self-examination. The implication is perhaps that Orwell has undergone this examination himself and has come to recognize any latent anti-Semitism as irrational but still there.

It is interesting to compare his conclusion here with his review in *The Observer* (November 7, 1948) of Jean-Paul Sartre's *Portrait of the Anti-Semite.* He takes issue with the book's title, with its reference to "*the*" anti-Semite, implying that all anti-Semites are the same, largely confined, according to Sartre, to the "petty bourgeois" class. For Orwell, Sartre has merely replaced one scapegoat with another, objectifying not only the anti-Semite but also the Jew.

In his memoir of Orwell, his good friend T. R. Fyvel notes that MALCOLM MUGGERIDGE was surprised that so many Jews would have been present at Orwell's funeral, "because he was, at heart, strongly anti-Semitic." Fyvel, a Jew who had experienced anti-Semitism throughout his life, disputes this idea. However, he does suggest that Orwell's attitude on the "Jewish question" was ambivalent. Fyvel then summarizes the points that Orwell makes in this essay. But he finds that Orwell's attempts to explore the subject did not get very far: "European anti-Semitism was much too large, too old, too historic, too complex a problem for his type of amateur social research" (181). Fyvel then goes on to discuss a disagreement the two had over Orwell's essay "Revenge Is Sour," in which Fyvel took him to task for his relative indifference to the Holocaust and his characterization of an American officer who features prominently in the essay as "the Jew." He describes Orwell' reaction to the criticism as "sheer astonishment . . . but I think he took my point about language. He never again referred to anyone simply as 'the Jew'" (182).

WORK CITED

Fyvel, T. R. *George Orwell: A Personal Memoir.* New York: Macmillan, 1982.

"Arthur Koestler"

Essay first published in his *Collected Essays* (1946), American title: *Dickens, Dalí and Others* (1946). The essay was originally written for the journal *Focus,* which did not publish it until after its appearance in book form.

SYNOPSIS

Koestler is one of a very small group of European writers who have experienced living under totalitarian rule. No English writer has undergone this experience. As a consequence, there is "in England almost no literature of disillusionment about the Soviet Union." In Koestler's case, his specific focus is on the Moscow purge trials. He has written five novels that have been published in English. Three of them are set primarily in prisons, yet all of them are imbued with the atmosphere of a nightmare.

Orwell considers the earliest of these *The Gladiators,* a historical novel based on the story of Spartacus and the slave revolt that occurred in 65 B.C. The revolt fails because of a recalcitrant faction among the former slaves, but as Orwell sees it, the story fails to confront the novel's central problem of the corruption of revolutionary ideals by the reality of power. In *Darkness at Noon,* Koestler's masterpiece, the focus is more psychological than political. This novel approaches true tragedy in its account of the old Bolshevik Rubashov, who confesses to crimes he has not committed. It is not torture that forces him to confess but the fact he is a man who has been hollowed out. In the course of his career as an agent of the party, he has committed a whole range of crimes in the name of the revolution. But, unlike the "new men," of the party, he has memories of prerevolutionary life and of the moral values that were erased by the revolution. Here, Orwell suggests, Koestler is on the verge of asserting that revolution itself is a corrupting process, but he does not cross that line explicitly.

His next book, *Scum of the Earth,* is an autobiographical account of his experiences of prison life in Spain and later his internment as an enemy alien in France and England. *Arrival and Departure,* his next book, advances the idea that personal neuroses may lie at the root of the revolutionary's motivation. Nevertheless, his main character obeys an instinctual urge to fight against the evil of fascism, which renders his motivation essentially irrelevant.

Orwell points out that Koestler sees himself as a "short-term pessimist." Although rejecting revolution, he still clings to the ultimate socialist illusion of an earthly paradise. Thus he sees Koestler falling back on his basic hedonism, in retreat from Orwell's alternative view, which is to abandon the idea "that the object of life is happiness." He concludes with the reminder that "all revolutions are failures, but they are not all the same failures." Orwell's comments on the apparent failure of revolution have played a pivotal role in many discussions of *Animal Farm.*

"Art of Donald McGill, The"

An essay first published in *Horizon* (1941) and later included in *The Collected Essays of George Orwell* (American title: *Dickens, Dalí, and Others*) in 1946. This essay is one of Orwell's pioneering studies in the field later known as POPULAR CULTURE.

SYNOPSIS

The topic of this essay is the "penny or twopenny postcards with their endless succession of fat women in tight bathing dresses," illustrating a joke, invariably a low joke. The master of this genre is Donald McGill, who is not only the best, but also the most representative figure in this field. To examine his work is to encounter the type in its purest form. His postcards are distinguished by their "overpowering vulgarity," both in the jokes and the drawings. Their subject matter is almost exclusively devoted to one of the following topics: sex, home life, drunkenness, WC jokes, interclass snobbery, stock figures, and politics. The largest of these categories, by far, is the sex joke, which adheres to two conventions: "Marriage only benefits the woman" and "Sex appeal vanishes at the age of twenty-five." Home life's two conventions are that "there is no such thing as a happy marriage" and "no man ever gets the better of a woman in an argument." The two abiding conventions of drunkenness are that "all drunken men have optical illusions" and that "drunkenness is something peculiar to middle-aged men. Drunken youths or women are never represented." For WC jokes, the two conventions are that chamber pots are inherently funny "and so are public lavatories."

In the category of interclass snobbery, the working class and the upper class are the preferred targets of these jokes, indicating that the audience are members of the better-off working class and the poorer middle class. Stock figures include Scotsmen, lawyers, and two holdovers from the Edwardian age, the "masher" and the "suffragette." The "Jew joke" has disappeared with the rise of Hitler. Political jokes tend to reflect an old-fashioned radicalism circa 1900.

The heart of the appeal of these postcards is their obscenity. Their "dominant motif . . . is the woman with the stuck-out behind." But these cards are not intended to be pornography. Rather they are a parody of pornography, examples of what might be called the Sancho Panza view of life. The Sancho Panza/Don Quixote relationship symbolizes the duality that exists within each of us. Don Quixote represents the part of each person that aspires to nobility of spirit, while Sancho represents the material body, the fat little man within, whose goal is to indulge his senses and to stay alive. To continue to exist, society must exert a rigorous control over Sancho Panza. In fact, in our society, one of the few places where Sancho Panza is allowed to express himself is in comic postcards. Another is in the music halls. The fact that they seem vulgar or ugly is precisely the point. They are the modern versions of the Saturnalia, the holiday spirit when the ordinary rules governing society are suspended or ignored. In Shakespeare's time, the low humor of clowns and bumpkins was integrated into the serious plays, but in our time it is preserved only in those postcards. As a result, they speak for an important "corner of the human heart."

COMMENTARY

Susan Watson, who served as housekeeper and guardian of Orwell's son, Richard, after the death of Orwell's first wife, Eileen, recalled an occasion when Orwell invited his aunt NELLIE LIMOUZIN to his flat and showed her his collection of Donald McGill postcards. The fact that he was a collector adds to the seriousness of his interest in the seemingly lighthearted subject. He had for some time wanted to explore popular culture with a view to seeing what its conventions reveal about society. In 1936, he wrote of this interest to his friend, the well-known anthropologist GEOFFREY GORER. "I have often thought it would be very interesting to study the conventions, etc., of books from an anthropological point of view." By 1940 the notion of books had expanded to other cultural forms. In a BBC program on "The Proletarian Writer," the discussion turned to popular forms of poetry, such as limericks and advertising jingles, to which Orwell added "Yes, and don't forget the jokes on the comic colored postcards, especially Donald McGill's. I'm particularly attracted to those." A year later, he published this essay, his first incursion into a form of popular culture in order to demonstrate the role it played in society. A striking feature of the article is its lack of condescension. Although he does not indicate in the essay that he is a fan, he treats his subject with the respect that he believes it deserves. At one point, he compares the similarities of its conventions to Greek tragedies. At the conclusion, he invokes the low comic figures in Shakespeare's serious plays, such as the porter in *Macbeth* and the gravedigger in *Hamlet* (although he doesn't actually mention these plays). All of this adds to the principle that underlies cultural studies, that popular culture should be approached with the same respect as high culture.

Reinforcing this idea further is the invocation of Sancho Panza as a metaphor for the view of life represented by the postcards. It might be said that Orwell had already worked these ideas out in his 1939 novel, *Coming Up for Air*. In many respects, George Bowling, his protagonist, is the embodiment of the Sancho Panza view of life, a fat little man trapped in a deadening marriage, looking for a temporary escape. Among those who have heaped praise on this essay, when it first appeared in a collection of Orwell's essays, are two somewhat surprising early reviewers. The first is the mandarin prose stylist Harvard professor Harry Levin: "The greatest literature derives its wholeness, he [Orwell] knows, not only from the intransigent intellectuality of Don Quixote but from the easygoing vulgarity of Sancho Panza. Tense modernity has banished the latter to the subterranean realm of the comic postcard, and thither Orwell enterprisingly pursues it" (218). The other is the conservative satirist Evelyn Waugh, whose review declared: "'The Art of Donald McGill' is, perhaps, the masterpiece of the book" (213).

WORKS CITED

Levin, Harry. Review of *Dickens, Dalí and Others. The New Republic,* May 6, 1946. Reprinted in *George Orwell: The Critical Heritage,* edited by Jeffrey Meyers, 215–218. London: Routledge, 1975.

Waugh, Evelyn. Review of *The Collected Essays of George Orwell. Tablet.* April 6, 1946. Reprinted in *George Orwell: The Critical Heritage,* edited by Jeffrey Meyers, 211–215. London: Routledge, 1975.

"As I Please"

The running title of a column in *TRIBUNE* written by Orwell from December 3, 1943, to April 4, 1947. In that period, he wrote 80 columns, touching on a riotous range of topics, whose index occupies five double-columned pages in volume 20 of Peter Davison's *Complete Works of George Orwell.* He usually discussed no more than one or two topics in each column.

Orwell wasted no time in provoking his largely left-wing readers into hitting back at his opinions. He began his first column with a description of the obnoxious behavior of American soldiers stationed in England. Among his observations was the comment, "The general consensus of opinion seems to be that the only American soldiers with decent

NATIONAL UNION OF JOURNALISTS

7 John Street, Bedford Row, London, W.C.I

'Phone : HOLborn 2258 Telegrams : Natujay Holb, London

This is to certify that

Mr. GEORGE ORWELL

of The Tribune

is a member of the T. & P. Branch of the National Union of Journalists.

Leslie R. Aldous Branch Sec.

(Address) 66, Priory Gdns., N.6.

Member's Sig.

George Orwell's 1943 National Union of Journalists card *(Orwell Archive, UCL Library Services, Special Collections)*

manners are the negroes." One respondent eviscerated every phrase in this sentence, concluding with the observation that "I'm afraid I must diagnose the decent manners in many negroes as a projection of their servility—and as such, highly lamentable, much more lamentable to me than the bumptiousness of white soldiers." This was the beginning of a wonderfully invigorating feature of these columns, in which his readers gave as good as they got, with the result that "As I Please" became the most controversial feature of *Tribune.* His most provocative column came in reaction to the 1944 Warsaw uprising, in which the Soviets made no attempt to support the Polish rebels and the English left-wing press followed the party line, defending the Soviet inaction and defaming the rebels. In his column, Orwell concentrated on the automatic acceptance of the Soviet interpretation of the events in Warsaw. He reminded "English left-wing journalists and intellectuals" of the fate that awaited them: "Don't imagine that you can make yourself the boot-licking propagandist of the Soviet regime, or any other regime, and then suddenly return to mental decency. Once a whore, always a whore."

Although many of his columns distressed the editorial board at *Tribune,* its editor ANEURIN BEVAN never tried to censor or control Orwell's writing. In her review of *Orwell in "Tribune": As I Please and Other Writings,* Kate McLoughlin offers a breezy, 21st-century view of the man behind "As I Please":

> Their author comes across as temperate, meticulous, preachy, humorous, occasionally (as when considering the use of "infer" for "imply") splenetic: a decent, Dickens-reading, trivia-appreciating, hobby-horse riding, very English old buffer. When he wrote the last of them, Orwell was forty-four.

WORKS CITED

McLoughlin, Kate. *Times Literary Supplement,* November 3, 2006, 28.

Anderson, Paul, ed. *Orwell in "Tribune": As I Please and Other Writings.* London: Methuen, 2006.

BBC writings

Orwell worked at the BBC from August 1941 to November 1943, writing and producing broadcasts for the Indian Section of the BBC Eastern Services Department. His basic tasks involved writing scripts that were variously described as newsletters, news reviews, and news commentaries. These included weekly newsletters, broadcast to India, Malaya, and Indonesia in English. It is probable that much of these texts were similar but not identical. Some of these English scripts were read on air by Orwell himself. In addition, he prepared scripts that were translated into the Indian dialects Bengali, Marathi, Tamil, and Gujarati. With the exceptions of a few fragments, these have not survived.

Of course, everything that was read on the air had to pass the scrutiny of the wartime censors. The censorship and the generally bureaucratic character of the BBC were bad enough for someone of Orwell's temperament, but worse was the sense that the reports were reaching a very small share of the already small number of short-wave radios in India.

In addition to the more than 200 news scripts he wrote during his 27 months at the BBC, he also produced a number of individual programs for the Eastern Services. Some of these were adaptations of existing stories and plays, such as "The Fox," adapted from a story by IGNAZIO SILONE. The story is set on a pig farm, but it is not an animal fable and therefore in no sense would have served as a source of *Animal Farm*. Another script is an adaptation of an H. G. WELLS's short story "A Slip under the Microscope." Still another is his adaptation of *Macbeth*, his favorite Shakespearean play. In his commentary, he calls *Macbeth* "Shakespeare's most perfect play."

Shortly before he left the BBC to become the literary editor of *Tribune*, he adapted the Hans Christian Andersen fairy tale "The Emperor's New Clothes," which Orwell considered his most successful adaptation. But the program he was most proud of was VOICE, a six-episode poetry magazine on the air.

Orwell wrote for the BBC both before and after his tenure as a producer in the Eastern Service Department. Three months before signing on, he delivered a talk on the Gerard Manley Hopkins poem "Felix Randal" under the heading "THE MEANING OF A POEM." In 1946, he wrote two radio plays, "The Voyage of the Beagle" on Charles Darwin, and for the BBC Children's Hour "Little Red Riding Hood," the denouement of which finds a woodcutter slitting open the belly of the wolf and grandmother and Red Riding Hood emerging unscathed. In 1947 he adapted *Animal Farm*, produced by his friend RAYNER HEPPENSTALL.

"Benefit of Clergy: Some Notes on Salvador Dalí"

An essay in response to reading Dalí's autobiography, *The Secret Life of Salvador Dalí* (1942). Intended for *The Saturday Book*, 1944, this essay had an ironic publishing debut. It was included in the printing of the book, but at the last minute, the publishers decided that they might be accused of obscenity and proceeded to excise Orwell's contribution, although retaining the title in the table of contents. The irony rests in the fact that the obscenity lay in Orwell's description of Dalí's book, which he was condemning for its obscenity.

SYNOPSIS

Orwell begins with the observation that autobiographies that never reveal "something disgraceful" about their subjects cannot be trusted. On the other hand, when the autobiographer is obviously stretching the truth or presenting fantasies as reality, he may be unintentionally revealing a truth about himself. Such is the case with Salvador Dalí's memoir. Some of the incidents Dalí records are simply incredible if taken as literal truths; others are sensationalized distortions of ordinary experience. They add up to a picture not only of the man but of his age. Examples of fantasies represented as real include his "delirious joy" in kicking his three-year-old sister in the head, flinging another little boy off a bridge, putting a wounded bat into a pail, and later, when he sees the dying bat being eaten by ants, putting the bat, still covered with ants, in his mouth and biting it in half.

Consistent with the perverse imagination of these recollections are the pictures that made Dalí the enfant terrible of expressionist art—his best-known pictures, many of which are included in his book. Among the lurid vices Dalí claims to have indulged in, necrophilia is very prominent; corpses, skulls, and decomposing bodies regularly recur in his pictures, notably in his "Mannequin rotting in a taxicab." The mannequin depicts the dead body of a girl, over whose face and breast large snails are crawling.

Orwell argues that behind Dalí's modernist rebel posturing is a turn-of-the-20th-century sensibility. In English terms, he is an Edwardian artist at heart, but he is driven by the need to reassure himself "that he is not commonplace." To avoid the fate of being ordinary, he has used his art to "escape: into wickedness." Orwell concedes, that

Dalí is an excellent draftsman, which is to say that as an artist he is competent; however, as a man he is deplorable.

Dalí's behavior raises the question of the responsibility of the artist to his society. There are those who would argue that the artist should be exempt from the moral claims of the community. They are asking for the aesthetic equivalent of *Benefit of Clergy* (the medieval principle that members of the clergy were exempt from being tried by a secular court). This extraordinary privilege is sometimes invoked in the belief that the artist is ahead of his time and therefore not to be judged by the standards that apply to other members of society. Orwell makes it clear that he is not suggesting that either Dalí's pictures or his book should be banned. To be sure, Dalí's art invites psychological analyses of the man. But the appeal of such art raises sociological questions about the society or segment of society that seems to accept it. A Marxist critic would have a ready-made explanation that Dalí's popularity is a clear sign of bourgeois decadence now entering its final stage, but that is too general an answer. More to the point is to recognize that pictures such as "Mannequin Rotting in a Taxicab" are "diseased and disgusting" and to proceed from there to examine their appeal.

COMMENTARY

In this essay, Orwell comes to grips with a problem that he has encountered before, notably in INSIDE THE WHALE, the role of the artist/writer in society. In the case of Henry Miller and his indifference to social and political responsibilities, he allowed that a case can be made for the artist's becoming detached and uninvolved if that is where his artistic conscience dictates he should be. Dalí, however, presents a much less acceptable possibility. For Orwell, he is not a true artist but an exploiter, whose purpose is to call attention to himself while capitalizing on the shock value of his work. The objection to Orwell's characterization, raised by at least one critic, is that although many might agree with Orwell's estimate of Dalí's art, this essay does not demonstrate that Orwell is capable of rendering a knowledgeable opinion on the subject.

WORK CITED

Vervoort, P. "'Benefit of Clergy': Opposition to Salvador Dalí" In *Orwell x 8: A Symposium,* edited by J. M. Richardson, 67–92. Winnipeg, Alberta: Ronald Frye, 1986.

"Bookshop Memories"

Brief essay first published in *Fortnightly* (1946), recalling his experiences working at Booklovers' Corner in London from October 1934 to January 1936.

SYNOPSIS

A secondhand bookstore is a magnet for all sorts of eccentrics, of which "two types of pest" are guaranteed to show up. One is a "decayed type of person, smelling of bread crumbs," who tries to sell books of no value; the other is a person who has books put aside or put on order, promising to return and never does. For the latter, merely the illusion that they were buying the books gives them some gratification.

Bookstores also offer various sidelines, secondhand typewriters, used stamps, and sixpenny horoscopes. The main sideline, however, is the lending library, in which you rent a book for a few cents. The best-selling author in the lending library world is Ethel M. Dell, well-known author of women's novels. Men, on the other hand, prefer detective stories. As for the classic English novelists, nobody borrows their books. Another feature of borrowers: They don't like short-story collections.

Orwell asks himself if he would like to own a bookshop, and his answer is no. The principle reason is that working in a bookstore destroys one's love of books. First is the moral problem of having to lie about books. The other is that the pleasure—"The sight, the smell, the feel" of a book is lost when you are surrounded by thousands of dusty ones.

COMMENTARY

Orwell's work at the Booklovers' Corner near Hampstead Heath formed the basis of several chapters of his third novel, *Keep the Aspidistra Flying*. In the novel, the protagonist loses his job at the respectable bookstore where we first meet him, and he descends into bookstore hell, working for Mr. Cheeseman, a man who "had never in his life read a book himself, nor could he conceive why anyone could want to do so."

Orwell's coworker at Booklovers' Corner was JON KIMCHE, who recalled enjoying the work while Orwell carried out his tasks with "moody anger." On the other hand, it proved to be a good place for a young bachelor to meet women, such as KAY EKEVAL, his girlfriend until he met his future wife EILEEN O'SHAUGHNESSY.

"Books vs. Cigarettes"

A short essay, published in *Tribune* on February 8, 1946, and reprinted in *Shooting an Elephant and Other Essays* (1950), on the relative value of books. Orwell confronts the prevailing notion that purchasing books is far too expensive a hobby for most working-class people. The notion that "twelve and sixpence" for a book is beyond the means of average people derives from a failure to see the expenditure in the broader context of average daily allowances for other commodities.

First, Orwell catalogs his large personal library to determine how much he has spent over the course of a fixed period of years on books. Having arrived at an approximate total, he reduces the amount to a yearly figure of some 25 pounds. On the surface, the total may seem costly. Compared to other yearly expenses, however, he determines that such an expenditure on books is far less than the average man spends on tobacco.

"Boys' Weeklies"

Essay published as one of three in *Inside the Whale and Other Essays* published by Victor Gollancz on March 11, 1940. It appeared at the same time in the March 1940 issue of *Horizon*.

SYNOPSIS

Visit a news agent's shop in a poor area of any city in England, and you will find, in addition to the daily papers, a vast array of twopenny weeklies devoted to a single subject. It is extraordinary that so many of these exist, and their existence provides some interesting insights to the thoughts and feelings of the common people of England, more so, say, than best sellers, which cater to a middle-class audience, or to films and radios, because these forms of entertainment are basically forms of monopolies that don't have to cater to a specific niche audience. But the small weeklies operate with a very distinct audience, and to exist they must reflect the minds of their readers.

In that connection, Orwell asserts that he will be looking at popular weeklies written for boys. Two of the oldest of these are *Gem* and *Magnet*, which for 30 years have specialized in stories of public-school life, focusing on 14- to 15-year-old boys. The plots center around a group of good boys and their conflicts with a gang of bad boys at the school. A standard situation is one in which one of the good boys is accused of doing something wrong, but rather than squeal on the real miscreants, he suffers in silence. There are two subjects that are never introduced in these stories: sex and religion.

The source of the attraction these stories hold for boys is the glamour associated with elite public schools, and particularly their snob appeal. In the stories, a few characters are regularly identified by their aristocratic titles, or are we told directly of their parents' wealth, so that we hear of boys who receive five pounds a week of pocket money. The question Orwell wants to address in this connection is who reads these weeklies? Not the boys at the elite public schools, once they reach the age of about 12 years. The readership consists of teenagers, including girls not just in England but throughout the British Empire. These stories play a significant role in the fantasy lives of these young readers. The secret of their success is that "the characters are so carefully graded as to give almost every type of reader a character he can identify himself with." Thus, the characters range from the high-spirited athletic type to the scholarly type, or the boy who does not engage in games and high jinks but has some special talent that comes in handy in resolving plots. Of particular importance is the scholarship boy, with whom readers from poor homes can identify themselves. For the same reason, the cast of characters usually includes figures from Ireland, Scotland, Wales, and Australia.

The politics of *Gem* and *Magnet* are based on two principles: that "nothing ever changes" and "foreigners are funny." Ideologically, it is still the world of 1910. As for the international situation, although England is now on the brink of war (mid-1939) there is no sign of it in these stories.

But lately *Gem* and *Magnet* have been losing popularity as a newer group of boys' weeklies have emerged on the scene, moving away from the school setting into a wide variety of story types, notably adventure stories and science fiction. One striking difference is that the recent trend has thrown the emphasis on one dominating individual hero, as opposed to the group ethos of the *Gem/Magnet* stories. Here we see the influence of American magazines of this type: "The American ideal, the he-man, the tough guy . . . who puts everything right by socking everybody else in the jaw . . ." But like *Gem* and *Magnet,* the new weeklies operate on the assumption "that the major problems of our time do not exist . . . that the British Empire will last forever."

Orwell then compares the stories in boys' weeklies with those written for slightly older young women who have entered the workplace. Superficially, these stories appear more realistic and less sensational, and they include advice columns in which genuine problems are discussed. But the stories always end happily; someone who has lost a job gains a better one; the rival for a boyfriend's affection is routed.

It is true that these are escapist literature for teenagers and are essentially harmless, but they all reinforce an implicitly conservative message. Today's sophisticated adults carry with them attitudes and beliefs that they absorbed from their childhood and teenage reading, one of which is that the "British Empire is a sort of charity-concern which will last forever." One wonders why there are no weeklies from a left-wing perspective. The answer is that the wealthy press lords who control these publications would never permit it. As a result, ". . . boys' fiction above all, the blood and thunder stuff which nearly every boy devours at some time or other, is sodden with the worst illusions of 1910."

COMMENTARY

In the course of his essay, Orwell mentions that the author of the stories in *Magnet* was "Frank Richards" and in *Gem* the author is "Martin Clifford," but he goes on to doubt that over a period of 30 years any one person could be writing those stories every week. Shortly after the publication of the essay in *Horizon,* the magazine printed a detailed refutation of Orwell's article from Frank Richards. Richards (the pen name of Charles Hamilton) claimed that he was in fact the author of all of the *Gem* and *Magnet* stories. His stinging, angry reply answered Orwell's charges with wit and style. The substance of his defense, however, only justified Orwell's view of his political naïveté and old-fashioned Toryism. He concludes with a dismissal of Orwell's idea of a left-wing boys' paper: "Boys' minds ought not to be disturbed and worried by politics" (*CW,* XII, 85).

A few months later, Orwell received a letter from a children's book writer Geoffrey Trease, discussing the idea of a boys' weekly that was a "little more 'left' and also a little less out of date than the present ones." As for Richards, Orwell comments that "it's well nigh incredible that such people are walking about." (*CW,* XII, 156–157). The prospect of a left wing boys' paper was not developed, largely because of the severe paper shortage that set in on England during the war years. For an interesting discussion of one example of left-wing children's literature, see the Later Criticism section of the ANIMAL FARM entry.

"Boys' Weeklies" has come to be regarded as a pioneering effort, along with "THE ART OF DONALD MCGILL" and "RAFFLES AND MISS BLANDISH," in the sociological analysis of POPULAR CULTURE.

WORK CITED

The Complete Works of George Orwell. Edited by Peter Davison. Volume 12. London: Secker & Warburg, 1998.

British Pamphleteers

A two-volume collection of English pamphlets, for which Orwell wrote an introduction. The first volume was published in 1948 by Alan Wingate. This volume of pamphlets covered the period from the 16th century to the late 18th century, or in Orwell's words, "from the Reformation, with which English pamphleteering may be said to have started, to the war of American Independence." Although Orwell is listed as coeditor of volume I, all of the editing and selecting was the work of his friend Reginald Reynolds, to whom Orwell gives full credit in his introduction. He did not live to see volume 2, which was published in 1951, containing an introduction by the historian A. J. P. Taylor.

SYNOPSIS

Orwell's introduction begins by making it clear that the editorial work has been done by Reynolds, whose task was complicated by having to decide what constitutes a pamphlet. As a genre, the pamphlet is often confused with any small booklet published in paper covers. A true pamphlet, Orwell argues, is a text of anywhere from 500 to 10,000 words and which sells for a few pennies, and regardless of its subject, constitutes a protest of some sort. Pamphleteering exists most prominently in a society in which dissent is relatively common, always recognizing that all regimes in the 16th and 17th centuries were oppressive by modern standards. Thus, in a contemporary totalitarian state, pamphleteering is virtually impossible. Even in those earlier days, pamphlets were generally seen as a form of underground literature, the authors of which were either anonymous or used pen names. It is no accident that a mere four pamphlets in this volume cover the period from 1714 to 1789. The preceding 150 years were the great age of English pamphleteering; at stake were two great conflicts that concerned every citizen: the Catholic/Protestant and the feudalism/capitalism struggles.

Orwell asserts that although modern society has seen a vast increase in the publication of pamphlets, it has also seen a considerable decline in quality. One reason for this is the general decay of the English language. To illustrate his point, he contrasts a passage in a pamphlet written by his old publisher VICTOR GOLLANCZ with a passage on a similar subject by 16th-century pamphleteer John Aylmer. He is quick to point out that Gollancz's prose is a perfectly acceptable example of modern English and in some ways more precise than John Aylmer's, but the rich, down-to-earth, metaphor-laden prose of Aylmer shows how much we have lost in our language. Another problem with the modern pamphlet is that the majority are produced by parties or organizations, while the early pamphlets were the products of individuals airing a grievance, attacking an enemy, or proposing a plan. As the outlet for a distinctly individual perspective, the pamphlet serves as a "footnote or marginal comment on official history." It exists as an alternative view, a minority view, which the modern state has become more and more efficient in suppressing. As a result, he points out, "At any given moment there is a sort of all prevailing orthodoxy, a general tacit agreement not to discuss some large and uncomfortable fact." Orwell cites as an example the postwar expulsion of 12 million Germans from East Prussia and the Sudetenland, which the majority of the British people are not even aware of. What is needed now is a revival of the pamphlet, not as the expression of a political party but as that of an individual with the ability to employ the pamphlet as a significant social and literary vehicle of free expression.

COMMENTARY

As with comic postcards, Orwell was an ardent collector of pamphlets. He began collecting in 1935 or 1937. By 1947, he estimated that he owned between 1,200 and 2,000, some of which were rare. He stored them in classified boxes, and each box had a list of the contents attached. After his death, in accord with his wishes, the pamphlets were donated to the British Museum (now the British Library), where they have been cataloged and made available to the public. Orwell described himself on one occasion (disparagingly) as not a novelist but a pamphleteer, a term also used by V. S. Pritchett in his review of *Nineteen Eighty-Four.* In addition, some of Orwell's work did appear in pamphlet form, such as "POETRY

AND THE MICROPHONE" (*The New Saxon Pamphlet*, No. 3).

The Lion and the Unicorn has sometimes been referred to as a pamphlet, but it is, by Orwell's definition, too long, fitting more precisely the term *booklet.* Both as a reader and a writer, Orwell had more than an ordinary interest in the pamphlet. In 1943, he wrote a conglomerate review of 15 pamphlets, which he divides into eight categories: anti-left and crypto-fascist, conservative, social democrat, communist, Trotskyist and anarchist, nonparty radical, religious, and lunatic. He goes on to bemoan the current state of pamphlet writing, since he feels that the pamphlet ought to be *the* literary form of an age like our own. For that purpose, the category that is most likely to produce a renaissance of pamphlet writing is "the non-party radical" (*CW*, 14, 300–303).

Burmese Days

Orwell's first novel, published in the United States by Harper's in 1934 and then a year later in London by Victor Gollancz. The novel is notable for its ambitious attempt to incorporate one individual's struggle to achieve authentic self-realization within the corrupting context of European colonialism.

HISTORICAL/BIOGRAPHICAL BACKGROUND

Burma (now Myanmar) came under British rule in 1885 and was declared, for administrative purposes, a province of India. The Burmese proved to be a relatively tranquil colonial population until 1919. That year, the British government, in response to the Gandhi-led campaign for greater power, passed the Government of India Act, providing local reforms in India, but not in Burma. An outpouring of protests, particularly among Buddhist monks and students at Rangoon University, greeted this discriminatory treatment, followed by a nationwide student strike. Eventually, the strike was called off, but many students refused to return to British-run schools to enter so-called national schools. The same year (1919), the entire Burma/India situation was exacerbated by the Amritsar Massacre, in which British troops opened fire on a crowd of protesting Indians in the city of Amritsar, killing 379 civilians and wounding 1,500. Forced to resign his post, the British commander who had ordered his troops to open fire on an unarmed crowd, General Reginald Dyer, returned to England and received a hero's welcome by conservative politicians. (In chapter 2 of *Burmese Days,* the English Club members echo those sentiments about Dyer.) In 1923, the British government agreed to extend the Indian reforms to Burma, but by then, the damage had been done. The young had awakened, no longer content to be treated as inferiors in their own country.

The opening line of Orwell's essay SHOOTING AN ELEPHANT ("In Moulmein, in Southern Burma, I was hated by large numbers of people. . . .") suggests the extent of the bitterness that existed between the local population and the British occupiers during his five years in Burma. He had arrived in 1922 to assume a doubly despised role: He was not only an Englishman but also an English policeman. He had chosen Burma rather than India, because he had family connections still living there, including his maternal grandmother Thérèse Limouzin (see HALLILEY, THÉRÈSE). He also had some Eurasian cousins, the children of two uncles, William and Frank, who had married Burmese women. These relatives lived in Moulmein, a relatively sophisticated city, not at all like the small-town atmosphere of the novel's Kyauktada, the model for which was Katha, Orwell's last posting before returning to England.

The Burmese experience converted the young man, fresh from the cloistered, bookish world of Eton (he was 19 when he arrived in Burma) into a lifelong opponent of IMPERIALISM, the intensity of which, as he admitted, was rooted in guilt for his role in the oppression of the Burmese people. But the conversion did not take place overnight. For much of his time there, he was ambivalent, torn between the desire to "drive a bayonet into a Buddhist priest's guts" and attempts to understand and appreciate the Burmese, their culture. He was particularly struck by the natural environment. As he confessed in the autobiographical section of THE ROAD TO WIGAN PIER, "[t]he landscapes of Burma, which, when I was there so appalled me, as to assume the qualities of a nightmare . . . stayed so hauntingly in my mind that I was obliged to write a novel about them in order to get rid of them." Over a period of time, he came to hate his job, doing "the dirty work of Empire." That hatred comes through clearly in the novel.

Burma won its independence from England in 1948, but since 1962, it has been ruled by military regimes. At present it is a de facto police state, with government spies and informers a pervasive presence in a reasonable approximation of *Nineteen Eighty-Four.* One measure of the government's oppression is the fact that the works of George Orwell have been banned, with the single exception of *Burmese Days.* In *Finding George Orwell in Burma* (2004), Emma Larkin describes her visit to present-day Myanmar in an attempt to trace the steps of Blair/Orwell. While visiting Katha (the novel's Kyauktada), she used a sketch of the village that Orwell had made, indicating the locations of the English club and other spots. She was also able to locate the building that was Orwell's house during his stay. Adding to the interest of her findings is the fact that she was being spied on by government agents throughout her visit. It was as though the setting of his first novel had been transformed into that of his last.

SYNOPSIS

Chapter I

Enter the villain—U Po Kyin, subdivisional magistrate of Kyauktada, a small town in upper Burma. U Po Kyin sits on his veranda early in the morning. Although it is only the month of April, the prospect of blazing midday heat is already here. U Po Kyin is dwelling on his past life. He recalls the day he witnessed, as a "naked pot-bellied child," the British troops marching into Mandalay, a sight that sent him fleeing in momentary panic. He recognized almost immediately that these tall invaders could not be beaten; they must be joined. At the age of 20, he had "a lucky stroke of blackmail" that enabled him to buy a position as a government clerk. Once there, he joined a ring of clerks who were stealing government property. When he learned that some clerks were slated to be promoted, he wrote a letter denouncing his fellow clerks and was promoted for his treachery. Now, as a subdivisional magistrate, he will probably be promoted to deputy commissioner. In the meantime, he uses his magistrate position to enrich himself in a variety of ruthless and treacherous ways. He never takes bribes on one side in a case, rather he accepts bribes from both sides and decides the case on its merits. As a result he has acquired a reputation for fairness. This morning he is checking up on his latest scheme with his underling, Ba Sein. Ba Sein is the trusted clerk of Mr. Macgregor, the deputy commissioner of the district. He shows U Po Kyin a copy of the *Burmese Patriot,* a disreputable "rag" that contains a scurrilous attack on Macgregor, accusing him of having sired nine Burmese children and of not having supported any of them. The article has been written by Hla Pe, a young man, hoping that U Po Kyin will recommend him for a clerkship. The story is a tissue of lies, but it is U Po Kyin's intention to spread the story that it was written by Dr. Veraswami, the local physician and the superintendent of the jail. U Po Kyin is determined to destroy the doctor by convincing the Europeans in the village that the doctor is not loyal to the crown. He plans to begin an anonymous letter writing campaign denouncing Veraswami, beginning by ascribing the article in the *Burmese Patriot* to him. When Ba Sein points out that Veraswami has a strong ally among the English, timber merchant Mr. Flory, U Po Kyin predicts that "Flory will desert his friend quickly enough when the trouble begins." Having set his villainous plot in motion, the enormously obese magistrate devours a massive breakfast, served to him by his wife, Ma Kin. Ma Kin chides him for his plot against Veraswami, a good man. A pious Buddhist, Ma Kin warns her husband that he must be careful to acquire merit in the hereafter by supporting the local priests and other acts of charity. U Po Kyin agrees, confident that he has enough credit to do very well in future incarnations.

Chapter 2

On the same morning, we meet the Mr. Flory, referred to as a friend of Dr. Veraswami in the previous chapter, as he prepares to leave his house. John Flory is a 35-year-old man of average height and of ordinary looks, except for a large blue birthmark that covers the left side of his face. He is extremely self-conscious about this disfiguring mark. From his house at the top of a slope, he has a view of the town of Kyauktada, with its population of 4,000 Asians and seven Europeans. The center of life for those seven is the European Club, in which direction Flory is headed. Entering the club, he meets Westfield, the district superintendent of police; Maxwell, the divisional forest officer; Lackersteen, the manager of a local timber firm; and Ellis, the manager of another timber firm. Although it is only a little after nine o'clock, Lackersteen is already drunk, a sign that his wife is not nearby. Ellis, whose sharp Cockney voice and intimidating anger dominates the conversation, reads a notice from Macgregor announcing that the question of opening club memberships to Asians will be on the agenda of their next meeting. The Kyauktada club is one of the few remaining European clubs that has never admitted a non-European. The notice enrages Ellis, who is a fiercely foul-mouthed racist. He accuses Flory of being in favor of the club's admitting Dr. Veraswami, and Flory, clearly intimidated, denies this. The group is then joined by Macgregor, a good-natured but somewhat feckless man in his 40s. With him is Mrs. Lackersteen, who whiningly introduces two prominent subjects: the heat and the incivility of the natives, capped by the comment ". . . in some ways they are getting just as bad as the lower classes back home." Ellis then defiantly confronts Macgregor with his memo regarding opening admittance to non-Europeans, but Macgregor maintains that they're postponing the discussion until the next meeting. Secretly, Macgregor is not in favor of the idea, but he is being pressured by his superiors to conform to the general practice.

The discussion leads to the question of the continuing threat to the future of the British Raj in India and Burma. In the eyes of some, the days of the empire are numbered. Die-hards like Ellis, however, insist that all that is needed is the kind of "pluck" that General Dyer exhibited at Amritsar. All agree that "poor Dyer" had been betrayed by the politicians back home. (See Historical/Biographical Background.)

At this point, Flory has had enough. He has been listening to the same comments spoken by the same people countless times. About to burst with frustration, he leaves the group. After he is gone, Ellis comments "Exit Booker Washington, the niggers' pal." Westfield offers a limp defense of Flory: ". . . he is not a bad chap. Says some Bolshie [Bolshevik] things at times. Don't suppose he means half of them." By the time they all disperse, the blinding sunlight has made movement all but impossible for any living thing except the lines of ants along the ground and the circling vultures in the sky.

Chapter 3

After leaving the club, Flory pays a visit to Dr. Veraswami's house. The doctor's pleasant, shade-filled veranda is well stocked with English books, as Veraswami is a great admirer of English culture. Upon arriving, Flory unleashes a string of invective directed at his fellow club members. Veraswami will have none of it. The English are the "salt of the earth," considered to be the great administrators who have produced such marvels in India, the noble spirit and camaraderie of English gentlemen. To speak of them as Flory has is to indulge in seditious talk. Flory replies that he doesn't want to see the English leave Burma. He wants to remain here to make money. What he cannot tolerate is the hypocrisy that insists that this country is part of the "white man's burden . . . the lie that we are here to uplift our poor black brothers instead of to rob them." The doctor replies that it is not a lie, that the English do more than take profits. They build roads, hospitals, schools, combat disease and plagues, and, perhaps most important, bring "law and order, unswerving British justice and the Pax Britannica," all exemplars of modern progress. Flory responds that uprooting of native traditions and customs is a heavy price to pay for progress.

Then the discussion shifts to personal matters. Veraswami reveals that he is the victim of a developing conspiracy designed to ruin him. The figure behind the plot is U Po Kyin, who intends to spread malicious lies about him through an anonymous letter-writing campaign. Veraswami's only hope is to be elected to membership in the club, which would put him beyond U Po Kyin's accusations.

He asks Flory to propose his membership. Flory does not agree to propose the membership, but he does agree to vote for him. Although secretly disappointed, the doctor expresses his gratitude for Flory's support. He also warns Flory to be on guard that he might become a target of U Po Kyin's slanderers.

Chapter 4

It is the same day, now four o'clock. Flory is awakened from his afternoon nap by his servant Ko S'la. Flory and Ko S'la had been together since his first day in Burma. Ko S'la was not a good housekeeper, but he was fiercely loyal to Flory, whom he regarded as "childless and easily deceived." He tells Flory that he has a visitor, "the woman," his disparaging term for Ma Hla May, Flory's Burmese mistress. She complains of his neglect of her and of her lack of money. At first he rejects her, but soon, in a rather automatic fashion, the two have sex. Afterward, Flory feels ashamed of himself and becomes conscious of his birthmark, an instinctive reaction whenever he has a sense of shame. Ma Hla May tries to arouse him again, acting on the belief that sex lends her an increasing power over a man. After giving her five rupees and calling her a prostitute, Flory forcibly ejects her from his room. At a loss for anything to do, he takes a two-mile walk to a hidden grotto-like pond. Stripping off his clothes, he enters the pool and feels the familiar pang whenever he encounters natural beauty—the pain of being alone, of not having someone to share beauty with. On his way back, he gets lost and, with the help of a man driving a bullock cart, finds his way back to the main road. He returns home, washes, has dinner, and prepares to visit the club and get drunk.

Chapter 5

Later that night, Flory is awakened by a barking dog. There is no possibility of going back to sleep because of the guilt he feels over his behavior at the club. The slanderous article about Macgregor has been brought into the club, and Ellis has concluded that it was written by Veraswami. He insists that they all sign a statement of support in which they declare their firm opposition to considering native membership in the club. Flory, in an act of complete cowardice, agrees to sign the statement. His unwillingness to go against the majority is related to a lifelong sense of inferiority rooted in his birthmark. In school, his nickname was Blueface, and later it was Monkey-Bum. After school, his parents paid his way into a job with a timber firm in Burma. He has been there for 15 years. In that time he has become an avid reader but a bitterly lonely man, the loneliness intensified by his growing sense of the evils of imperialism. He has grown particularly intolerant of his English colleagues. Living with them is "stifling, stultifying . . . a world in which every word and every thought is censored." A member of this group is permitted any excess. He can be a lazy, cowardly drunkard as long as he adheres to the Pukka Sahib code. So one retreats to the inner world of the mind, despising the outer self and the people with whom one associates. If only there were someone to share thoughts and feelings with—a wife.

Chapter 6

Flory receives an anonymous letter, denouncing Veraswami, accusing him of, among other offenses, being a member of the Nationalist Party and the author of the article about Macgregor in the *Burmese Patriot.* Faced with the choice of showing the letter to Veraswami or otherwise making it public, he chooses to tear it up and say nothing, thereby adhering to the cardinal precept of the Pukka Sahib code: not to become involved in disputes among the natives.

As soon as he does, he hears a woman's cry—hers is an English voice. Rushing to the source of the scream, he discovers a young woman who is terrified by the sight of a water buffalo staring at her. Striding up to the buffalo, he gives it a smack on the nose, and it turns away. The young woman throws herself into Flory's arms, still shivering with fright. When she's recovered, she tells him that she is Mr. and Mrs. Lackersteen's niece, having arrived the prior evening by train. He invites her to sit and talk on his veranda. She stuns him with the news that she has come to Burma not from England but from Paris, where her mother lived as an artist. In the course of the conversation, which is dominated by Flory, he interprets her polite acquiescenses as proof that he and she share the same love of reading and of nature, that in essence they are soul mates. When Ma Hla May appears on the veranda demanding to know who this woman is, Flory, speaking Burmese, tells her to leave immediately or he will have her beaten mercilessly.

Chapter 7

This chapter is devoted to the back story of Elizabeth Lackersteen. Both of Elizabeth's parents are dead. Her father was a tea merchant and was intermittently successful. During World War I, he experienced a surge of prosperity, which enabled him to send his daughter to a very expensive boarding school. This made a lasting impact on her character. Mixing with the very rich, she developed fixed beliefs, summarized in two words: *lovely* and *beastly*. *Lovely* referred to all things expensive, elegant, and aristocratic; beastly covered anything cheap, boring, and requiring effort. When her father died of influenza, the beastly came to dominate her life. Her mother was left with an income of 150 pounds a year; she was a hopelessly impractical woman, however, convinced of her own superior sensibility, which she most recently expressed in the notion that she was an artist. Thus, the move to a garret in Montparnasse, where she would mingle with other bohemians while trying (unsuccessfully) to get by on three pounds a week. Elizabeth had to take a job teaching English to a banker's family, while fighting off the banker's advances. After two years, her mother died, and she soon received a cable from her uncle and aunt inviting her to join them in Burma. A follow-up letter from Mrs. Lackersteen made it clear that the prospect of finding a husband there was very good. When Elizabeth returns from the visit with Flory, she gives them a complete account of the morning, concluding, as an afterthought, with the appearance of Ma Hla May.

Chapter 8

That evening, after carefully choosing his clothes and getting a haircut from the local barber, Flory meets Elizabeth at the club and invites her out for a walk. They come upon a pwe, which, Flory explains, is a kind of play, "a cross between a historical drama and a revue." Standing in back, they are invited by U Po Kyin to sit with him. Genuinely interested in and enjoying the presentation, Flory is so busy explaining to Elizabeth the significance of the performance, he is oblivious of the fact that she is intensely uncomfortable sitting in the midst of Burmese and longs to be back in the club with other white people. She stands up and abruptly leaves, with Flory following her penitently. Before entering the club, they agree not to mention their attendance at the *pwe*, which would put Flory in a bad light. During the evening, Ellis and Westfield suggest to Flory that he is being set up as a potential husband, with marriage being the sole purpose of Elizabeth's visit to Burma. He refers to the "meat market," in which English girls are shipped to India and Burma "like carcasses of frozen mutton." Flory's protests do nothing to deter Ellis's smutty talk.

Chapter 9

In the next two weeks, the enmity between U Po Kyin and Veraswami heats up, turning the native Kyauktadans into two factions, the more powerful one being U Po Kyin's. Also, there are rumors of a nationalist uprising planned in the neighboring village of Thongwa. As a result, a detail of Indian troops led by an English officer will soon be sent to the area.

Meanwhile, Flory has sent Ma Hla May away permanently, giving her a hundred rupees. It was clear to Ko S'la and the other servants that Flory is planning to marry. He has even taken to attending church on Sundays.

Chapter 10

Flory's efforts to create a more meaningful relationship with Elizabeth are continually thwarted. They see each other every day, but their friendship is based on superficial chatter. His positive comments about Burmese people and culture seem strange to her. That he appears to like these people is odd enough, but for him to want her to like them is really going too far. Typical of this failure to see eye to eye occurs when Elizabeth sees Flory engaged in a conversation with two Eurasians, Francis and Samuel, both the sons of English missionary fathers. When she comments that "only a very low kind of man would - er—have anything to do with native women . . . ," he agrees with her, but then he remembers a Eurasian girl he had seduced and then abandoned 10 years ago. One subject that they do agree on is hunting, and they look forward to a hunting expedition together.

Chapter 11

During a walk with Elizabeth, Flory once again tries to interest her in the native customs. He persuades her to visit the crowded local bazaar, with its rich aromas and hordes of people. Once again, as in the *pwe* incident, he is blithely unaware of her negative reaction to the scene. When she complains of the heat, he persuades her to visit the Chinese grocer in the bazaar, Li Yeik, who will serve them a beverage. As they are about to enter his shop, Flory is stopped by a man who hands him a note from Ma Hla May, in which she demands 50 rupees. Flory instructs the man to tell Ma Hla May that if she attempts blackmail, he will cut her off completely. In the grocer's shop, they are offered a cup of green tea, which, to Elizabeth, "tastes exactly like the earth." A naked infant crawling on the floor comes near them and, panicked by the strange white faces, begins to urinate on the floor. Aghast, Elizabeth flees the shop, with Flory following sheepishly behind. He recognizes that, once again, his efforts to make her aware of his real interests in life have resulted in failure. At the same time, he realizes he is hopelessly in love with her. Finally she is mollified when their conversation turns to trivial subjects like the weather and dogs. They part amicably, looking forward to a hunting expedition.

Chapter 12

U Po Kyin is boasting to his wife, trying to impress her, since she is the only person in his life who is not afraid of him. Filled with high spirits, he explains that the 18 anonymous letters denouncing Veraswami are having their intended effect. This is particularly true of the last letter sent to Macgregor, relating to the escape from the local jail. The escape had been arranged by U Po Kyin, who had bribed the warden with 100 rupees. Thus, U Po Kyin is able to write a letter predicting the escape, ascribing it to the doctor and sending the letter as soon as the escape occurred. The fact that the letter predicted the outcome lent it more credibility in the eyes of Macgregor.

But even more significant is U Po Kyin's latest ploy. The rebellion that appears to be forming in the village of Thongwa is being subsidized by U Po Kyin, who had paid for and distributed so-called bullet-proof jackets, which the natives believe will protect them from English bullets. Just as the rebellion is about to start, U Po Kyin will arrest the ringleaders, thus appearing as the hero who has prevented the uprising. Of course, there may be some fighting, resulting in the deaths of the fools wearing their impregnable jackets, but what of that, because Po Kyin views them as "a pack of superstitious peasants." As the hero, U Po Kyin will then suggest that Veraswami was the mastermind behind the rebellion, saying, "He will be ruined for life." When U Po Kyin's wife protests that he seems to be glorying in villainy for its own sake, he replies that he does indeed have a goal in mind. He has learned that, in a short while, the European club will be forced to admit a native member. With the doctor out of the way, he is the logical candidate. Ma Kin is stunned by the revelation. Never in her wildest dreams did she imagine that she, a peasant born in a bamboo hut, would one day be sitting wearing shoes and stockings and "talking to English ladies in Hindustani."

Chapter 13

Flory visits Veraswami at the hospital, where he sees the impossible conditions under which the doctor labors. There are too many patients, and most of them are unwilling to submit to any type of operation out of fear of being cut open. Retiring to Veraswami's house, Flory tries to apologize for signing Ellis's notice on the club bulletin board, but the doctor dismisses the apology as unnecessary. He tells Flory of U Po Kyin's plot to foment a rebellion and then take credit for crushing it, meanwhile connecting Veraswami's name to it. To offset this plan, Flory promises to put up the doctor's name for membership in the club. As a member, his "prestige" would be unassailable. Having agreed to do the right thing, Flory wonders why he would suddenly be willing to take a risk, small though it was, to violate the code of the Pukka Sahib. He realizes it is because of Elizabeth. Her very presence has returned him to the spirit of freedom of thought and speech.

Returning to his home, he is greeted by the sight of Ma Hla May, hysterically pleading to be taken back. Groveling on the floor and kissing his feet, she insists that her life has been ruined, that she is an outcast and impoverished despite the 100 rupees Flory had given her shortly before. Despite himself, Flory feels guilty, gives her another 50 rupees, and watches her leave.

Chapter 14

Flory and Elizabeth are in two separate canoes headed upriver to a small native village. From there, they track through the jungle to a clearing, where Flory shoots a few pigeons. At first, Elizabeth is too excited to hit anything, but soon she successfully shoots a sitting bird. The whole experience is immensely exciting to her, as is her admiration of Flory's hunting skills. Later, Elizabeth shoots a bird in flight. She and Flory rush to the spot where the bird has fallen. The two are kneeling hand in hand. Flory draws her to him but stops; his awareness of his birthmark inhibits him. Then they see a leopard. The tracking and final shooting of the leopard reveal the depth of feeling Elizabeth brings to the hunt. The experience creates an unstated bond between the two. By the end of the day, it is clear that Flory will ask Elizabeth to marry him.

Chapter 15

It is the evening following the hunt. Elizabeth has come to the club with the Lackersteens, following an upsetting incident. While she was dressing for dinner, Mr. Lackersteen entered the room, ostensibly to hear more about the hunt, and made a gross pass, pinching her leg. Realizing that continuing to live in a house with a lecherous uncle would be intolerable, she is eager accept a marriage proposal from Flory. That afternoon's hunt had left her inclined to say yes, in any case. Of course, she has lingering doubts, particularly about Flory's somewhat highbrow way of speaking, but her uncle's pass—undoubtedly the first of many to come—has tipped the scale. She will say yes when the question is asked, probably that very evening. When she and Flory meet at the club, they walk outside, admiring the moon, and very soon embrace and kiss. But instead of proposing to her immediately, he feels impelled to describe the overwhelming sense of loneliness of one who is exiled from his native land. He goes on to speak of his desperate need to have someone with whom he can share his deepest thoughts and desires. This lengthy preamble leads up to "Will you . . .," but then he's interrupted by the voice of Mrs. Lackersteen, which is then followed by an earthquake that throws the two of them to the ground. Picking themselves up, they enter the club to share in the excited conversation about the quake. The proposal is postponed until the next day.

Chapter 16

The next morning, Flory heads for the club, hoping to complete his aborted marriage proposal, when he encounters a new arrival, Lt. Verrall, dispatched to Kyauktada at the head of a detail of Indian soldiers in anticipation of a possible rebellion. Verrall is handsome, young, and an arrogant snob. Sitting on a horse, he oozes aristocratic superiority from every pore. He demonstrates his excellent horsemanship as he practices spearing tent pegs from his horse, securing a hit each time. Just then, Flory sees Elizabeth emerging from her uncle's house. He makes a decision. He asks permission to try tent-pegging on one of the other horses. He waits until Elizabeth comes closer to the scene, and then, mounting the horse, he signals the horse to run. Immediately, he finds himself flying in the air and landing painfully on his shoulder, directly in front of Elizabeth. He calls out to her, but she passes by without even glancing at him. His fall had been caused by the saddle's having been loosened by one of the Indian soldiers, who is no doubt pleased to see an Englishman bloody and battered.

Chapter 17

That night, bruised and more than usually self-conscious about his face, Flory encounters Ellis and Westfield, which triggers a quarrel about the doctor, referred to by Ellis as "very slimy." Flory, most of his attention drawn to the door in anticipation of Elizabeth's entrance, declares that he will propose Veraswami's membership at the next meeting. Immediately afterward, the Lackersteens enter the club. All three are dressed in their best formal clothes. As an accessory to the clothes, Mrs. Lackersteen is sporting a ludicrous upper-class accent.

Elizabeth completely ignores Flory. When he finally gets a chance to ask her what he has done to offend her, she refuses to reply, implying that there is nothing between them that would warrant an explanation. Flory, however, refuses to accept her lack of response, finally provoking her to lash out, "I'm told that you are keeping a Burmese woman." Flory is stunned, at a loss to explain how Elizabeth could have learned. The answer lies in the evening before the earthquake. While Flory and Elizabeth were in the garden, Mrs. Lackersteen was reading the civil list, which gives the annual income of every civil servant in Burma. It occurred to her to look up Lt. Verrall, who was arriving the next day. She was amazed to see next to his name, the words "the honorable." The possibility of a marriage of her niece to "the honorable" swept before her eyes. In a desperate attempt to abort any marriage proposal that might be taking place, she called out Elizabeth's name. Her timing was impeccable, mightily assisted by the earthquake that followed. Later that night, Mrs. Lackersteen, with an air of great solemnity, broke the news about Flory and Ma Hla May.

As Flory walks home, his spirits crushed, he meets Ma Hla May, who is working outside his house. She screams that she needs more money or she will keep screaming until they hear her at the club. He gives her 25 rupees and his gold cigarette case. After she leaves, he ponders the possibility that someone is putting her up to this blackmailing behavior.

Chapter 18

Flory returns to his work in the jungle the day after Elizabeth's rejection. As a result, he is ignorant of the tales being spread about him and his "Bolshie" beliefs. Elizabeth now realizes her uneasiness with Flory's ideas derived from the fact that he was that hated being, a "highbrow." Flory throws himself into his work, which had virtually come to a standstill in his absence. Meanwhile, Mrs. Lackersteen's campaign to bring together Lt. Verrall and Elizabeth is making no progress. Verrall proves to be a formidable snob, the son of a peer but not rich, and he is interested in only two things: clothes and horses. He holds the world in contempt, with the exception of cavalry officers and polo players. His contempt extends to women, but his good looks and beautiful clothing draw them like moths to a flame. He occasionally takes advantage of their willingness to be seduced and then abandons them without a qualm. Only when he is confronted by Mrs. Lackersteen thrusting Elizabeth before him does he consent to visit the club. At the club that night, the highlight of the evening is the sight of Verrall and Elizabeth, dancing flawlessly to a gramophone record. Verrall pays exclusive attention to Elizabeth, ignoring the other members. Before leaving, he arranges to go riding with her in the morning. Elizabeth and Mrs. Lackersteen are up until midnight, shortening her aunt's riding habit for her to wear.

Chapter 19

As April moves closer to May, the Burmese heat becomes almost unendurable. At the club, Verrall continues to treat everyone but Elizabeth with aristocratic disdain. The two young people, less affected by the heat than the middle-aged club crowd, go riding every evening. Elizabeth, who has always been fond of horses, now becomes totally absorbed by them and by Verrall, the paragon of a cavalry officer. Inevitably, their relationship moves to the kissing and embracing stage.

Meanwhile, Flory, determined to win back Elizabeth, leaves his jungle camp and, with his servants, returns to Kyauktada. He intends to present her with the leopard skin he had left at the prison to be cured. He visits Veraswami, whose other position is as supervisor of the prison. The doctor informs him that preparation of the skin had been botched. The prisoner who was so expert in the curing of animal skins was the same person who had escaped aided by U Po Kyin. Nobody else was capable of doing the task well. The skin is not only dried and mottled but it also gives off an offensive odor. Flory nevertheless takes the skin to the Lackersteens. Dressed in her riding clothes, Elizabeth looks even more desirable than Flory remembers. He finds himself bereft of words, and the tiger skin—with its scarred surface and noxious odor—makes a dismal present. Dismissed from the house, he watches from a distance as Lt. Verrall and Elizabeth ride off into the jungle. Later, as he is negotiating a purchase with a book seller, he sees the two riderless horses making their way back to the village. He concludes that the horses got loose because Verrall and Elizabeth are making love. Driven to distraction by the mental images of the two lovers, he races home to finish off a bottle of whiskey. After passing out, he wakes in the middle of the night to find a local prostitute, whom his servant Ko S'la had hired to console him. He reacts by bursting into tears.

Chapter 20

The next morning, Flory returns to camp and several days later receives a letter from Veraswami: U Po Kyin's plot to take credit for suppressing the revolt that he himself instigated has gone according to plan. The "rebellion" was a comically undermanned, ill-prepared fiasco. The rebels consisted of seven men. U Po Kyin's men, joined by Mr. Maxwell, who had heard of the rebellion, had easily captured the group. One of the seven tried to run away and was shot and killed by Maxwell. The villagers have shown ill will toward Maxwell as a result. Macgregor, Lt. Verrall, and Westfield sped to the scene, but by the time they arrived, it was all over. They found U Po Kyin lecturing the villagers on the evils of rebellion. As a result, the villainous magistrate is now looked upon by the English as a hero. The result is certain to mean more trouble for Veraswami. While the weeks pass, gossip about Elizabeth and Verrall grows apace. Mrs. Lackersteen does her best to remind Elizabeth indirectly of the importance of a young girl's finding a husband. If not the seemingly unattainable Verrall, then she must remember she has a second choice, Flory.

On another front, unbeknownst to the major characters (including U Po Kyin), there are stirrings of native discontent, suggesting the possibility of another genuine rebellion in the area.

Chapter 21

It is the first of June, the day of the club meeting. Everyone is present except Maxwell, who has given his proxy to Ellis. Macgregor opens the meeting with a boring financial report, and Flory, gazing out a window, is struck by a group of natives navigating a sampan across the river that the club overlooks. Then Macgregor proceeds to the question of membership. He asserts that the commissioner's position is that if the vote of the club against opening membership is unanimous, the present membership can stay as it is; but if it is not unanimous, then one non-European will be automatically inducted as a member. It appears that the unanimous vote will carry the day, but Flory stands up and proposes Dr. Veraswami for membership. Flory's announcement produces a hate-filled harangue from Ellis and milder, but still negative, reactions from the others.

In the midst of the argument, their attention is diverted by the call of a native directing them to look down over the veranda. The barge that Flory had seen was now docked by the club. The natives carry a large object in a sheet up to the club and place it at the feet of the club members. Uncovered, the object turns out to be the hacked-up body of Maxwell, who has been killed by relatives of the man Maxwell had shot.

Chapter 22

Maxwell's death causes a stir not simply in Kyauktada but throughout Burma. The murder of a white man is an unspeakable act that must be avenged. The funeral in the Kyauktada cemetery is attended by the entire white population, with the sole exception of Lt. Verrall, who practices his horsemanship, oblivious of the nearby funeral. After the funeral, Westfield, the police superintendent, leaves the town to pursue Maxwell's killers. He commands Verrall to go with him, explaining to others that it would be good for Verrall to do some work, for a change. Ellis, enraged at Maxwell's death, strides to his office, his bad temper exacerbated by the prickly heat from which he suffers. Passing a group of teenage boys insolently smiling at him, he yells after them, "What are you laughing at, you young ticks?" One of them replies, "Not your business," whereupon he raises his cane and slashes it across the boy's eyes. A brief fight ensues, in which Ellis gets the best of them. He reports the incident to Macgregor as an unprovoked attack. That evening, the club members, Flory included, are startled to discover that a large, angry crowd has gathered in front of the building. When Macgregor goes to address them from the front porch, he is told that the crowd is demanding that he turn over Ellis to them. The boy he hit is now blind, and since he will never receive justice in a white man's court, the crowd wants to punish Ellis themselves. When Macgregor angrily refuses, they begin to hurl a volley of stones, hitting Macgregor and the others. The club members bolt the doors as they retreat from the porch. The din becomes increasingly ominous. The members are at a loss as to what to do. The military police appear to be helpless. Elizabeth suffers a slight injury while her aunt is screaming hysterically. Elizabeth pleads with Flory to do something. He realizes that the rear of the clubhouse is only a few paces from the river. If he can reach the water and swim up the river to police quarters, perhaps he can mobilize them. Macgregor gives the command to open fire on the crowd. Flory jumps down from the rear veranda and succeeds in reaching the water. Swimming up to the police barracks, he sees that the police are trying to stop the crowd from the rear and getting swallowed by the overwhelming numbers of natives. Finally reaching the second in command in Verrall's absence, he instructs him and his men to retreat to their barracks to get rifles and ammunition. He instructs the police to fire high over the heads of the crowd, and to fire all at once. The volley creates a great roar, followed by another, as the crowd disperses in front of the club. Flory walks in that direction, where he encounters Veraswami, who has been valiantly trying to restrain the crowd. He also encounters U Po Kyin arriving on the scene in an effort to claim some credit. As he approaches the clubhouse, it begins to rain. The rainy season has begun.

Chapter 23

The next day, Westfield and Verrall return with two prisoners arrested for the killing of Maxwell. The rain continues to come down at a furious pace. Flory is treated as a hero at the club, and he uses the opportunity to tell Macgregor of Veraswami's loyal efforts to restrain the crowd. He has a partial reconciliation with Elizabeth, who, however, continues to go out riding with Verrall, notwithstanding the fact that the lieutenant has given her no indication of a proposal. Meanwhile, U Po Kyin is enraged over the outcome of the rebellion and Flory's heroic status, which all but guarantees Veraswami's membership in the club. But after reflecting on it, the magistrate devises a new plan, which is designed to discredit Flory. Flory has returned to camp, and Verrall has suddenly stopped seeing Elizabeth and no longer visits the club. After three days of no word, she and her aunt are waiting at the club when a young man enters to announce that he is the new head of military police, replacing Verrall, who at this moment is boarding the train to Mandalay. The two women race out the club door and, the rain pouring down on them, hurry to the station just in time to see the train pull out ten minutes early. The station master explains that Verrall had insisted on the train's leaving early. The only question was whether he had demanded this in order to avoid Elizabeth or two furious Indian grain merchants, to whom he was in debt for his horses' feed. Later, Mrs. Lackersteen consoles herself with the knowledge that at the coming Sunday's church services, Flory will be there, back from camp.

Chapter 24

The church service—held only once in six weeks—is well attended by the European community and a few Eurasians, such as Francis and Samuel. Flory had met Elizabeth earlier at the club where he asked her if Verrall had gone and, hearing her reply that he had, took her in his arms. It was clear that they would be married, perhaps at the next church service. As the service begins, Flory is sitting across the aisle from Elizabeth, for the first time confidently exposing his birthmark to her. As the service proceeds, he daydreams of his future life with Elizabeth—a new life, an end to the dreary, lonely, pointless existence he has been leading. Suddenly, the service is interrupted by someone screaming his name. It is Ma Hla May, dressed in dirty, tattered clothes and with her hair hanging down. She is screaming that she has been vilely mistreated by Flory. Finally, she is dragged away by Francis and Samuel. Throughout the ordeal, Flory stares straight ahead, but his face has grown "so rigid and bloodless that the birthmark seemed to glow upon it like a streak of blue paint." Elizabeth is appalled by the scene, but what is most repellent to her is his birthmark. "She hated him now for his birthmark. She had never known till now how dishonorable, how unforgivable a thing it was."

Of course, Ma Hla May's outburst was the latest example of U Po Kyin's scheming. He had coached her before her performance and paid her well. After the service, outside the church, Flory makes one last desperate attempt to explain to Elizabeth, but she reverts to her earlier position that his behavior means nothing to her. But when pushed to answer the question of whether she might in time consent to marry him, she replies "never." She might have been able to forgive his past, but she could never forget the look of his face in the church: "It was, finally, the birthmark that had damned him." Her revulsion sprang from the deepest part of herself. As Flory returns home, he realizes that, after Elizabeth, there is no possibility of his returning to his old life.

He takes out his automatic pistol and a clip of cartridges. He calls his dog, Flo, into his bedroom, and instinctively aware of some evil intent, refuses to enter and has to be dragged in. Flory then calls her to him, and as the creature crawls toward him, he fires a bullet into her skull. He then tears open his coat and, pressing the muzzle of the gun against his chest, pulls the trigger. Ko S'la sends for Veraswami, but Flory is already dead. The birthmark has all but completely faded, leaving only the faintest stain. Veraswami has a violent spasm of grief when he examines the body. Once he recovers, he tells Ko S'la to bury the dog. Flory's suicide will be reported as an accident that occurred while he was cleaning his gun. "It shall not be written on his tombstone that he committed suicide," Veraswami says.

Chapter 25

Flory's funeral takes place the next day. The official verdict is that his death was an accident, but no one believes it, as suicide is fairly common among the English in Burma. The death of Flory has several unfortunate effects. It enables U Po Kyin to continue his slanderous campaign against Veraswami, who now lacks his most important ally. The doctor is eventually demoted, on the grounds of being "untrustworthy," and he is transferred to a hospital in Mandalay. Ko S'la receives 400 rupees from Flory's estate, but his fortunes steadily decline. Ma Hla May ends up in a brothel in Mandalay, regretting her time with Flory and the money from him that she should have saved. Later, U Po Kyin becomes the first Asian member of the club and makes a good impression on the others. He is eventually promoted to deputy commissioner and leaves Kyauktada. At his retirement, he is honored by the government for his service. Three days later, before he can enact his plans of atoning for his sins, he dies of a stroke. Elizabeth ends up marrying Macgregor and the two live happily together; she proves to be a model Pukka Memsahib.

COMMENTARY

The novel's epigraph, from Shakespeare's *As You Like It* ("This desert inaccessible / Under the shade of melancholy boughs"), suggests that at least one important element in the story will be the scenery of Burma, with its exotic, intimidating flora and fauna and its suffocating heat. It is interesting to compare this epigraph with "John Flory: My Epitaph" part of some early sketches for this novel that Orwell wrote in the late 1920s:

> JOHN FLORY
> Born 1890
> Died of Drink 1927
>
> Here lie the bones of poor John Flory;
> His story was the old, old story.
> Money, women, cards & gin
> Were the four things that did him in.
>
> He has spent sweat enough to swim in
> Making love to stupid women;
> He has known misery past thinking
> In the dismal art of drinking.
>
> O stranger, as you voyage here
> And read this welcome, shed no tear;
> But take the single gift I give,
> And learn from me how not to live.

Aside from exhibiting a satirical and somewhat callous attitude toward the protagonist, this jaunty first sketch reveals a superficial view of Flory, a hint that the author was not fully engaged with his subject at that time. In that respect, he did well to abandon the first attempt, returning to it a few years later. Another advantage of the chosen epigraph is that it points up a basic motif of *Burmese Days:* loneliness. John Flory, the novel's tortured protagonist, is a desperately lonely man. As he attempts to describe his life to Elizabeth, "the foreignness, the solitude, the melancholy! Foreign trees, foreign flowers, foreign landscape, foreign faces. . . . This country's been a kind of solitary hell to me . . . and yet I tell you it could be paradise if one weren't alone." Flory is also trapped in a role that he wants to reject, that of the Pukka Sahib, the agent of an imperialism he detests. But, in his longing for human contact, he cannot desert the despised colonialist world of the English club, partly because of a deep-seated sense of inferiority, rooted in the birthmark that mars his face. Flory's birthmark causes him to approach people sideways, maneuvering "to keep the birthmark out of sight." Although he realizes that he is morally and intellectually superior to the other club members, he also sees these "dull louts" as his superiors: ". . . at least they are men in their oafish way. Not cowards, not liars. Not half dead and rotting." "Half dead and rotting" might well be his description of his face. Still, he is not completely in despair but enmeshed in ambivalence. He seizes the chance to resolve that state when he falls in love with Elizabeth Lackersteen, whom he mistakenly sees as a potential soul mate, "someone who would share his life in Burma—but really share it. . . . Someone who would love Burma as he loved it and hate it as he hated it." The problem is that Elizabeth is just another Memsahib in the making, as the last line of the novel indicates.

Elizabeth notwithstanding, Flory is doomed, carrying his mark of Cain upon his face. The system that imperialism has created leaves little possibility of any other result. The novel weaves together the political theme with the personal. As the critic Frederick Karl put it, "*Burmese Days* contains conflicts sufficiently dramatized to raise social protest to literature. . . . As Orwell recognized in writing this novel, tragedy must be conceived in individual and not social terms" (Karl, 157).

The problem for some readers is that the psychological focus dilutes the social protest. As the marxist critic Terry Eagleton has argued, it lacks a firm commitment to anti-imperialism, both on the part of Flory and his author: ". . . *Burmese Days* is really less a considered critique of imperialism than an exploration of private guilt, incommunicable loneliness, and a loss of identity, for which Burma becomes . . . little more than a setting" (Eagleton, 17). Even critics with less of a political orientation than Eagleton would doubtless agree, although some would maintain that the novel is even less a critique of imperialism than of the hypocritical, "white man's burden" cant that imperialism spawned. Flory admits that, like any other Englishman, he is in Burma to make money, but what is unendurable is living a life in which one is not free to speak what one believes to be the truth. In its focus on Flory and the world of the club, the novel sees imperialism primarily in terms of its impact on the colonizers while thrusting the colonized into the background.

The opening chapter brings on the stage the subdivisional magistrate, U Po Kyin. He is a villain of comic-book proportions, a bribe-taking, blackmailing, treacherous, lecherous schemer who has risen within the colonial system by betraying his colleagues and slandering his rivals. Enormously obese, he looks the part as well as acts it. As a character, he belongs with the Asian villains of the popular literature of the time, such as Saxe Rohmer's Dr. Fu Manchu, although, as Jeffrey Meyers points out, in appearance at least he bears a strong resemblance to the figure of Doramin in Joseph Conrad's *Lord Jim* (Meyers, 67). The fact that U Po has such success as a parasite living off the colonial system is itself a damning comment on the system. U Po's ultimate goal, the prize that will cap his career, is membership in the Kyauktada European Club, which prides itself on never having admitted a non-European member. Now however, the club is under pressure from above. The reform policies of the British government have extended to the Englishman's sanctuary, the "spiritual citadel, the real seat of British power," the club. The other candidate for membership is Flory's good friend Veraswami, who, ironically enough, would be an ideal choice, since he shares the same notions of English superiority that the members do. An avid reader of English literature, Veraswami wants to join the club so he can participate in what he imagines to be intellectual discussions of high culture. The contrast between Veraswami's imagination and the dreary reality could not be more stark. The club members include Macgregor, the nominal head, capable of a few Latin phrases and a number of boring anecdotes; Westfield, the police superintendent impatiently expecting trouble from the natives that will enable him to crack a few heads; Maxwell, easygoing but too quick on the trigger; Mr. and Mrs. Lackersteen, a drunken lecher and a social-climbing schemer who are desperately trying to marry off their niece. But the one character who stands out from this crowd is the fierce racist, Ellis, whose intensity and motiveless malignity strips the veneer from the imperialist lie to expose its rock-like core. Ellis is an intimidator, and early in the novel, Flory wilts under his tirade.

In chapter 2 we have our first look at the club and its attitudes, summed up in Ellis's reference to "poor Dyer." In 1919, General Rex Dyer was the commander of a force of troops sent in to quell the political disturbances in Amritsar, a city in northwest Punjab, India. When 2,000 people gathered in an unauthorized meeting, Dyer ordered his troops to open fire for 10 minutes, killing 379 people and wounding 1,500. The next day, Dyer issued punitive regulations, among which was an order requiring Indians to crawl on their stomachs whenever they passed a place where Indian youth had attacked a British woman. Forced to resign, Dyer returned to England, where he was treated like a hero by conservatives in Parliament. All the other members join in an expression of pity for "the martyred general." Barely able to stifle his rage, Flory abruptly leaves the club. In an effort to right the balance, at this point, the authorial narrator qualifies his satire of the club members, suggesting that their life was not easy: "Living and working among Orientals would try the temper of a saint." Presumably, Orwell was recalling his own nonsaintly experiences in Burma. The imperialist argument is carried on in the next chapter in which the anglophilic Veraswami defends the English from Flory's attacks. Veraswami insists that the English have been a civilizing influence, but Flory replies, "We're not civilizing them, we're only rubbing our dirt on to them."

The sordid aspect of Flory's life is depicted in the opening of chapter 4, where he is at home, attended to by his longtime servant, Ko S'la, who sees Flory as a boy who must be coddled, and by his mistress, Ma Hla May, who sees him as a customer. Both are agents in the disintegration of his character, contributors to his lethargy, self-indulgence, and subsequent sense of guilt. But later in the same chapter, Orwell departs from the realistic, satiric tone of the novel to engage Flory in a lyrical interlude that emphasizes the natural setting and Flory's relationship with it. He takes a stroll into the jungle area to immerse himself in a hidden pond. It is clear that the pond serves a cleansing purpose for Flory, a temporary reprieve from the prison of his life. Watching a beautiful green pigeon perched on a branch, he is struck by the painful reminder that "beauty is meaningless until it is shared. If he had one person, just one to share his loneliness."

The critic Lynette Hunter points out the discrepancy between the narrator's moving and beautiful description and Flory's reaction. Instead of responding to the beauty, Flory seizes on its negative implication—the fact that he is alone—indulging in sentimental self-pity. He cannot find the proper language "because he is caught in the clichés, the conventional vocabulary and phrasing of the world he wishes to leave" (Hunter, 25).

A green pigeon reappears in chapter 14 when Flory takes Elizabeth on a hunting expedition. By this point, Flory has already fallen in love with Elizabeth, visualizing her as a lifelong companion, someone with whom he can share—and therefore relish—the beautiful aspects of life in Burma. That he is totally deluded in this belief has become obvious. Elizabeth is a conventional, pretty, young woman whose life has been shaped by the financial ups and downs of her father's business. For two years of her father's most "up" period, she had attended an exclusive girl's prep school and rubbed shoulders with the children of the rich. That was the highlight of her life. The low point was spent in Paris with her widowed mother. The move to Paris was to enable the mother to pursue her career as a bohemian artist, one of the mother's many pretensions. Living, and forced to work, in virtual poverty, she longs for middle-class security. Her stint in Paris has left her with a particular distaste for the arts and intellectual discourse. All of this is lost on Flory, who has already made two disastrous attempts to introduce her to native customs and culture.

The hunt, on the other hand, has the opposite result. Elizabeth is thrilled by the hunt and by Flory's performance as a hunter: "If only he would always talk about shooting, instead of about books, and art and that mucky poetry." When Flory later shoots two green pigeons, he shows them to Elizabeth, commenting on their beauty. But she can only feel envy that he, and not she, had shot them. Much of the hunt is presented through Elizabeth's consciousness, and there is no doubt of the mixture in her blood of shooting and killing and sexual passion. Later, Verrall will stir the same or even greater passion in connection with horse riding. In depicting the conjunction of sex and violence in Elizabeth, Orwell is clearly tipping his hat to a writer he very much admired, D. H. LAWRENCE.

Elizabeth's rejection of Flory plunges him into despair, which has at least the salutary effect of leaving him with nothing left to lose and with it the freedom to defiantly advance Veraswami's name for club membership. At precisely that moment, the members become aware of an angry mob surrounding the club, demanding that Ellis, who earlier had caned a boy across the eyes, blinding him, be handed over to them. In this crisis, Flory proves to be the bravest, most effective member of the club. He leads the police in the dispersal of the crowd and becomes the hero of the English, and is reunited with Elizabeth, who has been deserted by Verrall. He is on the brink of realizing his dream when Ma Hla May's denunciation in the church brings his world crushing down on him. Little wonder that in reviewing the book, when it first appeared in 1935, Sean O'Faolain, the Irish novelist, commented that "poor Flory hasn't a dog's chance against his author" (51). Orwell appears determined to suggest that working within the larger system, derived from the fact of imperialism, you cannot have it both ways. Flory wants to be a rebel and he wants Elizabeth, the perfect embodiment of colonialism. Her rejection of him finally rests upon her recognition of his birthmark, seeing it for the first time as the mark of an outsider, someone who will never be "one of us." She perceives what he had never allowed himself to see, that the marriage of the two of them would be a dismal failure.

In his essay on the novelist GEORGE GISSING, by way of praising Gissing as "a true novelist," Orwell defines what he means by the term *true novel.* It is one in which at least two characters, and probably more, are described from the inside with credible motives [that] come into conflict. By that definition, *Burmese Days* comes closer to his ideal than any of his other novels. For although British imperialism plays an important thematic role in the novel, it constitutes the context that conditions but does not control the psychological drama at center stage. There stands the enigmatic John Flory, a man who carries with him the outward sign of his alienation, a blue birthmark that discolors half of his face. Acutely self-conscious of its "hideousness," Flory allows its presence to form the core of his sense of self. It was the central feature of his childhood and youth. In prep school, he was the object of a satiric couplet, "New tick Flory does look rum / Got a face like a monkey's bum," from which he acquires the nickname Monkey-Bum. The birthmark dictates—or he allows it to dictate—significant decisions. Thus, when he is on the verge of kissing Elizabeth, he asks her if she is put off by it, a question guaranteed to put her off.

In the pivotal final scene at the church, when Ma Hla May disgraces Flory and humiliates Elizabeth, the birthmark assumes a significance that moves the novel to another level. In a move of tragic hubris, Flory, the confident groom-to-be, sits across the aisle from Elizabeth, exposing for the first time the birthmark to her view. When Ma Hla May's performance is finished and she is removed from the church, Elizabeth looks across the aisle at him:

> His face appalled her, it was so ghastly, rigid and old. It was like a skull. Only the birthmark seemed alive in it. She hated him now for his birthmark. She had never known till this moment how dishonouring, how unforgivable a thing it was.

Later, she realizes she might have been able to forgive him:

> But not after that squalid scene, and the devilish ugliness of his disfigured face in that moment. It was finally the birthmark that had damned him.

In describing his earlier career as a writer in "WHY I WRITE," Orwell speaks of his intention of writing "naturalistic novels that end unhappily," which certainly describes *Burmese Days,* except for the birthmark. It is as though he cannot quite resist the impulse to plow beneath the naturalist surface as a nod in the direction of symbolism.

Orwell, whose own history in Burma was close enough to Flory's, decided after five years to leave. Had he stayed 15 years, as Flory did, he might well have met the same fate. But Orwell had available another possibility denied to Flory, the conviction, which had been within him since childhood, that he would become a writer.

CHARACTERS

Ellis, Mr. Local manager of a timber company, "a tiny wiry-headed fellow with a pale sharp-featured face" and "a queer wounding way of speaking." Ellis is a rabid racist with a vicious tongue, and his racism runs deep, which gives him the power of intimidation over other club members. His encounter with a group of Burmese students, in which he slashes his cane across the eyes of one of the boys, triggers the native rebellion that Flory is able to quell.

Flo Flory's dog, whose name suggests a certain identification with her master, which is underlined when Flory shoots her before shooting himself.

Flory, John The novel's protagonist, a 35-year-old manager of a timber company adjacent to the small town of Kyauktada in northern Burma. He is the odd man out among the six other English people in Kyauktada, looked at askance for his "Bolshie" views and his friendship with Dr. Veraswami, an Indian who is the local physician. Flory is miserably unhappy, and above all, lonely, after 15 years in Burma. He has nothing but contempt for his fellow Englishmen but is at first afraid to speak up for Veraswami when the question of Burmese membership arises. He falls in love with Elizabeth Lackersteen, who is visiting her aunt and uncle. At first receptive, she later hears of his Burmese mistress and rejects him when a handsome aristocratic officer, Lt. Verrall, arrives on the scene. Flory regains the respect of everyone after he manages to suppress a rebellion. He reconciles with Elizabeth, who has been deserted by Verrall, but his marriage plans are ruined when his former Burmese mistress appears in the middle of a church service and creates an ugly scandal. Rejected again by Elizabeth, he shoots himself.

The key to Flory's character is a disfiguring birthmark, a source of shame since his childhood. It symbolizes the ostracization and alienation he has always felt in his relation with others.

Kin, Ma Wife of the villainous U Po Kyin. A devout Buddhist, she worries about her husband's evil deeds, fearing that he will be dreadfully punished in the hereafter. A simple woman with no pretensions, nevertheless, even she is impressed by the prospect of membership in the European Club.

Kyin, U Po Villainous submagistrate in Kyauktada, who has risen from lowly beginnings by means of bribe-taking, slander, treachery, rape, and fomenting trouble that he can attribute to others. His target in the novel is Dr. Veraswami, the upright Indian physician against whom he has launched a slanderous letter-writing campaign. Later, he zeroes in on John Flory, bribing Flory's ex-mistress to disgrace his name in the middle of a church service. His plan is to have himself chosen as the first Burmese member of the club. He is successful in this, having convinced the English that Veraswami is untrustworthy. Later, he is promoted to a higher position and leaves Kyauktada, and then, after his retirement, he receives a special honor for his work. Shortly thereafter, he dies.

Lackersteen, Elizabeth Attractive young Englishwoman in her early twenties who is left stranded after the deaths of her parents. She comes to Burma at the invitation of her aunt and uncle, hoping to find a husband in a world where white women are rare. She is courted by John Flory, whose skill she admires, but whose "high-brow" and artistic conversations put her off. When the arrogant, aristocratic Lt. Verrall arrives on the scene, Elizabeth rejects Flory—only to later be rejected by Verrall. Flory's heroism in foiling an insurrection reconciles the two. But the final, fatal disruption occurs when Flory's former mistress causes a disgraceful scandal. After Flory's death, Elizabeth marries Mr. Macgregor, and the two live a contented colonial life.

Lackersteen, Mr. Manager of a timber firm, an alcoholic and lecher, to whom his wife acts as a mother with a miscreant child. His niece, Elizabeth, fends off his attempts to seduce her.

Lackersteen, Mrs. Elizabeth's aunt, who schemes to have her niece marry well, first with John Flory, and then with Lt. Verrall, and then back to Flory when Verrall deserts Elizabeth. Foolish and vulgar, for all her social-climbing pretensions, Mrs. Lackersteen is exceeded in her unattractiveness only by her husband.

Macgregor, Mr. Deputy commissioner of the Kyauktada district and secretary of the European Club. He is a large, genial man in his early forties, who, acting on orders from above, tries (against his own personal preferences) to orchestrate the admission of a non-European member into the club. He bravely but ineffectively confronts the rebellious mob at the doors of the club. After John Flory's death, Mr. Macgregor marries Elizabeth Lackersteen.

Maxwell, Mr. Acting division forest officer. He is a young Englishman, who, during a round-up of a group of would-be rebels, shoots and kills one of them who is trying to flee. Shortly after, relatives of the man he killed murder him, slicing up his body and dumping it at the door of the European Club.

May, Ma Hla John Flory's Burmese mistress, who, after having successfully manipulated him throughout their relationship, is cast aside when Flory falls in love with Elizabeth Lackersteen. With the assistance of U Po Kyin, she enacts her revenge, playing the abused, impoverished victim of Flory's cruelty during an Anglican church service. She later becomes a prostitute.

Sein, Ba Macgregor's chief clerk, who also spies for U Po Kyin. His access to Mr. Macgregor's papers enables him to pass on important information regarding the club and other matters to the villainous submagistrate.

S'la, Ko John Flory's somewhat lazy but consistently loyal personal servant. He and Flory are the same age (35) and have been together for 15 years. In that time, Ko S'la has matured and become a man, acquiring wives and children. Flory has remained a child, in Ko S'la's eyes, naive in dealing with Burmese people, and particularly with his mistress, Ma Hla May, whom Ko S'la despises.

Veraswami, Dr. Indian physician at the local hospital and a supervisor of the jail, Dr. Veraswami is an intense admirer of the British and an avid reader of English literature. He and John Flory share a close friendship based on their mutual interests. With Veraswami, Flory can express his hatred of colonialism and his contempt for his fellow Englishmen in Kyauktada. Veraswami, however, always defends the English. He becomes the target of U Po Kyin's campaign to destroy his reputation so that U Po Kyin, and not he, will be elected to membership in the club. After Flory's death, the campaign succeeds, and the doctor is demoted and transferred to Mandalay.

Verrall, Lieutenant Commander of military police temporarily assigned to Kyauktada, Lt. Verrall is a study in narcissism. The handsome scion of an aristocratic family, he treats everyone around him with icy contempt. He toys with, and presumably seduces, Elizabeth, before running out on her. His only real love is for his horses and, of course, for himself.

Westfield, Mr. District superintendent of police. A typical club member in his prejudices, Mr. Westfield is frustrated when he misses out on real action, such as the uprising when the club is besieged. A point in his favor is that he is not fooled by U Po Kyin.

WORKS CITED

Eagleton, Terry. "Orwell and the Lower-Middle-Class Novel." In *George Orwell: A Collection of Critical Essays,* edited by Raymond Williams, 10–33. Englewood Cliffs. N.J.: Prentice-Hall, 1974.

Hunter, Lynette. *George Orwell: The Search for a Voice.* London: Open University Press, 1984.

Larkin, Emma. *Finding George Orwell in Burma.* London: Penguin, 2004.

Karl, Frederick. *The Contemporary English Novel.* New York: Farrar, Straus, 1962.

Meyers, Jeffrey. *A Reader's Guide to George Orwell.* Totowa, N.J.: Littlefield, 1971.

O'Faolain, Sean. Review of *Burmese Days.* Reprinted in *George Orwell: The Critical Heritage,* edited by Jeffrey Meyers, 50–51. London: Routledge, 1975.

"Catastrophic Gradualism"

A brief essay/review of Arthur Koestler's *The Yogi and the Commissar,* a collection of his essays, of which the title essay had created a considerable stir. For Koestler, the figures of yogi and commissar represented two attitudes toward progress and change. Orwell's review was printed in *C. W. (Common Wealth) Review* side by side with a review of the same book by a communist journalist, Reg Bishop, who took the position opposite to Orwell's. In the United States, Orwell's review first appeared in Dwight Macdonald's *Politics* (September 1945).

SYNOPSIS

Orwell opens his discussion by introducing a new term, *catastrophic gradualism,* to describe a theory that he sees coming into view. Simply put, it is the idea that significant historical progress can be achieved only through a process that involves "blood-shed, lies, tyranny and injustice." Thus, among other things, the theory represents a convenient justification for the reign of Joseph Stalin. In the long run, according to Stalin's supporters, his crimes will be seen as a necessary tactic on the principle that "you can't make an omelette without breaking eggs." This, in substance, is the argument put forth in a review of Arthur Koestler's *Yogi and the Commissar* by Kingsley Martin in the *New Statesman.* Martin was responding to Koestler's point that the underlying principle of the commissar is that "the end justifies the means," to which Koestler opposes the Eastern view that the end is unknowable, all that matters is the means.

Orwell argues that Koestler is not, as is commonly thought, privileging the Eastern over the Western view but championing a synthesis of the two views. In practice, it means that the West has to learn the necessity of conquering the will to power, which has corrupted all revolutions. We are now, Koestler argues, at the point where a pivotal decision must be made to abandon power politics. The individual can overcome the will to power through contemplation, but the contemplation of the yogi has its limitations in that it removes one from the field of action, the service of the community. At this point, Orwell points out that Koestler's essay was written before the dropping of the atomic bomb. The atomic bomb created one of history's turning points. The prospect of nuclear war puts us in the gravest possible danger, adding to the urgency of Koestler's message that there must be "a change in the individual heart." In this respect, Orwell concludes, the yogi is superior to the commissar, but it must be a mode of contemplation that extends out to society.

It is clear from this brief review that, however unpredictable his stands might be on the major issues of the second half of the 20th century, Orwell would have been an active supporter of nuclear disarmament.

"Censorship in England"

Short essay on the state of censorship in England in the late 1920s. Orwell published this essay—his first professional published work—in the French journal *Monde* on October 6, 1928. No English original of the work exists. Orwell's English copy was translated into French by H. J. Salemson. Peter Davison's *Complete Works of George Orwell* (10,

117–119) includes an English version of the essay translated from the French by Janet Percival and Ian Willison.

SYNOPSIS

Orwell begins the essay by describing the types of censorship one is likely to encounter in England. In the theater, all plays must be submitted to a government official before they are permitted to open. This censor can ban a play completely or require certain changes before licensing a performance. Books are not censored before publication but may be suppressed after a public outcry or a campaign. Most of the censoring process has to do with sexuality, not politics.

The 18th-century novel was filled with ribaldry and raw humor, but by Dickens's time, prudery had become the order of the day. The difference between the two centuries lies in the fact that the puritan middle class—the merchants and factory owners—came into power and could exert their will over the general populace. Censorship is a hopelessly outdated institution, and recent evidence suggests that its end may be in sight.

This essay marks Orwell's first professional publication. Two months later, his "A FARTHING NEWSPAPER" appeared in G. *K.'s Weekly,* his first professional publication in English.

"Charles Dickens"

Essay first published in 1940 in a collection of three essays by Orwell under the title *Inside the Whale.* It was reprinted in 1946 in another essay collection, *Critical Essays,* the American title of which was *Dickens, Dali and Others.* This is an example of what Orwell called "sociological" literary criticism, which focuses on the author's work and ideas in their social and historical contexts. This essay is generally recognized as Orwell's finest piece of literary criticism.

SYNOPSIS

Orwell begins by noting that Dickens is a "writer worth stealing," which is precisely what some of his critics have done. He has been represented as a near-Catholic by Catholics and as a revolutionary by Marxists. He has also been widely identified as a "proletarian writer." In fact, there are few proletarians in his novels, nor is he a revolutionary, intent on overthrowing the system. "The truth is that Dickens's criticism of society is almost exclusively moral." Capitalism, for example, is not the target of his anger; it is human nature that is the enemy. Dickens's view is a deceptively simple one: "If men would behave decently, the world would be decent." Thus Dickens's works are filled with a recurrent figure, "the good rich man." However, even this character type undergoes diminishing stature in Dickens's later novels, only to be resurrected in *Our Mutual Friend* in the character of Boffin whose generosity puts everything to right.

One social evil that Orwell does not focus on is child labor. In *David Copperfield,* when Dickens deplores 10-year-old David's having to work in a blacking factory, he zeroes in on the iniquity of a talented boy doing slave labor. He makes no general statement about other boys, talented or not, suffering the same fate. He was equally unresponsive to the trade-union movement.

As for revolution, his treatment of the reign of terror in *A Tale of Two Cities* is as "a monster . . . begotten by tyranny that always ends by devouring its own instruments." Rejecting both violence and politics, Dickens places his faith in a better world through education. He was a tireless critic of oppressive power wielded in the classroom. He does not, however, believe in changing the educational system but in changing the hearts of those in power. In any case, "No English writer has written better about childhood than Dickens."

Dickens was a product of the urban middle class, like H. G. Wells, a writer who resembles him to some extent, although, unlike Wells, Dickens does not focus on the future. Dickens exhibits a "rather sloppy love" of old objects, but he shares with Wells a preference for the petit bourgeois to the exclusion of the aristocratic and proletarian classes.

Dickens's childhood experiences left him with a strong fear of poverty. Despite his sympathy with the working class, he is repelled by the thought of being a member of the lower class. Most of his heroes are young gentlemen, such as Nicholas Nickleby, Pip, David Copperfield, and Martin Chuzzlewit. One interesting feature of some of the novels is the author's attitude toward sex or marriage between classes. A striking example is the reaction of David Copperfield to Uriah Heep's intention to marry Agnes Wickfield. David is almost overcome by the notion of "seizing the red hot poker out of the fire and running him through with it." Orwell acknowledges that Heep is odious, independent of his class, but he insists "it is the thought of the 'pure' Agnes in bed with a man who drops his aitches that really revolts Dickens." As for the servant question, Dickens's picture of the ideal servant, such as Sam Weller in *The Pickwick Papers,* is that of a person who has a devotion to the master that is feudal.

Dickens had no difficulty in writing about ordinary people. What he did not write about, as an isolated urban man, was the nature of work. He was able to describe something that exists already but not the process that brings it into existence. He was not "mechanically minded." His heroes are not really interested in their work. Business and politics are ethically dubious, science uninteresting, and agriculture beyond the pale. The only exception to the hero's indifference to work is David Copperfield, the novelist.

Orwell imagines that, at this point in the essay, readers may be inclined to feel impatient with his exclusive focus on Dickens's message, virtually ignoring the literary achievement. But the message is important. "All art is propaganda," but that is not all that art is. In Dickens's case, the artistry is present in the abundant fertility of his imagination. That imagination is the source of those extraordinary minor characters who people the plots, stealing scenes whenever they appear. They are the source of the claim that Dickens is "only a caricaturist." But these caricatures mysteriously come to life and frequently remain in the memory of readers who long ago have forgotten the plots. That is also the case with Dickens's exuberant prose passages. Frequently, these rich, profuse passages are technically artistic flaws, violating the credibility of the characters who speak them, but there are no rules in novel writing. For any work of art, there is only one test worth bothering about: survival. Dickens has survived not only as a classic, but he also continues to be a popular writer with a wide appeal among ordinary people.

The difference between Dickens and a novelist like Tolstoy is that Tolstoy's characters grow in the course of his novels, "struggling to make their souls, whereas Dickens's people are already finished and perfect." Not to say that Tolstoy is superior to Dickens, but that he's merely different, and ". . . one is no more obliged to choose between them than between a sausage and a rose."

Dickens is at heart a moralist, which is the source of his greatness: "You can only create if you *care.*" His message is to behave decently. He is not out to change the society—to overthrow capitalism, for example—but to change the capitalist, or any person who is oppressing others. He is always with the underdog, with the exception of the ending of *David Copperfield,* in which he seems to be extolling the doctrine of success.

The secret of his popularity is his "native generosity of mind," which has enabled him "to express in a comic, simplified and therefore memorable form the native decency of the common man." Orwell concludes by describing the mental image he carries of Dickens's face, "the face of a man about 40, with a small beard and a high color. He is laughing . . . the face of a man who is *generously angry*—in other words of a 19th-century liberal, a free intelligence, a type hated . . . by all smelly little orthodoxies which are now contending for our souls."

COMMENTARY

In 1938, Orwell's wife Eileen wrote a letter to Francis Westrope, owner of the bookstore where Orwell had worked in 1934 and 1935. She was writing from Marrakech, asking Westrope to send them some of Dickens's early novels. She mentioned that they had been reading and re-reading *Our Mutual Friend* so devotedly that they were "competent to pass the most searching examination on it" (Shelden, 312–13). That close reading was to pay off a few months later, when Orwell wrote this essay, his longest and finest example of literary criticism.

Orwell had serious doubts about the value of literary criticism, as he indicated in his essay

"WRITERS AND LEVIATHAN," "I have often had the feeling that even at the best of times literary criticism is fraudulent, since in the absence of any accepted standards whatever—any *external* reference which can give meaning to the statement that such and such a book is 'good' or 'bad'—every literary judgment consists in trumping up a set of rules to justify an instinctive preference." As a result, Orwell practiced what he considered a type of "sociological criticism," relating a given author and his works to their social and historical contexts while also being conscious of the modern reader's context. But, as George Woodcock points out, Orwell's best criticism is also profoundly personal, so that his approach to his subject represents a "passionate engagement" (238). Orwell's devotion to Dickens is not uncritical. He takes him to task for his old-fashioned plots, riddled with coincidence; for his sentimentality; for his "piling up of detail on detail, embroidery on embroidery"; and for his neglect of the working class.

Numerous readers and critics have commented on the similarities between Orwell's Dickens and Orwell himself, particularly his identifying Dickens as a moralist, deeply suspicious of "-isms."

WORKS CITED

Shelden, Michael. *Orwell: The Authorized Biography.* New York: HarperCollins, 1991.

Woodcock, George. *The Crystal Spirit.* London: Jonathan Cape, 1967.

Clergyman's Daughter, A

Orwell's second novel, published by Victor Gollancz in March 1935 and by Harper & Brothers in New York in August 1936. This work represents his first and only attempt to portray a female protagonist. To his credit, Orwell was the first to recognize and acknowledge that his attempt failed.

HISTORICAL/BIOGRAPHICAL CONTEXT

In the broadest sense of the term, the historical context of the novel is the emergence of secularism and the weakening of religious belief, a phenomenon that had been developing in Western Europe since the 17th century. The decline of religion had been accompanied and, to a significant extent, precipitated by the rise of scientific thinking. The most dramatic expression of this development in England occurred in 1859, with the publication of Charles Darwin's *On the Origin of the Species,* offering an account of the evolution of mankind that rocked the already-fragile foundations of all religions. Less dramatic but equally serious was the socioeconomic thesis put forth by Karl Marx, which characterized religion as "the opiate of the people."

Also in England, within Christianity itself, there were the conflicting divisions of sects challenging the authority of the Church of England, calling for disestablishmentarianism, an end to the practice of government support of that church. Added to these difficulties was the practice known as the higher criticism, by which the authority and stability of biblical texts were scrutinized and questioned by scholars. Another issue dividing the Church of England, emerging from the opposite of the disestablishment faction, was the Oxford Movement, an effort to return the Church of England to the Catholic rituals of the Middle Ages. In the novel, Victor Stone, the schoolmaster at St. Athelstan's, represents a frivolous example of this movement.

In the atmosphere that followed World War I, the doubts of the 19th century laid the groundwork for the secular materialism of the 1920s and '30s. As the cynical Mr. Warburton puts it in *The Clergyman's Daughter,* the modern world's rendering of the famous passage in St. Paul's Epistle to the Corinthians ("the greatest of these is charity") would replace the word *charity* with *money.* Orwell was fond enough of this idea to use it as the epigraph to his next novel, *Keep the Aspidistra Flying.* Not a believer himself, Orwell nevertheless saw the loss of religious faith in the post–World War I world as a crucial problem, depriving many people of a sense of meaning in life.

Orwell wrote *A Clergyman's Daughter* between January and October 1934, while recovering from an attack of pneumonia he had suffered the previous December. His recuperation took place at his parents' home in Southwold, Suffolk. The description of Knype Hill in the opening chapter is based heavily on Southwold. The hop-picking scenes in chapter 2 derive not only from his experiences but also from his writing about them. His article "Hop Picking," published in December 1931, the result of his engaging in the activity earlier that year, is a direct source of the descriptions in the novel. Similarly, the recounting in chapter 4 of Dorothy's dreadful experiences at the Ringwood School bears some relation to Orwell's stint as a teacher from April 1932 to July 1933 at the Hawthorns High School for Boys in Hayes, a suburban town that is the model for South Bridge, the location of the Ringwood School. While at Hawthorns, Orwell wrote and directed a play, *Charles II.* Like Dorothy, he also made the armor and costumes, "suffering untold agonies with glue and brown paper . . ." as he wrote in a letter to his friend Eleanor Jaques.

As for the experimental, surrealistic depiction in chapter 3 of the homeless gathered in Trafalgar Square, it was an effort inspired by the Nighttown episode in James Joyce's *Ulysses,* a book that Orwell read in 1933 and by which he was profoundly impressed. As a source, Joyce's novel proved to be a mixed blessing.

That the character of Warburton exhibits features corresponding to those of his author seems less farfetched in the light of the recent revelation of Orwell's attempted rape of JACINTHA BUDDICOM. In the original manuscript, he had written that Warburton had tried to rape Dorothy, later amending it to ". . . making love to her violently, outrageously, even brutally." Another, admittedly thin, piece of evidence supporting the association of character and author is the fact that one of the names assumed by Eric Blair on his tramping excursions was "Edward Burton."

In October 1934, Orwell finished the novel and submitted it for publication. He had strong reservations about its quality, but he was in dire financial straits, living at his parents' home in Southwold and feeling that he had made a mess of a good idea. The only part of the novel that he took some pride in was his experimental third chapter, as mentioned above. As he wrote in a letter to his friend BRENDA SALKELD, "There are whole wads of it that are so awful that I really don't know what to do with them." His publisher, Victor Gollancz, worried about a possible libel suit, passed the manuscript on to his lawyer and to his coeditor, Norman Collins, both of whom recommended publication with minor revisions. Collins's report contains some interesting observations about the book's author. In fact, Collins might qualify as Orwell's first Freudian critic:

> I know nothing about Orwell, but it is perfectly clear . . . that he has been through hell, and that he is probably still there. He would certainly be a plum for a practicing psycho-analyst. There is in his work, either latent or fully revealed, almost every one of the major aberrations. . . . (Crick, 165).

Gollancz did publish the book, after Orwell agreed to some minor changes.

SYNOPSIS

Chapter 1, Part 1

On a chilly August morning, the alarm clock in Dorothy Hare's bedroom goes off at 5:30 A.M., awakening her from a deep, troubled sleep. Dog-tired, she wants nothing more than to snuggle under her blanket, but she leaps out of bed and shuts off the alarm lest its continued ringing wake her father. Then begins her morning ritual: kneeling to say the Lord's Prayer, heading down to the kitchen to light the fire—setting a kettle over it for her father's shaving water, back upstairs for a penitential cold bath. She detests cold baths; it is for that very penitential reason she makes it a rule to take all her baths cold from April to November.

While still in her bath, she looks over her to-do list for the day. Dorothy is a woman of 27, the only child of Charles Hare, the rector of St. Athelstan's Anglican Church in Knype Hill, Suffolk. Since the death of her mother, Dorothy has assumed all the "dirty work" of a pastor's life: visiting, consoling, and counseling parishioners, as well as running the rectory, dealing with tradesmen, and paying the bills. In that connection, high on her list of tasks for the day is "must ask father for money." Cargill, the local butcher, has not been paid for seven months, and his bill now amounts to more than 20 pounds, a figure that constantly gnaws at her nerves. She returns to the kitchen to bring her father's shaving water to his room, where she is rebuked by him for being seven minutes late. Then she is off on her bicycle to the church for Holy Communion service. During the service, Dorothy's mind occasionally wanders, and, as a result, she carries a pin, which she uses to punish herself for her sinful behavior. One example occurs when it is time to receive communion. The only other communicant is old Miss Mayfill, whose "ancient, bloodless face" contained a particularly repellent mouth, from which an under lip "slobbered forward, exposing a strip of gum and a row of false teeth as yellow as the keys of an old piano." Gazing at that mouth, Dorothy prays that she will not have to drink from the chalice *after* Miss Mayfill. The next moment, "in self-horror," she realizes that her wish is not only un-Christian, but it is also blasphemous. "She drew the pin from her lapel and drove it into her arm so hard that it was all she could do to suppress a cry of pain. Then she stepped to the altar and knelt down meekly on Miss Mayfill's left, so as to make quite sure of taking the chalice after her." Kneeling there, Dorothy is on the verge of not taking Communion, convinced that she is so unworthy of receiving the Lord. But a sudden shaft of light above the church pierces the morning clouds and splashes through the trees outside, "filling the doorway with green light." The exquisite greenness evokes in her a profound religious serenity that fills her heart. She drinks joyfully from the chalice, undeterred by the aftertaste of Miss Mayfill's lips.

Chapter 1, Part 2

Knype Hill is a town of some 2,000 people, more than half of whom are employees of the Blifil-Gordon sugar beet company. St. Athelstan's stands at the highest point; halfway down the hill is the rectory. Both church and rectory are in advanced stages of decay, a fact that the Reverend Hare refuses to recognize, just as he continually ignores the unpaid bills piling up and preying on Dorothy's mind. Her father is a man of "unfailing ill humor . . . disgusted and infuriated" by everything about the modern world. He had been born into an upper-class family. As the second son, he was slated for a career in the church, since the first son inherited the property. A man with an ill-disguised contempt for the "lower classes," he fares just as poorly with his peers. As a result, the membership in his church has steadily declined over the years, the congregation shrinking from 700 when he arrived 23 years ago to 600 at the present time. He has failed to conduct his church according to one of two existing courses—that of Anglo-Catholicism, the extreme legacy of the 19th-century Oxford movement or, at the other end of the ecclesiastical spectrum, the modern relativistic low-church style, maintaining that one religion is as good as another. When Dorothy finally summons up the nerve to ask him for money, particularly to pay some part of the butcher's bill, he adopts a familiar old aristocratic excuse, "Doesn't everyone owe money to his tradesman?" an occasion for him to reminisce about his days as a student at Oxford.

Chapter 1, Part 3

Later that morning, as Dorothy bicycles into town, she is stopped by Proggett, the church's sexton. Proggett explains, as he does regularly, the problem of the bells in the church tower. Only one of them still functions; seven others have come loose from their hinges and are lying on the floor of belfry, severely straining its floor. He reports that "the floor's a-busting underneath 'em." When Dorothy suggests that they ask Miss Mayfill for the money to move the bells, Proggett prudently points out that if Miss Mayfill becomes aware of the danger the bells represent, she will never set foot in the church again. With this added burden on her mind, Dorothy proceeds into town where a political rally is in progress for the election of Blifil-Gordon, the owner of the beet refinery, to Parliament. There she bumps into the local rake, Mr. Warburton. He is a recent addition to the town, a painter with an independent income and the father of three illegitimate children. Warburton delights in shocking Dorothy with his clever mix of satiric and sexual comments. At one point in the past, he had moved beyond the merely verbal. Two years ago, shortly after first moving to Knype Hill, he invited Dorothy to his home for tea. At the time, he was passing himself off as a widower with two children—later, it became clear when his "housekeeper" became pregnant that she was the mother of his two children. At tea, Warburton delighted Dorothy with his witty, sophisticated talk, and then he suddenly tried to force himself on her. His effort amounted to an attempted rape, but she successfully fought him off. The incident put her on guard but their friendship survives, although Warburton, completely unrepentant, continues to try to make physical contact whenever they meet. Although Dorothy genuinely dislikes his physical presence, she harbors a fondness for Warburton not just for his witty, blasphemous conversation but also for "a species of sympathy and understanding which she could not get elsewhere." Warburton invites her to dinner at his house that evening to meet his guest, Ronald Bewley, the author of *Fishpools and Concubines,* which he describes as "real high-class pornography." Warburton assures her that Bewley's wife will also be there, "Full chaperonage. No Tarquin and Lucrece business this evening." After they part, Dorothy is accosted by the town's chief scandalmonger, Mrs. Semprill. Mrs. Semprill's "stories were not only dirty and libelous . . . they had nearly always some monstrous tinge of perversion about them." In her dedication to expose others, "she had been instrumental in breaking off not less than half a dozen engagements and starting innumerable quarrels between husbands and wives." When Dorothy finally breaks away from her, she realizes that since Mrs. Semprill lives directly across the way from Warburton's house, Dorothy will be the subject of gossip tomorrow.

Chapter 1, Part 4

Later that morning, Dorothy is busily engaged in the pastoral care that is her father's responsibility. Visiting the church's parishioners in their cottages, helping with chores, ministering to the sick, offering consolation and counsel to all, Dorothy is particularly sensitive to the various odors arising from the cottages, particularly the strange smells emanating from old Mr.Tombs's house. Mr. Tombs slept under what appeared to be a fur rug, which, on closer examination, proved to be the 24 cats he maintained. Today, Dorothy visits Mrs. Pither, a woman in her seventies who is suffering from rheumatism. In addition to engaging in a discussion of Mrs. Pither's favorite topic, heaven, Dorothy also helps draw a day's supply of water from her well, and applies some liniment to Mrs. Pither's "large, grey-veined, flaccid legs." On her way home, Dorothy stops by a meadow and finds herself overcome by "a mystical joy in the beauty of the earth . . . all the riches of summer, the warmth of the earth, the song of birds, the fume of cows, the droning of countless bees, mingling and ascending like the smoke of ever-burning altars." When she realizes she is kissing a stalk of fennel, she immediately checks herself. Is she falling into the heresy of nature worship, "mere pantheism"? She uses a rose thorn to inflict punishment on herself. As she prepares to leave, the local Catholic priest, Father McGuire, passes by, deliberately snubbing her. The priest and her father are not on speaking terms. Nor does her father speak to the local Congregationalist, Methodist, or Fundamentalist preacher.

Chapter 1, Part 5

At the parish school, Victor Stone, the intense, young schoolmaster, is directing a rehearsal of *Charles I,* a school play about the English king who was beheaded by Parliament in 1649. Dorothy is present, it having fallen to her (as it always does) to make the costumes, using as her material glue, pins, and brown paper. With two weeks to go to opening night, she faces an overwhelming task in creating all the costumes, swords, shields, breast plates, helmets, and especially, most dreadfully from Dorothy's point of view, jackboots needed to enact the English Civil War. After rehearsal, she sits at her sewing machine, desperately trying to keep up, while Victor Stone pleads with her to persuade her father to have a procession next month. Victor is a staunch member of the right wing (the Anglo-Catholic segment) of the church, in love with the rich pageantry and music that Anglicanism retained after the break with Rome in the 16th century. Dorothy follows her father in his belief that, although the Church of England is Catholic, not Protestant, the emphasis on ritual in the Roman church is overdone. She cuts short her discussion when she realizes that she must be home in time to prepare an omelet for her father's lunch.

Chapter 1, Part 6

It is after 10 P.M. on the same day. Dorothy has been on the run all day and is now sitting in a large, comfortable chair in Warburton's house. She has discovered that the other expected guests, the novelist Bewley and his wife, were not coming. What she does not know is that these people do not exist, they were invented on the spot by Warburton in order to lure her to his house. She realizes she should be leaving now, but the chair is comfortable and she is so tired that she's having trouble getting to her feet. Besides, Warburton has engaged her in a clever theological argument. Now Warburton makes his move, approaching her chair from behind, stroking her arms. She protests and insists on leaving. As she walks down his path to her bicycle, he tells her he is leaving with his children for France the next day. He tries to coerce a kiss from her, she reminds him that Mrs. Semprill is probably taking this all in. Reflecting on his advances, she is reminded of her secret, the fact that "she really could not bear it. To be kissed or fondled by a man—to feel heavy male arms about her and thick male lips bearing down upon her own—was terrifying and repulsive to her." It was not that she disliked men, particularly if, like Warburton, they had a sense of humor and interesting ideas. But too many men made it clear that they were only interested in one thing. *All that* was her term for it. She has been proposed to five years earlier by a sincere and decent curate at a neighboring parish. "How gladly she would have married him if only it had not been for *all that!*" She traces the roots of her frigidity to her childhood, ugly scenes between her mother and her father and to some old steel engravings of satyrs pursuing nymphs, which marred her childhood and left a permanent mark. Arriving home, exhausted, she remembers the jackboots and forces herself to begin cutting and pasting after warming the glue pot.

Chapter 2, Part 1

The second of this five-chapter novel opens on a strange new world—strange, that is to Dorothy, who comes to consciousness on New Kent Road, a London street. Dressed in clothes she's never seen before, she has no sense of where she is, how she got there, and more importantly, who she is. Looking into a mirror of a local store, she does not recognize the face but accepts it as hers. She passes by a newsstand with posters proclaiming the story of the missing "rector's daughter" but the words make no impression. Finally, she reaches a logical conclusion, "Of course, I've lost my memory."

She meets three young people, two men and a woman, wearing backpacks and speaking in Cockney dialects that Dorothy finds difficult to understand. When they learn that she has a half-crown (about 65 cents), they invite her to join them. They are looking for work picking hops, used in the brewing of beer, in Kent. The spokesman for the three is Nobby, whose spirited language is liberally sprinkled with the word *mulligatawny*. The other two are Charlie and Flo, who are a couple. With Dorothy's half-crown they plan to take the two-penny tram to Bromley. From there it will be two days' hike to the hop-picking farms.

Chapter 2, Part 2

The narrator explains that seven days have elapsed between the night Dorothy has fallen asleep working on the costumes and her encounter with Nobby and his friends. That period is lost forever. Meanwhile, the prospect of reaching the hop fields seems to be a receding goal, as the four young people have to zig-zag their way, always begging for food at every door they pass or stealing fruits and vegetables from orchards and fields. The frustration and fatigue leave Flo and Charlie, two young city dwellers who are not accustomed to life on the road, openly resistant. The group runs into an old Irishwoman, Mrs. McElligott, who suggests they try a farm five miles away. Then they fall into a discussion regarding the scandal of the "rector's daughter," during which an exhausted Dorothy almost falls asleep, rousing herself when hearing words like *rector* and *church*. But fatigue wins out as she falls back to sleep in the open air. The next morning, Charlie and Flo refuse to move, so that only Dorothy and Nobby make the five-mile trip to the farm Mrs. McElligott mentioned. After waiting for hours, they are told there are no jobs, and when they return, they discover that Charlie and Flo have deserted them, stealing Dorothy and Nobby's food and equipment. Late that evening, their luck finally turns when they are taken on at a nearby farm. Dorothy collapses in a straw-filled hut for single women pickers into a deep, luxurious sleep.

Chapter 2, Part 3

Dorothy and Nobby settle into the life of hop picking: waking up at 5:30 A.M., cooking breakfast over a fire—tea, bacon, and bread fried in the bacon grease; and cooking another meal—same ingredients—to take with them for lunch. Once in the field, they began the process of tearing off the hops, trying to separate them from the leaves and stalks. The bines contain minute thorns that eventually cut into the skin, but once the blood flows freely, they can pick without pain. At noon, they have an hour's break for lunch, then more picking until five or six P.M. Looking back later, Dorothy would always recall the long afternoons, the hot sun and rich aromas of the fields, the hypnotic quality of the work, which took hold of you and absorbed you, "[B]ut mostly she would remember the singing of the pickers chanting over and over a few select tunes, melancholy songs of unrequited love." At the end of the workday they return to camp, making an effort to clean up at least their hands before supper—tea, bread and bacon along with a four-penny worth of meat from the local butcher or whatever food Nobby was able to steal from the owner. After eating, they sit around huge fires, singing old songs and nodding off to sleep.

Chapter 2, Part 4

On Sunday, the one day off, Dorothy, having cooked a meal consisting almost entirely of food stolen by Nobby, is dozing in the sun like a contented animal when Nobby drops in her lap a tabloid scandal sheet containing an account with her picture—the "rector's daughter." But her mind is so bathed in Sunday-afternoon stupor that she falls asleep without reading it.

Chapter 2, Part 5

The following Sunday, Nobby is arrested for his wide-ranging food thefts. As he is led away by the police, he winks at Dorothy, showing his indomitable spirit and good humor as he heads for jail. For Dorothy, the shock of his arrest shatters her fragile sense of herself. "It was as though a bubble in her brain had burst. . . . Her memory was coming back to her, that was certain, and some ugly shock was coming with it." She retrieves the paper that Nobby had passed on to her a week earlier. Now with a painfully alert awareness, she reads the scandal rag's account, most of it based upon the eyewitness of "Mrs. Evelina Semprill." Mrs. Semprill reports seeing Dorothy embracing Mr. Warburton, before driving away with him, dressed in scanty attire "and under the influence of alcohol." Now fully recollecting her past, she dreads what has been done to her reputation, but she has complete confidence that her father will defend her. She writes him a long letter explaining what has happened and asking him to send clothes and two pounds for her fare home.

Chapter 2, Part 6

On the third day after posting the letter, she goes to the local post office expecting a reply. When no letter is there, nor on the next day, she writes a longer letter and waits five days for a reply, but no letter arrives. She realizes that her father has rejected her. But she also has another realization: that not once since regaining her memory has she resorted to the "very source and center of her life," prayer, that with all she has been through, she has not the slightest impulse to pray. Even more surprising is the fact that her failure to pray does not mean all that much to her. "Prayer, which had been the mainstay of her life, had no meaning for her any longer." Right now she had to think about her future, since the hop picking season was coming to a close. She continues working in the fields, now with a new partner named Deafie, an old tramp but an excellent picker. On the last day of picking, the male pickers celebrate by tossing the females into the bins. That evening the pickers all gather around a huge fire, hands clasped singing "Auld Lang Syne." The next day, after being paid, Dorothy leaves with the Turles family on the "hoppers' train" to London.

Chapter 2, Part 7

In London, she has no luck finding a room because of the contrast between her bedraggled appearance and her educated accent. She finally finds a place at Mary's, a semibordello. Trying to find work as a servant, she applies for 18 jobs and always encounters the distrust engendered by her educated accent. After a week, and two more fruitless letters to her father, she finds herself homeless, with the weather becoming increasingly colder, as she roams the streets and arrives at Trafalgar Square.

Chapter 3, Part 1

This chapter represents a departure from the straightforward, realistic, third-person narrative that characterizes the rest of the novel. Part I is written as though it were the script of an expressionist play, with stage directions, dialogue, spoken by various characters we have already met in the novel (Mrs. McElligott, Charlie, Deafie, and Dorothy herself) commingled with characters whose history can only be guessed at (Mr. Tall Boys, Mrs. Bendigo, Mrs. Wayne, Ginger). The setting is Trafalgar Square in the late evening, early-morning hours when the homeless gather looking for some protection from the cold as they try to sleep on the square's benches. One of the purposes of the scene is to capture the cacophony of dialects and verbal dissonance as they converge into a plea for recognition of their humanity. The visual equivalent of the verbal occurs when they form a pyramid on the bench, a "huddled mass," with their only protection from the cold being their newspaper posters. Awake at 4:30 A.M., they must wait in line outside Mr. Wilkins' cafeteria, which opens at 5:00, where four of them share a breakfast of one large tea and one doughnut, and the golden chance to sleep in a warm room until 7:00. Thus, an episode presented in surrealist fashion finishes on a note of harsh reality.

Chapter 3, Part 2

Dorothy drifts for the next 10 days as a homeless beggar, often spending more sleepless nights in Trafalgar Square. After a point, she is recognized as a regular, and she and Mrs. McElligott are arrested in a routine roundup of beggars. Relieved to be spending the night in a relatively clean, warm place, she crawls to the cot in her cell and falls asleep for 10 hours.

Chapter 4, Part 1

The scene shifts to Knype Hill and Dorothy's father. His predictable first reaction to his daughter's disappearance is rage over the inconvenience she has caused him, forcing him on one occasion to make his own breakfast. Once Mrs. Semprill's version of events hits the newspapers, depicting him as "a broken old man," he writes Dorothy off, his none-too-generous heart "hardened beyond possibility of forgiveness." This attitude persists until he receives Dorothy's letters from Kent. Then he writes to his cousin, Sir Thomas Hare, asking him to help Dorothy find a job in London. Sir Thomas dispatches his butler, Blyth, to find her and bring her back to his house. Blyth tracks Dorothy down to the jail and meets her when she is released. Blyth brings her back to Sir Thomas's house and installs her in one of the bedrooms. After meeting Dorothy, Sir Thomas arranges through his solicitor to have her employed as a schoolmistress at Ringwood House Academy for Girls, in Southbridge, a suburb of London. Dorothy, skeptical of her ability to teach any subject, is aware of the irony: In the past few weeks, she had been unable to obtain the lowliest of jobs, and here she is finding an apparently desirable one in three days. It reminds her of Mr. Warburton's favorite observation that if you substituted the word *money* for *charity* in St. Paul's epistle to the Corinthians, it would have 10 times as much meaning as the original.

Chapter 4, Part 2

The headmistress of the Ringwood school is Mrs. Creevy, a woman of few words. In their interview, she makes it clear that her only interests are the fees she extracts from the parents of the students. Education itself is not mentioned, except to speak about emphasizing the "moral side." It is clear that Mrs. Creevy is an ignorant, grasping, miserly tyrant who will make Dorothy's life at the school miserable. For class preparation, Mrs. Creevy shows Dorothy three lists of names. The first list includes the children of parents who pay their fees promptly. These are never to be "smacked." The second group lists the children of the "medium payers," whose parents pay but usually have to be dunned and pressured. These students can be smacked but not in a way that might leave marks. Mrs. Creevy's preferred form of punishment is to twist their ears, because it's painful but leaves no mark. The third group are those whose parents are two terms behind in payments—and to them you can do anything "short of a police court case." Alone with her class, Dorothy discovers they have learned virtually nothing, except for two subjects, handwriting and basic arithmetic. Handwriting is particularly stressed, because the neat specimens of flowery passages that the students copy in their notebooks make a good impression on their poorly educated parents.

Chapter 4, Part 3

Soon Dorothy finds herself moved by her students and fired by the determination to educate them. She comes to realize that the students respond to situations in which they play an active role, creating papier-mâché models in geography and cutting out illustrations representative of historical periods and affixing them to a chart, which, unfolded, symbolized historical progress. All these developments in class bring Dorothy a sense of happiness that even "the beastliness of living in Mrs. Creevy's house" cannot entirely undermine.

Chapter 4, Part 4

Dorothy's honeymoon with her students is a short-lived one. First, there are individual complaints from one or two parents about her new teaching methods, but the parents rise up in a body when they discover her ultimate iniquity. Almost all the parents are nonconformists (not members of the Church of England but of more fundamentalist Protestant sects). A delegation of them come to the school to protest the fact that in teaching *Macbeth,* Dorothy has not only chosen a text that includes the word *womb* (MacDuff was "from his mother's womb / Untimely ripped") but who has actually explained its meaning to the class. When Dorothy responds that "the children wouldn't have understood the play if I hadn't explained!" the group spokesman puts the case more forcefully, "We don't want them to understand. . . . We don't send our children to school to have ideas put in their heads. . . . We try to bring our children up decent and save them from knowing anything about the Facts of Life."

Having disposed of the Shakespeare problem, the parents weigh in with the complaints that Dorothy has been neglecting practical subjects like business arithmetic and handwriting. After they leave, it is Mrs. Creevy's turn to lay down the law, insisting on a return to her ways of teaching, always guided by her one fundamental educational principle: "There's only one thing that matters in a school and that's the fees." Thoroughly humiliated, Dorothy agrees to conform to Mrs. Creevy's demands. As the chapter proceeds, the authorial voice intrudes, maintaining that Mrs. Creevy is merely giving voice to "what most people in her position think but never say." In other words, too many private schools are run strictly for profit by people who know nothing about education, and such schools are not inspected by authorities.

Chapter 4, Part 5

The next day, Dorothy begins to reintroduce the old curriculum: copying passages in writing, learning the capitals of the English counties, "practical" arithmetic, French phrases, all to be learned by rote. Gradually the students begin to turn against Dorothy, misbehaving as much out of revenge as out of boredom. The effect on Dorothy's nerves is powerful, as the full horror of living under Mrs. Creevy's tyrannical rule is brought home to her. The only respite from the nerve-racking weeks that follow the *Macbeth* incident is attendance at the local Church of England services. Although Dorothy's loss of faith is complete and total, she nevertheless finds in the familiar phrases and actions of the liturgy precious moments of peace that keep her from completely falling apart. As the term comes to an end, the behavior of her class becomes increasingly hostile. Some students deliberately act up so that Mrs. Creevy has to come in to discipline them and humiliate Dorothy. Finally, she snaps and, against her most basic principles, delivers one student a full-scale smack across her face.

Chapter 4, Part 6

As the holidays begin, Dorothy receives a letter from Warburton, indicating that he has only recently returned to Knype Hill and learned about the scandal involving the two of them. He has been making every effort to contradict the story, including confronting Mrs. Semprill and reducing her to "hypocritical snivelings." He reports that Dorothy's father misses her very much. He has been forced to pay off all his debts. His creditors confronted him en masse at a meeting in the rectory. It seems that only Dorothy's presence "could keep the tradesmen permanently at bay." Warburton goes on to news about himself, but at that point Dorothy tears up the letter, annoyed at its light tone, considering his partial responsibility for her plight.

A few days later, she hears from her father, who encloses two pounds in his letter. After some perfunctory inquiries as to her health and well-being, he launches into complaints about problems at the church with indirect references to missing Dorothy's help but no request for her to return. Reading the letter, Dorothy is filled with longing to return home. With school now in recess, she has more time to herself, spending her free hours on long, solitary walks or reading in the public library alongside the homeless men lingering there to avoid the cold. The only friend she makes is Miss Beaver, also a schoolmistress, whose room in a boardinghouse provides an occasional haven for Dorothy. Over a cup of tea, she and Miss Beaver work the daily crossword puzzle in the paper. When the new term starts, she finds disciplining the students an easier task because she is ruthless from the beginning, not making the mistake of "treating them like human beings." Even Mrs. Creevy becomes less monstrous, leading Dorothy to hope that she might be due for a raise. On the final day of the term, Mrs. Creevy pays her off and then tells her off: She is to pack up and leave. She is fired, to be replaced by a teacher who will be bringing with her a few students. Utterly shocked, Dorothy takes her leave, intending to look for another teaching job in the London area.

Chapter 5, Part 1

No sooner has she closed the gate at Mrs. Creevy's when she encounters a telegraph boy delivering a telegram for "Miss Millborough." The telegram is from Warburton: Mrs. Semprill has been sued for libel and is completely discredited. Dorothy's reputation has been restored, and her father wishes to have her return immediately. Warburton also indicates that he will be picking her up that day. A short while later, Warburton appears in a taxi, rescues Dorothy's luggage from Mrs. Creevy's house, and whisks her off to the London station. On the way, he explains that Mrs. Semprill had been successfully sued by the local bank manager and has been forced to leave town. After a good lunch they take the train—first class at Warburton's insistence—to Knype Hill. Rather than speak of her adventures, she tells him about something more important—her loss of faith. Warburton insists that she never really was a believer. As a clergyman's daughter, he argues, she had sold herself a bill of goods until the strain of self-deception became too strong. That is why, he suggests, she lost her memory. Dorothy replies that the important point is not *when* she lost her faith but *that* she has lost it. How does she go on now that "the whole world is empty"? But she appears to accept the possibility of pretending to be a believer so as not to tamper with others' beliefs. A world without God is a world without meaning, and such a prospect is bad enough for her without inflicting it on others.

Warburton tires of the discussion at this point. He has another project in mind, that he and she be married. He sketches Dorothy's future if she does not marry him: Her father will last for another 10 years and then die, leaving her without a penny. She will have engaged in endless, thankless chores, sat through "interminable church services," having lost her youth, ending up as a poor, withered old maid. The bleak picture of her future almost convinces her, but the moment he tries to take her in his arms, "a wave of disgust and deadly fear" goes through her. Her sexual frigidity is too powerful to be overcome. She resists, and Warburton accepts her rejection with perfect aplomb. As for the future, she will continue to behave as she has in the past in the interest of being useful. She will still be an outwardly conforming Christian, but certain private expressions of her faith, such as the use of a pin to punish herself, will cease.

Chapter 5, Part 2

It is a week later, and Dorothy is back performing her pastoral duties and tending to her father's whims. He still refuses to accept her amnesia explanation, but otherwise their relationship remains unchanged. Within herself, however, she still grapples with the important truth that could not be evaded, "Either life on earth is a preparation for something greater or more lasting, or it is meaningless, dark and dreadful." At this point, the author's voice assures us that Dorothy has unconsciously hit upon the answer to her problem in simply "doing what is customary, useful and acceptable." Dorothy will pursue the daily tasks, such as the one she is now working on, preparing the costumes for another church festival, working in the pervasive aroma of the glue pot.

COMMENTARY

From the moment the alarm goes off in Dorothy's room in the first chapter, we are impaled on the cross of self-sacrificing drudgery surrounding Charles Hare, her clergyman father. Dorothy, the only child of the widowed rector, serves as the *de facto* pastor of the dwindling flock at St. Athelstan's Anglican Church. She does everything except officiate at services and deliver sermons (although she types the latter). With all the chores and cares on her shoulders, we might expect her to be resentful and bitter. Instead, the most intense feeling she exhibits is a severe sense of guilt, which she appeases by sticking herself with a sharp pin. Dorothy appears to be a candidate for sainthood, except that her saintliness resembles, ironically enough, the kind of behavior people had in mind when, after his death, they referred to Orwell as a saint, a nonreligious, long-suffering, selfless truth teller (see the "Afterlife" section of part 1 of this book). But Dorothy's religious truth has left her prey to all the self-interested citizens of Knype Hill, of which her father is at the head of the line.

The one episode in which something like a religious, as opposed to ecclesiastical, experience occurs when Dorothy interrupts her chores for a moment to admire some roadside flowers. Kneeling among them, she pulls a leaf of fennel, inhaling its aroma:

> Its richness overwhelmed her, almost dizzied her for a moment . . . her heart swelled with sudden joy. It was that mystical joy in the beauty of the earth and the very nature of things that she recognized, perhaps mistakenly, as the love of God.
>
> . . . She began to pray, and for a moment, she prayed blissfully, ardently, forgetting herself in the joy of her worship. Then, less than a minute later, she discovered she was kissing the frond of the fennel that was still against her face . . . Was it God she was worshiping, or was it only the earth? . . . She had been betrayed in to a half-pagan fantasy . . . mere pantheism.

The incident bears a strong resemblance to a scene in a later novel, COMING UP FOR AIR, in which the protagonist George Bowling stops by a roadside and finds himself overwhelmed by the aroma of primroses. His reverie is interrupted by an approaching car. Both scenes suggest that, to the extent that Orwell, whose love of nature is well documented, harbored religious feelings, he associated them with the beauty of the natural world.

But when challenged by her womanizing, atheist friend Warburton (their friendship is another of the novel's improbabilities), she puts up a firm defense of traditional Christian beliefs. The only apparent crack in her armor occurs when Warburton tries to force himself on her. The authorial narrator explains that she is sexually frigid, the consequence of some version of a primal scene she has witnessed as a child. Here, Orwell is flagrantly sparing of any details that might make this alleged trauma remotely credible. The suspicion grows, sounded out resoundingly by the feminist critic Daphne Patai, that Orwell, having invented a female protagonist, does not know what to do with her, with the result that he "moulds her into a cipher" (Patai, 97) Perhaps *cipher* (the same word is used by Peter Quennell in an early review of the novel) is too strong a term, but Dorothy is an extremely passive character. Dominated by her father, perhaps in imitation of her mother, who, until her death, also did the "dirty work" of the parish, she is manipulated by a poor parishioner, Mrs. Pither; hounded by creditors; tricked and molested by Warburton; conned out of her last half-crown by her hop-picking companions; brutally exploited by the headmistress Mrs. Creevy; and humiliated by the school's parents. Even on the central issue of her loss of faith, she decides not to let that cataclysmic event have any influence on her behavior. She will go about, as she imagines millions have before her, as an observant Christian in practice but a nonbeliever in her heart.

During her amnesiac phase in chapter 2, Dorothy adopts the name of her father's housemaid, Ellen, and the last name Millborough from a neighboring borough that houses an Anglo-Catholic church whose employment of Catholic rituals had irritated her: "You could hardly see what's happening on the altar, there are such clouds of incense." Presumably, her unconscious is affirming her status as her father's servant, but her identity is still cloudy and unclear. Hop picking offers her a brief respite. GEORGE WOODCOCK maintains that the finest section of the novel is the description of the hypnotic appeal of working in the hop fields that Dorothy experiences: "It is a time of renewal through a descent, almost in a Jungian sense, into the soothing waters of half-consciousness." But the idyll ends with the arrest of Nobby and with Dorothy's recovery of her identity. "From this point joy drains out of the book, and vitality with it" (Woodcock, 111). For this section, Orwell borrowed heavily from his 1931 essay "Hop Picking." His partner in the actual picking was a man named Ginger, the original of Dorothy's Nobby. A character named Ginger makes a brief appearance in the Trafalgar Square scene in chapter 3.

The controversial chapter 3 speaks to another feature of Orwell's complexity as a novelist. He had come of age at a time when the dominant mode of "serious" literature was modernism, with its focus on the inner life of the isolated, often alienated, individual consciousness, reflected in poetry in T. S. Eliot's "The Love Song of J. Alfred Prufrock" and in fiction in Virginia Woolf's *To the Lighthouse.* For Orwell, however, modernism at its best is represented by James Joyce's *Ulysses,* partly because the consciousness that Joyce chose to represent was that of a common man, Leopold Bloom, immersed in the daily routines of an ordinary day, but whose inner reality, his spirit or soul, emerges irrepressibly. In one chapter, Joyce took his experiment with the stream of consciousness a step further in the famous Nighttown sequence. Adopting features of surrealism and the Freudian theory of dreams, Joyce strove to represent not simply the consciousness but the Freudian/Jungian unconscious in all its seemingly chaotic confusion. In chapter 3, Orwell borrows from the Nighttown episode. Written as if it were the script of a play or film in the expressionist style, the scene can be taken as a semidream, semihallucination, semirealistic montage, the three styles colliding with and collapsing on one another—rendered through the consciousness of Dorothy. The figures parading on stage constitute a representative cross-section of down-and-outers, the insulted and the injured of modern society. At one point they congregate to form a pyramid with their bodies, like the penguins in Antarctica, creating faint protection from the cold.

This often maligned episode has an able defender in the linguistic critic Roger Fowler. He points out that the scene is an experiment in polyphony, that is to say, the representation of simultaneous speech. Reading the chapter in a linear fashion, rather than as overlapping and interweaving dialogue, we lose its impact. "The overall effect . . . is like the babble of a lot of people in one space, the so-called 'cocktail party effect' where everything is a blur except what you choose to concentrate on" (Fowler, 117). Fowler also provides a detailed and cogent analysis of the various idiolects of the individual speakers.

The point is to directly represent the hallucinatory, nightmarish quality that is Dorothy's sense of the scene. As an artistic experiment, the scene may be viewed as flawed and derivative, but it reflects more care and artistry than its reputation suggests. Something like its effect appears in a work that predates both Joyce and Orwell by three centuries: the mad declamations that take place on the frozen heath among Poor Tom, the Fool, and King Lear. That being said, the fact remains that the episode, unlike the comparable scenes in *King* Lear or *Ulysses,* does nothing to advance the plot nor to deepen our sense of the protagonist.

As chapter 4 opens, the scene shifts to Knype Hill and to the reaction of Dorothy's father, who has not been as cold and unresponsive as we may have imagined. However, confronted with Dorothy's plight, as revealed in her letter to him, he shifts the burden to someone else, in this case, his cousin the baronet, Sir Thomas Hare. This gives Orwell the opportunity to shift the narrative mode into Dickensian realism. Sir Thomas is a product of the mold Orwell classifies in his essay "CHARLES DICKENS" as "the good rich man," whose intervention constitutes, in this case, a temporary rescue of the protagonist. A more powerful and prominent example of Dickensian caricature, however, is the egregious Mrs. Creevy, who in the ranks of evil schoolmistresses, is second only to Mr. and Mrs. Wackford Squeers of Dotheboys Hall in *Nicholas Nickleby*. Mrs. Creevy is not only ignorant, mean-spirited, hypocritical, and miserly, but she is also a snoop, comparable in that respect to Mrs. Wisbeach, Gordon Comstock's landlady in *KEEP THE ASPIDISTRA FLYING*. She has her world under surveillance, not comparable, given her gender, to Big Brother but perhaps to Big Nurse of *One Flew over the Cuckoo's Nest*. Despite her presence, however, Dorothy discovers in herself the makings of a gifted teacher, capable of transforming the rote-riddled pseudocurriculum of the Ringwood school into active learning. Seeing her students coming to life before her eyes, she begins to see teaching as "more than a mere job, it was—or so it seemed to her—a mission, a life-purpose." This is notable as the first evidence of her choosing an active role, a suggestion that teaching will not only add purpose but the possibility of redefining herself. But this possibility is shattered when she is attacked by nonconformist parents for her teaching innovations, particularly for explaining the meaning of the word *womb* in *Macbeth*. Her humiliation by the parents is an effective scene, marred by the author's intrusion in an editorial voice, denouncing the lack of supervision and regulation of second-rate, third-rate, and fourth-rate public schools.

In the final chapter, the *deus*, whose death or disappearance is Dorothy's central concern in the novel, reappears as the deus ex machina, in the form, ironically enough, of the atheist Warburton, who comes to Dorothy's rescue just as she has been summarily fired and thrown out by Mrs. Creevy. His marriage proposal, which may or may not be sincere, is notable not for what he offers her but for what he is saving her from, a life of drudgery and penury, the latter a certain fate after her heedless father dies. Her refusal can be seen, in the words of one critic, as the act of "a rebel in reverse." Rejecting the meaninglessness of the modern world, ". . . she flees into a bankrupt past to escape her age" (Connelly, 67). On the other hand, the case can be made that the choice of living a life imbued with Christian values, as opposed to Christian beliefs, is completely in accord with the author's own convictions. His agnosticism notwithstanding, Orwell was a strong advocate of "religionless Christianity."

Generally regarded as Orwell's weakest novel, *A Clergyman's Daughter* has been the object of a variety of negative critical comments, none more sweeping and dismissive than those of the author himself. In a letter to his friend BRENDA SALKELD, one of the prototypes of the novel's heroine, Dorothy Hare, Orwell dismisses the book as "tripe." A year later, in a letter to the American novelist HENRY MILLER, he referred to it as a "bollox." As late as 1945, he instructed his literary executor that it not be reprinted.

Critics have lamented the novel's implausible plot and its failure to delineate with any depth or distinction the central character. As to the structure, its lame transitions from one chapter to the next reveal the hand of a fledgling novelist still learning his trade. Nevertheless, for all its failings, it is a much more interesting work than many better crafted, more modest novels. Orwell here takes on a big subject, bigger than the colonialism of *Burmese Days* and refuses to sugarcoat it, either in the direction of traditional religion or of triumphant humanism. We are alone in the universe, a fact that sucks the joy out of life. "Either life on earth is a preparation for something greater and more lasting, or it is meaningless, dark and dreadful." His capacity for "facing unpleasant facts" was never more in evidence than here.

Of the five chapters that make up the novel, the first and last, set in Knype Hill, find Dorothy performing the same actions in the same manner. Externally, it is as though nothing has happened; the only significant change has been an internal one: She has lost her belief in God and in the immortality of the soul. That is the essence of the story. What occurs in chapters 2, 3, and 4 seems to many to have little bearing on her loss of faith. She views the hardships, the social injustice, the iniquity of malicious individuals, such as the despicable

Mrs. Creevy, as merely temporary phenomena, petty disturbances compared with the void that opens up at the prospect of the meaninglessness of human existence. As she explains to Warburton on the train taking them back to Knype Hill:

> These things don't really matter. I mean, things like having no money and not having enough to eat. Even when you're practically starving—it doesn't change anything inside you. . . . It's beastly while it's happening of course, but it doesn't make any real difference; it's the things that happen inside you that really matter. . . . Things change in your mind. And then the whole world changes, because you look at it differently.

Dorothy's loss of faith is not a consequence of her experiences in the picking fields or in the fourth-rate public school in which she teaches. Nor is it a result of the semirealistic, semiphantasmagorical scene in Trafalgar Square, which can be seen as an expression rather than as a cause of that loss. Therein lies a major problem, the sense that the hop-picking, homelessness, and schoolroom scenes, all part of Orwell's recent experiences, were subjects he wanted to write about and chose to attach to Dorothy's story rather than having events naturally unfold. In the same vein is his employment of the amnesia ploy—notoriously prevalent in the history of modern soap operas, but even in Orwell's time, a hoary device. The novel's chief flaw lies in the disparity between its major theme and the failure to recognize that such a theme requires a commitment to a deep psychological or spiritual study of the main character.

As might be expected from a critic whose general thesis is that religious belief, or lack of it, plays a central role in all of Orwell's work, Christopher Small gives *A Clergyman's Daughter* a particularly close reading. He asserts that "Dorothy, we may say, is Orwell," the female protagonist permitting the author to express a softer, more tender part of himself. Small then suggests a deeper need on Orwell's part, to give expression to his own felt loss of God. Small cites as evidence Orwell's letters to his girlfriend ELEANOR JAQUES during the period he was writing the novel. He describes his friendship with an Anglican curate in Hayes, the suburb where he was working as a teacher. The curate is "High Anglican but not a creeping Jesus and a very good fellow." Orwell writes that, by way of doing research, he has been regularly participating in services at the curate's church, thereby giving Jaques the impression that he was putting on a pious act in order to get material for the book. But Bernard Crick interviewed the widow of the curate, who was "indignant at the idea that he was not a genuine believer. . . . He washed up after Church Guild meetings and often took tea or supper with them in their kitchen, helping with domestic tasks for the church, chopping firewood and filling coal-buckets," leaving Crick with the questions, ". . . which friend was he deceiving? Or was he uncertain himself?" (Crick, 142). Small contends that, as in the case of Orwell's tramping excursions, the choice of disguise reveals an "underlying feeling" of loneliness and loss. Dorothy is her author's "proxy, and much more than that, his soul" (Small, 60). In short, Dorothy's dilemma is her author's, in which he unwittingly exposed himself not as a believer, but as one profoundly wounded by his loss of belief.

Another critic interested in the religious theme is Alan Sandison, who aims to locate Orwell within the tradition of Protestant individualism derived from Martin Luther. Sandison's chief example of his thesis is *Nineteen Eighty-Four,* compared to which he considers *A Clergyman's Daughter* "a tentative and superficial exploration of 'faith and no faith,' as blatantly experimental in its credal position as it is in its conglomerate literary style" (Sandison, 127). But he goes on to make the interesting point that Orwell's best writing appears when he describes Dorothy's desire for faith, as in her reflection, "And given only faith, how can anything else matter? . . . Every act is significant, every moment sanctified, woven by faith into a pattern, a fabric of never-ending joy." In contrast, according to Sandison, his descriptions of the loss of faith are lifeless and flat. (Of course, one might argue that that is precisely what they should be.)

Putting aside the theme of the loss of faith, the other problem with Dorothy is that, unlike Orwell's male protagonists, she fails to mount a rebellion against a society that imprisons the individual's spirit. Of course, the rebellion of the other protagonists, John Flory in *Burmese Days*, Gordon Comstock in *Keep the Aspidistra Flying*, George Bowling in *Coming Up for Air* and, most notably, Winston Smith in *Nineteen Eighty-Four*, always ends in one form or another of failure: Flory, in suicide; Comstock, in recognizing that finally one has to do business with the money-god; Bowling, in discovering that you can't go home again; and Smith, in learning to love Big Brother. As failures they might be classified as antiheroes, but their failures are less significant than the vitality they exhibit in their struggle.

George Woodcock zeroes in on the social issue, designating "the central Orwellian theme of personal alienation, caused by the class system" in which the main character, seeking to liberate himself, undergoes a metamorphosis that involves the substitution of a new *persona* for an old self (Woodcock, 103). In regard to Dorothy, the key phrase in this description has to be "seeking to liberate himself" (the masculine pronoun may indicate that he has forgotten Dorothy or deliberately excluded her precisely because she does not fit the mold). For Dorothy does not seek "liberation"; it is thrust upon her, and she discovers in it only a "rootless freedom."

The cyclical structure of the novel reveals that she ends as she begins, having lost the one element that made life worthwhile. In that connection, one female critic's view of the novel and its main character strikes a resonant note:

> In fact, the dominant idea left by the novel is not of faith or loss of faith but of resilience, and it gives a powerful portrayal of this, despite its faults as fiction. The resilience shown is that of a duty-minded upper-middle-class person, like Orwell himself and, to that extent, Orwell and Dorothy are one. Dorothy, however, is a female protagonist and Orwell, whose ideas about women were conventional and unthoughtful, makes her resilience take the form of a passive acceptance that his male protagonists do not show (Gardner, 43).

Orwell borrowed from G. K. Chesterton the category of good/bad books, books like *Uncle Tom's Cabin*, that, however deficient from an aesthetic standpoint, had a positive effect on society. *A Clergyman's Daughter* might be seen as an example of a bad/good book, one whose "bad/goodness" taught its author both his limits as a novelist and his potential as a writer able and willing to go where angels fear to tread.

CHARACTERS

Beaver, Miss A schoolteacher, whom Dorothy meets at the library in Southbridge during her Christmas holidays. She is described as "a prim little woman with a round body, a thin face, a reddish nose, and the gait of a guinea-hen." The two lonely women form a fragile friendship, sharing cups of tea while working on crossword puzzles together. Twenty years of teaching have yielded Miss Beaver a bed-sitter in a rooming house, a salary of four pounds a week, and a collection of photographs from a holiday taken many years ago. Miss Beaver is a withered, forlorn embodiment of the future awaiting Dorothy.

Blifil-Gordon The proprietor of Knype Hill's sugar-beet factory. In his description of Knype Hill, Orwell writes in chapter 2 (part 1) that the town was divided between the largely agricultural south and the industrialized north side dominated by the sugar-beet factory and the "vile yellow brick cottages" that housed the factory workers. The town might be said to stand for North and South England, and Blifil-Gordon for the industrial capitalist.

Blyth The butler, "confidant and intellectual guide" to Sir Thomas Hare, the muddleheaded cousin of Dorothy's father. Receiving the rector's request to locate and find a job for Dorothy, Sir Thomas turns the task over to Blyth, who brings Dorothy from the courthouse—she had been arrested for begging—back to Sir Thomas's house. Blyth, whose voice "never rose above a whisper," bears a slight relationship to one of Orwell's favorite characters, P. G. Wodehouse's Jeeves.

Creevy, Mrs. Headmistress of the Ringwood House Academy for Girls, where in chapter 4,

Dorothy undergoes a surge of happiness as a successful and innovative teacher, which later turns into humiliation and defeat. Mrs. Creevy is an extraordinarily malignant figure. One would have to look to Mr. and Mrs. Wackford Squeers, the proprietors of Dotheboys Hall in Dickens's *Nicholas Nickleby*, to find her equal. Cruel, ignorant, and miserly, she operates on one educational principle: "After all, the fees are what matter." And she applies this principle in her treatment of the students. The ones whose parents are good payers are never to be smacked; the children of the medium payers can be smacked occasionally, but not so as to leave a mark: the bad payers' children, however, can be smacked at will. When Dorothy's educational innovations get her in trouble with some of the parents, Mrs. Creevy humiliates her in front of them and forces her to return to the school's boring, rote-learning curriculum. Finally, Mrs. Creevy dismisses Dorothy at the end of the term, giving her no notice and no references, and being careful at the same time to cheat her out of her full pay.

Deafie An old man who becomes Dorothy's hop-picking partner after the arrest of Nobby. He makes a brief appearance in the Trafalgar Square scene, singing a line of an obscene ditty.

Ellen The maid of all work in the household of Charles Hare. Dorothy chooses the name Ellen when she loses her memory.

Hare, Dorothy The protagonist of the novel, Dorothy is the overworked, religiously scrupulous daughter of a Church of England rector. Driven to distraction by her many responsibilities and the unwanted sexual advances of a charming but predatory friend, she loses her memory, whereupon she joins a group of young people off to pick hops in Kent. Later she finds herself among a group of huddled homeless people in Trafalgar Square. Rescued by a distant relative, she lands a teaching position at a dreadful private school, presided over by a vicious headmistress, Mrs. Creevy. Returning home, Dorothy confronts the fact that she has lost her faith and with it any sense of meaning in life. Nevertheless, she resolves to continue to observe the duties and rituals of a clergyman's daughter in the interest of being useful to others. In compiling his portrait of Dorothy, Orwell drew upon his private life. BRENDA SALKELD, a platonic girlfriend and the daughter of a clergyman, who resisted Orwell's amorous advances, formed the basis of his portrait of Dorothy.

Hare, Charles Dorothy's father, a man born 200 years too late, "disgusted and infuriated by the modern world." Not even his daughter's disappearance and apparent disgrace can shatter the shell of self-absorption in which he is encased. When he receives Dorothy's letters from the hop-picking fields, begging for help, he delays sending her money. Instead, he writes his cousin Sir Thomas Hare, who through his mysterious but efficient butler, Blyth, locates her and brings her back to Sir Thomas's house. Charles finally shows some long-repressed feeling, sending Dorothy £2 while still refusing to consider that she is telling the truth. When her name is cleared and she returns home, he reverts immediately to his old ways: ". . . when you've taken your bag upstairs, just bring your typewriter down here, would you? I want you to type my sermon."

Hare, Sir Thomas A wealthy cousin of Dorothy's father, he is "a good-natured, chuckle-headed man," whose distinguing feature is "an abysmal mental vagueness." Already embarrassed by the family association with the "rector's daughter" of tabloid fame, he instructs his butler, Blyth, to find Dorothy and bring her to his home lest she get into more trouble and create more scandal. When he meets Dorothy, he is surprised to see that she is not the vamp he anticipated but a well-spoken "spinsterish" girl. Through his solicitor, he finds a job for Dorothy as a teacher in a private school for girls.

Mayfill, Miss The ancient resident of a crumbling mansion located near St. Athelstan's church. She and Dorothy are frequently the only two communicants on weekday services, which results in a particular problem for her. Miss Mayfill's decayed condition is particularly evident in the area of her mouth, so that she tends to slobber when she takes Communion. Having had the un-Christian thought that she wants to drink from the chalice before Miss Mayfield does the overly scrupulous Dorothy immediately feels guilty and thus makes a point of drinking after the old woman.

McElligot, Mrs. An older Irish hop picker who advises Dorothy and her companions where they might find work (chapter 2). Later she joins a discussion among the pickers of the "rector's daughter" scandal, explaining, "She was carrying on wid a man 20 years older'n herself . . ." She reappears in the Trafalgar Square segment in chapter 3. She and Dorothy walk around the city trying to keep warm. When they come back to the square, they try to form a pyramid of bodies in an effort to fight off the midnight cold. At 5 a.m. in Wilkins Café, she explains how the three of them can share a cup of tea, and then put their heads on the table and sleep for two hours. Later, she and Dorothy are arrested for begging. In court the next day, Dorothy is released after 12 hours, but Mrs. McElligot, a repeat offender, is sentenced to seven days.

Nobby Dorothy's irrepressible companion during her hop-picking experiences (chapter 2). Nobby, whose favorite expresson is "mulligatawny," sports "a mat of orange hair cropped short and growing low on his head." At one point, he makes a sexual pass at Dorothy but holds no grudge when rebuffed. "He had that temperament that is incapable of taking its own reverses very seriously." He refuses to become dispirited, even when his companions Flo and Charlie abscond with his and Dorothy's belongings. Once they find work, Nobby spends his spare time stealing fruit and an occasional chicken. He gives Dorothy a copy of a scandal sheet containing her story. A week later, he is arrested for theft and carried off to jail, grinning and winking as he goes. As soon as he leaves, she recovers the unread newspaper and reads the story containing her picture. Nobby's last gift to her is her memory.

Nobby appears to be an adaptation of the real-life figure of Ginger in Orwell's essay "Hop Picking." As Ginger, he reappears in the Trafalgar Square scene.

Proggett Sexton at St. Athelstan's church, who would "poke around the church . . . Gloomily noting a cracked stone here, a worm-eaten beam there and afterwards . . . coming to harass Dorothy with demands for repairs." Proggett's most pressing concern are the loose bells lying on the belfry floor and liable to crash down into the church at any moment.

Semprill, Evalina Scandalmonger whose distorted and aberrant sexual imagination has adversely affected many of the residents of Knype Hill. Spying on Warburton and Dorothy, she spreads the rumor that the two have run away to Paris. Her version of events makes its way into the tabloid newspaper accounts of the "rector's daughter." She is finally exposed and forced to leave town when she is sued for libel by a local banker.

Stone, Victor The schoolmaster at St. Athelstan's, Victor is a young man in his twenties, "a restless, intelligent, little creature . . ." with a gift for dealing with children, but his real interest is church ritual. He not only urges Dorothy to talk her father into having more processions, but he is a regular letter writer to the *Church Times*, engaging in obsessive and obscure, controversial exchanges. When Dorothy returns after eight months away, she finds little change. There was to be a school pageant for which she must make the costumes, and Victor had had a controversy in the *Church Times*, which he won decisively.

Tallboys, Mr. A denizen of Trafalgar Square, a former Anglican clergyman who performs a black mass, real or imagined, in the course of Dorothy's evening at the Square.

Turle Family A family of East End Londoners, who befriend Dorothy and Nobby when they first arrive at the hop-picking farm. Later on the last day of the season, Dorothy returns with them to London, spending the night at their flat.

Warburton, Mr. Dorothy's atheistic, hedonistic friend, prone to challenging her religious beliefs while trying to seduce her. He invites her to his house, ostensibly to meet his friends but when she arrives he is alone. When his effort to overwhelm her fails, he follows her outside, thus providing ammunition for his neighbor, the town scandalmonger, Mrs. Semprill. The next day he leaves to travel abroad, the same day that Dorothy disappears. Mrs. Semprill reports to the town and the tabloid press that the two have eloped together. When Warburton returns from Europe some months later, he tries to restore Dorothy's reputation and to write to her when the scandalmonger is driven out of town on another charge of libel. He brings Dorothy back from the hellish school just as she has been dismissed. On the train back to Knype Hill, he proposes to Dorothy and is rejected to his surprise since he is unaware of her sexual frigidity. He takes the rejection in stride. The suggestion that at least some features of his personality derived from Orwell himself is supported by one of the aliases Orwell used when he would go tramping, Edward Burton. Another similarity lies in his attempts to seduce women by overpowering them. See JACINTHA BUDDICOM.

WORKS CITED

Connelly, Mark. *The Diminished Self: Orwell and the Loss of Freedom* Pittsburgh: Duquesne University Press, 1987.

Crick, Bernard. *George Orwell.* Boston: Little, Brown, 1980.

Fowler, Roger. *The Language of George Orwell.* New York: St. Martin's, 1995.

Gardner, Averil. *George Orwell.* Boston: Twayne, 1987.

Patai, Daphne. *The Orwell Myth.* Amherst: University of Massachusetts Press, 1984.

Sandison, Alan. *George Orwell: After 1984.* Dover, N.H.: Longwood Academic, 1986.

Small, Christopher. *The Road to Miniluv: George Orwell, the State and God.* Pittsburgh: Pittsburgh University Press, 1975.

Woodcock, George. *The Crystal Spirit.* London: Jonathan Cape, 1967.

Coming Up for Air (1939)

Orwell's fourth novel, featuring his most engaging protagonist, a 45-year-old, overweight insurance salesman, with a passion for his boyhood and an Orwellian ability to pinpoint the shallowness of modern life. The novel is structured in four parts. Part 1 is set in 1938, in which George narrates his present everyday life, his suburban house, two-child family, penny-pinching wife, and his job as an insurance salesman. Part 2 takes the reader back to the village of Lower Binfield, where George recounts the significant scenes of his childhood from the late 1890s to his joining the army in 1914, his postwar job hunt, and his marriage to the woebegone Hilda ("Right from the start, it was a bust"). Part 3 returns to the present and George's decision to return to Lower Binfield for a secret holiday, the dream-shattering reality he encounters there. Part 4 depicts his painful return to his suburban prison.

BIOGRAPHICAL/HISTORICAL CONTEXT

After their escape from Spain and return to England in 1938 (see *HOMAGE TO CATALONIA*), Orwell and his wife Eileen settled back in the village of Wallington.

But shortly after, Orwell became seriously ill, hemorrhaging blood from his lungs. In March, he was admitted to Preston Hall, a sanitorium in Aylesford, Kent, where doctors diagnosed a tubercular lesion on his left lung. While recuperating, he had the opportunity to rediscover one of the joys of his childhood, fishing. For health reasons, he and Eileen decided to spend the fall and winter months in Marrakech, which was part of French Morocco at the time. The Orwells arrived on September 28, 1938, the day before the signing of the Munich Pact, in which British Prime Minister Neville Chamberlain and French Prime Minister Edouard Daladier caved to Hitler's demands and ceded the Sudetenland in northwest Czechoslovakia to Germany. Although the Orwells disapproved of Chamberlain's diplomacy in general, they appeared to accept the Munich Pact as at least a temporary reprieve. One of the reasons for their position was the outcome of the Spanish Civil War, which was coming to a conclusion with the triumph of General Franco's forces and a victory for fascism. Fearing that a war with Germany would produce a similar result, Orwell adopted a pacifist position. But if *Coming Up for Air,* which he began writing at precisely this time, is any indication, he recognized and was haunted by the inevitability of a war that he thought would be fought on English soil. Narrator George Bowling offers a chilling forecast of this impending war:

> I can hear the air-raid sirens blowing and the loudspeakers bellowing that our glorious troops have taken a hundred thousand prisoners. I see a top-floor-back in Birmingham and a child of five howling and howling for a bit of bread. And suddenly the mother can't stand it any longer, and she yells at it, "Shut your trap, you little bastard!" and then she ups the child's frock and smacks its bottom hard, because there isn't any bread and isn't going to be any bread. I see it all. I see the posters and the food-queues, and the castor oil and the rubber truncheons and the machine guns squirting out of bedroom windows.

By January 1939, Orwell had completed his first draft. He typed the final draft aboard the ship that returned the couple to England in late March of that year. Upon arrival, he turned in the finished manuscript to his publisher, Victor Gollancz. Five months later, on August 23, the Hitler-Stalin Pact put an end to Orwell's pacifist phase. A week later, Hitler invaded Poland, forcing France and England to declare war on Germany. The apocalyptic visions anticipated in the novel were about to be tested by reality.

SYNOPSIS

Part 1, Chapter 1

The novel's first-person narrator, speaking from his bathroom as he prepares his morning bath, announces that "the idea" first came to him the day he got his new false teeth. But he digresses in order to introduce himself. His name is George Bowling. He is a 45-year-old, overweight (his nickname is Fatty) insurance salesman. He describes himself as a typical jolly, plump, outgoing type that is usually "the life of the party." Lately, however, he's been feeling morose, the result of having to wear a set of temporary false teeth while waiting for his permanent set to be ready. Today is that day, and he is taking off from work to pick up his new teeth at his dentist's office in London. Another prospect for the day involves a secret he has kept from his wife, Hilda, and their two children: He has won 17 pounds betting on a horse from a tip given to him by a fellow worker and is wondering how best to spend it.

At this point, his bath is interrupted by his son, seven-year-old Billy, desperate to use the toilet. He is forced to hurry and does an inadequate job of drying himself, leaving a soapy patch on his neck. At breakfast, the children squabble, Hilda worries about school bills, and George teases Hilda for buying the cheapest marmalade. He then leaves the house to take the train to London.

Part 1, Chapter 2

George walks to the train station of West Bletchley, a typical suburban development outside of London, consisting of "long rows of little semi-detached houses," each one identical to the others. To Bowling's eye, the houses resemble the cells in a vast prison, part of a "huge racket" called the Hesperides Estate operated by the Cheerful Credit Building Society. Before boarding his train, he stops in a shop and witnesses a shopgirl being reprimanded by the manager. Bowling realizes the girl looks at him with hate because he was a witness to her humiliation.

Part 1, Chapter 3

On the train, Bowling is addressed by another passenger as "Tubby," as though a fat man doesn't have any feelings. In fact, he concedes, there's something about being fat that precludes deep feelings, at least that's the image that emerges in popular novels and films. But inside every fat man is a thin man struggling for expression.

Meanwhile, a plane that has been glimpsed overhead reappears; it reawakens thoughts of impending war, which are never very far from George's thoughts these days. When war comes, it will probably be a surprise attack: "If I was Hitler, I'd send my bombers across in the middle of a disarmament conference."

Part 1, Chapter 4

After tasting and rejecting a revolting lunch at a so-called milk bar, George passes a newsboy shouting the headline story of the day: a woman's leg found in a parcel in the waiting room of a railway station, which only adds to his disgust with modern life. He feels somewhat better after getting his new teeth from the dentist and enjoying a couple of pints in a nearby pub. But walking up the Strand, puffing a fresh cigar, he thinks about the throng of people around him. He imagines how they'll look in a few years once the war has begun, everyone thin from the shortage of food, the air-raid sirens sounding, and the loudspeakers spewing propaganda about the victories of our glorious troops. Then he spots a headline poster referring to King Zog and triggering a memory of his parish church in Lower Binfield 38 years earlier. Now he is seven years old at a Sunday-morning service with his mother. The two men who lead the psalm singing are Shooter, the local fishmonger, and Wetheral, the undertaker, the two representing Sihon, king of the Amorites, and Og, the king of Bashan. Particularly vivid is the recollection of Wetheral's powerful bass voice as Og, which seems to summarize something called church, an essential element in the texture and meaning of life in Lower Binfield. A moment later, he is back in the real world of 1938, with its "posters and petrol stink and the roar of engines." But he realizes that Lower Binfield in 1900 is his real world.

Part 2, Chapter 1

"Before the war!" George's reminiscences use this phrase to establish that the time he is evoking takes place before 1914, the beginning of World War I, the event that changed the social and cultural core of English life. But Bowling, born in 1893, takes it back a bit further to the Boer War in South Africa (1899–1902), when English imperialism overstepped its limits and took the first steps leading to the dissolution of the British Empire. He recalls his hometown of Lower Binfield, nestled in a valley bordered by the Thames River on one side and a hillside on the other. His father's shop, a feed and grain store, was located on the main street. In his recollections it is always summer, on a lazy afternoon or at dinnertime. He walks through town and countryside with his brother Joe, older than he by two years, the two of them "minded" by Katie Simmons, a poor 12-year-old from a large family who is paid a small wage to take the two boys for their walks. Like the rest of her family, Katie never went to school. She became pregnant when she was 15 and eventually married a gypsy. Years later, Bowling passes a gypsy caravan, and he sees her, looking twice her age, "a wrinkled up hag of a woman . . . shaking out a rag mat."

Part 2, Chapter 2

Market Day in Lower Binfield was Thursday, when the local farmers arrived in town. In the evening, everyone would converge on the local pub, including the recruiting sergeant who would stand the young farm lads to drinks and lend them money to keep drinking. The next morning, the young farmer is marched off to the army, having signed the necessary paperwork in exchange for a shilling. The recruiting story reminds Bowling of the arguments between his father and his uncle Ezekiel over the Boer War. Ezekiel was a liberal, an outspoken critic of the conservative government. Father was quiet, soft-spoken, no match for Ezekiel in an argument. Bowling's mother's domain was the kitchen, in which she thrived with the help of advice from *Hilda's Home Companion,* a weekly women's magazine she read faithfully. Another of Bowling's memories is the sound of bluebottle flies buzzing on summer afternoons. They were pests but preferable to today's sound of bombing planes.

Part 2, Chapter 3

The local grammar school was four miles away, so he and his brother spent the years from ages six to eight at a preschool, run by an incompetent old woman who was incapable of controlling the children. Boys, in particular, played truant regularly. His brother Joe became a member of a gang, called the Black Hand, who engaged in all kinds of mischief. On one occasion, Joe and his friends take off from school in order to go fishing. When George begs to go with them, they refuse. He follows them anyway and, after some rough handling of him, they relent and allow him to fish nearby. This is his first time fishing. As it turns out, he is the only one to catch a fish that day, and the joy and excitement of that catch is burned into George's memory. Unfortunately, the catch is interrupted by Brewer, the grouchy old farmer who owns the land. He chases the boys away, landing a couple of good whacks from his stick on George's legs. Despite this disappointment, the day has been a triumph for young George: his first catch, and his introduction to the joy of fishing. Added to that was George's sense that he has undergone a transition. His experience as one of the gang marked his growth from being a kid to being a boy.

Part 2, Chapter 4

Bowling covers his grammar school years, 1901 to 1909, from the time he was eight to 15 years old. He was good at math and science, and there was some talk that he might win a scholarship, but for boys of his class—the sons of shopkeepers—school was not nearly as important as it was for upper-middle-class children. What really stands out in his mind about those years is fishing. Most of these memories focus on the pool at Binfield House, the old estate that overlooked Lower Binfield, deserted 20 years earlier by its owners. Old Hodge, the caretaker of the estate, reciprocating a favor done by George's father, permits him to fish the pond, provided he brings no other boys with him. On one occasion, George explores the outer extension of the pond, covered by bushes. Penetrating the bushes, he discovers another smaller but deeper pool that has been long forgotten. Here, the fish are enormous: "I stood there without breathing, and in a moment another huge thick shape glided through the water, and then another and then two more close together. The pool was full of them." George is overwhelmed by this secret find. Catching any one of these giants would require stronger tackle than he could possibly afford to buy. He resolves to steal the money if necessary, in order to get the equipment needed to catch these giants but in fact never returns to fish the hidden pond. "Almost immediately after, something turned up to prevent me, but if it hadn't been that, it would have been something else. It's the way things happen."

Part 2, Chapter 5

Continuing his thoughts on fishing, George confesses that despite the fact that "nothing I've ever done has given me quite such a kick as fishing . . . after I was sixteen, I never fished again." His reason behind it is that, in our contemporary English culture, "We don't do the things we want to do." The only time he came close to fishing again occurred while he was serving in France during World War I. His outfit has been pulled back from the trenches for a brief rest before returning to the front. Exploring the French countryside, he and a fellow soldier discover a pond filled with fish. They spend the rest of the day desperately trying to piece together some suitable tackle and bait, and plan to sneak away for a day's fishing, but the next morning at roll call, the outfit is ordered to ship out immediately to another part of the front line. After the war, "like everybody else I was fighting for a job, and then I'd got a job and the job had got me." Once on vacation with his penny-pinching wife and two children, he mentioned that he would like to spend some time fishing, but, when his wife discovered the initial cost of the equipment, the idea became out of the question. The clincher to her argument was that for "a great big grown-up man" to want to go fishing is to be acting like a baby. His two children take up the charge, chanting that their dad is a baby.

Part 2, Chapters 6

Bowling recalls that besides fishing, he was also an avid reader, first of the boys' penny weeklies and later of books such as *Sherlock Homes, Dracula* and *Raffles.* "I read the stuff I wanted to read, and I got more out of them than the stuff they taught me at school." Although his parents would have preferred that he read "good books," they were impressed by his love of reading, a striking contrast to Joe, who hated books. George says that he is still an avid reader, a member of the LEFT BOOK CLUB and up-to-date on the current best-sellers, But no reading experience matches that of those early years when a boy has his first encounters with the adventure stories in the boys' weekly magazines. Remembering how he lay on sacks of grain his father stored in a loft in the yard, living vicariously the life of

Donovan the Dauntless or some other hero, George recalls that time as "bliss, pure bliss."

Part 2, Chapter 7

Three days after George saw the giant fish in Binfield Hall, his father announced that his business was suffering badly from the competition of a big retail chain store, Sarazins. As a result, George would have to leave school to take a job as an assistant at the local grocery store. He worked at the store for five years. In the meantime, his father's business and health deteriorated. One of the contributing factors to the family's woes was George's brother, Joe, who had become a local thug. One night, Joe broke into his father's till, took out eight pounds, presumably booking passage for America. His behavior was a severe blow to the parents' morale.

In 1913, George began "walking out" with Elsie Waters, a clerk in the local draper's shop, and a warm and passionate young woman. The relationship blossoms into a full sexual affair when George brings her with him on a Sunday afternoon to the pool at Binfield House. After some preliminary kissing, George hesitates, suddenly remembering the hidden pool with the giant fish. He wavers, torn between teenage lust and his desire to see the pond, and the desire for his first sexual experience wins out.

1913 gives way to the summer of 1914, the end of an epoch. The small tradesmen of Lower Binfield and every other town in England are feeling but not comprehending the winds of change. These changes were not like any other, for they signaled the loss of something truly precious, the sense of continuity. "It's easy to die if the things you care about are going to survive." Although the generation of George's parents did not recognize it at the time, most of them having died without having to cope with it, traditional England begins to disappear in August 1914, when England declares war on Germany. Two months later, George joins the army; five months after that, he is in the trenches in France.

Part 2, Chapter 8

George is injured by an enemy shell and evacuated to a hospital on the south coast of England. After recuperating during the winter of 1917, he is sent to an officer training camp; the casualty rate among junior officers in the British army is extraordinarily high, and "anyone who wasn't actually illiterate could have a commission if he wanted one." In the rigid class structure of pre–World War I Britain, the movement into the officer class of a shopkeeper's son would have been a monumental one, but in the social upheaval created by the war, "nothing seemed strange in those days." While at officer training camp, Bowling receives a wire saying that his mother is dying (his father had died a year earlier). By the time he secures a home leave and arrives in Lower Binfield, his mother has died. He confesses that he felt grief over the deaths of his mother and father, but what primarily occupied his thoughts was how dashing he looked in his officer's uniform. Finishing up at officer training, he expects to be returned to the trenches, where he would doubtlessly end up, like so many second lieutenants, as cannon fodder. Instead, by a bureaucratic quirk so common in war, he is assigned as a secretary to Sir Joseph Cheam, in charge of rations and food storage. From there, he is assigned to check over the supplies at Twelve Mile Dump, on the west coast of Britain. When he arrives, he discovers only "eleven tins of bully beef." When he reports back his finding, he is told to remain there, as the officer in command at the dump. He lolls in this isolated outpost for the duration of the war, spending most of his time reading and thinking. The result for him and millions of others is the recognition that the war is "an unspeakable idiotic mess" producing nothing but "a wave of disbelief" in authority.

Part 2, Chapter 9

The experience of having been an officer creates a major problem for George and many others in the postwar world. Having achieved the social distinction that a commission carries in the wider world, they find it impossible to return to their old status. In Bowling's case, such a return would mean opening a grocery shop of his own, but for a former officer, becoming a shopkeeper, like his own father, would be a large step down socially and economically. Thus, in postwar Britain, the job market is flooded with returning veterans who feel cheated, disoriented, and often desperate. Bowling has the advantage of knowing what job he wants and would be good at—traveling salesman. He begins by taking a job that pays commission only, no salary, and even there he does reasonably well. Then, one day, he encounters his old commander, Sir Joseph Cheam, who recommends him for a job with the Flying Salamander Insurance Company, at which George is still working 17 years later, earning seven quid ($35) a week.

Part 2, Chapter 10

George recounts the story of his marriage to Hilda Vincent, whose father is a member of the Retired Anglo-Indian Officials class. This is a group who, as members of the Raj in India, acquired aristocratic poses and attitudes, but were retired and returned to England on minimal pensions, and thus mired in genteel poverty. George confesses that he was "vaguely impressed" by Hilda's family lineage, which had included "majors, colonels, and once even an admiral." But the present representatives of the Vincent family are a lifeless, feckless bunch. The marriage is, "right from the start . . . a flop." The problem, according to George, is that Hilda takes no joy in life. George admits that he has been unfaithful, but Hilda makes him pay for his pleasure when she discovers his transgressions, as she usually does. What keeps Hilda going is her friendship with her neighbors Mrs. Wheeler and Miss Minns. Hilda and Mrs. Wheeler shop for bargains and sales. One of Mrs. Wheeler's finds is the Left Book Club, which offers savings of one-third on the regular price of certain books.

Part 3, Chapter 1

One evening, Hilda is attending a lecture sponsored by the Left Book Club with Mrs. Wheeler and Miss Minns, and George decides to go along, although he chooses to sit in the back by himself. The speaker's topic is "The Menace of Fascism," and the speech is a litany of fascism's many evils. George, making an effort to put himself inside the speaker's head, recognizes the man is impelled by one motive: hatred. The speaker's vision—what he sees as he talks is "a picture of himself smashing people's faces in with a spanner . . . [wrench] and it's all O.K. because the smashed faces belong to fascists." After the speech, four young men (three regular communists and one Trotskyite) are continuing an argument. One of them asks George if he would be willing to fight in the event of war. His response: "In 1914 we thought it was going to be a glorious business. Well, it wasn't. It was just a bloody mess. You keep out of it."

He decides to pay a visit to an old friend, a retired public's schoolmaster, Porteous, who has rooms nearby. Porteous is a classical scholar and exudes "the classy Oxford feeling of nothing mattering except books and poetry and Greek statues, and nothing is worth mentioning since the Goths sacked Rome." For George, a visit to Porteous is usually a cherished retreat from the sordid reality of everyday life. But when George brings up the specter of Hitler, Porteous dismisses him as "ephemeral," assuring George that Hitler and Stalin will "pass away," but "the eternal verities" will not pass away. When Porteous reads a poem, the same poem in the same manner that he read the first time George had visited him, George realizes that Porteous is dead, incapable of change. All the people who think that England will never have to change and will always be what it is now are in for a powerful shock. The thought that occurs to him just before falling asleep is "why the hell a chap like me should care."

Part 3, Chapter 2

While driving in the countryside on the way to a business appointment, George stops to admire a patch of primroses. He notices among other beautiful sights of nature, the red embers of a recent camp fire. Looking at the embers and the flowers George realizes that at this moment he is *happy*, certain that "life is worth living." What brings about this sensation is the dying embers, more alive in their death throes that any living thing. Why, he wonders, don't we all take the time to really look at nature, to step off the treadmill? Instead, we are in this insane pursuit that will soon end in war. But even war and its horrors won't be a match for what may follow, living in a fascist or Stalinist state, where the sense of inner peace and happiness he is feeling today will vanish ". . . if the rubber truncheon boys get hold of us." He proceeds to pick some primroses but immediately throws them away when another car appears on the road. The car is filled with young people who would probably sneer if they saw the flowers. As they pass, he pretends to be closing his fly, so as to appear that he has stopped to urinate. Can't have people thinking they were seeing a fat man in a bowler hat, picking primroses. At that moment the idea occurs to him of going back to Lower Binfield.

Back in his car, he calculates that he can arrange to take a week off and, with the £12 remaining from his bet, enjoy a quiet, peaceful week in his hometown. Among other things, he will get in some fishing time, perhaps in the hidden pond he'd discovered at Binfield House. It as an opportunity to restore his nerves before the hard times began, war or another depression, desperate rushing to and fro, "everlasting din of buses, bombs, radios, telephones bells." Of course, Hilda would eventually find out that his story that he was in Birmingham on business was a lie, but he could live with the consequences. Meanwhile, he already had a great feeling, particularly about the hidden pond near Binfield House. It might be still there, undiscovered, with those huge fish, now even bigger.

> You know the feeling I had. Coming up for air! Like the big sea-turtles when they come paddling up to the surface, stick their noses out and fill their lungs with a great gulp before they sink down again among the seaweed and the octopuses. We're all stifling at the bottom of a dustbin, but I'd found the way to the top.

Part 3, Chapter 3

It is Friday, June 17, and George is on his getaway, the first day of his surreptitious vacation. He has told all the appropriate lies: explained to Hilda that he will be staying in Rowbottom's Hotel in Birmingham, got a fellow salesman, who will be traveling to Birmingham to post a letter George has written to Hilda, addressed from Rowbottom's. His tracks pretty well covered, he enjoys the roadside scenery but still has the nagging feeling that he is being pursued by Hilda and the children, Mrs. Wheeler and Miss Minns, the top executives of the Flying Salamander Company, his fellow employees, his neighbors in suburbia, the home secretary, Scotland Yard, Hitler and Stalin on a tandem bicycle, Mussolini, and the pope—they are all shouting:

> There's a chap who thinks he's going to escape! There's a chap who says he won't be streamlined! He's going back to Lower Binfield! After him! Stop him!

But nothing can stop him now. This was the idea that first entered his mind on the morning he stood before his mirror thinking of his new false teeth.

Part 4, Chapter 1

As he approaches Lower Binfield, he climbs a hill. At the top, the town, nestled in a valley, will come into sight. Already he sees a number of houses where there were once only woods. When he reaches the top, his reaction is, "Where is it?" The Lower Binfield he knew has been swallowed up by brand-new houses, which stretch out in every direction. At one end stand two very large factories and a few others, where in the past the only large commercial building had been a brewery. On the way down, he notices a very large new cemetery, the country churchyard having apparently become too crowded. Before the war, the population of the town had been 2,000; now, George estimates, it must be at least 25,000. Old Lower Binfield has all but disappeared, swallowed up by the invading army of newness. Only when he locates the High Street does he begin to recognize the homes and shops, but when he reaches the old marketplace, he is shocked to see that the horse trough is gone. He registers at the George, the local hotel and pub, and is offended that the clerk shows no sign of recognition when he gives his name.

Part 4, Chapter 2

After lunch, George strolls over to visit his father's shop, to find that it is now Wendy's Tea-Shop, done up in a fake antique style. He sits at a table where his father's armchair used to be. George tries to engage the hostess in conversation, but she ignores him. From there, he visits the churchyard cemetery, locating his father's and mother's graves. He has no reaction, because his memories of them are of their being alive rather than dead. He then enters the church and, for the first time since his return, sees that nothing has changed, except that there are no people. As he examines his family's pew, he is approached by the vicar, Old Betterton, who has been vicar since 1904. He gives George a tour of the church, not recognizing who he is. George explains why he doesn't reveal his identity to the vicar: To George, as a youth, Betterton had appeared to be an old man. When George knew him, the vicar was about 45, the age George is now. The thought that George looks as old to the young people as the vicar looked to him in his youth frightens him.

Back at the hotel, he tries to pick up a woman, and she cuts him dead. In the pub, he discovers that even the beer does not taste the same, the local brewery having been taken over by a national company. He also hears that a local stocking factory is now making bombs and that a large military airport has been built nearby, which accounts for the numerous planes overhead. It upsets George to realize that the war he came to temporarily escape has followed him to Lower Binfield. When George inquires about Binfield House, he is told that it is now a sanatorium for mental patients.

Part 4, Chapter 3

George wakes the next morning with a hangover. Exploring the town the next day, he sees a crowd of children rehearsing for an air raid. They are led by a Miss Todgers, who looks to be in her element, playing soldier. The children are carrying a large banner printed with the warning BRITONS PREPARE in large letters. In the rear of the parade are children carrying another banner, proclaiming WE ARE READY, ARE YOU? From his point of view, it's an example of the government campaign to get the people to accept the inevitability of war. Later, he buys a rod and tackle with the intention of going fishing. The next day, Sunday, he heads for Burford Weir, the regular fishing spot on the Thames. He is appalled that the secluded spot has become a local resort area, crowds of people, ice cream vendors, tea shops, and so many people fishing that no one is catching anything. The water itself is now brown and dirty, filled with cigarette ends and paper bags. George leaves in disgust, but before he goes he weighs himself on a penny weighing machine and discovers that he has put on four pounds in the last three days.

Part 4, Chapter 4

Later that day, George follows a woman through town because, although he does not recognize her, there is something familiar about her. When she turns, he has a better view of her face and soon realizes she is his old lover, Elsie Waters. He continues to follow Elsie, a "round-shouldered hag, shambling along on twisted heels."

When she turns into a "mangy" tobacconist's shop, he follows her, pretending he wants to buy a pipe. When he gets a close look at her, he realizes her face has collapsed into the face of a bulldog. He has a moment of guilt, realizing that he treated her badly years ago in failing to write to her while he was serving in the army. On the other hand, he rationalizes that he probably meant nothing special to her. Later, he goes to a pub, playing darts and drinking too much.

Part 4, Chapter 5

Awakening with yet another hangover on Monday, George realizes that for the past three days, he has been drinking too much. He recognizes that he hasn't found the thing he came back home to look for, but he is determined to keep looking. He resolves to visit that secret pond near Binfield House. It might still be there intact, which would make the whole trip worthwhile. He drives his car to a certain point near the house and then continues on foot, passing certain landmarks that reassure him that things have not changed. But as he approaches the pond, he sees a sign indicating that it has become the Upper Binfield Model Yacht Club, where young boys are sailing model boats. Overlooking the pond, where there used to be dense woods, he discovers a large group of houses, "one of those sham-Tudor colonies." He strikes up a conversation with an elderly resident who proceeds to boast about the pro-nature design of the colony and of the superiority of its residents ("three-quarters of us up there are vegetarians"). George asks about another pond that used to be there. The resident looks a little squeamish and reports that the pond was drained in order to serve as a rubbish dump. George walks over to examine the once-mysterious pool. The water had been drained off, leaving a round hole some 20 or 30 feet, and "already it was half full of tin cans." That does it for George: "I'm finished with this notion of going back to the past. . . . Coming up for air! But there isn't any air. The dustbin that we're in reaches up to the stratosphere."

Thoroughly disillusioned, George returns to his hotel in time to hear the last words of an S.O.S. on the radio "where his wife, Hilda Bowling is seriously ill." He concludes that Hilda has learned that he is not in Birmingham and that this "emergency" is a ruse to send him hurrying back home. Doubtless it was Mrs. Wheeler who had put Hilda up to it.

Part 4, Chapter 6

The next morning, after breakfast, George strolls out to the marketplace. Glancing at the sky, he sees a squadron of military planes looming overhead. A few seconds later, he hears a sound that he immediately recognizes as the whistle of a falling bomb. With the instincts he had developed in military combat 20 years earlier, he throws himself to the ground. He lies there waiting for the next explosion, convinced the town is under a surprise attack by the German Air Force. He looks up at what seems to be a herd of pigs running down the High Street, and only after a moment or two recognizes that it is the local schoolchildren in their gas masks. He soon learns that the bomb was dropped accidentally by one of the British planes flying overhead. The bomb had fallen and wiped out a greengrocers on the street where Uncle Ezekiel's shop had been. One building had an entire wall removed and looks like a dollhouse on the upper floor; the ground floor, however, is just a pile of debris, from which a leg, with the trouser still on, protrudes. George returns to his hotel to check out. To George, the bombing was a fitting end to a thoroughly disappointing trip, but George feels he has gained something: the "power of prophecy." He sees not only the terror and chaos of the approaching war but also of something even worse later:

> The bad times are coming, and the stream-lined men are coming too. What's coming afterwards I don't know, it hardly even interests me. I only know that if there's anything you care a curse about, better say good-bye to it now, because everything you've ever known is going down, down, into the muck, with the machine-guns rattling all the time.

Part 4, Chapter 7

Just as he arrives back in West Bletchley, his pessimistic sense of doom is dissolved in pragmatic reality, as his "ordinary habits of thought" return. He begins to think that Hilda really may be seriously ill. To his surprise, he finds that he really cares. Rushing home, he dashes into his house to find his two children in their pajamas, asking to see their presents, which he is supposed to be bringing back. He then turns to see the dreaded Hilda coming in the front door. He tries to take the role of the injured party by accusing her of playing a trick designed to bring him home early. It soon becomes clear that she was not the Hilda Bowling to which the S.O.S. referred. Hilda then has her turn, as she hands him a letter from a firm responding to her own letter, asserting that Rowbottom's Hotel had closed two years earlier. Why had she written to the hotel in the first place? It was a suggestion of Mrs. Wheeler. George realizes that he has only three choices. He can tell her the truth and try to convince her to believe him, tell her he had a spot of amnesia, or let her continue to think he was with another woman and suffer the consequences. "But damn it! I knew which one it would have to be."

COMMENTARY

Coming Up for Air is the only Orwell novel to employ a first-person narrator. From his point of view, the experiment was a failure, since the form caused him to impose his own point of view too often on the narrator. But many readers would disagree, feeling that George Bowling's voice is a distinctive and accurate reflection of his trade and his class (son of a small-town shopkeeper, who served as an officer but not, of course, a gentleman in World War I). Despite Bowling's distinctiveness, however, he shares with the protagonists of Orwell's three earlier novels, John Flory in *Burmese Days,* Dorothy Hare in *A Clergyman's Daughter,* and Gordon Comstock in *Keep the Aspidistra Flying,* the same condition. George Bowling is a man profoundly alienated from the modern world or, as he sees it, the prison in which he exists. But George's estrangement is more severe, because he is also alienated from himself. He is conscious of two Georges, symbolized by the body of a fat George, which has imprisoned the thin one, struggling to escape. Although the fat man is beginning to show signs of weakness, he still clings to the value of being fat: People tend to like fat people more, for they are seen as more friendly and easier to get along with, valuable traits in a salesman. Nevertheless, he has become increasingly aware of that thin inner self that he has lost touch with.

George has not always been fat, so he is conscious of the thin man within. Adding to this is the fact that George is picking up his set of false teeth. Now even his teeth are not real. George is in danger of becoming as artificial as the suburban world he inhabits. Most of us think of suburbia as a post–World War II phenomenon, and to a large extent, that is true. But Orwell's instincts as a social analyst predate the suburban revolution, enabling him to see in its earliest stages a pattern which would not only change the character of the city but, as this novel will vividly demonstrate, transform the rural small town.

George's housing tract is a prewar model of the suburban phenomenon that was to erupt after the war. Looking at the identical houses in identical rows, he develops his prison image further. The homeowners are really prisoners because they don't own the land on which the houses sit. Secondly, they are chained to a sixteen-year mortgage, thus the office-worker class, under the illusion that it has moved up, is imprisoned by the fact that it has much more to lose than does the working class. The fear of losing it all turns the suburban middle class into social and political conservatives. In his analysis, George is careful to include himself when he concludes that "we're all bought, and what's more we're bought with our own money."

On the train to London, George dwells on another source of his malaise, as he sees a bombing plane flying overhead. War is coming; the anticipation of enemy bombers destroying London had been a recurring motif three years earlier in *Keep the Aspidistra Flying*. Here it has become part of a more concrete vision, of Hitler choosing the initial attack during a disarmament conference. (Something like this was to occur in December 1941, when the Japanese attacked Pearl Harbor while Japanese diplomats were in Washington on a peace mission.)

But George's thoughts immediately return to another subject: his fatness. In some respects, being heavy has been a positive feature of his life. The image of the cheerful, convivial, overweight salesman, always ready to share a joke or anecdote over a pint at the local pub (the figure of George Flaxman in *Keep the Aspidistra Flying* is an example of the stereotype) has sustained George socially and professionally, but the inner man—the George within, "a hangover from the past"—is, as the novel's epigraph puts it, "dead but he won't lie down."

To George, the American-style diner where he has lunch in London perfectly embodies the values of the world in 1939, a place in which "food doesn't matter, comfort doesn't matter, nothing matters except slickness, shininess and streamlining. Everything's streamlined these days, even the bullet Hitler's keeping for you." This is a world of surfaces and shapes that cover up the true nature of things. Thus, the frankfurter that George orders is revealed in the first bite to be made of fish:

> It gave me the feeling that I'd bitten into the modern world and discovered what it was really made of . . . When you come down to brass tacks and get your teeth into something really solid, a sausage for instance, that's what you get. Rotten fish in a rubber skin, bombs of filth bursting inside your mouth.

Here the glossy surfaces of art deco architecture fuse with the lethal efficiency of the fascist war machine. Right or wrong, the association is much more effective because the language that gives expression to it belongs to its average man. Adding to the impact of the description is the reference to rotten fish. In a novel in which fish and fishing play a central positive role, the notion of rotten fish encapsulates the theme of the corrupting power of modern life.

What follows is George's Proustian movement. In the "overture" to *Swann's Way*, the first volume of Marcel Proust's epic *In Search of Lost Time*, the middle-aged narrator, Marcel, experiences an involuntary memory from his childhood when he tastes a madeleine cake dipped in tea. In George's words, "some chance sight or sound or smell, especially smell, sets you going, and the past doesn't merely come back to you, you're actually *in* the past." And being in it, George realizes, is where the real—which is to say, the thin—George, belongs. It is worth noting that for Orwell himself, the process reversed itself. He was a chubby boy who grew into a skeletal adult—a "Don Quixote" in the mind of more than one of his friends. But the Don Quixote exterior can be misleading, as Orwell demonstrates in his essay "THE ART OF DONALD MCGILL." Don Quixote is always accompanied by Sancho Panza, a creature who wants no part of the Don's heroic self-sacrifices and noble ideals. Sancho Panza is a little, fat man who wants to indulge in the pleasures of the flesh and get by without being detected by a society determined to keep him in prison. That sense of society's menacing presence at his back is literally reproduced part 3, chapter 3, when everyone from his wife to Hitler and Stalin, the latter two on a tandem bicycle, seems to him to be in hot pursuit as he heads for his hometown. George's return to Lower Binfield will be a quixotic quest, conducted not by Don Quixote but by Sancho Panza.

The first seven parts of chapter 2 cover the years of George's early childhood (the late 1890s) to his enlistment in the army in 1914. Among his earliest memories is the first-class row that Father and Uncle Ezekiel had "over the outbreak of the Boer War," an echo perhaps, of the Christmas dinner argument over Parnell in the opening pages of James Joyce's *A Portrait of the Artist as a Young Man* (1914). Uncle Ezekiel, sharper-witted than Father, identifies the Boer War as an example of British imperialism at work, scoffing at the high-minded motives that government propaganda attributed to the British aggression. In Ezekiel's stance, we see the origins of George's general skepticism regarding authority. Another interesting feature of the chapter is the account of the dismal fate of Katie Simmons, his early babysitter. Her life constitutes an exemplary picture of a member of the impoverished class that would have evoked eloquent outrage from George Orwell. But George Bowling records it with a simple "poor Katie." The comment serves as an example of Orwell's ability to stay in the character, something he's not always able to do in the novel.

Chapter Two provides a picture of Lower Binfield on market day and portraits of George's mother and father. George's father bears a strong resemblance to the father of Gordon Comstock in *Keep the Aspidistra Flying*. Both men are unsuited to their life's work and are not particularly successful; both die before their businesses fail completely. George's mother is a woman whose life does not really extend beyond her kitchen. The feminist critic Daphne Patai argues that George's description individualizes the father, while "Mother however, is simply Woman" (165). How adequately Patai supports this assertion is at least open to question. One point that George does make is that what little discipline the children experienced came from their mother. Their father "was really much too weak with us." As a result, his older brother, Joe, becomes a delinquent, eventually stealing money from his parents and running away from home.

This chapter also introduces fishing, a central theme of the novel. At the age of eight, George had already developed a passion for the pastime without ever having experienced it. His initial catch is interrupted by the owner of the pond where they are trespassing, but even that interruption cannot encroach on his happiness. The boys spend most of the day marauding through the countryside, causing trouble and brutalizing small animals. Daphne Patai correctly characterizes these actions as early-stage male initiation rites and goes on to assert that they valorize cruelty in the movement from being a "kid" to being a "boy" (169). It is clear that it is George Bowling's view and not at all clear that it is George Orwell's. In any case, it is not valorizing boyhood to assert the following:

> Then Joe found a late thrush's nest with half-fledged chicks in it in a blackberry bush. After a lot of argument about what to do with them we took the chicks out, had shots at them with stones, and finally stamped on them. There were four of them, as we each had one to stamp on. . . . It's a kind of strong, rank feeling, and it's all bound up with breaking rules and killing things.

This suggests an elemental truth, not, as Patai would argue, directed against women per se, but an expression of a primordial instinct for violence, reflected in the line from *King Lear*: "Like flies to wanton boys are we to the gods, they kill us for their sport."

George continues to discuss the importance of fishing to him. One reason, he suggests, is that fishing is "somehow typical" of the world that existed before World War I. In those days, all the streams and ponds seemed to be stocked with fish. "Now all the ponds are drained and when the streams aren't poisoned with chemicals from factories they're full of rusty tins and motor-bike tires."

George discusses his other childhood passion, reading. Boys' penny magazines are the subject of one of Orwell's better-known essays, "BOYS' WEEKLIES." The fantasy world of George's reading collides with reality, when his father, his business failing because of a newly arrived chain-store competitor in town, tells him he is taking him out of school so that he can begin earning money, working at the local grocery store. The fact that his father's announcement occurs soon after George's discovery of a secret pond with giant fish, which provides an excuse for George's not returning to the pond, raises some questions. Does the incident record the fact that George is simply another victim of the "money-world," forced into a job for financial reasons that will leave him alienated from his true calling? Or had George, in coming upon the pond, been an interloper, an intruder into an Eden-like world, much like the Sarazin's chain store, imitating their medieval namesakes, by besieging the holy land, his father's store? Or is George's failure to return to the pond a retreat from its absolute perfection, perhaps because he is terrified by the prospect of perfection? The lure of the pond might take him outside the ordinary world, a calling to some vocation to be different.

After being wounded at the front, George is sent to a hospital camp near Eastbourne, on the southern coast of England. Eastbourne was the location of St Cyprian's, Orwell's prep school, notoriously commemorated by him in one of his most famous essays, "SUCH, SUCH WERE THE JOYS." George makes a reference to "the slap-up boys schools" in Eastbourne, whose students would occasionally visit the hospital, handing out cigarettes and candy to the "wounded Tommies." After his recovery, he is sent to officer's training school. The experience of being a "temporary gentleman" has an impact on him that puts going back to a shopkeeper's life out of the question, but more important, he becomes aware of the shifting sands underlying the seemingly rocklike solidity of English social structure. Instead of being eternal in its make-up, as it had seemed in prewar Lower Binfield, George now sees the whole business as "just a balls-up."

His description of post–World War I England is one in which the competition for jobs among returning veterans is intense and bitter. Landing one at the appropriately named Flying Salamander Insurance Company (the salamander is noted for eating members of its own species), it becomes his permanent home. Orwell based his description of George's job on information he received from John Sceats, an insurance man (and a socialist) to whom he had sent queries. One example of a change is that Orwell "raised" George's salary from five to seven pounds a week. This type of detail reminds us that whatever moral or didactic purpose he had in mind, Orwell was determined to be true to one article in the code of realistic novelists: to stay close to the facts.

George's account of his courtship of his wife, Hilda, is a melancholy tale for which Orwell drew on his own family history. Like Eric Blair, Hilda is the product of a genteel, "poverty stricken officer class," Anglo-Indian family. (Of course, "poverty stricken" hardly describes the Blair family, but living on a pension would certainly exclude luxuries such as a university education.) Hilda's parents live in a small house furnished with the bric-a-brac typical of the vanished life of the Raj. To George, it is a strange, unknown world and socially a step up from his shopkeeper class. Not long after the marriage, he discovers that Hilda "lacks any kind of joy in life." Coming from a family that exists on an always-diminishing pension or annuity, girls like Hilda develop "a fixed idea not only that one is always hard up, but that it's one's duty to be miserable about it." Again it is doubtful that Orwell is describing his own family life, since his mother appears to have been a high-spirited, resourceful woman.

Part 3 brings us back to the present—Europe on the brink of war. Here, Orwell takes the opportunity to bite the hand that feeds him in his depiction of the LEFT BOOK CLUB lecture. Founded by Orwell's publisher Victor Gollancz, the club published, at significantly reduced prices, a monthly book selection. One of these in 1937 was THE ROAD TO WIGAN PIER. The Left Book Club's version of this text included a critical preface by Gollancz, anxious to avoid Orwell's treatment of middle-class socialists from giving offense to club readers. The treatment of the anti-fascist speaker at the club is another example of Orwell's independent thinking. George enters into the speaker's mind to see what he sees, "a picture of himself, smashing people's faces in . . . fascist faces, of course . . . it's all O.K. because the smashed faces belong to fascists." It is clear here, and in George's later remarks to three young men at the lecture, that he is clinging, although in near-despair, to a pacifist position in relation to the coming war.

When George stops by a roadside to admire the spring flowers, he also notices the dying embers of a camp fire. At that moment he experiences an epiphany, a recognition that life is worth living when you achieve the sense of inner peace he is having at that moment. It invokes a connection with the novel's epigraph, a line from a popular song: "He's dead, but he won't lie down." George is teetering on the brink of happiness comparable to his first glimpse of the hidden pond beyond Binfield House. He bends down to pick some primroses, acutely conscious of his body, including his false teeth, which he removes for a moment so that he can feel whole, "the sort of feeling of wonder, the peculiar flame inside you." But when he hears another car coming down the road, he throws the primroses he's picked over a hedge. Can't have the passengers looking at "a fat man in a bowler hat holding a bunch of primroses."

At that moment of self-betrayal, he conceives the notion of going back to Lower Binfield, an ominous sign that it will prove to be a bad idea. George's moment of truth has become his moment of *hubris*, underscored by his invocation of the book's title *Coming Up for Air*. But he fails to recognize that you cannot find peace in the past, only in the present moment, such as he has just experienced but thrown away. The earlier moments of epiphany—at the pond and in France—were spoiled by economic need, the attraction of sex, or the exigencies of war. This time it is the awareness of his body that contributes to a sense of shame.

The return to Lower Binfield is a predicable disaster. The village has been swallowed up by housing developments and factories. Where there once were 2,000 residents, there are now 25,000. The building that was both his home and his father's business has become a quaint, "arty" tea shop. The only recognizable place is the churchyard, filled to the brim with graves, requiring a separate cemetery on the outskirts of town. Inside the church, he runs into the vicar, the same man who had been vicar in George's childhood. At the time, he would have been 45—George's age now—and back then, he looked ancient to the young George. Now the vicar is about 65 and actually looks younger in Georges eyes. What is disturbing is that George realizes he must look ancient to young people. It is yet another lesson for him in the distortions that time is capable of producing.

George's attempts to re-experience the joys of fishing produce his most powerful frustrations. The local fishing spot on the Thames has become a noisy honky-tonk playground, where the fishermen compete with "rowing boats, canoes, punts, motor launchers full of young folk . . . screaming and shouting. . . ." The next day, he tries his luck at the secret pond near Binfield House, only to discover that it has been drained and converted to a trash dump. This may or may not be a comment on the decline of religious faith, but it is central to George's view that there is a break with the sense of fundamental continuity. After summarizing some of the evils existing in the old days, George identifies the essential element that sustained life in the village.

> And yet what was it that people had in those days? A feeling of security, even when they weren't secure. More exactly, it was a feeling of continuity. All of them knew they'd got to

> die, and I suppose a few of them knew they were going to go bankrupt, but what they didn't know was that the order of things could change. Whatever might happen to themselves, things would go on as they'd known them. . . . It's easy enough to die if the things you care about are going to survive. You've had your life, you're getting tired, it's time to go underground—that's how people used to see it. Individually they were finished, but their way of life would continue.

The *coup de grace* for the past occurs on George's last day in Lower Binfield. A British bomber accidentally drops a bomb on, appropriately enough, the heart of the old section of town. Summing up his bitterly disappointing experience, George employs a combat image: "I'd chucked a pineapple [hand grenade] into my dreams and . . . the Royal Air-force had followed up with five hundred pounds of T.N.T." In a sense, George's flight back to Lower Binfield had been an attempt to escape temporarily from the oncoming apocalypse, but he finds that it has followed him (or even worse, that he has brought it with him). Back in London, he saw the crowds on the street as "sleep walkers." Only he, apparently, is fully conscious of the calamity to come: "We're all on a burning deck and nobody knows it except me." He has carried that image with him. But as critics have pointed out, as fearful as he is of war, even greater is George's dread of what will come afterward, the world of *Nineteen Eighty-Four.*

CRITICAL RECEPTION

In *Coming Up for Air,* Orwell wrestles with a number of fundamental themes. The degree to which he succeeds in resolving or even realizing them is debatable, perhaps, but not the fact that he engages them. In terms of the novel's central metaphor, the hero is aware of the dark and deep waters of a hidden pond that contains the largest fish, but, unconsciously he retreats from the possibilities, or choices, that the pond may present. In *The Road to Miniluv* (1975), the critic Christopher Small offers an explicitly Christian interpretation of this scene and of the novel as a whole. He sees fishing as an act whose central importance lies in its example of "making a personal connection." "The 'monstrous' still uncaught, and perhaps, un-catchable fish that swim in the deep pool. . . . in the dark place among the trees, waiting for me all these years. And the huge fish gliding around it. Jesus! (100)" Small acknowledges that the last word may be "no more than a casual profanity" (the complete quote is "Jesus! If they were that size thirty years ago, what would they be like now?"), but he poses the possibility that the giant fish represent "the living Christ, the self, uncaught, whose word is like a sword; of the devastating effects of denial and separation. But neither George Bowling nor Orwell was able to interpret it" (100). Stripped of its specifically Christian reading, that is to say, taken as a nonsectarian evocation of a powerful "lost" religious or spiritual experience, Small's reading deepens our understanding of the novel. While remaining a confirmed agnostic, Orwell never wavered in his conviction that the decline in religious belief constituted the great moral crisis of the 20th century. One of the novel's many unanswered questions resting at the heart of *Coming Up for Air* lies in the answer to the question of why George never returns to the pond until it is too late. Is his failure simply the result of circumstances beyond his control: his father's failing business, his distraction by the imminence of his first sexual experience, the cataclysm of World War I, which separated him from any conscious connection with the pond, his wife's characterization of him as a baby in his desire to go fishing, or it is a hidden failure of nerve, as an existential critic might phrase it, the evasion of choice at critical moments. Not returning to the pond, throwing the primroses away, may be seen as spurious choices summarized by the growth of the fat man encroaching upon the thin one.

The fishing note is elaborated further in the incident in which George and a fellow soldier discover a pond filled with fish, providing another example of the use of fishing as a thematic instrument. The pond behind the front line, like the one at Binfield House, bypassed in the death-dealing world of war, offers George a temporary escape from "the noise and the stink and the uniforms and the officers and the saluting and the sergeant's voice. Fishing is the opposite of war." Of course, in the most strict literal sense, fishing might be seen as war on another species, but such an interpretation overlooks the fact that the fish we catch survive by eating other fish, that fishing is part of the natural process of life. The rod and reel are precise metaphors for the connecting links to the foundations of existence.

A number of critics, particularly Jeffrey Meyers, have pointed out that one of the important models for the book is James Joyce's *Ulysses* (1922), whose hero, Leopold Bloom, demonstrated to Orwell that it was possible to represent an ordinary man—"a good man," as Joyce characterized Bloom—embodying "the solitude in which a human being lives." Orwell's version of Bloom, George Bowling, is, like Joyce's character, a middle-aged, overweight salesman, but the two characters differ profoundly in the depth of emotion and sympathy that Bloom is capable of and that, at best, is barely evident in Bowling. Perhaps the difference is suggested in the connotations of the two names: the suggestion of "rooted in nature" of the word *Bloom* as opposed to "moving along a hard surface" of *Bowling*. One point Orwell would have noticed is that Bloom "exists" in a prewar Edwardian world (*Ulysses* is set in 1904).

The other classic 20th-century novel that *Coming Up for Air* suggests is Marcel Proust's epic *Remembrance of Things Past,* or, as the recent translation reads, *In Search of Lost Time.* Both titles come close to capturing two major sections of the novel, parts 2 and 4. In part 2 ("Remembrance"), George Bowling movingly weaves his memories of his hometown, Lower Binfield, without lapsing into sentimentality. Part 4, on the other hand ("In Search"), treats George's actual return, in which he discovers not only that his treasured past has been invaded and overwhelmed by the present but looks ahead to the dreaded future, as a British plane accidentally drops a bomb on, appropriately enough, the old section of Lower Binfield. In this respect, the focus falls on the iron hand of history, the modern force that has become one with its central symbol, the machine. George Bowling, the representative ordinary man, knows that the days of the individual, of the boy at the fishing hole, are over. What lies ahead looks ominously like the world of *Nineteen Eighty-Four.*

But the great majority of readers and critics have stressed the sociopolitical dimension of the novel. As George Woodcock argues in his study of the novel, Bowling's romantic quest to recapture a vanished past has left him "without illusions about the past or hopes for the future. . . . No way out from the prison of one's class or one's time into the freedom of an idiosyncratic self." However, the novelist and critic David Lodge comes at the novel at an interesting if somewhat oblique angle. Locating Orwell as one of the important realistic novelists of the 1930s, he suggests that these writers were rejecting the "obscurity, allusiveness, and elitism of the modernist-symbolist tradition in favor of a more politically aware and directly communicative approach" (190). In Orwell's terms, he saw himself as being "outside the whale," committed to social justice, unlike (his example) the novelist Henry Miller, who has opted to remain "inside the whale," viewing the world from the secure womb-like vantage point of the whale's belly, observing but choosing not to concern himself with the state of the world. (See INSIDE THE WHALE.) As if to illustrate how this difference affected literary styles in the period, Lodge draws on the distinction, first elaborated by the linguist Roman Jakobson, between metaphor and metonymy. To Jakobson, metaphor governs the human brain's selection of words, while metonymy guides the arrangement of these words. As an example of the distinction, Lodge points out the differences between George Bowling's reminiscences and those of the narrator of Marcel Proust's modernist classic, *In Search of Lost Time.* "Proust's evocations of the past are drenched in metaphor, George's are catalogues of literal facts" (191). An example would be George's recollection of Sunday service in the local church: "How it came back to me! . . . The sweet corpsy smell, the rustle of Sunday dresses, the wheeze of the organ and the roaring voices, the spot of light from the hole in the window creeping slowly up the nave." Lodge points out that Orwell's metonymic style is of course consistent with George's "ordinary man" character. But he goes on to argue, citing the episode of the hidden pond, that there is a "mythopoeic, metaphorical level" in the novel "buried under the ordinary prosaic surface" (Lodge 192). One might put it that inside the realistic novelist that Orwell saw himself as, and for the most part was, there may have been a symbolic modernist writer struggling to escape.

CHARACTERS

Bowling, George A middle-aged insurance agent who longs to escape his boring life, living in a suburban development with a nagging, brooding, joyless wife and two unappealing children. Thoroughly bored by his present life, he is even more dismayed by the future, in which an inevitable second world war now looms. During World War I, he was wounded and promoted to lieutenant but then, instead of returning overseas, he was sent to a deserted spot in Wales, where he sat out the war principally reading books. After the war, he secured a job as an insurance salesman, married Hilda, and settled into his humdrum existence. One day, while glancing at a headline, he has a Proustian recollection of times past that plunges his mind back to a Sunday service in his parish church. Using money he won by betting on a horse, he heads back to his hometown in an effort to recapture some of the happiness and fulfillment he knew as a child growing up in the years before World War I. The visit turns into a complete disaster as he finds his bucolic village transformed into a modernized town, with factories and housing estates that have all but obliterated the small village of his memory, the population of which has increased tenfold. To top it off, on the last day of his visit, a Royal Air Force bomber mistakenly drops a bomb on the old section of town, which suggests to George that the coming war will put the finishing touch on modern civilization's destruction of the past. He returns home, beaten but unbowed: "He's dead, but he won't lie down."

Bowling, Hilda The unhappy wife of George Bowling, who, like her creator, is the product of an Anglo-Indian family that barely made ends meet on the pension of a colonial civil servant. As a result, she is preoccupied with money worries, having married George with the expectations that he would be a greater success in business than he turned out to be. Adding to that disappointment is the fact that George has been unfaithful in the past. As a result, Hilda is convinced that his brief return to Lower Binfield was in fact an adulterous tryst with an unknown woman.

Bowling, Mrs. George's mother, a devoted wife, a good cook, and an organized, if not overly clean, housekeeper. She lived the life of "a decent, God-fearing shopkeeper's wife" and was fortunate not to know that she "lived at the end of an epoch," which concluded with the start of World War I.

Bowling, Samuel Father of George Bowling. He owns a corn-and-seed shop in Lower Binfield. His business suffers when a large chain-store competitor, a harbinger of the future, moves into town. Worn down by financial problems and the perfidy of his older son, he dies of pneumonia while George is away in the army.

Bowling, Ezekiel The independent-minded older brother of George's father, Uncle Ezekiel owned a boot shop in Lower Binfield. An "old fashioned nineteenth century Liberal," he opposed the Boer War as another example of rapacious British imperialism. He was a self-taught reader of serious literature, so that his brother was no match for him in a political argument. When Ezekiel died, he left his brother the money he needed to keep his failing business going.

Bowling, Joe George's ne'er-do-well older brother who runs away to America after stealing money from his parents.

Brewer Local farmer who chases George and the Black Hand gang off his land, where they have been fishing. He reports them to their parents, and they are all given a hiding.

Cheam, Sir Joseph George's commanding officer during the war, who chooses him as an assistant because, although he is an officer, George is not a gentleman and therefore is willing to work. After the war, George runs into him again and, through him, lands a job at the Salamander Insurance Company.

Grimmett, Mr. The local grocer, at whose store George goes to work at the age of 16. A devout Baptist, a town councilor and a shrewd businessman, Grimmett teaches George what he needs to know in order to open his own store one day.

Hodges The cranky old caretaker of Binfield House, a decaying mansion, whose grounds include two fishing ponds. In return for a favor that George's father has done, Hodges permits George to fish there.

Lovegrove, Sid Leader of a children's gang, the Black Hand, that George longs to join; he succeeds in doing so after a successful fishing experience.

Mellors A coworker of George, a devout believer in astrology, and a dedicated horse player. Following the advice of a book, *Astrology Applied to Horse-Racing,* he bets on a certain horse and implores George to do the same. When the horse wins, George puts his winnings, £17, in the bank, determined to have some fun with the money.

Minns, Miss Friend of Hilda Bowling and Mrs. Wheeler. A tall, thin woman living on a small fixed income, the repressed daughter of a clergyman, who "sat on her pretty heavily while he lived." She has joined up with the other two women out of sheer loneliness. Miss Minns seems in many respects to represent the kind of life Orwell might have imagined for Dorothy Hare, the protagonist of *A Clergyman's Daughter.*

Old Betterton Vicar of the Anglican church in Lower Binfield since 1904. In George's childhood, Betterton was in his mid-forties and seemed ancient to young George. On his return, George meets the vicar and realizes that he is now the age that the vicar was then, and that he must now appear old to young people. The vicar, now in his sixties, does not recognize George.

Porteus A retired schoolmaster whom George Bowling likes to visit occasionally. Porteus is a classical scholar immersed in the worlds of Greece and Rome and who regards contemporary events as passing phenomena, not worthy of serious consideration. George comes to see him as a man who, locked into the past, has stopped thinking, refusing to acknowledge the reality of the present. Some have seen in him a portrait of Orwell's tutor at Eton, ANDREW GOW.

Shooter A fishmonger who, along with Wetherall, led the singing of psalms at church services in George's youth. Shooter would lead off with a shout, only to be overwhelmed by Wetherall's booming bass. When George visits the cemetery during his return to Lower Binfield, he finds that the graves of Shooter and Wetherall are opposite each other, just as their pews were in church.

Simmons, Katie The 12-year-old babysitter of George and his brother, Joe, in their early years. She takes the boys for walks. Katie is from an impoverished family and suffers the typical fate of the poor. She becomes pregnant at 15, and years later, George sees her standing "in the yard of a squalid hut shaking the dirt out of a rug and looking twice as old as her 27 years."

Todgers, Miss Helena Local leader of the ARP (Air Raid Precautions) in Lower Binfield. George describes her as "the kind of tough old devil with grey hair and a kind of kippered face that's always put in charge of Girl Guide detachments, YWCA hostels and what-not." She is in her glory directing local schoolchildren at air-raid practice. When a bomb is accidentally dropped on the town, she has all the local children wearing gas masks as they run for shelter.

Waters, Elsie George's first lover. An attractive young woman, she works in a local shop. The two have their first sexual encounter on the day he takes her to a secluded spot near the mysterious pond he discovered. After he leaves for the army, he neglects to maintain their relationship. On his return to Lower Binfield 20 years later, he finds himself following a slatternly, overweight woman to a tobacconist's shop. It turns out that it is Elsie, who is married to the owner of the shop. Making a purchase from her, he sees that she does not recognize him, for which he is grateful.

Wetherall A joiner and an undertaker, the possessor of a powerful bass voice. He and the fishmonger Shooter led the congregation in singing psalms at Sunday services. Wetherall had an overwhelming sound that was particularly effective singing the psalm of Og, the king of Bashan. It is his voice that George hears when he has his Proustian recall from hearing newsboys shouting about King Zog.

Wheeler, Mrs. Friend of Hilda Bowling, a widow with a grievance against men. George considers her a bad influence on Hilda. She is always pursuing some fad, as long as it is something you can do for free or next to nothing. Mrs. Wheeler has dragged Hilda and their other friend into theosophy, spiritualism, and the Left Book Club. It is Mrs. Wheeler who convinces Hilda to check on George's alibi when he goes back to Lower Binfield.

Wicksey, Mr. Headmaster of George's grammar school, nicknamed "Whiskers," who thought highly of George's ability and spoke of the possibility of George's receiving a scholarship to a redbrick university.

Witchett, Mr. Chairman of the meetings of the Left Book Club, also secretary of the local branch of the Liberal Party, "a mild looking chap with a pink baby's bottom kind of face that's always covered in smiles.

WORKS CITED

Lodge, David. *The Modes of Modern Writing.* Ithaca, N.Y.: Cornell University Press, 1988.

Meyers, Jeffrey. *Orwell: Wintry Conscience of a Generation.* New York: Norton, 2000.

Patai, Naomi. *The Orwell Mystique: A Study in Male Ideology.* Amherst: University of Massachusetts Press, 1984.

Small, Christopher. *The Road to Miniluv.* London: Gollancz, 1975.

Woodcock, George. *The Crystal Spirit: A Study of George Orwell.* London: Cape, 1967.

"Confessions of a Book Reviewer"

A brief essay first published in *Tribune* (1946) and reprinted in the United States in *The New Republic* in 1946.

SYNOPSIS

Orwell opens with a portrait of an ink-stained wretch in a squalid bed-sitter, clearing a space for his typewriter on a shaky table, littered with cigarette butts and tea cups. This man is a writer trying to eke out a living as a book reviewer. An editor has sent him a parcel of books for an omnibus review of five works totally unrelated to each other. Three of these books deal with subjects he knows nothing about, and the review is due in 24 hours. Working all night, he will manage, helped by some ready-made clichés of book reviewing, to meet the deadline with a few minutes to spare. Meanwhile, a new batch of books will arrive, demanding immediate attention.

Such is the "thankless, irritating, exhausting job" of a professional book reviewer, that is, someone who reviews at least 100 books a year. The fact is that the great majority of books published are "worthless." However, the influence of the publishing industry—though not as powerful as it once was—dictates the policy of journals' reviewing more books than they should. Also the public relies on a quick summary of a number of books rather than a sustained review of one. So the reviewer has to meet the demand that eventually turns him into a hack. "He is pouring his immortal spirit down the drain, half a pint at a time. The heart of the problem lies in the assumption that all books must be reviewed. As it is, the regular reviewer is reduced to writing snippets on a number of books, which eventually "reduces him to the crushed figure" described above. However, as poor as the book reviewer is, he is better off than the film reviewer, "who cannot even work at home."

COMMENTARY

Orwell reviewed books for more than 20 years and for a good part of that time was desperately dependent on the supplementary income that came from reviewing. Thus, it is possible to see autobiographical elements, however exaggerated, in his description. For a period in 1940 and 1941, he reviewed not only books but also plays and films for *Time and Tide* magazine, so even his reference to the poor film reviewer who has to leave his flat is probably a personal recollection. See FILM REVIEWS and THEATER REVIEWS.

"Decline of the English Murder"

A short essay first published in *Tribune* (1946). According to Orwell, a favorite Sunday afternoon activity of the average Englishman or woman is to read about a famous murder in the Sunday paper. The great age of English murders—"its Elizabethan period"—fell between 1850 and 1925. There were nine famous murders during that time, and their stories have been told and retold in a variety of forms. Of these nine, the great majority involved using poison, the murderer being either the husband or the wife of the victim. A composite example typifying this form of homicide might be one in which a highly respectable middle-aged man, after painfully wrestling with his conscience, murders his wife, freeing himself to marry another woman, one with whom he has been having an affair. The murder would be carefully planned, but some minor detail the man had failed to anticipate would trip him up. Thus, the events would have a dramatic, ironic quality, which would make the story memorable.

Contrast this classical model to the typical murder of the present day. The two murderers in the recent "Cleft Chin Murder" were a couple of drifters, a man and a woman, looking for a cheap thrill. On the first night they met, they stole a truck and deliberately ran over a girl bicyclist. Later they killed another girl and a taxi driver, whom they robbed. After their arrest and conviction, the man, an American army deserter, was hanged, but the woman escaped the death penalty. The story itself and the resulting public clamor for her death are reflections of the "brutalizing effects of the war" on the general population. As for the murderers, the fact that the man was an American and the woman, one "who had become partly Americanized," suggests that the prevailing influence of Hollywood films have created a harsher modern England, where murder has become a casual experience. For that reason, this murder will not have the lasting appeal of the classical murders of an earlier age.

"Decline of the English Murder" bears comparison to Orwell's "Raffles and Miss Blandish," in that both call attention to a serious change in English culture. In the case of "RAFFLES AND MISS BLANDISH," the focus is on the crime novel as represented by the contrast in the two stories. Raffles is a gentleman burglar who is also a splendid cricket player, which is to say he plays by the rules, adhering to the code of Edwardian England except for an occasional theft. In contrast is the sadistic and violent contemporary novel *No Orchids for Miss Blandish,* which appears to abandon all standards of decency in the name of realism. This development in fiction is matched by crime, in fact. It is not coincidental that *No Orchids* is set in the United States and written in the popular hard-boiled style.

Orwell's sense of the deleterious effect of American influence on English life was a consistent minor theme in his essays and novels. He made several negative references to the presence of American soldiers during the war and, in *KEEP THE ASPIDISTRA FLYING,* to the spread of American advertising techniques.

Dickens, Dalí, and Others: Studies in Popular Culture

The title of the American edition of Orwell's first collection of essays, published in England as *CRITICAL ESSAYS.* Both English and American editions were published in 1946. The collection includes the following essays: "CHARLES DICKENS" (1939); "BOYS' WEEKLIES" (1940); "WELLS, HITLER, AND THE WORLD STATE" (1941); "The ART OF DONALD MCGILL" (1941); "RUDYARD KIPLING" (1942); "W. B. YEATS" (1943); "BENEFIT OF CLERGY: SOME NOTES ON SALVADOR DALÍ" (1944); "ARTHUR KOESTLER" (1944); "RAFFLES AND MISS BLANDISH" (1944); and "IN DEFENSE OF P. G. WODEHOUSE" (1946).

In the latter half of 1949, Orwell prepared notes on most of his major publications, including information on foreign translations and reprints. His entry on *Critical Essays* states that there is no difference in text between the English and American versions, except that the American edition "has bad misprints" and that he has marked the errors in a copy somewhere among his books. He also mentions some misquotations, specifically in the essay "Rudyard Kipling." Orwell suggests that future reprints should include a reply to his essay "Boys' Weeklies" by Frank Richards, one of the writers for boys whom Orwell cites in his essay.

Down and Out in Paris and London

Orwell's first book, published by Victor Gollancz in January 1933. *Down and Out* has been variously described as memoir, reportage, autobiography, travel diary, and autobiographical fiction. In 38 loosely knit chapters—or vignettes—the book chronicles Orwell's experiences among society's outcasts, first in Paris and later in the hop fields and flophouses of greater London.

HISTORICAL/BIOGRAPHICAL CONTEXT

In the late 1920s, Europe was still suffering from the effects of the disastrous world war that had crippled national economies and ignited fierce hostilities and upheavals, both within and among nations. The idealism represented by the efforts of men like the U.S. president Woodrow Wilson had run into the Old World's cynicism and New World's self-interested politics. The Treaty of Versailles testified to the continuing credo that the spoils of war belong to the victor. Wilson's dream of a League of Nations that would put an end to future wars was doomed from the beginning when his own country refused to join it. The result was a continent, in which, viewed against the stability of pre-1914 Europe, "mere anarchy" had been loosed. In Italy, Benito Mussolini consolidated his power as he moved to transform the nation into an efficient and ruthless military regime. In the Soviet Union, Joseph Stalin took the first steps in his dictatorship by expelling (and later murdering) his rival, Leon Trotsky. In Germany, the young National Socialist Party fared poorly in the 1928 election but left Adolf Hitler still confident of his ability to exploit the German people's anger at the humiliation of their country by the victors. The French refusal to remove their troops from the Rhineland long after the war's end was a festering source of German resentment.

In England, the General Strike of 1926 brought the country to a standstill. The strike had begun with management's lockout of the coal miners, the consequences of which would still be evident 10 years later when George Orwell would record his view of the miners' life in *The Road to Wigan Pier*. The coup de grace that finished off the '20s occurred in October 1929, when the stock market on Wall Street collapsed, sending calamitous shock waves around the globe: "America sneezed and the world caught a cold."

In August 1927, Orwell returned to England from Burma via Marseilles and Paris. By October of that year, having followed through on his intention of resigning from the Burma police and dedicating himself to becoming a writer, he set out to explore the lower depths of English society, the world of itinerant tramps. In his first attempt to explore this "undiscovered country," he dressed himself in rags to experience their life from the inside. In this he had a literary guide, a book titled *The People of the Abyss* by the American novelist and journalist JACK LONDON. In 1902, London had lived among the poor in London's East End in an effort, as he put it, "to know how those people are living there, and why they are living there, and what they are living for." Sharing London's view, Orwell also had a personal motive. As he expressed it in the autobiographical section of *The Road to Wigan Pier,* he wished to atone for his role as an agent of imperialism while in Burma. The English tramps "were the symbolic victims of injustice, playing the same part in England as the Burmese played in Burma." Guilty over his participation in the subjugation of a free people, Orwell decided to take up the cause of the poor and dispossessed by joining their ranks. "Once I had been among them and accepted by them, I should have touched bottom—this is what I felt: I was aware even then that it was irrational—part of my guilt would drop from me."

The following spring, he moved to Paris, by that time the home of the Lost Generation, young artists and writers from Europe and the United States who went to Paris to breathe the air of artistic freedom and experimentation (or, in many cases, simply to have a good time). As Orwell, looking back from 1940, put it in his essay "Inside the Whale": "During the boom years when dollars were plentiful and the exchange-value of the franc was low, Paris was invaded by such a swarm of artists, writers, students, dilettanti, sight-seers, debauchees and plain idlers as the world has probably never seen."

He stayed at a hotel on the rue du Pot de Fer (the rue du Coq d'Or in *Down and Out*). For a year and a half, he lived and worked there, writing regularly, but with little success, fiction, novels, and short stories. But he did produce a number of articles for French and English publications. In March 1929, he was hospitalized for two weeks with the flu, an experience he was later to capture in his essay "HOW THE POOR DIE." A short time later, the remaining money he had saved was stolen, forcing him to look for a job. The theft provides the springboard for the central action of the Paris section of the book, since it alters the narrator's stance from observer of, to participant in, the life of a down-and-outer.

Readers of *Down and Out* might infer that its narrator was cut off from all social contacts and living from hand to mouth against a background of outcasts, dodgy communists, beggars, and con men. For the several weeks that he worked as a plongeur in Hotel X, this was likely the case. However, Orwell was never without resources in Paris. For much of his stay, he lived in a fairly respectable though bohemian area of Paris's Left Bank. Unknown to him at the time, his schoolmate CYRIL CONNOLLY spent several months living only a few streets away. Orwell's aunt, NELLIE LIMOUZIN, also lived in Paris during his time there, and their correspondence from that period reveals that he visited her regularly.

Orwell completed a draft of the book in October 1930 under the title *A Scullion's Diary*. This version dealt exclusively with his time in Paris. He submitted the manuscript—running to 35,000 words—to Jonathan Cape, but the publisher deemed it too short. Orwell subsequently expanded the draft and resubmitted it. Cape again rejected it. More than a year passed before his next attempt at publication, during which he substantially revised the structure and content of the book. On the recommendation of his friend RICHARD REES, Orwell submitted the manuscript to Faber and Faber, whose principal reader at the time was the poet T. S. ELIOT.

In February 1932, Eliot wrote to Orwell to explain his rejection of the manuscript. "It is decidedly too short, and particularly for a book of such length it seems to me too loosely constructed, as the French and English episodes fall into two parts with very little to connect them." From Eliot's description, the manuscript is likely to have resembled the version eventually published. Dejected by repeated refusals, Orwell abandoned the manuscript and gave it to his friend MABEL FIERZ, asking her to destroy it, adding as a bitter note, "save the paper clips." A strong believer in Orwell's talent, Fierz ignored his request and delivered the manuscript to the literary agent LEONARD MOORE, badgering him into reading it. Moore was sufficiently impressed and submitted it to the left-wing publisher VICTOR GOLLANCZ, who accepted it on the condition that some minor changes be made.

Orwell proceeded to make the necessary revisions—changes in names and places, and the removal of indecent language were principal among them. At this point, he requested that, out of deference to the middle-class sensibilities of his parents, the book be published under a pseudonym.

Proofs of the manuscript arrived in November, with a tentative publication date of January 1933. Still to be resolved were the title and the pseudonym. Gollancz had suggested *Confessions of a Down and Out.* Orwell balked at the title, but compromised by suggesting *Confessions of a Dishwasher.* A compromise was struck with the title *Down and Out in Paris and London.* Orwell wrote to Moore about his decision for the author's name. "As to a pseudonym, a name I always use when tramping etc. is P. S. Burton, but if you don't think this sounds a probable kind of name, what about Kenneth Miles, George Orwell, H. Lewis Allways. I rather favour George Orwell" (Crick, 147).

Down and Out in Paris and London was published on January 9, 1933. The first edition ran to 1,500 copies and sold for just under nine shillings. Initial sales were promising. Later in January, a second press run of 500 was printed, and an additional run of 1,000 was printed a month later. Sales eventually leveled out, but Gollancz claimed not to have remaindered any of the stock. The first American edition by Harper and Brothers appeared in June 1933 in an edition of 1,750 copies, of which 383 were remaindered. A French edition was published by Gallimard and translated by R. N. Raimbault and Gwen Gilbert, with a preface by the author. The book enjoyed something of a renaissance in 1940 following the publication of a cheap Penguin edition of 55,000 copies. Inexplicably, the book was classified on the cover and in the Penguin catalogue as fiction. This was eventually corrected in later Penguin editions.

Orwell's first published book would later run through several English and American editions. In addition to the French edition, the book was translated into Czech (1935), Danish (1954), Italian (1966), Dutch (1970), Norwegian (1970), Spanish (1973), Swedish (1973), German (1978), Serbian (1984), and Finnish (1985). Perhaps the most important reissue of the book came in 1986 with the publication of the *Complete Works of George Orwell* edition, edited by Peter Davison. This volume reinstated the numerous omissions insisted upon by Gollancz. Many of the omissions were restored, according to Davison, on the basis of footnotes contained in the French edition.

Orwell's grim descriptions of filthy conditions in many of Paris's best restaurants elicited a letter of protest from one Humbert Possenti, a restaurateur claiming 40 years of experience. He wrote to *The Times* from Piccadilly's Hotel Splendide on January 31, 1933: "Such a disgusting state of things as he describes in such places is inconceivable," adding that "the kitchens of large and smart restaurants . . . are cleaner than those of most private homes." The letter prompted a response from Orwell, who claimed that the portions of the book objected to refer not in general to smart Paris eateries but rather "to one particular hotel, and as Possenti does not know which hotel this was he has no means of testing the truth of my statements."

SYNOPSIS

Chapter 1

It is seven in the morning, and Madame Ponce is screaming at one of her boarders about squashing bugs on the wallpaper. Orwell begins his account of life in Paris with this sketch to describe something of the atmosphere of the rue de Coq d'Or, where he lives in a small hotel. The street is narrow and rather squalid, and it comprises mostly cheap hotels with small bistros on the ground floors. The hotels lodge an eclectic mix of people, including Polish, Italian, and Arab immigrants. All in all, Orwell concludes, the street is a "representative Paris slum."

Orwell lives in the Hotel des Trois Moineaux, a five-story building divided into roughly 40 small rooms, which are invariably dirty and infested with bugs. Despite the filth, the rooms have a homelike feel. Madame F., the owner of the hotel, charges a low rate of 30 to 50 francs a week. The lodgers come and go without much notice, appearing for a week and then disappearing. They seldom have luggage, and they represent a variety of trades, from cobblers to prostitutes.

This diverse group of indigents includes a variety of eccentric characters such as the Rougiers, whom Orwell describes as "an old, ragged, dwarfish couple." They sell postcards along the boulevard St. Michel, which depict various chateaux in France's Loire Valley. Then there is Henri, a tall, sad-looking man. Once a respectable gentleman,

Henri suffered an unhappy end to a love affair, resulting in a heroic binge and a stint in jail. He now works in the Paris sewers. Other eccentrics include R., an English man who spends half the year in England and the other half drinking four liters of wine (six on Saturdays) per day, Monsieur Jules, a Romanian with a glass eye (but who refuses to admit it), and an old rag merchant named Laurent. These and many other odd characters all contribute to the story, but the principal character in this narrative is Poverty. The hotel is the setting for a story that offers an "object lesson" in poverty.

Chapter 2

The bistro on the ground floor of Orwell's hotel consists of a cramped room with brick floors and wine-sodden tables. Half the residents of the hotel meet each night for drinking, singing, games, and "extraordinarily public love-making." Visitors often hear rather interesting tales told by the patrons. One such conversation involves a young man named Charlie, educated and from a good family, who had run away and survived on money sent occasionally from home. Charlie recounts a story about his brother's visit to Paris, where he had come on his parents' orders to see Charlie and take him out to dinner. Charlie gets his brother drunk and steals all his money. He then looks for a brothel. An old woman answers the door and admits Charlie after charging him 1,000 francs. The old woman leads Charlie to a staircase leading down to the basement, and she tells him that he can do anything he wants with the girl below without interference.

At the bottom of the staircase, Charlie finds a bedchamber decorated in red with a large bed, upon which a young woman of perhaps 20 lies cowering. The girl tries to evade Charlie, but he catches her by the throat and forces himself upon her. The girl cries for mercy, but her protests only make Charlie laugh. He continues his assault vigorously and believes that, but for the law, he would have murdered the young girl. The moment of love, as Charlie calls it, is fleeting, like all human happiness. When he has finished, he feels an overwhelming sense of revulsion at his actions and sympathy for the weeping girl. He leaves the bedchamber without looking at the girl and walks home penniless and alone. He concludes his story by saying that it was the happiest day of his life.

Chapter 3

After reviewing his financial situation, Orwell discovers that he has only 450 francs saved, with an additional 36 francs a week that he earns from teaching English. He pays his rent two months in advance and begins looking for a job, thinking that the remaining 250 francs would be more than enough to carry him through until he secures employment. Orwell experiences a setback in his plans after the arrival at his hotel of an Italian of disreputable appearance. The Italian manages to make several duplicate keys for other rooms (including Orwell's) and systematically robs the other boarders before disappearing. Orwell loses all his money except 47 francs that he had left in a pocket of his pants. He then revises his plan and attempts to live on six francs a day.

The robbery forces Orwell to face his first real experience of poverty, a situation that everyone instinctively fears. He perceives that the condition of poverty is much different than he had expected. Poverty compels him to be secretive about his financial situation. Orwell goes out at mealtimes, as though he will go to a restaurant, but instead he loafs in the Luxembourg Gardens before smuggling home a meal of bread and margarine. He discovers many hidden obstacles to maintaining a budget of six francs per day. A bug in the milk that is boiling over the spirit lamp spoils one meal. To avoid meeting a prosperous friend, he ducks into a café and so must purchase something. Poverty teaches Orwell what it means to be hungry. A diet of bread and margarine makes it difficult to pass shop windows filled with all kinds of extravagant foods. He also discovers the boredom of being poor, because he has no money for entertainment of any kind, and his hunger leaves him with barely enough energy to rouse himself out of bed.

Orwell exhausts his savings of 47 francs after three weeks and even pawns some of his clothing for a small pittance. His rent is coming due and he foresees difficult days ahead. One redeeming quality of poverty, he discovers, is its propensity to annihilate the future. The poor can think only about immediate circumstances. However, poverty does offer a kind of consolation: When you have truly hit bottom, you discover "you can stand it. It takes off a lot of anxiety."

Chapter 4

He descends further into poverty when the two students he tutors in English decide to give up their studies. He packs up all but a few articles of clothing and makes another trip to the pawn shop, but not before informing Madame F. One cannot take clothing out of the hotel without permission. Orwell expects to receive 200 to 300 francs for the clothes and packing case, but he gets only 70 francs. A few days later, however, he unexpectedly receives 200 francs from an article he had previously published. He pays 200 francs toward the next month's rent, though it could mean he would have to go several weeks with very little food. Now desperate for money, Orwell must find employment. He remembers a friend named Boris, a Russian waiter who had previously offered to help him out if he was ever in trouble.

Orwell had first met Boris in the public ward of a hospital and describes him as a "big soldierly man of about 35," who was once good-looking but who has now grown fat from lying too long in a hospital bed. Boris's parents were killed during the Russian Revolution and Boris had served in the Second Siberian Rifles during the World War I. After the war he came to Paris and eventually worked his way up to the position of head waiter at the Hotel Scribe just prior to his illness. He hoped one day to open his own small bistro on the Right Bank.

Boris had often talked of his period of service in the military as the best time of his life. He never abandoned hope that he would one day be rich enough to open a restaurant of his own. Most waiters, Orwell would discover, thought this way about the future—perhaps to justify their work as waiters. Boris also told amusing stories about his life as a waiter. One can die poor, he explained, or one can strike it rich. The life of a waiter is a gamble, because one stands or falls on tips, which are sometimes quite large. Orwell listened to Boris's stories over games of chess in the public ward. Boris also encouraged Orwell to give up writing, which he called Bosh, and to become a waiter; he even offered to help him find a job if he ever required one. Orwell resolves to take him up on his offer.

Chapter 5

Orwell tracks down Boris at a shabby hotel, and the patron directs him upstairs. Boris is naked and asleep in a cramped attic apartment furnished with only an iron bed and a rickety washstand. His old friend wakes and explains that he shares the room with a Jew, who lets him use the room and pays him a few francs a day to satisfy a previous debt. Boris sleeps on the floor at night. When his roommate leaves in the morning, he moves to the bed. Boris is obviously starving, so Orwell runs out for bread. The meal cheers Boris up considerably.

After his meal, Boris assures Orwell that they have good prospects for employment. He knows about a new Russian bistro that will open soon. In the meantime, they leave the apartment at midday for a small café on the rue du Rivoli that serves as something of an employment bureau and meeting place for hotel employees looking for work. After two hours, they move on to the Hotel Scribe to speak to the manager, but he never appears. They return at nightfall to Orwell's hotel and eat a dinner of bread and chocolate. Boris again grows animated by the food and returns to the topic of their certain future success, even waxing on about the adventures they will have as waiters in Nice or Biarritz. Too tired to walk home, he falls asleep on Orwell's floor.

Chapter 6

Orwell and Boris have no success in their search for employment. The mixture of Orwell's inexperience and Boris's bad leg makes many prospective employers dismiss them on the spot. They enroll at agencies and answer advertisements, but nothing materializes. Orwell receives a notice about an Italian man looking for an English teacher. He borrows Boris's coat and uses what little money he has left for bus fare to get to the agency, only to discover that the Italian has changed his mind and left the country. Desperate for money, Boris writes to a former mistress for assistance; she responds sweetly that she cannot help but is certain their fortunes will improve soon.

The lack of money continues to frustrate them. They take their meals in Orwell's room; they subsist principally on bread, milk, cheese, and potatoes cooked into a soup over a spirit lamp. On some mornings, Boris collapses in despair and refuses to look for work. On other days, Boris and Orwell while away the day with chess or reading old newspapers.

Chapter 7

Orwell finally runs out of money and endures three days without food. On the first, he borrows a fishing rod and tries to catch his dinner in the Seine. He considers pawning his overcoat on the second day but decides instead to stay in bed reading. His hunger makes him almost completely inert. On the third day without food, he goes to Boris to see if he can share in his daily allowance of two francs from the Jew, but he finds Boris in a rage. The Jew has refused to pay him any more money. They decide to pawn their overcoats, but they must get Boris's things out of the hotel without the patron seeing them. Orwell manages to get to the pawnshop, but the broker refuses to accept any item not wrapped in something. Orwell returns to Boris, and they attempt to smuggle his suitcase past the patron. While Boris distracts him with conversation, Orwell sneaks out, but the broker again refuses to accommodate him because he has no identity papers. Frustrated and hungry, Orwell retrieves his papers and goes to a different pawnshop nearer to his hotel, only to find the shop closed until the afternoon. Orwell finds a five-sous coin while walking the streets to kill time; adding this to his remaining five sous, he purchases a pound of potatoes and returns to Boris to boil them up for their dinner.

At four in the afternoon, Orwell returns to the pawnshop and has another stroke of luck. Instead of the 10 or 20 francs he expects to get for the overcoats, he receives 50 francs; with their newfound wealth, they purchase bread, wine, meat, and alcohol for the spirit lamp. Boris resolves after his dinner to look up a friend who owes him money, but they quarrel violently for hours before going on a drinking spree that exhausts Boris's entire share of the money from the overcoats. He spends the night at the house of another Russian refugee, and Orwell returns to his hotel with eight francs and plenty of tobacco in his pocket.

Chapter 8

Boris turns up later with 20 francs, which he has borrowed from a Russian refugee. He also hatches another plan to earn money, this time by taking advantage of Orwell's writing skills. He knows about a secret group of communists looking for someone to write articles for a Moscow daily paper. Orwell initially objects to participating, because he had gotten into some trouble with the Paris police after they discovered him leaving the offices of a communist weekly paper. Boris eventually convinces him to meet with the group. The communists occupy rooms above a laundry shop, and Orwell and Boris arrive to find the way barred by a large Russian man demanding a password. The communists tell them that they must bring a parcel of laundry with them the next time they come to avoid drawing the attention of the police. They eventually get waved in and enter a shabby and sparsely furnished room with a tattered poster of Lenin hanging on one wall.

Boris talks briefly with another large Russian man in shirtsleeves, obviously the head of the group, who requires a membership fee of 20 francs. Boris gives him five francs as a down payment, and the man interrogates Orwell about his qualifications. Eventually satisfied, he explains to Orwell that he will send word by mail in a day or two with further instructions. Boris and Orwell leave the laundry shop and spend the next several days checking the mail for news from the communists, but nothing ever arrives. After a few more days, they return to the laundry shop to find the upper rooms abandoned. The shopkeeper downstairs says that the Russians left some days before without leaving any word of their future whereabouts. Orwell determines that they have been the victims of a scam, and that the group of "communists" has probably already set up shop elsewhere to bilk other unsuspecting Russian refugees out of the 20-franc membership fee. He does admit that the business about bringing a parcel of laundry was a nice touch.

Chapter 9

Boris and Orwell search for work over the next three days, while their money quickly runs out. They have two possible opportunities for employment: the first, at Hotel X in the Place de la Concorde; the second, at the forthcoming Russian bistro, owned by a Russian refugee who has recently returned to town. Boris takes Orwell to meet him at the still-unfinished restaurant. The man—a fattish, dignified sort—promises them positions as soon as the restaurant opens. He expects to open in two weeks' time, and Boris receives this news with renewed optimism for the future. Orwell, however, remains skeptical.

For the next two days, Boris and Orwell survive on bread rubbed with garlic. They still have no success in their job search, and Orwell's money eventually runs out. He spends another day in bed without any food. That night he awakens to shouts outside his window. Boris rouses him out of bed and tells him that he has found work at Hotel X. He also throws up a loaf of bread that he smuggled out of the hotel. Boris tells him to meet each day at the Tuilleries during his afternoon break, and he will bring whatever food he can smuggle from the hotel. Orwell meets him for the next three days and eats the scraps of food out of newspaper wrappings. When a *plongeur* (dishwasher) suddenly leaves his job at the hotel, Boris recommends Orwell for the position.

Chapter 10

Orwell arrives the next morning at Hotel X, a large building with a classical façade. The service staff enters the hotel by a small door leading into the hotel's lower floors. At the door, an Italian man holding the title of *chef du personnel* (or staff manager) interviews him about his qualifications. Initially put off by his lack of experience, the man decides that Orwell could be useful for helping the other staff practice their English; the hotel's clients are mostly Americans. Through a vast series of underground corridors, which remind Orwell of the lower decks of a steamship, the Italian leads him to a small, stiflingly hot cellar with a sink and some gas ovens. A waiter—also Italian—advises Orwell to mind his work and threatens to make things difficult for him if he slacks off.

Orwell starts working immediately—his job entails washing dishes, cleaning the employee dining room, and fetching meals for the waiters, among other things—and his shift lasts from 7 A.M. to a quarter past 9 P.M. Fetching meals requires the greatest effort, as the kitchen is hot almost beyond bearing. Twelve chefs tend the fires and roundly curse Orwell when he makes the slightest mistake. At 4 P.M. the *chef du personnel* returns and tells Orwell to take a break until five. He has no time to leave the hotel, so he settles for sneaking a cigarette in the bathroom. The hotel prohibits smoking by the staff.

At a quarter past nine, the Italian waiter tells Orwell to come upstairs for his dinner, a fair meal consisting of the leftovers from the higher employees' meals and a ration of two liters of wine. The waiter tells Orwell about his life, and they generally get along well. Orwell thinks that he will like his new position and hopes that the job will last, since he was only hired as a temporary replacement. He later gets his wish when the *chef du personnel* stops him on his way out to offer a permanent position. Resolved to honor his promise to work at the Russian bistro, Orwell declines in favor of a two-week position, but the hotel has no such contract. That night he recounts the event to Boris, who explodes in anger over Orwell's honesty. He convinces Orwell to return to the hotel and beg for the permanent position. Orwell notes that he should not have worried about inconveniencing the hotel, as the owner would never think twice about firing employees if it suited him.

Chapter 11

Orwell works six days a week at Hotel X—four days in the cafeteria with Boris, one day assisting the waiter on the fourth floor, and another substituting for the woman who washes up in the dining room. The cafeteria is in a small, hot cellar crowded with equipment. The cafeteria's other staff include Mario, an "excitable Italian," and a small "animallike" man called the Magyar. Every two hours, the workload grows frantic. Orwell and his companions send meals to waiters on the upper floors by way of two dumbwaiters. Apart from the physical strain, work in the cafeteria exacts a heavy toll mentally because each of the staff members must remember so many details. During periodic lulls in activity upstairs, the cafeteria staff cleans counters, sweeps the floors, and polishes the brass. Often they fall behind in their work during busy periods, but Mario keeps them in line. A veteran employee of 14 years, he possesses an astonishing ability to manage multiple tasks.

The cafeteria shift breaks at 2 P.M., and the staff emerges from the basement to relax in a nearby bistro if they have any money. At 4:45 P.M., the cafeteria shift resumes for the dinner rush, and Orwell can barely describe the chaos of this period of the day, during which 200 to 300 hundred hotel guests order individual multicourse dinners. By 8:30 P.M., the rush is over, and the staff has only to clean up the cafeteria until the shift ends at about 9 P.M.

After his first week at Hotel X, Orwell needs a holiday and gets drunk with his friends at the bistro below his hotel. Early the next morning, the night watchman from the hotel shakes him awake and tells him that he is needed to fill in at the hotel. Still reeling from his drinking binge, Orwell reluctantly agrees. He soon discovers that within an hour of his working the shift, the hangover vanishes. Like a Turkish bath, the heat of the hotel cellar leeches the alcohol out of his system.

Chapter 12

Orwell spends two days each week helping the waiter on the fourth floor. These are his best days at the hotel. The waiter, an engaging and handsome youth of 24, had worked his way up to that position from the bottom of the hotel business. Orwell's worst day at the hotel is Sunday, when he has to fill in for the old woman who washes up in the dining room. The shift lasts for 13 hours, and the poor quality of the cleaning supplies makes the work slow and ineffectual. Apart from washing, Orwell also has to fetch meals for the waiters and serve them at the table, during which the waiters often treat him with considerable insolence. Orwell notes that he sometimes has to use his fists to get any civility from the waiters.

Orwell's vantage point near the dining room on these days gives him new insight into the hotel business and the lives of waiters. The filthy washroom stands only a few feet from the finely appointed dining room where wealthy patrons take their meals. The waiters often wash up in water that holds clean dishware, as they transform themselves from the sweating, harried creatures in the back hallways to the gliding, sophisticated servers in the dining room.

Chapter 13

At Hotel X, Orwell is introduced to the class structure that exists among the staff. All hotel employees conform to an elaborate caste system. Each employee—from the manager down to the lowly *plongeur*—enjoys specific privileges, as well as rates of pay. Waiters, cooks, cellar men, and *plongeurs* all steal food at a rate that corresponds to their rank of importance. Employees also steal from each other. The doorkeeper is perhaps the most wanton thief in the hotel. Orwell calculates that he has lost nearly 114 francs to the doorkeeper in six weeks' time.

He also notes that specific jobs in the hotel seem to correspond to different races. Office employees, cooks, and sewing women are invariably French. Italians and Germans make up the majority of the wait staff. *Plongeurs* come from a variety of ethnic groups—Middle Eastern, African, European. Apart from racial differences, hotel employees differ as to their personal backgrounds. Some have arrived in France without passports and are working illegally. Others are well educated and come from prosperous families. Some of the staff are even thought to be spies. The strangest character in Orwell's experience is a Serbian hired on as a temporary worker for the day. The Serbian worked well until midday, after which he blatantly shirked his duties, even going so far as to smoke openly in the back hallways—something expressly forbidden. The Serbian insults the manager vulgarly when confronted and loses his job. Boris asks for an explanation of his behavior, and the Serbian explains that the hotel must pay a full day's wages for anyone who works past midday. His shift ends at two, and he feels disinclined to work any longer than he has to for the same wage. The Serbian adds that this method has worked at hotels all over Paris, but it has the disadvantage of only being able to work once at any given hotel.

Chapter 14

Orwell begins to understand the principles by which the hotel operates. The chaos that occurs at mealtimes is actually a normal consequence of this type of work. Meals must be prepared on demand, and there are usually many people demanding them at the same time. The hotel staff often quarrels and hurls insults and curses at each other, but this, too, serves a specific purpose. Such behavior allows them to blow off steam. As a result, they work harder and more efficiently.

Perhaps the most important quality among the staff is the pride they take in their work, which differs with respect to the various jobs at the hotel. Cooks consider themselves artists. Orwell calls them the most workmanlike and the least servile. They possess amazing memories and know instinctively when to prepare each dish. Waiters, on the other hand, excel at being servile. Their work gives them the mentality of a snob rather than a workman. Being in such close proximity to the wealthy, the waiters identify with the rich and adopt their high-handed manners. Many waiters make an excellent living, so much so that some of them on the Grand Boulevard pay for the privilege of working at a café. Even among the lowly *plongeurs* there exists a level of pride in their work, but it is "the pride of the drudge." Put another way, it is the pride a man takes in knowing that he is up to any task, no matter how difficult. The plongeur has no escape from his job. He never makes enough money to save, and he works too many hours to train for another vocation. The goal of a *plongeur,* rather, is to become known as a *debrouillard,* or a resourceful person.

Hotel X succeeds because the staff members know their jobs and carry them out conscientiously. The weakness, Orwell notes, exists in the difference between what the customer pays for (good service) and what the employees provide (the appearance of good service). Behind the service doors, the hotel is a filthy place. The food is served with the appearance of artistry and cleanliness, but it is prepared with little regard for sanitation. The cooks and waiters finger the food indiscriminately. Food that has been dropped on the floor is wiped and served to the guests. As Orwell explains, "The hotel employee is too busy getting food ready to remember that it is meant to be eaten." As to the owner of the hotel, the patron engages in wholesale swindling with respect to the quality of products and their prices. The food is of inferior quality, but patrons pay top prices. In fact, the patrons (mostly Americans) are particularly easy to swindle.

Chapter 15

Orwell hears unusual stories from the staff at the hotel, often involving a disreputable cast of dope fiends, debauchers, and thieves. Valenti, the young waiter from the fourth floor, tells Orwell an unusual story from his past.

Compelled by extreme poverty to go without food for five days, Valenti had no strength to get out of bed or to wash himself. On the fifth day, his extreme hunger forced him to take an unlikely step. He noticed a faded print of a woman on the wall of his room. Thinking that she must be Saint Eloise (the patron saint of the quarter), Valenti decided to pray for help. As he prayed, he promised to burn a candle for her if his prayer were answered. Five minutes later, a friend arrives, a portly peasant girl named Marie, to check up on him. She was alarmed by his condition and asked if she could help. They looked around the room for something to pawn and discovered an oil bidon, which Valenti could return for a deposit of three and a half francs. Marie returned the oil bidon and brought back food for Valenti. After his meal, he decided to send Marie out for cigarettes with the little money left over, but he remembered his promise to burn a candle for Saint Eloise. He showed the picture on his wall to Marie, who began to laugh hysterically. She informed him that the picture does not in fact depict Saint Eloise but rather Suzanne May, a prostitute after whom the hotel was named. Valenti decided that he didn't need to burn a candle for a prostitute and sent Marie out for cigarettes.

Chapter 16

Orwell and Boris decide one day to visit the Russian bistro, the Auberge de Jehan Cottard, where they have been promised jobs. No further work has been done on the interior, and in fact the owner asks to borrow five francs from Orwell. He insists that the restaurant will be ready in two more weeks and introduces them to the new cook, a large Russian woman who claims to have been a singer.

In the meantime, Orwell's life at the hotel continues, and he begins to adjust to the daily routine. He gets up quite early and fights for a place on the metro among all the other working-class folk. Then he descends into the hotel cellar to work until two in the afternoon. In the interval before his afternoon shift, he usually sleeps. If he has money he goes to a bistro. Most of the *plongeurs* spend their break in this manner. Some visit a nearby brothel on the rue de Sièges, which charges low rates and is a favorite among hotel workers.

On his days off, Orwell lounges in bed until noon. After lunch and a few drinks, he goes back to bed. Sleep becomes more than a necessity for a *plongeur.* It is a profound pleasure. To illustrate this point, Orwell recounts the story of a murder that took place outside his hotel. The victim lay on the street with a broken skull. Orwell sees the three murderers fleeing down the street. Some of the guests go down to see if the man is alive, but they soon return to their beds. Working people, Orwell explains, have no time to lose over a murder. The job at Hotel X has taught Orwell the importance of sleep, just as poverty has taught him the importance of food.

Chapter 17

Orwell usually spends his Saturday nights at the bistro below his hotel. The small brick-floored room is usually packed with 20 people or more, and the noise is deafening. The revelers sing "La Marseillaise" or the "Internationale," in groups or individually. Everyone is happy with the world and their place in it. At midnight, a hush falls over the crowd as Furex, the Limousin stonemason, rises for his expected speech. Furex works hard all week and drinks himself blind on Saturday nights. Madame F. keeps an eye on Furex to prevent him from wasting all his money on drinks. While he is sober, Furex is a devoted communist, but after a few liters of wine, he becomes a violent patriot. When sufficiently drunk, he stands and gives a patriotic speech in the same manner and using the same words each time, at one point even partially undressing to reveal a scar he received during the Battle of Verdun. People from all over the quarter would come to the bistro to watch this spectacle. Sometimes the other patrons bait Furex. After convincing him to sing "La Marseillaise," a few of the strongest men hold his arms while the peasant girl Azaya shouts "Vive l'Allemagne!" at a safe distance. Furex turns purple with rage, but he can do nothing. Finally exhausted, he grows limp or sometimes is sick from the wine. The next day, he appears quiet and civil with a copy of the communist paper *L'Humanité.*

After midnight, the serious drinking begins. Some patrons continue to sing, but most talk loudly about love affairs, fishing in the Seine, or the coming workers' revolution. The mood becomes more contemplative as the night wears on. By one in the morning, the patrons are no longer happy. Madame F. begins to water the wine, patrons grow quarrelsome, and the girls run the risk of too much attention from drunken men. Patrons soon begin to drift out. By half past one, the world is no longer a good place, and the patrons see themselves as nothing more than underpaid working people who are shamefully drunk. Some head into the yard to be sick, while most go home to sleep for 10 hours or more. The Saturday-night drinking binge, the interlude that made their lives worth living, is over.

Chapter 18

On another such Saturday night at the bistro, Charlie, whose sordid story is recounted in chapter 2, rises to demand the crowd's attention for a story. Hard up and with no food for three days while waiting for money to arrive from home, Charlie grows desperate for a way to get food. The woman he lives with, an uneducated peasant named Yvonne, complains ceaselessly about her hunger. In a moment of self-described brilliance, Charlie remembers that the government maternity hospital provides free meals for pregnant women. He convinces Yvonne to pretend that she is pregnant by putting a cushion in her dress. The plan works perfectly. Yvonne receives hearty meals each day and manages to smuggle a little extra food home for Charlie until his money arrives.

A year passes, and Charlie is out walking with Yvonne. They meet a nurse from the government maternity hospital who recognizes Yvonne. The nurse asks how she is and if her baby was a boy. Yvonne says no. "A girl?" the nurse asks. Yvonne says no again. The nurse grows perplexed, and Yvonne is on the verge of confessing the deception. At the last moment, Charlie intercedes by saying that Yvonne had given birth to twins. The nurse is delighted and embraces Yvonne in congratulations.

Chapter 19

After five or six weeks at Hotel X, Boris disappears one day without explanation. When Orwell meets him later that evening, Boris tells him that the Auberge de Jehan Cottard will open the next morning and that Orwell should give his notice at the hotel. Orwell quits the Hotel X and shows up at the restaurant the following morning to find it locked. He searches for Boris and finds him in bed with his new mistress. Boris explains that the restaurant still needs a few minor alterations. Later that morning, they unlock the restaurant and discover that very little has actually been done since the last time they were there. The kitchen still needs furnishing, and the electricity and water have not yet been connected. The restaurant appears to need at least 10 days of work before it can open, and the owner is still short of money. The staff has apparently been engaged early in order to get them to do the alterations without pay.

Despite Orwell's alarm, Boris remains hopeful. He has retrieved his coattails from the pawnshop and believes that everything will arrange itself. The bistro begins to take shape as Boris and Orwell begin to clean it up. A third employee, the waiter Jules, does little to assist them. He is a Magyar and a communist and prefers to tell stories while the others work. The cook sometimes looks in on things but weeps when she sees the poor state of the kitchen. Meanwhile, the owner manages to disappear quickly whenever money is needed for the restaurant. The staff is instructed to tell anyone who is looking for him that he has gone out of town. Orwell's money begins to run out, and he is back to eating dry bread. Jules gets angrier each day over the delays and tries to convince Orwell not to work.

After 10 days spent in this fashion, Orwell is once again penniless and desperate. He is behind on his rent, and on the 10th day he must go without food or tobacco. He asks the owner for an advance on his wages, and the owner promptly disappears. Unwilling to face the manager at his hotel, Orwell spends the night on a bench in the boulevard. His luck turns on the following day. The owner of the restaurant reaches an agreement with his creditors, and the kitchen furnishings (stoves, pots, and pans) arrive. Orwell also receives an advance and enjoys his first hot meal in nearly two weeks. Workmen are brought in to finish the alterations, which are made hastily, and the tables and linens are assembled. The owner has cut corners in the dining room. Instead of baize, smelly army blankets are used under the table linen. The entire staff works late that night to prepare for the opening. Orwell and Jules miss the last metro and spend the night on the bistro floor. They wake in the morning to the sight of two large rats nibbling on a ham in the dining room, which Orwell considers an inauspicious sign.

Chapter 20

At the newly opened Auberge de Jehan Cottard, Orwell holds a position similar to that at Hotel X, though the premises and equipment are far inferior. Orwell learns just how dismal conditions can get at many small restaurants in Paris. The kitchen is filthy and small with no baking oven. Joints of meat must be sent out to a nearby bakery. The kitchen also has no larder, so vegetables and meats have to be stored in a shed in the yard, and animals raid it at will. When he is washing the pots and pans, Orwell has to make do with only cold water. He wipes the congealed grease off the dishes with bits of newspaper. The owner has difficulties with many of his creditors, so the linens often get delayed at the cleaners. The inspector of labor takes issue with the lack of any French employees at the restaurant, but Orwell speculates that the owner has probably bribed him out of causing any problems.

In these conditions, Orwell works nearly 18 hours each shift. As the head waiter, Boris works even longer hours. Orwell eventually settles into a routine at the restaurant that makes his life at Hotel X seem easy in comparison. He gets up early each morning and takes the metro to the bistro. The shift begins with food preparation and washing up, but each task seems to be preempted by other tasks, and nothing ever seems to get finished on time. The stress of these conditions creates friction among the staff. Orwell has terrible quarrels with the cook, who has nervous breakdowns several times a day. The bistro opens at 11 A.M. Until then, the day moves at a manageable pace. During the lunch rush, however, the pace becomes chaotic. The waiters have a moment of calm between three and five in the afternoon, but Orwell and the cook must work furiously to prepare for the dinner rush. They survive without breaks by drinking strong tea, which they keep brewing throughout the day.

By 5 P.M., the chaos begins again. The owner keeps the same long hours as the rest of the staff, but he does very little work beyond standing all day at the bar and greeting the guests. His wife does most of the managing of the bistro. At 10 P.M., Orwell takes his dinner with the cook and washes up as much as possible before leaving for the last metro home. If he misses the last train, he sleeps at the bistro. The owner often stops him on his way out to give him a glass of brandy, a small compensation for the day's labors.

Chapter 21

Orwell continues his busy schedule at the bistro for the next two weeks, with a slight increase in hours as it grows in popularity. The hours at the bistro have begun to take a toll on him physically. He has almost no time to attend to personal matters or even read a newspaper. He decides to write to his friend B. in London to see if he can find a job for him in England. After the first week at the bistro, the employees are no longer on speaking terms with one another, and the quarrels grow more frequent and petty. Orwell fights with the cook over the placement of the kitchen garbage can. Orwell quarrels even with Boris.

Meanwhile, the kitchen becomes filthier and the rats grow more bold. Orwell wonders if there is a restaurant in the world dirtier than the Auberge de Jehan Cottard. The rest of the staff assures him that there are worse places, and despite its filthiness, the bistro becomes a modest success. All the initial customers are Russian refugees, but soon other foreigners show up. One day, the first French customer arrives, and he receives special treatment. The quality of a bistro, he notes, is measured by how many French customers it attracts. The next night the Frenchman returns with a few friends. Orwell speculates that the bistro owes its success to the sharpness of its knives, an essential feature of all successful restaurants.

Orwell hears back from his friend B. in London, who informs him that a position is available for someone to look after a disabled youth. Orwell imagines an easier life somewhere in the countryside, where he can get more sleep. B. includes five pounds to cover the cost of passage to England and to retrieve his things from the pawnshop. Orwell gives one day's notice at the bistro, which catches the owner off-guard. He comes up 30 francs short in Orwell's wages but offers him a glass of expensive brandy to make up the difference. Orwell later learns that the bistro has engaged a capable Czech *plongeur* to replace him.

Chapter 22

Orwell reflects on the life of a Paris *plongeur*—not just the physical details but the possible social significance. The *plongeur* is little more than a modern slave, working his life away at tasks that lack any essential meaning. He makes only enough to keep himself alive, while offering almost no opportunity for marriage and even less leisure time for real thought. If he could reflect on his situation, he would not remain a *plongeur*. He continues to exist, like every other sort of drudge, because modern civilization creates the conditions that perpetuate such work, but the work itself is not necessary to civilization. Many assume that manual labor is necessary in and of itself, but it may exist only to create a false sort of luxury.

The life of a *plongeur,* in Orwell's estimation, resembles that of a rickshaw driver or a quarry pony.

Old and often diseased, rickshaw drivers work endless hours, much like *plongeurs.* They work like this, Orwell concludes, for no other reason than that Orientals consider walking to be vulgar. Quarry ponies also work like drudges all day and suffer the stings of the whip. Rickshaw drivers and quarry ponies, like the Paris *plongeurs,* provide only minor convenience, which means little next to the misery they endure. Orwell poses a question: Is the *plongeur* any more necessary to civilization and its luxuries than rickshaw drivers or quarry ponies? Large hotels and restaurants provide only the appearance of luxury, and their services are never better than what can be found in a private house. None benefits from the existence of the *plongeur* except the proprietors of hotels and restaurants who grow rich off the profits. Smart hotels provide services for which patrons pay exorbitant prices but which they never really wanted.

If the *plongeur* provides only essentially meaningless services, why should he continue in this way of life? Orwell suggests that society's desire to perpetuate meaningless work is based on a fear of the mob. If the working classes had no work, they might become dangerous. They might even find a way to rise above their social class and become a threat to the upper classes. Fear of the mob, Orwell suggests, is based on a false distinction between the rich and the poor that anyone would see through if they spent any time among the poor. Rich and poor people differ only with respect to their incomes. "To sum up. A *plongeur* is a slave and a wasted slave, doing stupid and largely unnecessary work. He is kept at work, ultimately, because of a vague feeling that he would be dangerous if he had leisure."

Chapter 23

After his final day at the Auberge de Jehan Cottard, Orwell sleeps for nearly 24 hours. He spends the next two days cleaning up and getting his clothes out of the pawnshop. He puts on his best suit and returns to the bistro to splurge on an English beer. Boris regrets that Orwell has left just as the bistro has become successful. Orwell would later learn that Boris was making 100 francs a day and had set up a new mistress. Orwell spends another day walking through the quarter to say good-bye to old friends. Charlie tells Orwell a story about the famous miser Roucolle who once lived in the quarter. Orwell knows that the story is probably a lie, but he finds it entertaining nonetheless. Roucolle had died a few years before Orwell arrived in Paris, but he had been frequently discussed. He was an uncompromising miser who survived on damaged vegetables and cat's meat and who wore newspapers for undergarments. He used wainscoting from his hotel room for firewood despite having a personal fortune of half a million francs.

As the story goes, a Jew comes to the quarter one day with a scheme to buy cocaine and sell it for a large profit in England. A young Pole introduces the Jew to Roucolle. It takes several weeks for the Jew to convince Roucolle to part with 6,000 francs for the cocaine. The Jew delivers the cocaine and disappears. News of the transaction circulates in the quarter, and the police arrive the next morning at Roucolle's hotel and begin searching the rooms on the lower floor. The Pole pleads with Roucolle to get rid of the cocaine, but he refuses to lose his investment. He finally submits to hiding the cocaine in tins of face powder, which he then displays prominently to avoid suspicion. The police later arrive and search the room thoroughly, but they find nothing. The inspector examines the tins, and Roucolle can barely contain his fear. Suspicious of Roucolle's behavior, the inspector arrests him and the Pole and sends the tins to the lab for analysis.

Under interrogation, Roucolle alternately weeps, moans, and prays, to the amusement of the police officers. The results of the analysis of the tins come back after an hour, and a police officer informs the commissioner that the tins contain face powder, not cocaine. Roucolle and the Pole are subsequently released. The Jew had swindled Roucolle with a scheme that he had employed successfully throughout the quarter. While the Pole is grateful to be free, Roucolle grieves for the loss of his money. He suffers some kind of stroke after three days and dies two weeks later.

Chapter 24

Orwell books a third-class ticket on a steamer to Tilbury, England. Aboard the ship, he meets a Romanian couple traveling to England for their honeymoon. His joy at returning home leads him to tell elaborate lies about the beauty of his country. After his dire poverty in Paris, England seems to him a kind of paradise. When he lands at Tilbury pier, he notices the confusion on the faces of the Romanian couple, whose first view of the idyllic England described by Orwell is an ugly stucco hotel. Orwell next visits his friend B. about the job caring for the disabled youth. He finds, however, that the family has gone abroad for a month. He leaves before asking B. for a loan of more money. After spending most of the day in the streets, Orwell looks for a place to sleep. He has only 19 shillings and six pence. After paying for a cheap room at a family hotel, he has only 12 shillings left. In the morning, Orwell stores his belongings at the station cloakroom. He takes one of his suits to a rag shop in Lambeth and trades them for a cheaper set of clothes and a shilling. His new clothes are filthy, and Orwell notices the difference in how people treat him. Men on the street call him mate, and the women avoid him "as though he were a dead cat."

Orwell walks the streets until the evening and then looks for a place to sleep. A man on the street directs him to a house in Waterloo Road with the sign "Good Beds for Single Men." Orwell pays a shilling for a bed, but he finds the accommodations filthy. The sheets on the bed reek of sweat. Six men are already in bed. During the night, Orwell wakes frequently from the noise of the other boarders. He gets only about an hour of sleep all night. In the morning, Orwell sees more clearly the filth of the room. The washbasin is caked with sludge, and he decides to leave the house without washing. He walks to a coffee shop on Tower Hill for tea and bread with margarine, which is known throughout London as tea and two slices. A sign on the wall near his table warns against pocketing the sugar packets. After Orwell pays the bill, he is left with 8 shillings and two pence.

Chapter 25

Orwell's supply of money covers his expenses over the next four nights. He travels east and spends the first night at a lodging house in Pennyfields. The house accommodates between 50 and 100 men, and they are lodged in groups of 15 to 20 men per dormitory. Well managed by a deputy, the house turns a good profit for the owner, as houses of this type generally do. The fee for a night's residence is either nine pence or a shilling. A shilling buys a little more room between beds. All lodgers have access to the downstairs kitchen, where they can use the kitchen fires for no additional charge. In return, the lodgers take alternate turns cleaning the kitchen and the dormitories. A man named Steve holds the position of Head of House and arbitrates all disputes among the other lodgers.

The lodgers often gather in the kitchen for games, singing, or washing their clothes. The kitchen is a dim and stiflingly hot place. It is common among the lodgers to share food with each other, particularly with the men out of work. One of the most indigent of the lodgers, a man called Pore Brown, regularly received support from the other lodgers. Several old-age pensioners lodge at the Pennyfields house, and Orwell is impressed with one of them for his ability to survive on 10 shillings a week. Orwell spends much of his time during the days walking the streets, and he notes the differences between the people in England and those he saw in Paris. He notes that English people have less individuality than the French, they are less often drunk, and they are more likely to lounge around on street corners. Orwell is fascinated by the people he sees in neighborhoods throughout London: the pretty East London women, the Orientals at Limehouse, the Salvation Army services in the East India Dock Road. He even sees two Mormons attempting to address a mostly hostile crowd. On Middlesex Street, a harried mother argues with her unruly child. Orwell finds all this unusual after his long exile in Paris.

On Orwell's last night at Pennyfields, a quarrel erupts between two lodgers. An elderly man harangues a younger, stronger one for well over five minutes. He calls him all kinds of vulgar names and threatens violence while the other lodgers look on uncomfortably. Finally spent from his exertions, the old man collapses in exhaustion. Orwell later learns the cause of the quarrel: Someone had stolen the old man's supply of bread and margarine, which means that he must endure several days with nothing to eat. The younger man had taunted him about it. The next day, Orwell moves to a cheaper lodging house in Bow, as he only has one shilling and four pence left. The accommodations in Bow are far inferior to Pennyfields. The dormitory sleeps six men to a room, and the floor is covered with large beetles. During the night, a drunken man gets sick on the floor near Orwell's bed. Orwell notes, however, that the owners of the house were nice sorts and always ready to offer a cup of tea to any lodger at any time of the day or night.

Chapter 26

After a breakfast of tea and two slices and the purchase of half an ounce of tobacco, Orwell has only a halfpenny. He is not yet willing to ask B. for another loan, so he decides to look for a casual ward in Romton. He arrives late in the afternoon and meets an Irish tramp. The tramp is surprised when Orwell offers him some tobacco. He has not had a proper cigarette for a long time. The Irishman tells Orwell that the Romton casual ward—called a spike—is not as bad as some in other parts of the country, and he invites Orwell to join him for tea. A young woman distributes free tea and buns to tramps in the afternoon in exchange for leading them in prayers.

They go to a tin-roofed shed, where a long line of tramps is queued outside, waiting for admittance. Inside the shed are 30 or 40 hard chairs, a harmonium, and a gory-looking crucifix. The woman passes out the tea and buns and then leads the group of tramps in prayer and the singing of hymns. Though they are clearly not interested in salvation, the tramps do their best to follow along. Outside they grumble about having to pray for their meal. Orwell observes that the young woman has no wish to humiliate the men. She sincerely believes that the prayers and hymns are good for the men's souls, and the tea is excellent: ". . . we ought to have been grateful—still we were not."

Chapter 27

Orwell and the Irishman arrive at the Romton spike at 6 P.M. It is a dismal brick building in the corner of the workhouse yard surrounded by high walls and spotted with barred windows. The other tramps waiting for entry comprise a variety of ages and types, from hardened tramps to out-of-work clerks. While they wait, the tramps smoke and share stories about conditions in other spikes around the country. Each spike, Orwell discovers, has its advantages and disadvantages, and the seasoned tramps know each of them like the backs of their hands. They follow a circuit from spike to spike, particularly in the winter, because no tramp is allowed to stay at the same spike more than once in the same month. When the gates to the spike open, the tramps register their name, their trade, and their age. They must also include information about where they have come from and where they intend to go next. Orwell lists his trade as "painter." A spike official asks each tramp if they have any money, as it is prohibited to enter a spike with more than eight pence. If discovered by the officials, the money is confiscated. The tramps who have money, therefore, smuggle it into the spike in packets of tea or sugar. They also hide it in their personal papers, which are never searched.

After registration, each man is led into the spike by an official called the Tramp Major and the porter. The spike consists of a lavatory, a bathroom, and a long row of stone cells. The place has the look and smell of a prison. The tramps then file into the bathroom six at a time to be searched. They are not allowed to bring tobacco into the spike, but if they manage to smuggle it in successfully, they are allowed to smoke. The tramps often hide the tobacco in their boots. When they strip down for the search, they transfer it to their coats. The scene in the bathroom during the searches is repugnant. The men huddle, naked and filthy, in a small room with only two bathtubs. Fresh water is allowed only to men having a complete bath. Those not opting for the full bath often have to wash in water that other men have used to wash their dirty feet. After bathing, the porter ties the tramps' belongings into bundles and issues workhouse shirts. A dinner of bread smeared with margarine is brought over from the workhouse along with a pint of unsweetened cocoa. Each man is then assigned to a sleeping cell. If he has a friend with him, they bunk together. Otherwise, the men are assigned to other tramps. The cells are eight feet by five feet with eight-foot ceilings and a barred window at the top of one wall.

The door to the cells has a spy hole. The men are locked in for the night. Orwell is shocked to discover that the cells have no beds. The men must sleep on the stone floor.

Orwell and the companion assigned to him make themselves as comfortable as possible. It is necessary to use some of the blankets as a bed, but it is too cold not to use most of them for warmth. Sleep comes only in short intervals because of the hardness of the stone floor. Shortly after midnight, Orwell's companion makes sexual advances towards him, which Orwell easily rebuffs. However, Orwell cannot sleep for the rest of the night. Instead, he spends the night talking to his companion about the latter's life. He has been out of work for three years. His wife deserted him after he lost his job, and he has been away from women for so long that he barely remembers what they are like. Homosexuality, he adds, is quite common among tramps. In the morning, the porter unlocks the cells and wakes the men. Only one basin of water is provided for the men, so Orwell decides to forgo washing up. Breakfast consists of more bread and margarine, after which the men assemble in the yard to peel potatoes. Then each man is inspected by the workhouse doctor, primarily to detect signs of small pox. The tramps have every sort of ailment, but the exam is merely a formality. The doctor does nothing for any of the other diseases among the men. After the inspection, the men get their belongings back and receive a meal ticket worth six pence at cafes along the route they identified during registration on the previous night. Most men cannot read, so "scholars" (men who can read) must tell them how to use it. As Orwell had become better acquainted with the Irishman, whose name is Paddy Jaques, they decide to travel together to the spike in Edbury, 12 miles away. They stop at a café in Ilford to use their meal ticket and discover that the tramps are routinely cheated out of three or four pence of the value of their tickets by the café owners.

Chapter 28

Over the next two weeks, Orwell gets to know Paddy well. He offers an account of Paddy's life, as it seems to be fairly representative of the lives of tramps throughout England. A tallish man of about 35, Paddy has the look of a tramp even from a distance, though he dresses somewhat better than most men on the road. He carries a razor and a boot brush. Raised in Ireland, Paddy served two years in the military during World War I before landing a job at a metal-polish factory. He had been laid off from the factory two years prior to meeting Orwell. Ashamed of being a tramp, he had nonetheless picked up all the characteristics of the typical tramp. Paddy horded cigarette ends and collected food that he found along the street, though he was always willing to share with Orwell. Paddy was not a thief, though hunger and opportunity often tempted him. He also had two recurring themes of conversation: the humiliation of being a tramp, and the best way to obtain a free meal. Orwell finds Paddy's ignorance limitless and appalling. Paddy could read, but he hated books. He carefully guarded his store of matches, preferring to get a light from a stranger than to waste any of his precious stock.

Orwell identifies self-pity as the key to Paddy's character. Paddy spends a considerable amount of time complaining about his situation and envying those in better circumstances. He looks at women with a mixture of longing and hatred. Young and pretty women are so far above his station, but prostitutes are a constant source of desire. Paddy most desires employment, and the sight of a working man fills him with bitterness. He blames all foreigners, whom he refers to collectively as dagoes, for unemployment in England. Despite his prejudices, Orwell finds Paddy a good fellow, always eager to share his last bite of food with a friend. He would have been an able worker, Orwell speculates, if his diet of bread and margarine had not ravaged his health.

Chapter 29

While traveling to Edbury, Orwell tells Paddy that he can borrow more money from his friend in London. Paddy does not wish to miss out on a free meal, however, and the two continue on to the spike in Edbury. The spike there is much the same as the one in Romton, though all tobacco is prohibited. The Vagrancy Act allows tramps to be prosecuted for a variety of infractions, including smoking, but authorities generally just throw men out of the spike for breaking the rules. At Edbury, the men are not required to work, and the cells are a bit more comfortable. Meals consist of the familiar bread and margarine, but the men at Edbury receive tea instead of cocoa. The Tramp Major sells extra rations of tea in the morning and pockets the money. Each tramp receives bread and cheese for his midday meal when he leaves the spike. Orwell and Paddy take their meals and leave Edbury for London. Once there, they must wait eight hours for the lodging house to open. They have no money and nowhere to go, but they must keep on their feet. Tramps are not allowed to sit anywhere in the street. They can find no open churches to rest in, and the libraries have no available seats.

At six that evening, Paddy and Orwell go to the Salvation Army shelter. Beds cannot be purchased until 8 P.M., but they can enter if they buy cups of tea. Orwell finds the Salvation Army hall uncomfortably clean and cold. It is filled with decent-looking men seated on long wooden benches. The walls feature numerous signs that list prohibited behavior—especially gambling. Orwell is struck by the dreariness of the hall in comparison to the spikes. The broken-down men who frequent the Salvation Army still believe that they will reclaim their respectability. Two foreigners play chess without a board by calling out their moves. Another man breaks out in blasphemies whenever the officers in the hall are out of hearing, though Orwell later discovers him in a back room praying for help. He was obviously on the verge of starvation. After paying for their beds, Orwell and Paddy have five pence left over, which they spend on cheap food at a bar in the hall.

At 10 P.M. an officer marches up and down the hall blowing a whistle to announce the night's curfew. At seven the next morning, the officers shake those men not already awake. The routine, Orwell notes, is the same in all Salvation Army lodging houses. Though cheap and clean, these places operate too much like workhouses. Some even require the men to attend religious services. In Orwell's opinion, the Salvation Army thinks so much like a charitable organization that they cannot run a decent lodging house without making it stink of charity.

Later that morning, Orwell visits B.'s office and gets a loan of two pounds. Free of their money troubles temporarily, Orwell and Paddy spend the day in Trafalgar Square looking for one of Paddy's friends. They stay that night at a lodging house in a back alley of the Strand. It is an evil-smelling place and a regular haunt of "nancy boys." Orwell witnesses a strange exchange in the kitchen that night. A naked newspaper seller barters with another man to purchase his clothes. After settling on a price, the newspaper seller puts the other man's clothes on and gives him a few copies of his newspaper to cover himself. The dormitory is dark and crowded with about 15 beds, and it reeks of urine. As Orwell tries to fall asleep, a man leans over and introduces himself as a fellow Etonian. He had apparently noticed Orwell's educated accent earlier in the day. He begins to sing the Eton boating song but gets quickly shouted down by the other boarders. After producing a bottle of cherry brandy, the man falls heavily across Orwell's bed. Paddy helps the man back to his bed, where he climbs in fully dressed and with his boots on. About 50 years old, the man is fairly well dressed—the brandy alone indicated that the man was not as hard up as he seemed. Orwell considers it likely that he has come to the lodging house for the nancy boys. Orwell wakes later in the evening to discover the man next to him trying to steal his money from under his pillow, all the while pretending to be asleep. He tells Paddy about the attempted theft the next morning. Such thefts are apparently common occurrences in lodging houses.

Chapter 30

In the morning, Orwell again accompanies Paddy to look for his friend, a man named Bozo, who works as a screever (pavement artist). Paddy thinks that they might find him in Lambeth, but they eventually track him down on the embankment near Waterloo Bridge. He is busy copying an image of Winston Churchill in chalk from an original drawing in a penny notebook. Bozo is a small man, hook-nosed with curly dark hair and a badly deformed leg. Considered by most to be a Jew, Bozo vigorously denies this and calls his nose Roman. He also prides himself on his alleged resemblance to the emperor Vespasian. Bozo talks in a heavy but understandable cockney accent. Paddy and Orwell stay for a while with him, and Bozo gives an account of his life. He describes himself as a serious screever (one who uses proper colors, like a painter). He specializes in political and sporting cartoons. He shows Orwell his notebook and explains that he bases his drawings on current political events. He does no cartoons about socialism, because the police will not tolerate it. When the weather is fair, Bozo can make as much as three quid between Friday and Sunday. Accounting for rainy days when he cannot work, Bozo clears about a pound a week. The key to his success is to change his pictures frequently, because people are more likely to stop and pay. Bozo observes that foreigners pay more generously than Englishmen, and nobody pays if you have too much money already in the hat. Screevers generally stay 25 yards apart so as not to infringe on one another's business. Bozo points out another screever nearby who he claims frequently steals his ideas.

Orwell considers Bozo an interesting fellow and is anxious to see more of him. Paddy and Orwell meet Bozo later in the evening and travel with him to a nearby lodging house in Lambeth. Bozo walks with a wooden cane and carries his box of chalk over his shoulder. He grows quiet while they walk, and Orwell notices that he is looking at the stars. Bozo points out the star Aldebaran and says it looks like a "great blood orange." Orwell is astonished at his knowledge of astronomy as Bozo points out the principal constellations. He explains that he often looks at the stars and watches for meteor showers. Just because a man is on the road, Bozo says, doesn't mean he cannot think about something other than food. Orwell responds that life on the road seems to steal a man's intellect. Bozo insists that as long as a man remembers that he is free inside his head, it doesn't matter whether he is rich or poor. Orwell listens with great attention, as Bozo is the first person he has ever heard say that poverty does not matter. Orwell sees much of Bozo over the next few days because the rain prevents him from working, and he learns more about his background. Bozo is the son of a bankrupt bookseller. At 18, he began working as a house painter. He served three years in the military in France and India during World War I. Back from the war, he found work as a house painter in Paris and stayed there for several years. He had saved some money and was engaged to be married to a French woman. When his fiancee was crushed and killed by an omnibus, Bozo went on a weeklong drinking binge. He eventually returned to work but fell 40 feet from a ladder and crushed his leg. He received only 60 pounds in compensation and returned to England, where he quickly exhausted his money. He tried to sell books in a Middlesex Street market before settling down to work as a screever.

During Orwell's acquaintance with Bozo, the screever owns only the clothes on his back, his drawing materials, and a few books. He dresses much like a beggar but with the addition of a tie and collar, which he patches with bits of fabric from his shirttails. His injured leg is getting worse and will probably need to be amputated. In Orwell's opinion, Bozo is bound to end up a beggar and die in the workhouse. Despite his situation, Bozo never feels sorry for himself, never bothers to save any money, and expects society to take care of him when he runs out. Bozo thinks of himself as an enemy of society and does not flinch from the possibility of turning to crime if such a course would ever be necessary. He accepts charity as his right, provided that he is not required to express gratitude. On principle, he never picks up cigarette ends and therefore considers himself above the common lot of beggars. He is better educated than most beggars, speaks tolerable French, and occasionally reads works by Emile Zola, Shakespeare, and Swift. He uses vivid, memorable language and has managed to keep his mind alert. He is also an embittered atheist, which Orwell describes as someone "who does not so much disbelieve in God as personally dislike him." While sleeping on the embankment, Bozo sometimes looks at the planets Mars and Jupiter in the night sky and thinks that others are sleeping on embankments on those planets. He has a theory that life is difficult on Earth because it is poor in the necessities of life. Mars, with its harsh climate, must be poorer still. If you are imprisoned for stealing six pence on Earth, the penalty must be far more serious on Mars or

Jupiter. Bozo, in Orwell's estimation, is an exceptional man.

Chapter 31

Bozo's lodging house, a large place with accomodations for 500 men, charges nine pence per night. It is a well-known meeting place for tramps, beggars, and petty criminals. Orwell meets an assortment of characters of many races. Among this motley group is a former doctor who now sells newspapers and dispenses medical advice for a few pence. Another man writes fraudulent letters appealing for financial support for his ailing wife. At the lodging house, Bozo teaches Orwell about the different begging techniques used throughout London. Some beggars make as much as five pounds a week. The most prosperous of the London beggars are the street acrobats and photographers. Organ grinders also make a fair living, but most of their earnings come from working in small cafés and pubs. One of the organ grinders, a friend of Bozo's named Shorty, tells Orwell about his trade. He considers himself an entertainer rather than a beggar. He and his partner take in two or three pounds a week. Bozo introduces Orwell to a screever who actually has a background in art. He had studied art in Paris and submitted his paintings to the Salon. His specialty is copying versions of the Old Masters in chalk on the pavement.

This artist got his start in the trade when his family was starving because he could sell none of his paintings. He stopped to watch a screever, and when the man ducked into a pub for a quick drink, the desperate artist took the screever's place and began drawing. He earned nine pence from the gathering crowd. When the screever returned, the artist explained that he had to make money for his family. They went together to the pub for a drink, and the artist has been a screever ever since. With the money he makes and the small sums his wife brings in by sewing, the artist and his family just survive. The artist explains to Orwell that the worst thing about being a screever is the cold. A close second is interference from the authorities. He once copied Botticelli's *Venus,* a nude, on the sidewalk, only to have a churchman insist that he remove what he called an obscenity. On another occasion, a policeman rubbed out another nude drawing with his foot. Bozo has often suffered interference from the police, and he takes great care to avoid drawing anything that might cause trouble.

Screevers hold a somewhat exalted position among beggars. Beneath them are the singers of hymns and those who sell items such as matches, bootlaces, or envelopes full of lavender. These types make very little money. They are merely beggars that make an appearance of providing a service. The laws against begging in England create this absurd situation. If a person asks for two pence from a stranger, they can be turned in to the police and receive seven days in jail. If someone makes a nuisance of themselves by singing hymns or selling trinkets, they are thought to be following a legitimate trade.

Orwell's experiences lead him to see beggars as human beings, something that society as a whole does not do. Society makes a distinction between beggars and the regular working class. Beggars are considered outcasts, like prostitutes or criminals. The distinction between beggars and working men depends on how one defines work. Beggars work as hard as any laborer, though their work may be meaningless to society. Nothing that beggars do, Orwell concludes, deserves the scorn that society exhibits towards them. They are reviled only because they do not make a decent living. People in general judge work on the basis of the profit it accrues. "Money is the grand test of virtue." If a beggar earned 10 pounds a week, then he might achieve some sort of respectability. Seen in a certain light, a beggar is merely a businessman making his living any way he can. His only mistake is that he has adopted a trade that can never make him rich.

Chapter 32

In his travels with tramps and beggars in London, Orwell has learned something of the slang and curse words they regularly employ. What follows is a kind of glossary of London slang: A *gagger* is a general term for a tramp or a street performer; the *chanter,* a street singer; the *clodhopper,* a street dancer. Other slang terms refer to everything from particular parts of the city to denominations of English currency. The city of London is often referred to as Smoke. The terms *spike* and *lump* refer to a casual ward. Money earned from begging is often called a *drop,* presumably referring to dropping coins in a hat or other receptacle. Half crowns are called *tasheroons,* while a *deaner* or *hog* denotes a shilling. When a tramp is compelled to sleep out of doors, he calls this a *skipper.* Some of the slang that Orwell learns can be found in larger dictionaries, and he explores some possible etymological derivations for certain words. London slang changes rapidly. Examples from 19th-century literature are no longer used. Heavy cockney accents, which Orwell notes were first mentioned in literature in Herman Melville's *White Jacket,* have changed significantly, and the rhyming slang that was once popular in the streets of London has become virtually extinct.

Curse words have also changed over the years. The term *bloody* is hardly ever used by tramps and beggars, though it is still a popular term among the educated classes. Orwell's extended discussion of vulgar language is hindered by the heavy edits adopted by his publisher. He finds swearing in England a mystery. Words once used to create shock—usually terms for private things like sexual functions—have now become divorced from their original meanings. Insults follow the same pattern. Orwell notes that men in England do not often curse in front of women. This is not the case in Paris, where men often employ the crudest language no matter who the audience might be. Orwell finds it disappointing that someone more capable than he has not attempted a more detailed study of the subject of slang and cursing or that no annual publication of such terms has been compiled that could shed more light on the formation, development, and eventual obsolescence of such language.

Chapter 33

Orwell's most recent loan from B. lasts for 10 days, primarily due to Paddy's thriftiness. He teaches Orwell how to live on half a crown per day. Paddy and Orwell also try to earn a little extra for themselves, but jobs are difficult to find and queues of men wait hours each day for them. One of the more coveted jobs is distributing handbills. Paddy and Orwell stay on at Bozo's lodging house, and their lives during this period are characterized by a crushing boredom. They spend most days in the kitchen reading old newspapers. It rains frequently and the kitchen smells foul. Paddy complains tirelessly about their idleness. Many unemployed men desire work more strongly than they do money. Orwell remembers little about this dull period except his conversations with Bozo.

One evening, a slumming party invades the lodging house. The group consists of a man in a clerical frock, a woman with a portable harmonium, and a youth with a crucifix. They hold an impromptu religious service in the kitchen. The men in the lodging house peaceably ignore the trespassers and continue their conversations. The group eventually leaves without incident, priding themselves, Orwell is certain, on their courage to attempt to convert the heathen. Paddy explains that such groups visit lodging houses several times a month. Orwell is insulted that some people feel that they have a right to preach to you if your income falls below a certain level.

Orwell's money begins to dwindle again. He has only one shilling and nine pence. He puts aside 18 pence for their night's lodging and buys tea and two slices for himself and Paddy. Still hungry after their meal, they go to a church near King's Cross station that gives free tea to tramps once a week. They find a line of perhaps 100 men when they arrive. The doors open, and the men are led to the upper gallery by a clergyman and a group of young women. A church service follows the tea, with the regular congregation sitting below. A few of the tramps manage to leave before the service begins, but the majority remain in the upper gallery. The tramps misbehave during the service in shocking ways. They talk loudly and flick bread crumbs from their tea on the congregants below. Orwell physically restrains one of the tramps from lighting a cigarette. He is surprised by the display, but he considers that this is the tramps' way of exacting revenge on the church for their charity. The minister addresses the last five minutes of the service to the tramps, and he adopts a suitable fire-and-brimstone approach. Orwell is intrigued by the scene at the church. It is normal for tramps to disdain the source of the charity they receive. That they did it so unabashedly suggests to Orwell that they felt a greater sense of boldness because they outnumbered their benefactors.

Later that day, Paddy manages to earn an extra 18 pence. This will cover expenses for one more night at the lodging house. At half past eight the following morning, Paddy leads Orwell down to the Embankment. He knows a clergyman there who distributes meal tickets to tramps. A long line of men had formed under Charing Cross Bridge, and they were tramps of the lowest order. Some were dressed in rags tied to their bodies by rope. The clergyman, a young and pudgy man, soon emerges and quickly distributes the meal tickets without waiting to be thanked. As a result, the tramps are genuinely grateful. The tickets could be redeemed at an eating house close by for six pence worth of food. However, the owner of the eating house only provides four penny worth of food for the tickets. This kind of swindle occurs regularly all over London. Paddy and Orwell spend that evening in the lodging-house kitchen. Bozo shows up a little later, having made no money at screeving and having finally to resort to outright begging. He managed to collect eight pence but is still one pence short of the price of a bed. He decides to sell his razor to make up the difference. After the sale, he joins Paddy and Orwell at the kitchen fire and begins to laugh. He explains that he sold his razor without first having a shave.

Chapter 34

Orwell and Paddy run out of money and decide to stay at the spike in Cromley. They arrive too early to enter the spike, so they walk a few miles further to a plantation where they can rest. Several other tramps join them, and one of the men manages to light a fire. The tramps begin to tell stories about life on the road. A burly tramp named Bill talks about his aversion to work. He could get work if he wanted, but after his first paycheck, he would go on a drinking binge and get fired. Bill is known as a moocher—someone who does no work but sponges off others. He explains to Orwell the advantages and disadvantages of mooching in various towns in England. Bill's life seems to consist of mooching, drunkenness, and periodic jail sentences for begging. Another tramp shares a ghost story about the Cromley spike. A man once smuggled a razor into the spike and committed suicide. The Tramp Major discovered him in the cell and broke the corpse's arm trying to open the door to get to him. As an act of revenge, the man's ghost haunted the cell. Anyone who slept in the cell would die within a year. One grisly story related by two ex-sailors describes the unfortunate death of a tramp who stowed away on a steamer. Hidden in a packing crate, the man suffocates to death when the crate he occupies is accidentally stored at the bottom of the pile in the ship's hold. His body is not discovered until the end of the voyage, by which time the corpse had already started to decay. These stories set the tramps to talking about history, and Orwell notes that their knowledge comes not from books but rather from an oral tradition that must have passed down from generation to generation.

Paddy and Orwell spend that night at the spike in Cromley, where they see and hear nothing from the alleged ghost, and set out the next morning at ten. They leave Cromley in the company of seventeen other tramps and head toward the spike in Lower Binfield. During the trip, a fight breaks out between two tramps, and the other men gather to watch. One of the combatants loses his cap in the brawl. The men see his white hair and realize that he is quite a bit older than his opponent in the fight, and so they intervene on his behalf. The brawl is later determined to be the result of a theft of food—a common reason for fighting among tramps.

The tramps arrive at the spike in Lower Binfield quite early, and Paddy and Orwell find work chopping up crates for firewood. They earn 10 and six pence and purchase bread and tobacco, leaving them with five pence between them. Paddy suggests that they bury the money before entering the spike and retrieve it the next morning. The Tramp Major at Lower Binfield has the reputation of being a bully, and they do not want to risk the confiscation of their money. Tramps often sew their money into the lining of their clothes, but if they are caught, they can face prosecution. Paddy and Bozo tell an interesting story about an Irishman who tries to hide his money from a Tramp Major. The man gets stranded in a small village with 30 pounds in his pocket. Looking for a place to stay, he consults a tramp, who advises him to go to the workhouse. The Irishman could have easily paid for a room in the village, but he chooses to pretend to be a tramp to get a bed for free. He sews the 30 pounds into his clothes. Meanwhile, the tramp he consulted sees an opportunity. He asks the Tramp Major for permission to leave the spike early the next morning, at which time he leaves in the Irishman's clothes (and consequently with his 30 pounds). When the Irishman complains about the theft, he is sentenced to 30 days in jail for entering a spike under false pretenses.

Chapter 35

Orwell and the other tramps wait on the village green for the spike to open. Several of the residents watch the men with a mixture of curiosity and fear. A clergyman and his daughter come to view the tramps briefly before scurrying away. The group of tramps consists of about 12 men and one woman—the first female tramp Orwell has ever seen. He describes her as a "fattish, battered, very dirty woman of sixty." She does not mix with the other tramps and clearly considers herself more respectable than the others in the group. Because it is a Saturday, the tramps will be confined in the spike through the weekend. The spike opens at six that evening, and Orwell registers his profession with the Tramp Major—a former soldier—as a journalist. Impressed by this, the Tramp Major asks if Orwell is a gentleman, to which he replies that he supposes so. Such is the strength of that word that Orwell receives preferential treatment through the duration of his stay at the spike. He is not searched upon entering, and he gets a clean bath towel—an unheard-of luxury in a spike. By seven in the evening, the tramps have eaten their tea and two slices and are locked into their cells. Each tramp gets a private cell with a bedstead and a straw mattress. Though the cell is more comfortable than other spikes, it is unbearably cold, and the men get only about an hour or two of sleep during the night. After breakfast the next morning, the tramps are confined in a small room for the rest of the day, with nothing to do but smoke furtively when the Tramp Major is not watching. Again, Orwell benefits from his designation as a gentleman. He is selected with a few other men for a job in the workhouse kitchen.

Orwell finds very little to do in the kitchen and decides to hide out in a storage shed, where several workhouse paupers have assembled to avoid the morning church service. They talk to him about life in the workhouse. The uniforms that the paupers are required to wear seem to cause the most concern among the men. If they could wear their own clothes, they would not object so much to life in the workhouse. Orwell takes his lunch in the workhouse kitchen, and it is the largest meal that he has eaten since his first day of employment at the Hotel X in Paris. The paupers explain that they eat well on Sundays, but they generally starve the rest of the week. After his meal, Orwell washes up the dishes in the kitchen. He is appalled by how much food is thrown away after each meal. It is apparently the policy of the workhouse to discard the food, even though the spike is filled with starving men. At three in the afternoon, Orwell rejoins the other tramps. He strikes up a conversation with a young tramp—a carpenter by trade—who comes to the spike when his hunger compels him. He explains that he is on the road because he has no money for a set of carpentry tools. Orwell mentions the appalling waste of food in the workhouse kitchen, but the young carpenter shows no sympathy. He says that conditions cannot be too good at spikes. If they were, the spikes would attract even more worthless sorts. The carpenter refers to the other tramps as scum. Orwell contradicts the young man, but he keeps insisting that the tramps are nothing but scum. Orwell finds it interesting how the man has disassociated himself from his fellow tramps.

The evening meal arrives at six that evening and consists of stale bread and drippings. The tramps spend that night in the workhouse dormitory to keep them separated from the new arrivals at the spike. The dormitory is a barnlike structure with 30 beds set close together. A tub serves as a common chamberpot for the room, which reeks of urine. The older tramps in the group make it difficult for the other men to sleep during the night. They cough and get up frequently to use the chamber pot. However, the crowded room is much warmer than the cells, and the tramps manage to get a little more sleep than they otherwise would. After their medical inspection the next morning, the tramps begin to disperse from the spike. Paddy and Orwell head north toward London. After they start on the road one of the tramps comes running out to catch them. He wants to return the cigarette he borrowed from Orwell: "One good turn deserves another—here y'are."

Chapter 36

Orwell records some general thoughts about tramps. They are a queer sort in his view. They number in the tens of thousands and maintain a rootless existence as they wander the country from spike to spike. Orwell suggests that one cannot understand the life of a tramp without abandoning certain prejudices against them. Tramps are generally considered to be dangerous and desperate men. Such prejudices, however, obscure the real issue, which involves the vagrancy laws in England. Society provides a number of explanations about why men turn to a life on the road. Tramps are considered by many to be lazy men with no desire to work. They live on the road to better facilitate their desire to beg and steal. Moreover, one book on criminology suggests that tramps are a throwback to the nomadic stage of human history. Orwell suggests that the real reason that a man becomes a tramp is that the laws in England compel him to adopt that lifestyle. Unless a man with no income or resources receives support from a parish, he must seek that support from the casual wards. Since he can only stay at a particular casual ward once in any given month, he must take to the road and travel to other spikes in other villages.

In Orwell's experience, tramps are neither dangerous nor predominantly drunkards. With very few exceptions, they do not willingly become social parasites. Englishmen have too keen a sense of the sinfulness of poverty to willingly become tramps—though there are examples of what he calls sturdy tramps, or men who appear quite healthy and well fed. Orwell does not argue that all tramps are idealized characters. They are, rather, just normal human beings. If they are worse off than other men, their situation is the result—not the cause—of their way of life. Orwell also attempts to dismantle the prejudice that tramps deserve the hardships that they face on the road. As he sees it, there are three specific evils inherent to life on the road. Tramps experience an almost unmitigated hunger, because the casual wards provide only the meanest form of food, often not more than stale bread and margarine. Tramps also have no access to women. Few women travel in their circles, and women of the higher classes will have nothing to do with a tramp. Thus they are forced by circumstances to adopt a celibate lifestyle unless they can afford the few shillings it costs for a prostitute. This in turn leads to a greater incidence of homosexuality among tramps, as well as a few isolated cases of rape. The lack of any legitimate sexual outlet, according to Orwell, is devastating to a man's self-respect. The third evil of life on the road is enforced idleness. The vagrancy laws in England compel tramps to spend their days walking and their nights locked in a cell. In short, tramps in England lead an almost entirely futile existence. A tramp expends enormous amounts of energy walking throughout the country for a place to sleep and a few scraps of food. That energy could more properly be applied to agriculture or some other meaningful task.

Orwell considers a number of options that could be instituted to improve the lives of tramps. Aside from making the spikes more hospitable—which Orwell notes has been done in certain areas of England—the key to improvement is to provide some kind of honest labor. Orwell suggests that the casual wards might operate a working farm or simply a kitchen garden. Each man who stays at a spike could be required to give an honest day's work for his room and board. The produce of the casual ward farm could then be used to feed the boarders. England could also revise its law against a man staying in a spike only once in a month. As long as they work at the spike, men could stay as long as they liked. Then the casual wards could work toward becoming self-sufficient, and the tramps could settle down in one place—thus ceasing to be tramps. Orwell admits several drawbacks to his proposed plan, but he insists that any improvements must incorporate some version of his suggestions.

Chapter 37

Tramps have several options for sleeping accommodations when they have no money to purchase a bed at a lodging house. Some tramps choose to sleep outdoors, on the Embankment. Paddy has given Orwell an apt description of this experience. Tramps must arrive early in order to secure a bench to sleep on, and they must try to fall asleep as early in the evening as possible. By midnight the weather is generally too cold for sleep, and the police wake the tramps at four in the morning and send them on their way. Orwell's own experiences on the Embankment support Paddy's description, but it is better than not sleeping at all. Tramps who spend the night on the streets can sit down, but the law forbids them to sleep. Paris has no such prohibition, and people sleep in the Metro stations, under bridges, and on benches in squares.

In London, there are the following options: The two-penny Hangover; the four penny, Coffin, which offers a room with a wooden box with a plastic tarp that serves as a blanket. A night in the Coffin is quite cold, and the boxes are infested with bugs.

Then there are the many common lodging houses that vary in price between seven pence and a shilling and penny. The best of these are the Rowton houses, which offer private cubicles and excellent bathrooms. If cleanliness is important, the Salvation Army hostels are a good choice for lodgings. They cost seven to eight pence and vary in quality. Lodgers also must pay extra for a bath. Salvation Army beds are generally comfortable, but they are placed too close together and do not provide good sleeping conditions. Ordinary common lodging houses are also plentiful in England, but they are uniformly dirty and uncomfortable. The only advantage of these accommodations is their warm kitchens, where some kind of social life is possible for tramps. Few lodgings for tramps accommodate couples, and it is not uncommon for a husband and wife to sleep in different lodging houses.

Orwell claims that there are at least 15,000 people living in common lodging houses. They provide a fair value for a man making at least two pounds per week. The downside, however, is that he pays money to sleep in these establishments, and sleep is virtually impossible. The dormitories are crowded and noisy, with chronic coughing and people with bladder problems that force them to wake frequently during the night. In general, boarders at common lodging houses get only five hours of sleep in a night. He suggests that government legislation could improve the conditions in lodging houses by requiring better beds, sheets, and blankets. Dormitories could also be divided into cubicles to provide privacy. Owners of lodging houses, however, would object to such improvements. Less crowding would mean less profit. Orwell concludes that the government should do something to make the conditions in lodging houses more hospitable for boarders.

Chapter 38

After leaving the spike at Lower Binfield, Paddy and Orwell earn half a crown by weeding and sweeping one of the villager's gardens. They pass the night at Cromley before walking back to London, where they eventually part ways. Orwell borrows another two pounds from his friend B., and his money troubles are over for the eight days that remain before the family with the disabled youth returns to London. The job turns out to be more difficult than Orwell had anticipated, but it is much better than spending nights at the spike or working at the Auberge de Jehan Cottard in Paris.

Paddy leaves London for Portsmouth to find a friend who might have a job for him. Orwell never sees him again, but he later hears a rumor that Paddy had been run over and killed. It is possible, however, that the man killed was not Paddy but someone else. Orwell also hears news of Bozo. He was given 14 days in jail in Wandsworth for begging. Here Orwell ends his story, which he calls a trivial one. He hopes, however, that the descriptions of his experiences have been interesting—perhaps like a travel diary. The world he describes is what awaits anyone in England who becomes penniless. Orwell expresses the hope one day to explore the down-and-out world in greater depth and to know characters such as Paddy more intimately. Orwell admits that, at best, he has only seen the fringes of poverty. He nonetheless cites a number of lessons he has learned during his travels among the poor. He will never think that all tramps are drunken scoundrels. He will not be surprised that unemployed men seem to lack energy nor expect a beggar to be grateful for a handout. He will never support the Salvation Army. He will never pawn his clothing. He will also always accept a handbill and never enjoy a meal at a smart restaurant.

—Philip Bader

COMMENTARY

The experiences recounted in *Down and Out* occurred or were heard about over a period of three years (1928 to 1931). As rendered and reshaped in the book, they take place over four months, three in Paris and one in London. In reality, the earliest of these adventures occurred in London in 1928 before the move to Paris. The account of that experience was published as "The Spike" in the *Adelphi* in 1931, later incorporated as two chapters in the book. Reshaping disparate experiences into a chronologically sequenced narrative marked one of Orwell's departures from strict fact. Another was the inclusion of certain anecdotes that were, at the least, of doubtful authenticity, although they were probably stories told by the characters to whom they were attributed. Two examples are Charlie's sexual fantasy (chapter 2) and his account of the death of the miser Roucolle (chapter 23). Thus, *Down and Out* is a mixed genre, in large part true in detail but altered in the interest of maintaining a coherent narrative flow or injecting an interesting anecdote. The most significant deviation involves the return to England, where the narrator is plunged immediately into the tramp world. In fact, on his return, Orwell went to his parents' home, staying there for several months while he wrote the Paris section of the book. Then he set out on a series of tramping expeditions, punctuated by periodic returns to the homes of relatives or friends. It should be remembered that this was a man in continually frail health. To have voluntarily submitted to these privations, even on an interrupted basis, indicates not dilletantism, but its opposite, a reckless heroism, or as some would have it, masochism. The result, in any case, is a document revealing the lives of a group of people, whose experiences would have otherwise gone unnoticed.

In the opening scene, the reader is thrust into an early morning street quarrel between a resident and the madame/manager of a rundown hotel, which soon expands to include other residents as they throw open their shutters to join in. The opening elliptical sentences ("The rue du Coq d'Or Paris, seven in the morning. A series of furious, choking yells from the street.") read like stage directions or the script of a film by René Clair. Already, the reader may guess that he or she is being positioned to view the action directly, without any authorial guidance, but a few sentences later, he appears, reassuring us, "I sketch this scene just to convey something of the spirit of the Rue du Coq d'Or."

Modern readers might well think that they need no quasiapologetic reassurances, since they are very familiar with the rhetorical technique of showing, not telling. But the book's original readers were viewing the experience from the other end of the telescope. For the fledgling writer, the opening is a daring innovation, dispensing with the authorial narrator, "refining him out of existence,' as James Joyce put it in *Portrait of the Artist as a Young Man,* the point being to let nothing, not even the voice of author, come between the reader and the experience depicted.

The book as a whole is an interesting example of Orwell's willingness to experiment with various rhetorical devices, while still hewing closely to the traditional forms of narrative. Thus in the first chapter he is soon back on a traditional track, describing the various individuals staying at the hotel, including "Furex, a Limousin stone mason." The province of Limousin was not only the ancestral seat of his mother's family but their name as well. If the stonemason reference is a private allusion or inside joke, its point has been lost.

Near the end of chapter 1 he reveals that his subject is poverty. He is attempting to explore what it is like to be poor, how the condition of poverty governs one's life, casting a shadow over one's experiences and shaping one's basic attitudes. In this effort, Orwell's style will play a central role. In the opening passage, for example, he thrusts the reader into the reality of an impoverished life. The quarrel between Madame Monce, the manager, and her tenant relates to her charge that he is guilty of squashing bugs on the wallpaper, instead of throwing them out the window "like everyone else." The phrase "like everyone else" introduces the reader into a norm of impoverished life. It is designed to be a representative anecdote: In the Hotel des Trois Moineaux, everything is infested with bugs, but there is a right way and a wrong way of dealing with them. Such a place conjures up eccentricity, and its people are given a wide berth (provided it does not extend to the wallpaper). Eccentricity is another outgrowth of poverty, as various people, pushed to extremes, resort to bizarre and complex coping strategies.

All the hotels on the rue feature a ground-floor bistro, which is the common meeting ground for tenants and neighbors. It is there one gathers on a Saturday night, drinking until oblivion or the dawn arrives, listening to tall tales, outright lies, and exotic fantasies, which create a community of the poor, a family, similar to Harry Hope's saloon in Eugene O'Neill's *The Iceman Cometh.* We are conscious of the narrator living on the fringe of this group, an observer as well as participant. He is on the outside looking in, because he is not yet poor. He has enough to live on for a month, but that all changes when his room is robbed. Now he begins a life in which he tries to exist on six francs a day (approximately 25 cents):

> It is altogether curious, your first contact with poverty. You thought it would be quite simple; it is extraordinarily complicated. You thought it would be terrible; it is merely squalid and boring. . . . You go out and look into shop windows. Everywhere there is food insulting you in huge wasteful piles. A sniveling self-pity comes over you at the sight of so much food . . . You discover that a man who has gone even a week on bread and margarine is not a man any longer, only a belly with a few accessory organs.

The persistent use of the second person narrative pulls its readers further into the experience, forcing them not just to learn about poverty but to share it. It is a use of the second person that embraces both the first and the third as well.

Reaching out for help in navigating this strange new world, he contacts Boris, son of wealthy parents, former captain in the czar's army, forced by the revolution to flee the Soviet Union. Boris has survived in postwar Paris, working himself up in hotels from *plongeur* (dishwasher) to waiter in the main dining room. But when he calls on Boris, he finds him in dire straits, having lost his job. Boris is one of the distinctive characters who populate the book, a free spirit whose zest for life testifies to the proposition that down is not necessarily out. His London equivalent is Bozo, a sidewalk artist, although Bozo is more thoughtful and articulate. Boris is a passionate, mercurial spirit, summed up in the word *paradox*: On one hand, he is exuberant that he has a patron saint looking out for him; on the other, he is plunged in despair, giving vent to his czarist officer's anti-Semitism. The adventures of the pair as they look for work are both serious and comic. Their plight is often desperate, but the two men display an odd-couple, comic relationship in which Boris's "leads" consistently prove to be dead ends, usually resulting in the fine mess characteristic of a Laurel and Hardy film. As a consequence, there is a comic brio that underlies the grim descriptions of poverty in the Paris section. This is true, as well, of the Saturday-night bistro scenes, where the high spirits that reign until about 1:30 in the morning gradually give way to a melancholic end-of-the-party *tristesse.* Even in the hotel kitchen scenes, although here the comedy is more ironic, even satiric, we are conscious of vitality, of life, that is stronger and more powerful than in the London scenes.

Eventually, Boris finds an opening as a dishwasher for the narrator at a luxurious hotel. There the narrator not only encounters life at the bottom of the heap, but he is also reintroduced to the pervasive power of class. Among the staff, the class system is alive and well, more persistently present, more stringently adhered to than in the society at large. From the *patron* at the top to the *plongeurs* and, below them, the *cafetiers,* the hotel observes rigid caste rules that make the regular society look anarchic. As an example, the *plongeurs* are not permitted to wear a mustache because the waiters cannot have a mustache. The deep roots of class consciousness will be a theme of *THE ROAD TO WIGAN PIER,* here, it is implied and observed not analyzed. The message of part 1 is that the condition symbolized by the *plongeur* is that of a slave, a person whose entire existence, with the exception of the Saturday-night saturnalia, is devoted to work. And society's perpetuation of this condition is the result of fear. The poor must be kept busy, just trying to survive, or else they will rise up and wreak revenge on the middle and upper classes. The irony is that the fear is based on ignorance. If they came to know the impoverished, they would recognize that their fears are misplaced.

When the scene shifts to London, the subject of the book shifts with it. The Paris section is concerned with poverty as a condition endured by people at the bottom of the working class, who at least have the stability of a place to live. In England, the subject is not simple poverty but a condition experienced by the special class known as tramps. The difference between Paris and London is the difference between poverty and homelessness. The Hotel des Trois Moineaux was—bedbugs, dirt, and all—home. The desperation of a 17-hour-a-day job was relieved by Saturday night in the bistro. For the tramps, there is no home, no job, no Saturday night. We learn that, in England, the continuous movement of tramps is not a function of their choice but a consequence of the Vagrancy Laws, which prohibit them from staying more than one night a month in any particular public shelter. Thus, a tramp's day is spent walking from one town or one section of a large city to another. As a result, the myth of the tramp as an irresponsible nomad who can't stay in one place because of an inherent wanderlust has grown to be accepted as truth.

The contrast between Paris and London is also embodied in that between Orwell's two closest companions, the irrepressible Boris and the deeply repressed Paddy. Both men are exiles from their native countries, with Paddy displaying the cautious, conciliatory manners of a true colonial, while Boris exhibits the self-assurance of the upper middle class. Thus, Boris: "Ah but I have known what is to live like a gentleman, *mon ami.* I do not say it to boast, but the other day I was trying to compute how many mistresses I have had in my life and I made it out to be over two hundred." Paddy, on the other hand, speaks "in a whimpering, self-pitying Irish voice. . . . It was malnutrition and not any native vice that had destroyed his manhood." More to Orwell's taste is Bozo, the sidewalk artist, defiant, intelligent, independent. Bozo refuses to accept society's judgment on him as a slacker, a sinner, and a failure. Pointing to his temple, he declares, "I'm a free man in here."

Orwell concludes with a plea for recognition of the common humanity of the tramp. Man is a social animal, and the tramps have been thrust out of society, treated like aliens and exiles; they are men who, despite being brutalized by society, are not brutes. Brutalization falls on the shoulders of respectable citizens who, like the blinkered colonialists in India and Burma, are oppressed by their own oppression.

One of the striking features of *Down and Out,* given Orwell's later reputation, is its notable absence of a political, as opposed to a social, consciousness. He advocates reform, but they are the reforms of a 19th-century liberal rather than the social upheaval of a revolutionary. In the early 1930s, Orwell had not yet attached himself to a political cause. He was still at the stage that he identified with Charles Dickens in a 1939 essay, in which he concludes that Dickens was a "moralist, not a politician. . . . All he can say finally is 'Behave decently,' which is not . . . necessarily as shallow as it sounds."

The Indian critic Alok Rai calls attention to the absence of a political creed, "It is . . . with a slight sense of shock that one realizes how little there is of politics in Orwell's writings of the years 1930–35" (53). Rai goes on to point out that these were the years of intense political consciousness, when various forms of radicalism were being espoused by writers. All the more surprising to him that Orwell "seems to take the tramps (and indeed the whole subworld) for granted and gives little hint of any protosocialist desire to reorder society in such a way that there are no more tramps and derelicts ceaselessly in quest for food" (54). A more recent political critic, Bernard Schweizer, sees the apparent lack of a political statement in *Down and Out* as a result of Orwell's "infatuation with narrative," in which he seems, in the Paris section of the book, more interested in telling a good story than in making any ideological commitment:

> As a rhetorical achievement, the text is superb; as an episodic story, the book has its bright moments (even though it is rather loosely plotted). But as a testimony to foreign living and working conditions, the text offers no more than pointers and subjectively filtered impressions (22).

Schweizer is somewhat more forgiving in relation to the London section, citing Orwell's plea that tramps be treated with respect as an example of the book's "socially revisionist appeal":

> The political significance of *Down and Out* is thus enhanced in the same measure as its infatuation with narrative diminishes to make room for a more pragmatic, documentary approach to travel writing as a form of social critique (24).

In a sense, Orwell implicitly confirmed these criticisms in his famous statement in "WHY I WRITE" (1946): "Every line of serious work I have written since 1936 has been written, directly or indirectly, against totalitarianism and for democratic Socialism." It was the experience of the Spanish civil war that "turned the scale and from then on I knew where I stood," he said. However, what is not stated but clearly evident through his development as a whole, is that he had been approaching the turning point from the time of his Burmese experience. He had grown into socialism. (Whether or not he later outgrew it is a celebrated, controversial question.) In defense of Schweizer's position, it should be noted that Schweizer is treating the book as an example of travel literature and specifically, as his subtitle denotes it, "The Politics of Travel Writing in the 1930s." As a result Schweizer adopts a dismissive attitude toward the "good story," implying that you can have one or the other but not both. Even so, Schweizer's and Rai's critiques of *Down and Out* would seem to be a case of criticizing a kitten for not being a cat. In any case, the effort to have both, to integrate art and politics, is central to Orwell's creative efforts as a writer. Schweizer concedes as much in his judgment of *Homage to Catalonia* as the place where "the representation of spiritual and political experience and their ideological contextualization substantially fuse."

No such questions were raised by the first reviewers of the book, such as the Irish-American novelist James T. Farrell, who characterized it in The New Republic as "genuine, unexaggerated and intelligent, adding that the individual "portraits and vignettes . . . give the book interest and concreteness" (47). The poet C. Day Lewis reviewed the book for *Adelphi,* asserting "The facts he reveals should shake the complaisance of twentieth century civilization if anything could; they are 'sensational,' yet presented without sensationalism" (43).

One of the finest tributes to the book is the judgment of a man with whom Orwell shared an off-again, on-again appreciation of each other's work, the American novelist HENRY MILLER. In a *Paris Review* interview published in 1962, Miller characterized *Down and Out* as "a classic," adding, "For me, it's still his best book" (181).

CHARACTERS

Azaya One of the Saturday regulars at the bistro, "a great, clumping peasant girl who worked fourteen hours a day in a glass factory." She is an active participant in the baiting of FUREX every Saturday night.

B. Orwell's mysterious benefactor. B. lends him money on a number of occasions and finds him a job caring for a mentally impaired child in England.

Boris A Russian émigré and a former member of the czar's army who is living in Paris in the aftermath of the Bolshevik Revolution. Boris is "a big soldierly man of about thirty-five," hampered by an arthritic leg, now working as a waiter whenever he can find work. He and Orwell support each other in their efforts to survive while looking for a job. At first, they find work at a posh hotel, Boris as a waiter, and Orwell as a dishwasher, or a *plongeur.* Boris convinces Orwell to quit the job at the hotel for one at a soon-to-be-opened Russian bistro, which ends up opening later than planned, leaving the two destitute for a while. Eventually, Orwell quits the bistro job to return to England, leaving behind Boris, who is content with his new job.

Bozo A pavement artist with an independent and sometimes defiant view of society. His chalk drawings are generally political cartoons. As a young man, he lived in Paris, where he worked as a house painter. He was engaged to a young woman who later died in an accident, and Bozo fell while painting, injuring his foot.

Bozo demonstrates an interest in and a knowledge of the stars and planets, which impresses Orwell. He admires Bozo's personal integrity, the fact that, as difficult as life has been, it has not undermined the fact that Bozo is the model of "a free man."

Charlie A young man of exceedingly youthful appearance, educated, and from a good family. He survives on money sent periodically from home. Charlie spends most of his time talking about himself to anyone who is willing to listen. His favorite topic is what he calls love, although his anecdote suggests it is a sadistic form of that emotion. Charlie's story about the happiest day of his life, during which he steals money from his brother and forces himself upon a young prostitute, is as lurid as it is unconvincing. In chapter 23, Charlie recounts to Orwell the story of the miser Roucolle. Charlie is referred to in passing in the London section of the book, when Orwell meets a clergyman who distributes meal tickets to a group of tramps. The youthful clergyman reminds Orwell of Charlie.

Chef du Personnel An Italian man in charge of the staff at Hotel X. He hires Orwell as a dishwasher despite his lack of experience, because Orwell may be able to help the staff improve its spoken English.

Cook At the Auberge de Jehan Cottard, the cook is an overworked, frazzled Russian woman who is in charge of the kitchen. On her break, she collapses in a dustbin, moaning and crying. She constantly berates Orwell, giving him one contradictory order after another. After he leaves to return to England, Orwell learns that she has been fired.

Etonian, Old An inebriated man in a London lodging house who surmises from his accent that Orwell went to Eton, as he did. He begins to sing the Eton boating song but falls into a drunken stupor.

F., Madame The proprietress of the Hotel des Trois Moineaux and the bistro bartender on Saturday night. She keeps a watchful, compassionate eye on Furex and makes sure he is put to bed when he passes out. As the night wears on, she waters down the wine, probably for economy as well as to limit the somewhat-wild drunkenness that may ensue.

Furex A stonemason who lives at the Hotel des Trois Moineaux. Although he is a sincere communist, when he is drunk, he becomes a fierce patriot. Every Saturday night, he delivers the same speech about being wounded at the battle of Verdun, partially undressing to show his wounds and capping off the speech with a rendition of "La Marseillaise." Then the crowd begins the ritual of tormenting him by shouting German slogans and disparaging France, while two men hold him down. Eventually he passes out and is carried off to bed. On Sunday morning, he reappears calm and restrained, carrying his copy of the communist paper *L'Humanite.* Furex is a native of the province of Limousin in central France, which is the ancestral home of the Limouzin family, Orwell's matrilineal ancestors.

Head Cook The boss of the kitchen at the luxurious Hotel X who regularly curses out the *plongeurs.* When Orwell, in his inexperience, makes a mistake, the head cook remarks, "Well, Monsieur l'Anglais, may I inform you that you are the son of a whore?"

Henri A tenant at the hotel, whose downfall resulted from an unhappy love affair. Once a gentleman, he now works in the Paris sewers.

Jaques, Paddy The Irish tramp who teams up with Orwell during his final tramping excursion. A "good fellow, generous by nature," he also exhibits some of the faults of a tramp, "abject, envious, a jackal's nature." Paddy's experience on the road proves immensely helpful to Orwell as he tries to navigate the life of a tramp. He is particularly helpful in managing the art of surviving on very little money. When they part, Paddy heads for the prospect of a new job. Orwell hears later that he died after being run over by a car but is doubtful that the report is true. "Jaques" seems an odd choice as an Irish name. It may have something to do with the fact that Orwell's romantic interest at the time was Elinor Jaques.

Jules The second waiter, after Boris, at the Auberge de Jehan Cottard. An ardent communist, he is an outspoken critic of the Patron. Part of his job is to shop at the local grocery store and flirt with the grocer's wife, ensuring continued credit for the restaurant.

Maria A character in a story the waiter Valenti tells Orwell about his experience of acute hunger. On his fifth day without food, he prays to a picture of Saint Eloise on his wall to provide him with food. Maria, a "big fat peasant girl" and "very stupid," but also "a good sort," visits him and is horrified by his disheveled, unhealthy appearance. While looking through his room for something to sell, Maria discovers an oil bidon for which Valenti can receive a deposit of more than three francs upon its return. He sends Maria to collect the deposit and to purchase food. After his meal, Valenti considers sending Maria out for cigarettes with the remaining money, but he remembers his promise to light a candle to Saint Eloise, the patron saint of the quarter. He explains the situation to Maria, only to discover through her that the image on the wall of his hotel room is not that of Saint Eloise but rather a depiction of the famous prostitute for which the hotel is named. Valenti and Maria have a good laugh about the mistake, and she goes out to buy his cigarettes.

Marinette "A thin, dark Corsican girl" and a Saturday-night regular at the bistro, where her specialty is belly dancing.

Mario An "excitable Italian" who is in charge of the cafeteria at Hotel X. His years of experience have made him an invaluable member of the staff.

Monce, Madame Manager of the hotel directly across the street from the Hotel des Trois Moineaux. Her street quarrel with a lodger provides the opening scene of the book.

Paddy See JAQUES, PADDY

Patron Russian owner of the Auberge de Jehan Cottard on the rue du Commerce. A former colonel in the czar's army, to Orwell he looks "like a cheat, and, what was worse, an incompetent cheat." The restaurant opens only after a long delay. The Patron does a good job of looking the part of a patron, but he never does any real work.

R. An Englishman who spends half the year in England and the other half in the bistro, quietly consuming vast quantities of wine.

Roucolle An old miser and the subject of a story told by Charlie. Roucolle is persuaded by a Jew to buy a large stash of cocaine. Shortly after the sale is made, the police arrive at his hotel to search for illegal drugs. Roucolle is forced to hde the cocaine in a tin of face powder. The police confiscate the tin and arrest him, and they send the tin to the lab for analysis. The results confirm that the contents are indeed face powder, and Roucolle is released. Rather than being pleased at having avoided a stay in prison, Roucolle is in despair over the loss of his money. He suffers a stroke and soon dies.

Rougiers An old couple living at the Hotel des Trois Moineaux, who eke out a living selling post cards on the Boulevard St. Michel of chateaux in the Loire Valley.

Serbian Temporary worker at Hotel X, who works well until noon but then stops working. As a result, he is fired, but he always receives a full day's pay because he worked until noon.

Shorty A London street accordion player, who earns about two pounds a week and considers himself an entertainer rather than a beggar.

Tramp Major An official at an English spike who supervises the running of the place and interrogates the tramps.

Valenti A young waiter at Hotel X who tells Orwell the story of Saint Eloise.
(See MARIA.)

WORKS CITED

Crick, Bernard. *George Orwell: A Life.* Boston: Little, Brown, 1970.

Farrell, James T. *"Down and Out in Paris and London."* In *George Orwell: The Critical Heritage,* edited by Jeffrey Meyers, 46–7. London: Routledge, 1975.

Hitchens, Christopher. *Why Orwell Matters.* New York: Basic Books, 2002.

Lewis, C. Day. *"Down and Out in Paris and London."* In *George Orwell: The Critical Heritage,* edited by Jeffrey Meyers, 42–3.

Miller, Henry "Interview with Henry Miller." *Paris Review,* 1962.

Meyers, Jeffrey, ed. *George Orwell: The Critical Heritage.* London: Routledge, 1975.

Rai, Alok. *George Orwell and The Politics of Despair.* Cambridge: Cambridge University Press, 1988.

Schweizer, Bernard. *Radicals on the Road: The Politics of English Travel Writing in the 1930s.* Charlottesville: Virginia University Press, 2001.

English People, The

Booklet published in 1947, although it was written three years earlier as part of a series called "Britain in Pictures." Its wartime provenance is evident in its patriotic tone. Publication was delayed, however, until 1947. Shortly before his death, Orwell stipulated that *The English People* not be reprinted, along with *A Clergyman's Daughter, Keep the Aspidistra Flying,* and *The Lion and the Unicorn.* The booklet is divided into six sections: "England at First Glance," "The Moral Outlook of the English People," "The Political Outlook of the English People," "The English Class System," "The English Language," and "The Future of the English People."

SYNOPSIS

England at First Glance

The prevailing image among foreigners of the typical English person used to be that of an aristocrat sporting a monocle, that is, a member of the upper classes. But the war has brought to England's shores a huge number of foreigners, principally refugees from Europe and soldiers from the United States. A foreign observer arriving here without prejudices would probably notice the following characteristics of the English common people:

Artistic insensibility Evident in the general acceptance of the destruction of the beautiful countryside by industrial expansion and the need for housing.

Gentleness, respect for legality Reflected in orderly queues, unarmed police, and the lack of a revolutionary tradition.

Suspicion of foreigners The English people's difficulties with foreigners is a consequence of their diet, wholly alien to continental cuisine, and their reluctance to learn a foreign language, especially French, which seems, to the average Englishman, snobbish and unmanly.

Sentimentality about animals Notably expressed in the growing appearance of dog cemeteries, a side effect of the declining birth rate among English humans.

Hypocrisy Brazenly on view in the gap between the laws governing gambling, drinking, prostitution and profanity, and the actual practices of the people. Also evident in the professed attitude toward British imperialism.

Exaggerated class distinctions Diminishing in recent years, but the great gap is still evident in the class dialects of spoken English.

Obsession with sports Reflected in the lionization of sports heroes and the persuasive practice of football pools, which, during the depression, "did more than any other one thing to make life bearable for the unemployed."

Were he to put together these features, would our hypothetical observer emerge with a reliable picture of the English of today, and how would it compare with the reality of English life? From all accounts not very well, leaving open a further question: "Do such things as national cultures really exist?"

The answer to that question is that the notion of a consistent English character from the 16th century on is probably a myth, but Orwell adds, "myths which are believed in tend to become true." Thus the behavior of ordinary people during the blitz suggests that they were living up to one major myth, symbolized by the national emblem of "the Bulldog," acknowledging that other nations excelled them in art, music, philosophy, and theory, and were content to be the home of the poets and the scientists. As a result, the foreign observer might conclude that "a profound, almost unconscious patriotism and an inability to think logically are the abiding features of the English character. . . ."

The Moral Outlook of the English People

Since the beginning of the nineteenth century, organized religion has undergone a steady decline in England. The remnants of traditional religion are evident in a "vague theism . . . and an intermittent belief in life after death. . . ," but practices such as church attendance and Bible reading have all but disappeared. One religious value English common people retain is the rejection of the power principle, the worship of power that underlies all the modern "-isms." (It is important to note that the Marxist version of socialism in England attracts mostly middle-class adherents, not working class people.)

For the common people, the central English folktale is "Jack, the Giant Killer," the basic story of the triumph of the underdog. Recent history has shown that the people have sided with the weaker side even when it was not to their advantage, as, for example, in the Irish fight for independence in 1916. More ambivalent is the English attitude toward crime and violence. The downside is that the prevalent attitude is "ignorant and old fashioned," and the upside is that "if Al Capone were in an English jail, it wouldn't be for tax evasion."

The English people are not puritanical. In the 19th century, some workers were browbeaten into behaving like their Calvinist bosses, but that era seems to have passed. The alcoholism generated by cheap gin and other liquors did constitute a serious problem, and the temperance movement was justified until it tried to abolish all liquor, thus separating the working man from his pint and, more importantly, from his pub, "one of the basic institutions of English life. . . ."

Free speech is by and large a reality in England, but freedom of the press is another matter. The power of the press lords means that the large-circulation newspapers pretty much follow the party line of their owners. The people are basically uninterested in theoretical discussions of politics. They have one underlying touchstone: a moral entity, "vaguely described as decency." With that basic foundation, they have withstood the appeal of the "-isms," even in the darkest days of World War II.

The Political Outlook of the English People

The English are not only ignorant of political theory, but they also lack a real understanding of their own political system. The distinction between the two major parties, Labor and Conservative, has blurred, as England and the rest of Europe have moved toward a planned economy, which is to say toward the left. But this is a pragmatic move, not an ideological one. Distrust of ideology is still endemic among English people. The one political term they do employ is *democracy*. Orwell's historical example of what a democracy is not would be the German invasion of Russia in 1941: "The German people woke up to find themselves at war with a country that they had been on friendly terms with on the previous evening." This would never have happened in England. For the English, the government is known as "they." They are in charge, but they are not necessarily trusted. And when they step over the line, they are removed. As for the monarchy, the abdication of Edward VIII in 1936 may have wounded it fatally, but another long reign, like that of Victoria or of George V, might make the crown once again "an appreciable factor in politics."

The English Class System

The unique feature of the English class system is not its unfairness, since distinctions between upper, middle, and lower classes exist in almost every nation, but that it is an anachronism, as becomes clear when you examine the subdivisions within each class. In the case of the upper class, for example, the old aristocracy, families extending back to the Middle Ages, has all but disappeared. What passes for old families today are those who became rich in the Renaissance and in the eighteenth century. These families set up the ideal of the country gentleman with a value system that placed style and tradition above the crass commercialism of the urban rich. Something like this distinction exists among the middle classes, in which the upper middle class is identified not by their income as much as by their manners, speech, and "to some extent, outlook." One characteristic of the upper middle class is their tendency to make major financial sacrifices for the education of their children.

Recently, there has developed a "classless" middle-class figure—the technician or scientist who tends to disregard the past and, as a result, doesn't think of him- or herself in terms of class. As for the working classes, there is a wide gap between the better-paid working-class people and slum dwellers.

One ongoing result of class distinctions is the generally held opinion that the upper classes are better equipped to rule the country, a notion reinforced by the example of Winston Churchill during World War II. This may be a form of snobbishness, but in any case it has been offset by an increased leveling of class distinctions, a process that was sped up by the war years. Also, the resemblance of cheap, mass-produced clothing has given, at least on the surface, a more uniform look to the general population. Other social levelers include popular entertainment, paperback books, and restaurant chains.

All of this does not mean that class differences are disappearing, but one trend seems permanent: the merging of the working and middle classes. Where all this is leading is impossible to determine. Some maintain that individual freedom, of the type that the English people enjoy, depends upon a defined class structure, that freedom and equality are not compatible. Be that as it may, the people seem to want equality.

The English Language

English is a language with a large vocabulary and a simple grammar. Its vocabulary is enhanced by the practice of transforming parts of speech. Thus, nouns are regularly used as verbs, which substantially increases the number of verbs. Also, some verbs can field a large number of meanings by adding certain prepositions, and some nouns can be turned into adjectives by adding suffixes, such as *-ful* and *-like.* Adjectives can be made more flexible by adding nouns, as in *lily white* and *coal black.* English also borrows words freely from other languages, such as *alias, alibi, garage,* and, more recently, *blitz.*

English grammar has very little inflection. Verbs, for example, have only the root inflections: third person, singular, present, and past participle. The other distinctive feature of the language is its broad range of tones, from headlines to lyric poetry. Its simplicity qualifies it as the modern lingua franca, which it is on its way to becoming. The disadvantage of its easy accessibility is that it makes it difficult for the English people to discipline themselves sufficiently to learn a foreign language. Another important fact about using this language, either spoken or written, is that its essence cannot be captured by a series of rules. Nevertheless, certain guidelines are worth noting, chiefly the avoidance of worn-out phrases and dead metaphors. Technical jargon has a corrupting effect on the language, but the chief contaminant is BBC English, because of its wide impact. As a result, English is becoming anemic; it is no longer being enriched from below; it is now being strangled from above by the BBC.

For decades, English has been borrowing from the United States, and particularly its rich lode of slang. This is partly because of its inherent vitality but also because American terms have no class connotations. Although many Americanisms enliven the language, they tend to disallow words that have a history in favor of simple usefulness, so street names in many American cities tend to be numbers. On the whole, the English should try to resist the American influence while continuing to borrow "its best words."

The Future of the English People

It is unlikely that England will play a leading role in international power politics in the future. There is, however, a slim chance of its serving as a model of behavior through the English "habit of not killing each other." England might serve as the leader of western Europe, mediating between "Russian authoritarianism on the one hand and American materialism on the other." But for this to happen, a minimum of four developments need to take place: an increased "birth rate, more social equality, less generalization, and more respect for the intellect." The declining birth rate is an economic problem and can be solved by rewarding large families by providing housing, tax breaks, and free education. Greater equality can be expedited by narrowing the gap in salaries between the top and bottom. Also needed is a more democratic educational system: All children up to the age of 10 or 12 should attend the same schools. After that, they can be separated according to skills and natural ability. This should be accompanied by removing "the class labels from the English language" through teaching a national, standard English that is free from a class association.

Culturally as well as politically, England is London-centric. This centralization has a dispiriting effect on the rest of the country, particularly the agricultural areas. We should encourage regional pride. Scotland and Wales should be more autonomous, and provincial universities should be more heavily subsidized. As for the lack of respect for intellect, the pervasive contempt of the average person for the highbrow, has resulted in English intellectuals' becoming consistently hostile to their native country. Thus, we have a serious weakening of the cultural fabric. But the intellectual atmosphere can be improved through the improvement of education and by recognizing the educational potential of radio, film, and the press.

To summarize the tasks facing the English people:

> They must breed faster, work harder, and probably live more simply, think more deeply, get rid of their snobbishness and their anachronistic class distinctions, and pay more attention to the world and less to their own backyards. Nearly all of them already love their country, but they must learn to love it intelligently. They must have a clear notion of their own destiny and not listen either to those who tell them that England is finished or to those who tell them that the England of the past can return.

The fulfillment of these tasks cannot occur unless the people assume the power that is rightfully theirs. All through the war years, they have been promised this power. Now is the time to redeem those promises.

COMMENTARY

Much of *The English People* covers territory very similar to Orwell's earlier booklet *The Lion and the Unicorn,* published in 1941. The principal difference between the two lies in Orwell's intention. The earlier work was an argument designed to make the case for a socialist government in order to win the war at a time when England was in real danger of losing it. By the time he was writing "The English People" in late 1943 and early 1944, Orwell was clearly aware that the war was being won—and with a conservative government at the helm. At that point, he would have to admit that he was wrong about the war but right in arguing that there had been a shift to the left on the part of the English people. That shift was confirmed in the 1945 Labor Party victory in a national election. In any case, from the publisher's standpoint, *The English People* was meant to be a celebration of English virtues, one of a series titled *Britain in Pictures,* in which the text would be complemented by artists' renderings of representative scenes. In effect, the series was designed to produce a feel-good experience, leaving the readers to exclaim, "Aren't we wonderful?" Orwell's answer, characteristically, is, "Yes, but . . ." As an early warning shot, he begins the opening section, "England at First Glance," with a negative characteristic—"artistic insensibility"—establishing his credentials as a plain speaker. However, he follows that negative with—as he makes clear—a much more important virtue: gentleness. He continues this pattern of alternating weaknesses and strengths throughout. The readers sense that they are dealing with an honest broker who brings with him a lively, offbeat point of view. He is not your conventional spokesman, as he demonstrates in his summary of "abiding features of the English character . . . A profound, deeply rooted patriotism and an inability to think logically." But lest it be thought that the two cancel each other out, he includes one name that, for him, exemplifies this paradox—"Shakespeare"—knowing full well that this is the supreme compliment to pay an English audience. He keeps this audience in a state of uncertainty, never knowing whether it's going to be whipped or praised.

Orwell's second section, "The Moral Outlook of the English People," touches on some of his recurrent themes: the loss of religious belief among common people, the economic roots of 19th-century puritanism, and what he considers the bedrock foundation of English morality, decency. *Decency* is a term that he acknowledges is vague, but its existence is affirmed by the people's refusal to be carried away by contending ideologies.

In section 3, "The Political Outlook of the English People," Orwell describes the popular movement toward a planned economy. He sees it, however, as a pragmatic move rather than an ideological one on the part of the people. The ideological commitment extends only to the term *democracy*. As for the monarchy itself, although seriously wounded by the abdication of Edward VIII in 1936, it still elicits a powerful symbolic emotion among the common people, particularly when the monarchy enjoys a long reign. Here, as elsewhere, Orwell betrays his own sentimental attachment to the monarchy, seeing in its symbolism an important connection with the past.

In "The English Class System"—section 4—Orwell reveals that, the House of Lords notwithstanding, "England has no real aristocracy": that is, families who can trace their roots back to the Middle Ages. What passes for "old families" were early capitalists who acquired their wealth from the late 16th to the 18th centuries. Nevertheless, they did continue the practices of the earlier families in becoming country gentlemen.

Within the middle class there exists a significant divide between the professional subgroup and people "in business," to the disadvantage of the latter. The working class has been going through a process in which they have become politically more opposed to the upper class while culturally more tolerant, and both developments are an indication of the blurring of class lines. The bringing together of classes during the war in organizations such as the HOME GUARD and the firewatchers brigades, in addition to the armed forces, has had a positive effect on class relations. Other factors include industrial improvements that have resulted in mass-produced housing, furniture, and clothing, made possible by installment purchasing. In Orwell's 1939 novel, *Coming Up for Air,* George Bowling, the protagonist, rails against these very developments as examples of the homogenization of English society and the deadening consequences of a machine-made world. What had intervened was a catastrophic war, in which the "dead men" depicted in the novel came to life.

In "The English Language," the fifth section, Orwell touches on points he would later deal with in greater detail in "POLITICS AND THE ENGLISH LANGUAGE," his well-known 1946 essay. He makes the case for a short and simple vocabulary, saying "concrete words are better than abstract ones," and calls for alert awareness when a tired phrase or dead metaphor hovers into view. He makes a strong point in tying the anemic state of present-day English to the class system. He maintains that the language is no longer being fed by the working class, whose language is rooted in material objects rather than in abstract ideas. He also sends out warning signals about the linguistic invasion that accompanied the arrival of American soldiers during the war. It's fine, he argues, to borrow American terms, but not to the extent where they "modify the actual structure of our language." This last phrase smacks of the very vagueness he warns against, since he says nothing further about it.

In the final section, "The Future of the English People," Orwell tackles what he sees as four fundamental issues that England must confront if it expects to play a major role in international politics. The first of these is the declining birth rate, for which he suggests a number of policies that are as elaborate as they are unworkable. Here, he fails to foresee a more obvious solution: the immigration of large numbers of people from the former colonies of India, Pakistan, and the West Indies. His flexible mind never stretched far enough to the extent of redefining the "English" race itself. This same immigration phenomenon would add a new dimension to the class question. He recommends decentralizing British life, including giving more local power to Scotland and Wales. He does not mention Northern Ireland, however, possibly anticipating the hot spot that area was to become.

Reviews of *The English People* were generally favorable. In the complete works, Peter Davison has included the comments of Charles Humana in *Freedom* (October 18, 1947), who pointed out Orwell's principal message, "that of Britain leading a European bloc in the face of a Russo-American Stalemate" (*CW*, XVI, 228). Humana suggests that Orwell is perhaps unconsciously calling for a British Empire, rooted in a version of a "master race." Whether Orwell perceived the threat implicit in his remarks, he was careful to include the "The English People" among his works that he wished not to have reprinted.

WORK CITED

The Complete Works of George Orwell. Vol. 16. Edited by Peter Davison. London: Secker & Warburg, 199–228.

"Farthing Newspaper, A"

Essay published in *G. K.'s Weekly* on December 29, 1928. Orwell describes the publication of a new Paris newspaper, *l'Ami du Peuple,* which sells for an unusually small price and which claims, in ubiquitous mission statements posted throughout the city, that its editorial aims are philanthropic and revolutionary rather than commercial. The journal promises to defend the freedom of the press, fight for a better standard of living, and battle the powerful commercial and political trusts. In September 1789, Jean-Paul Marat (1743–93) introduced a radical paper, *l'Ami du Peuple,* with which he helped incite the French to revolt against the monarchy. The adoption of this title for the 1928 version of *L'Ami du Peuple* most certainly attempted to cash in on the historical significance of this name and its connection to social and political revolution. As Orwell is quick to point out, however, such a connection would be less than accurate.

M. Coty, the publisher of the newspaper, is a prosperous businessman and the proprietor of other popular journals, including *Figaro.* In other words, he is part of the powerful commercial and political trusts that the paper sought to attack. Orwell also claims that the paper is actually "anti-radical and anti-socialist, of the good-will-in-industry, shake-hands-and-make-it-up species" (*CW,* 10, 119). Its growing success, moreover, would eventually result in the failure of other newspapers, thereby stifling freedom of the press.

"A Farthing Newspaper" was the first professional writing published by Orwell in England, and though it is not exclusively socialist in its tone, the article does reveal a suspicion of big business and capitalism. In addition, Orwell displays the iconoclasm and irony that would become principal elements of his later journalism. Perhaps more significant, Orwell uses this article to address the importance of a free press, an issue that informs virtually all of Orwell's writings.

WORK CITED

The Complete Works of George Orwell. Vol. 10. Edited by Peter Davison. London: Secker & Warburg, 119–121.

Film Reviews

After writing THEATER REVIEWS for several months in 1940 for *Time and Tide* magazine, Orwell agreed to review films as well. As with his theater reviewing, he showed no particular aptitude for judging movies. Most of his reviews were written in haste and in fairly general terms. Thus, in his first film review (October 5, 1940) of the Hollywood film *The Doctor Takes a Wife,* he notes the film's "vivid American dialogue [that] makes up for the banal plot." He has a good time with the famous tearjerker *Waterloo Bridge* (November 23, 1940), reporting the conversation of two matrons sitting behind him, which was more interesting than the dialogue on the screen. In his review of the anti-Nazi film *Escape* (January 25, 1941), he deplores its preposterous plot but acknowledges its grimly accurate account of the individual's struggle against a "totalitarian state." Reviewing Preston Sturges's

The Lady Eve (May 24, 1941), starring Barbara Stanwyck, Henry Fonda, and Charles Coburn, he applauds the acting, dialogue, and direction while questioning the psychological probability of the main characters' being attracted to each other.

He is quietly impressed by *Brigham Young* (January 18, 1941), a film that concentrates on the heroic journey of the Mormon community, after being persecuted in and driven out of Illinois to reach their permanent home in Salt Lake City, Utah. "The film is pro-Mormon, the polygamy being played down as much as possible. . . . an interesting example of the way in which important events lose their moral color as they drop backwards into history." His review of *Quiet Wedding* (February 8, 1941) applauds its "entirely English"—"not a single American voice in it"—atmosphere, depicting the "country gentry" in a film that is no less charming, though it is depicting a world that will probably not survive the war. Orwell's general attitude toward films is perhaps best summed up in his review of *One Night in Lisbon* (August 16, 1941), a wartime drama: "What rot it all is. What sickly enervating rubbish . . . and yet as current films go, this is a good film."

The film that he devotes the most serious attention to is Charlie Chaplin's *The Great Dictator* (December 21, 1940). He comments on the strong facial resemblance between Chaplin and Hitler, which forms the basis of the plot in which Chaplin plays two roles, the ruthless dictator Hynkel and a poor little Jewish barber, who is Hynkel's exact double. In the climactic moment in the film, when the meek little barber, assumed to be Hynkel, delivers a passionate defense of democracy, Orwell characterizes the speech as "tremendous . . . one of the strongest pieces of propaganda I have heard for a long time." It is one of history's sharpest ironies, he suggests, that Chaplin, the little guy who's always getting knocked down by bigger bullies, should bear such a strong resemblance to the all-powerful superman, who is bent on ruling the world. Little wonder that Chaplin's films have been banned in Germany. "If our government had a little more imagination, they would subsidize *The Great Dictator* heavily and would make every effort to get a few copies into Germany. . . ." When Orwell wrote those words, he could not have imagined that the English and American governments would ultimately follow his advice. His two satires, which at that point were, if anything, only seeds germinating in his mind—*Animal Farm* and *Nineteen Eighty-Four*—were used in government-sponsored propagandistic films.

Orwell's film reviews are reprinted in volumes 12 and 13 of *The Complete Works of George Orwell*, edited by Peter Davison (London: Secker & Warburg, 1998).

"Good Word for the Vicar of Bray, A"

Essay first published in *Tribune*, April 1946.

SYNOPSIS

Orwell recalls a visit to the vicar of Bray's church in Berkshire. The churchyard contains a "magnificent yew tree" planted by the vicar himself. It strikes Orwell as ironic that a man who is famous for having been a time server should have been responsible for a beautiful tree that has brought pleasure to people for years. He is reminded of Thibaw, the last king of Burma, a murderer and a drunkard who planted tamarind trees along the streets of Mandalay, which offered relief from the hot sun for many years.

At this point, Orwell digresses to speak of a woman, described by John Aubrey, the 17th-century writer, in his *Brief Lives*: The woman, Mrs. Overall, the wife of a Cambridge professor of theology, was "extensively unfaithful" to her husband. In his account of Mrs. Overall, Aubrey includes a ribald poem. Orwell concludes that, like the vicar, Mrs. Overall is a less-than-proper person but has nevertheless brought pleasure and joy to the readers of this poem.

Digression over, Orwell returns to his real subject: the planting of trees. He advocates the practice of planting, particularly hardwood trees, as a way of making a gift to future generations at very little cost. Such an act would have an impact far greater than any other good or bad deed one might do. He cites his own experience at Wallington. In

1936, he planted five fruit trees, seven rose and two gooseberry bushes, at a cost of 12 shillings, 6 pence. They are all healthy and thriving, including one apple tree, a Cox's Orange Pippin, that looked like a weakling when he planted it.

Orwell's one regret is that he has never planted a walnut tree. He is not suggesting that one can fulfill all his obligations as a citizen by planting trees and bushes, but he does recommend doing so each time one commits an antisocial act. As a result, despite the evil you do in your lifetime, you might end up as someone whose life had a positive impact on society after all.

COMMENTARY

Although it is lighthearted in tone, this essay reveals a serious attitude on Orwell's part—his love of nature and his concern for preservation. Usually these concerns take a negative form: deploring the destructive effects of industrialism and suburbanization, which is a major theme of COMING UP FOR AIR. But here, as in Winston Smith's dream of "the Golden Country" in *Nineteen Eighty-Four,* the emphasis is positive, an exhortation to plant and grow for posterity, if not for the present. Implicit in the appeal but not obvious are the pleasure and sense of gratification that comes from the work itself. In his conclusion, he is not above stealing an appeal that originates in Judeo-Christianity, and perhaps in all religions: that of atoning for one's sins by good deeds.

"Hanging, A"

Essay first published in *Adelphi,* August 1931. A short but brilliant and powerful piece of writing that ranks as one of Orwell's finest essays. In *Adelphi,* the name of the author is given as Eric A. Blair, as 1931 was two years before he was to settle on the name George Orwell.

SYNOPSIS

In the sickly light of early morning, the prisoner, a Hindu, is led from his cell on death row. He is a small, "puny wisp of a man" with a comical mustache. His guards, towering over him, link a chain to his handcuffs through their belts. The superintendent of the jail, impatient to have this execution over with, urges the head guard to speed up the process, since the other prisoners cannot be fed until after the hanging.

The narrator, who is present in some official capacity, is part of the procession following the prisoner and his guards. Their progress is halted when, seemingly out of nowhere, a stray dog playfully runs and jumps up on the prisoner, trying to lick his face. It takes several minutes for the guards to snare the frisky dog and lead him away. They resume their march to the gallows, now about 40 yards away. At one point, the prisoner steps aside to avoid a puddle. The narrator records his reaction: "It is curious but till that moment, I had never realized what it means to destroy a healthy conscious man . . . the unspeakable wrongness of cutting a life short when it is in full tide." He was one of us, a creature still capable of normal functions, including those of the mind—remembering, anticipating, and reasoning—and shortly those powers would be gone.

When they reach the gallows, the guards push him up the ladder. Then the hangman climbs up to tie the rope around his neck. At this point, the prisoner begins to call out to his god, Ram, repeating the word continuously, as if it were a chant. Even when the hangman places a hood over the prisoner, the sound of "Ram" continues, rattling the nerves of guards and observers, who want the thing to be over with. Then the order is given and the prisoner disappears through the trap door. The dog gets loose and races over to the body, but stops and retreats to a corner. The observers, including the narrator, walk under the gallows to examine the body, dangling toes-down, slowly revolving on the rope.

On the way out of the prison, the head guard explains that this hanging went very well. Sometimes the prisoner resists, as in the case of one man who held on to the bars of his cell so fiercely it took six guards to dislodge him. He kept resisting even when the guards tried to reason with him, reminding him of all the trouble he was causing them. The narrator and the others laugh uneasily at the story and then move to the superintendent's car to have a drink, about a hundred yards from where the dead man is hanging.

COMMENTARY

There is some question about the factual basis of this essay. MABEL FIERZ, a close friend of Orwell, claimed that he told her he had never attended a hanging. On the other hand, in the autobiographical section of *THE ROAD TO WIGAN PIER,* he writes, "I watched a man hanged once. It seemed to me worse than a thousand murders." For some readers, doubt about whether the essay is an eyewitness account or a short story with a first-person narrator weakens its impact. This is not at all the case with the novelist and critic David Lodge. Lodge argues that it doesn't matter whether Orwell actually witnessed a hanging or not. He argues that "A Hanging" is literature, not journalism. The difference lies in a host of formal elements in the essay. He points out that the essay has been rigorously stripped of external references to the location of the prison, the name of the prisoner, the crime with which he has been charged, and the dates of the events. All these are details that a proper reporter would have included in the first paragraph. In "A Hanging," these things are unimportant, but they would be critical elements in a journalist's report. In literature the key detail is the prisoner's stepping aside to avoid the puddle. This event, Lodge contends, reveals "the paradoxical relationship between the concepts of death, life, and time in the context of capital punishment" (15). We all die, but we don't experience our death. Executions, however, perversely try to create that experience for the condemned, but ordinary life—puddles and dogs and chants—gets in the way, interrupting the process as a form of protest.

George Woodcock's sensitive reading of this essay focuses on its animal imagery, suggesting that the interrupting dog represents "the world of nature" breaking in to condemn "the unnatural proceedings of men" (67–68). Both analyses serve as reminders that Orwell might well be considered a forerunner of the 1960s phenomenon known as the New Journalism, in which a basically factual report is enhanced by the addition of literary features.

WORKS CITED

Lodge, David. *The Modes of Modern Writing.* Ithaca, N.Y.: Cornell University Press, 1977.

Woodcock, George. *The Crystal Spirit.* London: Jonathan Cape, 1967.

Homage to Catalonia

Orwell's third, and commonly considered his finest, nonfiction, full-length book, published in April 1938 by Secker & Warburg. The book was not published in America until 1952, by Harcourt, Brace; this version contained an important introduction by LIONEL TRILLING.

HISTORICAL/BIOGRAPHICAL CONTEXT

For many years, both before and after the 40-year rule of Francisco Franco, Catalonia had been an autonomous region in northwestern Spain. At the outset of the Spanish civil war, its capital, Barcelona, was the center of a successful resistance to Franco's military uprising in the region. The keys to that success were the local working-class "militias," formed by various trade-union factions, the anarchist Confederación Nacional de Trabajo (CNT) and the socialist Union General de Trabajadores (UGT). Some CNT members also joined the smaller PARTIDO OBRERO DE UNIFICACIÓN MARXISTA (POUM), while Communists generally served in the UGT. Since the CNT had played the critical role in the victory, they were the dominant group in the city at the time of Orwell's arrival there.

In December 1936, Orwell finished the final draft of *THE ROAD TO WIGAN PIER,* freeing him to cover the war as a journalist or—possibly at the back of his mind all along—to participate in the fight against fascism directly as a soldier. In order to get press credentials, he applied in London to Harry Pollitt, the general secretary of the British Communist Party, Pollitt refused to help. Orwell then turned to the INDEPENDENT LABOUR PARTY (ILP), which agreed to provide him with the credentials to cover the war for their journal, the *New Leader*. Bearing a letter to JOHN MCNAIR, the ILP

Members of POUM (Partido Obrero de Unification Marxista) unit assembled at the Lenin barracks in Barcelona, Spain, January 1937. Orwell is partially obscured in the extreme rear. *(Orwell Archive, UCL Library Services, Special Collections)*

representative in Barcelona, he left England a few days before Christmas, stopping off in Paris before entering Spain.

While in Paris, he paid a visit to American novelist HENRY MILLER, who advised him not to go to Spain out of a sense of obligation. Miller's morally indifferent attitude to events in Spain disturbed Orwell sufficiently that he later wrote a long essay, "INSIDE THE WHALE," reflecting on the role of the writer in society, with particular attention to Miller. After receiving travel documents from the Spanish embassy, Orwell left Paris for Barcelona on December 26. There he delivered his introductions to John McNair, who arranged men and materials for the ILP, which operated in close collaboration with the POUM. Orwell's affiliation with the POUM would cost him dearly in later months, but at the time, he had no understanding of the complex political relationships among the anti-Franco factions. "When I came to Spain, and for sometime afterwards, I was not only uninterested in the political situation but unaware of it," he would write later in chapter 5 of *Homage*. Orwell had arrived in Spain to fight against fascism and for common decency. The political infighting that would ensue between the Communists and the POUM militias caught him by surprise and ultimately put his life in great danger, the details of which he includes in the closing chapter of *Homage*.

The Communists—the largest and the best funded of all the militias—insisted on a strategy of defeating Franco first, before moving toward a radical social revolution. The POUM insisted on the immediate establishment of a revolutionary government, such as the one operating in Barcelona when Orwell first arrived there. At the time, Orwell largely agreed with the Communist position: "The communists had a definite practical policy, an obviously better policy from the point of view of the common sense which looks only a few months ahead." But the Communist response to the POUM's dissenting opinion was to begin a ruthless campaign of suppression, including murder and imprisonment of their allies. Their enmity toward the POUM had been intensified by the latter's open and defiant denunciation of the "Show Trials," then being conducted in Moscow.

The betrayal of the POUM had a profound effect on Orwell. As he wrote to his publisher Victor Gollancz while still in Spain in May 1937, "I hope I shall get a chance to write the truth about what I have seen. The stuff appearing in the English papers is largely the most appalling lies—more I can't say, owing to the censorship. If I can get back in August I hope to have a book ready for you about the beginning of next year." Orwell had at the time been recovering from a near-fatal bullet wound to the throat that he received on May 20, 1937. He planned to seek his discharge papers and prepare for his return to England. But upon returning from the hospital to the Hotel Continental in Barcelona, his wife, Eileen, who had followed him to Barcelona to work in the ILP office, was waiting for him in the lobby. She walked up to him and whispered that agents were waiting to arrest him. The purge of anarchists and POUM militiamen had begun.

It is likely that Orwell had been taking notes for his book about Spain while in the trenches. He is known to have kept a journal—which was seized, along with photographs and newspaper clippings, when police conducted a search of his wife's hotel room in Barcelona. Orwell and Eileen eventually fled Spain for France, and with considerable difficulty. They returned to Wallington in early July, at which time Orwell began work on *Homage to Catalonia.*

Concurrent with his work on *Homage,* Orwell also asked *The New Statesman* and *Nation* if they would be interested in an article on Spain. He sent them the essay "SPILLING THE SPANISH BEANS." It was rejected, but he published it in two parts in *The New English Weekly* on July 29 and September 2, 1937. Then the *New Statesman* asked him to review Franz Borkenau's *The Spanish Cockpit,* based on his experiences in Spain, including a stint in a communist prison. Orwell called it the best work published on the Spanish war. Borkenau, like Orwell, found uncomfortable equivalences between Stalinism and fascism. Orwell's review, which included many of his own opinions about the Communist betrayal in Spain, was rejected by *New Statesman* editor Kingsley Martin. "The reason," he explained to Orwell in a letter, "is simply that it too far controverts the political policy of the paper." Orwell found a more willing publisher in *Time and Tide* in July. These two rejections were forerunners of things to come, as Orwell suffered a blacklisting from the English leftist press.

Orwell's conflicts with many of London's left-wing publications—all of whom feared that his attacks on communism and the Soviet Union would undermine the Republican cause—did not bode well for the future of his own book on Spain. In London, he found the city's leftist intellectuals engaged in a war of words. Anyone remotely affiliated with the POUM and critical of the Communists became the object of vicious political attacks. Articles and interviews in the Communist *Daily Worker* increasingly suggested that POUM militiamen were not merely Trotskyist dupes but collaborators with the fascists. The *Daily Worker* printed a long statement by FRANK FRANKFORD, who had served in the same ILP unit with Orwell. According to the article, Frankford claimed he had witnessed carts from the POUM camp crossing the fascist lines at Alcubierre, and said it was generally understood that the POUM was supplying the fascists with weapons. Two days later, the paper issued a correction, at Frankford's request, to say that he could not be sure that the carts actually crossed the lines. Both John McNair and Orwell responded to Frankford's charges in letters to *The New Leader.* After a point-by-point refutation of Frankford's alleged charges, Orwell suggested that he allowed the slander to be printed under his name in order to "save his skin," that is, to get out of prison in Barcelona. Orwell's account was cosigned by 14 other members of the ILP unit. Interviewed by Bernard

Crick in 1979, Frankford denied ever "having written the statement or even having signed it" (Crick, 439, n. 63).

It was in the midst of this political upheaval among the English Left that Orwell worked on his manuscript of *Homage to Catalonia.* His slant on events in Spain would lead to more attacks and allegations. In fact, they would lead to his publisher Victor Gollancz's refusal to publish *Homage to Catalonia.* Gollancz had written in early July, in response to Orwell's description of the content of his proposed book on Spain, to say that he felt the work would "harm the fight against fascism." The perceived unwillingness of many to hear (or let others hear) the truth about Spain affected Orwell deeply. "People who ought to know better have lent themselves to the deception on the ground that if you tell the truth about Spain it will be used as Fascist propaganda," Orwell wrote in "Spilling the Spanish Beans."

Shortly after Gollancz's refusal, Fredric Warburg contacted Orwell and expressed interest in a book about Spain. The two met on July 8, and Orwell said that he would likely have a finished manuscript by the end of the year, despite his writing commitments, which were considerable during this period. Orwell participated actively in defending himself and others against ideological attacks, largely coming from the *Daily Worker.* "These people are well aware that I am writing a book about the Spanish war and would, if they could, get me written off beforehand as a liar, so as to discredit anything I say," he wrote to his agent Leonard Moore in August 1937. Nonetheless, Orwell finished a draft of *Homage* in December and completed work in early January 1938. *Homage to Catalonia* was published on April 25, 1938.

SYNOPSIS

Chapter 1

Orwell begins with a personal portrait of an Italian militiaman, whose person and appearance capture something of the spirit of Barcelona and the significance of the events occurring there. The anarchist militias control most of Catalonia, and the city of Barcelona has the appearance of a functional classless society. Despite the general high spirits of the Spanish people, the city itself is in shambles from the fighting. Food stores are scarce, and the streets and buildings have sustained significant damage. At night, the town is kept dark for fear of air raids, but the streets are filled with the sound of revolutionary songs.

A similar turmoil affects the troops of the militia. Orwell is stationed in the Lenin Barracks, where he waits with other soldiers until enough men can be assembled and trained to be sent to the front. With the exception of drilling in the parade grounds, the men of Lenin Barracks receive very little in the way of practical training. Many have no knowledge of firing or loading a rifle, and equipment and uniforms are scarce. Orwell does learn something of the spirit of the Spanish people. He notes their overwhelming generosity and decency. He also recognizes the disorganization, lack of discipline, and extreme youth of many of the recruits, some of whom have enlisted for the money and the food.

After many delays, Orwell's militia receives its orders. With little equipment available, they assemble in the barracks square under torchlight and, to the sound of revolutionary songs, march through the town, accompanied by the cheers of bystanders waving revolutionary flags. At the station, the ill-equipped militia boards a train for the Aragon front.

Chapter 2

The train arrives in Barbastro, a small village well behind the front lines and teaming with militiamen. Orwell's company travels by lorry first to Siétamo, a hotly contested village that repeated shelling has reduced to rubble. Later that evening, the company arrives in Alcubierre, about three miles from the front, and they bunk in a mule stable on dirty chaff. The town has sustained little damage from shelling, but the streets are filled with mud, refuse, and human waste.

For the next two days, the militia waits for the arrival of weapons. The front lines are relatively quiet, with most of the activity limited to the occasional influx of fascist deserters. Most of these soldiers are not regular troops but rather young conscripts who happened to be serving their military term at the outbreak of hostilities. Hungry, ill-equipped, and young, the deserting troops are barely distinguishable from the militiamen of Orwell's company.

Supplies of rifles arrive on the third day in Alcubierre. Rusty and damaged, the 40-year-old German Mauser rifles are barely functional. Each man receives a rifle and 50 cartridges of ammunition; after a cursory introduction on loading and disassembling the rifles, the troops form ranks and leave for the front. GEORGES KOPP, a Belgian volunteer and *commandante* of Orwell's company, leads the militia to a mountaintop position across a valley from the fascist forces. Along the way, Orwell despairs of the disorganization among the militia and the youthfulness of most of his comrades. Stories from his youth about the trench fighting during World War I make Orwell fear what he will find at the front. The reality, however, proves to be far different.

Separated from opposing forces by a wide ravine, the POUM positions ring a mountaintop, with shallow dugouts and a parapet providing the only cover. The captain of the militia to be relieved by Orwell's company, named Levinski but called Benjamin by his men, greets the reinforcements and shows them around the front line. Though the distance between the opposing forces is too great to fire the rifles with any accuracy, both sides trade a few stray shots. One young boy sustains the group's first casualty when his corroded rifle explodes in his face as he fires it. When sentries from Orwell's company take their positions for guard duty, they begin firing eagerly but with little reason across the ravine. Orwell joins them after being encouraged by his comrades and notes that this is the first time he has fired a weapon at a human being. Orwell is dismayed by the essential stalemate between the fascist troops and the POUM militia, both of which occupy safe positions too distant from each other to offer much chance of engagement.

Chapter 3

The principal concern for the troops of Orwell's company is keeping warm. The enemy poses only a minor threat at night when they might decide to make a surprise attack. The front line itself zigzags across flat mountain peaks above a wide valley. The daily routine for Orwell and his company consists primarily of collecting firewood, serving sentry duty, digging trenches, and performing patrol duty. Their current position had once been the scene of fierce skirmishes, but now both sides seem content to hold the positions they have captured, due in part to the low supplies of ammunition.

At night and during misty weather, patrols are sent into the valley between the opposing positions. Few volunteer for this duty, but Orwell likes wandering through the dark valleys, even at one point going as far as the fascist lines. Upon his arrival at the front, Orwell receives the rank of corporal and takes command of a squad of 12 men. The troops, however, show little discipline and often fall asleep on guard duty. The militia system at that time, and for many months following, functions along political lines, though the militias attempt to re-create the classless ideal among the ranks. All soldiers draw the same pay, and the only real distinction in rank is between an officer and a nonofficer. Orwell notes that, despite the lack of training within the militias and the general disfavor with which journalists looked upon them, the militias held their lines while the regular Loyalist army forces trained in the rear.

While firewood remains a constant need and water is closely rationed, most other items (like food, cigarettes, and candles) remain in good supply. The chief struggle is accepting the boredom of life along the front. The fascists and militias each hold essentially impregnable positions. Each side also suffers from a lack of ammunition. Orwell also notes that political reasons, which he did not perceive until much later, prolong the delay in fighting. The militias possess few functional weapons, generally aged rifles built from odd parts and shoddy hand grenades that kill the throwers almost as often as the targets. Helmets, bayonets, pistols, and a variety of other useful gear are rarely available. When fighting does occur, casualties in Orwell's company are frequently the result of accidents, malfunctioning weapons, and poor training.

Chapter 4

Orwell is transferred to a company of English volunteers from the Independent Labour Party who arrive in Alcubierre and take up positions along a mountain ridge at Monte Oscuro, to the west and in sight of Zaragosa. Among them is BOB SMILLIE, whose later death in Valencia would deeply affect Orwell. The company also includes a dozen Spanish machine gunners. Orwell's new post sits somewhat closer to the fascist lines, but the distance still prevents much engagement with the enemy position. The fascist troops comprise mostly Spaniards, but deserters report the presence of a few German noncommissioned officers. Near the front lines is a tract of unoccupied land to which both the militias and the fascists send patrols.

The weather remains clear and cold, and the soldiers among the militia are required to function for long periods without much sleep. Basic supplies such as candles and matches become scarce, and water comes in small quantities by donkey from Alcubierre. At Monte Pocuro, along the Zaragosa front, Orwell has few occasions to fire on enemy positions. The principal weapon here is propaganda. Both sides try to demoralize each other by screaming slogans or misrepresenting the quality of rations in an attempt to convince soldiers to desert. These methods prove surprisingly effective on the fascists.

In February, a fascist airplane drops leaflets over Orwell's position, which announce the fall of Málaga. The news sparks a halfhearted attack by fascist forces, during which most of the militia's weapons malfunction. This is Orwell's first experience under direct and intense fire, and he is humiliated to discover that he feels horribly frightened, thinking each moment about what part of his body might be struck by an enemy bullet. A few days later, news reports carry stories about the attack, in which they embellish the details on both sides. This experience teaches Orwell to distrust any such future reports, and he even questions the news about the fall of Málaga. In coming days, however, the fall is verified; from these reports, it seems likely that the capture of the town by Italian forces was accomplished through betrayal. The Loyalist forces were allowed to evacuate the town, while civilians were indiscriminately killed. Orwell begins to have his first serious misgivings about the war. In mid-February, Orwell and all POUM forces in the area join other militias preparing to besiege Huesca.

Chapter 5

Orwell's new position at Huesca, where once again the anti-Franco forces seem more intent on containing the enemy than defeating them, increasingly brings to his attention the political divisions on the Republican side. Upon his arrival in Spain, Orwell had no interest in the political side of the conflict. He simply wanted to fight against fascism and for "common decency." His choice to serve in the POUM militia is a matter of expediency, as he possessed letters of introduction to the group from the Independent Labour Party. The various political divisions within the anti-Franco forces merely exasperate Orwell, who naively believes that all parties aligned against fascism are fundamentally socialist in orientation.

The political foundation of the Spanish civil war has been obscured in Orwell's estimation by the nature of Franco's revolt against the Spanish government. Unlike other fascist leaders, Franco rose to power in what amounted to a military mutiny, which enjoyed the support of the Spanish aristocracy, the church, and what Orwell identifies as the liberal bourgeoisie. In opposition to Franco, the Spanish working classes and trade unions organized and armed themselves for revolution. They seized land and factories, and they destroyed churches and banished or killed priests, contributing to the impression among foreign press that Franco was resisting a communist revolution in Spain.

In early skirmishes, fascist forces were defeated primarily by poorly armed troops composed of members of the working class and trade unions. The resistance in Catalonia, more than in other parts of Spain, was clearly intent on promoting a socialist agenda through collectivization of industry and the organization of a worker's government and a worker's militia. The revolutionary nature of the resistance to Franco received little attention outside of Spain. Orwell suggests that this deception occurs particularly because of the influence of the Soviet Union, whose position as chief arms supplier to the anti-Franco forces allowed them considerable political leverage, but capitalist nations that have significant holdings in Spain also have no interest in reporting any news that suggests a socialist revolution in Spain. Such an event, if it were to occur, would threaten their investments. It was in the interest of both the Soviet Union and the English governments, in Orwell's estimation, to distort the facts as to what was happening in Spain.

For several weeks, during lulls in the fighting, Orwell hears endless discussions about the shifting political situation in Spain. The three most prominent political viewpoints belonged to the Marxist militia, the Communist brigades, and the anarchist faction, all of which have different agendas in the fight against Franco. These differences would eventually spill over into the press and spark a prolonged and vicious feud among the antifascist forces, particularly between the Communist brigades and the POUM. What began as a disinformation campaign in the press would lead ultimately to an active suppression of POUM members, who were initially attacked for ideological differences before being branded as outright traitors. While Orwell has some sympathy for the Communist position—win the war first, and then focus on the revolution—he discovers over time that this is simply a cover, that the Communists were doing their level best to prevent any kind of socialist revolution in Spain.

Disunity among the anti-Franco forces weakens their position. Orwell speculates that weapons were intentionally withheld from the anarchist and Marxist militias for fear that they would retain them for revolutionary purposes after Franco's defeat. The Communist emphasis on nonrevolutionary, or democratic, victory in Spain essentially kills the fervor among working classes outside of Spain, who had previously supported the revolutionary action against Franco with money and troops. In the early months of his involvement in the war, Orwell does not see the outcome of all these theories. He is chiefly concerned with the perpetual inaction and the feeling that he has not done his fair share of fighting. He resolves to join the Communist brigade when he returns to Madrid from the front. He notes that, although all this time he was very critical of the POUM position, he never suffered for it. His comrades were completely tolerant of his minority opinion. All this time, Orwell never officially joined the POUM, but in hindsight, after the persecution of group members begins in later months, he comes to wish that he had.

Chapter 6

Still in Huesca, Orwell continues with the daily grind of patrols, digging trenches, and enduring wind, rain, and occasional snow. He sees no direct action against the enemy except for occasional stray bullets and random but inaccurate shelling. Patrols sometimes infiltrate the no-man's land between the two positions to look for signs of activity. The troops in Orwell's militia are now slightly better armed than before, but no action against the fascist positions is ordered until six weeks pass. Then the militias stage an assault on a section of the fascist line, but the attack is compromised when one of the militiamen's grenades falls short. Alerted to the attack, the fascists open fire and drive the militias back. By March, the militias are running short of food and ammunition. Orwell's wife, Eileen, arrives in Barcelona and sends him packages of tea, chocolate, and tobacco whenever she can acquire them. Orwell leaves the front for 10 days at the end of March to treat an infected hand. During his stay in the hospital, someone steals most of his personal possessions, including a camera and all his photographs. He recuperates for a few days in the battle-damaged village of Monflorite, near the front. There he discovers signs of the coming spring: subtle changes in the weather as well as peasants cultivating the fields that used to belong to landowners loyal to Franco. In the village graveyard, he is surprised by the almost complete absence of religious iconography. He suggests that the revolutionary fervor of Catalonia has spelled the temporary destruction of the influence of the church.

Orwell returns to his unit on the day they advance their position to within a few hundred yards of the fascist lines. Nearly 600 troops make the move and dig 1,200 meters of trenches under the cover of darkness, without alerting the enemy. The next morning, when the fascist sentries spot the new lines, they open fire with machine guns and rifles, killing several militiamen but not as many as if they had been more organized and thought to employ artillery. Orwell spends that night in a barn, where he and a group of militiamen, awaiting attack orders, rest on piles of human and animal bones that swarm with rats. The attack is called off, as is one scheduled for the next evening. While waiting to be useful to the war effort, Orwell listens to the anarchist militias attacking fascist positions near Huesca. Along several approaches to the city, the militias construct barricades and firm up their defenses, while the fascists rain artillery shells upon them and snipers pick off a few individual men.

Chapter 7

Orwell volunteers for a diversionary attack with 14 other militiamen. One evening, at midnight, they move through rain-filled trenches to a farmyard near the fascist lines. There, they learn that their mission is to penetrate the lines and seize a series of trenches. Simultaneously, a group of shock troops will attack an adjoining position connected by a communication trench. After a delay of more than an hour, the men march single file toward their target. The rain and the terrain make a silent approach difficult, but Orwell and his companions make it through the outer perimeter without detection. As they breach the inner perimeter, however, fascist sentries open fire with rifles and grenades. An intense firefight follows, while Orwell is caught between enemy fire ahead of him and friendly fire to the rear. After a pause in the action from the fascists, Orwell and the rest of the militiamen charge the trench and drive them out. While the men search the trench for ammunition and other supplies, Orwell spots a retreating fascist and gives chase with his bayonet; the man soon outruns him and Orwell returns to his group.

Though initially driven back, the fascists begin to regroup and fight their way back. The shock troops fail to capture their end of the trench, and Orwell's group is ordered to retreat. In the darkness, the men have difficulty distinguishing the enemy troops from their own. As dawn approaches, the militiamen are in complete disarray and scrambling for the POUM lines without knowing precisely where they are. Some men mistakenly run directly toward the fascist lines, from which pour heavy rifle fire and grenades. Orwell's group finally reaches their lines as dawn breaks, and they learn that an otherwise botched assault is judged a success by their commanders. The purpose of their mission was to divert fascist troops from Huesca to facilitate an attack by the anarchist militias.

Chapter 8

The weather begins to warm up as summer approaches. A group of Andalusian soldiers joins Orwell's regiment, and while their political affiliations might be cause for speculation, their skill at rolling the dry and inferior Spanish tobacco—the only type available—is undeniable. At midday, the heat is almost unbearable. Two English volunteers die of sunstroke, and the rest of the men are plagued by mosquitoes, lice, and rats. Another lull occurs in the fighting as the POUM and fascist lines trade occasional sniper fire. The anarchist position along outside Huesca, which had sustained heavy casualties, remains in place. They manage to block the road and guard it with machine-gun nests. The fascists, however, construct a sunken road adjacent to the road that accommodates the arrival of occasional supply trucks. Deserters inform the militiamen that Huesca has large supplies of ammunition but little food. It is in no danger of falling to the anti-Franco forces. The Republican government would later wage a massive land and air assault on Huesca, but even this could not dislodge the fascists.

Orwell has now been on the front lines for nearly four months. He reflects on the limited contributions he has made to the fight against Franco. He has seen only limited fighting and feels isolated from events happening elsewhere in Spain, particularly in Madrid. His time at the Aragon front, however, has provided an education that he could not have acquired in any other manner. The POUM militia to which he is attached has brought him a keen and personal understanding of socialism. The militiamen have created a relatively classless society, in which all members are, or feel, equal. The militias, in Orwell's view, are truly revolutionary, and socialism is the default political position, while capitalism is almost universally reviled. "One had breathed the air of equality," Orwell says of his experiences during the four months on the line. For him, the militias represent a microcosm of the classless society for which they are fighting to achieve. The unpleasantness of life in the trenches fades in later months, though his memories of it remain vivid. The sights, sounds, and faces of his comrades have taken on considerable importance in Orwell's memories. On April 25, Orwell and his comrades are relieved by a new section of militiamen. They hand over their rifles and equipment and march back to Monflorite. After a short rest, they travel—first by truck and then by train—to Barcelona, where they arrive the following afternoon.

Chapter 9

Orwell notices immediately a difference in the atmosphere of the city. The revolutionary spirit so prominent in prior months has vanished. The people seem to have lost interest in the war, and the social divisions that once appeared on the verge of elimination are now reappearing. Those in the militias were initially motivated by the belief that they would be fighting for social equality. As it becomes evident that such a future in Spain is remote, the number of volunteers for the militias declines sharply. The influence has shifted to the government-established Popular Army, which operates in a different manner than the militias. The Popular Army maintains strict distinctions between rank, pay, uniforms, and equipment among its members—the lack of such distinctions had been a distinguishing feature of the militias for Orwell. To combat the growing apathy toward the war, the government has instituted conscription. Barcelona's distance from the principal fronts of the civil war might explain the public's waning interest. The local population thinks more about food shortages than the outcome of the war, though most hope that Franco will ultimately be defeated. Now back in Barcelona, Orwell notices that most politically minded people speak more about the growing divide between communists and anarchists than the threat from Franco of a fascist government.

In Orwell's absence, the militias have become unpopular, where a political campaign in favor of the Popular Army has begun. Its streets once filled with workers singing revolutionary songs and believing that a true socialist society was imminent, Barcelona now exhibits strict class divisions. The streets now teem with smartly dressed people. Expensive restaurants cater to the wealthy classes, while the majority of the city's residents struggle to procure basic necessities. Workers' patrols, previously responsible for civil security, have been dissolved by the government and replaced by the prewar police force. Orwell uses the shortage of tobacco to illustrate the social shift taking place in the city. Throughout Spain, tobacco is in short supply. Profiteers in Barcelona, however, have found a way to smuggle in expensive foreign tobacco, which they sell at exorbitant rates at smart hotels that serve the city's wealthy class. Barcelona has not suffered the physical ravages of the war like other cities in Spain, and Orwell suggests that the natural camaraderie that exists among people in difficult circumstances no longer exists. The case is much different in Madrid, the civil war's principal front, where deprivations and the dangers of war drive people together despite their differing economic backgrounds.

In his first week back in Barcelona, and despite his awareness of growing social inequalities, Orwell takes advantage of as many luxuries as he can afford—good food, wine, and American cigarettes. He also searches for a revolver, which is impossible to acquire in the militia, though more useful in the trenches than a rifle. The government refuses to issue revolvers to militiamen, but the city's police officers and officers in the Popular Army carry them. After considerable effort, Orwell purchases a revolver from an anarchist. He also makes preliminary arrangements to transfer out of the POUM militia, hoping to join a unit that will serve on the Madrid front. To get to Madrid, Orwell discovers that he must join the communist International Brigade, which requires a recommendation from a Communist Party member. A friend agrees to help him join, but he decides to take a week of rest first before returning to the war. Had he joined immediately, Orwell speculates, he would have missed witnessing the fighting that subsequently broke out in Barcelona and thus would not have been in a position to refute the "official story" of events.

Beneath the revived capitalist atmosphere of Barcelona, Orwell sees a growing hatred between those who desire a true socialist revolution in Spain—the workers' militias—and the Communists who want to prevent it. The government has begun to make efforts toward disarming militia members in Barcelona, many of whom hold key industrial positions controlled by the trade unions. Rumors abound of violence breaking out sporadically between the anarchist CNT and the communists of the larger and better-equipped Partido Socialist Unificado de Cataluna (PSUC). A May 1 demonstration planned by two key workers' groups—including the CNT—to show solidarity among the workers is called off by the government. Orwell had intended to march in support of the POUM, but he is relieved at the cancellation because the demonstration would likely have ended in violence.

Chapter 10

The unrest in Barcelona, long hinted at since Orwell's return to the city, erupts on May 3, when a group of government Civil Guards attack the city's telephone exchange, under the control of the anarchist militia (the CNT). The assault follows a decree by the government that requires the CNT to hand over its weapons. Orwell hears gunfire break out throughout the city but initially has no idea what has caused it. The streets empty, and many POUM members head for the headquarters to receive their orders. Throughout the city, barricades go up, and the various militia factions take up positions to guard the city buildings under their control. In the next five days, the militias square off against the Civil Guards and the forces of the PSUC. Orwell verifies that his wife—staying at the Hotel Continental in Barcelona—is safe, and he spends the better part of a week on guard duty at POUM headquarters in a tower across the street. He leaves his post only periodically to search for food. The city is thrown into chaos as gunmen fire indiscriminately at anyone in the streets. Weapons and ammunition are scarce, and twice Orwell has the rifle that was issued to him at POUM headquarters taken from him.

Orwell meets Georges Kopp and discovers that the militia has been ordered to adopt a defensive position in the fighting and not engage the Civil Guards unless fired on by them. Amid the swelling violence, Orwell and the rest of the city struggle to understand who is fighting whom and for what reason. Word begins to circulate that the government in Valencia has dispatched 6,000 Assault Guards to quell the fighting in Barcelona, and in response, the POUM will divert 5,000 troops from the Aragon front to stop them. After a few days of fighting, Orwell learns from Kopp that the government is planning to outlaw and ultimately suppress the POUM. Orwell and the handful of men guarding the headquarters prepare for an all-out assault by hoarding what little fresh water is available and securing the building's perimeter. Orwell expects a long, pitched battle and decides to get some rest before it begins. When he wakes, his wife is at the headquarters with him. Something of an armistice has taken effect throughout the city. The Ramblas—the wide central street that runs through the city—is filled with people, and shops have reopened.

The respite is short-lived, as fighting again breaks out later that evening. At the Hotel Continental, where Orwell and his wife take their meals, a collection of militiamen, communists, journalists, and dozens of men, women, and children, hoping to escape the fighting in the streets, have gathered. Suspicions run high as everyone suspects everyone else of being a spy for one group or another. By the end of the week, the fighting appears to have ended, and the government begins to broadcast the message that the city's population should stay at home as much as possible and anyone found in possession of a weapon on the streets after a certain hour will be arrested. The shops begin to open again, and people return to the streets. The Assault Guards from Valencia arrive suddenly that evening. Well dressed and equipped with new weapons, the Assault Guards begin regular patrols of the city.

The guards at POUM headquarters discover that they have left six rifles in the tower across the street. Orwell and a Spanish youth volunteer to retrieve them in the evening and secretly return them to headquarters. They face arrest if they are discovered in possession of the rifles. The two eventually retrieve the rifles, concealing them individually in their trousers. The following morning, the Assault Guards are out in force in the streets. Orwell is impressed with their discipline and the quality of their equipment. He notes that the police force and the Assault Guards are far better equipped than the militias, despite the fact that they have not been stationed at the front. The Assault Guards get on well with the people in Barcelona, but brief spots of violence break out with anarchist militia members. When some of the troops searching people in the streets discover a CNT militia card, they tear it up and stamp on it, provoking some anarchists to retaliate.

The fighting in Barcelona has given the Valencia government an excuse to assume greater control of the city, once firmly in the hands of the workers. The government intends to disband the militias and absorb them into the Popular Army. Barricades are removed throughout the city, though the ones in front of Communist-controlled buildings are allowed to remain. The police seize CNT weapons, and the anarchist newspaper *La Batalla* suffers heavy censorship. Meanwhile, the communist media suffers no censorship, publishing inflammatory articles calling for the suppression of the POUM, which they declare to be a fascist organization. The "official" or Communist version of the past week's fighting describes it as a fifth-column fascist uprising initiated by the POUM.

Communist newspapers from abroad begin to arrive in Barcelona, and they are filled with partisan and largely untruthful accounts of the unrest in the city. These reports are written by journalists well removed from the events they purport to describe. Asked at this time by a Communist friend whether he still intends to join the International Brigade, Orwell says no because it might mean taking up arms against the Spanish working classes. He senses that the brewing political situation in Barcelona will require taking a side. As the fighting has subsided, the CNT releases prisoners taken during the week. The Civil Guards, however, refuse to release captured workers and in fact continue to arrest innocent workers and foreign citizens, including an English friend of Orwell's.

Having described his personal experience during the internecine fighting in Barcelona, Orwell prepares to analyze the reasons behind it in order to combat the overwhelmingly untruthful accounts that are circulating widely. He offers a warning to readers with no interest in the political controversies that exist between the various antifascist groups and suggests that they skip the next chapter. He concludes ominously by saying that the fighting in Barcelona is far more significant than might appear at first glance.

Chapter 11

Orwell admits that no completely accurate and unbiased account of the Barcelona fighting is possible, but he proposes to explain the things he witnessed firsthand and the accounts of those he deems reliable. He locates the source of the outbreak of violence in the growing tension between communists and anarchists in the city that reached its climax in May 1937. The government's announcement that all private arms should be surrendered gave a clear indication that they intended to build up a nonpolitical or nonrevolutionary police force from which the working classes, specifically the anarchists, would be excluded. Their next move would be to seize control of key industries controlled by the workers' trade unions.

The government's attack on the Barcelona Telephone Exchange on May 3 convinced many that they had initiated an all-out war on the anarchists with the assistance of the PSUC. Simultaneous with the assault on the telephone exchange, the Civil Guards seized other strategically located buildings. Word spread among the working classes that they were being attacked, and fighting erupted in the streets, though mainly defensive in nature. Orwell witnesses no workers storming buildings and no use of artillery during the fighting. Orwell also notes that there was no fixed plan for the revolt. CNT and UGT leaders exhorted the population to resume their normal lives and avoid aggravating the situation. The fighting stopped on May 6, and the following day, the assault troops from Valencia arrived. The government then demanded that all nonregular troops surrender their arms. The death toll for the week of fighting was officially set at 400, with 1,000 wounded. Orwell considers these figures inflated.

The fighting in Barcelona, Orwell suspects, has had little or no impact on the war against Franco, though he admits that it is impossible to say with certainty. The negative consequences—Valencia's assumption of power in Barcelona, the breakup of the militias, and the suppression of the POUM—would have happened in Orwell's view regardless of events. The question of whether the CNT members who took to the streets gained or lost because of the fighting is to Orwell a more important question. Since the outbreak of civil war in Spain, the workers' militias had been losing direct control of the state, which was slowly being centralized and which would ultimately have ended with state or private capitalism. The resistance of the CNT might have slowed this process. Orwell denies the widely disseminated claim that the uprising was a preconceived plot to overthrow the government, except that everyone in Barcelona seemed to expect that violence would eventually erupt. While a few smaller groups added a revolutionary tinge to the fighting in Barcelona, they did so after the fighting started. The CNT leadership disavowed the uprising initially to preserve their involvement in the government and to prevent rupturing their efforts at reconciliation with the UGT. In addition—though this was not widely known at the time—the CNT feared foreign intervention if the working classes had captured the city. British warships had arrived in the harbor during the fighting, ostensibly to protect British interests. Orwell considers it likely that they would have intervened in the event of a working-class takeover.

The POUM had actively participated in the uprising to protect their interests. There is also evidence that some members supported a pamphlet circulated by a group called Friends of Durutti, which advocated a workers' takeover of the city. The pamphlet is something of a mystery to Orwell, as no one was able subsequently to find a copy of it. Ultimately the POUM leadership tried to restrain the workers and limit their activity to defensive actions. They ordered no attacks and principally manned barricades protecting POUM-controlled buildings. The anarchist newspaper *La Batalla* also carried warnings for militiamen not to leave the front to participate in the uprising. In the end, there was no concerted effort to overthrow the government, according to Orwell. The workers' actions were in response to what they believed was an attack by local police. Orwell also dismisses the idea that the uprising was an attempt by communist factions to smash the power of the CNT.

The events in Barcelona were widely discussed in the foreign press, where the uprising was characterized as an insurrection by anarchists and Trotskyists who stabbed the Spanish government in the back. In the English press, the Spanish government's attempt to disarm the CNT was presented as an effort to acquire much-needed arms for the men fighting at the Aragon front. Both the CNT and PSUC were caching weapons, though no attempt was made to disarm the communist group. In addition, the local police force and civil guards serving at the rear of the front had plenty of new weapons and equipment that could have been diverted to the front. A natural antipathy existed between the communist factions and those of the anarchists, exacerbated when the communist ranks swelled with the introduction of numerous foreign communists, many of whom expressed a desire to liquidate the ranks of the anarchists after Franco fell.

The attack on the telephone exchange was simply the last straw in Orwell's view. Reports that the Civil Guards were attempting to seize buildings that the workers had previously won during earlier fighting—buildings of significant sentimental importance—rallied the workers. A natural enemy of the anarchists, the Civil Guards were linked in many people's minds with capitalists and wealthy landowners. They were also of doubtful loyalty to the antifascist side, as many had been known to defect to Franco when attacked. Orwell concludes that the blame for events in Barcelona cannot fall on one side. It was portrayed that way because the revolutionary parties never had any influence in the foreign press, which systematically denigrated them.

Orwell admits that his analysis of events is biased, though he has tried to be objective. Such efforts at fairness were never made in the communist press, whose reporting on events became the most widely accepted. Orwell exhorts his readers to look at the issue from all sides and with equal skepticism. Because of communist influence, the POUM became the sole scapegoat for the bloodshed in Barcelona, and they were labeled by the Communists as Franco's fifth column engaged in a fascist plot. An excerpt from a *Daily Worker* article illustrates this point. Orwell counters this assertion by explaining that the POUM had too few members and too little influence to perpetrate such a plot, and the POUM stronghold at Lérida was in no way involved in the events of Barcelona, which they would have been if they were in league with Franco. Moreover, the allegations presented in the communist press were based on no concrete evidence.

The events leading up to the fighting in Barcelona, as reported in the communist press, also reveal a systematic misrepresentation of facts. Orwell provides numerous excerpts to show the distortions, which he believes were designed to stir up hatred against the POUM. Communist newspapers frequently published information—numbers of POUM forces—that could have been useful to the fascist side and compromised the war against Franco. One particularly egregiously distorted report claimed that POUM militiamen were playing soccer with fascist troops when in fact they were fighting and suffering heavy losses—including many of Orwell's friends—at the hands of the fascists. Had the government not been under the influence of the communist factions, they would never have allowed such reports to be circulated in Spain.

Such allegations against the POUM, in Orwell's opinion, defied common sense. The POUM militiamen all had revolutionary and antifascist histories. Jacques Maurin, a leader of the POUM, had been one of the first people to warn the government about Franco's impending revolt, and the POUM was one of the first groups to form militias in Catalonia and Madrid. Orwell witnessed no fascist activities during his months with the POUM, though he admits that their stance on revolution in Spain may be seen to have divided the government—a much different charge than collusion with the enemy. When the POUM was declared an outlaw organization in mid-June 1937 by the newly established Negrín government and its leaders were arrested, the communist press quickly produced alleged evidence of a preconceived plot. Six months after these arrests, however, no formal charges had been lodged and no evidence was produced to support the arrests. More to the point, many government officials disputed the allegations. An international delegation even determined that the charges were false. They discovered that the arrests of POUM members were not ordered by the government but rather by the local police force acting on its own authority and influenced by the communist factions. The actions against the POUM were tolerated, Orwell suggests, because of fear of offending the Soviet Union, the principal military supporter of the Republican cause. The fact that the international delegation could not gain admittance to the communist-run secret prisons in Barcelona, despite having a signed order from the ministers of prisons and justice, illustrates the extent of their influence.

Orwell addresses the charge of Trotskyism widely leveled against the POUM, which he feels rests on a misunderstanding of the term. It is used in three ways: to describe one who believes in world revolution as opposed to socialism in one country, a member of the organization of which Trotsky is the head, or a disguised fascist who poses as a revolutionary to engage in acts of sabotage against the Soviet Union or to subvert left-wing forces. The POUM could be said to correspond to the first definition, though numerous left-wing organizations could as well. No connection existed between the POUM and Trotsky, except that some members were former associates—a fact that was exploited often by the communist press. The third common definition is rooted in the Stalin-initiated purges in Russia during the 1930s, when anyone who disagreed with Stalinism was branded a traitor. Such allegations amount in Orwell's view to little more than libel. Orwell justifies his extended analysis of the suppression of the POUM because he believes that such distorted press campaigns are capable of doing irreparable harm to the antifascist cause. They also represent a split in the worldwide working-class movement. Hope for the working class depends on the ability to discuss the issues reasonably and truthfully. The libel perpetrated by the communist press serves only to silence honest debate.

Chapter 12

Orwell returns to the Aragon front about three days after the fighting ends in Barcelona, but his attitude toward the war has changed. The ideological war carried out in the press has spread disillusionment among the antifascist forces. Orwell perceives that the war is following a predictable course. The Caballero government would eventually fall—

which it did a few weeks later—and be replaced by a more right-wing and communist-influenced government, which followed when the Negrín government took power. If Franco was not ultimately defeated, the power of the workers' unions would be broken, and Spain would institute a dictatorship. Despite his reservations, Orwell still considers the government worth fighting for, if only to prevent Franco from assuming power. The spread of fascism haunts Orwell, and he claims to enjoy the prospect of checking its seemingly unchecked progress. In later months, Orwell would come to respect the Negrín government, though he believes firmly that the only way to prevent fascism from taking root in Spain is socialist revolution.

Still stationed outside Huesca, Orwell receives a promotion to the rank of *teniente*—the equivalent of a second lieutenant in the British army—with about 30 men under his command. The militias have seen only light fighting, but snipers from the fascist trenches—on higher ground than those of the POUM, pose a threat. Orwell's 29th Division had established a rifle nest in a patch of tall grass close to the enemy lines. Stationed in the nest, Orwell takes several shots at the enemy without ever knowing if he has hit the mark, but he is confident that he will. To his surprise, the opposite is true.

After ten days back at the front, Orwell becomes a casualty of the Spanish civil war while stationed one morning at a dangerous corner of the fascist lines. During a conversation with the sentry on duty, Orwell sustains a clean rifle shot through the throat. As he crumples to the ground, he is not immediately sure of the location or extent of his injuries, and he feels no pain. His men attempt to stanch the bleeding and call for a stretcher, on which Orwell is carried to the rear of the lines. His initial thought is that he will die. He thinks of his wife and feels resentment over having to die. He also wonders if the sniper who shot him knows that he was successful.

While on the stretcher, Orwell's right arm—initially paralyzed—begins to hurt. This provides some reassurance that he will not die. A field doctor temporarily dresses the wound and gives Orwell a shot of morphine before sending him to the hospital at Sietamo—a poorly constructed staging area where patients are queued for transport to Barbastro or Lerida. The pain in Orwell's right arm increases steadily, and his mouth fills with blood. Soldiers from his unit arrive to strip him of all weapons, ammunition, and other equipment before the items are stolen by the hospital staff.

Orwell arrives at Barbastro later that evening, and he learns from the harrowing ambulance ride why so many soldiers die in transit. Apart from bad roads, little care is taken to secure the wounded with straps to prevent them from falling out of their beds. From Barbastro, Orwell arrives by train in Lérida and spends a week in the hospital—a large, crowded place full of soldiers with ghastly injuries. Within days, Orwell is able to walk short distances with his arm in a sling. He has sustained some internal injuries from falling after he was shot, and his voice is gone; otherwise, the wound in his throat gives him no pain. The hospitals Orwell has seen have competent doctors and a good cache of medical supplies, but they are used primarily as casualty clearing stations. Patients rarely get much treatment unless they are too injured to be moved. Some patients, Orwell notes, spend many days before receiving any treatment beyond a change of bandages. The nurses are poorly trained, and the patients are neglected; surprisingly, the food is excellent, if not a little too heavy for wounded men.

Orwell next moves on by train to Tarragona, where he cables Eileen to announce his arrival. En route, Orwell and the other casualties pass a transport train full of Italian soldiers from the International Column. The scene impresses Orwell, who remembers vividly the faces of the proud men and the barrels of the field guns. He learns later that these men were the heroes of the Battle of Guadalajara, but that most of them were subsequently killed some weeks later during an assault on Huesca. At Tarragona, Orwell makes more progress toward recovery, even walking alone on the beach. Nearly two weeks after being shot, Orwell finally has his wound examined thoroughly by a doctor, who explains that the bullet passed cleanly through the neck, just missing the carotid artery but damaging one of his vocal cords. The doctor advises that he will never get his voice back, though this proves not to be the case when his voice returns suddenly after a few months. A damaged nerve in his neck has produced the nagging pain in his right arm. The doctors in Tarragona consider him something of a curiosity and lucky to be alive. He can't help but think it would have been luckier not to have been hit at all.

Chapter 13

Orwell spends his final weeks in Spain navigating the increasingly treacherous atmosphere of Barcelona, which swells with fear, suspicion, and uncertainty. The communist factions have steadily gained influence after the fall of Caballero's government, and no one in the city doubts that there will be political reprisals. Rumors circulate that the new Negrin administration will ultimately compromise the war against Franco. They give no real support to the Basque city of Bilbao under siege by profascist forces. The CNT issues flyers that warn people to be on their guard against an unnamed party (presumably the communists) planning a coup d'etat. Police informers crowd the streets, and the jails slowly fill with arrested anarchists and POUM members.

Foreigners serving in the International Column are being arrested by the hundreds, though most will be ultimately repatriated to their countries of origin. Assault troops and the Civil Guards patrol the streets, and PSUC buildings still retain their barricades. Orwell receives a warning not to show his POUM militia card for fear of arrest. Anarchist newspapers *La Batalla* and *Solidaridad* are being heavily censored by the government, and food is again in short supply throughout the city. Orwell has difficulty describing the atmosphere because he can find no corollary in England. The controlling authorities in Barcelona have initiated a campaign to eliminate everyone who disagrees with their policies. The Stalinists control the city, and therefore anyone branded a Trotskyist is in immediate peril.

Orwell stays at the Sanatorium Maurin—where he receives electric-shock treatment for his arm—in a suburb of Barcelona called Tibidabo, but he visits Barcelona during the day. He and his wife decide to return as quickly as possible to England. Having been designated as medically unfit to return to the front, Orwell still needs to finalize his discharge papers, which requires a visit to the Medical Board at a hospital near the front and a visit to the POUM headquarters at Sietamo. There, he encounters Georges Kopp, who believes that Huesca is on the verge of falling to the workers' militias. In fact, the city does not fall, and the antifascist forces sustain heavy casualties. At the headquarters, Orwell is initially issued a rifle and ordered to prepare for duty as a reserve militiaman. He is willing to fight despite his still-healing wound, but he fears going back into combat. Ultimately, Orwell never receives orders to go to the front, and after several trips to hospitals, he receives the necessary paperwork for his discharge. Orwell's attitude toward Spain has changed during his months of service and on the eve of his return to England. He is more observant about his surroundings. Cities—like Barbastro—that previously struck him only as bombed-out wrecks now seem more interesting. With his discharge papers in hand, Orwell feels more like a human being. Spain has always had a powerful hold on his imagination, and he had wanted to visit for many years. After several months of fighting, he was seeing it seemingly for the first time.

Back in Barcelona, Orwell decides to stay the night at the Hotel Continental with his wife instead of returning to the Sanatorium Maurin. She is waiting for him in the hotel lobby, and she whispers in his ear that he must leave the hotel at once. In his absence, the POUM has been suppressed and its members indiscriminately arrested, already in jail, or in some instances summarily executed. In a quiet café, away from the hotel, Eileen explains recent developments in the city. Andres Nin, the leader of the POUM, has been arrested, and anyone affiliated with the organization in any way is at risk for arrest. Wounded militiamen are said to have been taken from their hospital beds to prison. Authorities are also seizing buildings and other property belonging to the POUM. No news of these events has reached the militias at the front. Reports appear in the Valencia newspapers—including one claiming to expose a fascist plot by the POUM to undermine the Republican government—but nothing appears in the Barcelona press. Orwell sees the first stories about the suppression of the POUM in British newspapers that arrive in Barcelona a few days later.

Mass arrests continue over the next few months, during which the local police act independently of the government, even arresting high-ranking officers within the antifascist ranks. A group of police officers from Barcelona arrest Jose Rovira, leader of the 29th Division in which Orwell served, at the Aragon front. When a protest is filed with the Ministry of War, it is discovered that the government and the chief of police had not been informed of Rovira's arrest. Orwell finds it particularly disturbing that the militiamen on the front know nothing about events in Barcelona. They continue to risk their lives, while behind them their comrades are being thrown in jail and called traitors. Orwell wonders how the information could have been kept from them. The motive for secrecy, he suggests, is to keep them fighting, as a large-scale attack on Huesca was in the works.

Several of Orwell's friends have managed to avoid arrest. Others, like Georges Kopp, are not so lucky. On a special mission to Barcelona for the Ministry of War, Kopp is arrested in the Hotel Continental. No move had been made by police against Eileen. He considers that she is being used as a decoy to draw him out into the open. However, the police do raid her room and search it thoroughly. They confiscate his diaries, books, and newspaper clippings. To avoid arrest, Orwell stays away from the hotel and sleeps on the streets. He makes arrangements with his wife to get their passports in order for the journey out of Spain. To leave the country, they will require passport stamps from the chief of police, the French Consulate, and the Catalan immigration authorities. Orwell sets out in the evening to find a place to sleep, and he settles on a pile of rubble in a burned-out church.

Chapter 14

Orwell wakes early the following morning, but he must wait several hours for the shops to open. He notices that all former POUM buildings now fly the Republican flag. At the end of the Ramblas, a group of shabby POUM militiamen sleep in chairs set out for the bootblacks. Fresh from the front, they have only recently learned about the danger they face in the city. While militiamen are hunted vigorously during the night, they enjoy relative safety during the day. A few days pass before Orwell and his wife meet at the British Consulate, along with two English friends, John McNair and Stafford Cottman, who will travel with them out of Spain. He learns from them that another friend—Bob Smillie, whom Orwell had learned was under arrest some weeks before—has died in prison, allegedly from appendicitis. News of Smillie's death hits Orwell hard. Smillie was only 21 and had given up a promising career at Glasgow University to fight in Spain. He was tough and dedicated, and his death was entirely unnecessary.

Following their trip to the consulate, Orwell and his wife visit Kopp in prison. In good spirits, Kopp asks Orwell to recover a letter from the Ministry of War that was taken from him when he was arrested—a dangerous task for Orwell, though one that might make things considerably easier for Kopp. Orwell leaves his wife at the jail and heads for the Department of War. After considerable effort, he finds the office Kopp identified and speaks to an aide-de-camp of the official in possession of the letter. In explaining his reason for coming, Orwell admits that he served with the POUM, thereby putting himself in considerable danger. Instead of arresting Orwell, the aide-de-camp escorts him to the office of the chief of police and retrieves the letter Orwell seeks. Prior to leaving, the man approaches Orwell and shakes his hand—a small gesture, but one that means a great deal to Orwell. Having lived for several weeks in an environment where he could be arrested at any moment and charged as a fascist spy, to Orwell this small kindness is a momentous event.

Orwell sleeps that night with McNair and Cottman in the empty lot of a derelict building. The following afternoon, Orwell and his wife make a final visit to Kopp. They would discover later that he had been moved to a secret prison run by communists and that he was probably executed. Until they depart for the border, Orwell's safest course is to try to pass as a wealthy tourist. He and Eileen—along with McNair and Cottman—frequent smart hotels in areas of town where they are not likely to be recognized. After considerable effort, they get their passports back from the British Consulate and make preparations to leave. On the morning of their departure, Eileen slips away from the Hotel Continental without being seen, and the group boards a train for France. Orwell manages to send a letter to the Department of War on behalf of Georges Kopp, but he never learns whether anyone received it. Months after returning to England, he still has no direct information about Kopp's fate.

The journey to France passes without incident. Detectives aboard the train take Orwell and his companions for wealthy travelers and do not ask them about their papers. At the passport office near the border, they are searched from head to foot. None of their names appears on the card index of wanted suspects, and they cross unhindered into France. The shock of being on peaceful soil requires a period of adjustment for Orwell. He buys tobacco and enjoys his first cup of tea with fresh milk in several months. McNair and Cottman depart for Paris, and Orwell continues on with his wife to relax on the shores of the Mediterranean Sea. They spend three troubling days in the coastal village of Banyuls, as neither can stop thinking about Spain. In fact, both feel a strong desire to return to Spain, despite the fact that they would most certainly be arrested if they were to do so.

Orwell feels some difficulty in conveying his impressions of Spain now that he is free of the war. The sights, sounds, and smells stay with him vividly. The war has left him with evil memories of Spain, but he feels fortunate to have experienced what he did. He conveys his best wishes to the militiamen he had known in the trenches, most of whom are probably languishing in prison. Despite his considerable suffering, Orwell states that he has been left with a stronger belief in the decency of human beings. He concludes his account with a warning. He hopes that he has not misled anyone with his characterization of events. He acknowledges that everyone writes in a partisan way, despite their efforts at objectivity. He urges his readers to be aware of his partisanship and to read his account—and any other accounts of events in Spain—with the same discerning eye. Orwell travels north to Paris with his wife before landing in the south of England, which he describes as "the sleekest landscape in the world." He revels in the scenes of his youth and the familiar English traditions. He also feels that his country seems to be ignorant about what is happening elsewhere in the world and caught in a deep sleep that will end only with the coming roar of bombs.

—Philip Bader

COMMENTARY

Regarded by many as the book that exemplifies Orwell's style at its best, *Homage to Catalonia* exhibits a vivid, elegant clarity that enables the reader to see and feel, and not just read about, the world it presents. For Orwell personally, the six-month experience in Spain certainly ranked among the most important of his life, its significance reinforced, not weakened, by the fact that it was both the best and worst of times for him. That contradiction is mirrored in the different styles in which the book is written. On the one hand, Orwell employs a style appropriate to the documentary aim of the book: careful, simple, "transparent" prose, as in his description of leaving Barcelona for the front:

> The train was due to leave at eight, and it was about ten past eight when the harassed, sweating officers managed to marshal us in the barrack square. I remember very vividly the torchlit scene—the uproar and excitement, the red flags flapping in the torchlight, the massed ranks of militiamen with their knapsacks on their backs . . . and the shouting and the clatter of boots and tin pannikins, and then a tremendous and finally successful hissing for silence; and then some political commissar, standing beneath a huge red banner and making us a speech in Catalan. Finally they marched us to the station, taking the longest route, three or four miles, so as to show us to the whole town. . . . The train pulled out of Catalonia at the normal wartime speed of something under twenty kilometers an hour.

Frequently, however, he escalates realism to a level that the linguistic scholar Roger Fowler calls sordid realism, or naturalism, employing a dry, ironic undertone to communicate, for example, the experience of life in the on the front lines during the winter months:

> A life as uneventful as a city clerk's and almost as regular. Sentry-go, patrols, digging; digging, patrols, sentry-go. On every hill-top, fascist or Loyalist, a knot of ragged, dirty men shivering around their flag and trying to keep warm. And all day and night the meaningless bullets wandering across the empty valleys and only by some rare improbable chance getting home on a human body.

Then there is the mixture of styles in which the realist exterior is penetrated by a romantic subtext, capturing the revolutionary spirit, not in the abstract language of ideology but in the concrete, particular details that bring abstractions to life. A famous example is the opening-page description of an Italian militiaman, whose physical features and dress are sketched in the best tradition of descriptive realism:

> He was a tough-looking youth of twenty-five or six, with reddish yellow hair and powerful shoulders. His peaked leather cap was pulled fiercely over one eye. He was standing in profile to me, his chin on his breast, gazing with a puzzled frown at a map which one of the officers had open on the table.

Orwell then goes on to read into these details attitudes and values ("The face of a man who would commit murder and throw away his life for a friend") such as a novelist might invent for a character. The reader's reaction to this mix is similarly complex. On the one hand we accept the objective reality of the militiaman, while recognizing the subjective, not necessarily literal, reality of him as a representative man. Similarly, Orwell's account of their shaking hands ("It was as though his spirit and mine had momentarily succeeded in bridging the gulf of language . . . meeting in utter intimacy") which suggests an identification of himself with the Italian soldier. Certainly, in his reckless behavior at the front and in the ends to which he goes to save Georges Kopp (chapter 14), Orwell qualified as a man who would throw away his life for a friend. This subjective truth is thus confirmed and illustrated by Orwell's later behavior.

The word that comes to mind in the opening pages is *spontaneity*. Arriving in Barcelona, Orwell has come upon a revolutionary society, one in which red-and-black posters are everywhere, tipping is forbidden by law, and no one says "señor" or "don" but "comrade," conveying "a feeling of having emerged into an environment of equality and freedom." Caught up in the spontaneity, he joins the POUM, ". . . in that atmosphere, it seemed the only conceivable thing to do." It is possible that joining up may have been in the back of his mind all along. After all, as he wrote later in the essay "MY COUNTRY RIGHT OR LEFT," he belonged to the generation too young for World War I (in 1918, he was 15), who always felt they had missed out on something, as dreadful as it was. But World War I was clearly a massive "swindle," a slaughterhouse brought on by incompetent old men on both sides. The Spanish civil war was "the good fight," pitting idealists against fascists. But the impression that his joining up was an impulsive act is important in establishing his credibility as a man in motion, someone who is not content just to call it as he sees it, but also, in the right circumstances, to join it.

That credibility is sustained in his unromantic accounts of the total lack of proper training and equipment in the POUM militia. But his dismay about the inadequate, undisciplined preparation for war only adds to the sincerity of his later conversion to the belief that the anarchists were "the best fighters among the purely Spanish forces."

Another convincing aspect of Orwell's narration is his account of his initial sympathy for the communist argument of "war first, revolution later." He backed that opinion with action, planning to transfer to the International Brigades, despite the warnings he received from his comrades and friends. But all that changed when he returned on leave to Barcelona in May, walking right into a small civil war, when the newly reconstituted police force tried to size the telephone exchange, which up to then had been controlled by the POUM allies, the CNT. In that battle, POUM was basically on the outside looking in. He conveys with an unfailing sense of authenticity, the fact that the whole affair was a complete surprise to the POUM leaders. What followed was the great crime that he would never forget or forgive. The fighting was represented to the world as a POUM insurrection, functioning not only as Trotskyites, but in conspiracy with Franco. The lie, soaked up by a credulous left-wing press all over the world (one exception, noted by Orwell, was the *Manchester Guardian*), precipitated a systematic, Moscow-directed suppression of POUM, involving the arrests and, in some cases, the murder of many of its members. One of the many ironies of Orwell's experience is that the Soviet orders to crush the POUM were given in December 1936, the same month that he first arrived in Barcelona. At the same time he was falling in love with the POUM, the wheels of its destruction were being set in motion.

The book's combination of autobiography, history, politics, and propaganda posed severe structural problems. Orwell admitted having little understanding of the political complexities underlying the war in Spain, and he would take considerable pains in examining their bearing on its fate. In Spain, "the real weapon was not the rifle, but the megaphone." The view of the historian Hugh Thomas is that "*Homage* is very perceptive about war. Nevertheless it is very misleading about the Spanish Civil War" (151).

Orwell interrupts the narrative in chapter 5 to explain what he has only gradually come to realize about the fight against Franco. "It was above all things a political war. No event in it, at any rate during the first year, is intelligible unless one has some grasp of the inter-party struggle that was going on behind the government lines." What follows is a protracted and somewhat distracting analysis of the many antifascist factions, which Orwell warns may not suit the tastes of all his readers. "If you are not interested in the horrors of party politics, please skip; I am trying to keep the political parts of this narrative in separate chapters for precisely that purpose."

Chapter 9 involves a key shift in the narrative. It is reflective, opening as it does with a lengthy reference to his time in Burma. He has left behind the boredom and filth of the front lines and returned to Barcelona on leave, only to find that the revolutionary spirit so appealing to him on his arrival in Spain has vanished. "For under the surface-aspect of the town, under the luxury and growing poverty, under the seeming gaiety of the streets, with their flower stalls, their many-colored flags, their propaganda posters, and thronging crowds, there was an unmistakable and horrible feeling of political rivalry and hatred." This contrasts sharply with the largely democratic and socialist operations of the militia at the front. Chapter 10 amplifies the sense of a reversal in the revolution in Spain, as war on the streets of Barcelona breaks out among the various political factions. This is the seminal event in Orwell's narrative. It would be reported on in the English and communist press with, in Orwell's view, no correspondence to actual events. His need to set the record straight compels him to again adopt an editorial approach in the following chapter to unravel the political side of events.

Chapter 11 includes quotations from press clippings and extended refutations by Orwell of erroneous conclusions by biased reporters. It is perhaps the most tedious yet interesting chapter of the book, and it foreshadows many of the themes that Orwell would return to in *Nineteen Eighty-Four,* particularly with respect to the mutability of historical fact. This chapter marks Orwell's transition from a free-willed political revolutionary to an unwitting pawn in a complex and irrational power struggle. The difficulties of his changed position are driven home first by a bullet through the throat in chapter 12 and then in chapter 13 by learning that he was wanted by the police for his affiliation with the POUM. The book's concluding chapter chronicles the Orwells' narrow escape from Spain: the difficulties obtaining travel documents, their evasions of authorities attempting to arrest them, and the humiliating retreat across the border to France, leaving behind comrades who would ultimately be imprisoned or killed.

Another irony lies in the fact that, although he was unaware of it in his lifetime, he had good reason to take the purge of the POUM personally. Three weeks after their escape into France, "ERIC BLAIR *and his wife* EILEEN BLAIR," described as "rabid Trotskyists," were reported to the Tribunal for Espionage and High Treason in Valencia, the seat of the republican government at the time. Peter Davison points out that had they still been in Spain, "they would surely been imprisoned, if not actually executed, and Orwell's health being what it was, he might well have suffered Bob Smillie's fate" (*CW*, 11, 33). Bob Smillie was a young ILP comrade, whom Orwell admired and who died in a Spanish prison, either from neglect of a serious medical condition or by execution. "As Orwell put it in *Homage*, "Smillie's death is not a thing I can easily forgive." And he never did.

Another such victim was ANDREAS NIN, the POUM leader who was imprisoned and tortured by the communists in an attempt to have him confess to treason. His refusal to betray his comrades short-circuited an attempt to stage a series of show trials in Spain matching those in the USSR. As a result, Nin was either murdered on direct orders from Moscow or left to die in prison.

But anger and the desire for revenge were not the only emotions with which Orwell came away from Spain.

> When you have had a glimpse of such a disaster as this. . . . the result is not necessarily disillusionment and cynicism. Curiously enough the whole experience has left me with not less but more belief in the decency of human beings. And I hope the account I have given is not too misleading. . . . beware of my partisanship, my mistakes of fact and the distortion inevitably caused by my having seen only one corner of events. And beware of exactly the same things when you read any other book on this period of the Spanish war.

Such candor and honesty might easily be seen as one more rhetorical ploy by a master rhetorician, but it much more likely is a reflection of confidence by a man who tells the truth as he sees it. He concludes with a tribute to England and a warning to the English, "sleeping the deep, deep sleep, from which we shall never awake until we are jerked out of it by the roar of bombs."

Although clearly the most important, *Homage* is not Orwell's only contribution to the literature of the Spanish civil war. He also wrote four separate essays—the two most important being "Spilling the Spanish Beans" (1937) and "LOOKING BACK AT THE SPANISH CIVIL WAR" (1942). He also reviewed eleven books on the subject. To a large extent, he and a few others, such as ARTHUR KOESTLER and FRANZ BORKENAU, were voices crying in the wilderness, not just ignored but contemptuously dismissed. The controversy over the overall conduct of the war still goes on, but the evidence that what Orwell saw in Barcelona was in fact what happened there and that what was reported were vicious lies now seems incontrovertible. As Lionel Trilling, in his introduction to the American edition of the book in 1952, put it:

> He told the truth, and told it in an exemplary way, quietly, simply, with due warning to the reader that it was only one man's truth. Its particular truth refers to events now far in our past . . . It does not matter the less for that—this particular truth implies a general truth, which . . . will matter for a long time to come. And what matters most of all is our sense of the man who tells the truth (xxiii).

CRITICAL RECEPTION

Homage to Catalonia was a commercial failure on its publication. It sold only about 500 copies during Orwell's lifetime, and an American edition did not appear until 1952. Whether this can be attributed to a general boycott on political grounds, as Orwell was to claim, is uncertain but plausible. The book did receive largely positive contemporary reviews, though many of them were written by friends or those with compatible ideological perspectives on the war in Spain.

GEOFFREY GORER, an anthropologist and a friend of Orwell's, reviewed the book for *Time and Tide,* calling it "a book to read; politically and as literature it is a work of first-class importance" (123). John McNair—who was with Orwell and his wife, Eileen in their escape from Spain—spares no punches: "The chapters in which he describes the bitter and unscrupulous attacks made on the POUM amount to the slow unfolding of an unanswerable case, beside which the slanders and abuse which were used sink to their real level of lying propaganda" (125–126).

WORKS CITED

Crick, Bernard. *Orwell: A Life.* Boston: Little, Brown, 1980.

Fowler, Roger. *The Language of George Orwell.* New York: St. Martin's Press, 1995.

Gorer, Geoffrey. "*Homage to Catalonia.*" In *George Orwell: The Critical Heritage,* edited by Jeffrey Meyers, 121–123. London: Routledge, 1975.

McNair, John. "*Homage to Catalonia.*" In *George Orwell: The Critical Heritage,* edited by Jeffrey Meyers, 124–126. London: Routledge, 1975.

Meyers, Jeffrey, ed. *George Orwell: The Critical Heritage.* London: Routledge, 1975.

Orwell, George. *The Complete Works of George Orwell.* Vol. 11. Edited by Peter Davison. London: Secker & Warburg, 1998.

Thomas, Hugh. "*Homage to Catalonia.*" In *George Orwell: The Critical Heritage,* edited by Jeffrey Meyers, 150–151. London: Routledge, 1975.

Trilling, Lionel. Introduction to *Homage to Catalonia.* New York: Harcourt, 1952, v–xxiii.

"How the Poor Die"

Essay published in *Now* in November 1946; reprinted in *Shooting an Elephant and Other Essays* (1950). *Now* was an anarchist journal edited by Orwell's friend George Woodcock, who recalled that in 1946, on the heels of the popularity of *Animal Farm,* editors all over England and America were offering large fees for articles by Orwell. The fact that Orwell gave it to Woodcock reflected a man who did not forget his friends at the impoverished little magazines that sustained him when he began writing in the 1930s.

While in Paris in March 1929, Orwell was admitted to the public ward of the Hôpital Cochin in Paris with a severe case of influenza. This essay describes his treatment—and in certain instances, his abuse—at the hands of doctors and nurses who had difficulty recognizing patients as human beings.

SYNOPSIS

The processes of admission, treatment, and discharge (or death) at a public hospital produce increasing levels of humiliation. Patients undergo a rigorous preadmission interview, despite the severity of their condition. In Orwell's case, he spent 20 minutes filling in forms before being compelled to take a bath and walk across a lengthy courtyard—barefoot and with a high fever—in the cold of a Paris winter.

Finally, Orwell is given a bed in a cramped, foul-smelling room with little space between patients. In the bed across from his, a patient is being cupped, or undergoing the practice of popping glasses drained of air on the back of a patient's back. The vacuum raises a large blister. Then the doctor and his aide come to Orwell and perform the same process on him. This is followed by a hot mustard poultice tightly wrapped around his chest, where it remains for fifteen excruciating minutes. For the rest of his two-week stay, he is regularly prodded and tapped by medical students, who imitate their

Hôpital Cochin, the Parisian hospital where Orwell was confined for two weeks with influenza in 1929, an experience he described in the essay "How the Poor Die" *(Photo by William Herman)*

teachers in refusing to recognize that the objects before them are human beings. He offers as an example a patient in his ward with a diseased liver, regularly put on display in the middle of the ward. As his case is discussed, the doctor pushes and pulls his body, but never speaks directly to him or acknowledges him in any way.

A few days later, that same patient dies, his body left lying in the ward for some time. Looking at him, Orwell reflects that it is worse to die a "natural" death in old age than to die violently when you are middle-aged. It is particularly terrible to die in a pauper's ward. Orwell leaves the hospital as soon as he can, not waiting for a formal discharge.

It is true, he admits, that hospitals have improved over the past 50 years. The two major factors have been anesthetics and disinfectants, along with the national health service. These represent important steps in democratizing medical care. Still, the fear of hospitals is very strong among the poor and a submerged fear even among the rest of us. Most of us still think, "it is a great thing to die in your own bed," but he adds his own opinion: "It is still greater to die in your own boots." For Orwell, the fear of hospitals is reflected in his recollection of the Tennyson poem "The Children's Hospital," which he heard as a child and which came back to him while he was a patient in "Hospital X."

COMMENTARY

Orwell had more hospitalizations in his lifetime than most people, but he would have had many more had he not so stubbornly resisted going to the hospital. All of these were related to his lungs, except for his two hospital stays in Spain, one for an infected hand and the other for a bullet through his neck. As he grew older and the diseased lungs grew harder to ignore, he resigned himself more to being a patient.

Orwell died, at the age of 46, in a hospital. However, his death occurred just six months after the publication of *Nineteen Eighty-Four,* so it might be said, with some justice, that he died with his boots on.

WORK CITED

Woodcock, George. *The Crystal Spirit.* London: Jonathan Cape, 1967.

"In Defense of English Cooking"

Brief essay on the merits of English cuisine, first published in *The Evening Standard* in December 1945.

SYNOPSIS

Orwell contends that foreigners and nationals alike malign English cooking as either appalling or derivative. This charge is simply untrue. He proceeds to list items of uniquely English cooking, from Yorkshire pudding and kippers, Devonshire cream, muffins and crumpets, and innumerable puddings, to a rich array of cakes and biscuits. Also, there is the variety of ways of cooking potatoes, much more creative than simply frying them. Then there are the many sauces, great cheeses and English bread. The English "have no cause to be ashamed of our cookery." The problem, at least as far as foreign visitors are concerned, is that you can't find this food outside of a private home. An English restaurant is a rarity in England. Expensive restaurants are usually imitation French, and for inexpensive fare, one goes to Greek, Italian, or Chinese eateries. Since we are still subject to rationing, there is not much we can do about this, but as soon as rationing ends, we should see a renaissance of old English cooking, both at home and in restaurants.

COMMENTARY

The date of this essay, December 1945, marks the beginning of the postwar austerity period in England, a time when good food was even less available than during the war. But Orwell's optimistic message declares that English cooking will once again prosper, despite current deprivations, just as England itself will return to its former state after the devastation wrought during World War II. Orwell also links his discussion of food with the issue of national identity. The lists of unique delicacies reflect the singularity of England and its people. Orwell adds a political dimension to the essay when he states that the best English cuisine is found not in restaurants but in poor working-class homes. He locates the center of English identity and strength in the common Englishman and Englishwoman, a theme that recurs often in Orwell's essays and novels.

People who lunched regularly with Orwell were frequently struck by his odd palate. The gusto that he would bring to eating strange concoctions that emerged during the heavy rationing period of World War II left them dazed. On the other hand, he could be quite particular about home cooking. In COMING UP FOR AIR, George Bowling's evocation of his mother's cooking no doubt reflects Orwell's idea of good home cooking: "Enormous meals—boiled beef and dumplings, roast beef and Yorkshire, boiled mutton and capers, pig's head, apple pie, spotted dog and jam roly-poly—with grace before and after."

"In Defense of P. G. Wodehouse"

Essay first published in *The Windmill* (July 1945). This essay is a striking example of Orwell's swimming against the tide, adopting an unpopular opinion, signaled by its "In Defense . . . " title. In two other essays, "In Defense of the Novel" and "In Defense of English Cooking," Orwell has stronger clients and an easier case to make.

SYNOPSIS

Wodehouse was captured by the Germans in the summer of 1940 while he was living in his villa in Belgium. One year later, he was living in a hotel in Berlin, having agreed to do nonpolitical broadcasts for German radio. The five broadcasts he did seemed to make light of the discomforts of having been an internee of the Germans: "There is a good deal to be said for internment. It keeps you out of the saloon and helps you to keep up with your reading."

The news that the famous and extraordinarily popular writer was doing broadcasts sanctioned by the Nazis caused a great stir in England. One local library banned Wodehouse's books. The BBC banned his lyrics, and letters to the press consistently denounced him as a traitor and a fascist.

One of the broadcasts Wodehouse gave was an interview with an American correspondent in Berlin, before America's entry into the war. The journalist later published an account of the interview, in which he made two points as to why the Nazis chose Wodehouse to do the broadcasts. The first was that he "made fun of the English," and the other that Wodehouse was still living in the past.

Orwell disagrees with the former comment. But he completely accepts the view that Wodehouse is living in a pre-1925 world. Wodehouse's favorite subject is the English aristocracy, but it is wrong to think of him as a satirist of aristocrats, although he did create the clueless Bertie Wooster, a figure who would be totally lost without his man Jeeves. But the attitude is softer than satire. It is more "a mild facetiousness covering an unthinking acceptance." Bertie is a throwback to the pre–World War I period. Bertie Wooster, if he ever lived, was killed in 1915.

Given this frame of mind, Wodehouse exhibits a complete "lack of political awareness." As for fascism, he was, like the great majority of the English people, almost totally unaware of its presence and its nature. He was equally unaware of the developments that took place during his internment: Dunkirk, the fall of France, the Battle of Britain, the Blitz. He had no idea of the perilous nature of the war from England's point of view.

In the meantime, the war had become a "people's war" in England, and it suited the authorities to offer up a scapegoat rich man, a role that Wodehouse conveniently filled. But it is "morally disgusting" to see the postwar hunt going on in France and elsewhere for "collaborators," mostly because it turns out to be a hunt for the little rats while the big ones get away.

COMMENTARY

In the summer of 1945, the appetite for revenge was being fed in an indiscriminate fashion. Having witnessed it as a correspondent in the closing days of the war, Orwell found himself questioning the value of such reactions. In "Revenge Is Sour," he comments on the mistreatment of a Nazi by a Jewish soldier but does not entirely escape the charge of minimizing the Holocaust. However, in

Wodehouse he has a better defendant. He exhibits an impressive knowledge of this prolific writer's body of work, demonstrating that Wodehouse has always been a political innocent, still inhabiting the Edwardian world of Orwell's childhood. The code of behavior at that time was rooted in the "public-school morality" that Wodehouse captured in his early works. Then Wodehouse moved to the United States, where he became a writer of lyrics and the "books" of Broadway musicals, but he continued to turn out the comic novels of English life for which he is famous. In all this time, he never showed the slightest interest in politics.

In volume 17 of *The Complete Works*, Peter Davison summarizes two letters from Wodehouse to Orwell thanking him for his defense, noting that his critical observations on his work was a "masterly bit of work and I agree with every word of it." Six years later, in a letter to Denis Mackail, Wodehouse recalled the essay as "one long roast of your correspondent" (63).

"In Defense of the Novel"

Essay published in *New English Weekly* in November 1936

SYNOPSIS

As a literary genre, the modern novel has suffered a loss of prestige. While there remain "a few contemporary or roughly contemporary novelists whom the intelligentsia consider it permissible to read," the general lot of published novels, which Orwell calls "good-bad" novels, are increasingly ignored. Orwell is not concerned here with the larger debate of whether the novel is still a viable literary art form. He assumes that it is, and that it is worth saving.

But saving from what? The principal cause of the novel's decline is the utter disdain readers have for the "blurb-reviews" (brief quotations from reviewers) that appear on the back covers. These vapid exclamations of unqualified and exaggerated praise put intense pressure on readers to agree with a reviewer's opinion of a book, the majority of which will not measure up. "When all novels are thrust upon you as works of genius, it is quite natural to assume that all of them are tripe."

Misleading reviews have their source in the nature of the book trade. Reviews are tied to publisher advertising, and bad reviews lose advertising revenue. Publishers and reviewers, however, participate in this swindle unwillingly and of necessity. "The hack-review is in fact a sort of commercial necessity, like the blurb on the dust-jacket, of which it is merely an extension." The publisher must sell books, and the reviewer must earn his wage, but the real difficulty is the assumption that "every novel is worth reviewing."

Reviewers get their parcel of novels for review, and the majority will inspire no thoughts whatsoever. In order to sell his work, the reviewer must say something about the plot of the novel and its relative merits. The real evil, however, is that the reviewer "is expected not only to say what a book is about but to give his opinion as to whether it is good or bad." Accomplishing this task requires a standard of measurement, against which the bulk of contemporary novels would fall short.

Orwell suggests a remedy. A new periodical, "which makes a specialty of novel-reviewing but refuses to take any notice of tripe, and in which the reviewers are reviewers and not ventriloquists' dummies clapping their jaws when the publisher pulls the string," would provide a point of comparison that may eventually lead to the decline of the hack reviews. Next, a new system of grading novels must be employed. Good books—and bad books—are good and bad on different levels. "This is the fact that the hack-reviewer has made it his special business to obscure." Such a system would allow reviewers to qualify their praise or damnation of a book.

In order to make such a system work, reviewers would need a healthy appreciation of the novel as an art form and an interest in the technique and subject matter of novels. Orwell suggests that amateur writers may provide more reliable evaluations. "A man who is not a practiced writer but has just read a book which has deeply impressed him is more likely to tell you what it is about than a competent but bored professional." This proposed system may not drive the blurb writers from the field, but the availability of quality reviews could repair some of the damage to the novel's prestige.

The current outlook for those who love the novel, as well as for those who write them, is bleak. Intelligent readers shun them, and respected novelists turn to other genres. As a result, the genre suffers. Orwell does not agree that the novel as a genre is in danger of elimination. It is, however, at risk of declining into "some perfunctory, despised and hopelessly degenerate form."

COMMENTARY

In his essay "CONFESSIONS OF A BOOK REVIEWER" (1946), Orwell elaborates on the craft of the book reviewer. "It not only involves praising trash . . . but constantly inventing reactions towards books about which one has no spontaneous feelings whatever." This essay relates what "In Defense of the Novel" does not mention. Orwell had spent many years reviewing books under the same conditions the hack-reviewers he criticizes suffered. It is Orwell's attempt at "coming clean" in an industry by which he profited but which he nonetheless despised.

Orwell's unusual suggestions for improving the state of novel reviewing, such as instituting a grading process, are less interesting and less practical than two other ideas mentioned in the essay. The subject of "good-bad" books, the topic of a 1945 essay of the same name, reveals many of Orwell's opinions about the function of literature and demonstrates that he was no literary snob. Orwell's suggestion that a more honest review of a novel may be had from an amateur has considerable bearing on the kinds of reviews he wrote.

"In Front of Your Nose"

A short essay published in Tribune in March 1946.

SYNOPSIS

Recent comments in the press have called attention to the inability of the coal industry to produce as much coal as is needed by the country because of the shortage of mine workers. At the same time, and in the same paper, you can find statements to the effect that we cannot afford to admit foreigners to work in the mines, because that might result in unemployment in the industry.

This is an example of a common mode of thinking, and the psychiatric term for it is *schizophrenia*: "the power of holding simultaneously two beliefs which cancel [each other] out." Orwell then proceeds to list examples of people acting as if something were true that they know "in another part of their mind" to be false. One is the recent history of Hong Kong. The British government knew that English control of Hong Kong would be lost once the war with Japan began. Rather than face that fact, however, the government sent a completely inadequate number of troops to defend the city. They were promptly captured when Hong Kong fell to the Japanese early in World War II. In the late 1930s, all reasonable people believed that the English had to stand up to the Germans, but in 1937 the Labour Party voted against a draft. As a result, the British Army was no match for the Germans in the early months of the war.

Another is the assertion that contraception is an enlightened idea, as it could solve the problem of high unemployment, but at the same time the people who take that position must realize that a dwindling birth rate will be catastrophic for the nation as we know it.

Another example is the newly formed United Nations. Everyone knows that if it is going to control the production of armaments, it has to have access to the armament sites of every country. Two or three major countries have never accepted these conditions. In effect, the UN's power to ensure world peace has been doomed from the beginning, but many informed people actually think it is going to succeed.

Avoiding reality seems to be a universal trait. In democratic societies, it is carried along by the need to win over the will of the majority, but it also exists in totalitarian societies, where there is no need to ensure popular consent. Thus, the Russian people have been told for years that they are better off than those in the West, even when it was obviously not true. Seeing what's in front of your nose requires constant self-discipline. One aid in that struggle is to keep a diary of your opinions about important issues. Without that check, we all tend to forget the foolish opinions we once held. A diary also helps when we make a correct prediction, because it shows *why* we were correct.

While people in their private lives may be fairly realistic, they tend to become illogical creatures when making political judgments. It must be that they feel their political judgments "will not have to be tested by reality."

COMMENTARY

The striking feature of this essay is its formation of an idea that was to appear in an enlarged and more malevolent form as "doublethink" in *Nineteen Eighty-Four.* Within a few months of the publication of this essay, Orwell reported that he had completed the first 50 pages of the novel, which would appear to confirm that doublethink was an idea very much on his mind. It is interesting to note that in his examples, he chose one, in which his own doublethink showed itself. He was certainly among those who knew that Hitler was a menace, but in his case he adopted an antiwar position, which he maintained through 1938 and most of 1939, until the Hitler-Stalin Pact in August 1939 turned him around.

"Inside the Whale"

The title essay in Orwell's first collection of essays (1940). The essay itself deals with the American writer HENRY MILLER (1891–1980) and his refusal to commit himself to any social or political cause.

HISTORICAL/BIOGRAPHICAL CONTEXT

The question of the responsibility of the artist to the society in which he lives is an ancient one, comparable in some respects to the roles of the philosopher or scientist. Clearly, as a citizen the artist has the same obligations as everyone else. He or she cannot claim exemption from the duties and laws of his land. The question is whether the obligation should extend to his or her art.

Earlier, in 1935, Orwell had reviewed Henry Miller's *Tropic of Cancer,* praising it as a "remarkable book," which appears to suggest "that if one stiffens oneself by the contemplation of ugliness, one ends by finding life not less but more worth living." At the time of the review, and for years after, *Tropic of Cancer* was banned as pornography.

In 1936, on his way to fight in the Spanish civil war, Orwell stopped off in Paris, where he visited Miller and was shocked to discover that the American was completely indifferent to the struggle in Spain. Before they parted, Miller gave Orwell a jacket, which Orwell wore throughout his four months in Spain, but, as Miller's biographer put it, Miller would have given it just as willingly to a supporter of General Franco.

SYNOPSIS

The essay begins with a description of Henry Miller's novel *Tropic of Cancer.* When the book was first published in 1935, it was immediately censored because of its obscene language and frank sexuality. However, Orwell maintains that the book is not pornography but a remarkable attempt to present a world, the "down and out" segment of bohemian Paris. But Miller's portrait differs from others in that it does not imply a criticism of modern life or a protest against social injustice. Instead, it celebrates the life it depicts, somewhat in the fashion of another American writer, Walt Whitman, with one important difference. Whitman's acceptance of his civilization was built on an affirmative vision of "democratic vistas" extending into the future, while Miller is accepting an age of decay, an "epoch of fear and regimentation." Miller has adopted the position of the average man, content to manage his private life, knowing he has no control over the public sphere. In this respect, he is swimming against the tide of current literary fashion. Since the beginning of the 1930s, he asserts that literature has become increasingly political, and the times seem to demand that a writer be committed to a social and political agenda.

Looking back at the literary scene between 1910 and 1940, Orwell traces some discernible patterns. The poetry of A. E. Housman, for example, appealed to young people (like Orwell) born around the turn of the century. Its attraction lay in the poet's ability to evoke the countryside, and to suggest an anti-Christian sentiment, which appealed to the rebel inside every public-school boy. In the 1920s, however, a new type of literature emerged in the persons of JAMES JOYCE, T. S. ELIOT, D. H. LAWRENCE, and others. Although these writers were hardly a movement, they shared a type of pessimism that focused on modern culture while more or less ignoring politics. With the onset of the Depression, a new generation of writers has emerged that is not only political but "Marxised," creating a leftist orthodoxy: "The idea had begun to gain ground . . . that a writer must either be actively 'left' or write badly." Among the leading figures of this new leftist school are the poets W. H. AUDEN, STEPHEN SPENDER, C. Day Lewis and Louis MacNeice.

Having lost faith in patriotism and religion, these writers have "flocked into or toward the Communist Party. It was simply something to believe in." But having come from the "soft-boiled emancipated middle-class," they had no experience of what totalitarian communism really entailed. A case in point is a line from Auden's poem "Spain," in which Auden expresses the tasks that must be accepted by the "good party member," which include: "the conscious acceptance of guilt in the necessary murder." The phrase *necessary murder* could only be used by someone who has no conception of what "murder" really means. Here it is used by the type of man "who is always somewhere else when the trigger is being pulled."

What the history of the 1930s teaches us, Orwell concludes, is that no writer worth his salt should accept the discipline of a political party. Writing literature is an individual act that can only be negatively influenced by orthodoxy, of any type, which returns us to the subject of Henry Miller. "When I visited Miller on my way to Spain, he informed me that I was a fool to become involved in the civil war "from a sense of obligation." Miller acknowledges the "impending cataclysm," but he doesn't care. Miller compares the intensely personal, subjective writing of the diarist Anaïs Nin to Jonah inside the whale's body. No doubt many people find the idea of being returned to the womblike belly of a whale comforting. Miller is one of these, with the difference that his whale is transparent, so that he can see what's really happening, but not deluding himself that he can do anything about it. This is the height of irresponsibility. Now (1940) we are moving toward an age of totalitarian dictatorships, in which freedom of thought will come to an end, and with it, literature as we know it. Miller's response to this crisis is quietism. For him, the writer's only choice in the future will be to get inside the whale. Miller, with all his flaws, has provided the only alternative to the disintegration of Western Civilization: "Accept it."

COMMENTARY

It is clear that the experience of Henry Miller—both the man and his work—represented a severe shock for Orwell. Here is a powerful, original writer who shares Orwell's vision of the imminent collapse of Western culture, but feels no obligation to do anything about it, not even to the extent of being saddened by it. His "acceptance" of the modern world seems to Orwell to be inexcusable but provocative, forcing him to consider the role of the writer in society. To Orwell, it was clear, as he was later to put it in "Why I Write," that "it was invariably when I lacked a political purpose, I wrote lifeless books . . ." But he realizes that this was not true for apolitical writers such as T. S. Eliot or Edgar Allen Poe, and clearly not for Henry Miller.

In part 2, he sketches a brief outline of English literature from 1910 to 1940. The dominant theme for the period of World War I was the war itself, but the main concerns of Georgian poetry—as represented by A. E. Housman—were nature, nostalgia, and self-pity. (It is odd that he should overlook the work of a writer from this period who was very important in his own development, H. G. WELLS.) With the advent of the 1920s came the formalist revolution. Yeats, Eliot, Joyce, and D. H. Lawrence, all of whom share a profoundly pessimistic view of the modern world. Yeats's "The Second Coming" stands as a perfect example of the mood, an apocalyptic vision of the future and a repudiation of the present. Orwell views the group coming of age in the 1930s—particularly the poets W. H. Auden, Stephen Spender, C. Day Lewis, and Louis MacNeice, as examples of the spoiled, middle-class university elite, seduced by the illusion of Soviet communism, who have made antifascism their single goal. In his indictment of this leftist group-think, he looks at Auden's poem "Spain." While acknowledging that "the poem is one of the few decent things that have ever been written about the war," he zeroes in on the phrase *necessary murder* with icy precision, "it could only have been written by a man for whom murder is at most a *word*." Auden was sufficiently stung by the critique that he revised the line to read "the fact of murder." (Somewhat later, after his religious conversion, he excluded the entire poem from an edition of his collected poetry.)

In the face of a totalitarian future, Orwell feels that "quietism" is a form of defeatism. It expresses not only Miller's position but the only viable alternative available in the coming dark age. Miller's work is "negative, unconstructive, amoral" but, unfortunately, credible. This essay pinpoints a central dilemma of Orwell's. He is absolutely committed to the goal of making political writing an art, yet when he examines the position of a writer he admires, he seems to recognize that the nonpolitical artist may be adhering to a darker truth: Evil exists and there is nothing to be done about it. There seems to be a realization on Orwell's part that he is caught in a self contradiction.

He may have resolved that double bind as he looked at Miller's subsequent career. As he pointed out in a 1942 review of Miller's work post–*Tropic of Cancer*, ". . . in a period like the present a contempt for politics and a regard for one's own skin lead one automatically away from a place where anything interesting is happening" (CW, 218–219).

WORK CITED

The Complete Works of George Orwell. Edited by Peter Davison. Vol. 14. London: Secker & Warburg, 1998.

Keep the Aspidistra Flying (1936)

Orwell's third novel. Like its predecessors, *BURMESE DAYS* and *A CLERGYMAN'S DAUGHTER*, it focuses on a main character who rejects his or her society's norms. In this case, the rejection takes the form of a crusade—a war on money and on the civilization that worships it. But the novel presents a more complicated picture than that of a heroic rebel fighting the good fight (an image, as it happens, that many people hold of Orwell himself), but of a recognition that in our political and ideological commitments we are often, as the principal character admits, "objectifying our own feelings." Thus, the novel has a dual focus: offering a social analysis of the commercial world while exploring the psychological roots of its main character, sparing neither one the sharp satiric gaze of its author. Insofar as his principal character bears some of the traits of Orwell himself, it indicates that he was also a remorseless, if ultimately forgiving, self-critic.

HISTORICAL/BIOGRAPHICAL CONTEXT

Set in 1934, written in 1935, and published in 1936, the novel is set in the middle years of the Great Depression, the worldwide economic crisis that resulted in widespread poverty and unemployment. In addition, although economic questions occupied the forefront of the average person's concern, the threat of war was never far from the surface of their consciousness, many of whom were beginning to realize that the monstrous world war they had lived through might in fact be merely the first act in an ongoing drama. These were the years in which the "intermission," in what historians now see as a single world war, beginning in 1914 and ending in 1945, was coming to a close. It was also a time that witnessed the birth and growth of two forms of totalitarianism, COMMUNISM and FASCISM, both about to engage each other in the SPANISH CIVIL WAR.

For 15 months, from October 1934 to January 1936, while he was writing *Aspidistra,* Orwell worked as a part-time clerk in Booklovers' Corner, a bookstore near Hampstead Heath. Unlike his protagonist Gordon Comstock, however, he had no trouble integrating his writing with the demands of the job—in fact he thrived under the discipline it imposed: Up early to open the shop, then returning home for at least three uninterrupted morning hours of writing before returning to work from 2:00 to 6:30 p.m. Also, far from the bitter alienation and loneliness Gordon experiences, his creator was enjoying a growing reputation as a writer to be watched, while leading an active social life, crowned by meeting and falling in love with his future wife Eileen O'Shaughnessy. Of course, as any novelist would, he drew upon his experiences for various incidents, but the burning indignation that oozes from Gordon would have to have been an emotion recollected in tranquility, summoned up from Orwell's "Down and Out" period three years earlier, when publishers were routinely rejecting the manuscript of that book.

Note on Money Terms

In 1936, the English pound (slang term, *quid*) was exchanged at the rate of $5. A shilling (slang term, *bob*) was the equivalent of 25 cents, A *crown* was five shillings and a *half crown,* two shillings, sixpence ("two and six"). A *florin* was two shillings. A *threepenny* bit, a very small coin (slang term, "Joey"), made so much of in the opening chapter, was three cents. Thus, Gordon Comstock's weekly salary at the advertising agency is four pounds, 10 shillings (approximately U.S. $22.50), his salary at McKechnie's bookstore is two pounds ($10) and his salary, working for the miserly Mr. Cheeseman is 30 shillings ($7.50).

SYNOPSIS

Epigraph

The epigraph is a parody of St. Paul's strictures on charity (1 Corinthians xiii), in which he speaks of the fundamental importance of charity ("Though I speak with the tongues of angels and men and have not charity. . . ."). In this version, wherever the word *charity* would appear, it has been replaced by *money.*

Chapter 1

The date, November 30 (Saint Andrew's Day), 1934. The place, McKechnie's, a small bookstore in North London: Gordon Comstock, a 29-year-old clerk at the store, pouts, dwelling on his inability to make ends meet on his skimpy salary. At this moment he is wrestling with the problem of how to make four cigarettes last for two days, smoking cigarettes being an essential condition for any writing he hopes to do in the evening after work. The lack of money for cigarettes is a particularly painful example of Gordon's most passionate conviction: that the modern world is ruled by the "money god," who governs every human act and event, even that of writing poetry. A concrete example, as far as Gordon, is concerned, is the fact that all the money he has in his pocket (five and a half pence) contains a *Joey,* a coin given to him as change by a shop girl as a sign of her contempt for his bedraggled condition. To Gordon, the coin is worthless, because using it to buy something would betray his poverty.

Physically unprepossessing and socially alienated, Gordon is bored and depressed by his job. He looks around at the 7,000 books in the store and realizes he has grown to hate them, including one, *Mice,* a book of poems he himself had written two years earlier. "He hated the whole lot of them . . . the mere sight of them brought home to him his own sterility. For here he was, supposedly a writer, and he couldn't even write." He walks to the front of the store to gaze out on the street scene, blighted by the advertising posters fluttering on the fence across the street. (Advertising is going to assume a major role in this story, just as, by 1934, it had already assumed in modern life.)

Gordon's bitter thoughts are regularly interrupted by his mental tinkering with one stanza of a poem he is trying to finish and with the comings and goings of browsers and buyers. According to the type of customer, Gordon adjusts his manner and style of speech, all the while despising both the customer and his own insincerity. The customers fit various stereotypes: the self-styled literary ladies visiting the lending library, the "nancy-boy," and the "feminist," used as terms of contempt (reminding the reader that the novel is a creature of its time). He reflects for a moment on his good friend Ravelston, the editor of the socialist journal *The Antichrist,* and of Rosemary, Gordon's girlfriend, who professes to love him but not enough to sleep with him.

After dismissing from the store an impoverished old beggar and his wife, he sees in them the typical "throw outs of the money-god. All over London, by tens of thousands, draggled beasts, creeping like unclean beetles to the grave." A painfully shy young man purchases a book of poems by D. H. Lawrence, leaving Gordon alone again in the shop. Overcome by the urge to smoke, Gordon lights up, despite his vow to save his cigarettes for the evening, a betrayal of principle that further darkens his mood. Gazing out the window, he sees the "grayish reflection of his face in the pane" and the shabby figures walking by, which evoke for him two lines from Baudelaire's poem "Ennui." His personal pessimism takes on an apocalyptic tone, ". . . our civilization is dying. But it isn't going to die in bed. Presently the aeroplanes are coming," dropping bombs. He imitates the sound of the imagined planes, "a sound, which, at that moment, he ardently desires to hear."

Chapter 2

Returning from work, Gordon finds the rooming house where he lives even more depressing than the bookstore. Presided over by Mrs. Wisbeach, "one of those malignant, respectable women who keep boarding houses," it is a dingy, airless place.

In the hallway, he searches in vain for letters, either from publications where he has submitted his poems or from Rosemary, who has not written to him in several days. As he moves toward the stairs, he meets his fellow lodger Flaxman, a hearty, back-slapping traveling salesman for the Queen of Sheba Toilet Requisites Co. He invites Gordon for a drink at a local pub. Although dying for "a pint of Guinness," Gordon refuses, knowing he has but two pence to his name. Although aware that Flaxman would gladly treat him to drinks, he is determined not to depend on another's charity. He proceeds to his room, where he encounters his bête noire, the sole decorative item in the room, "a sickly aspidistra plant." For Gordon, the plant's ubiquitous presence in front windows all over London marks it as the perfect embodiment of lower-middle-class English life.

Soon after, he is called down to dinner by Mrs. Wisbeach for her usual scanty and unappetizing meal. Back upstairs, he proceeds to his nightly ritual, preparing a clandestine cup of tea, forbidden by the landlady and requiring extraordinary skill to manage successfully. Feeling a little better from the tea, he attempts to do some writing. He had planned to spend the evening working on "London Pleasures," a long poem he has been struggling with for two years. He had originally conceived of the poem as a kind of modern epic of some 2,000 lines, describing one day in London. But it had proven too big a job. Nevertheless, he persists, in defiance of the money-god, for it is an article of faith with him that money—or rather the lack of it—is the principal cause of his writing failure. However, tonight is one of those increasingly rare moments when he feels he might do some good work. No sooner does he begin than the he becomes aware that Mrs.Wisbeach is delivering the evening mail. He hears her footsteps on the stairs and fervently prays for a letter either from a publisher or from Rosemary, but the landlady's steps soon fade, along with his desire to write. Shortly after, the remaining oil in his lamp gives out. He crawls under the covers to escape the cold. The last image before falling asleep comes from the headlights of a car in the street, briefly illuminating a leaf of the aspidistra, "shaped like Agamemnon's sword."

Chapter 3

The chapter opens with an account of Gordon's family. Gordon's paternal grandfather Samuel Comstock was "a tough old scoundrel," whose impact on his 11 children consisted of "crushing out of them any spirit they might have ever possessed." Included among the old man's victims was Gordon's father "a depressed and therefore depressing" chartered accountant, only fitfully successful in his career. Although they can ill afford it, his parents are able to send Gordon to a "third rate" public (in the United States, "private") school. Of course, there is not enough money for Gordon's only sibling and older sister, Julia, to have the same opportunity: "It seemed only natural that 'the girl' should have been sacrificed to 'the boy.'" Having been stigmatized as one of the "poor" children at the school, Gordon, at the age of sixteen, develops a theory of money: "One could possess money or despise money; the one fatal thing is to worship money and fail to get it." Having been told by his teachers that he would never succeed in life (he is an indifferent student), "he would refuse the whole business of 'succeeding.'" The following year his father dies and Gordon takes a job for the sake of his mother, who is in ill health. Living with his mother and his doting sister, who works long hours in a tearoom, he bides his time. Four months after his mother's death, he quits his job, hoping to drop out of the money world and devote himself to writing. He soon discovers that there can be no writing without money. Finally, he is thrown back on his family—aunt, uncle and particularly Julia—off whom, with occasional pangs of conscience, he selfishly sponges. Finally, he finds a job in the newly rising field of advertising at the New Albion Publicity Company. When someone notices that he has published a poem, he is promoted by Mr. Erskine, managing director of the company, to the position of assistant to the chief copywriter of the firm, Mr. Clew. Early on, Gordon exhibits a conspicuous talent for writing clever magazine ads for a new deodorant, put out by the Queen of Sheba Toilet Requisites Co. But Gordon sees his success as the real trap, a "good job." He is also privately horrified to find that he is very good at writing ad copy.

To the dismay of family and friends, he again quits his job, this time being careful to line up a part-time position at McKechnie's. Shortly after, his book of poems, *Mice,* is published and receives generally good reviews. *The Times Literary Supplement* declares it shows "exceptional promise." But this proves to be the high point of Gordon's war against money. What now, two years later, he has come to recognize is that the damage done by a salary of two pounds a week lies in its effect on the brain and the soul, "mental deadness and spiritual squalor." He is going the same route as all the other members of the Comstock family, a fact that has brought Julia to near despair. She had invested all her hopes in the prospect that Gordon would be the family member who would break the chain of failure. She and Gordon are the only two grandchildren of old Samuel. The family is dying without leaving a trace of having lived.

Chapter 4

In a rare good mood, Gordon approaches the house of the critic Paul Doring, where he has been invited to a literary tea party. He looks forward to the party as a relief from another of the life-killing by products of poverty—loneliness. He pictures himself too poor to engage in normal social intercourse, too conscious of being overlooked because of poverty. His thoughts turn to his long poem, *London Pleasures.* He has been making real progress toward its completion, possibly in two or three months, another reason for his high spirits. When, however, he discovers no one at home and no other guests waiting outside the house, his high sprits turn to fury. He concludes that his host changed the date of the party and did not bother to tell him because, as someone with no money, he simply didn't count. He spends the next hours walking all over the city, his anger matched only by piercing loneliness as he observes the throbbing life of London. As he walks he is overcome by the knowledge that he has been fooling himself about his poem: It is no good; it will never be finished; he was a fool to imagine otherwise. He plunges on for miles, passing pubs and tea shops and movie theaters filled with warmth and comfort and the promise of relief from loneliness. As he approaches home, he peeks in at the local pub, the Crichton Arms, where he spots Flaxman at the bar. He starts to enter, knowing that Flaxman would willingly lend him the price of one or two pints, but he turns away at the last moment, repeating the first commandment of the moneyless: "Never let other people buy your drinks for you." Stumbling home, cold, tired, and hungry, he opens a letter from a journal to which he has sent a poem, only to find a rejection slip. Totally frustrated, he sits down and writes a letter to Rosemary, who has not written to for five days, obviously, he reasons, because he has no money. He must hit back at somebody. His letter, unsigned, consists of one sentence: "You have broken my heart."

Chapter 5

Gordon pays a visit to Ravelston, that is, he gets as far as the sidewalk in front of Ravelston's house and throws a pebble against the window, thus avoiding actually entering his flat. The flat is "unconsciously upper-class," its very lack of pretentiousness intimidating Gordon so that he is reluctant to enter it. Ravelston, like Gordon, is striving to escape his class, except that in Ravelston's case the class is the aristocracy. A committed socialist, he is the editor and publisher of *Antichrist,* a journal that mixes politics and belles lettres, whose editorial policy is often motivated by charity. "Practically anything got printed in *Antichrist* if Ravelston suspected that its author was starving." Thus it gives him special pleasure to inform Gordon that the next issue of *Antichrist* will include one of his poems, "the one about the dying prostitute."

The two men pretend that they have already eaten dinner, saving Gordon the embarrassment of admitting he can't afford dinner. Ravelston already knows, although he can't understand why, that his paying for Gordon's meal is out of the question. Instead, they head for a dingy working-class pub, where Gordon can afford to buy one round of beer. At the pub, Ravelston makes a brave effort to fit in but commits the faux pas of ordering two whiskies in a bar that has only a beer license. The two fall into their usual topic of conversation, the corrupt and demoralizing conditions of modern life. Ravelston sees the modern malaise as the advanced stages of the imminent death of capitalism, a prelude to the triumph of socialism. Gordon is skeptical of the socialist ideal, fearful that it will produce a society of mindless conformity, such as is depicted in Aldous Huxley's *Brave New World* (1932). He takes a step further, dismissing all political talk as examples of "objectifying our own feelings" and saying that our ideas "are all dictated by what we've got in our own pockets." Ravelston replies that Gordon's phrase is the very essence of Marxist thought, the economic foundation of all ideology, but Gordon thunders back that you cannot understand poverty as an abstract idea. You have to experience the "squalid meanness" of it all. He cites the snub he received from Doring and moves on to the even more personal subject—the way women react to a man who is poor. To a woman, a poor man is "dishonored. He has sinned against the aspidistra."

When Ravelston asks him if he has a girlfriend, Gordon distorts the truth about Rosemary, depicting her as a callous, tormenting creature who would fall into his arms if he had more money. When he discovers they can never find a place to be alone, how their dates consist of cold, rainy walks, Ravelston offers to lend him 10 pounds to take his girl out. Gordon, sorely tempted, refuses. After the two friends part, Ravelston goes home to find his girlfriend, Hermione Slater, a rich, self-indulgent, society type with no social conscience, waiting for him. The two head out for a late dinner at Ravelston's favorite restaurant, Modigliani's. There he orders a juicy steak, which he consumes with "guilty joy," the same phrase used to describe Gordon's pleasure in chapter 1 as he prematurely smokes one of his last cigarettes.

Gordon returns to his room, where he opens a letter from Doring, indicating that the day of the party had been changed ("We did tell you, didn't we?") and inviting him to another party. Although he's not certain whether Doring told him about the change, he chooses to think the worst. Rather than waiting till morning, when a clearer head might prevail, he writes and immediately posts a reply:

> "Dear Doring,
>
> With reference to your letter, Go and—— yourself."

Chapter 6

"The Woman business!" Driven by sexual desire, Gordon prowls the streets, thinking of sex—with women in general, with Rosemary in particular. She had not written him in eight days. It was clear she wanted nothing to do with him. In his fixated fashion, he understands why: He has no money. "No money, therefore no hold. What holds a woman to a man except money?" Of course, one might always get married, but marriage is the ultimate trap, tying you to a job and a lifetime of "nagging, burnt meals, children crying and thunder of embattled mothers-in-law." But neither marriage nor keeping a mistress is possible on two pounds a week. Thinking of Rosemary, he turns into a local street market and runs into her, wearing a particularly becoming hat. She was on her way to see him to express her anger at the "beastly" one-sentence letter he had sent. Consistent with his self-centered state of mind, he replies, "What beastly letter?" After describing Rosemary as a sensible, lively, attractive woman in her late twenties, the authorial narrator anticipates the reader's question—what does she see in him?—by describing her love for him as a mystery to herself. The two met at the New Albion agency, where Rosemary is an illustrator. They have been seeing each other for two years. Although, along with everyone else, she thought his quitting his job sheer folly, she accepted his decision. What she has not accepted is his repeated attempts to sleep with her. But one glance at his bedraggled, unshaven face and worn-out, buttonless clothing dissipates her anger at his childish letter.

She follows him to a dark, deserted alley for some passionate kisses, the passion being Gordon's contribution, while Rosemary's is closer to compassion. When he urges her to sleep with him, she says yes, but she refuses to specify the time or place. Rosemary is the product of a large (14 children), lively, middle-class family, profoundly magnanimous but reluctant to give up her sexual innocence. Her refusal sends Gordon off on a sophistical rant, accusing her of holding back because of his poverty. When his tirade extends to blaming all women for being in league with the money god, she bursts out laughing, which sets off the "merry war," a verbal battle of the sexes that is a regular feature of their meetings that both delight in. The mutual pleasure is spoiled when Gordon refuses to let Rosemary take him to dinner. Confounded by his obstinacy, she breaks down in tears. At this moment, they embrace and Gordon senses her capitulation. This time, her body tells him she is ready to have sex. They agree to spend next Sunday in the country. Gordon goes home, confident that on Sunday they will have sex for the first time—weather permitting.

Chapter 7

Gordon and Rosemary begin their trip to the country on a high note, financed in part by the latest of a series of loans from his spinster sister, Julia. (Gordon's strict rules prohibiting borrowing from others do not apply to family members. Family members, particularly doting older sisters, don't count.) Thanks to Julia's five shillings, he has a total of 14, which he calculates should be enough for two round-trip tickets; two bus fares; some cheese, bread, and beer at a pub; and a pack of cigarettes. The day is warm and the couple extremely happy as they stroll through the woods, exclaiming at the beauty of the surroundings. They become so engrossed in their surroundings, they are a little late leaving the woods to search for a place to have lunch. They soon pass up a pub as unsuitable and discover their mistakes when they find others with early Sunday closing hours already in force. Finding nothing else open, the desperately hungry hikers are forced to stop at a hotel, where the food is bad as well as expensive and the waiter contemptuous. They know what they've walked into but are completely intimidated by the atmosphere. When it comes to order the bread, cheese, and beer, Gordon loses his courage and asks for the lunch menu. He also orders a bottle of wine. The bill leaves Gordon with exactly eight pence left in his pocket, and the fares home still to be paid for.

Nevertheless, determined to try to salvage the day, the two find a well-hidden piece of earth, where they will consummate their relationship. Rosemary removes her clothes and lies back expectantly, but she pulls away horrified as Gordon attempts to enter her. He is not wearing a condom. Refusing to admit his thoughtlessness, he blames their need for contraception on their lack of money. The moment is spoiled and the two dress in silent anger at each other. As they trudge home, a former couple, now two separate individuals, Rosemary dwells guiltily on her reaction and offers to give herself to him right on the spot. Gordon says he has something more important to discuss, something dreadful. He must ask her to pay their fares back home. Rosemary can barely believe what she's hearing, that during the entire length of their return walk he's been brooding about asking her for money. She regards the whole idea as completely absurd, whereas for him the lack of money is fundamental to his identity as a man. Again he repeats his principle, "I can't make love to you when I've only eightpence in my pocket."

Back in London, after he had to endure the humiliation of her giving him money for the fares, they part at Rosemary's Underground station, but after he has gone a short distance, he feels a hand on his arm; she has thrust into his coat pocket a pack of cigarettes, purchased from a tobacconist. On his way home, he hits upon the last two lines of the poem he has been working on, a catalogue of the powers of the money-god in human affairs, who "lays the sleek estranging shield/ Between the lover and his bride."

Chapter 8

Five days after the Sunday outing, Gordon receives a check for $50, an unheard-of sum for a poem, from the *Californian Review,* an American magazine. His first thought is to give half of it to his sister, Julia, a partial repayment for all the money she has given him over the years. He races to the bank, where his check is converted to ten pounds cash, five singles and a fiver. Stowing the latter into an envelope, he promises himself that he will soon mail it to Julia. Meanwhile, to celebrate his good fortune, he invites Ravelston and Rosemary to dinner. Insisting that the restaurant be a good one, he chooses Ravelston's favorite, Modigliani's. He spends most of the afternoon in the pub across the street from the bookstore and then takes a cab to the restaurant. The cab driver, aware that he has a "live one" in Gordon, stops not at the restaurant but in a nearby pub where he and Gordon have a few more drinks. By the time he reaches Modigliani's, he is "well-oiled." He orders an expensive bottle of wine and proceeds to drink most of it. Alarmed at the money he is spending and the amount he's drinking, Ravelston and Rosemary try talking sense into Gordon, whose behavior is beginning to attract attention at nearby tables. Ravelston's attempts to pay for the dinner are stridently rebuffed, as Gordon insists that this is his party and proceeds to order another bottle of wine.

Paying the bill (with tip, four pounds) has a momentarily sobering effect, but not enough to deter him from insisting on taking a cab to the Cafe Imperial for a nightcap. A blast of cold air on the ride awakens him to the image of Julia's face and the knowledge he is about to squander her five pounds. Guilt-stricken, he flees back to his drunken state. He orders the driver to stop in front of a liquor store and jumps out of the cab, emerging a moment later with an open bottle of Chianti, which he brings with him into the café. They leave the noisy, crowded café shortly after arriving because Gordon wants to hit the pubs before closing time. On the street, he drags Rosemary to a spot where, treating her like one of the prostitutes cruising the area, he is so insulting and boorish that she slaps his face before leaving him on the street. Ravelston, attempting to appease him, takes him into a pub where he proceeds to down a quart-sized mug of beer and then orders a second. Incapable of swallowing the second quart, he spills it all over himself and others at the crowded bar. Ravelston drags him away from the pub and proceeds to look for a cab. Left alone for a few moments, Gordon engages a couple of prostitutes in conversation. When he returns with a cab, Ravelston tries to be firm with Gordon. But constitutionally incapable of firmness, especially when confronted with the prospect of offending two of society's downcast victims, he allows himself to be dragged along to a sleazy hotel, where Gordon, too drunk for sex, passes out with a last swig from his Chianti bottle, but not before noticing that the "mean, dreadful room" contains an aspidistra.

Chapter 9

Awakening the next day, head throbbing, body racked with pain, Gordon finds himself in a jail cell, charged with drunkenness and assaulting a police officer. Apparently he had left the hotel and was reeling through the streets, Chianti bottle still in hand, when he was stopped by the police. At that point, he swung out and hit a sergeant on the ear. Before appearing in court, he is visited by Ravelston and his boisterous fellow lodger Flaxman, who learned about the incident when Ravelston came to the boarding house, delivering the news to an outraged Mrs. Wisbeach. Ravelston declares that he is going to pay Gordon's fine, but Gordon insists he'd rather rot in jail. In court he is fined five pounds paid, as promised, by Ravelston, who brings Gordon back to his flat. Although he is finished at Mrs. Wisbeach's, there is still hope that Mr. McKechnie, a strict teetotaler, does not know the truth. Flaxman has already spoken to him, explaining that Gordon is down with the flu. However, in the neighborhood newspaper, there is a full account of Gordon's binge, making his firing inevitable.

Still occupying a room in Ravelston's flat, Gordon undergoes a few days of humiliation, vainly looking for a job. At one point, Rosemary visits the flat, takes one look at Gordon's deteriorated condition and collapses in tears, but he wants neither tears nor pity. He has now sunk to a new level: "the sub-world of the unemployed." However, Rosemary has come to announce that she is quite certain that New Albion would be happy to take Gordon back, and at a salary of four pounds a week. Gordon angrily rejects the idea. She protests that he just wants "to sink—just *sink.*" He replies, "I'd sooner sink than rise." She leaves in despair. Eventually, Gordon accepts a job, clerking in a two-penny lending library, specializing in cheap sensational novels, grouped under headings such as Sex, Crime, and Wild West. The owner, Mr. Cheeseman, is a character out of a Dickens novel, "a sinister little man, small enough to be called a dwarf." He knows about Gordon's drunken spree and is delighted to have something to hold over him. The salary is 10 shillings less than the two pounds he was starving on, but Gordon is perversely delighted. ". . . ten bob nearer the mud. It was what he wanted."

Chapter 10

Gordon's new job is one of "inconceivable futility," simply registering borrowed books and collecting two pence for each. When there are no customers, he spends his time reading the trashy stories, enabling him to make recommendations to customers. Mr. Cheeseman, his tightfisted boss who is convinced Gordon must be cheating him, is interesting, a man who has no regard for books and who never reads them, in fact, but who makes a good living selling rare editions, ". . . he seemed to know by the mere feel of a book whether it was valuable or not." Gordon's new lodging, near the store, is located in an alley, his room a filthy garret with a sloping roof and a skylight. The old landlady Mother Meakins is the opposite of the nosey, overbearing Mrs. Wisbeach. Here you can do as you please. Dirt and dust and bugs are everywhere, the perfect spot for someone like Gordon. His only problems are the annoying letters from friends and relatives exhorting him to reform, or expressing pity, in either case trying to tie him to a world "from which he was trying to escape." Ravelston visits him, appalled by the bugs, the smell, the unwashed cups and dishes, pleading with him at least to move to a more acceptable place, but Gordon's indifference makes it clear that "their friendship is at an end," his sponging on Ravelston while he lived with him "has spoiled everything. Charity kills friendship."

Rosemary and Julia are more persistent. They have banded together, hoping their combined efforts will bring him to his senses. Rosemary had gone to see Mr. Erskine at New Albion and convinced him to rehire him. Gordon responds by accusing her of going behind his back. Julia's case is even more difficult since she has no appreciation for his literary ambitions, nor any idea of how living in a slum and isolating himself could have any relation to writing poetry. One night, while he's lying in his bed in a semistupor, he is visited by Rosemary, who climbs into bed with him, forcing him to have sex with her, "without much pleasure." She does so, he recognizes, not out of passion but "magnanimity, pure magnanimity." After it is over, she dresses and leaves, feeling "dismayed, disappointed, and very cold."

Chapter 11

Winter has given way to spring, and Gordon has settled further in to his squalid life at the bookstore and boarding house. Left unanswered are letters from Rosemary, Julia, and Ravelston. He views them all as obstacles, distractions from his main goal, "to sink down in the ultimate mud" until Rosemary appears at the store one day to announce that she is pregnant. The choices are clear: marriage with Gordon returning to New Albion, or marriage with Gordon persisting in his life of poverty. (This would require Rosemary's returning to her parents' home and living off them) and the third choice, abortion. The latter could be arranged apparently for five pounds. For Gordon, the equation of a child's life with five pounds brings the reality directly home: abortion is out of the question. The only problem is the decision to marry with or without his return to New Albion. Rosemary asserts that such a decision will be his to make. She insists that, above all, she wants him to "feel free." Gordon tells her that he will make his decision that night.

He closes the shop early and stops in at a public library. First, he goes to the reference section, looking for a book on pregnancy. The illustrations of the fetus at various stages of gestation confirm his rejection of abortion. Then he moves to the periodicals section, where he looks first at the ads in an American magazine and then at an English one, to both of which he reacts with total disgust. This was the type of "muck" he would be producing at New Albion.

But he knows in his heart that his mind has been made up all along. He calls up Rosemary to tell her he will go to New Albion the next day to ask for his job back. Delighted, she tells him she will wire him four pounds to buy clothes that will make him look presentable. On his way home, he realizes that this decision was inevitable. Even if there had been no pregnancy, something else would have brought him back. The path of renunciation he has been choosing was possible only for saints, and "he was no saint." Passing the lower-middle-class houses, with their lace curtains and aspidistra plants, he realizes that the people in those houses have chosen life, with all the limitations imposed on that life by the money-god. These people have a simple dignity, their "points of honour," busy being born, begetting, working, and dying, all the while keeping the aspidistra flying. "The aspidistra is the tree of life, he thought suddenly." As a final gesture, he takes the manuscript of *London Pleasures* from his pocket and pushes it between the bars of a sewer drain.

Chapter 12

Rosemary and Gordon are secretly married in the Registry Office. Gordon had wanted a church wedding, but Rosemary "had put her foot down." Ravelston is their witness, but Julia, the only other person who knows of the wedding, was unable to get the day off from the tea shop. Rosemary intends to keep working for the next few months, while Gordon is busily ensconced at New Albion. He and Mr. Warner, a go-getting Canadian with advertising experience honed in New York, have teamed up to launch a "monster campaign" for Flaxman's firm, the Queen of Sheba Toilet Requisites Company. The company had decided to market a new product and they needed a catchy slogan. In a stroke of genius, Warner has come up with a two-letter phrase "that would rankle in the public consciousness like a poisoned arrow": P. P. (for "Pedic Perspiration"). Gordon supplies the texts for the ads, "harrowing little stories, each a realistic novel in one hundred words." It appears that his struggles to find the mot juste as a poet have equipped him "to use words with the economy that is only learned by years of effort."

After the wedding, the couple and Ravelston have lunch, not at Modigliani's of bitter memory but at a charming, inexpensive Soho restaurant. Later they return to their new apartment, a top-floor flat near Paddington Station. They love everything in the flat, but for Gordon it lacks one essential item, an aspidistra plant. He insists they go out and buy one immediately. Rosemary strenuously resists, but, after a long quarrel, she relents. As they descend the staircase, she suddenly stops to report that she has just felt the baby move. Standing a step below, Gordon kneels and presses his head against her belly: Despite all prior indications to the contrary, the Comstock family is alive and kicking.

COMMENTARY

The parody of Saint Paul in the epitaph underscores a central theme of the novel, the idea that the modern world is dedicated to the worship of the "money-god," but it becomes obvious as the reader engages the text that this theme needs no underscoring in a novel whose protagonist is obsessed with this very idea. A closer look at the parody reveals that many of the "money" substitutions do not work; they lack relevance. ("Money suffereth long and is kind; money envieth not; money vaunted not itself, is not puffed up, does not behave unseemly, seeketh not her own, is not easily provoked, thinketh no evil. . . ."). A possible conclusion is that the parody, like the novel, cuts both ways: mocking both those who worship the money-god and those who, like the novel's protagonist, in professing to hate it, in fact overestimate it.

Encouraging the view that the novel is more experimental than is usually recognized are two stylistic features that Orwell employs. These are now fairly common practices in fiction, but in 1935, they were still relatively new, their possibilities having been brilliantly exploited in James Joyce's *Ulysses* (1922), a novel that had a powerful impact on Orwell. One technique is known as free indirect style, which employs traditional third-person, past-tense narration while placing the reader inside the character's mind, using spoken language appropriate to the individual. Here is an example of Orwell's use of it in the first chapter:

> Dull-eyed, he gazed at the wall of books. He hated the whole lot of them, old and new, highbrow and lowbrow, snooty and chirpy. The mere sight of them brought home to him his own sterility.

Here the first sentence is straight narration, and the rest free indirect style. Another more-radical stylistic feature is interior monologue or stream of consciousness. In this case, third-person narration disappears, and we are directly inside the character's head, in the present tense, as illustrated in Roger Fowler's *The Language of George Orwell*:

> Two lines from a poem struggled for birth in Gordon's mind.
>
> Sharply the something wind -for instance threatening wind? No better menacing wind blows over. No sweeps over, say. The something poplars—yielding poplars. No better, bending poplars. Assonance between bending and menacing? No matter. The bending poplars, newly bare. Good.

Here, the first sentence is straight third-person narration; the rest, present-tense phrases, or sentences, examples of interior monologue or stream of consciousness (Fowler, 145–147). There are some passages in *Aspisdistra* in which three styles are juxtaposed in one paragraph:

> His eye fell again on the ad posters across the street.
>
> He almost wanted to laugh at them. They were so feeble, so unappetizing. As though anyone could be tempted by *those*. Like succubi with pimply backsides.

Here the first sentence is straight third-person narration; the second and third, free indirect style, and the last two, interior monologue. The difficulty raised by this mix of styles, particularly with the free indirect style, is that it is sometimes not clear whether the words are spoken by the authorial narrator or the character. Thus when terms like "nancy-boy" and "feminist" appear, they clearly reflect Gordon's attitude toward homosexuals and feminist women. Do they also reflect Orwell's? Many critics would say, and have said, yes, emphatically, adding that Orwell has taken advantage of the ambiguity inherent in the style to foist off on his main character his own prejudices. Others would say it is clear throughout a good portion of the book that Orwell is satirizing the opinions and the behavior of his main character, for example, his obsession with money, his self centeredness, his behavior to his girlfriend, his treatment of his sister. Orwell, they maintain, must at least be given the benefit of the doubt in the grey areas. Regardless of what Orwell himself, thinks, his character, who has very few good words for anyone, is very likely to exhibit a negative attitude about nearly everyone. Others would add that a book written in 1936 will inevitably contain some language or ideas that contemporary readers will balk at. In any case, on the basis of chapter 1, it appears that Orwell intends the portrait of Gordon to be a satiric treatment of the aspiring romantic poet, aloof, indifferent, and bored to the extent that he looks forward to the bombing of London as something he would welcome.

How legitimate is Gordon's critique of the money world? Some have complained that Orwell leaves us in the dark finally. Clearly, Gordon has hold of at least a partial truth, even if he has magnified it into a worldview. The view has been expressed before, and among those who seem to come closest to Gordon is Friedrich Engels, coauthor of *The Communist Manifesto,* as quoted in Alex Zwerding's *Orwell and the Left*: "Then came money, that universal commodity for which all others could be exchanged. But when men invented money they little suspected that they were creating a new social power, the one universal power to which the whole of society must bow" (65). Gordon's problem is that he is using the money-god as a crutch designed to avoid responsibility for his rebellion against a family he despises. As the family's last great hope of success, he is exacting revenge on them, as evidenced by his treatment of Julia. It is only the prospect of creating a new family that brings him back from the mud.

The movement in chapter 2 from the bookstore to his living quarters is clearly a social and psychological descent for Gordon. At the store, he is, if not the master of his domain, at least from the vantage point of the customers and browsers, the man in charge, knowledgeable about books, and subtly contemptuous of the clientele. At the boarding house, however, he has none of these advantages, occupying the least-desirable room (top-floor rear) and easily intimidated by his landlady from hell, Mrs.Wisbeach ("wise bitch?"). His rejection of his oversized neighbor Flaxman's offer to visit the local pub takes on a wider significance when we learn later that the firm for which Flaxman works, the Queen of Sheba Toilet Requisites Co., is the same one for which Gordon had been writing copy when he threw over his job at New Albion. Orwell would appear to be having fun with the idea that good-natured Flaxman is the unwitting agent of the temptress queen, or perhaps a modern, plump Jack Falstaff trying to lure back Prince Hal from the path of righteousness. Gordon's lone triumph of the evening—a mock-heroic portrait of Gordon as Romantic rebel—is his successful campaign to make himself a surreptitious cup of tea under the nose of the all-watchful Mrs. Wisbeach, who appears to be an early, domesticated sketch of *Nineteen Eighty-Four*'s Big Brother. (For a more upbeat account of tea brewing, see Orwell's prescriptions in his brief essay "A NICE CUP OF TEA").

The pattern of irresoluteness that we saw in Gordon when he surrendered to his desire for a cigarette in the store, emerges here, when he is distracted from working on his poem by the sound of Mrs. Wisbeach's delivery of the late evening mail. When she passes by his room without stopping, he is so upset, he can no longer continue to work, another indication that Gordon's dedication to his poetry is something less than total. The chapter ends with the illuminated stem of the aspidistra in his room, gleaming "like Agamemnon's sword," suggesting that there is more vitality in the sickly plant than in the poetry of its adversary, that the aspidistrian sword is mightier than the Comstockian pen.

Chapter 3 deepens the perspective from which the reader views Gordon. We see him as a Comstock, the last hope of a family in which hope is a scarce commodity. (Gordon's last name may be an ironic reference to Anthony Comstock [1844–1915], an American crusader against pornography, the founder of the Society for the Suppression of Vice. The irony may be directed against Gordon, who is another crusader against the ultimate vice, money.) On the other hand, Orwell may have in mind the Comstock Lode, the famous Nevada silver mine. The discovery of a rich vein of silver in the 1850s touched off a furious rush to the site. Henry Comstock sold his share for a pittance some years before the discovery, thus making him an ideal candidate for membership in Gordon's family. The Comstock family consists of the 11 children of Grandfather Samuel Comstock, a fierce tyrant who crushed his children so effectively that only one of them, Gordon's father, produced any children. Another possible relation to Anthony Comstock, the old man's effect on his children seems to be one of sexual repression. The rest employed what little energy they could muster in futile attempts to achieve commercial success in life, all of them fated to fail. Gordon's father, forced by his father into a business (chartered accountancy) for which he was unsuited, never achieved any success.

Nevertheless, his parents squeaked by in "shabby genteel" fashion, bordering on abject poverty in order to send Gordon to a "third rate" public school, where the majority of boys were richer than he. "Probably the greatest agony one can inflict on a child is to send it to a school among children richer than itself." Here, Orwell evokes his bitter experience at St Cyprian's prep school, which he attended from 1910 to 1916 on a partial scholarship for talented boys with limited income. His sense of economic inferiority was only one of the torments experienced there and recorded in his famous essay "SUCH, SUCH WERE THE JOYS."

The humiliation Gordon suffers from abuse by his wealthier fellow students leaves a powerful mark on him. At 16, he declares a secret war on money. Unfortunately, he never outgrows this adolescent view. When his father dies, Gordon is two years away from graduation, and his mother and sister insist on his finishing school. They undergo additional hardships to pay his fees. Eventually, he accepts a job in the advertising agency. Gordon's (and presumably Orwell's) contempt for advertising is rooted in its growing power in creating a consumer culture, but also in its ability to distort language in the fashion of *Nineteen Eighty-Four's* Newspeak.

Chapter 4 intensifies the picture of Gordon as the alienated outsider, a stranger not only in the world of London, but in his own inner world. Before he arrives at the critic Doring's house, his spirits are buoyed by the prospects of a "padded armchair under his bum, and tea and cigarettes and the smell of women—you learn to appreciate such things when you are starved of them." One measure of his, for him, high spirits is his tinkering with the new poem he has been working on in the bookstore as well as his optimism about finishing his long epic, *London Pleasures*. But his fragile self-image is easily fractured by the slightest mishap. Thus his understandable disappointment at finding no one at home turns to paranoid fury as he interprets of the look he receives from a servant girl in the house next door:

> He looked a fool. . . . And suddenly it came to him that that girl knew all about him, knew that the party had been put off and everybody except Gordon had been told about it—knew that it was because he had no money that he wasn't worth the trouble of telling. She *knew.* Servants always know.

Nursing his paranoia, he unleashes his anger on himself and his poetry; "His empty, silly poems!" He then proceeds to walk the length and breadth of London until anger and self-hatred are replaced by the experience of hunger, cold, and fatigue. Unstated but implicit is the suggestion that his walk though the city is an enactment of the basic idea underlying *London Pleasures:* capturing a day in the life of London, presumably as Joyce did in *Ulysses.* Unlike Gordon, Joyce's hero Leopold Bloom, although, as a Jew, technically an outsider in Dublin, enters into the life of the city, refusing to be deterred by imagined snubs of servant girls and barroom bullies. Extending this analogy a bit further, Gordon no doubt would prefer to think of himself as Stephen Daedalus, the aspiring artist yearning to fly above the entangling nets of society. Still another interesting contrast between Bloom and Gordon is their profession. Bloom is an advertising canvasser. Rather than disdaining the business, he accepts it wholeheartedly, his head filled with jingles and slogans. Gordon's priggish response to the common life is a reaction that leaves his nose pressed to the window of a pub, peering at the by now emblematic Flaxman in the midst of life. The bitterness of his experience might have been redeemed had we seen him returning to his room and incorporating the day into *London Pleasures,* adding richer ironic resonance to the title. As it is, his injured pride or narcissism prevents him from translating social rejection into literature, if only as grist for the mills of satire. At this point, the reader may begin to harbor the suspicion that Gordon's commitment to writing is a superficial one. When he finally arrives home, instead of enriching his poem, he writes a self-pitying, childish letter, attempting to wound Rosemary.

The figure of Philip Ravelston, whom we first meet in the fifth chapter, is modeled on RICHARD (later Sir Richard) REES, Orwell's good friend and, in the 1930s, coeditor of *Adelphi,* a journal of politics and literature that published a number of early poems and essays by Orwell. In his study of Orwell's work, *George Orwell: Fugitive from the Camp of Victory,* Rees cites two reasons why *Aspidistra* "deserves close attention. The first is that it marked the end of the first period of Orwell's writing. The year 1936 was a turning point in his career. And second, for its points of similarity with *1984* . . ." (32). By "first period," Rees is referring to the years 1930 to 1936, during which Orwell wrote *DOWN AND OUT IN PARIS AND LONDON, BURMESE DAYS, A CLERGYMAN'S DAUGHTER* and *Aspidistra.* All these works, while dealing with significant social questions such as poverty, imperialism, and loss of religious belief, deal with an alienated protagonist, a loner, but they lack a specific political orientation. It is only after the completion of *Aspidistra* and his experience in Spain that Orwell became committed to socialism as a viable and realistic political force. Prior to that period, Orwell maintained an essentially apolitical independence, at one time characterizing himself as a "Tory anarchist," combining a deep distrust both of capitalism and government with a profound distaste for the vulgarity and callousness of modern culture. In this respect, Orwell was far from being alone among 20th-century modernist writers. Allowing for their individual differences, "Tory anarchist" might be a term applicable to W. B. YEATS, D. H. LAWRENCE, and Ford Madox Ford. Thus, in the pub discussion between Gordon and Ravelston, Gordon expresses his apolitical creed, dismissing socialism for its routinizing of life: "Four hours a day in a model factory, tightening up bolt number 6003 . . . Community-hikes from Marx Hostel to Lenin Hostel. Free abortion clinics on all the corners. All very well in its way, of course. Only we don't want it." (The inclusion of abortion clinics in Gordon's catalog will prove to be relevant later in the novel.) His answer to Ravelston's question, "What *do* we want?" is the apolitical "God knows. We only know what we don't want." That is as far as Gordon takes it. Orwell would in the ensuing years accept socialism as a political creed while still retaining the "Tory anarchist" as a second voice within him. Rees's description "He was conservative in everything but politics" is partially true, particularly of Orwell's last days, but he still reserved a spot for the rebel in society, even when, as in Gordon's case, the rebel lacks not a cause but the self-knowledge and discipline needed to serve a cause.

In the last two, contrasting, scenes of chapter 5, we see Ravelston's capitulation to Hermione Slater, his stereotypical society girlfriend, the embodiment of what Tom Wolfe in the 1960s would call "radical chic": "I know you're a socialist. So am I. We're all Socialists nowadays." If Ravelston's commitment to his socialist cause is marred by compromise and contradiction, what are we to make of the zealous, true believer Gordon? Despite the doubts about not having been told of the change in date of Doring's party, refusing even to look at his papers to see if the original letter was there, he translates Doring's reasonable letter into an opportunity to give full vent to his paranoia. His furious reply leaves little doubt that, at a barely discernible level of consciousness, Gordon is engaged on a self-destructive path, playing at being a victim but in fact choosing defeat.

In the view of feminist critic Daphne Patai (*The Orwell Mystique: A Study in Male Ideology*), the opening paragraph of chapter 6 "is a perfect expression of Gordon's androcentric vision" (115).

> The woman business! What a bore it is! What a pity we can't be . . . like the animals—minutes of ferocious lust and months of icy chastity. Take a cock pheasant, for example. He jumps up on the hens' backs without so much as a with your leave or by your leave. And no sooner is it over than the whole subject is out of his mind. . . . He is not called upon to support his offspring either. Lucky pheasant. How different from the lord of creation, always on the hop between his memory and his conscience!

Although Patai recognizes that these are Gordon's thoughts and not necessarily Orwell's, she sees it as an example of Orwell's concentration on the male figure to the exclusion of any comparable attention to the woman's point of view, and there is no doubt that many readers at this point would agree. Nevertheless, the passage in question is clearly satiric in intent and execution. Gordon is here exposed in all his self-centered, adolescent male arrogance. Even were it to be shown (by citing, for example, the recent revelation involving JACINTHA BUDDICOM) that Orwell in this passage is recollecting an attitude he had held as a young man, it is still being treated satirically. One of the problems with Patai's book is that you would never guess from reading it that Orwell had a sense of humor, although it is, to be sure, a distinctly male sense of humor.

In any case, Rosemary's appearance in the novel is a welcome one to readers beginning to tire of the one-note melody on money that Gordon has been holding. Orwell may have realized the pitfall involved in rendering the consciousness of an obsessive character, recognizing that sooner or later the reader is going to lose patience. Ravelston and Rosemary in chapters 5 and 6 serve as foils, reminding us that there are rational alternatives to Gordon's views. In Rosemary's case, she and Gordon make a game of the male/female argument, the stuff of comedy at least since Shakespeare. The term "merry war" is a phrase from *Much Ado about*

Nothing, and refers to the quick-witted exchanges between Beatrice and Benedick in that play. The recognition that it is a game the two have created, enabling them to engage in an exchange in which the only weapon is a sharp wit. (*A Merry War* became the title of a British film version of *Aspidistra* released in 1997. See below: FILM ADAPTATION.)

The game ends abruptly when Gordon refuses to accept Rosemary's offer to pay for their dinner. At this point the "game" is over, and Gordon is deadly serious: If he were to let her pay for his dinner, she would despise him. When they reconcile and Gordon knows that she is now willing to sleep with him, he realizes that "at this moment he loved her but did not desire her. His desire could only return at some future time when there was no . . . consciousness of four and four pence in his pocket to daunt him."

The connection between money and sexual desire has been suggested throughout the novel. At this point, it is becoming more pronounced and more apparent that Gordon's money obsession is more deeply entrenched in his psyche than the reader anticipated.

In chapter 7, in which Gordon and Rosemary's countryside tryst turns into a shambles, is, for Gordon, just another example of the pervasive power of money to govern even sexual experience: "It's the money. It's always the money." But it's not the lack of money that caused him to forget to buy a condom. His 14-shilling budget would have allowed for that purchase. The fact that he forgets to acquire the "estranging shield" suggests either that he is, as we have seen, completely self-centered, with no regard for the danger in which he would be placing Rosemary (indicated in his initial response, "You don't think I'd go in for that kind of thing, do you?"), or that Gordon's commitment to failure extends to sex as well as to other areas of his life. The second sense corresponds with the view of the psychoanalytic approach of the critic Robert Smyer, who argues that Gordon's behavior is rooted in a fear of sexual inadequacy, evidenced by his thought on the brink of making love, "He wanted to have had her, he wished it were over and done with. It was an effort, a thing he had to screw himself up to." Smyer argues that Gordon's dropping out of society is motivated by a desire to achieve a childlike sexual innocence. Thus, his commitment to poverty necessarily involves freedom from adult heterosexual contact (and Oedipal guilt) since there are, in Gordon's view, only two alternatives: "Serve the money god or do without women." The only exception to the rule, as Gordon dimly perceives, is Rosemary. Although he sometimes lumps her together with all women, which is to say "all servants of the money-god," she manages to transcend his rigid categories just often enough to create some reasonable doubt in his unreasonable mind.

The last two lines of Gordon's poem ("lays the sleek, estranging shield / Between the lover and his bride) offers an interesting example of the problems that sometimes arise in trying to distinguish Gordon's view from Orwell's. From one angle, Orwell seems to be satirizing Gordon's final couplet, blaming his faux pas on the money-god. However, Orwell's good Catholic friend CHRISTOPHER HOLLIS takes an entirely different view, arguing that this passage constitutes Orwell's "first attack on the philosophy of contraception . . . it is a central feature of his indictment of the dreary Comstock family that, above all other failings, they never reproduced themselves." (74) The complete poem is printed at the end of the chapter. In support of Hollis's thesis, the same poem, with minor variations, was printed, under the title "Saint Andrew's Day" in *Adelphi,* the journal edited by Richard Rees, in November 1935. Its author is identified as George Orwell.

Another autobiographical note struck in this chapter is revealed by the poet RUTH PITTER, a friend of Orwell's. In a BBC interview relating to Orwell, she made the following observations:

> [Ruth]: "You know, he would go out and hadn't any money, and was fit to die of chagrin if I put my hand in my pocket and put money in his hand. He hated it, poor soul."
>
> [Interviewer]: "There's a long passage in one of his novels . . . where he goes for a walk in the country with a girl and then they decide to get a cup of tea and the only cup of tea is in a

pretentious place—a set tea—so he had to borrow money to get home."

[Ruth]: "Must have been that time. There was thin, melting snow on the ground and we went for an awful long walk all around the countryside . . ." (Coppard and Crick, 72).

When Gordon receives the astounding fee of $50 from the *Californian Review* (Orwell's sly point: Only rich Californians would, in the middle of the Great Depression, dream of paying so much for a poem), he keeps uppermost in his mind the decision to give the money to Julia, who, over the years, has given him 10 times that amount. "It was a vaguely distasteful thought, however." The sentence has an ominous ring. From this point on, whenever he thinks of what he will do with his 10 pounds, he has to remind himself that it is five, not 10, pounds at his disposal. Even when he is completely drunk, the image of Julia comes to his mind. His horrendous treatment of Julia may be the most damning feature of his personality, lending credence to the view of the critic Nicholas Guild that Gordon's war on money is "born of his revulsion against the genteel poverty of his spiritless relatives and of his own sense of inferiority" (78). Julia, the older sister and substitute mother, represents the family and preeminently falls under the category that "family don't count" when it comes to borrowing money. Although the comment sounds dismissive, the fact that family exists as the exception to any rule Gordon holds in regard to money is an index of its importance. Gordon's behavior exhibits a kind of childish acting out that masks real anger, as though he were using his drunken binge to exact revenge on his real and, in the case of Rosemary and Ravelston, his extended family.

Robert Smyer's psychoanalytic interpretation of the novel looks at the brothel scene in this chapter for its Oedipal implications. According to Smyer, Gordon's coming into money exposes him to adult sexuality which his poverty has preserved him from, but in the brothel scene:

Gordon, about to accompany one of the whores to her room, sees an older client leaving, "a family man," and thinks "his predecessor. In the same bed probably." Now Gordon proves to be a helpless child, incapable of sex, "not the criminal usurper of an older man's bed" (65). This type of interpretation often raises cries of dismay, but of course the point of psychoanalytic criticism is that it is usually the author's (or character's) unconscious intention that is being examined. In this case, Smyer is examining the relationship between sexual guilt and Gordon's out-of-control behavior.

"And by Jove, tomorrow we were sober!" The opening line of the next chapter should dispel any temptations to view Gordon's plight as a serious fall from grace. But the lighthearted irony soon gives way to a depressingly detailed account of the physical and mental agony of Gordon's monumental hangover and his subsequent spiritual decline. The arrivals of Ravelston and particularly that of Flaxman bring a breath of fresh air into the jail. Not that the visit is appreciated by narcissistic Gordon, too sealed off in his self-induced misery to express any gratitude for their help. As the situation deteriorates further with the loss of his job and a place to live, Gordon's failure to help himself—along with his angry reaction to Rosemary's inquiring at New Albion as to the possibility of his return there—suggests that he has some distance to go before he declares an end to his self-imposed martyrdom, if that's what it is.

By now, Gordon's strategy seems to be clear: He is determined to fail. The good fortune that arrived in the form of a $50 check opened up a dangerous possibility: that of succeeding, not by selling out to the money-god but by becoming a successful writer. He had paid lip service to this possibility, but his deep sense of inferiority made him rule it out. His impulse may be to rid himself as fast as possible of the evidence of that outcome. Beyond that lies what the French call *nostalgie de la boue,* the urge to wallow in the mud, the desire to explore what life is like at the bottom. Obviously, this was an emotion not foreign to the author of *Down and Out in London and Paris,* but unlike Orwell, who was never very far from his typewriter, Gordon abandons writing. He is now committed to what the critic David Kubal calls the mystique of failure: "But the mystique of failure is nothing more than a reveling in self pity, an adolescent gesture of defeatism, designed to avoid responsibility" (Kubal, 17).

A biographical source for the drunken incident is recorded in *Orwell Remembered* (1984) in an interview with KAY EKEVAL, Orwell's girlfriend prior to his meeting Eileen O'Shaughnessy:

> "He tried to get himself imprisoned once in order to study prisons. I heard in the end that he became a prison visitor."
>
> *"Was that when you knew him? How did he try and get himself into prisons?"*
>
> "He bashed a policeman or something like that when he was drunk."
>
> *"When you read* Keep the Aspidistra Flying *did you recognize that . . . ?"*
>
> "Oh yes, well I think most of the people who knew him in those days felt that there was something of themselves in that book because a lot of the incidents were things that I recognized, like the party when he spent all the money he'd got for an article or something. There were about five or six people there and he treated us all to a great slap-up meal and then he got completely drunk—that was the time he assaulted the policeman" (Coppard and Crick, 101).

The first words of chapter 10 ("Under ground, under ground!") pinpoint Gordon's arrival at his desired destination. The words evoke the theme of Fyodor Dostoevsky's classic story "Notes from Underground" (1864), a work that had a profound influence on 20th-century literature; adapted to a racial theme, for example, in Richard Wright's *The Man Who Lived Underground* (1942, 1944) and Ralph Ellison's *The Invisible Man* (1952); and elsewhere regarded as a fundamental text of literary existentialism. The nameless narrator of the Russian tale is a despised and self-despising bundle of contradictions, which he continually examines, stripping away his shallower motivations trying to arrive at a core in himself. He is perversely proud of his failure to experience love, consistency, or self-control. He rails at the smug complacency of his time, a world governed by the unchallenged belief in scientific progress. He speaks of himself as a mouse rather than as a man, acutely conscious of the ultimate insult: not even being noticed by others. Nursing his grievances, he retreats to his nasty, stinking underground hole, where he can record in his diary his everlasting spite.

In the 20th century, the Underground Man embodied the principle of freedom, understood in the existentialist sense, as a value greater than rational self-interest. Gordon's "filthy hole" inverts the underground motif in favor of a garret, a more appropriate dwelling for a romantic image of the starving poet. The distinction may also reinforce the difference in intensity between the Underground Man and Gordon. Orwell's friend CYRIL CONNOLLY once cited the difference between Orwell and himself as, "I was a stage rebel. He was the real thing" (163). The same may be said of the difference between Dostoevsky's defiant rebel and Gordon. Gordon lacks the former's ruthless capacity for self-examination. One measure of that difference is that Gordon is in one sense perversely pleased with his condition. For one thing, he knows that he can go back, rejoining the lower-middle-class world he rejected. More important, as we learn in the next chapter, ". . . it was what, in his secret heart, he had desired." Orwell's Underground Man has neither the intensity nor the depth of Dostoevsky's extraordinary rebel. Nor is he a saint. But he does exhibit the potential for self-awareness that holds out hope.

In the meantime, he has even acquired a fondness for his miserly, cynical new employer, Mr. Cheeseman. The two share an attitude about the supreme importance of money. Gordon, of course, is no miser, but the vow of poverty he has taken is the obverse of the miser's vow of acquisition. Both are testifying to the all-powerful, overwhelming presence of the money-god.

The movement of the action from winter to spring is the first hint of changes to come. As if conscious of a literary cliché in the wings, the narrator relates that the shift has no impact on Gordon. He is dismissive of the poetic tradition, from Chaucer to the present, in praise of spring. In any case, in the slums of London, spring is barely distinguishable from winter. Having disposed of the cliché by mentioning it, Orwell then shamelessly reintroduces it along with its venerable cousin, the pregnancy from one's first sexual encounter. When Rosemary delivers the news of the baby, Gordon's first reaction—"a disaster"—is radically altered when she suggests the possibility of an abortion: "That pulled him up. For the first time he grasped, with the only kind of knowledge that matters, what they were talking about. The words 'a baby' took on a new significance. They did not mean anymore an abstract disaster, they meant a bud of flesh, a bit of himself down there in her belly, alive and growing."

When he leaves the shop on his way to the library, he sees an ad that he imagines is an omen of the coming war. He realizes for the first time, in a complete reversal of his attitude at the end of chapter 1, that he does not want this war. Clearly, "this 'baby business' has upset everything." He now has something to live for. At the public library, one more time, he explores alternatives, the pictures of the fetus and the ads in the women's magazines: women as the bearers of life or as the handmaidens of the money-god. For the first time, he recognizes that he had always wanted to go back. Even if there had been no baby, he would have eventually returned to the money world. "For it was what in his secret heart, he had desired. To abjure money is to abjure life."

What are we to make of Gordon's conversion (or capitulation) at the end of the novel? Some critics view its ending as the book's most striking flaw. Not a few readers have expressed dissatisfaction with Gordon's surrender. For them, it is too easy, too quick, his glorification of the lower middle class and his celebration of the aspidistra as the "tree of life" are mere rationalizations from a character who is all too capable of self-deception. An interesting example of this approach is evident in the existentialist interpretation of Michael Carter, who argues that Gordon's initial error was to rebel by using a built-in excuse, the money world. He could then assert that he was pushed into his choice by the egregious values of that world. Thus, he evades the responsibilities for his actions and continues to evade them until faced with the problem of paternity. He frames his final choice as "no choice" (138). Carter goes on to maintain that in representing Gordon's choice as inevitable, Orwell has denied him the genuinely free choice that marks the authentic self.

The fact that Gordon has been satirized consistently throughout appears to undermine his critique of the money-worshipping society he sets himself against. For some, this basic ambivalence is directly traceable to its author, leaving the reader unsatisfied. Viewing the ambivalence from a Marxist perspective, the political critic Terry Eagleton argues that confusion results from the fact that Orwell portrays Gordon as immature and self-indulgent, while at the same time depicting his poverty as powerfully real. Eagleton accuses Orwell of fluctuating between Gordon's paranoia and the reality of his experience, thus fudging the reader's reactions. In his discussion with Ravelston in chapter 5, for example, Gordon asserts: "All this about Socialism and Capitalism and the state of the modern world and God knows what. I don't give a—for the state of the modern world. If the whole of England was starving except myself and the people I care about, I wouldn't give a damn." This apparent rejection of collective political action, written before Orwell's commitment to democratic socialism, does not sit well with readers like Eagleton, but again, this is Gordon's position, not necessarily Orwell's.

Viewing the novel from another perspective, some critics point to the biographical fact that while he was writing *Aspidistra,* Orwell met, fell in love with, proposed to, and later married Eileen O'Shaughnessy, a woman whose devotion, like Rosemary's, imposed no obligations on him. These biographical events might account for the "happy ending" that some see as being tacked on to a realistic story that logically calls for Gordon to end his days in the mud. But it is also possible that, unlike John Flory, the protagonist of *Burmese Days* whose story ends in suicide, to Orwell, Gordon is basically a comic figure and the structure of the novel is basically comic satire. As such, Gordon comes to the self-discovery that in his rebellion he has become a pretentious, self-glorifying ass, convinced of his own specialness. As a comic hero, he needs to discover, and finally does, that his protestations notwithstanding, his real purpose is the procreation of the race, a humbler but truer role that, like an aspidistra, survives even in the most unhealthy environments. As a Comstock, he needs both to imitate and reform the reign of his grandfather, a man of prodigious procreative power (having had 11 children) and who became a tyrant, thereby almost bringing about the extinction of the line. Gordon's progeny will benefit from the lesson he has learned: Fight the good fight, but don't lose sight of your frail humanity. In short, he comes to terms with the fundamental law of comedy, the fact that, as Shakespeare's Benedick puts it, "The world must be peopled."

CHARACTERS

Cheeseman, Mr. Gordon's employer, a miserly, somewhat unscrupulous book dealer, not without some Dickensian appeal.

Comstock, Gordon The protagonist of *Aspidistra,* he abandons his job in an advertising agency, the New Albion Publicity Company, in order to drop out of the money rat-race and pursue a career as a poet. Trying to survive as a bookstore clerk on a salary of two pounds a week, he soon discovers that embracing poverty enslaves the soul as well the body. His life is further complicated by a paranoid strain, in which all of his problems, many of them self-induced, are attributed solely to his lack of money. When his fortunes go from bad to worse as the result of a drunken spree, it only confirms his desire to sink into the mud. Finally, the heroic efforts of the woman who loves him bring him to a reconciliation with the "money-god," as he returns to the advertising job at which he excels. But the real turning point in his life is his impending paternity, which enables him to achieve self-understanding.

Comstock, Julia Gordon's long-suffering, spinster sister, who has always accepted her role as the supporting player in the drama of Gordon's life. When the Comstock family can afford to send only one child to prep school, she uncomplainingly defers to their choice, Gordon. She takes a job as an assistant in a tea shop, a position she holds for many years without ever being paid what she is worth. The little money she manages to save is always "borrowed" by Gordon, who exhibits very little remorse in sponging off her on the grounds that "family don't count." Her work in the tea shop corresponds to the job held by Orwell's younger sister, AVRIL BLAIR.

Comstock, Samuel Gordon's dictatorial grandfather, who is long dead, but his powerful influence on his children is still very much a presence in the novel.

Flaxman, George A fellow lodger in Mrs. Wisbeach's boarding house and a salesman for the Queen of Sheba Toiletries, the once and future account that Gordon works on at the advertising agency. Flaxman is temporarily estranged from his wife and family, but that doesn't interfere with his social life, which centers on the local pub he frequents every night, suggesting that Gordon join him. When Gordon wakes up from his binge to find himself in jail, he is visited by Ravelston and Flaxman, the latter of whom cheerfully recommends a remedy for hangovers. Some have seen in him a portrait modeled on Humphrey Dakin, Orwell's brother-in-law, who described himself as a "pub man."

McKechnie, Mr. The owner of the first bookstore where Gordon works. A teetotaler, he fires Gordon when he learns of Gordon's drunken binge.

Meakin, Mrs. The opposite of Mrs. Wisbeach, a landlady who is a life-affirming representative of the working class. She offers Gordon an undesired but inescapable gift, an aspidistra plant.

Ravelston, Philip Gordon's editor, an overly tolerant companion, and a wealthy socialist. Incapacitated to a certain extent by his guilt over being rich, he allows himself to be dragged along on Gordon's notorious binge. Nevertheless, he exhibits "a kind of fundamental decency" throughout, bailing Gordon out of jail, allowing him to live in his flat for several weeks, and never entirely giving up his efforts to bring his friend to his senses. At the end, he is the witness at the wedding of Gordon and Rosemary. To an extent, the model for his character was Orwell's friend, Sir Richard Rees.

Warner, Mr. Account executive, a Canadian, who joins New Albion after five years experience on Madison Avenue. Warner comes up with the brilliant idea of "P. P." (for Pedic Perspiration, or smelly feet). On his return to the agency, Gordon becomes the chief copy writer for the P. P. campaign.

Waterlow, Rosemary The girlfriend and ultimately the wife of Gordon, she is a breath of fresh air in the intense, fixated world that is his consciousness. Her commitment to him is as resolute and selfless as his is wavering and egoistic. It may be clutching at the name straw to suggest that her final triumph indicates that in her, Gordon has met his Waterloo.

She is regarded by many as Orwell's most successful female characterization, exhibiting some of the high-spirited vitality and forbearance of the woman he met while writing the book, his future wife Eileen O'Shaughnessy.

Wisbeach, Mrs. Gordon's nosy, controlling, stingy, and ever-watchful landlady. The embodiment of oppressive middle-class prejudices, she effectively bullies Gordon, finally expelling him from her house.

FILM ADAPTATION

A Merry War (1997) Director, Robert Bierman; producer, Peter Shaw; screenplay, Alan Platter. Starring Richard E. Grant (Gordon Comstock) and Helena Bonham Carter (Rosemary Waterlow).

Drawing on the novel's underlying romantic comic structure, screenplay author Alan Platter and director Robert Bierman throw the emphasis on the relationship between Gordon and Rosemary, and on Gordon's aspiration to be a serious poet. In the process, Gordon's obsession with the money-God is muted, and along with it goes much of the novel's satiric edge. Thus the film is both more enjoyable and possibly less interesting than the novel. One of the film's striking deviations is that the major characters are less beaten down and more assertive than their counterparts in the novel. Gordon gives as good as he gets from Mrs. Wisbeach and the insolent waiter at the country hotel. Rosemary shows similar spirit in her relations with Gordon and with her supervisor at the advertising agency. Even poor Julia is properly sassy both with Gordon and her overbearing boss. Clearly, it was decided that an audience six decades and at least one cultural revolution after the setting of the novel would have little patience with three passive victims, perhaps dismissing them as wimps.

WORKS CITED

Carter, Michael. *George Orwell and the Problem of Authentic Existence.* Totowa, N.J.: Barnes & Noble, 1985.

Connolly, Cyril. *Enemies of Promise.* London: Routledge and Kegan Paul, 1938.

Coppard, Audrey and Bernard Crick, eds. *Orwell Remembered.* New York: Facts On File, 1984.

Eagleton, Terry. "Orwell and the Lower-Middle-Class Novel." In *Exiles and Emigres: Studies in Modern Literature,* 76–108. London: Chatto & Windas, 1970.

Fowler, Roger. *The Language of George Orwell.* New York: St. Martin's Press, 1995.

Guild, Nicholas. "In Dubious Battle: George Orwell and the Victory of the Money-God." In *George Orwell.* Bloom's Modern Critical Views, edited by Harold Bloom, 77–84. New York: Chelsea House, 1986.

Hollis, Christopher. *A Study of George Orwell: The Man and His Works.* Chicago: Regnery, 1956.

Kubal, David. *Outside the Whale: George Orwell's Art and Politics.* Notre Dame, Ind.: University of Notre Dame Press, 1972.

Patai, Daphne. *The Orwell Mystique: A Study in Male Ideology.* Amherst: Massachusetts, University of Massachusetts Press, 1984.

Rees, Richard. *George Orwell: Fugitive from the Camp of Victory.* Carbondale: Southern Illinois University Press, 1962.

Smyer, Richard. *Primal Dream and Primal Crime: Orwell's Development as a Psychological Novelist.* Columbia: Missouri University Press, 1979.

Zwerdling, Alex. *Orwell and the Left.* New Haven, Conn.: Yale University Press, 1974.

"King Charles II"

School play written and directed by Orwell. This brief—its running time was half an hour—two-act play was written by Orwell in 1932 for his students at HAWTHORNS PRIVATE SCHOOL. The school produced the play sometime before Christmas 1932. Seventy years later, the Compass Arts Theatre staged another production of the play on April 4, 1992. Peter Davison, editor of the *Complete Works of George Orwell,* notes that the play survived because one of the original cast members, Geoffrey W. Stevens, preserved his copy of the script. His name, written by Orwell, appears on the top of two pages of the typescript.

Interestingly, the play appears to adopt a resoundingly royalist position. Cromwell is not a character, but he is alluded to in a very negative fashion. Perhaps this was done to please the conservative tastes of the school's parents or was merely an expression of the Tory aspect of Orwell's "Tory radical" political self-definition at the time. In "THE LION AND THE UNICORN," while describing the features of a future socialist England, he maintains that the House of Lords should be abolished but the monarchy be retained.

"Lear, Tolstoy and the Fool"

An essay published in *Polemic* in March 1947, now regarded as an important contribution to Shakespearean criticism and a striking example of metacriticism, the critique of a critique.

SYNOPSIS

Orwell opens with the observation that the pamphlet "Shakespeare the Dramatist" (1903), written by the great Russian novelist Leo Tolstoy (1828–1910), is difficult to find in an English translation. As a result, he will begin by summarizing the Russian's argument. Tolstoy always had difficulty appreciating Shakespeare, but it was only after reading the complete works that he came to the conclusion that the English dramatist is not only overrated, but also that his reputation as an unmatched genius is "a great evil." To illustrate his point, Tolstoy selects for analysis *King Lear,* widely regarded as one of, if not *the,* greatest of his plays. He proceeds to summarize the play's plot, commenting on its inconsistencies and the lack of motivation of its chief characters and their failure to achieve any "individuality of language." By way of contrast, Tolstoy then examines Shakespeare's main source, an earlier play, *The Chronicle History of King Lear,* and finds the latter "incomparable and in every respect superior to Shakespeare's adaptation." Tolstoy concludes by asserting that what is true of *Lear* is true of the entire Shakespearean canon. Shakespeare was a failure both as an artist and a thinker. In the latter capacity, Shakespeare belongs in the company of those who believe "the end justifies the means." Great art, says Tolstoy, must deal with a subject that is "important to the life of mankind, it must be the product of a profound emotion on the part of the author and it must exhibit true technical mastery that can instill in its audience a profound emotional and intellectual response."

Tolstoy then moves to an explanation of why Shakespeare has come to be idolized by so many for so long, suggesting a type of mass hypnosis—that, plus the fact that the degradation of modern life is accurately reflected in his plays. The specific form the degradation takes lies in the absence of a religious dimension, without which great art cannot exist. As to the origin of Shakespeare's great fame, Tolstoy blames the Germans. German professors—aided to a significant extent by their famous poet Goethe—elevated Shakespeare to compensate for their own lack of good dramatists.

Orwell begins his response by asserting that one cannot objectively demonstrate that Shakespeare is either good or bad. The only real test of literary merit is survival, the test of time. But one can look at Tolstoy's critique and make a judgment about it. It is filled with misrepresentations, which suggest that Tolstoy has "willfully misunderstood" many passages in *King Lear,* so that one can only suspect that he held an "especial enmity towards this particular play." That enmity may be rooted in a similarity between Lear's story and Tolstoy's life.

"When you think of Lear, you are likely to envision in your mind's eye an old man . . . with flowing white hair and beard . . . wandering through a storm and cursing the heavens in company with a fool and a lunatic." Tolstoy regards the fool and his puzzling comments as an example of the play's incoherence. Orwell, on the other hand, sees the fool as central to the play's design. His is the voice of sanity counterpointing Lear's rages and the monstrous deeds that are being enacted onstage. Tolstoy's objection to the fool is symptomatic of his objection to Shakespeare. The fool is an example of Shakespeare's profligate genius, his attention to the processes of life, his concern with crowding onto his canvas the rich details that bring a picture to life. Tolstoy, at the time he is writing his critique, is very near the end of his life, interested only in "the parable," its message as to how we ought to live our lives. Blinded by this narrow perspective, Tolstoy misses the rich range of human feeling that abounds in *King Lear.* Shakespeare was no philosopher or great moral teacher, but each of his major tragedies do focus on a central theme. In *King Lear,* that theme is renunciation. Lear renounces power at the beginning of the play, and when he discovers that others will take advantage of his lack of power, he falls into a rage and a madness motivated by revenge. In the end, he recovers his sanity but is crushed anew by the death of Cordelia. Here, Orwell delivers his main point: the striking similarity between Lear and Tolstoy himself.

Near the end of his life, Tolstoy "renounced wealth, fame and privilege," adopting a type of Christian anarchism and asceticism. Tolstoy imagined that his renunciation would bring about happiness, since he had come to see happiness as the result of "doing the will of God . . . casting off all earthly pleasures . . ." But what he discovered was that he "was driven to the edge of madness by people . . . who persecuted him *because* of his renunciation." Orwell suggests that in this final phase of his life, Tolstoy may have exchanged "one form of egoism for another." In this case, he argues that Tolstoy's Christian commitment is self-interested and hedonistic because it rejects the human struggle in favor of the nirvana of an afterlife in heaven.

In any case, it is not the ideas of Shakespeare that account for his preeminence but his language, which is "a kind of music, a deep and powerful source of joy—at least to native speakers of English. Tolstoy's attack on Shakespeare demonstrates that he is, in fact, attempting to exert power, to kill the enjoyment others find in the plays. As it turns out, however, his efforts are all for naught. Shakespeare is still the acknowledged master, under whose shadow even *War and Peace* and *Anna Karenina* fall.

COMMENTARY

In August 1949, five months before his death, Orwell wrote to his publisher Fredric Warburg to propose a new collection of his essays. In addition to two that he hoped to write in the near future on George Gissing and Joseph Conrad, he cites six already-published essays. First on this list is "Lear, Tolstoy and the Fool," an indication of his high regard for the piece. He was not mistaken. Time has shown this to be not only one of his finest essays but also an important contribution to Shakespearean criticism, as witnessed by its inclusion in Frank Kermode's anthology *Four Centuries of Shakespearean Criticism* (1965).

More notable than his demolition of Tolstoy's argument (after all, a rather easy target) is his analysis of *Lear.* Characteristically, he eschews the inflated rhetoric of much Shakespearean criticism of the period in order to focus on the play's vitality, the range of its characters, and the richness of their language. As was his custom, Shakespeare invests that vitality equally among his evil characters and his good ones, such as the bastard son, Edmond, and Lear's faithful follower, Kent. But Orwell does not deal with these two, choosing to focus on the fool and his "central role" in the play. The fool is an excellent choice, both in the seeming excess of his rhymes and riddles, and, on the other hand, the painful realism of his advice to Lear, reminding him that, in his act of abdication, Lear has played the fool.

A measure of how well Orwell hit a bull's-eye in identifying renunciation as the play's subject is reflected in a well-known essay by his former BBC colleague and friend WILLIAM EMPSON. Empson's "Fool in Lear" accepts Orwell's view that Lear's renouncing the things of this world is a roundabout way of retaining them, thus making "a fool of himself on the most cosmic and appalling scale possible." Empson points out that not only is Orwell correct in zeroing in on the theme of renunciation, but he is also apparently the first person in the history of *Lear* criticism to do so (125). Another tribute to Orwell's insight is offered by the critic and philosopher Stanley Cavell.

> It is, perhaps, of the nature of Orwell's piece that one finds oneself remembering the feel of its moral passion and honesty, and the clarity of its hold on the idea of *renunciation* as the subject of the play, without being able oneself to produce Orwell's, or one's own, evidence for the idea in the play—except that the meaning of the entire opening and the sense of its consequences assume, as it were, a self-evidence within the light of that idea. . . . Orwell's writing, here as elsewhere, is exemplary of a correct way in which the moral sensibility . . . exercises its right to judge an imperfect world, never exempting itself from that world (75n).

A flaw in the essay occurs at the end when Orwell moves out of literary criticism to attack pacifists and anarchists, who, removing themselves from the dirty world of politics, assume the right to bully everyone else into agreeing with them. Not surprisingly, when Orwell submitted the essay to Dwight Macdonald's *Politics,* Macdonald, a staunch pacifist, suggested cutting this section of the essay and in fact never did publish it. As for anarchism, Orwell's good friend and an anarchist George Woodcock turns his approach to Tolstoy and Lear back on Orwell. Woodcock argues that he, too, like Lear and Tolstoy, had pursued the path of renunciation in giving up his career with the Burmese police and descending into the lower depths of society, in the belief that he could overcome the divisions of class—a belief that he discovered was mistaken. Woodcock makes the same point in reference to Orwell's essay on Jonathan Swift, "POLITICS AND LITERATURE." He maintains that in Orwell's biased treatment of anarchism, he is "criticizing a tendency within himself . . . trying to discipline his own strong emotional feeling for a doctrine which his realistic and rational self recognized to be . . . impractical in any foreseeable future" (244–45).

WORKS CITED

Cavell, Stanley. *Disowning Knowledge.* Cambridge: Cambridge University Press, 1987.

Empson, William. *The Structure of Complex Words.* Ann Arbor: University of Michigan Press, 1967.

Woodcock, George. *The Crystal Spirit.* London: Jonathan Cape, 1960.

Lion and the Unicorn: Socialism and the English Genius, The

A booklet published by Secker & Warburg in February 1941. This was the first pamphlet in a series called Searchlight Books. The aim of the series was to make the case for a socialist government to prosecute the war.

HISTORICAL/BIOGRAPHICAL BACKGROUND

With the fall of France in June 1940, Britain braced itself for the next phase of the war, the Battle of Britain. German plans to invade England involved first massive bombing attacks that would demoralize the English people and pave the way for a relatively easy invasion. But in the ensuing air war, the British turned out to be formidable foes, their fighter planes, Spitfires and Hurricanes, proved equal if not superior to German Messerschmidts, and their "secret weapon," radar, enabled them to inflict serious damage on German bombers. What has to be considered the finest minutes of their "finest hour" occurred on September 15, 1940, when the Royal Air Force (RAF) shot down 60 German bombers. As a result, the Germans postponed their plans for a seaborne invasion, while continuing to bomb English cities in the campaign known as the blitz. In February 1941, when this pamphlet was published, the blitz was an ongoing everyday danger, and the possibility of invasion still loomed on the horizon.

Eager to play an active role in the war, Orwell, who now rejected the PACIFISM he had earlier entertained (reflected in his 1939 novel, *Coming Up for*

Air), tried desperately to enlist in the military but was decisively rejected on the grounds of poor health. He joined the Local Defense Volunteers, later renamed the HOME GUARD, and took its existence very seriously, seeing in it perhaps the English version of the POUM militias that he had joined in Spain. In collaboration with his friend TOSCO FYVEL, he planned a series of booklets (Searchlight Books) that dealt with issues of the war and which the two men would coedit. Orwell's *The Lion and the Unicorn* would be the first. Under the circumstances, it is not surprising that the pamphlet contained, among other things, a rousing tribute to patriotism. The pamphlet is divided into three parts: "England Your England," "Shopkeepers at War," and "The English Revolution."

SYNOPSIS

Part 1, "England Your England"

The booklet begins with a characteristically striking Orwellian opening sentence, "As I write, highly civilized human beings are flying over head, trying to kill me." If they succeed, he adds, they will not experience any qualms, because they are doing it in the service of their country. Such is the power of patriotism. "Christianity and international Socialism are as weak as straw in comparison with it."

Now, in the second year of World War II, the notion that all human beings are basically alike is true only in a very broad sense. Even casual observation demonstrates that human behavior differs significantly from country to country. England, for example, differs from Europe, not to mention from the rest of the world, in a host of ways, having developed its own particular and peculiar culture. Right now, in the middle of a great war, it is vitally important to find out what England is. Among some obvious examples are these: England does not produce great artists or musicians or abstract thinkers. On the other hand, the English cherish their individual liberty and their privacy ("Nosey Parker" is "the most hateful of names"). Its working class is less puritanical, less overtly religious than its middle class. But one feature that all classes seem to possess is a gentleness, a dislike of violence, of militarism and war. The English are patriotic, but not in a jingoistic fashion. They are, however, hypocritical about their empire, which is ruled by a sword but a "sword which must never be taken out of its scabbard."

But any generalizations about the English must take account of the differences in class. England is famous for its class consciousness. Of course, as in all societies, the common people display a tendency to live against the grain of the middle class. But common to all classes is a fierce patriotism that unites them in times of crisis, an "emotional unity." In this respect, British society resembles a family, a "Victorian family . . . in which the young are generally thwarted and most of the power lies in the hands of irresponsible uncles and bedridden aunts. . . . It has its private language and its common memories, and at the approach of an enemy it closes its ranks."

One of the surprising developments in recent English history has been the decay of the ruling class, best illustrated by the inept leadership of the English governments of the 1920s and '30s. This is also true of the army, which has always been staffed at its highest levels by the ruling class, who are incapable of change. As a result, they invariably prepare for each war by assuming it will be "a repetition of the last."

The past two decades have also impacted two other classes. One is the middle class, which once formed the backbone of the empire—the young men, either military or commercial, who administered the empire. Centralization of control now resides in London, with the result that onetime "empire builders were now reduced to the status of clerks." The other is the left-wing intelligentsia, who have adopted an automatic anti-English posture, always distancing themselves from anything that smacks of patriotism. This is a disturbing development, now more than ever, when intelligent patriotism is desperately needed.

Another feature of modern life is the redefinition of middle class: modern technologically advanced society has required a large number of managerial, technical, and professional workers, and they are drawing fairly large salaries. This new version of the middle class has influenced the working class. This is the beginning of the end of class privileges, a process that will be hastened by the war. Eventually, the class distinction will be eliminated, but the basis of national culture will remain: "England will still be England . . . having the power to change out of recognition and yet remain the same."

Part 2, Shopkeepers at War

The blitz continues, and although we can still win this war, these are dark times, brought about largely as a result of capitalism. If we had a socialist economy, we could have put all of our resources into producing the armaments and military equipment necessary to carry out a full-scale war. Like socialism, fascism—at least as it exists in Germany—is capable of controlling the entire economy. Private owners continue to own businesses and factories, but they are really just managers, employees of the state, taking orders from the government. The difference between the two is that socialism strives for a state made up of "free and equal human beings," while Nazism takes inequality as a fundamental law of life. Hence, Germans are depicted by Hitler as members of a superior race destined to rule the world. On the other hand, British capitalism operates on one fundamental principle—profit. Thus while Hitler has spent the last seven years building "the most powerful war machine the world has ever known," England has been doing business as usual, selling vital raw materials such as tin and rubber, to Germany. As a result, when the fighting broke out, the English were hopelessly outgunned and outmanned, leading to the disastrous 1940 retreat from Dunkirk. But the British public learned a lesson from this defeat. They now realize that a planned economy is far more effective than the "free-for-all" of laissez-faire capitalism, in which the profit motive is supreme.

Making the change from capitalism to socialism requires a power shift away from the ruling class, that is, the wealthy and those "who step into positions of command by right of birth." These people are, of course, patriotic Englishmen, but their anti-fascist zeal has always been diluted by their greater fear of communism. Thus at moments of crisis, "they are likely to falter, pull their punches, do the wrong thing." We need a revolution, with or without bloodshed, not necessarily involving a change of government, but requiring the abolition of special privileges. We need to put into effect an "equality of sacrifice." The war will probably go on for another three years. These will be extremely difficult times, and the working class will, as always, be the ones most affected, but, to carry on, they must be able to see to see the rich being asked to make the same, and in regard to taxes, even greater, sacrifices.

There is no danger of a "fifth column"—an organized group of traitors—appearing in England. Nor is it likely that Germany can win simply by bombing. They will have to invade, and that would create problems they don't want. More probably the Germans will offer an armistice with terms that would disguise their intentions. It would probably end in a Quisling type of government. This would appeal to the followers of Sir Oswald Mosley (leader an English fascist paramilitary group), and the Communists (this was written while the Hitler-Stalin pact was still in force), and the pacifists. None of these groups, alone or in concert, is large enough to have a direct impact on the war, but they might become "half-conscious" supporters of a phony peace. But the real danger will occur when the rich, who do not want to pay the supertaxes that war imposes, capitalize on working-class discontent and build support for a "surrender disguised as peace."

Part 3, The English Revolution

In England, we are undergoing a quiet revolution that began a few years ago, but whose pace has accelerated with the war. In order to win the war, we must have a socialist government, but to bring this about, we must first examine the failure of English socialism. In England, socialism is represented by the Labor Party, but the Labor Party has never been able to effect real change because it is riddled with internal contradictions. It has been incapable of offering a real socialist program, only a "timid reformism," contented to be the political arm of organized labor and little more. Now, however, we are faced with our greatest crisis. "We cannot win the war without introducing socialism, nor establish socialism without winning the war." The war has made it possible for the first time to be both "revolutionary and realistic." Here is a practical six-point socialist program that could be submitted to the people of Britain for consideration:

1) *Nationalization of Property, Transportation and Major Industries* Ownership would shift to the state, with former owners acting as managers. In agriculture, there would be a less sweeping change, with farmers retaining ownership of a portion of the land.
2) *Limitation of Incomes* This would introduce a minimum wage and establish the principle that the highest wage be fixed at no more than ten times the minimum.
3) *Reform of the Educational System* The school system would be made available to all students, according to their ability. The degree to which public school education is a training in class consciousness and snobbery would be abolished. Access to universities would be open to all capable of success there.
4) *Dominion Status for India* This would make India a partner rather than a colony, but it must be accompanied by the freedom to secede it so chooses. If India has the choice, it will refuse independence for at least some years.
5) *Formation of an Imperial General Council,* "In which the coloured people are to be represented." (See Orwell's essay "NOT COUNTING NIGGERS.")
6) *Formation of an alliance with China, Abyssinia and other nations victimized by fascism*

Admittedly, this is just a rough outline, but it represents a direction toward the goal of English socialism. If we successfully hold off a Nazi invasion, within a year we will see the rise of this new form of socialism. It will assimilate most of the past but make radical changes where necessary. For example, it will abolish the House of Lords but let the monarchy stand. It will not dissolve the empire but transform it into a confederacy of socialist states. It will attack "foreign neutrals" (such as Spain). This prophecy is based on the conviction that we cannot win this war unless we make it a revolutionary war. ". . . It is certain that with our present social structure, we cannot win."

The tendency on the left for the past 20 years has been to sneer at the word *patriotism.* But the nationalist spirit is deeply rooted in human beings in totalitarian as well as democratic states. Those who argue that there is little difference between fascism and capitalist democracy are completely deluded. The limited democracy that exists in England requires only that we extend it. That is why we must be willing to turn the war into a revolutionary war. If we do and are defeated any way, we will still have the memory that will never be completely erased: England must be true to itself not by standing still to fight the war but by moving forward through revolution.

COMMENTARY

The opening line of the essay sets the tone of rueful, realistic optimism and broad mindedness. "As I write, highly civilized human beings are flying overhead trying to kill me." The German aviators are, of course, patriots, another example of the power of patriotism as a motivational force. The strength of patriotic feeling has never been better demonstrated than in the reaction of the English public to the blitz. Orwell then explores the other distinctive characteristics that constitute Englishness, the special feelings for flowers and gardens, its antimilitarism contradicted, to some extent, by its hypocrisy about the British empire, its deep belief in the rule of law, and, perhaps most important, its gentleness.

He then moves on to consider the problem caused by the decay of the ruling class. The product of the public schools, members of the ruling class have a deeply imbued patriotism but their eyes are fixed upon the past. It is clear, on the other hand, that any revolution that wishes to reject the past completely will never succeed in Orwell's view. Traditional English culture has to form the foundation of the new order. Thus, for example, although official Christianity—as represented by the established Anglican church—might pass away, Christian ethics and morality would be preserved.

In "Shopkeepers at War," the second section of the pamphlet, he argues that "war is the greatest of all agents of change," particularly, when it is a "people's war." Clearly, this one is. Centralized control of planning and industry is necessary to win the war but also to bring about a postwar England of justice and equality. But that will only be possible through a democratic socialism, one in which "the mass of people are living roughly upon an equal level, and have some kind of control over the government."

The apparent success of Nazism, which calls itself "national socialism" but is in fact a form of capitalism, "borrows from socialism such features as will make it efficient for war purposes." But both capitalists and workers are completely controlled by the Nazi party, with its goal being control of the entire world. For all the evil it has engendered, Nazism has demonstrated one positive thing: the power of a planned economy. Democratic socialism would put that power to work for good instead of evil. As for the capitalists, the real threat is that they might be in favor, as the war goes on, of a phony "truce," which will leave their privilege untouched while the rest of us are enslaved.

Section 3, "The English Revolution," argues that the revolution Orwell speaks of has already begun. It has been slowly evolving since the 30s, but the disaster of Dunkirk has speeded it up. We have only a limited time to move to a planned, wartime economy, essential if we are to win the war, . . . "the war has turned socialism from a textbook word into a realizable policy." What follows is his six-point program, the first three dealing with domestic issues and the final three with the empire.

The reaction to the booklet was mixed. On the one hand, it sold well, some 10,000 copies and its patriotic tone registered with readers. On the other hand, many had serious reservations about advocating radical social transformation while the Nazi wolf was at the door. In a way it was a replaying of the argument between the POUM and the communists during the Spanish civil war. On the other hand, like POUM, Orwell was asserting the case for a simultaneous revolution/war, maintaining that only a socialist planned economy could mobilize English industry to match the Nazi war machine. His argument that the revolution was already under way was confirmed, if we add the word "revolution" to the June 1945 victory of the Labour Party right after the victory in Europe and before the defeat of Japan. The Labour's party brand of socialism was less than Orwell had hoped for but it was a definite step in the right direction.

On one point, he was unequivocally right. It had been a "people's war" and, in it, the people had found their voice. Written in haste, *The Lion and the Unicorn* may have been "slapdash," as V. S. Pritchett characterized it. Orwell had been wrong on many points, which he acknowledged in his December 1944 London letter to *Partisan Review:* "I fell into the trap of assuming that the war and the revolution are inseparable. There were excuses for the belief, but it was a very great error. For after all, we have not lost the war . . . and we have not introduced socialism."

But the more general goal of the booklet is to lay out a scheme of what a genuinely English socialism might look like; one that emerges from the inherent nature of the English people as opposed to the theories of European intellectuals, or their English clones, the "intelligentsia." At this moment of supreme crisis, with the threat of a German invasion looming on the horizon, he appealed to the English people to rally around the profound emotion that transcends class distinctions: patriotism.

Included in his conception is the recognition of a "new class," the technical expert, what James Burnham characterized as the "managers." These people must be cultivated, not alienated. In his review of *Lion,* the American critic DWIGHT MACDONALD zeroed in on the distinctive feature of Orwell's approach to his subject, calling it "impressionistic rather than analytic, literary rather than technical, that of the amateur, not the professional" (191). He acknowledges that Orwell's critique of left-wing intellectuals is justified, but he accuses him of overreacting, retreating "to the kind of common-sense Philistinism, which Orwell embraces in matters of theory, seems to me even less calculated to preserve the values we both want to preserve than the sectarian Marxism it rejects" (194). Orwell may have taken that criticism to heart when he listed *The Lion and the Unicorn* as one of his works that he did not want to have reprinted.

WORK CITED

Macdonald, Dwight. "*The Lion and the Unicorn.*" In *George Orwell: The Critical Heritage,* edited by Jeffrey Meyers, 191–194. London: Routledge, 1975.

"Literature and the Left"

A short essay published in *Tribune* (June 1943). Here, Orwell once again skewers his favorite target: the doctrinaire Left.

SYNOPSIS

It is not only the blimpish Right but the orthodox Left that harbor a profound distrust of the highbrow. This is particularly true in their treatment of writers who experiment with the traditional forms of literature. For the "good party man" writers, such as James Joyce, D. H. Lawrence, W. B. Yeats, and T. S. Eliot are "bourgeois intellectuals" and therefore "bad writers." Eliot, in particular, is damned for being a reactionary.

It is perfectly legitimate for left-wing critics to insist on the view that all art exhibits a social/political message, but they go badly astray when they transform a political judgment into a literary one. When they don't agree with the message, the critics condemn the art. In the early 1930s, a group of poets led by W. H. Auden tried to write what, in effect, was left-wing propaganda, some even joining the communist party, but when "they would not or could not turn themselves into gramophone records, they were thrown out on their ears."

As a result of this philistine error, socialism has alienated literary intellectuals. This is particularly true among the young writers currently coming of age. Some of the best of these are pacifists; a few have fascist leanings; hardly any are interested in socialism.

COMMENTARY

In his essay, Orwell cited Shakespeare as a writer who "perhaps was, even by the standards of his own time, reactionary. . . ." Peter Davison includes as a supplement to this essay a letter by Kenneth Muir, later to be known as a distinguished Shakespeare scholar. Muir takes exception to Orwell's characterization. He grants Shakespeare's orthodoxy in his early career, but argues that, after 1600, Shakespeare became increasingly skeptical of authority. Muir cites as evidence *Measure for Measure,* as in Isabella's strong depiction of "Man, proud man / Dressed in a little brief authority," *King Lear*'s great indictment of injustice in society, and the treatment of the theme of money in *Timon of Athens,* which includes a speech on gold that was quoted and praised by Karl Marx (*CW,* 15, 127).

WORK CITED

The Collected Works of George Orwell. Vol. 15. Edited by Peter Davison. London: Secker & Warburg, 1998.

"Looking Back on the Spanish War"

Essay printed in 1942 in abridged form in *New Road,* a short-lived journal, edited by Alex Comfort. In its complete eight-part form, it was published in a collection of Orwell's essays, *England Your England* (1953), and in the American edition of that collection, titled *Such, Such Were the Joys* (1953).

SYNOPSIS

Part 1

Orwell begins by recollecting the sounds and smells and shapes of things in his first week of training in Barcelona. He recalls the names and faces of seven of his fellow soldiers, two of whom were "mere riff-raff" and who probably deserted to the other side. The others, he assumes, are all dead by now. He speaks of the "essential horror of army life," highlighted by the experience and smell of the latrines. Such memories remind you of "the reality that the justice you are fighting for, although a morale booster, never overcomes the fact that you are usually too angry, or frightened, or cold, or, above, all, too tired to bother about the political origins of the war." It is important to underscore this point, because the left-wing intelligentsia, who, before the Spanish civil war began, would have hooted down any suggestion that a war could be a serious crusade, swallowed whole hog "stories of freshly wounded men clamoring to get back into the fighting." These were the same people who shifted from antiwar to prowar, according to the party line. They did it effortlessly because they were removed from the reality that war is evil but sometimes the lesser evil. He sums up his position with an epigraph: "To survive you often have to fight, and to fight you often have to dirty yourself."

Part 2

In connection with the last point, consider atrocities. In the Spanish civil war, both sides were guilty of atrocities, although the fascists committed a greater number than the republicans. But the point is that belief or disbelief in atrocities is so often determined by one's political convictions. Such fluctuations should not cause us to take a relativist attitude towards atrocities. The rape of Nanking by the Japanese and the killing of Jews by the Nazis were in fact true atrocities, not events that are suspect because the British government uses them as propaganda.

Part 3

Orwell recalls two incidents from the war. "The first involved myself and another man advancing close to the enemy lines as snipers, hoping to pick off a soldier or two just before the break of dawn. We stayed too long and were getting ready to dash back to our lines when suddenly an enemy soldier apparently carrying a message for an officer ran along the parapet holding his pants up with one hand as he ran. I did not shoot him because he was holding his pants up. I had wanted to shoot a 'fascist' but a man who is holding up his trousers isn't a fascist; he is visibly a fellow creature, similar to yourself, and you didn't feel like shooting at him." This is the sort of thing that regularly happens during a war.

The second incident involved a ragged, dark-skinned, barefooted boy probably of Arab descent. When Orwell reported the theft of cigars from his bunk, the officer in charge accused the boy, who said little in his own defense. He had a fatalist air as he was ordered to strip naked. He was innocent, but his innocence did not erase his sense of shame: That night, Orwell took him to the movies and gave him some brandy and chocolate, but the attempt to make up for his shame with presents was inadequate.

Orwell writes that later, acting as a noncommissioned officer, he ordered a man to a post, and when he refused, Orwell began to drag him along. Others interfered, saying that Orwell had no right. Soon he had a crowd around him, some supporting him, others opposed. The brown-skinned boy sprang into the middle of the circle, vigorously defending Orwell. The point is that in ordinary times, the breach between the boy and Orwell would never have been healed, but in Spain in 1936, generosity of feeling was relatively easy. It was "one of the byproducts" of revolution, though in this case only the beginnings of a revolution and foredoomed to failure."

Part 4

Of all the fantastic lies that surround the Spanish civil war, the most flagrant and notorious is the myth, propagated by the European reactionary and Catholic newspapers, of the presence of a large Russian army in Spain. What Orwell is worried about is the fact that lies such as this will be perpetuated. The implication of this is the possibility that has appeared with totalitarianism, that a ruler or ruling group will control the past as well as the present: "If the leader says . . . 'it never happened'—well, it never happened. If he says that two and two are five—well, two and two are five." Perhaps it is morbid to speculate on the nightmare of a totalitarian world, but the problem is that we have been nursed on the theory of the happy ending. There is just as much historical evidence for the opposite. Think of the slave empires that endured for thousands of years. Think of the hundreds of millions of slaves who have lived and died, leaving no records of themselves.

Part 5

The working-class formed the core of the resistance to Franco, as they are the most reliable enemy of fascism but only in the long run. They may be taken in for a while by fascism's promises, but they soon discover that fascism cannot raise their standard of living. But the working-class struggle is a natural, organic development, like a growing plant reaching inexorably for the light. The Spanish civil war was finally a class war. If it had been won by the working class, it would have enriched the lives of common people everywhere, but it was lost.

Part 6

By the summer of 1937, it was obvious that the republican forces could not match Franco's army without assistance from foreign governments such as those of England and France. The fascists were stronger, better equipped, and more efficient. The only chance the republicans had was foreign aid, but the "mean, cowardly, hypocritical. . . . British ruling class did all they could to hand Spain over to Franco. . . ." And the Russians acted in a contradictory fashion, offering some help and then deserting the republic. It may have been simply a case of ineptitude on Stalin's part. Whatever the motivations of the various governments concerned, the result is crystal clear: ". . . the Nazis knew what they were doing and their opponents did not."

Part 7

Orwell recalls two other memories of the war: One was of the wounded soldiers in a hospital ward, singing a song with a refrain that speaks of a resolution to fight to the end. The other memory is of the Italian soldier he described in the opening of HOMAGE TO CATALONIA. The Italian soldier represents the entire class of workers throughout the world who ask only for the basic minimum of a decent life:

> Enough to eat, freedom from the haunting terror of unemployment, the knowledge that your children will get a fair chance, a bath once a day, clean linen reasonably often, a roof that doesn't leak, and short enough working hours to leave you with a little energy when the day is done.

Orwell closes with the poem he dedicated to the Italian soldier, which concludes with the oft-quoted final two lines, "No bomb that ever burst / Shatters the crystal spirit."

COMMENTARY

The opening section of the essay sets out to deglamorize a war that had been promoted by leftist propaganda as "the good fight," a particularly noble and just war. Orwell accepts the idea that the fight was justified, but it was first and foremost a war, and like all wars, it was a dirty, exhausting, evil business made tolerable only by its status as a lesser evil.

The second section follows up on the evils of war by commenting on atrocities. He maintains that the fact that both sides were guilty of atrocities during a war should not mislead us into a judgment that they cancel each other out. It is also true that both sides also use atrocities as a propaganda weapon, but the evidence is clear that the atrocities of the Nazis and the Japanese armies were far greater crimes than those of their opponents.

In part 3, he discloses two incidents designed to offer a personal view of war as he experienced it on the Aragon front in 1937. He speaks of his decision not to shoot an enemy soldier who was running while trying to hold his trousers up. He establishes the notion that a simple human gesture can trump the view of a man as the enemy. In another incident, he describes a comrade, a young boy whom he inadvertently humiliated and whom he eventually apologized to and tried to make amends. When some of the men under his command later accused Orwell of acting too aggressively with a recalcitrant soldier, the boy defended him. He sees the boy's defense as an example of the power of a war atmosphere to cut through the essential pettiness of ordinary life.

In part 4, he considers the fact that the victor in a war usually controls the "official story" of that war. Thus, Franco's forces will write histories of the civil war, spreading the falsehood that the republican forces were assisted by large numbers of Russian troops. In fact the Russians sent advisers and weapons, but no troops. This is an example of a ruling group controlling the past as well as the present. This, he argues, is the terrible feature of a totalitarian government. As an example, Orwell cites a ruler asserting that two and two equals five, and it being accepted as true. This is the prospect that he famously develops, using the same example in *Nineteen Eighty-Four.*

In part 5, he argues that the working class, although it may be attracted by promises in the short run, is ultimately the natural enemy of fascism. Attempting to characterize the developing consciousness of the working class, he invokes the metaphor of a growing plant: "stupid, but it knows enough to keep pushing upwards towards the light . . ." It is a romantic conception, one that Orwell, priding himself as a realist, would ordinarily shun, but the experience of Barcelona in December 1936, the spectacle of "the working class in the driver's seat," made a permanent impression to which he clung even at the darkest moments of *Nineteen Eighty-Four*: "If there is any hope it lies with the proles."

Part 6 deals with the role of international politics on the outcome of the war. Franco's army consisted of professional soldiers, trained and disciplined, as opposed to the factory workers and peasants fighting for the government. But it was the support of Germany and Italy that guaranteed Franco's victory. What remains a puzzle is the failure of England and France to come to the aid of the republic. Orwell maintains that the English failure was inexplicable because everyone knew the coming war with Germany was inevitable.

At this point, Orwell is engaged in his own rewriting of history. In 1938, far from assuming the inevitability of war, he had taken a pacifist position, and as one of his letters (November 1938) suggests, he had not only supported Chamberlain's action at Munich but also saw English rearmament as a mistake: "I admit that being anti-war probably plays Chamberlain's game for the next few months, but the point will come when the anti-wars of all complexions will have to resist the fascising [sic] processes which war-preparation entails" (*CW*, XI, 240). At this point, he was still banking on the internationally popular antiwar movement in England and France extending to the Soviet Union. If such a movement can be mobilized, he believes that "Hitler will be done for." He was cured of this illusion the following year by the signing of the Hitler-Stalin pact.

Part 7, the final section, recounts his meeting with an Italian soldier at the Lenin barracks in Barcelona. This encounter is described in moving detail in the opening chapter of *Homage to Catalonia*. Here, he uses this representative of the "working class of Europe" in contrast to the notable figures who have backed fascism. The irony is that some of these people censure the working class for being materialistic, when every one of them enjoys the material comforts that they criticize workers for wanting. He acknowledges that there may be fundamental moral and intellectual changes required to bring about a safer, more just world, but first we must deal with the issues of poverty and backbreaking labor before moving on to larger questions.

WORK CITED

The Collected Works of George Orwell. Edited by Peter Davison. Vol. 11. London: Secker & Warburg, 1998.

"Marrakech"

Essay published in *New Writing*, edited by John Lehmann (Christmas 1939).

SYNOPSIS

Orwell opens with a description of a funeral, attended by a group of wailing men and boys (no women) and a horde of flies attracted by the corpse who is not in a coffin but merely wrapped in a large rag, carried on a wooden bier by his friends to the burial ground. The friends chop out a parcel of lumpy dirt about one foot deep. The grave that results is simply an unmarked mound of dirt.

Walking through the town, you are reminded that the swarming brown masses belong to a colonial empire in which their value as individuals goes virtually unrecognized. "They rise out of the earth, they sweat and starve for a few years and then sink back into the nameless mounds of the graveyard. . . ." The Jewish quarter in town is just as impoverished as the rest of the place, but rumors abound, nevertheless, about their secret riches.

Morocco is a desolate wasteland for the most part. Lacking any alternative, the native population engages in backbreaking, primitive labor in the attempt to cultivate the land. Native women carry enormous burdens. On their backs, the donkeys, who are terribly mistreated, are made to carry impossible weights until they collapse and die, at which time they are tossed into a ditch and torn to shreds by hungry dogs. The irony is that while the horrible mistreatment of donkeys elicits the observer's sympathies, the human beings—particularly the old women—are not even noticed. "People with brown skins are next door to invisible."

Watching a troop of Senegalese soldiers, Orwell catches the eye of one who looks at him with "profound respect." The young boy has been taught that the white man is his superior, "and he still believes it." But Orwell and every white person who looks at a parade of powerfully built black soldiers have but one thought, "How long before they turn their guns in the other direction?"

COMMENTARY

Not surprisingly, Orwell's essay begins in the descriptive mode but very soon turns into a commentary on imperialism and the racism that renders the native an "invisible man." It concludes with a premonition of the end of empire, the long line of black soldiers scattering the white birds, "glittering like scraps of paper."

The brief description of the treatment of donkeys will remind readers of the fate of Boxer, the carthorse in *Animal Farm.*

"Meaning of a Poem, The"

Radio talk given on the BBC (May 1941), reprinted in *The Listener,* June 1941.

SYNOPSIS

Orwell begins by reading "Felix Randal," a sonnet written by GERARD MANLEY HOPKINS. He acknowledges that it is a "difficult poem," describing the life and death of Felix Randal, a blacksmith who moves from being a strong, healthy man to his old age, weakened by disease and weeping like a child. Orwell then explains that he chose this difficult poem because it exemplifies the great importance of sound, of musical effects in poetry. Hopkins is a poet celebrated for his ability to extract "astonishing beauty" from his arrangements of words. As an example, the last line of this poem describes Felix Randal in his prime, shoeing a carthorse: "Didst fettle for the great grey dray horse his bright and battering sandal."

Orwell explains that the final word was chosen because it rhymes with *Randal,* but the word does more than that. It elevates the poem, transforming pathos into tragedy. "*Sandal* connotes, for an English reader, Greece and Rome, an association reinforced by the meter of the final line, which is a hexameter, the meter of Homer and Virgil." Orwell goes on to speak of the fact that Hopkins was a Catholic priest and a man living at the end of the 19th century, when the rural way of life—represented by the village blacksmith—was passing away. Thus, the poem exhibits a Christian view of death as tragic, a feeling that permeates the poem. Also Hopkins's use of predominantly Saxon vocabulary merges with the Christian emotion. "The two fuse together, inseparably, and the whole is greater than the part." None of this explains why the poem is the source of such pleasure, a pleasure that is increased, not lessened, by the attempt to interpret it.

COMMENTARY

Orwell's explication of "Felix Randal" demonstrates his sensitivity and range as a literary critic. Normally, his criticism is, as he would put it, sociological or author-oriented. These two approaches are evident here in his depiction of the poem's reflection of the passing of the rural English village and in his stressing the relevance of the fact that Hopkins was a Catholic priest. But the striking aspect of the critique is the importance he assigns to its formal elements; principally, the sound of the words, ". . . the astonishing beauty of its sound-effects. . . . the music of the poem." His conclusion masterfully blends the formal analysis with the sociological, all done in a straightforward, simple style, unclotted with technical terms.

One particularly poignant biographical point emerges in a letter from Orwell to the poet STEPHEN SPENDER, describing an experience while fighting in the Spanish civil war.

> I sometimes feel as if I hadn't been properly alive since the beginning of 1937. I remember on sentry-go in the trenches near Alcubierre I used to say Hopkins' poem Felix Randal, I expect you know it, over and over to myself to

pass the time away in that bloody cold, & that was about the last occasion when I had any feeling for poetry. (*CW,* 11, 130–131)

This essay demonstrates that the loss of feeling he speaks of was only temporary.

WORK CITED

The Collection Works of George Orwell. Vol. 11. Edited by Peter Davison. London: Secker & Warburg, 1998.

"Moon under Water, The"

Short essay published in the *Evening Standard* on February 9, 1946. The essay's title is taken from the name of Orwell's favorite public house, though he soon makes it clear that no such establishment exists.

Orwell outlines 10 qualities that make the Moon under Water superior to other drinking houses, most of which relate to its atmosphere. The location (on a side street but near a bus stop) provides easy access and egress without attracting the attention of rowdies and drunkards. The architecture and furnishings are substantial and real, and they conform to what Orwell calls "the solid, comfortable ugliness of the nineteenth century." The Moon under Water has a good fire in winter and plenty of room for its patrons, with several bars and an upstairs dining room. Patrons can talk comfortably with no interference from a radio, a piano, or excessive noise. The barmaids, all middle-aged women, know the patrons by name and take a personal interest in their lives. The pub sells such conveniences as tobacco, cigarettes, aspirin, and stamps, and no fuss is made over the use of the telephone. The pub does not serve dinner, but patrons can get an assortment of foods at the snack counter, and they can purchase a good lunch at a reasonable price six days a week in the upstairs dining room. Unlike most pubs in London, the Moon under Water serves draught stout. They also take care to serve their drinks in appropriate vessels: handled glass, pewter, and china mugs. A sizable garden connects to the pub and features large trees, tables and chairs, and an area reserved for children to play. The presence of children in the pub marks an important distinction for Orwell, which prevents pubs like the Moon under Water from turning into "mere boozing shops instead of the family gathering-places that they ought to be."

Orwell concludes the essay by revealing what he expects any Londoner to know, that no such pub as the Moon under Water exists. Most pubs possess only a few of his preferred qualities, and one has as many as eight out of 10. Orwell then asserts that he would be glad to know from his readers of any pub that comes close to his ideal. Peter Davison, the editor of *The Complete Works of George Orwell,* notes that a response was found among Orwell's collection of pamphlets, from a Yorkshire civil servant who claimed that a pub called Mason's Arms in West London might suit the writer. Davison further notes that the pub still exists.

WORK CITED

The Complete Works of George Orwell. Edited by Peter Davison. Vol. 18. London: Secker & Warburg, 1998, 98–109.

"My Country, Right or Left"

An essay first published in *Folios of New Writing* (Autumn 1940).

SYNOPSIS

Orwell begins with the observation that the past often seems more momentous than the present. A case in point is World War I, seen now in 1940 as an epic struggle because in our memories, major events are telescoped together, and we have been conditioned by books and reminiscences to elevate their significance. In fact, for his generation, "too young for the war" (11 years old in 1914), no single battle in the war was as significant as the sinking of the *Titanic* in 1911. For a young boy in a small town, the most memorable event of the early years of the war was the commandeering of all the horses in town by the army and the tears of an old cab man, watching his horse being taken away.

As a teenager near the end of the war, Orwell had shared in the general pacifism of his fellow students at Eton, writing off the war as "meaningless slaughter." But afterward, as the war receded into history, his "too young" generation became conscious of having missed something important. The reason for this feeling was that "most of the English middle class are trained for war from the cradle on, not technically, but morally." Part of the appeal of the Spanish civil war was that it offered an opportunity for those who had missed the Great War to experience it on a smaller scale.

As for the present war, the night before the Soviet Union and Germany signed a nonaggression pact, Orwell had a dream that the war had begun. The dream taught him two things about himself. The first was that, after years of dreading its arrival, he could feel relieved now that it was here, and second was the discovery that he was a patriot at heart, prepared to fight for his country. His reason is that "there is no real alternative between resisting Hitler and surrendering to him, and from a socialist point of view I should say it is better to resist." But beyond the rational motive is the fact that his patriotism is too deeply embedded for him to undermine his country. Furthermore, his form of patriotism is not that of a conservative. He is still committed to a socialist revolution, but one that will retain the essence of "the England I was taught to love" along with the spirit of democratic socialism.

COMMENTARY

The significance of this essay is that it marks Orwell's break with the antiwar movement and by extension the Independent Labour Party, which maintained the position that the fight against Hitler was a capitalist war. The central point in his shift was the dream he had on the night of the Russian-German pact in 1939. Now that the civilized world's two great enemies, Hitler and Stalin, were allied, the picture was stunningly clear. This alliance created havoc among the left, producing major defections from the British Communist Party. For Orwell, it confirmed his conviction that Stalinism and fascism were sisters under the skin. However, he insisted that his reaction was not a conservative one, such as that of Guy Crouchback, the Tory hero of Evelyn Waugh's *Men at Arms,* who enlists after the announcement of the pact because his two enemies have joined together. Orwell sees the patriotic impulse as the necessary foundation of the socialist society he envisions in the near future. Orwell was to work these propositions out in great detail the following year in THE LION AND THE UNICORN. However, in 1949, when he drew up instructions for his literary executor, he listed "My Country Right or Left" among his works that should not be reprinted.

Nineteen Eighty-Four

Orwell's final and most famous full-length work of fiction, published in 1949.

In ANIMAL FARM, Orwell had realized his goal of making political writing an art. (Although later generations would judge that he had already achieved that goal in an earlier book, HOMAGE TO CATALONIA, the recognition of that achievement did not occur in his lifetime.) The beast fable had provided him an ideal form to expose the Stalinist regime and to emphasize the danger of revolutionaries who are motivated by the lust for power rather than for justice. He chose to end *Animal Farm* with a parody of the Teheran Conference in 1943. The conference marked the first meeting of the Big Three, Joseph Stalin, Winston Churchill, and Franklin Roosevelt, who convened to discuss Allied strategy for the remainder of the war, which by that time (October/November 1943) pointed to victory in Europe within the next two years. But there surfaced in the course of the conference significant differences, over wartime strategy to be sure, but also over the nature and extent of the spoils to be claimed by the victors. It was clear that Stalin had designs on Eastern Europe, not as part of an overt empire, but as nominally independent countries with communist governments.

To Orwell, this move was a portent of the future, roughly outlined by the political theorist

Bob Flag (as Big Brother), John Hurt (as Winston Smith), and Richard Burton (as O'Brien) in a still from Michael Radford's film adaptation of *Nineteen Eighty-Four* *(Photofest)*

JAMES BURNHAM, who had predicted that most of the globe would be controlled by three superstates, with totalitarian governments ruled by a managerial class, "the Party." Although Orwell rejected most of Burnham's conclusions, he accepted the principle of the three superstates and the notion that they would be regularly at war with one another. In a 1948 letter to his editor Roger Senshouse, he discussed his intention in writing the book:

> What it is really meant to do is to discuss the implications of dividing the world into zones of influence (I thought of it in 1944 as a result of the Teheran Conference), & in addition to indicate by parodying them the intellectual implications of totalitarianism.

With *Animal Farm,* his target had been an existing, historical development. Here was a future prospect, one sufficiently dark and ominous to engage fully both his imagination and his intellect. He crafted a satire, designed not to predict the future but to zero in on a phenomenon that may have existed in the past in one form or another, but which had emerged full-blown in the twentieth century: TOTALITARIANISM.

One feature of totalitarian societies that particularly enraged Orwell was their systematic, organized lying. Having worked for the BBC as a propagandist during the war, he recognized and accepted the fact that all governments lie, but he also saw the distinction between the big lies and the little ones, and not only governments' lies but the conspiracy of lying he encountered among the English Left during the Spanish civil war, which imbued him with a lifelong rage. In *Nineteen Eighty-Four,* he imagines an all-out assault on truth by a government dedicated to controlling thought and language to the extent that a dissident thought would become literally inconceivable. His message for his readers is that preventing totalitarian rule is much easier than eradicating it after it has established itself. As Orwell himself pointed out, the critical turning point in *Animal Farm* occurs when the pigs claim the cow's milk for themselves and the other animals allow them to do it. There lies the first denial of the commandment that "All animals are equal."

Fueling Orwell's fear was the threat of a hot war between Anglo-America and the Soviet Empire that, in the end, would be inconclusive, leaving behind wrecked economies, such as Germany endured in the 1920s, which paved the way for Hitler's totalitarian takeover. One glance at England in 1948 gave a succinct preview of the aftershocks of war: a dreary, dispirited world of shortages, including scarcity of food, fuel, clothing, and manipulative wartime euphemisms like Victory Gin and Victory Coffee. In such a situation, the descendants of the present Labour Party, "tougher types" than the present leadership, while representing themselves as socialists (INGSOC) might in fact be sowing the seeds of totalitarian thought, particularly those committed to the belief that, as in the Soviet Union, the party's ends justified its means.

HISTORICAL CONTEXT

As has often been noted, Orwell did not have to look very far in imagining the London of *Nineteen Eighty-Four.* He found it in the London of 1948. As Peter Lewis describes it, "the era of post-war austerity, severe rationing, unrepaired bomb damage, shabbiness, weariness and shortages of such things as razor blades and cigarettes forms the dingy background of *1984*" (112). The war had effectively bankrupted England and the new Labour government had to face enormous problems as it began its efforts to nationalize major industries, such as coal and transportation.

In the broader context of international affairs, England aligned itself with Western Europe and the United States in the cold war against the Soviet Union and their Eastern European satellites while at the same time undergoing the process of dismantling its colonial empire. Adding to the dreariness and deprivation of the postwar world in the novel is the remembrance of the recent war itself. The periodic buzz bombs (V-1, V-2) that fell on England in 1944–45 (one of which destroyed the Orwells' flat while they were absent) left many Londoners with the sense that the war would never end. In *Nineteen Eighty-Four,* it never does. But a deeper concern had emerged: the prospect of an atomic war. For Orwell, the atomic bomb had done more than establish a new context for international military conflicts. As Orwell argued, nuclear warfare had also had increased the possibility of totalitarianism, since the acquisition of complex, expensive weaponry had historically tended to increase the power of the centralized state. The recent history of Italy, Germany, and Japan, along with the ongoing example of the Soviet Union and its East European satellites, had settled the question of whether totalitarian rule was possible. Still open—particularly in England, where a recently elected moderate socialist party had come to power, and in the United States, where the specter of James Burnham's "managerialism" loomed large—was the question of whether totalitarianism was inevitable. To make the public acutely aware that it could happen here, "here" being postwar England and its superpowerful Big Brother on the other side of the Atlantic, Orwell set the novel in London, an outpost of Oceania, where the basis of the currency is the dollar.

BIOGRAPHICAL CONTEXT

As early as 1943, a year before he began writing *Animal Farm,* Orwell made an outline of a novel he called *The Last Man in Europe.* But writing *Animal Farm* came first, which he finished in February 1944 while he continued to work as literary editor of *Tribune* and write a regular column, "As I Please," for that journal. In the spring of 1944, he and his wife Eileen adopted a baby boy, Richard, and that summer their flat was bombed, leaving his library in shambles. In early 1945, he went to Europe to cover the end of the war as a correspondent; while he was abroad, Eileen died suddenly. In summer 1946, he rented a farmhouse called Barnhill on the island of Jura, off the west coast of Scotland. In September of that year, he reported that he had done "about fifty pages" of his new novel. But he was by this time so over-extended with writing commitments that he referred to himself as being "smothered by journalism." By 1947, his health had deteriorated.

In December, he was admitted to Hairmyres Hospital, near Glasgow, diagnosed with tuberculosis and forbidden to do any writing. Among the treatments he underwent was one using an experimental new drug, streptomycin, which had to be imported from the United States. His condition improved, and he was able to write the essay "Writers and Leviathan." In July, he returned to Barnhill to work on the second draft of his new novel, which he finished in November 1948. At that point, he had undergone a couple of relapses and should have been in a hospital. Instead he set about retyping the entire manuscript, although his health was extremely frail. The effort was, in the words of his biographer Gordon Bowler, "a fatal error" (383). Shortly after submitting the retyped manuscript, he suffered a serious relapse and entered the Cotswold Sanatorium, in Cranham, Gloucestershire, in January 1949.

SOURCES

The major sources for *Nineteen Eighty-Four* are *We,* a satirical novel by the Russian writer EUGENE ZAMYATIN; the writings of the American political theorist JAMES BURNHAM; JACK LONDON's futuristic novel *The Iron Heel;* and a number of books by H. G. WELLS.

We is set in the "United State" sometime in the 26th century. Numbers by this time having replaced names, the main character is D-503, a mathematician loyal to his government but torn because of a disloyal act on his part: He has fallen in love with a woman, I-330. The world of *We* has no place for love, since love has no mathematical basis. It is a reflection of the disease known as imagination. I-330 is a secret dissident in this world, and it is she who shows D-503 what he will lose if he undergoes an operation to remove imagination from his system. The leader of the state in *We* is the Benefactor, who rules over a nation in which cleanliness and order are the chief virtues. The Benefactor convinces D-503 of the errors of his ways and orders the execution of I-330, which D-503 watches with equanimity.

Orwell first read *We* in a French translation from the Russian, and he campaigned to have the book translated into English, praising its critique of a world in which human beings are transformed into machines, gaining security at the price of their souls. In his attack on *Nineteen Eighty-Four,* Isaac Deutscher, the Marxist biographer of Lenin and Trotsky, implied that Orwell's use of *We* amounted to plagiarism, but in truth, Orwell's debt to *We* lies more in its generalized satirical dystopian form, with little borrowing of details. The genuine similarities between the two are quite few and indirect. On the other hand, Deutscher's charge may stand as an ironic rebuke to Orwell, who in his review of *We* in *Tribune* (1946) suggested that Aldous Huxley's *Brave New World* was "quite possibly a plagiarism" of *We.*

A more important source of the ideas as opposed to the format of *Nineteen-Eighty Four* was the work of James Burnham. Burnham first attracted wide attention with the publication of *The Managerial Revolution* (1940), a forecast of the political future, which maintained that capitalism was in its death throes, but that it would not be replaced by socialism. A new ruling class was coming into existence, whom Burnham termed "the managers"—business executives (not owners), technical experts, members of the military, and a wide range of specialists drawn from the professional class. This "managerial society," he predicted, will tend to be totalitarian, not democratic, in the interest of efficiency. The state will own the means of production, and, in that sense, it will be nominally socialist, but without any resemblance to the democratic socialist ideal championed by Orwell. In his next book, *The Machiavellians* (194), Burnham, taking a historical view, described the development since Machiavelli of the principle of power as lying at the root of all politics. In *The Struggle for the World* (1947), he argued that the atomic bomb had radically altered the world picture. Burnham predicted that the Soviet Union would soon possess the bomb, and the result would be a nuclear war. He advocated the formation of an alliance between the United States and Great Britain in a unified effort to defeat communism by, if necessary, a preventive atomic strike on the Soviet Union.

Orwell vehemently contested virtually all of Burnham's later conclusions. As William Steinhoff details in his excellent study *George Orwell and the*

Origins of 1984 (1975), Orwell rejected Burnham's overstatement of his case and his apocalyptic all-or-nothing approach to the future. But Orwell conceded that, in some areas, Burnham's prophecy had proved true. One of these was his prediction about the emergence of three superstates. In his essay "You and the Atomic Bomb," Orwell conceded that "Burnham's graphical picture of the world has turned out to be correct. More and more obviously, the surface of Earth is being parceled off into three great empires." In *Nineteen Eighty-Four,* those three states are represented as Oceania, Eurasia, and Eastasia.

Another important source was the work of Orwell's childhood hero H. G. Wells. Wells's projections into the future were generally sanguine in their celebration of scientific progress but more cautious in regard to social and political progress. According to Steinhoff, one Wells novel in particular that impacted Orwell's thinking was *When the Sleeper Awakes* (1910), in which a ruling class exploits the lower orders of society, feeding them with propaganda from loudspeakers on every street corner. Another influential Wellsian text was *The Island of Dr. Moreau* (1896), in which a mad scientist conducts experiments with animals, enabling them to exhibit human characteristics. Dr. Moreau shares with O'Brien a belief in the transforming power of pain: "[E]ach time I dip a living creature into the bath of burning pain, I say 'this time I will burn out all the animal. This time I will make a rational creature of my own'" (Quoted in Steinhoff, 9–10). Although the personal relationship between Orwell and Wells deteriorated in the 1940s, Wells exercised a formative influence on Orwell, which the latter acknowledged on a number of occasions.

Another writer to whom Orwell owed a debt was the American novelist and journalist Jack London. At the beginning of his career, Orwell looked to London's *People of the Abyss* (1903) as a model in writing *Down and Out in Paris and London.* London's futurist novel *The Iron Heel* (1907) depicts a fascist state, in which the power principle emphasized by O'Brien is acknowledged to be supreme both by the ruling party and the revolutionaries attempting to overthrow them. In *The Iron Heel,* the working class are called Proles, and the novel's title suggests a recurring Orwellian image. In *Coming Up for Air* as well as in *Nineteen Eighty-Four,* "a boot stamping on a human face is an image" used to describe the totalitarian future.

Steinhoff cites two other interesting possible sources: Cyril Connolly's short story "Year Nine," in which a man and a woman are guilty of the crime of falling in love in a society where love or friendship is outlawed and the citizens are under constant surveillance; and G. K. CHESTERTON's *The Man Who Was Thursday* (1908), whose hero is a man named Syme (unlike the linguist of that name in Orwell's novel, this Syme is a poet). Another strong influence on Orwell was a novel of his good friend ARTHUR KOESTLER, *Darkness at Noon* (1940), which demonstrated that a deeply political and passionately antitotalitarian fiction could also be a work of art.

Two nonfiction sources include a pamphlet by Boris Souvarine, a former prominent communist who left the party in the wake of Stalin's purge trials. His pamphlet *Cauchemar en U.R.S.S* (Nightmare in the USSR) provided a detailed analysis of the 1930s Moscow trials and of the torture techniques employed by Stalin's secret police. A book which may have contributed details to Orwell's novel is Julia de Beausobre's *The Woman Who Could Not Die* (1938, 1948). De Beausobre and her husband were imprisoned by the secret police in 1933. Shortly after, her husband was shot, and she was put in solitary confinement. She was driven "to the brink of madness" by the conditions in the prison and the endless inquisitions designed to force her to confess. In the course of those, she experienced, as does Winston Smith, the powerful connection that binds the "man who is tortured day in day out and the man who, day in, day out, tortures him." When she is transferred to a Siberian labor camp, she has to endure the ubiquitous rats crawling over her while she lies in bed. Another possible connection is her first name, Julia. Orwell did not publicly comment on her book, but it is listed as being in his personal library. Huxley's *Brave New World* (1932) has often been linked with *Nineteen Eighty-Four,* and the two books share a similar skepticism about scientific progress and the mind-numbing acquiescence that political culture can reinforce. But although both books are dystopian, *Brave New World* sees a future in which hedonism rules, southern California writ large. Orwell takes a much tougher view.

Jonathan Rose has uncovered some other potential sources, including Olaf Stapleton's *Darkness and the Light* (1942), a "future history" in which two superpower nations engage in war while retaining totalitarian control over their own citizens. Another minor source may have been Alfred Noyes's *Edge of the Abyss* (1942), a nonfictional account of the torpedoing of a ship carrying 100 children who were being evacuated to Canada. This may have been the source of the newsreel film of the bombing of children in a lifeboat, recorded by Winston in his diary. In 1940, Noyes published another novel, *The Last Man,* in which the protagonist, after experiencing a brief love affair, is tortured by a power-worshipping sadist. Still another possible, although long-distance, source is *1920: Into the Near Future* (1918), an anonymous collection of articles, satirical descriptions of First World War England, oppressed by a government obsessed with military victory. The objects of this satire were the "Oxford Pamphlets on War," in which prominent academics engaged in lies and distortions for propaganda purposes. One of these was by an Oxford don named O'Brien. However, Rose cautions, that there is no evidence Orwell read *1920.* Rose summarizes his observations by pointing out that there were about 200 antiutopian stories published between 1903 and 1945. Many of them shared similar conventions and stock characters, which an avid reader like Orwell would have absorbed. "Literary derivation is usually not a matter of one book 'influencing' another, like two billiard balls clicking together, but a process of collective reinforcement over a lifetime of reading" (Rose, 145).

One recent addition to possible influences on at least the title of *Nineteen Eighty-Four* is a futuristic poem written for the 10th annual reunion of her secondary school in 1934, depicting the lives of the classmembers 50 years into the future, 1984. The author of the poem was EILEEN O'SHAUGHNESSY, who two years later became the wife of George Orwell.

SYNOPSIS

Chapter 1, Part 1

On a chilly, windy April afternoon, Winston Smith returns to his apartment complex, called Victory Mansions. The elevator being, as usual, out of service, he climbs the seven flights to his apartment, noting on each landing the huge poster, depicting the face of a man of about 45 with a black mustache and eyes that seem to follow you as you move. The caption beneath it reads: "Big Brother Is Watching You." As he enters his apartment, the telescreen is on, as it always is. The telescreen is a two-way transmitter device capable of seeing and hearing activity in the apartment.

Gazing out his window, he can see, less than a mile away, the Ministry of Truth, towering over the shabby buildings surrounding it. This is the city of London, the capital of Airstrip One, an important province of Oceania. Winston works for the Ministry of Truth, one of the four ministries that dominate the London skyline. The four ministries constitute "the entire apparatus of government": the Ministry of Truth, in charge of news, entertainment, and education; the Ministry of Peace, which conducts wars; the Ministry of Love, in charge of law and order; and the Ministry of Plenty, which deals with the economy. As rendered in Newspeak, the official language of Oceania, the ministries' names are Minitrue, Minipax, Miniluv, and Miniplenty.

Winston has used his lunch hour in order to return to the apartment, and to offset his hunger, he gulps down a teacup of a nasty, acrid alcoholic drink known as Victory Gin. He then moves to a small table nestled in a tiny alcove that is out of range of the telescreen. From the table drawer he takes out an old, blank book that he surreptitiously bought in a junk shop in a disreputable quarter of town. When he bought the book, he had no conscious use for it, but now that he has it, he realizes that he intends to keep a diary. He begins to write the day's date: April 4, 1984, although he is not even certain of the year. He begins by describing a film he saw the previous evening, a war film depicting horrific death and destruction, wildly applauded by the audience, except for one Prole woman who protested the idea of showing such scenes to children. Winston stops writing because he has developed a cramp, but as he does he is aware that the reason he has started the diary today. It has something to do with an incident that occurred at work this morning. Winston had taken his seat along with all the other ministry workers to participate in the Two Minute Hate. Just before the hate began, he noticed two people sitting in the room. The first was "a bold-looking girl," wearing over her uniform a red sash, signifying her membership in the Junior Anti-Sex League. In the past, she had given him an intense glance that filled him with a mixture of uneasiness and fear. The other person was an important Inner Party member named O'Brien, to whom Winston was attracted because something in his manner suggested that he was not a typical party member. The hate began, as always, with the face of Emmanuel Goldstein, projected on a large telescreen. Goldstein had been a leader in the party in the early days, but he betrayed the party and managed to escape from Oceania. "Somewhere or other he was still alive and hatching his conspiracies . . . perhaps even—so it was rumored—in some hiding place in Oceania itself." He was said to lead an underground terrorist network, known as the Brotherhood, and to have written a book filled with foul lies about Big Brother, proclaiming his betrayal of the revolution. Behind his image on the screen marched a vast army of enemy Eurasian troops. Those sights unleashed in the audience a pent-up fury that swept like a wave over everyone. The girl who had glanced at Winston became so caught up in the mass frenzy, she threw a book at the screen, hitting the image of Goldstein in the face. Even stolid, unemotional O'Brien was sitting with his face flushed and his breast heaving. Winston found himself caught up in the furor, alternately venting his hatred of Goldstein and then of Big Brother. He managed as well to switch his hatred to the young girl behind him, whom he imagined beating to death, or raping, cutting her throat "at the moment of climax." He realized that he hated her because she was pretty, young, and desirable, and yet wore the sash of chastity. Finally, Goldstein's face faded, replaced by the figure of a Eurasian soldier, firing a machine gun, but that image faded as well, replaced by the calm, powerful image of Big Brother and the three slogans of the party:

> WAR IS PEACE
> FREEDOM IS SLAVERY
> IGNORANCE IS STRENGTH.

The audience now responded by chanting "B-B! B-B!" repeatedly. Although Winston joined in the chant he was always repulsed by this aspect of the hate, which showed in his eyes as he locked glances with O'Brien.

> I am with you, O'Brien seemed to be saying to him. I know precisely what you are feeling, I know all about your contempt, your hatred, your disgust. But don't worry, I am on your side!

The connection is broken immediately, but it is enough to suggest to Winston that he is not alone in his hatred of the party. Perhaps there is even some truth behind the myth of the Brotherhood.

Now looking down at his diary, he finds that he has written unconsciously the words "Down with Big Brother" over and over. His first instinct is to destroy what he had written, but he realizes that it is too late. His writing it is irrelevant; the crime lay in thinking it. *Thoughtcrime* was the word for it, and the Thought Police would inevitably catch him. They would yank him from sleep one night and he would disappear. His name would be erased from any record testifying to his existence. He would be, in a word, *vaporized.* He defiantly scribbles in his diary that he doesn't care that they will shoot him in the back of the neck: "Down with Big Brother." At that moment, he hears a knock at his door and, his heart pounding, he gets up to open the door.

Chapter 1, Part 2

To Winston's relief, the person at the door is a neighbor, Mrs. Parsons, the washed-out wife of a colleague of his at the Ministry. She has a clogged drainpipe in the kitchen and is asking Winston for help. He clears the drain, after which he has to deal with the Parsons' children, a boy and girl who are acting up because they couldn't go to the public hanging of some Eurasian soldiers in the local park. As he leaves their apartment, in the hall he is hit by a projectile in the back of the neck. He turns in time to see the Parsons boy, slingshot in hand, being dragged into the apartment by his mother. The boy shouts out to Winston, "Goldstein!" The Parsons boy and girl are typical of today's children, fiercely loyal to the party and suspicious of their parents, quite capable of denouncing them to the Thought Police.

Back in his apartment, he thinks again of O'Brien and of a dream he had seven years ago, when a voice in the dark had said, "We shall meet in a place that has no darkness." The voice was that of O'Brien. The telescreen announces a glorious victory against the Eurasians, which Winston recognizes as the prelude to bad news: The chocolate ration would be reduced to 20 grams. As he ponders the dreary hopelessness of his situation, he takes some solace in the fact that he is a thought-criminal. He is a dead man, but ". . . it became important to stay alive as long as possible." Washing his finger clear of a possibly incriminating ink stain, he returns to work, putting a grain of dust on the cover of his diary to determine whether it has been discovered.

Chapter 1, Part 3

Winston dreams of his mother, who, along with his father, disappeared in the early 1950s, victims in one of the purges of that decade. In the dream, his mother is cradling his sister in her arms as the two of them sink deeper below water while he looks down on them from above. There was a tragic dignity to her and his sister's deaths, one that would be impossible to duplicate in today's world governed by fear, hatred, and pain.

The dream shifts to a pasture near a hidden stream. The girl from the Fiction Department is walking toward him and, as she does, she tears off her clothes with a graceful defiance that seems to obliterate the world of "Big Brother" and to invoke another time. "Winston woke up with the word 'Shakespeare' on his lips." He comes awake to the sound of the telescreen alarm, which is followed by the summoning of 30- to 40-year-olds to calisthenics, "The Physical Jerks." Even before he begins, he is subject to a coughing fit that leaves him breathless. As he goes through the motions of exercise, in his mind he struggles to summon up the past. He dimly recalls the outbreak of a war, which included the dropping of an atomic bomb on an English city. Since that time, Oceania had always been at war, either with Eurasia or East Asia, but at the moment, the official party line is that we have always been at war with Eurasia. Winston knows that Eurasia had been an ally until four years ago, but there is no evidence to support that idea. All the records have been changed to agree with the party line. The party's view of the past is summed up in the slogan "Who controls the past, controls the future." The present intrudes itself on Winston when the telescreen barks at him that he must make a greater effort to touch his toes without bending his knees.

Chapter 1, Part 4

With a sigh, Winston begins his day on the job. It consisted primarily of rewriting "misreported" newspaper accounts, that is, any statements issued by the government that turned out to be false. Winston's revisions would then be collated with others from that day's paper and the revised issue would be printed and filed, while the original would be consigned to "memory holes," which lead to a furnace in the bowels of the buildings. As a result, the official record makes it clear that the party is always right. In another section of the Ministry, books are altered in a similar fashion. For Winston, the irony of all this falsification was that, when it came to statistics, the original figures were as false as the revisions.

Winston recognizes that he is merely the smallest of cogs in an enormous machine. His section, the Records Department, large as it was, was only one branch of the Ministry, which included, in addition to the ongoing reconstruction of the past, the production of a vast array of entertainment and information aimed at the proletariat population.

Winston's main task this morning is to revise a speech by "Big Brother," five months earlier, in which he conferred an honor on someone who is now an unperson, someone who never existed. The characterization "unperson" means that the individual has been executed for some unknowable reason, and his identity must be obliterated. Winston rewrites the copy by inventing the fictional figure "Comrade Ogilvy," whom he depicts as an ordinary soldier who had died in battle. Winston creates a brief biography for his mythical hero, a paragon of devotion to the cause. As he finishes his story, he is struck by the fact that this fiction will be transformed into a historical fact. He had had the godlike pleasure of creating a human being out of nothing.

Chapter 1, Part 5

Winston queues up for lunch at the Ministry's cafeteria. There he meets his friend Syme, who works in the Research Department. Syme is one of a vast army of linguistic scholars engaged in compiling the "Eleventh Edition of the Newspeak Dictionary." The two men receive their daily ration of "pinkish grey stew" and some bread, cheese, and coffee. For an additional dime, they purchase a cup of Victory Gin. Syme explains how the work on the dictionary is going. He and his colleagues are actively engaged in eliminating words, "cutting the language down to the bone." With adjectives, for example, they can eliminate both synonyms and antonyms. He cites *good* as an example, "if you have a word like 'good,' what need is there for a word like 'bad'? 'Ungood' will do just as well . . ." He goes on to observe that if you want a stronger word than *good,* you can use *plusgood* or, even stronger, *doubleplusgood.* Syme concludes his praise of Newspeak by claiming that its goal is the narrowing of thought, so that thoughtcrime will be impossible because the words that express it will no longer exist, words like *freedom.* It suddenly occurs to him that Syme is going to be vaporized, "he sees too clearly and speaks too plainly. The Party does not like such people." Winston and Syme are joined at their table by Parsons, who proudly relates how his daughter recently denounced a stranger to the Thought Police. Their conversation is interrupted by an announcement from the Ministry of Plenty claiming that the standard-of-living index has risen by 20 percent and that the chocolate ration was being raised to 20 grams a week. Winston is stunned to see that no one in the cafeteria seems aware that the ration had been *reduced* to 20 grams only yesterday. He wonders if he is the only one left with a memory.

Suddenly, he becomes aware that someone is staring at him from the next table—the dark-haired girl from the Fiction Department.

Chapter 1, Part 6

Winston is writing in his diary about his encounter with a prostitute three years ago, but it is interrupted by the thought of Katharine, his ex-wife. They have been separated for 11 years. Katharine was a perfect example of a party woman, having been carefully schooled in the antisex credo of the party. The party insisted that the function of the sex act is solely for reproduction, rightly recognizing that sexuality is a difficult force to control, an affirmation of sensual pleasure outside the party's control. Katharine insisted that they have sex regularly, but only as a duty to the party to have children. The physical act itself repels her. When they were not able to produce children, they separated. What was left to Winston was this furtive, fear-ridden encounter with a painted prostitute who turned out to be a toothless old woman.

Chapter 1, Part 7

Winston writes in his diary: "If there is hope, it lies in the proles." The proles, who represent 85 percent of the population, are the only class with the power to rise up and overthrow the existing tyranny. But they lack the consciousness to do so. The proles live in freedom, relative to members of the Outer Party. They live their lives unhampered by telescreens, secret police, and government spies because the party sees them as harmless, their minds dulled and inactive. While they focus on beer and football and raising children, they unthinkingly accept the party's depiction of the past as a time when proles were ruthlessly exploited by people called capitalists. They are continually told how much better off they are now, and there is no way of knowing whether that is true, Winston thinks, because the past has been erased.

He recalls one instance where he knew for certain that the past had been falsified. In the 1960s, the government had conducted sensational purges, in which one leading party member after another confessed to conspiring with Goldstein to overthrow Big Brother. The last of these so-called traitors were Jones, Aaronson, and Rutherford, who confessed to a wide range of heinous crimes. They were not executed, however, but released from prison. From that point on, they spent every day at the Chestnut Tree Café, sitting slumped before their gin glasses. Winston had seen them there once, listening to a song about betrayal. Rutherford had tears in his eyes, and Winston noted that Aronson and Rutherford had broken noses. The three were later rearrested and executed. Some years later, on the job, Winston came across a picture of the three men from a 10-year-old newspaper, showing them at a party conference in New York. The date of the paper was the same day that the men had confessed they were conspiring with the enemy in Siberia. Winston, completely fearful at the time, dropped the clipping down the memory hole. The recall of the incident reawakens in him a basic question about the falsification of the past. He records his dilemma in his diary, "I understand HOW: I do not understand WHY." The Party's ultimate goal is "to deny the evidence of your senses." He imagines that the party will one day proclaim "that two and two make five, and you would have to believe it."

The party operates on the assumption their greatest enemy is common sense, the belief in objective reality. But suppose everything is in the mind, and the mind can be controlled. This prospect suddenly raises the image of O'Brien before him. He instinctively feels that O'Brien agrees with him. He realizes that he is writing these thoughts "For O'Brien—*to* O'Brien." O'Brien would understand that, despite the sophisticated arguments that might be lodged against him, "they were wrong and he was right." He makes a final assertion in his diary that he feels summarizes his position: "*Freedom is the freedom to say that two plus two make four. If that is granted, all else follows.*"

Chapter 1, Part 8

Winston is walking through an unfamiliar area in London, realizing that he should be spending his time at the community center. Taking a walk by yourself would arouse suspicion of individualism, a heresy which, in Newspeak, was called *ownlife.* As he walks through the slums of a prole neighborhood, a rocket bomb explodes, and he is forced to fling himself down on the street coming close to being hurt. As he continues his walk, he remembers that he is near the junk shop where he bought his diary. As he walks on, he spots an old man entering a pub. The man must be at least 80 years old, and Winston is suddenly impelled to follow him into the pub and ask him about life before the revolution in the past. He gets no satisfactory answers from the old man and moves out into the street again, where he finds himself in front of the junk shop. Without looking for anything in particular, he enters the shop. The owner, Mr. Charrington, a man of some 60 years, remembers him but complains that there are few antiques left. As Winston looks around, he spots a small glass dome with a piece of coral inside, which he buys. The owner then suggests that there are more objects upstairs. As he enters the upstairs, he sees a place that looks ready to be lived in, featuring a large mahogany bed. The proprietor points out a framed picture of an old church, St. Clement's, which reminds Winston of a children's street game that named all the churches in London. As he leaves the junk shop, he spots a figure coming down the street. It is the girl from the Fiction Department. She looks at him squarely in the face and moves on down the street. He is convinced that the girl is spying on him. He has a momentary fantasy of following her and smashing her head in with the glass dome he is carrying. Instead, he returns home, anticipating the arrival of the Thought Police.

Chapter 2, Part 1

At work, Winston, on his way to the men's room, encounters the same girl with dark hair again. With her arm in a cast, she stumbles and falls and Winston, although still suspicious of her, stoops to help her up, seeing that she is in real pain. As he does, she slips a small scrap of paper into his hand and proceeds on her way. He is profoundly unsettled by this move, still suspecting that she is a Thought Police spy—he makes no attempt to read the note until he is back at his desk after mixing it with a pile of papers. When he finally does read it, he is startled to discover the message: "I love you."

It is only when he is lying in the dark at home that he is able to consider the situation rationally. He believes she is telling the truth, a fact that leaves him determined to stay alive as long as he can. He must get in touch with her quickly but without being detected on the telescreen. He determines that the safest way to communicate with her is at the cafeteria. A week goes by before the opportunity ever presents itself, when he trips up a man who is headed for the table where she is sitting alone. Without looking at each other, they agree to meet after work at Victory Square, where there is always a large crowd. At the square, the crowd is exceptionally large, having come to see a truck convoy carrying Eurasian prisoners of war. Crushed together by the crowd, they arrange to meet on the following Sunday afternoon in the countryside outside of London. Their hands lock together for a full 10 seconds before they part.

Chapter 2, Part 2

On Sunday, the two meet at the appointed spot but do not speak until she leads him further into the woods to an enclosed clearing. The woman, named Julia, speaks of the party with complete contempt. When Winston asks her why she chose a middle-aged, unprepossessing man like him, she replies that it was something in his face. She knew just looking at him that he was "against them." As he surveys this spot in the woods, he realizes that it is the "Golden Country" of his dream, confirmed by her when she says there is a stream nearby filled with big fish. They return to the clearing and she, as in the dream, tears her clothes off. As they proceed to have sex, Winston asks her if she has done this before, and she answers "hundreds of times—well, scores of times"—always with members of the Outer Party, and the answer delights Winston, realizing that the party, too, has its inner weakness. After sex, they fall asleep. Winston awakens first and, looking at her naked body, perceives that their lovemaking had been more than pure love or pure lust. It had been a victory over the party. "It was a political act."

Chapter 2, Part 3

Before parting, they arrange to meet after work at an open market. At this and subsequent meetings, they speak to each other, strolling along as if they were looking at the wares on sale. Their next sexual encounter occurs in the belfry of an abandoned church tower in the countryside. There she tells him of her work in the Fiction Department, where novels are produced by machines. She also offers a theory of the party's politics of antisexuality:

> "When you make love you're using up energy; and afterwards you feel happy and don't give a damn for anything. They can't bear you to feel like that. They want you to be bursting with energy all the time. All this marching up and down and cheering and waving flags is simply sex gone sour."

Winston tells her of his marriage to Katharine and of the opportunity he once had to push her over a cliff. When Julia asks why he didn't do it, he says that in the long run it would not have made a difference. Julia protests that he is too pessimistic. He counters that from the moment you set yourself up against the party, you should think of yourself as dead. Julia answers that as long as you are alive, you should feel alive.

Chapter 2, Part 4

Winston is in the room above Mr. Charrington's junk store. Throwing caution to the wind, he has rented the room where he and Julia can conduct their affair. While he awaits her arrival he watches a sturdy prole woman hanging out diapers on a clothesline, singing as she works. The lyrics of the tune she sings are the product of a machine, called a versificator, which cranks out popular songs for the prole audience, but she sings it so well, it is transformed into something genuine. He thinks again of the folly involved in renting this room, virtually guaranteeing that they will be caught. His fears fade as he greets Julia, who has brought all sorts of delicacies, like real coffee and tea, leftovers from Inner Party members. As an added treat, she dons makeup she has bought in a prole shop, and the two fall into the room's large mahogany bed. Later Julia spots a rat and hurls a shoe at it. The presence of the rat has a traumatizing effect on Winston. He is subject to a recurring nightmare in which he is confronting in the dark some unbearable reality. He always wakes up without discovering what the horrible object is, but Julia's mention of a rat has triggered the same response. There the two luxuriate in the taste of the coffee Julia has brought. Winston, explaining to her why he loves the paperweight. "It's a little chunk of history they've forgotten to alter." When Julia asks about the picture of St. Clement's, Winston mentions the children's rhyme. To his surprise, Julia recalls a couple of lines, taught to her by her grandfather. Winston takes up the paperweight again and reflects that the room he was in is the glass dome, and he and Julia are the coral set in its heart.

Chapter 2, Part 5

At the Ministry, Syme has disappeared. On the first day of his absence, some people noted it. By the second day, no one mentioned him. Everyone is working overtime preparing for Hate Week. And at Winston's apartment house, Victory Mansions, preparations under the leadership of sweat-smelling Parsons are feverish. Meantime, the rocket bombs falling on London have increased, stirring anger against the Eurasian enemy. A huge poster of a Eurasian soldier firing a machine gun directly at the viewer is plastered over the entire city. Despite the frenzied pace, Winston and Julia have managed to escape to their hideout over the shop as much as seven times in the month of June. Winston's health is improving. The ulcerous vein above his ankle is less painful and his bronchial condition improved. Just knowing their secret room exists makes life endurable. On arrival at each visit, he has a brief chat with Mr. Charrington, who retrieves from his fading memory fragments of old nursery rhymes.

In bed, the two cling together, knowing that they will soon be discovered. On occasion, they speak of actively rebelling against the party. Winston tells her of his feeling about O'Brien, and she, operating on the assumption that everyone secretly hates the party, considers it possible, but she doubts the existence of an underground Brotherhood, regarding it as another fiction created by the party along with the myth of Goldstein. She even doubts the existence of the war against Eurasia, suggesting that the rocket bombs dropping on London were being fired by the government. But she is a pragmatic, here-and-now person, not upset by or even interested in Winston's account of the Rutherford, Aaronson, Jones affair. Winston tries to convince her that the past has been constantly revised so that history no longer exists. "Nothing exists except an endless present in which the party is always right." He speaks of the need to preserve some sense of reality to pass on to the next generation, but she answers that she has no interest in the "next generation. I'm interested in us." He replies, "You're only a rebel from the waist downwards," a remark that gives her great pleasure. Winston concludes that people like Julia manage to stay sane by ignoring or failing to understand the implications of party doctrine.

Chapter 2, Part 6

As Winston is walking down a corridor at the Ministry, he senses someone behind him. Turning, he sees O'Brien, who falls into step with him, chatting amiably about Winston's interest in Newspeak and his writing in general. O'Brien suggests that Winston might be interested in seeing the latest edition of the *Newspeak Dictionary,* of which he has an advance copy. He stops to write down his address, suggesting that Winston stop by his flat some evening. They part with Winston aware that he will visit O'Brien and that meeting will have fateful consequences.

Chapter 2, Part 7

In bed in their room, Winston awakes from a dream, his eyes filled with tears. The dream took place inside the dome of the glass paperweight and a gesture made by his mother and by the woman in the newsreel who tried to protect a young boy. Now, upon his awakening, it suddenly comes back to him that he thought he had murdered his mother. The experience he now suddenly recalls occurred in the 1950s. He was about 10 years old, living with his mother and younger sister. His father had disappeared some time earlier. It was a time of desolation caused by air raids, roaming street gangs, cities reduced to rubble and widespread starvation. He remembers himself as a sniveling, wheedling drain on his mother's nerves, determined to whine his way to more than his share of the family's drastically reduced rations. His desperate hunger had no regard for the needs of his mother or his baby sister, a two-year-old frail and ailing child. One day, a chocolate ration, the first of its kind in a long while, was issued. He insisted on being given the entire piece, whining and incessantly nagging until his mother finally broke the chocolate, giving him three-quarters and the baby the rest. Winston grabbed the piece out of the baby's hands and ran out the door—as he looked back, he saw his mother draw her arm around the child and pressed her to her breast. Somehow, as he fled from the house, he knew his sister was dying. When he later returned to the flat, he found that they were gone, vanished like so many others then and now. He sees his mother as one of the people of the past, one of those "governed by private loyalties. . . . What mattered were individual relationships. . . . not loyalty to a party or a country or an idea, they were loyal to one another." Now only the proles retain these values. "The proles had stayed human."

Julia wakes, and they discuss what might happen when they are caught by the Thought Police. He says the important thing is that neither one of them betrays the other. By *betrayal* he does not mean confessing. Confession is merely an act; what matters is feelings. If they could make the two stop loving each other, that would be betrayal. Julia agrees that they can never do that. They can get you to "say anything—*anything*—but they can't make you believe it." Winston is resolute, confident that whatever else they do, they cannot alter the feeling residing in the "inner heart," the "impregnable" part of the self.

Chapter 2, Part 8

The moment of decision has arrived. Winston and Julia are standing in O'Brien's study, having decided, somewhat rashly, to visit him together. Looking around them, they are clearly intimidated by the room as well as by the man sitting behind a large desk. After he dispenses with some routine work, he rises from the desk and presses a button, shutting off the telescreen. The act impresses Winston sufficiently to have him assert bluntly that they have come because they believe that O'Brien is part of a conspiracy against the party and that the two of them want to join this movement. He is interrupted by O'Brien's servant carrying a decanter containing a liquid, which they learn is wine. O'Brien fills their glasses including one for the servant, Martin, and proposes a toast "to our leader: to Emmanuel Goldstein." O'Brien then outlines the nature of the Brotherhood and begins asking questions to determine the lengths they will go to in pursuit of the overthrow of the party. To all of his questions, Winston answers yes, until he asks them if they are ready to separate and never see each other again, at which point Julia breaks in to say "No!" After an indecisive pause, Winston repeats Julia's "No." O'Brien appears to accept their answer. He then dismisses Martin, but not before asking him to memorize Winston and Julia's faces.

O'Brien then gives a brief and profoundly pessimistic account of the party's almost invisible structure and of their individual fates. "You will work for a while, you will be caught. You will confess, and then you will die." Their only hope lies in some indeterminate future.

Now it is time to leave. Julia will go first. Before she leaves, O'Brien proposes one more toast, asking what it should be—to the death of Big Brother, or to humanity, or to the future. Winston proposes "to the past." O'Brien agrees that the past is even more important. He suggests that the two of them leave separately. After Julia leaves, O'Brien inquires about their hiding place and Winston tells him of the room above the junk shop. O'Brien then tells him that he will shortly be surreptitiously receiving a copy of Goldstein's book. As they part, O'Brien suggests that if they do meet again it will be . . . Winston, recalling his dream, finishes O'Brien's thought ". . . in the place where there is no darkness." O'Brien invites Winston to ask one more question before he leaves. He asks O'Brien if he knows the old rhyme "Oranges and lemons say the bells of St. Clement's." And O'Brien completes the last line. As Winston leaves, O'Brien gives him a small white tablet to disguise the smell of wine on his breath.

Chapter 2, Part 9

On the sixth day of Hate Week, the day before the scheduled execution of 2,000 Eurasian prisoners, the word came down that Oceania was not at war with Eurasia, and had never been at war with Eurasia, a trusted ally—the enemy was East Asia. The consequence for Winston and the other members of the records department was a massive task of rewriting events with an entirely new cast of villains and geographical locations. Winston had to work 90 hours in five days, sleeping on cots in the Ministry. In the meantime, the Goldstein book had been delivered to him, but he had not time even to open it. Now that the crisis was over, he is free for 15 hours. He heads for Mr. Charrington's shop. Despite his fatigue, he is filled with anticipation. In their room, he opens the book, *The Theory of Oligarchical Collectivism* by Emmanuel Goldstein. The title of the first chapter is "Ignorance is Strength." Its opening sentences proclaim that throughout history there have been three classes of people, "the high, the middle, and the low," and that these groups are "entirely irreconcilable." Winston then jumps around to chapter 3, "War Is Peace." It describes the events that followed World War II, when the Soviet Union gained control of Europe ("Eurasia") while the British Empire was absorbed by the United States ("Oceania"). A decade later, after continued fighting, "East Asia" emerged as a third superstate. These three powers are constantly at war, but the sides are always shifting, so today's ally may be tomorrow's enemy. The reasons for this continuous state of war are radically different from those of wars in the past in that none of these three superpowers can be beaten. They are all too evenly matched. The real basis for war rests on the fact that it is destructive. It is destructive of materials that would contribute to the welfare and comfort of the mass of human beings, to the elevation of their standard of living. That elevation would free people from drudgery, leaving them the opportunity to develop their intelligence and become socially and politically active. Such a movement would threaten the existing oligarchy. The other virtue of war is that it requires massive amounts of labor expended without bringing any material benefit to the society. It produces "a state of scarcity."

War serves one of the two principal goals of the superstate; first, to conquer the world. The second goal is "to extinguish once and for all, the possibility of independent thought." In pursuit of these two goals, the party enlists the aid of scientific research, in the first case to help create weapons of such destructive power that millions of people can be annihilated at a single blow; and in the attempt to wipe out independent thought, it looks to science to "get inside another human being and discover what he/she is thinking."

All three superpowers possess atomic bombs, and in the wars of the 1950s, they were frequently used, but the three governments soon realized that continued use would create a global wasteland in which their own power would be extinguished. As a result they continued to stockpile their weapons while tacitly agreeing not to use them. As a result, limited wars are conducted with the old weapons, with the exception of rocket missiles instead of bombers. But the important point is that these wars will never end. Permanent war ensures the status quo within each superstate. That is the true message behind the slogan "War Is Peace."

Winston's reading is interrupted by the arrival of Julia. After making love, Winston begins to read the book aloud to a sleepy Julia. After the opening passage in chapter 1, the chapter goes on to chart the history of the various ideologies that developed around the question of achieving an equitable social arrangement other than the high-middle-low structure. Socialism claimed to offer a solution, but various attempts to implement it resulted in the abandonment of the principles of equality and freedom. However, a quiet revolution took place in what were to become the three superstates. A new class, drawn from the middle and the upper strata of the low, came to power: the professionals, who brought technical skills and managerial expertise to the seats of power. A major source of this new power was the new tchnology, enabling the ruling class to shape the thinking of the public and "to keep its citizens under constant surveillance" through the use of various collecting devices, and most important, via two-way televisions.

The new superstates reconstituted themselves on a nominally "socialist" basis—"the abolition of private property"—but in fact, the party owns everything. The pyramidal structure of Oceanic society is as follows: At the top is Big Brother, omnipotent, all-seeing and immortal. Because he is not an individual, he is a symbol, the embodiment of the party. Beneath him are the Inner Party members, the brains of the party, two percent of the population. Below them are the Outer Party, about 12 percent of the population, the "hands" of the party. Finally there are the proles, 85 percent of the population, the blood and brawn of the party. One does not gain admission to the inner party by inheritance. A party member must have an instinctive sense of the party's will, but that sense can be enhanced by education. As a child, the future Party member first learns the technique of *crimestop,* the ability to abort any thought that is headed in a dangerous direction. From here the child moves on to acquire the skill known as *blackwhite,* the ability to assert that black is white in the interests of Party discipline, but also to believe that such is the case and "to forget that one has ever believed the contrary." These two educational steps are essential to the process known as *doublethink,* crucially related to the party's sense of the past. For the party, the past is not fixed and permanent; its reality is evident only in records. Thus the past is always being recreated to serve the interests of the party. As for people's memories, one can learn to "control reality," that is, to hold two contradictory beliefs in one's mind simultaneously and accepting both, "which is the basic definition of *doublethink.*" *Doublethink* is the foundation on which the party's power rests. The only question that remains is to examine the motive behind the development of "*doublethink* and the Thought Police and continuous warfare . . ."

At this point, Winston stops reading, realizing that Julia has fallen asleep. Reflecting on what he has read, he thinks that he understands how the present system came into being, but he has yet to learn why. One thing that has reassured him that he is not insane. He has been right in opposing the regime. With that thought, he falls asleep.

Chapter 2, Part 10

He wakes to the sound of a prole woman singing. Julia awakes and the two dress and move to the window to watch the prole woman at her clothesline. As he watches the woman, he becomes convinced that "if there was hope, it lay in the proles." The proles are still alive, but we are the dead. He says these words to Julia and she repeats them, when suddenly they hear a voice coming form behind the picture of St. Clement's on the wall, saying, "You are the dead." The voice orders them to stand still with their hands behind their heads, while the room is invaded by men in black uniforms, followed by Mr. Charrington, only now he has discarded his disguise of being an old man. He is a middle-aged man, alert and cold, a member of the Thought Police.

Part 3, Chapter 1

At first, Winston was brought to an ordinary prison, thrown in with regular criminals, thieves, drunks, prostitutes and black marketeers, along with a few political prisoners like himself. Now he is somewhere in the Ministry of Love in a cell, sitting on a long narrow bench under constant surveillance form four telescreens. At one point he is joined by the poet Ampleforth, guilty of leaving the word *God* in a Kipling poem he was editing, because he couldn't find a suitable substitute. Ampleforth is taken out shortly after, slated to go to room 101. Later, Winston is joined in the cell by Parsons, who was overheard by his daughter crying out "down with Big Brother" in his sleep. His daughter reported him to the Thought Police, for which, Parsons says, he is proud of her. After Parsons leaves, a number of prisoners come and go, including one skull-faced man who is clearly starving to death. When another man, Bumstead, tries to give him a piece a bread, a voice from the telescreen commands him to stop where he is. Then a guard enters and brutally beats Bumstead. Meanwhile, the starving man is told he must go to Room 101. Sometime after that, a door opens and O'Brien walks in. Winston thinks that O'Brien, too, is a prisoner, but then O'Brien steps aside to let a guard deliver a paralyzingly painful blow to Winston's elbow. O'Brien tells him not to deceive himself, that he has always known who O'Brien really was.

Part 3, Chapter 2

He is lying strapped down on a high cot. O'Brien is standing next to him with another man, holding a hypodermic syringe. He has endured an extraordinary range of pain, and he has confessed to a host of crimes. But he has not denied the reality of an objective past. Winston insists that some memory is involuntary, that it can't be controlled. O'Brien insists that Winston has failed to exercise the self-discipline that would make him capable of that control. O'Brien asserts that objective reality is an illusion: "Reality exists in the mind and nowhere else." He then reminds Winston that he wrote in his diary, "Freedom is the freedom to say that two plus two make four." O'Brien holds out four fingers and asks Winston how many fingers he sees. When Winston answer "four," O'Brien tells him that it is five, "What do you say?" When Winston answers four, he feels a jolt of pain. O'Brien repeats the question and with another answer of four, the escalating pain becomes so intense that Winston says "Five," but O'Brien is not satisfied. Eventually, the pain reaches a level that Winston really cannot determine how many fingers he sees. At that point, O'Brien cuts off the current and Winston experiences an injection that immediately replaces the pain with a blissful warmth. At that moment he feels an overwhelming love for his torturer. O'Brien then asks Winston why he thinks the party brings people here to torture them, explaining that it is done to cure them. The party does not make the mistakes of past torturers, the Inquisition, the Nazis, the Communists—they all created martyrs, who inspired more people to rise up against them. O'Brien explains that the party converts its heretics and turns them into genuine believers. His function is to convert the heretic to "make him one of ourselves before we kill him." Then, O'Brien's attendants place two large moist pads against Winston's temple. He experiences a blinding flash of electricity and a feeling inside his head as if a portion of his brain had been removed. O'Brien asks him a series of questions designed to determine if the treatment has worked and he is satisfied with Winston's answers. He now allows Winston to ask him some questions. His first question concerns the fate of Julia, and O'Brien replies that she was "a perfect conversion, a textbook case." His next two questions, about the existence of Big Brother and of the Brotherhood, receive ambiguous responses. Winston's final question is "What is in Room 101?" And he is told only that he already knows what is in Room 101. A needle is then inserted into Winston's arm, and he immediately falls into a deep sleep.

Part 3, Chapter 3

O'Brien explains to Winston that he has just completed the first stage of his "cure." The first stage is the learning phase, which must be followed by understanding and finally by acceptance. The second stage begins with Winston's being once again strapped down but tighter than before. O'Brien reminds him of his question about understanding the "how" but not the "why." Now he asks Winston to tell him why he thinks the party wants power. Winston realizes that O'Brien expects to hear an explanation based on the belief that humankind needs security, not freedom. The average person is incapable of self-government. As soon as he attempts this answer he feels an electric shock through his body. Then O'Brien gives him the correct answer, "The Party seeks power entirely for its own sake." He adds that the party is historically unique precisely because of its willingness to acknowledge this fact. The Nazis and Stalinists employed many of our methods but they were too cowardly to face up to their true motives: "The object of power is power."

Winston looks at O'Brien and sees fatigue registered in his face. O'Brien, reading his thoughts, tells Winston that the fatigue and decay he sees in O'Brien do not contradict what he is saying: The individual is merely a cell in the larger organism that is the party. Power resides in the collective, not in the individual. But if one can submit his individual will to the will of the party, the person becomes a part of a whole that is all-powerful.

A second point is that power is power over other human beings, not simply their bodies, but their minds. When you control the mind you control reality; "Reality is inside the skull." When Winston insists that you can't control the laws of nature, he is told, "We make the laws of nature." And, thanks to doublethink, we can contradict those laws anytime we please. Winston tries to think of the term for the fallacy inherent in O'Brien's logic. O'Brien, again reading his mind, supplies the term Winston is looking for, "solipsism. Collective solipsism, it you like"—but he denies its application to his ideas.

As O'Brien sees it, the future will consist of an increasingly more brutal world, in which humanist values will be suppressed under the reign of power. "If you want a picture of the future, imagine a boot stamping on a human face—forever." Pushed to his limit, Winston finally asserts that eventually the party will be be defeated by the "spirit of Man." O'Brien explains to Winston that he is the last man. He orders him to take off his clothes and stand before a three-sided mirror. When he looks at his emaciated, devastated face and figure in filthy rags, the image overwhelms him and moves him to tears. When O'Brien asks him if he can think of a single degradation he has not been reduced to, he answers that he has not betrayed Julia. O'Brien agrees, and when Winston asks when they will shoot him, O'Brien says not for some time yet, but "in the end we shall shoot you."

Part 3, Chapter 4

For Winston, life is becoming relatively easy. Still in a cell—an improved, more comfortable one, he is eating regularly, gaining weight, wearing clean clothes, and slowly acquiring the new knowledge O'Brien has imparted, accepting with equanimity all the party slogans, even formulating one of his own, "God Is Power."

On one occasion, he falls into a reverie in which he is walking in the Golden Country and has a momentary hallucination which causes him to cry out aloud Julia's name. Shortly after, O'Brien comes to his cell. He tells Winston that he has improved considerably on an intellectual level, but emotionally he has made no progress. He asks him if he loves Big Brother and when Winston replies that he hates him, O'Brien says that it is time for Winston to enter the final phase of his cure: He must love Big Brother. O'Brien pushes Winston toward the guards and instructs them: "Room 101."

Part 3, Chapter 5

Room 101 is located deep on the bottom floor of the Ministry of Love. The room contains, besides the chair to which he is strapped, two small tables. O'Brien enters. He tells Winston that the answer to his earlier question about what was in Room 101 is "the worst thing in the world," which varies according to the individual. The door opens and a guard enters carrying a case, which he sets down on one of the tables. For Winston, O'Brien explains, "the worst thing happens to be rats." O'Brien moves the box to a table next to Winston close to his face while clicking something on the cage. He explains that he has unlocked the first lever on the rat cage. When he places the cage over Winston's head he will release the second lever, freeing the two rats to attack his face. As the cage is descending over his face, Winston understands what he must say: "Do it to Julia, do it to Julia." Although he had the sensation of falling a great distance, Winston is conscious of hearing a click and knowing that the cage is being closed, not opened.

Part 3, Chapter 6

Winston is sitting in the Chestnut Tree Café, drinking Victory Gin and watching the telescreen. The news is not good. The war with the Eurasians (the war has always been with the Eurasians) was not going well on the African front. Winston spends most of his time at the café. One day he had run into Julia in the park and the two spoke to each other, each admitting that he/she had betrayed the other. She described the process which was exactly how Winston had experienced it: Don't do this thing to me, do it to the other. After that there is no love. The two walked away from each other, having nothing else to say.

He had a token job at the Ministry of Truth, but it was meaningless, a subcommittee's subcommittee charged with the task of determining whether to put commas inside or outside of quotation marks. The other members were people like him, ghosts who had gone through the cure. At the café, he has a brief recollection of playing Snakes and Ladders with his mother, but he pushes that "false memory" away. On the telescreen comes a great announcement: The conflict on the African front has resulted in a great victory for Oceania. Winston stays seated but he would like to be out in the streets celebrating. His great climactic moment has arrived. Gazing up at the majestic visage of the Leader now appearing on the screen, he has finally triumphed over himself. "He loved Big Brother."

Appendix, The Principles of Newspeak

Newspeak was the official language of Oceania. It was expected to have been codified and perfected in the eleventh edition of *The Dictionary of Newspeak.* The complete transformation of English into Newspeak would not occur until 2050.

In 1984, it was still in its formative stage. No one used it exclusively in their speech, but the process and the general outline of the new language was well under way. As the years passed, it was assumed that it would emerge as the only language to be used. Future generations of children, for example, would learn it in school to the exclusion of other languages.

The goal of Newspeak was to provide a vehicle of communication consistent with the principles and mental practices of Ingsoc at the same time that it would make any other way of expressing oneself "literally unthinkable." A key feature of Newspeak was its ability to limit thought. The process involved inventing new words, eliminating a large number of old words, and, in some cases, stripping an old word of some of its meanings. Thus, *free* could still be used in the sense of being rid of something undesirable, but it would have no political or intellectual connotation.

The vocabulary of Newspeak was divided into three categories. The A vocabulary included the words of everyday life—*run, dog, house,* etc.—with the difference that such words would be stripped of any metaphorical or ambiguous meanings. The B vocabulary consisted of compound words, designed both to carry a political meaning and to evoke a proper mental state in the person using them. Some examples are *crimestop* and *goodthink.* Many B words were designed to cover a broad range of eliminated terms, so that words like *honor, justice, democracy,* etc., would be covered by the B word *crimethink.* Many of these words had a harsh sound with equal stresses, producing a monotonous effect, ideally suited to "spraying forth opinions as automatically as a machine gun." The C vocabulary consisted entirely of scientific and technical terms. Those were similar to oldspeak terms, always, however, purged of any politically unacceptable meanings.

Newspeak's grammar was the same for all three categories. Its chief distinctions were interchangeable parts of speech (any given word could serve as a noun, verb, adjective, or adverb) and the use of the *un-* prefix to negate any word or the *plus-* prefix to strengthen any word. The past and past participle of any verb could be formed by an *-ed* suffix.

The overall effect was to render unorthodox opinions nearly impossible. Narrowing what could be thought reduced the possibility of political heresy. As for the language of the past, certain documents, such as the Declaration of Independence, would have to be eliminated, since it would not be possible to transcribe it into Newspeak. For appearances' sake, translations of Shakespeare and a few other great writers would be undertaken, but it would be a long, difficult task. Once the translation was made, of course, the original texts would be destroyed. For that reason it appeared that the final triumph of Newspeak would not be complete before 2050.

See "A Glossary of Newspeak" in the appendix.

COMMENTARY

Nineteen Eighty-Four begins quietly but ominously. The opening paragraph sends us indirect signals that something is not quite right, if not rotten:

> It was a bright cold day in April and the clocks were striking thirteen. Winston Smith, his chin nuzzled into his breast in an effort to escape the vile wind, slipped quickly through the glass doors of Victory Mansions, though not quickly enough to prevent a swirl of gritty dust from entering along with him.

The reference to April might suggest spring, new beginnings, as it does, for example, in the famous opening line of Chaucer's *Canterbury Tales.* On the other hand, readers might be reminded of a more recent opening line, from T. S. Eliot's *The Waste Land:* "April is the cruelest month . . ." As the story unfolds, both connotations surface: April proves to be a new beginning for Winston, but, ironically, one that ends for him in the cruelty of Room 101. The clocks striking "thirteen" indicates an alteration of language, the adoption of a more military terminology, a movement reinforced by the reference to Victory Mansions, while the "vile wind" and "gritty dust" hint that here the outer penetrates the inner, anticipating the telescreen in Winston's apartment as well as the basic strategy of a government that aims to invade and control the interior life of its citizens.

We are also given the name of the character Winston Smith. *Smith* offers no problem. It is the name of everyman. In the United States, *Joe Smith* was and is a common term, even a cliché, for an ordinary citizen. As for the first name, although it is logical that the 39-year-old Winston, born in England in 1944 or 1945, would have been named Winston, after the wartime prime minister, it also suggests that our Smith is a man of the past, a political figure who is also something of a writer and historian, perhaps the last of a dying breed. (From the vantage point of 1948, with a Labour government firmly in control after their electoral victory three years earlier, the ex-prime minister might easily have exemplified a dying breed.)

The stage is set for a dramatic conflict. In simple terms: It is Winston against the party. He takes a step which he recognizes as fatal when he begins to record his feelings in his secret diary. Keeping the diary seems to be simply an act of despair, a record that no one will read, destined to be vaporized along with its author. But he also knows, subconsciously at least, that this is not quite true. As he comes to recognize later, he is writing the diary "to and for O'Brien." He will have his reader.

In his entry, he records watching a movie newsreel the previous evening. He inadvertently draws a picture of people brutalized and filled with hate by the daily diet of war and cruelty they have been fed. His conditioning is such that he shares the audience's view. He describes their laughing at "a wonderful shot," the sight of a helicopter dropping a bomb on a lifeboat filled with children, and of a Jewish woman in the boat trying to protect a screaming child, her arms cradling the boy to her breast. The one exception in the audience is a prole woman, who is heard to cry out that such violence and cruelty should not be shown to children. It is a measure of Winston's own conditioning that he dismisses the woman's protest: "... the police turned her out and I don't suppose anything happened to her nobody cares what the proles say. . . ." Later, Winston recognizes that if there is any hope at all, it lies with the proles. But at the beginning, his rebellion is essentially a private and convenient form of suicide.

That there is something more to him is hinted at in the dream he has that evening, in which he watches from above as his mother and younger sister sink beneath the water. This part of the dream has been clearly triggered by the newsreel of the woman in the lifeboat. In the contrast between the newsreel and the dream, he recognizes the difference between today's world of "fear, hatred and pain" and the lost world in which death could be faced with tragic dignity "when there were still privacy, love, and friendship. . . ."

Thus a good portion of the novel is devoted to the application of the party slogan, "who controls the past, controls the future." Winston has been an active participant in this control. Part of him—the *Smith* in him, the wordsmith—even enjoys the challenge of creating, for example, a completely fictional character, Comrade Ogilvy, for whom he invents an imaginary, heroic life and death in order to replace an account of someone who is now an unperson.

Winston's conflict with the state moves to a second, deeper stage when he begins his affair with Julia. Julia had appeared in the same dream as his mother. She had approached him in a country setting, throwing off her clothes as she neared. The reckless, freedom-loving gesture seems enough to abolish the whole oppressive world he lives in. The dream is harshly interrupted by the voice of the telescreen summoning Winston to participate in the daily morning calisthenics required of all Outer Party members. When, thanks to Julia's courage and daring, they finally do meet and make love, he understands that, as an expression of freedom, sex is a political act. In the affair, "Winston discovers the supreme importance of uncomplicated human love and loyalty." When the affair is solidified by the seeming good luck of finding their own private room, a flicker of hope illuminates Winston's consciousness, associated with the strength and beauty of a prole woman who is singing while hanging out the wash. He has a second dream, dominated by the encircling maternal arm of his earlier dream, attempting to protect a child from being strafed and bombed by an enemy plane. This dream has triggered a childhood memory. After being given three-quarters of a chocolate ration, he had grabbbed the other quarter from the hands of his starving baby sister. He ran out of the room, but looking back, he saw his mother cradling his sister to her breast. It is clear that, on the personal level, the past is not the idyllic time imagined by George Bowling in *Coming Up for Air* or hinted at by Orwell in some of his essays, hints that caused Cyril Connolly, who knew him from childhood, to describe Orwell as "a revolutionary in love with 1910."

Only once in his dialogue with O'Brien does Winston have a chance to express an opinion that O'Brien accepts. When the latter proposes a toast at the meeting in his house, he suggests possible objects of the toast ". . . To humanity? To the future?" At this point, Winston interjects, "to the past," and O'Brien agrees, "the past is more important." A touch of that idyllic past seems to be present in the references to the old London church bells and children's street songs, but these allusions turn out to be simply tactics employed by Charrington and O'Brien to further ensnare Winston. The party controls the past.

For Winston personally, the past is also a source of guilt that needs to be expiated. That need may be a primary motive for his increasing recklessness as he moves from the diary to the affair with Julia, to approaching O'Brien about joining the Brotherhood. These rash acts are conducted in the spirit of nothing left to lose, but they also express the sense of something to atone for. But now the suicidal impulse has been replaced by a defiant affirmation, not simply a "no" to the party's war on the individual, but an assertion that it just might be possible to activate a resistance that could catch the attention of the proles.

The first step, he believes, is to move beyond flirtation with O'Brien, after the latter sends him a signal that appears to be unmistakable. The scene in which the lovers are initiated into the mysterious Brotherhood is layered over with religious symbolism, including the wine and the white wafer, ostensibly designed to cleanse one's breath, and the importance attached to "the book," i.e., Goldstein's treatise on oligarchical collectivism, the bible of the Brotherhood movement. Of course, their underground world, even the book itself, turns out to be an illusion constructed by the party to bring dissidents to a level of consciousness and conviction that will make them enemies worthy of being crushed, a suitable sacrifice to the god of power. For O'Brien, personally, Winston must seem a special challenge, particularly since he exhibits the instinct that is the most difficult to erase, a capacity for love. The challenge, however, is not to eliminate Winston's love but to transform it into the love of Big Brother. This is the reason that led the philosopher Richard Rorty to suggest that "after Winston and Julia go to O'Brien's apartment, *1984* becomes a book about O'Brien, not about twentieth century totalitarian states" (Rorty, 171).

Even allowing for the fact that Rorty may be overstating the case, it is certainly true that O'Brien is the second-most important character in the novel, after Winston. Therefore the question as to his human credibility is important, even if his essential role is symbolic. (Moby Dick, as it is said, has to be a believable whale before it can be anything else.) In this respect, O'Brien is given a distinctive feature, one that Winston finds particularly attractive, resettling his glasses on his nose. It is a very human gesture, and perhaps Winston sees in it a sign of flexibility, a recognition of the need to adjust, to acknowledge that he may not be seeing quite clearly. This is entirely the opposite of the raving fanatic we see in Room 101. Between the two extremes, O'Brien negotiates reality through his mastery of doublethink.

But while doublethink may provide us with a description of O'Brien's skill, it does not penetrate within; it does not give us a picture of O'Brien resettling the glasses of his mind. The argument that we should move from O'Brien's Irishness to his Catholicism and from there to his Jesuitical character is plausible but at a triple remove, tenuous. Even more that we should move from the first letter of Eileen's maiden name (O'Shaughnessy) to the first letter of O'Brien's as "a vehicle of guilt" (Porter, 70). In this respect, V. S. Pritchett's metaphorical description of Orwell's technique, ". . . he knows exactly where on the new Jesuitism to apply the Protestant whip" (Pritchett, 291) would be literally correct as well as metaphorically vivid.

The third important character is Julia, important not only individually but as the vehicle for the theme of sexual politics. Feminist critics have criticized Orwell for his characterization of Julia. To begin with, we are never given her last name, whereas all the male characters, except for Winston, Parsons, Syme, Charrington, Bumstead, Jones, Aaronson, Rutherford, and most notably, O'Brien, are known in the best British public-school tradition, only by their last names. The one exception is O'Brien's mysterious servant, Martin. One can justifiably deduce from this that first names are for women and the lower classes. More substantively, Orwell's depiction of Julia suggests that she is ". . . every man's most potent sexual fantasy . . . sexually liberated, healthy, a creature of instinct and emotion, but not intellect, a man-identified woman . . ." (Mellor, 118). Winston only confirms this view when he refers to her as "a rebel from the waist downwards," which she then confirms by laughing and hugging him. It, of course, in no way extenuates the case against Orwell to suggest that he modeled Julia on his soon-to-be wife Sonia, a sexual rebel whose most overt rebellious act was a habit of spitting at nuns in retribution for her repressive convent-school education. On the other hand, some feminist critics overlook the positive aspects of Julia. She takes the lead in the early stages of the affair and shows ingenuity and intelligent planning in trying to evade the thought police. It is Winston, not she, who conceives the rash idea of visiting O'Brien, and, once there, she, not he, who gives a resounding "no" to the question of whether they would, in the interests of the Brotherhood, be willing to separate and never see each other again. Only after a considerable pause does Winston ratify her "no." On the other hand, neither Julia nor Winston hesitates to acquiesce when O'Brien asks them if they would be willing to throw sulfuric acid in a child's face. This marks them as precisely the type of revolutionaries who become brutalized by the revolutionary act, propelled by the fatal doctrine that the end justifies the means.

Her response touches on the theme of sexuality and love in the novel. The principle, articulated by Winston but embodied in Julia, is that sex ". . . was a blow struck against the Party. It was a political act." Julia is a hedonist, to be sure, but she is also a pragmatist, personally courageous, appropriately distrustful of abstract ideology. Thus, she falls asleep listening to Winston reading aloud from Goldstein's book. But, as John Newsinger points out, here she is a model for the many readers who skip this section of the book, some no doubt, even having trouble with the title "The Theory and Practice of Oligarchical Collectivism."

It is not clear that O'Brien is telling the truth when he claims to have been one of its authors. It would be consistent with his tendency to assert that the party is always one jump ahead of its enemies. Goldstein's treatise is, as Winston discovers, an admirably clear example of *how* the party maintains its power, but on the brink of discovering "the central secret," the *why*, Winston stops reading and falls asleep. It is left to O'Brien to reveal that secret—power—or "power for power's sake." But O'Brien has a distinctive definition of power: "Power is in tearing human minds to pieces and putting them together again in shapes of your own choosing . . . power is not power over things but over men." For some readers, that answer leads to a deeply pessimistic conclusion. If power hunger is rooted in human nature, then despair would seem to be the logical reaction. Richard Rorty offers another possibility. He maintains that in O'Brien, Orwell is giving us a picture of the function of the intellectual in a future totalitarian state. For Rorty, the "central sentence of *1984* is O'Brien's statement 'the object of torture is torture.' That is, given the conditions operative in a state like Oceania, the only satisfaction available to a master of doublethink such as O'Brien is to engage non-doublethinkers with a similar intellectual orientation, in order to feel the pleasure of twisting and breaking the special, hidden, tender parts of a mind with the same gifts of his own" (187). Rorty maintains that "the last third of *1984* is about torturing, not about being tortured" (180).

Another extraordinary example of the continuing relevance of *Nineteen Eighty-Four,* is that the subject of torture, long delegated to peripheral organizations like Amnesty International, as restricted to despotic third-world governments, should reemerge as a tactic and topic of discussion, as a tool in allegedly furthering the goal of spreading democracy.

Rorty's interesting argument notwithstanding, many critics have seen the last part of the book, beginning with the arrest of Winston and Julia, as seriously flawed. Orwell himself agreed in a letter responding to a review of the book by Julian Symons: "You were right of course about the vulgarity of the 'Room 101' business, but I didn't know another way of getting somewhere near the effect I wanted." The question that emerges from that quotation relates to Orwell's intention. The presumed answer is to demonstrate how the party can get inside individuals, to transform them in thought as well as in deed.

The other attack on thought is through the manipulation of public language, and for that reason the novel has two endings: One focusing on the ravaged face of Winston and the other, near the conclusion of the Newspeak Appendix, when the anonymous author quotes the opening of the Declaration of Independence, indicating that the author of the appendix was living in a world where the Newspeak project has not succeeded and the principles of democracy were still alive.

CONTEMPORARY REVIEWS

In an early review, appearing soon after the publication date, the poet and critic Julian Symons began by making a distinction between novels that focus on interrelationships among characters and those that focus on "ideas about life and society." Orwell, he goes on to say, is clearly a novelist of ideas. Although he deplored the "school boyish sensationalism" of the torture scenes, Symons concluded with a tribute to the courage and intelligence which Orwell brought to questions concerning "the nature of reality and the terrors of power" (257). Within a week of the review's publication, Orwell wrote to Symons, thanking him and agreeing with him "about the vulgarity of the 'Room 101' business. I was aware of this while writing it, but I didn't know another way of getting near the effect I wanted" (Meyers, 251). From *The New Statesman and Nation,* whose editor, Kingsley Martin, was an enemy who had written a dismissive review of *Animal Farm,* Orwell might have anticipated a negative review. Instead, the reviewer V. S. PRITCHETT pulled out all the rhetorical stops: "I do not think I have ever read a novel more frightening and depressing and, yet, such are the originality, the suspense, the speed of writing and withering indignation that it is impossible to put the book down" (291). On the other hand, a reviewer for *Pravda,* I. Anisimov, denounced it as a "filthy book," one of many books written by "a whole army of venal writers . . . on the orders and instigation of Wall Street" (282).

In America, *Nineteen Eighty-Four* was reviewed in the *New Yorker* by Lionel Trilling and by his wife, Diana, in the *Nation.* Lionel Trilling's piece zeroed in on the "mystique of power" as the book's central target. Diana, on the other hand, while praising the book's brilliant conception, recorded her reservations about "something in the book's temper, its fierceness of tone and in the enormous pressure it exerts upon the reader" (261). Another prominent figure among "the New York intellectuals," Philip Rahv, chose to review the book at length in *Partisan Review,* calling it "far and away the best of Orwell's books." The only problem he saw in the book is that O'Brien's "power for power's sake" explanation seemed unrealistic in terms of O'Brien's psychology. He maintained that the Inner Party members would have to cling, as Dostoevsky's Grand Inquisitor does, to some more noble rationalization.

As to the literature-politics divide, all the reviewers acknowledged its literary flaws, but all pointed out that its greatness rested on its moral and political passion, not on its aesthetic achievement. Pritchett's comment ("He is the most devastating pamphleteer alive . . .") represents the ambivalence, giving Orwell the highest praise as a political writer, but not as a novelist.

SUBSEQUENT CRITICISM

Political interpretations of *Nineteen Eighty-Four* begin with its first reader, Orwell's publisher FREDRIC WARBURG. Warburg's prepublication memo to his staff describes the novel ". . . as a deliberate and sadistic attack on socialism and socialist parties generally. . . . It is worth a cool million votes to the Conservative Party" (104). In his memoir, written three decades later, Warburg regretted this remark, asserting that Orwell certainly did not intend it to be an attack on socialism. Warburg's first reaction derived in part from Orwell's use of Ingsoc as the name of the book's tyrannical ruling party. Orwell explained that the name *socialism* had provided a convenient umbrella term for such totalitarian entities as the Nazi (National Socialist) Party and the Union of Soviet Socialist Republics. But at the same time, he conceded that any highly centralized, collectivist form of government was vulnerable to the danger of totalitarianism. And, as he did in *Animal Farm,* he chose the Stalinist regime in Russia as his principal model, even while setting the novel in an England degraded to the status of "Airstrip One," an outpost of the Oceania Empire, whose real power center is indicated by the fact that the dollar is the basic currency. Orwell's broader point was that totalitarianism, already a given in Stalin's Russia, was a looming threat throughout a world learning "to live with the bomb."

But in the United States, the distinction between anti-Stalinism and antisocialism was generally lost or deliberately obscured. A *Life* magazine article summarized the book as "the cruel fate of man in a regimented left-wing police state which controls his mind" (Rodden, 26). At the other end of the spectrum, in England, the antisocialist view was reinforced by the far Left, many of whom also viewed the book as an attack on socialism. The well-known biographer of Trotsky and Stalin, Isaac Deutscher, saw it as an anticommunist tract, "an ideological super-weapon in the Cold War" (333), and spoke of "its underlying boundless despair" (342). Deutscher went on to impugn Orwell's integrity, asserting that he had plagiarized elements of Eugene Zamyatin's *We* (see "Sources," above).

The word *despair* reappeared regularly in criticism of the book. Underlying this view was the assumption that pessimism represents a flaw in a writer, a judgment that would condemn a number of the 20th century's greatest writers, such as Franz Kafka, Eugene O'Neil, and Samuel Beckett. But in a strictly political sense, pessimism is often viewed, at least on the Left, as a reinforcement of the status quo, a turning away from the possibilities of a progressive improvement in the struggle for justice and equality. In Orwell's work, that view is probably best expressed in the character of Benjamin the Donkey in *Animal Farm,* who views all change as a mirage disguising the fact that society is always made up of the dominators and the dominated. Benjamin's stance is a form of the "quietism" that Orwell ambivalently rejected in his discussion of HENRY MILLER in *Inside the Whale.*

This is the view put forth by Raymond Williams, who argued that "the warning that the world could be going that way [toward totalitarianism] became . . . an imaginative submission to its inevitability." Williams's point is that Orwell was guilty of the same thinking he criticized in JAMES BURNHAM, assuming that the present is an absolute guide to the future.

Alex Zwerdling's more nuanced view argues that the pessimistic strain is a result of Orwell's partial reliance on the argument of James Burnham, who maintained that the spread of totalitarianism was inevitable (see "Sources," above). For Zwerdling, Orwell always wrestled with the conflict of despair versus hope. He sees Orwell's hope as being based upon the belief that ". . . democratic societies can prevent the triumph of totalitarian methods," but it would be extremely difficult, if not impossible, to destroy totalitarianism after "it has established itself." Zwerdling concluded that Orwell may have been "sanguine about prevention but hopeless about cure" (106).

Orwell was writing in a democratic society, and his book served as a warning to that society: what might happen if the people, like the animals in *Animal Farm,* allowed tyranny to develop, even in its earliest stages. As for a future socialism of the ideal type he once believed in, Zwerdling suggests Orwell was, in fact, pessimistic. But his pessimism gave birth to a more realistic socialism after his death, one based on the need to confront the threat of power-hunger that seems to be inherent in human beings. John Newsinger's *Orwell's Politics* Looks at the question of Orwell's "despair" by acknowledging the defeat of Winston but then considers whether Winston's hope vested in the proles offsets his defeat, making the reader-oriented point: "these beliefs [in the ultimate triumph of socialistic ideals] inform the book but one suspects that their resonance very much reflects the extent to which the reader is in sympathy with them" (Newsinger, 129).

The critic Patrick Reilly takes a similar tack in declaring that Orwell is employing "a strategic despair . . . hope and salvation are not within the text because Orwell means us to seek those in the street not in the study . . . the text despairs so that we will not presume" (Reilly, 124–125).

A recent example of the continuing political relevance of *Nineteen Eighty-Four* is James Decker's treatment of the novel. Decker begins by reminding readers that the United States and the West in general are also targets of the satire. Oceania is clearly a projection of an American empire, indicating that the totalitarian threat exists independently of any particular ideology. Decker then moves to a consideration of the "end of history" concept generated by the historian Francis Fukuyama in the 1990s. After the collapse of the Soviet Union, Fukuyama argued that the triumph of liberal democracy over communism marked the beginning of the universal acceptance of democracy, vested in the principal of individual desire. The result will be a global utopia free of ideological strife. Decker argues that Orwell saw this possibility but recognized in it a fatal flaw that ". . . damages the very essence of humanity and transforms life into a perfunctory trudge toward undifferentiated existence" (Decker, 163). Orwell's warning of totalitarianism implicitly contains a recognition of the ongoing need for a society that fosters resistance.

There is an inevitable overlap between the political and the literary in the critical history of *Nineteen Eighty-Four,* where the traditional questions of plot, character, and style merge into considerations of theme. In that respect, very few critics approach the novel from an exclusively aesthetic or formalist perspective. An exception is Harold Bloom, who does not so much discuss *Nineteen Eighty-Four* as dismiss it. (Although in *The Western Canon* [1994] he includes *Nineteen Eighty-Four* and Orwell's essays [but not *Animal Farm*] in his appendix (p. 555) designating "canonical" modern works.) Nevertheless, Bloom has edited several critical collections on the novel and on Orwell, containing a number of excellent literary and political essays, in which his own introductions seem to recognize that the aesthetic is not the only standard, although it may be the most important, by which to judge *Nineteen Eighty-Four.*

Many contemporary critics recognize that *Nineteen Eighty-Four* is a satirical political novel, a hybrid requiring attention both to the political and the rhetorical features. The rhetorical elements refer to the techniques Orwell employs in order to heighten the consciousness of the reader. As with the other novels, an excellent example of the dual-focused approach to *Nineteen Eighty-Four* is GEORGE WOODCOCK. A lifelong politically committed anarchist, Woodcock was also a friend of Orwell's, but, equally important, he was a sensitive and perceptive literary critic. His treatment of *Nineteen Eighty-Four* concedes that Winston and Julia have been absorbed into the death-in-life, generated by O'Brien and the Party. Although Orwell stresses the strength and pervasiveness of the love of power, he maintains that the reader becomes aware of the satirical element in the portrait of O'Brien. Woodcock sees in O'Brien's confidence in the immortality of power an echo of Hitler's "boasts of the Millennial Reich," which three years earlier had fallen away into ashes . . ." (175). *Nineteen Eighty-Four* is, first of all, a satire on the world of 1948, with its built-in utopian tendencies. . . . and it is also a warning about a danger in the future. . . . "The hidden truth . . . that the love of power is stronger and more pervasive than any material or economic motive." (Woodcock, 174–175). The terms *satire* and *warning* have come to dominate criticism of the novel as opposed to the more popular, though never intended, *prophecy.*

In *Orwell's Fiction* (1969), Robert Lee announces his intention to treat Orwell as a "novelist" rather than a political commentator, but he wisely realizes that "one must consider the significance of the theme of the work." Lee sees "corrupted languages" as Orwell's supreme theme. He argues that the worst fate an individual can undergo is "the loss of consciousness—and Orwell specifically defines this as a result of the failure of language" (Lee, 155). Thus he sees the appendix, "The Principles of Newspeak," as the culmination of Orwell's dark view of the future.

In calling attention to the appendix on Newspeak and the fact that it is written in the past tense, Lee anticipated the views of recent studies that look at the appendix, not as a simple add-on but as a resolution to a novel that only seems to conclude with the words *the end.*

Anthony Stewart's treatment of the novel focuses on the Orwellian value of "decency," a moral characteristic. Stewart argues that the novel expresses finally a "mitigated optimism" (165), resting on three elements in the conclusion. Two relate to the appendix and the fact that it is written in the past tense, implying the failure of the effort of the party to perpetuate itself. Secondly, Stewart quotes Andrew Kennedy's comment on the built-in contradiction evident in the word *Newspeak* (Kennedy, 81). Kennedy's analysis is notable, also, as one of those rare items, a "theorized" critical study that is readable. His subtitle, "Deconstructing *1984*" explains his methodology: to show the internal contradictions in the text. One example is the statue of Cromwell in Victory Square. Earlier, we were told that all existing statues had been altered so that no one could read history from them. For Carl Freedman, the book exhibits an internal conflict of genres: the novel and a programmatic satire, which Orwell was unable to resolve, expressing itself politically as the conflict between activist political commitment and "quietist despair" (Freedman, 91). In her book-length study of the novel *The Orwell Conundrum* (1994), Erika Gottlieb concludes her argument that Orwell is affirming his faith in the ultimate triumph of "the spirit of man." with references to Newspeak. By destroying the word through the introduction of Newspeak, the Party makes "free thought" no longer a "deadly sin," only a "meaningless abstraction." As a result, the destruction of language must also eliminate the entire concept of heresy on which O'Brien depends for the exercise of his power (Gottlieb, 284–285) Here again, the Newspeak appendix emerges as a central issue in determing the meaning of the novel.

INFLUENCE

Orwell believed that "all literature is political," but he also acknowledged that some is more overtly political than other literature, and he certainly included *Animal Farm* and *Nineteen Eighty-Four* in that category. But he never imagined that these two works would have the powerful impact they did, an impact that was not only political but broadly social and cultural. As a result, in the avalanche of commentary that *Nineteen Eighty-Four* has provoked, there lies ample evidence to suggest that it is the most influential novel of the 20th century. In discussing the meaning, significance, and value of the work, literary critics have shared the stage with historians, political commentators, sociologists, psychologists, legal experts, philosophers, theologians, and linguists, all taking the novel's measure from their particular perspectives.

To this has been added the fact that *Nineteen Eighty-Four,* largely as a result of its "required reading" status in high school and college curricula, has emerged as "a linchpin of popular culture." From rock bands, whose repertoires are certain to include at least one reference to the book, to Big Brother T-shirts, the novel has secured a seemingly permanent place among the world of young adults. And not only in England and the United States, but in many countries in Europe and Asia. (A notable exception: Myanmar [Orwell's Burma], where it has been banned by the military dictators of that unhappy nation.) Its popularity raises an interesting hypothetical question: What would Orwell, whose essays on popular culture pioneered that field of study, have made of the popular phenomenon of *Nineteen Eighty-Four?*

With the fall of the Soviet Union, Orwell's principal but not sole target, the interest in the book might have reverted to the literary world, but that has not been the case. As the editors of a recent, largely nonliterary essay collection (*On Nineteen Eighty-Four: Orwell and Our Future* [2005]) have put it, "Orwell did not lose his power with the collapse of the Soviet system. Indeed, the new era of ever vigilant technology seemed to give new relevance to his ideas just when their specific political occasion had apparently vanished . . ." (Gleason, Nussbaum, 1). As its title suggests, the anthology's contributors deal with the question of what, if any, light *Nineteen Eighty-Four* sheds on the future development of issues as wide-ranging as the objectivity of truth, torture as a political weapon, thought control, technology, the invasion of privacy, and the relation of sexual repression to political repression, specifically the repression of women.

Clearly, the original source of the novel's enormous influence was the common tendency, particularly in the United States, to regard it as a prophecy. Orwell had specifically disavowed this "prophetic" interpretation in a press release he dictated from his hospital bed to his publisher Fredric Warburg. Warburg's notes read as follows: "I don't think *1984* is what will happen—but I do think, allowing for the fact that the book being parody, that something like it could happen . . . moral is, don't let it happen" (Warburg, 118). But Orwell's qualifications were overwhelmed by the sense that the book was predicting a future near at hand. Since 1984 was within the range of most reader's lifetimes, the accuracy of its so-called predictions would be easily verifiable. Critical in this respect was the book's title, providing not just a "near future" but a specific date. As a result, it took on a life of its own. The year 1984 became "an all-purpose target date" (Rodden, 258), as if it would mark an historical watershed. Indeed, a few religious groups viewed the date as confirming a biblical apocalypse, seeing August 1984 as the date set for the end of the world. Some Jewish Kabbalists, operating from the fact that in the Hebrew calendar 1984 corresponds to 5744 and that in the Kabbalist letter-for-number system, 5744 spelled out the word *destruction,* feared a similar final calamity (Rodden, 259–262).

When the fatal year came and went in pedestrian fashion, the prophetic interpretation receded in significance but was not completely dismissed. Two places where that lessening of interest did not occur were West and East Germany. Rodden provides an interesting account of German writers' reaction to Orwell and *Nineteen Eighty-Four.* Reading it surreptitiously right after *Animal Farm,* East Germans generally looked at Oceania as a portrait of their present condition; West German writers made similar connections, while at first repressing comparisons to Hitler's Germany. Two decades later, a new generation proved more open to acknowledging the novel's relevance to the Nazi regime while at the same time shifting their focus to the threat that technological progress represented for a democratic society. One German writer who repeatedly called attention to the peril of forgetting the ideological-historical context of *Nineteen Eighty-Four* was Gunther Grass. "It was Grass who described the 1980s as 'The Orwell Decade'" (Rodden, 301–303). Grass's recent self-revelation of his own past adds a piquant note to his reaction to the novel.

The story of how *Nineteen Eighty-Four* entered and altered the popular imagination of England, the United States, and, in a more restricted but perhaps more powerful way, eastern Europe during the cold war, has been successfully recorded in two books by John Rodden, *The Politics of Reputation* (1989) and *Scenes from an Afterlife: The Legacy of George Orwell* (2003). Rodden's accounts deal with the phenomenal growth of Orwell's reputation (or mythification) as a whole, but not surprisingly, *Nineteen Eighty-Four* plays the major role in that process.

Nineteen Eighty-Four first sounded a responsive chord along a broad range of Anglo-American culture. The original response was rooted in the fear of totalitarianism in general and communism or, more precisely, Stalinism, in particular. As with *Animal Farm,* the roles played by the British Information Research Department (IRD) and the American Central Intelligence Agency (CIA) were significant but by no means crucial in the achievement of that popularity. In one case, the CIA-sponsored 1954 film of the novel was a failure, both commercially and as a propaganda weapon, while the nonideological BBC television production in the same year attracted what at the time was the largest audience in the history of British television. The BBC production created a perfect storm of controversy, not over its political message but on account of the brutality of its torture scenes and the candor of its sexual scenes. The upshot of this controversy was a series of debates in Parliament. Here, too, the debates centered not on politics but on topics such as "Orwell, the novel, broadcasting censorship, and the lines between television violence and criminal behavior" (Shaw, 155). Thus, *Nineteen Eighty-Four* first surfaced among the "acknowledged legislators," ironically enough in relation to three issues that might be peripheral in the novel, but happened to be subjects of interest to Orwell: torture, representations of violence in popular culture, and censorship. Here was an early example of what has consistently been true in speaking of the influence of this work—how issues that appear in the background of the novel later emerged as significant in the culture and which the novel helps to clarify.

Thus when the Nobel Prize–winning economist Kenneth Arrow discusses "the economics of *Nineteen Eighty-Four,*" he brings a fresh viewpoint, looking at such seemingly inevitable drawbacks as unemployment under capitalism and shortages of goods under socialism. Although both systems have their inequities, capitalism has shown more flexibility. Socialism's challenge is to decentralize economic control, and by that standard, "the economy of *Nineteen Eighty-Four* is a miserable failure . . . Orwell caught beautifully certain trends imminent in our world and exposed them without complications" (Arrow, 45, 47). In "The Death of Pity," the philosopher Martha Nussbaum focuses on the "embracing maternal arm" in Winston's dreams and the "death of pity" not only in the novel, but in the post–September 11 posture of America in relation to the rest of the world.

One of the most chilling examples of the "misuse" of *Nineteen Eighty-Four* emerges in the accounts written by the prominent Stanford social psychologist Philip Zimbardo. In two long articles, written two decades apart, Zimbardo makes a strong case for his thesis that Jim Jones, leader of the of 1978 Jonestown experiment, which culminated in the mass suicide of more than 900 of its followers, "modeled his mind control tactics directly on those he learned from George Orwell's handbook for mind-controllers *Nineteen Eighty-Four*" (Zimbardo, 146). According to a former member of Jones's inner circle, "Jim talked about *Nineteen Eighty-Four* all the time." The group's leading entertainer composed and wrote a song titled "Nineteen Eighty Four," which was a Jones favorite. Zimbardo recounts the total mind control exercised by Jones in Jonestown. One example, echoing Winston's rat torture, occurred when a Jones follower confessed to a fear of snakes. He later was punished by being stripped and bound, so that snakes might crawl over him. Zimbardo suggests that as Jones treated Orwell's warning as an "operations manual," the Bush administration has "taken another leaf from Orwell," both in the conception and conduct of the Iraq war as illustrated by its manipulation of language and the scandal of Abu Ghraib prison. He concludes with a direct question: "Dear Mr. Orwell, did you really have to get so much right on what is proven so wrong for America?" (Zimbardo, 154). From this point of view, Orwell's warning has turned out to be something of a prophecy after all.

CHARACTERS

Ampleforth A colleague of Winston's at the Ministry of Truth. Winston encounters Ampleforth in prison, to which Ampleforth has been consigned. His crime: While preparing a Newspeak edition of RUDYARD KIPLING, he had not changed the word *God* in the original text because he needed a rhyme for *Rod.*

Big Brother The all-knowing, all-seeing, all-powerful leader of Oceania. Big Brother's appearance takes two forms. The first is as the face on enormous posters that dominate the city of London, posters on which the eyes of Big Brother seem to follow you as you move. The other appearance is on the telescreen at the climax of the Two-Minute Hate sections. As the hated Goldstein's face recedes, Big Brother's appears, saying something reassuring although the actual words cannot be heard. His appearance provokes a rapturous, religiously intense response followed by the the rythmic chanting of "B-B! B-B!" that Winston regards as subhuman. Goldstein's forbidden book asserts that Big Brother does not actually exist. He is a symbol that embodies the Party.

Bumstead A prisoner in the Ministry of Truth who is viciously beaten after he tries to give a crust of bread to another prisoner, who is starving. He shares the last name of Dagwood Bumstead a character in the cartoon and film series *Blondie.* Orwell reviewed a *Blondie* film during his stint as a film reviewer from 1940–41. Dagwood was famous for his midnight snack, which always consisted of an enormous sandwich.

Charrington, Mr. The proprietor of an antique junk shop, who appears to be a frail, aged man in his sixties. In his shop, Winston purchases a blank book, which he uses as a diary. He returns, buying a domed paperweight, and he examines a furnished room above the shop. The two men seem to share a reverence for the past, and Charrington agrees to rent out his room to Winston and Julia. Upon their arrest in the upstairs room, Winston discovers that Charrington is a young, fierce 35-year-old officer in the Thought Police.

Goldstein, Emmanuel A semimythical figure who functions as the all-purpose scapegoat for INGSOC propaganda. He is described as having "a long Jewish face, with a great fuzzy aureole of white hair and a small goatee beard . . ." He was a prominent member of the party, who betrayed its principles and is living in exile somewhere. In these details, he is clearly modeled, as is the character Snowball in *Animal Farm,* on the Russian revolutionary LEON TROTSKY. Goldstein has apparently written an attack on the party, *The Theory and Practice of Oligarchical Collectivism,* which Winston reads. The equivalent book by Trotsky was *The Revolution Betrayed* (1936). Winston is told later that the book he has read is a forgery, written by O'Brien and other members of the inner party.

Jones, Aaronson, and Rutherford A trio of disgraced former members of the inner party, who were arrested in 1965, confessed to their crime and waited out their inevitable execution sitting in front of a chess board at the Chestnut Tree Café. Eventually they were rearrested and executed. Winston once saw a newspaper photograph of the three men in New York at an international convention. The date of the newspaper corresponded to the testimony of the three men that they were in Siberia plotting with Goldstein on that date. The fate of the men clearly parodies the Stalinist purge trials of the 1930s.

Julia The girl from the Fiction Department at the Ministry of Truth, with whom Winston has a passionate, doomed love affair. She is described as an attractive, "bold looking girl of about twenty-seven, with thick dark hair, a freckled face, and swift, athletic movements." On the surface she is a zealous member of the Anti-Sex League and an obstreperous participant in the Two-Minute Hate sessions. In fact, however, she is a "rebel from the waist down," sexually promiscuous and filled with contempt for the party's discipline, very skillful in covering her tracks for secret trysts with Winston. A true hedonist, she is not interested in history or politics but in the love that develops between her and Winston. When the two are captured and separately tortured, each betrays the other, effectively killing the love they shared. After release from prison, they encounter each other in a park, two hollowed-out strangers anxious to be rid of one another. In some respects, Julia is thought to be modeled on Orwell's second wife, Sonia Brownell Orwell, who was in her youth a sexual rebel against her repressive Catholic boarding-school background.

Martin O'Brien's inscrutable servant, who brings in the wine and joins the group after O'Brien assures Winston and Julia that "Martin is one of us."

O'Brien A powerful member of the Inner Party, whose bearing and intellect exert an almost hypnotic effect on Winston. O'Brien arranges to have Winston visit his flat, thereby hinting that he supports Winston's opposition to the party. When Winston and Julia arrive at his house, they declare their true feelings and ask to be recruited into the underground movement known as the Brotherhood. O'Brien welcomes them as new recruits and tells Winston that he will soon receive surreptitiously a copy of Emmanuel Goldstein's forbidden book.

When, after his arrest, Winston first sees O'Brien, he thinks that O'Brien has been arrested as well, only to discover that his mentor will be his chief torturer, who will bring about Winston's "cure," which consists in bringing him to the point of loving Big Brother. The importance of O'Brien in the novel is strikingly asserted by the philosopher Richard Rorty. "After Winston and Julia go to O'Brien's apartment, *Nineteen Eighty-Four* becomes a book about O'Brien, not about twentieth century totalitarian states" (171). In other words, O'Brien represents what the intellectual might become in a future totalitarian world. In this respect, he is, in Rorty's opinion, "as terrifying a character as we are likely to meet in a book" (183).

Parsons, Mr. Winston's colleague at the Ministry of Truth and neighbor at Victory Mansions. Parsons is a zealous party member who works tirelessly on the preparations for Hate Week. He is arrested by the Thought Police when his young daughter hears him muttering anti–Big Brother slogans in his sleep. Parsons' devotion to the party is so total that he is proud of his daughter for betraying him.

Parsons, Mrs. A harried housewife and mother who asks her neighbor Winston to unclog a drainpipe in her kitchen. Mrs. Parsons is memorably described as giving "the impression that she has dust in the creases of her face." She is intimidated by her two vicious children, who belong to the police spies, which encourages them to report any politically incorrect behavior on the part of their parents.

Skull-faced man An anonymous prisoner in the Ministry of Love. He is starving to death, and when another prisoner, Bumstead, tries to give him a crust of bread, guards rush in and beat Bumstead. Then they inform the skull-faced man that they are taking him to Room 101, whereupon the man becomes hysterical, screaming that he would rather watch his wife and three children have their throats cut than to go to Room 101. According to Bernard Crick, this scene "verges on the ludicrous" (Crick, 38).

Smith, Katharine The separated wife of Winston, a woman who has been shaped by the party's puritanical repression of sex. Despite her frigidity, she insists that she and Winston have regular joyless intercourse since it is her "duty to the party" to produce children. By mutual agreement, the two live separately.

Smith, Winston An employee in the Records Department of the Ministry of Truth, whose work consists of revising and rewriting records and previously published reports, bringing them into conformity with the current thinking of the ruling party. At 39, Winston is an unprepossessing, frail figure, bothered by an ulcerated vein in his ankle and a persistent chest cough. Despite his frailty, Winston has taken a decisive step in opposition to the prevailing government. He has started to keep a diary. In addition, he begins an affair with a fellow employee, Julia, who shares his detestation of the party. Both are aware that it is only a matter of time before they will be arrested and killed, but they persist, thanks to Winston's discovery of a convenient trysting place above an old junk shop. Acting on hints given to Winston by O'Brien, a high-ranking government official, the lovers visit O'Brien's home and announce their intention to join the antigovernment underground. Deceived into thinking O'Brien is on their side, they are later arrested. In jail, Winston is tortured and lectured to by O'Brien, who explains that the party is motivated by one goal, power for the sake of power, and that the instrument of power is torture. Winston and Julia are both broken and reconstituted as empty shells. Finally, Winston succumbs to the condition that O'Brien has been driving him to: loving Big Brother.

Syme A colleague of Winston in the Ministry of Truth, Syme is a linguist, employed in the construction of the definitive edition of the Newspeak Dictionary, which, when completed, will render a discussion of heretical ideas impossible. Syme is enthusiastic about the progress of Newspeak and its capacity to "narrow thought." Syme speaks eloquently and intelligently about his project, but Winston thinks that he is too intelligent not to run afoul of the authorities. Shortly after his discussion, it becomes clear that Syme has been vaporized.

Tillotson A colleague of Winston at the Ministry of Truth who sometimes receives the same assignment, so that there exists a rivalry between them.

FILM AND TELEVISION ADAPTATIONS

Nineteen Eighty-Four (1953) American TV adaptation aired on September 21, 1953. This was an hour-long version, part of the CBS "Studio One" series. The cast included Eddie Albert as Winston, Lorne Greene as O'Brien, and Norma Crane as Julia. The adaptation was by William Templeton, directed by Paul Wickell, and produced by Felix Jackson. This presentation is powerful and straightforward, with no attempt to lighten the mood or suggest an optimistic theme. The *New Yorker* critic Philip Hamburger characterized the effect as "stunning," praising the setting and the acting, citing in particular Norma Crane's Julia, who "made me . . . believe that she was fighting literally for the very right to think and breathe and remain human amid the terrors of Oceania. . . ." (85).

Nineteen Eighty-Four (1954) BBC television adaptation that premiered on December 12, 1954. This version was adapted by Nigel Kneale, produced and directed by Rudolph Cartier. It included Peter Cushing as Winston, Andre Morell as O'Brien, Yvonne Mitchell as Julia, and Donald Pleasance as Syme.

This production first aired on a Sunday evening, a time when families watched television together, and created a furor in the press and among the public, the controversy finally reaching Parliament. Large numbers of viewers were horrified by the violence of the torture scenes and, to a lesser degree, shocked by the sensuality of the love scenes. The play was shown again four days later, attracting what was, at that time, the largest audience ever for a BBC drama. It was the first time the British public was confronted with the peculiar power of television: in effect, to carry the world's evil into their homes.

A slightly revised form of the 1954 version was aired in 1965, which had such a mild effect, it left commentators wondering what all the fuss had been about 11 years earlier.

1984 (1956) The first film version of the novel, produced in 1956, distributed by Columbia Pictures, adapted by William Templeton and Ralph Bettinson, directed by Michael Anderson, and produced by J. Peter Rathson. Cast included Edmond O'Brien as Winston, Michael Redgrave as O'Brien (renamed O'Connor in this production, which already had an O'Brien in the lead role), and Jan Sterling as Julia.

This production was hamstrung from the beginning by producers interested primarily in a commercial success. They insisted on shooting a "happy ending" as well as Orwell's. The "happy" version was designed for an American audience. It depicted Winston and Julia dying in each others arms, riddled with bullets, shouting, "Down with Big Brother!" (Rodden, 284). Michael Redgrave's appearance in the O'Brien role later took on an ironic twist with the revelation that his name appeared in ORWELL'S LIST. Despite the changes, the film was neither a commercial nor critical success. Sonia Orwell was so incensed by this production that she withdrew it and the two other *Nineteen Eighty-Four* films as of the mid-1970s.

Nineteen Eighty-Four (1984) Virgin Films Production, written and directed by Michael Radford. This production is generally regarded as the most successful adaptation of the novel. The cast included John Hurt as Winston, Richard Burton (in his last screen role) as O'Brien, Susanna Hamilton as Julia, and Cyril Cusack as Charrington.

Although widely regarded as the most effective and sophisticated of the film adaptations, this version also encountered internal obstacles. The producers, Virgin Films, insisted on hiring a rock group, the Eurythmics, to provide the film's musical background. The director, Michael Radford, had already commissioned a score, composed by Dominic Muldowney. The producers, however, exercised their "final cut" rights and combined the two scores. As a result, there exist different versions of the original with different musical scores.

In comparing the 1956 and 1984 versions, Erika Gottlieb argues that both films fall short of the novel, each one grasping half of the Orwellian whole—the 1956 version concentrates on the political dimension, and the 1984 focuses on the psychological drama. As a result, neither one captured the novel's insight that "the fatal threat implied in the *political* nightmare of totalitarianism is the indiviudal's inevitable and irrevocable

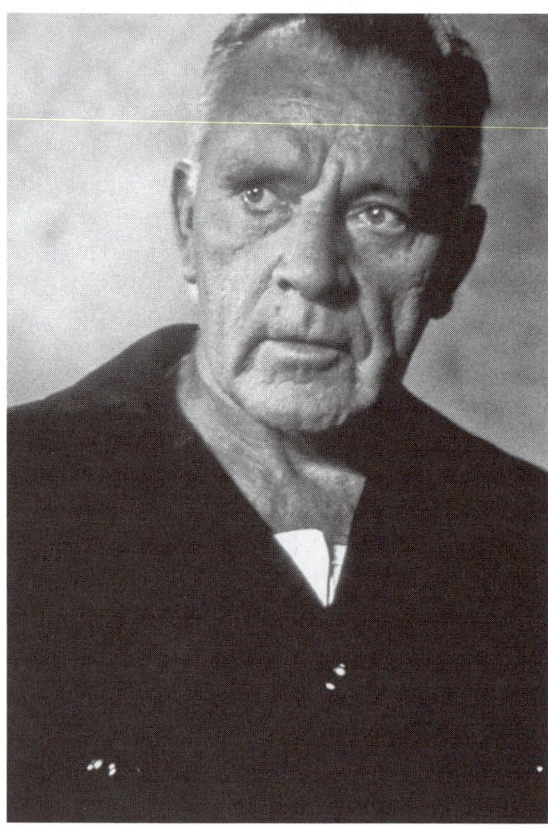

Richard Burton (as O'Brien) in a still from Michael Radford's film adaptation of *Nineteen Eighty-Four* *(Photofest)*

psychic disintegration" (Gottlieb, 259). Gottlieb takes a stern view of the 1984 director/adapter Michael Radford, accusing him of condescending to the book, which he described as "a political essay with a melodrama attached and some cardboard minor characters" (quoted by Gottlieb, 261). She concludes that while both versions fail to realize the full complexity of the work, the 1956 version hews more closely to the novel than the "deconstructed" 1984 version.

WORKS CITED

Anisimov, Isaac. Review. In *George Orwell: The Critical Heritage,* edited by Jeffrey Meyers, 282–283. London: Routledge, 1975.

Bloom, Harold, ed. *George Orwell's 1984.* New York: Chelsea House, 1987.

———. *George Orwell's 1984.* Updated Edition. New York: Chelsea House, 2007.

———. *The Western Canon.* New York: Harcourt Brace, 1994.

Crick, Bernard. "Reading *Nineteen Eighty-Four* as Satire." In *Reflections on America, 1984: An Orwell Symposum,* edited by Robert Mulvihill, 15–45. Athens: University of Georgia Press, 1986.

Decker, James. "George Orwell's *1984* and Political Ideology." In *George Orwell.* Updated edition. Blooms Modern Critical Views, edited by Harold Bloom, 133–144. New York Chelsea House, 2007.

Deutscher, Isaac. "*1984*—The Mysticism of Cruelty." In *Orwell's* Nineteen Eighty-Four, edited by Irving Howe, 332–343. New York: Harcourt Brace, 1982.

Gleason, Abbott, Jack Goldsmith, and Martha C. Nussbaum. *On* Nineteen Eighty-Four. Princeton, N.J.: Princeton University Press, 2005.

Gottlieb, Erika. *The Orwell Conundrum.* Ottawa: Carleton University Press, 1992.

———. "Orwell's Satirical Vision on the Screen: The Film Versions of *Animal Farm* and *Nineteen Eighty-Four.*" In *George Orwell: Into the Twenty-Fist Century,* edited by Thomas Cushman and John Rodden, 252–263. Boulder, Colo.: Paradigm, 2004.

Hamburger, Philip. "*Television: 1984.*" *New Yorker,* October 3, 1953, 84–85.

Howe, Irving. *Orwell's* Nineteen Eighty-Four: *Text, Sources and Criticism,* 2nd ed. New York: Harcourt, Brace, 1982.

Kennedy, Alan. "The Inversion of Form: Deconstructing *1984.*" In *George Orwell: New Casebook Series,* edited by Graham Holderness, Bryan Loughrey, and Nahem Yousaf. New York: St. Martin's, 1998.

Lee, Robert. *Orwell's Fiction.* Notre Dame, Ind.: Notre Dame University Press, 1968.

Lewis, Peter. *George Orwell: The Road to 1984.* New York: Harcourt Brace, 1981.

Mellor, Anne K. "You're Only a Rebel from the Waist Downwards: Orwell's View of Women." In *Nineteen Eighty-Four,* edited by Peter Stansky, 115–125. New York: W. H. Freeman, 1983.

Meyers, Jeffrey, ed. *George Orwell: The Critical Heritage.* London: Routledge, 1975.

Newsinger, John. *Orwell's Politics.* New York; London: St. Martin's Press, Macmillan Press, 1999.

Pritchett, V. S. Review of *1984*. In *Orwell's* Nineteen Eighty-Four, edited by Irving Howe, 291–292. New York: Harcourt, Brace, 1982.

Reilly, Patrick. Nineteen Eighty-Four: *Past, Present and Future.* Boston: Twayne 1989.

Rahv, Philip. "The Unfuture of Utopia." In *Orwell's* Nineteen Eighty-Four: *Text, Sources and Criticism,* 2nd ed., edited by Irving House, 310–316. New York: Harcourt Brace, 1982.

Rodden, John. *The Politics of Literary Reputation.* New York: Oxford University Press, 1989.

Rorty, Richard. *Contingency, Irony, and Solidarity.* Cambridge: Cambridge University Press, 1989.

Rose, Jonathan. "The Invisible Sources of *Nineteen Eighty-Four.*" In *The Revised Orwell,* edited by Jonathan Rose, 131–147. East Lansing, Mich.: 1992.

Shaw, Tony. "Some Writers Are More Equal Than Others: George Orwell, the State and Cold War Priviledge." *Cold War History* 4, no. 1 (October, 2003): 143–170.

Steinhoff, William. *George Orwell and the Literary Origins of* 1984. Ann Arbor: University of Michigan Press, 1975.

Stewart, Anthony. The *George Orwell and the Value of Decency.* New York: Routledge, 2003.

Symons, Julian. *1984.* In *George Orwell: The Critical Heritage,* edited by Jeffrey Meyers, 251–257. London: Routledge, 1975.

Trilling, Diana, Review. In *George Orwell: The Critical Heritage,* edited by Jeffrey Meyers, 259–262. London: Routledge, 1975.

Trillling, Lionel, "Orwell on the Future," *New Yorker,* June 18, 1949, 78–83.

Woodcock, George. *The Crystal Spirit.* Boston: Little, Brown, 1966.

Zwerdling, Alex. *Orwell and the Left.* New Haven, Conn.: Yale University Press, 1974.

"Not Counting Niggers"

A review of a book by Clarence Streit, *Union Now,* in the *Adelphi* in 1939. Orwell chose the deliberately provocative title to highlight the fact that this apparently sound call for a union among the western imperialist democracies against the Nazi threat could not succeed without regard for the opinion of six hundred million people of color subjected to imperial rule.

SYNOPSIS

Orwell comments on the war fever that is sweeping England in the summer of 1939. The book under review, *Union Now,* calls for a federal union of 15 nations to begin with and opportunities for more to join in the future. This union, consisting of the United States and all the democratic nations of Western Europe, in their combined strength would be enough to deter an attack by Hitler on any one of them. But the problem is that Streit assumes that the British and French colonies will continue to exist as they have for the benefit of the union. These colonies will be treated as "dependencies," which is to say that their vast population of colored people will have no say in this operation. Thus, the system of exploiting hundreds of millions of colonized people will continue as usual. In effect, the union would be working to defeat the evil of Nazism while reinforcing the evil colonial system, which is just as bad as Hitler's and much larger in terms of the number of people affected.

Negotiations are now going on between the Soviet and English governments that will probably result in an alliance against Hitler: The arms race will then continue on both sides. In a couple of years, there will develop in England a strong fascist movement. The only hope of preventing it is the emergence on an antiwar party that rejects both war and imperialism, but such a possibility seems remote.

COMMENTARY

At the time he wrote this review, Orwell was still clinging to an antiwar position consistent with that of the Independent Labour Party, which he had joined in 1938. At the conclusion of this review, he speaks of the possibility of a Soviet-English alliance against Hitler. Six weeks after the publication of this review, Europe was stunned by the signing of the Hitler-Stalin pact, in which the two enemies agreed to cooperate with each other. One week later, Hitler invaded Poland, and World War II began. As a result, Orwell quit the Independent Labour Party, abandoned his antiwar position, and became an outspoken critic of PACIFISM. Although Orwell still retained a strong anti-imperialist stand, his opposition took a lower priority than the Nazi menace. His work at the BBC exemplified this position. On the one hand, he still stood in favor of postwar independence for the colonies, but he felt that any such move would have to be postponed for the duration of the war. He felt that it was not only in England's interest to maintain the colonial relation, but also India's in particular. Orwell feared that if India fell into the hands of the Japanese, the Indian people would regret it. This is precisely what did happen to the people of Burma, who had the misfortune to come under Japanese control during the war. As for the proposed federation, it might be seen as the forerunner of NATO or the European Union.

"Notes on Nationalism"

An essay published in the first issue of *Polemic: A Magazine of Philosophy, Psychology and Aesthetics* (October 1945)

SYNOPSIS

Orwell announces his intention to use the term *nationalism* in a very broad sense, defining it as "the habit of identifying oneself with a single nation or unit, placing it beyond good and evil and recognizing no other duty than that of advancing its interests." He distinguishes it from patriotism, which he defines as "devotion to a particular place and a particular way of life . . . with no wish to force it upon other people." Patriotism is a defensive posture, unlike nationalism, which he considers aggressive, motivated by the desire for power. According to this definition, such movements as communism, political Catholicism, Zionism, anti-Semitism, Trotskyism, and fascism are types of nationalism.

Under this broad umbrella, nationalism can be seen as dominant strain among English intellectuals. It reveals itself in a prevailing tendency to make political, historical, or literary judgments, based not on the facts but on a priori judgments. Among English intellectuals, it is clear that communism, in the loose sense of the term that includes fellow travelers and many liberals, is the preferred form of nationalism, but there are many other types. For example, twenty years ago there was a form of political Catholicism associated with G. K. CHESTERTON, who, after his conversion, proselytized for his new belief in everything he wrote.

Although not all forms of nationalism are the same, there are certain distinguishing features of nationalist thought. One of these is, as in the case of Chesterton, *obsession*. Another is *instability*. English intellectuals exhibit this trait in their flagrant worship of the Soviet Union at the expense of their own country. A third feature is *indifference to reality*, most notable in the tacit acceptance of atrocities when they are committed by "our side." In the case of anti-Semitic nationalists, the extermination of the Jews in the war manages "to bounce off their consciousness."

Orwell now moves to try to classify the forms of nationalism as practiced by English intellectuals according to three categories: positive, transferred, and negative. He further divides positive nationalism into three subdivisions. The first are neo-Tories, people who refuse to accept fact that Britain has declined as a world power. The second group are Celtic nationalists, the movements in Ireland, Scotland, and Wales, that believe in independence for their countries. The third group of positive nationalists are the Zionists, whose American wing appears to be "more violent and malignant than the British."

Under transferred nationalism, Orwell lists, in addition to communism and political Catholicism, "color feeling," which among intellectuals takes the inverted form of believing in the "innate superiority of the colored races." Another subdivision is "class feeling," which, among middle- and upper-class intellectuals, is the belief in the superiority of the working class. The last category is pacifism. He admits that the majority of pacifists are "simply humanitarians who object to taking life . . ." but also that a small group of intellectual pacifists are attracted to "power and successful cruelty."

As for negative nationalism, Orwell cites Anglophobia, which he describes as endemic among English intellectuals, and anti-Semitism, which is not overt at this moment, in the wake of the Nazi crimes against Jews, but is nevertheless widespread among conservatives and, to a lesser extent, among the Left. A third form of negative socialism is Trotskyism, with its fixation on Stalin, making it a kind of mirror image of communism.

In summary, Orwell acknowledges that he has at times exaggerated, oversimplified, and generalized. This is because he has extracted feeling from attitudes that in individuals exist in an ambivalent form, part of a mix of sometimes contradictory thoughts and emotions. Undoubtedly there are people free from the nationalist virus. But the great majority of people harbor at least one principle that they will adhere to, no matter how it is contradicted by the facts. As for the English intelligentsia, they have been blinded by their rejection of patriotism and religion. But none of this should be seen as a retreat from the political world, for we have an obligation to engage it. Meanwhile, our particular nationalist biases must be struggled against, but this requires a "moral effort," an effort that, on the evidence of contemporary English literature, "few of us are prepared to make."

COMMENTARY

Orwell acknowledges that *nationalism* is an imprecise term for the phenomenon he is describing, but he can find no better term in English. Orwell begins by describing the nationalist psychology, one characterized by obsession, instability, and indifference to reality. These qualities enable one to simplify and order the complexity of the modern world, a world in which the old foundations of patriotism and religious belief have been pulled out from under them. The various *-isms* proliferating in modern society are the consequence of the intellectuals' version of the modern malaise. The intelligentsia, desperately trying to bridge the abyss of alienation, have created substitute religions that they hope will lend both meaning and solace to their lives. It might be said that Orwell's "substitute religion" was democratic socialism in its pure form, that is to say, as it existed in January 1937 in Barcelona, when he first arrived in that city. However, even there, he admitted that "there was much in it . . . I did not even like . . ." But unlike the typical nationalist he portrays, he acknowledges the imperfections, never abandoning his role as an unrelenting critic of his "faith." To do so requires a "moral effort," one "that few of us are prepared to make." It is worth noting that he uses the word *us*, indicating that he recognizes his own culpability in the condition he deplores.

Poems

"I am not a poet, only a novelist." Orwell wrote this in 1938 in response to a university librarian collecting poetic manuscripts. The *only* is an odd choice of a term for someone who had written three novels and three nonfictional works, the last of which, *Homage to Catalonia,* contained his best piece of book-length writing. He had also published a number of poems, but by that time he had concluded correctly that his gifts lay in prose, not poetry. Nevertheless, like many writers, he began writing verse and occasionally reverted to it later in life. The following is a chronological list of Orwell's poems.

"Awake! Young Men of England," *The Henley and South Oxfordshire Standard* (2 October 1914). An 11-year-old's call to arms.

"Kitchener," *The Henley and South Oxfordshire Standard* (21 July 1916). A 13-year-old's tribute to a military icon.

"The Pagan" (Autumn 1918), **"Our Minds Are Married, but We Are Too Young"** (Christmas 1918), **"Friendship and Love Are Closely Intertwined"** (Summer 1921). Three poems sent to Jacintha Buddicom that chart the progress of a romance that ended unhappily, as reflected in Jacintha's poetic reply to the last of these poems. (See part 1).

"The Wounded Cricketer (Not by Walt Whitman)" *The Election Times* No. 4 (3 June 1918); two Stanzas of **"The Youthful Mariner,"** *The Election Times* No. 4 (3 June 1918). Two poems published in an Eton student publication.

"After Twelve," *College Days* No. 4 (1 April 1919) 104; "Ode to Field Days" *College Days* No. 4 (1 April 1919) 114; "To A.R.H.B.," *College Days* No. 2 (27 June 1919) 42; "Wall Game," *College Days* No. 3 (29 November 1919) 78; "The Photographer," *College Days* No. 5 (9 July 1920). Five poems published in another Eton student publication, *College Days*. "Wall Game" was written as a parody of Rudyard Kipling's "If."

'The Lesser Evil', *Notes,* written between 1922 and 1927 in Burma; 'Romance,' *Notes,* written between 1922 and 1927 in Burma; 'When the Franks *Have Lost Their Sway,' Notes,* written between 1922 and 1927 in Burma; '*Here Lie the Bones of Poor* John Flory,' written winter 1927–28 or 1928–29. Four unpublished poems, all notably cynical, written while, or just after, Orwell was serving in the Burmese police.

'Sometimes in the middle autumn days,' *The Adelphi* (March 1933); 'Summer-like for an instant the autumn sun bursts out', *The Adelphi* (May 1933). Two poems in which the theme of death figures prominently.

"A dressed man and a naked man," *The Adelphi* (October 1933). Orwell's first poem that focuses on poverty and homelessness.

"On a Ruined Farm near the His Master's Voice Gramophone Factory," *The Adelphi* (April 1934). Expresses a sense of frustration at the inability to check the effects of industrialism on nature.

"St. Andrew's Day, 1935," *The Adelphi* (November 1935). Poem anticipating the onset of winter, the time when the tyranny of the "money-god" is most in evidence. In *Keep the Aspidistra Flying,* Gordon Comstock, the impoverished would-be poet, is depicted composing this poem. He completes the last stanza after his unsuccessful attempt to have sex because he has failed to bring a condom with him.

"A happy vicar I might have been," *The Adelphi* (December 1936). Orwell's lament over being born in the 20th century, perhaps thinking of his paternal grandfather, THOMAS RICHARD BLAIR, who led an apparently untroubled life as a country parson. Orwell quoted a part of this poem in his essay "Why I Write."

'The Italian soldier shook my hand' (1942). Orwell's best-known poem, originally printed in his essay "Looking Back on the Spanish War." It commemorates the incident described in the opening of *Homage to Catalonia,* in which Orwell briefly met and shook hands with an Italian volunteer, who seemed to embody the spirit of the fight against fascism. The phrase in the last line of the poem "the crystal spirit" was adapted by GEORGE WOODCOCK as the title of his book-length study of Orwell.

"As One Non-Combatant to Another: A Letter to 'Obadiah Hornbooke,'" *Tribune* (18 June 1943). A satiric verse responding to an antiwar satire implicating writers who engage in propaganda by the pacifist Alex Comfort ("Obadiah Hornbooke"). In a follow-up letter to Alex Comfort, Orwell conceded that although he had the better argument, Comfort wrote a better poem. The English poet Philip Larkin apparently did not agree, since he selected Orwell's poem for inclusion in *The Oxford Book of Twentieth-Century English Verse.*

'Memories of the Blitz,' *Tribune* (21 January 1944). A poem looking back at the blitz of 1940–41. Ironically, given the memorial tone of the poem, Orwell's flat was destroyed by a V-1 rocket months after the publication of the poem.

The texts of all of Orwell's poems as well as a few fragments are printed in *The Complete Works of George Orwell,* edited by Peter Davison, Vols. 10–19.

"Poetry and the Microphone"

Essay published in *The New Saxon Pamphlet* (March 1945). In part of the essay, there is a description of VOICE, the six broadcasts devoted to poetry by Orwell for an Indian university student audience on the BBC in 1942.

SYNOPSIS

Orwell begins by describing the format of the *Voice* programs which, whenever possible, featured contemporary poets reading their own poems, sometimes followed by a brief discussion. Each program would be organized according to a general theme, such as war. On some occasions, a poem would be framed by a piece of music. The musical setting helped to return lyric poetry to its roots as something to be heard as well as read. In fact, the idea of poetry as something printed, unconnected to the human voice and music, has no doubt contributed to the common people's rejection of it as difficult to understand at best and incomprehensible at worst. Radio is an ideal potential medium for poetry because, although it can reach a large audience, it is in fact "an audience of *one*." Each listener is alone or in a small group and feels that he/she is being personally addressed. But unlike the audience at a live poetry reading, the radio audience has no power to influence the writer's tone or delivery. But the very act of reading his or her poem aloud brings the poet into a new relationship with it, to think of it "as *sound* rather than as a pattern on paper." And it opens up the possibility on the receiving end of rescuing poetry from "its special position as the most hated of the arts." What is needed is a way of presenting poetry as something normal, not something "good for you." T. S. Eliot had suggested the music hall as a possible vehicle to normalize poetry. Orwell thinks radio is the best answer. If we can wrest control of it from the bureaucrats and install the people with real knowledge of the arts, we might see the presentation of all the arts enhanced through radio.

COMMENTARY

In addition to his successful *Voice* presentations, Orwell contributed to the poetic education of the radio audience with his "THE MEANING OF A POEM," a talk delivered on the BBC, reading and analyzing "Felix Randal," a poem by Gerard Manley Hopkins. Another contribution was his adaptation and analysis of his favorite Shakespearean play, *Macbeth*.

"Politics and the English Language"

Orwell's most popular and influential essay, "Politics and the English Language" stands as a key document in the movement for "linguistic plainness," the effort to purge English prose of pretentiousness and cant. (Originally published in *Horizon*, April 1946.)

SYNOPSIS

Orwell begins by taking as a given that "English is in a bad way," but he refuses to accept the notion that nothing can be done about it. Underlying the pessimistic view, he argues, is the notion that ". . . language is a natural growth and not an instrument which we shape for our own purposes." Stressing the crucial relationship between language and thought, he sees the two as interactive: Sloppy, imprecise thought results in vague, cliché-ridden language, and such language further intensifies poor thinking. Thus, cause and effect collaborate in an ongoing cycle that must be reversed. Modern written English is riddled with "bad habits" that spread the contagion of "foolish thinking." At stake are not just the fussy concerns of professional writers but an issue of great importance, "the political regeneration" of the society.

Promising to return to this point later in the essay, he offers five examples of poor writing. The first is a 53 word sentence containing five negatives (four *nots* and one *nothing*); the second, a sentence with two mixed, self-contradictory metaphors; the third, a "simply meaningless" collection of words; the fourth, a passage clotted with "stale phrases"; and the fifth, an expression of feeling with no concern for the words the writer uses to express it.

Orwell then proceeds to list four recurring features of bad writing:

Dying metaphors. As opposed to dead metaphors, which have become ordinary phrases ("foot of the hill"), dying metaphors have lost, through overuse, the ability to evoke a visual image in the mind of the reader ("no ax to grind").

Verbal false limbs. Adding extra words to verbs, using the passive voice, favoring noun constructions over gerund phrases ("by examination of" instead of "by examining").

Pretentious diction. Examples: foreign phrases ("deus ex machina"), Latinized words ("ameliorate"), Marxist polemics ("mad dog").

Meaningless words. Words like *democracy* and *freedom* emptied of their real meanings to refer to something good and *fascism* to mean something bad.

Following this catalogue of modern errors, Orwell caps his argument with his treatment of a verse from Ecclesiastes ("I returned and saw under the sun, that the race is not to the swift, nor the battle to the strong . . .") as it might be rendered in modern English ("Objective consideration of contemporary phenomena compels the conclusion that success or failure . . ."). Comparing the two versions, Orwell points out that the biblical text is crammed with visual imagery, its language concrete and detailed. The modern version contains not one vivid phrase, its language generalized and vague while offering a reduced meaning of the text. Acknowledging that the parody is exaggerated, he maintains "Still, if you or I were told to write a few lines on the uncertainty of human fortune, we should probably come much closer to my imaginary sentence than to the one from Ecclesiastes."

A writer striving to overcome the modern debasement of English should ask himself at least four questions about each sentence he writes: "What am I trying to say? What words will express it? What image will make it clearer? Is this image fresh enough to have an effect?"

At this point, Orwell returns to the question of politics and language. Political language can easily become the tool of dictators who institutionalize lying, deadening the spirits of the people subject to it. But even in democratic societies, language spoken or written by governments or members of political parties is almost always full of abstract generalizations, words that have lost any meaning they once had, and cloudy thinking. Official government documents employ euphemisms to camouflage ugly realities. It may be impossible to completely purify political language, but we can begin to reverse its influence by developing a critical attitude to our own writing and crying out when we it see it in others'.

COMMENTARY

Orwell has three aims in this essay: to demonstrate the debasement of modern English prose, to indicate the dangers such debasement holds for a free democratic society, and to suggest a strategy to combat those dangers.

Writing in 1946, the beginning of the cold war, Orwell was developing a heightened sense that this would be, to a significant degree, a war of words. A year earlier, he had produced, in *Animal Farm,* a vivid account of the power of language to corrupt and mislead a society. The lies of the propagandistic pig, Squealer, play a crucial role in the construction of the totalitarian state along with the ongoing alterations and reductions of the original Seven Commandments. This verbal chicanery and deceit testify to the total perversion of the animals' revolution. But Orwell was also fresh from his World War II experiences working at the BBC, where he had witnessed and, to some extent, participated in, a more subtle form of propaganda and manipulative news management. Of course, he recognized that propaganda was a necessary weapon in a war in which the very survival of England was seriously in doubt. Nevertheless, he was never very happy with the compromises with truth and the verbal trickery that he was sometimes asked to employ. As a result, he came away with a razor-sharp sense of the dangers of bureaucratic, official language, even among the "good guys."

But before addressing that problem, he devotes most of the essay to cataloging examples of the corruption inflicted on the language by people who should know better. At this point, the essay reads like a handbook on current usage along the lines of Strunk and White's *The Elements of Style,* skewering various forms of bad writing. More than 60 years later, it appears that some of the words and phrases he proscribes are still with us, including his pet peeve, the "not=un" construction, and the language seems none the worse for it. But on the whole, his criticism is valid and frequently entertaining. The high point occurs in Orwell's rendering of a passage from Ecclesiastes in modern bureaucratic English.

By this time, perhaps suspecting that he is having so much fun he has forgotten his main point, Orwell returns to the central topic: the language of politics. Political language, which includes the "official story" issued by governments, is fatally compromised by its preference for persuasion rather than truth. One of his examples reflects an uncanny anticipation of the language of the Vietnam War: "Defenseless villages are bombarded from the air, the inhabitants driven out from the countryside, the cattle machine-gunned, the huts set on fire with incendiary bullets: this is called *pacification.*" It is passages like this that cause readers to experience a shiver when reading Orwell. As for his conclusion—you can only reverse the evils of political language by curing yourself—it strikes many readers as weak, wishful thinking, thoroughly non-Orwellian. But the urgency of his message was already amplified and intensified in his unforgettable depiction of NEWSPEAK in *Nineteen Eighty-Four.*

In "Politics and the German Language," John Rodden vindicates Orwell's conclusion, citing the linguistic tactics of students in East Germany in 1989: "A powerful authentic language of the people rose up from the bureaucratic Dead . . . and it not only swept away Party *Ost*speak, but ultimately the Party and the Orwellian GDR, the German Doublethinking Republic" (79). Rodden's article forms a chapter in his *Scenes from an Afterlife: The Legacy of George Orwell* (2003).

"Politics vs. Literature: An Examination of Gulliver's Travels"

An essay first published in *Polemic (1946). Gulliver's Travels* was one of Orwell's favorite books of all time, but as a mature reader and critic, Orwell entertained serious questions about its author, Jonathan Swift, possibly because Swift is the classical English writer to whom he is most often compared. For both Swift and himself, the relationship between politics and literature was a critical issue.

SYNOPSIS

Orwell begins by tracing the changing image of Gulliver as he moves through the four parts of the *Travels.* In Book I, Gulliver appears as an ordinary, middle aged man, a practical unromantic figure. In Book II, he is essentially the same, although occasionally becoming a boastful chauvinist who inadvertently reveals his country's ridiculous habits. In Book III, he displays no chauvinism in his discussion with the learned fools of Lagado, and appears to be a person of a higher social class. Book IV presents him as a fierce misogynist, a man with a pathological hatred of the human race. In large part, these changes have been dictated by the settings of the story, but behind the various changes, Orwell maintains that we are hearing Swift himself savagely attack English society.

Orwell believes that a case can be made for seeing in Gulliver's adventures the story of Swift's political career. "Politically Swift was one of those people who are driven into a perverse Toryism by the follies of the progressive party of the moment." As a result, much of *Gulliver's Travels'* satiric target was the Whig Party, which dominated the England of Swift's day. His reactionary stance moved beyond politics in his opposition to scientific research. His rejection of science was so severe as to deny any value to curiosity or research at all. He had a reverence for the past, and particularly for classical Rome which corresponded to his hatred of his own age.

On the other hand, he was well ahead of his time in his detection of totalitarian trends, one example being the Houyhnhnms, whose society, founded on reason, never engaged in discussion, because the truth was always self-evident. As a result, conformity was so pervasive that in their vocabulary "they had no word for 'opinion.'" In other words, according to Orwell, they operated in a static society with "no freedom and no development." The world of the Houyhnhnms is governed by a narrow "reason," which does not allow for "love, friendship, curiosity, fear, sorrow, and—except in their feelings towards the Yahoos, who occupy the same place in their community as the Jews in Nazi Germany—anger and hatred."

Orwell argues that the Houyhnhnms inhabit an anarchistic society, in which reason is the governing principle. According to Orwell, Swift was a "Tory Anarchist" but underneath the political position lay a profound pessimism about human nature. The real purpose of Swift's description of the Houyhnhnms' world is to "humiliate Man." Lurking beneath that purpose may be the envy of a basically unhappy man whose unhappiness ultimately led to madness.

At this point, Orwell wishes to correct the impression that he is against Swift. He explains that despite his political and moral objections to *Gulliver's Travels,* he considers it one of the six greatest books of all time, a fact that leads to the subject of the relationship of one's agreement with a literary work and the enjoyment of it. The key word here is *enjoyment.* It is not simply a question of recognizing the artistic skill of a work that you disagree with. Enjoyment is a subjective feeling that "can overwhelm disapproval." This is because what he shows us is part of the truth, not the dominant part, as it is for him, but a part nonetheless. "The human body is beautiful; it is also repulsive and ridiculous. . . ." Swift forces us to see a basic, unpalatable truth of human beings and, because he possessed "a terrible intensity of vision," he produced "a great work of art."

COMMENTARY

Orwell received a copy of *Gulliver's Travels* as a present on his eighth birthday. It was one of the formative reading experiences of his life. That fact, at first glance, seems inconsistent with the negative tone of the essay. It may be that Orwell was aware of his too-close-for-comfort relationship with Swift, as signaled by his reference to the great satirist as a "Tory anarchist." This was the very phrase he used to describe himself in the early 1930s, prior to his commitment to socialism. In the essay, he used the term *anarchist* to make a recurring point about the totalitarian subtext of both anarchism and pacifism. The essay brought a sharp response from Orwell's anarchist friend GEORGE WOODCOCK, who asserted that Orwell has misrepresented anarchism, and he disputed Orwell's notion that public opinion is more oppressive than the law. In *The Crystal Spirit,* Woodcock argues that the closeness of Orwell's relationship to Swift, one extending back to Orwell's childhood, and their shared "Tory anarchist" philosophy were entangling roots that Orwell wished to rid himself of. "He attacked Swift's tendency to go to extremes precisely because he shared it and feared it in himself. It is ironic justice that Orwell's detractors should have accused him of the same anti-humanitarian bias he exaggeratedly imputed to Swift" (249). Woodcock is here referring to the views of those who read *Nineteen Eighty-Four* as a "cry of despair."

WORK CITED

Woodcock, George. *The Crystal Spirit.* London: Jonathan Cape, 1967.

"Prevention of Literature, The"

First published in *Polemic* (January 1946) and, in the United States, in the *Atlantic Monthly* (March 1947).

SYNOPSIS

Orwell reports on a P.E.N. Club symposium, commemorating John Milton's famous pamphlet on the freedom of the press, *Areopagitica.* Of the four speakers he heard there, only one of them spoke about freedom of the press. Orwell is not surprised by this development. Despite the end of World War II, censorship of varying types is still pervasive in the interests of national security. It is also true that many writers have had to do hack work in order to survive in an atmosphere where journalism is largely controlled by a few press lords. As a result, there are fewer and fewer writers willing to stand by their sense of intellectual integrity, to live by the words of the old hymn:

> Dare to be a Daniel
> Dare to stand alone
> Dare to have a purpose firm
> Dare to make it known

Nowadays, that hymn would be sung with the word *Don't* before each *dare.*

The particular argument against freedom of speech that Orwell wishes to confront is the charge that the individual is not a reliable source of truth because he is not acting within the confines of a larger truth. Currently, the chief representatives of this view are the communists. They have consistently held the position that speaking the truth should always be subordinated to the best interests of the Party. They frequently employ the argument that the truth would "play into the hands of" whatever enemy they are concerned about at a given time. As a result, "organized lying" has become a routine feature of life among communists and fellow travelers.

All totalitarian states are engaged in the abolition of objective truth. They argue that all so-called truths are relative in any case. This type of thinking has seeped into democratic societies, as well. In England, for example, press lords or movie producers or publishers control access, but far more debilitating is the subjective censorship writers impose on themselves. And this problem is not limited to political journalists. Imaginative writers, novelists, and poets who feel they must avoid certain subjects do damage to their "creative faculties."

This is particularly true in relation to prose writing. Totalitarian societies can accommodate poets more easily than prose writers. This is because in poetry the ideology is less significant than it is in prose. Prose literature, on the other hand, is "the product of rationalism, of the Protestant centuries." The best historical example of the negative influence of a totalitarian regime is the Catholic Church. The Middle Ages produced no prose literature of lasting value. Since the Middle Ages, "How many people have been good Catholics and good novelists?" Similarly, how many worthwhile novels have been published in the Soviet Union? We can reasonably assume that in a totalitarian takeover, prose literature—and ultimately, all literature—will perish. It will be replaced by film and radio. Perhaps there will be a device developed in which machines will write books, "low grade sensation fiction" for mass audiences. Books will be produced in assembly-line fashion, like Ford automobiles. As for the old literature—Shakespeare and Dickens, say—it will be either eliminated or rewritten.

What renders this bleak process even more depressing is that its supporters are drawn not from the English mass public, but from the intellectual elite. Among these are many scientists, a result of the fact that the work of scientists is highly valued in the Soviet Union, just as scientists were treated well in Nazi Germany. The need for scientific development has had one positive effect. It has deterred to some extent the denial of objective truth. "Two and two have to make four when you are. . . . drawing the blueprint of an aeroplane . . ." As a result, totalitarian societies tend to leave scientists free from the rigors of the party line. Despite this priviledged position, the scientist has to recognize his obligation to the community at large and join in the fight against totalitarianism.

In any case, Orwell concludes, we must all recognize that literature cannot exist without the freedom to assert an individual's truth: ". . . [T]he imagination, like some wild animals, cannot breed in captivity."

COMMENTARY

Orwell begins the essay with an anecdote drawn from the P.E.N. conference memorializing Milton's *Areopagitica,* one of the great pamphlets of English literature. Milton's theme was freedom of the press, a position closely associated with P.E.N. Therefore, Orwell detects in the conference's failure to address the subject evidence of the new climate of avoiding the question. He bluntly attributes this attitude to the influence of communists and their fellow travelers. They are aligned against the liberal tradition of allowing the individual to convey the truth as he/she sees it. Their justification lies in the conviction that the individual frequently fails to see the "big picture," which is to say, the Party line. Orwell then moves the argument out of journalism into literature—the novelist or short-story writer has his own form of truth, rooted in his own subjectivity. If he distorts his inner sense of truth in order to serve a political end, he is finished as an artist.

Orwell acknowledges that literature sometimes flourishes under tyrannical regimes, and he goes on to make some sweeping generalizations about poetry and prose. He insists that "it is broadly true that prose literature has reached its highest levels in periods of democracy and free speculation." Clearly he is overlooking the great period of the 19th-century Russian novel under the rule of czars, some of which, like Dostoevsky's *The Possessed* and Turgenev's *Fathers and Sons*, were political novels.

Another interesting aspect of this essay is that at various points, it touches on ideas that will reappear in *Nineteen Eighty-Four.* One of these is the theme of objective truth and the denial of it by adherents of "collective solipsism," as O'Brien names it in the novel. The notion that truth is located within the mind, in O'Brien's example, the mind of the Party, "its distinctive quality being 'doublethink,' the power of holding two contradictory thoughts in one's mind and accepting both of them." Another is the reference to a future in which books will be written by machines. *In Nineteen Eighty-Four,* Julia's job in the Fiction Department involves maintaining the machines that grind out popular fiction. Another is the practice of rewriting the past and the recurring Orwellian example of doublethink: Two plus two is five. Clearly, ideas are taking shape here that will be fully developed in *Nineteen Eighty-Four.* In fact, the essay and the novel share the same central theme: the threat that an all-powerful state poses for the individual.

"Raffles and Miss Blandish"

Essay first published in *Horizon* in October 1944, and in the United States, in *Atlantic Monthly,* November 1944. The title refers to two figures in popular novels that "glamorize crime." The first of these is Raffles, the hero of two novels by E. W. Hornung, *Raffles, A Thief in the Night* and *Mr. Justice Raffles.* The second is Miss Blandish, the victimized heroine of *No Orchids for Miss Blandish* (1939) by James Hadley Chase.

SYNOPSIS

Raffles, the gentlemen safecracker, remains one of the most popular characters in English literature, even though he has been around since 1900. As such, from a sociological standpoint he offers an interesting contrast with a recent popular crime novel that focuses on the criminal rather than on the detective. Orwell's purpose in juxtaposing the two is to highlight "the immense difference in moral atmosphere . . . and the change in the popular attitude that this probably implies."

The unique appeal of Raffles lies in the fact that he is a member of the upper class, a product of a public school. In the *Raffles* novels, he exhibits a social conscience—remorse for having "let down" his class—but no remorse about stealing from the rich. In this respect, his readers share his values. A telling indicator of his character is his talent as a cricket player. Not nearly as popular as football, cricket is famous for its ethical character, as expressed in the phrase "it's not cricket," which emphasizes form and style over winning or losing. His skill as a cricket player has opened the doors of high society to Raffles, but all that is lost when his thievery is exposed. He is cast out of paradise. The only redemption possible is to die a hero's death on the battlefield, which he achieves in the Boer War.

By today's standards, Raffles's adventures are noticeably low-key and lacking in sensationalism. Like many pre–World War I detective stories, the *Raffles* novels do not even contain many murders. This was an era when society still maintained standards, many of them foolish, but they lent a cohesiveness to English culture that has since been fractured.

By contrast, we have in 1939 the appearance of a best-selling crime novel, *No Orchids for Miss Blandish.* Set in the United States, the plot deals with the kidnapping of a wealthy man's daughter by a gang who are, in turn, killed off by a larger gang. This second gang collects the ransom but holds on to the victim, Miss Blandish, because one of its members, Slim, is attracted to her. Slim's mother, "the real brains of the gang," sees in Slim's attraction the possibility of curing his impotence. Aided by a number of sadistic torturers, Slim eventually succeeds in raping Miss Blandish. Shortly after, the gang is caught and eliminated, including Slim, who is killed after one last rape of his victim. The novel concludes with the suicide of Miss Blandish because, in Orwell's interpretation, "she has developed a taste for Slim's caresses." (In a footnote, Orwell acknowledges an alternative possible reason for the suicide: She is pregnant.)

The book, which has borrowed its main idea from William Faulkner's novel *Sanctuary*, is notable for another characteristic. Although written by an English author for an English audience, it is rendered entirely "in the American language." A summary of the action of the book reveals casual murders, an exhumation of a carcass, flogging, extreme torture, and the death of a masochist gangster who experiences an orgasm when he is knifed in the stomach. The novel is devoid of any decent human motivation or behavior. It is propelled by one force only: the worship of power.

The "American" character of this English novel reveals its link to the popular pulp fiction magazines (known in England as "Yank mags") that flooded the English market before the war. The separate English origins of this attitude can be traced to the detective stories of Edgar Wallace, who objected to amateur detective stories such as Sherlock Holmes. Wallace made his hero a Scotland Yard Official, the representative of an "all-powerful organization," tolerant of sadistic behavior on the part of the police. But Orwell acknowledges that even Wallace's brand of sadism is preferable to Chase's.

Chase follows the new school of American writers celebrated for their hard-boiled realism, whose credo might be summarized by the phrase "might makes right." This literary phenomenon is an expression of "the cult of power" that has surfaced in the forms of fascism and Soviet Communism. The truth of course, is that "the countless English intellectuals who kiss the arse of Stalin" are not different from the minority who gave their allegiance to Hitler or Mussolini. Although *No Orchids* exhibits no interest in political or social questions, it distills the modern world in which totalitarianism is a constant threat into a form that the average person can comprehend.

Orwell concedes that it is always possible he has been reading too much into the success of *No Orchids*. It may be just a fluke "brought about by the mingled boredom and brutality of war." Raffles has no moral code, either, but he does exhibit the social code of the gentleman. In *No Orchids,* "there are no gentlemen, and no taboos." We are left with no rules and no compass. There may be something to be said for "snobbishness," after all.

COMMENTARY

This essay is another example of Orwell's pioneering exploration of POPULAR CULTURE, looking at certain forms of so-called escapist literature, art, and other aspects of cultural expression to see what they reveal about the society that embraces them. In this case, he chooses the crime novel in which the focus is on the criminal and the vast moral gap between the novel of 1900 and that of 1939. Raffles embodies a society that has broken free of religious belief but adheres to a social code of ethics exemplified by "playing the game" (as in cricket), conducting oneself like a gentleman while breaking into safes. If there was a certain amount of hypocrisy there, it was a small price to pay for the civilized world, a world that was blown apart in World War I. Orwell sees it having been replaced by a world without standards, "the emancipated world of Machiavelli and Freud," which has unleashed the lust for power in which violence, brutality, sadism, sexual perversion, and power worship contribute to, or simply reflect, a world in which totalitarianism has arisen and, in Orwell's view, seems destined to triumph at least temporarily. He is particularly disturbed by the notion that books like *No Orchids* should be celebrated for their "realism." His own early novels were in the traditional realistic mode, but a realism in the sense of providing a recognizable picture of society and the attempted rebellion against it, staged by an individual. *No Orchids*' brand of realism offers a picture of brutal, deranged individuals contending for power in a moral jungle—not realism but nihilism. The high-mindedness of Orwell's critique is undermined by one observation, when he describes Miss Blandish's suicide as motivated by her having "developed a taste for Slim's caresses that she feels unable to live without him." Although, in a 1945 footnote, Orwell acknowledges another possible motive—that she is pregnant—he adheres to his original point. The sharp-eyed feminist critic Daphne Patai argues that had Orwell "been able to imagine Miss Blandish as a person," he would have recognized that her experience has invaded her "inner world." Like Winston Smith, she has undergone "a loss of self" (253). Of course, Patai may be guilty of begging the question as to whether a character in a novel of *Miss Blandish*'s quality could have an inner life. Nevertheless, the text offers more support for her interpretation than for Orwell's.

WORK CITED

Patai, Daphne. *The Orwell Mystique.* Amherst: University of Massachussetts Press, 1984.

"Re-discovery of Europe, The"

A talk given on the BBC Eastern Service, for which Orwell served as a producer from August 1941 to November 1943. This particular talk was aired in March 1942 and later reprinted in the BBC's *Listener* magazine, and finally included in *Talking to India,* an anthology of BBC Eastern Service talks edited by Orwell and published in 1943.

SYNOPSIS

Orwell recalls the teaching of English history when he was in school. History was seen as being divided into periods that dramatically differ, based upon arbitrary dates that signal radical changes, as when 1499 changed to 1500 and suddenly the Middle Ages became the Renaissance. This, of course, is an overly simplified version of the truth, but it is true that change does occur in history and in the history of literature, and occasionally it is a rapid change. He suggests, for example, that one can see the difference between pre-1914 literature and modern literature by looking at the poems of Rupert Brooke and those of T. S. Eliot, both of whom were writing only a few years apart. Similarly with the novelists of the first decade of the 20th century, H. G. WELLS, RUDYARD KIPLING, Arnold Bennet, and John Galsworthy, as opposed to JAMES JOYCE, ALDOUS HUXLEY, D. H. LAWRENCE, and Wyndham Lewis. The earlier group was committed to the idea of progress, social betterment, and the future. The younger group was apolitical or reactionary, repelled by the modern world and driven by aesthetic principles.

He then offers a comparison of the difference between some short stories of H. G. Wells and those of D. H. Lawrence. Wells's stories offer a largely optimistic picture of life, based upon his belief that science provides a golden key to the future, while Lawrence's stories offer a profoundly critical view of modern man, who has lost touch with his instinctual life. It is important to remember that World War I intervened between Wells's time and Lawrence's, and that the war "succeeded in debunking science, progress and civilized man." But even without the war, ". . . the biggest massacre in human history," Lawrence probably would have adopted the views he did.

Orwell moves to another comparison: John Galsworthy's *The Forsyte Saga* (1906–1922) with Joyce's *Ulysses* (1922). Both aim to give "a comprehensive picture of existing society." In the case of *Ulysses,* part of its importance is technical, its innovations in style, language, and format. But equally important is that Joyce's mind was influenced by a broadly based response to human history. Galsworthy, on the other hand, is a parochial writer primarily interested in the English upper middle class, seen from a narrow, contemporary point of view.

Orwell draws another brief comparison between Aldous Huxley's *Brave New World* (1932) and Wells's *A Modern Utopia* (1904), which points to a vast gap between the naïve belief in scientific progress of Wells and the disillusionment of Huxley. The modernist writers' revulsion against progress has had unfortunate political effects, driving them in some cases to Toryism or Fascism. But they have succeeded in breaking open the closed cultural circle of Wells, and enhanced English literature in the process.

COMMENTARY

This essay raises some puzzling questions. One of these relates to Orwell's discussion of the pre–World War I writers and those of the 1920s, without making any reference to the writers of the 1930s. This is odd because the 1930s writers are those with a specific political purpose. But it is not clear whether those writers might be said to derive from the 1920s modernists or the pre-1914 realists. In an earlier essay, Orwell did deal with the historical view of 20th-century English literature but without reference to its political orientation.

Another question raised by this essay relates to the fact that the writers whom Orwell characterizes as too English and too insulated from European influence are those who influenced him and in whose "school" his own novels are located. If H. G. Wells is parochial, what can we say of the author of *Burmese Days, A Clergyman's Daughter, Keep the Aspidistra Flying,* and *Coming Up For Air*? All his novels are in the traditional realistic mode, and all are saturated in "Englishness." One way to explain this paradox is to recall Orwell's disdain for his own fiction. Not until *Animal Farm* did he express genuine satisfaction with a fictional work of his own.

"Reflections on Gandhi"

A review of Gandhi's autobiography, *The Story of My Experiment with Truth* (1948), first published in *Partisan Review* (January 1949).

SYNOPSIS

Orwell begins by asking two questions about Gandhi: Was there an element of vanity in his presentation of himself as a weak, defenseless man, yet capable of bringing about the end of British rule in India? The second question is did he compromise his principles by entering the political arena, in which power and deception play critical roles? Gandhi's autobiography, which covers the years from his birth to the 1920s, suggests that he avoided both of the pitfalls implied by the two questions. At that time the British thought of him as "our man," someone they could manage or manipulate. So, too, did upper-class Indian society. But British administrators also genuinely liked and admired him.

Originally written for serialization in Indian newspapers, Gandhi's memoir makes it clear that, although he always exhibited a keen ethical awareness, he lacked a sense of direction until he acquired a religious philosophy. Western anarchists, pacifists, and others make a mistake in using Gandhi as a model because they fail to recognize that his message is not humanistic but religious, employing as it does the principle of "nonattachment" to earthly life.

Gandhi preached the doctrine of *Satyagrapha,* which has been translated as "passive resistance." Gandhi did not approve of this translation, preferring "firmness in the truth" as a more accurate rendering of the term. Despite his PACIFISM, Gandhi was honest enough to admit that in World War II, both sides were not the same. In relation to the question (according to Orwell, one usually evaded by pacifists during the war) "What about the Jews?" Gandhi was at least honest. In 1938, he said that the German Jews should commit mass suicide, and by so doing, awaken the world and the German people, to Hitler's true nature.

The truth is that Gandhi's effectiveness rested on the fact that open dissent and freedom of speech existed to a significant extent under British rule. You cannot and will not, for example, find a Gandhi equivalent in the Soviet Union. Yet he was successful in ending British rule, and that was an extraordinary achievement. The fact that it was done nonviolently was even more extraordinary, and it bodes well for future British-Indian relations. It must also be said, in the light of the threat of nuclear disaster, ". . . it is at least thinkable that the way out lies through nonviolence." Although Orwell confesses to an "aesthetic distaste" for Gandhi, he recognizes his honesty and ability as unique among world leaders.

COMMENTARY

This essay/review, written after Gandhi's assassination in 1948, represents a significant shift in Orwell's attitude to the great Indian leader. In earlier comments, particularly those written during the war, he had been sharply critical of Gandhi's pacifism and insistence on remaining neutral in the war between the allies and Japan. Added to those issues was Orwell's instinctual or, as he called it, "aesthetic" dislike of Gandhi. This attitude spills over in the skeptical opening of his essay ("Saints should always be judged guilty until they are proved innocent. . . ."). But the essay is much more positive in its estimation of Gandhi than his opening sentence would indicate. From Orwell's point of view, Gandhi never really understood the nature of totalitarianism, which would never have tolerated the nonviolent opposition he was able to mount against the British. Nevertheless, Orwell acknowledges Gandhi's successful role in winning Indian independence, and as George Woodcock points out, "Perhaps even more than the fact of Indian independence, what stood between the Orwell of 1942–4 and the Orwell of 1948 was the yet harder fact of the bomb over Hiroshima" (214). Orwell's remark that the atomic bomb had made it "at least thinkable that the way out lies through nonviolence" constitutes a major concession on his part as well as a measured tribute to Gandhi's influence. Orwell's concluding sentence sums up his ambiguous respect for the Indian leader.

> One may feel, as I do, a sort of aesthetic distaste for Gandhi, one may reject the claims of sainthood made on his behalf (he never made any such claim himself, by the way), one may also reject sainthood as an ideal and therefore feel that Gandhi's basic aims were anti-human and reactionary: but regarded simply as a politician, and compared with the other leading political figures of our time, how clean a smell he has managed to leave behind!

Ironically, this last sentence was cut, along with a number of other phrases in a government-sponsored reprint of this article. As Peter Davison, editor of *The Complete Works of George Orwell,* points out, the essay appears to have been tampered with for propaganda purposes. Thus, the changes are designed to give a more positive slant to Orwell's views (*CW,* 20, 11).

WORK CITED

The Complete Works of George Orwell. Edited by Peter Davison Vol. 20. London: Secker & Warburg, 1998.

Woodcock, George. *The Crystal Spirit.* London: Jonathan Cape, 1967.

"Revenge Is Sour"

Essay published in *Tribune* (November 1945).

SYNOPSIS

Orwell recounts an incident he observed while serving as a correspondent in Germany at the end of the war. He and another correspondent were being shown around a P.O.W. camp by a young officer in the American army, although the officer in fact had been born in Vienna and had escaped from Austria during the anti-Semitic persecutions of the 1930s. At one point, they came upon a group of former S.S. officers, one of whom had badly deformed feet. When the young Jewish officer approached the man, he kicked the misshapen feet and ordered the man to stand at attention, while the Jewish officer explained that this man had held a high civilian post in the S.S. and had been in charge of several concentration camps. He had been a Nazi party member since its early days. Thinking about the Jewish officer humiliating this S.S. man, Orwell wonders whether he found any satisfaction in it, and he concludes that he didn't. Orwell recognizes that "it is absurd to blame any Austrian or German Jew for getting his own back on the Nazis." Nevertheless, what Orwell derives from this and other postwar scenes is that revenge is an illusion, "an act which you want to commit when you are powerless . . . as soon as the sense of impotence is removed, the desire evaporates also." He goes on to argue that the fierce anti-German feeling in England has abated considerably and even more so among the allied armies of occupation. People we are accustomed to think of as monsters—Nazi leaders such as Goering and Von Ribbentrop—shrink down to human size once they have been captured. Sometimes the desire for revenge disappears when confronted with a concrete situation, like encountering the body of a dead German soldier. That one corpse can come to symbolize the 20 million corpses that the war has produced, leaving one with the realization that revenge is sour.

COMMENTARY

One of Orwell's Jewish friends, TOSCO FYVEL, describes a "serious argument" the two men had over this essay. Fyvel first notes that he reminded Orwell that, only in one dismissive sentence had Orwell mentioned the Holocaust, which Fyvel describes as "the greatest deliberate crime committed in man's history." Fyvel adds that Orwell compounded the insult by referring to the Jewish officer's action as "getting his own back." For Fyvel, there was no remote possibility of Jews' "getting their own back" for the murder of six million of them. Furthermore, he strongly objected to Orwell's frequent reference to the officer as "the Jew" or "the little Jew." Fyvel reports that Orwell was astonished at his reaction, but, Fyvel notes, Orwell never again used the word *Jew* in that generic sense in his published writing (179–180).

WORK CITED

Fyvel, *T. R. George Orwell: A Personal Memoir.* London: Weidenfeld and Nicolson, 1982.

"Riding Down from Bangor"

Essay first published in *Tribune* (November 22, 1946), reprinted with slight changes as "The World of *Helen's Babies*" in *The Literary Digest* (April 1947).

SYNOPSIS

The recent republication of *Helen's Babies* (1872), a book read by virtually every literate, English-speaking child born around the turn of the century, serves as a platform for some observations. The books we read when we are children create in our minds a distinctive geography, "a sort of false map of the world" that stays with us into adulthood. Certainly one of these is "America," an imaginary land, which in my childhood can be summarized by two pictures. One is of a barefoot boy sitting in a schoolroom that contains a large Bible and a woodpile that he has to keep full. The boy hopes to grow up to be president. The other is of a man in a large hat whittling a stick and emitting occasional pithy, laconic phrases. Orwell admits he also took much pleasure in reading girls' books such as *Little Women,* all of which gave him a picture of 19th-century America. *Helen's Babies* evoked a world very similar to *Little Women,* a world of "sweet innocence" and humorous gentility. In Orwell's mind, it is associated with a narrative song from that period, "Riding Down from Bangor." It tells of a young man, riding in a carriage, returning from some weeks hunting in Maine. As a result, he is sporting a "quite extensive" beard and mustache. Also in the carriage is an old couple and a young "beautiful maiden." When cinders fly into the carriage, the young man gets one in his eye. The young girl helps him extract it, and then the train enters a dark tunnel. When is comes out into the light, the girl is blushing profusely, since enmeshed in the young man's beard is a tiny earring.

Like the song, *Helen's Babies* exhibits a "sweet innocence" and "conscious gentility." The comic plot involves a young bachelor who agrees to look after his sister's two young children while she and her husband take a two-week vacation. He is driven to distraction by the escapades of the two young ones, but through them he ends up with the girl of his dreams. What is so surprising is that the society depicted here is so sedate: "Every action is governed by etiquette." Instead of the Wild West world of cowboys and Indians, this is a portrait of the Tame East in which "a society similar to Jane Austen's seems to have survived longer than it did in England."

The point is that underlying the apparent difference between America's Wild West and Tame East was "a common confidence in the future, a sense of freedom and opportunity." America in the 19th century was a place where the "twin nightmares" of the modern world—mass unemployment and encroaching governmental power—were not yet serious threats. It was "capitalist civilization at its best."

Road to Wigan Pier, The

Orwell's second nonfictional volume, *The Road to Wigan Pier* (1937), was the product of two months' research, observation, and personal interviews among the working classes—particularly coal miners—in Lancashire and Yorkshire.

HISTORICAL/ BIOGRAPHICAL CONTEXT

In February 1936, in a hotly contested general election, the Spanish people elected a popular front slate, a leftist coalition government, an event that would lead to the outbreak of civil war in July. In March, in open violation of the Versailles Treaty, Hitler sent German troops into the Rhineland, the area on the French-German border that had been demilitarized after World War I. In *The Road to Wigan Pier,* Orwell refers to this event only to mark its insignificance to the working men of northern England, when contrasted to their interest in the football pools. In England in 1936, foreign fascist threats took a backseat to the specter of widespread unemployment, especially in the northern industrial section of the country. Particularly hard hit were the coal miners, still reeling from the effects of a General Strike in 1926, which had ended unsuccessfully for the strikers. In the meantime, for the average working person in England, the bread-and-butter issues still occupied the center stage.

In early January 1936, following Orwell's completion of the manuscript for *Keep the Aspidistra Flying,* his publisher Victor Gollancz commissioned a new work, a study of the effects on unemployment on northern England's working classes. Given his experience with tramps, hop pickers, and other outcasts, Orwell would appear to be a logical choice for the task. There was only one problem: Gollancz was a committed leftist. A few months after commissioning the new book, he formed the LEFT BOOK CLUB, a book-of-the-month organization designed as a literary Popular Front equivalent, overseen by three-man editorial board: Gollancz himself, the economist Harold Laski, and the writer John Strachey. Strachey was a communist, and Laski and Gollancz were at least fellow travelers. Orwell, though sympathetic to the working classes, saw their problems in social terms and not yet in political ones. At this point of his life, he was skeptical of political -isms, instinctively unwilling to submit to any particular party's creed. Earlier he had described himself as a "Tory anarchist," a paradoxical combination of a revolutionary who still clung to a host of traditional values, specifically those that had structured his Edwardian childhood. But World War I, followed by the depression of the 1930s, had clearly undermined confidence in the capitalist system, and it seemed that the future held open only two possibilities: socialism or fascism. The logical choice for him seemed to be socialism, but as he made clear in chapter 5 of *Keep the Aspidistra Flying,* speaking through the voice of the protagonist, Gordon Comstock, there were too many features of socialism (and socialists) that he could not abide. (For Orwell, Soviet-style communism was not a viable alternative. By 1936, Stalin's show trials of Communist "traitors" had made that clear to him.) Within a year, inspired by the scene in Barcelona, where for the first time he witnessed a society in which "the working class was in the saddle," Orwell would declare himself a socialist. In hindsight, it is clear that he was inching his way toward socialism in this book, but not without first getting some things off his chest. In the process, he was guilty, in Part 2, of wild generalizations, self-contradictory arguments, and even some bad writing. But, for all that, the book remains, in Richard Hoggart's term, "unforgettable" (46).

By the end of January 1936, Orwell had given up his job at Booklovers' Corner in Hampstead, his flat in Kentish Town, and said good-bye to "my girl," Eileen O'Shaughnessy, whom he would wed shortly after his return. He left for Coventry by train on January 31 and spent the following five days traveling on foot and by bus to Manchester. There, he stayed with Frank Meade, a local union official. Meade suggested that he visit Wigan, putting him in touch with a miner named JERRY KENNAN, who in turn found him a room with another miner. After a few days, he left to take a room in a local tripe shop/boardinghouse, because "he wanted to see things at their worst." As the opening chapter of the book attests, he got his wish.

One feature of the original edition, not repeated until its appearance as volume 5 in Peter Davison's *Complete Works,* is the inclusion of 32 pages of photos, depicting the people and places of the industrial north in the midst of the depression.

The unpredictability of change is exemplified in the history of the Wigan Pier alluded to in the title. The pier, demolished long before the time of Orwell's visit, had been a "tumble-down jetty" that was used to load coal. As Orwell explained in a 1943 BBC interview, it had become a local joke to refer to Wigan Pier as a vacation spot, and the joke was picked up by music-hall comedians, "who had succeeded in keeping Wigan Pier alive as a byword, long after the place itself had been demolished" (*CW,* 10, 534). However, in the 1980s, the site became the home of "The Orwell Wigan Pier," which features not only a new pier overlooking a cleaned-up canal, but a museum and restaurants. Checking the name out on the Internet, Marjorie Sabin came upon a number of Web sites advertising a "restored and refurbished" heritage museum, and a hall, *The Orwell,* "the perfect venue for your private party or wedding." Sabin comments on the irony that a book which forces readers to "grapple with the social and historical reality of Depression suffering in the north of England" is now the raison d'être of a site offering "universal enjoyment" (243–244).

SYNOPSIS

Part I

Chapter 1

Beginning in medias res, Orwell describes himself awakening to the sounds of mill girls' wooden clogs, clanking on the cobblestones outside his window on their way to work He is staying at a combination tripe shop and lodging house in a room containing four beds. The cramped bedroom—actually a converted dining room—accommodates four lodgers, and Orwell must sleep with his legs curled up to avoid kicking the back of the man in the adjacent bed. The airless room has an unbearable smell, which one notices only after having spent some time outside of it. The boardinghouse has an indeterminate number of sleeping rooms and one decrepit bathroom. The kitchen/living room downstairs is heated by a central open fire, above which laundry usually hangs. The room is lit only by a skylight, as one side borders the shop and the other the larder, a dank, subterranean place where the owners, Mr. and Mrs. Brooker, store their tripe for the shop. A dingy couch sits near the door to the larder, and this is where Mrs. Brooker spends most of her time. She is an invalid, though no one seems to know the precise nature of her ailment. Near the center of the kitchen stands an old dining table covered in multiple greasy layers of tablecloth.

The shop is a narrow room with a large slab of counter space, on which Mr. Brooker prepares the tripe. The shop offers little more than tripe and tea, though cigarettes, bread, and tinned goods are also available. Mr. Brooker—out of work for the past two years—is a miner by trade, though he and his wife have for many years run various shops and other side businesses.

Meals at the Brookers are "uniformly disgusting." Mrs. Brooker's food is served to her on her sofa. She has a habit of wiping her mouth on her blankets or on strips of paper, which she leaves strewn on the floor for hours. Mr. Brooker, "an astonishingly dirty man," prepares most of the food for the boarders and invariably leaves a black thumbprint on the bread. The Brookers have some permanent boarders, including two old-age pensioners. The pensioners have given up their homes in compliance with the Means Test (rules governing the amount of public aid given to an individual). One of the pensioners suffers from a malignant disease—possibly cancer—and rarely leaves his bed except to pick up his pension money. The other pensioner, known as Old Jack, spent 50 years in the mines and seems to have no memories except those from his youth. Apart from the permanent boarders, the Brookers also host numerous commercial salesmen and advertising canvassers.

Orwell decides to leave the Brookers' place when he discovers a full chamber pot beneath the dining table one morning at breakfast. It is not simply the dirt and filth of the place that he objected to but rather "the feeling of stagnant, meaningless decay." Reflecting on his stay at the Brookers, he concludes that "It is a kind of duty to see and smell such places . . . lest you should forget that they exist; though perhaps it is better not to stay there too long."

Leaving Wigan by train, through a landscape dominated by slag heaps and belching chimneys, he sees a woman kneeling on the cold ground and trying to clear a clogged waste pipe with a stick. She is perhaps 25 years old but looks 40. He sees on her face a look of desolation and hopelessness, and he is convinced as, the train passes and she recedes into the distance, that it is wrong to assume that a lifetime in the slums has desensitized people to their fate. This woman knew all too well how miserable she was.

When the train reaches open country, the landscape regains some of its purity. It suggests to Orwell that the North is one great urban slum punctuated by "patches of cleanness and decency" interspersed between the muck.

Chapter 2

Orwell asserts via G. K. Chesterton that coal provides the foundation of modern civilization and that the coal miner occupies an exalted place in the order of things, though most people hardly consider their situation in this way. Part of Orwell's mission in the North is to evaluate of the life of coal miners, and any such study must include a visit to a coal face—the source at the bottom of a coal pit where the miners extract the coal. Though it is difficult to arrange, Orwell manages to organize a visit. He characterizes a coal pit in full operation as something like Hell, with the heat, the exertion, and the coal dust making the air virtually unbearable. The trip from the lift to the coal face is sheer agony. Bent double, neck craned to avoid overhead beams, the pain in his knees and thighs is excruciating. He moves at a slow pace so that the one-mile trip takes an hour. Arriving at the coal face, he finds a shiny black wall some three to four feet in height. The coal is sandwiched between layers of rock at the top and bottom. A conveyor used to move the extracted coal fills the air with an awful din. A half dozen men on their knees shovel the coal over their shoulders and onto the conveyor, which transports the coal to tubs and ultimately to the surface. These men—called fillers—impress Orwell with their strength and endurance.

A large part of a miner's work is simply getting to the coal face itself. The miners first take a cage lift—a steel box about the size of a telephone booth—to the bottom of the mine shaft. Once there, the miners often must travel a considerable distance, sometimes as far as three miles, to reach the coal face. Moreover, there are few places along the way where a miner can stand upright. The gallery that leads to the coal face cuts through solid rock. Wooden beams prop up the ceiling, and the ground is uneven and often covered with water. Tracks for the coal tubs add to the difficulty of walking, as the gallery narrows and miners are forced to walk in a stooped position. In some sections, they have to crawl on their hands and knees.

Orwell visits a few mine pits and feels that he has grasped the essentials of the processes going on below the ground. He explains the process of coal extraction with a colorful but apt metaphor. The process, he writes, is similar to "scooping out the central layer from a Neapolitan ice." Modern machinery has made the process easier by virtue of an electric coal cutter, a type of band saw that cuts horizontally while filling the pit with piercing noise and throwing coal dust into the air. Miners use the saw to cut into the rock above and below the coal seam before breaking up the coal with picks. In more difficult circumstances, miners drill holes into the rock, pack them with explosives, and cover them with clay. When the blasting or cutting is finished, miners remove the chunks of coal—sometimes as large as boulders—and place them on the conveyor. The coal is then moved to large tubs that travel up the main corridor of the pit to the mine shaft, where they are ultimately lifted to the surface. Above ground, miners sift the coal through screens and separate the shale, some of which is used as surfacing for belowground roads. The excess is dumped into piles called slagheaps on the surface. As the coal face recedes, new beams are installed and the conveyor is disassembled, moved forward, and reassembled. The cutting, blasting, and extraction are done in three shifts. The blasting takes place at night, as the law stipulates that it must be done only when no other men are working in the area. Orwell calculates that the fillers move approximately two tons of coal per hour, a workload that he calculates would kill him within two weeks.

The men working belowground represent for Orwell an alternative world, which people aboveground rarely consider. Coal mining plays a vital role in society. Every modern convenience depends upon it. Coal is an essential commodity, whether in peacetime or during war. Most people would agree, though they almost never question how it is obtained. Coal is a mysterious substance delivered at intervals to one's home. In Orwell's view, the coal miners below the ground drive the world above it. Some miners remember when mining processes were more difficult. Women were once used to pull the coal tubs with harnesses around their waists and chains running between their knees. They pulled the tubs even when they were pregnant. If the use of pregnant women were once again required, modern society would condone it. Such is the case, Orwell concludes, with all forms of manual labor, many of which are so removed from people's everyday experience that they have no conception of the hardships involved. Watching the miners at work makes Orwell doubt his belief in his intellectual superiority. Without the sweat and toil of the miners, the intellectuals would not remain superior. Poets, clergymen, writers of every sort, and revolutionaries owe the comparative comfort of their lives to men who break themselves belowground against the coal face.

Chapter 3

Anyone unfamiliar with mining would be taken aback by the sight of miners emerging from the ground. Despite the coal dust that clings obstinately to every part of their bodies, the miners' faces are ghostly pale from the bad air in the pit. The effect, however, wears off quickly in fresh air. Free of grime from the pit, miners look rather ordinary. They tend to be short, stocky and well muscled. The most distinctive feature is the blue creases in their faces, caused by coal dust getting trapped in open wounds that eventually get healed over with skin and remain fixed like a tattoo.

Above the ground after a shift, miners generally gargle fresh water to clear their throats of coal dust. Some wash before their meals. In Orwell's experience, most prefer to eat first. When they do wash, they are methodical. Some mining facilities have baths at the pithead where miners can bathe immediately after their shift. Such conveniences are rare because a coal seam is not permanent, and on-site baths are seen as an unnecessary and eventually a superfluous extravagance. Orwell contradicts the middle-class notion that miners would not clean themselves thoroughly even if baths were convenient. Where pithead baths exist, nearly all the men use them. Only among the older men, Orwell notes, does the belief persist that washing one's legs causes lumbago. In addition, the pithead baths are paid for out of the miners' welfare fund.

Miners have little time for personal hygiene—or anything else. Though their shifts run just under eight hours, they spend considerable time getting to the pit and then to the coal face. In mining districts, houses are in short supply. Many miners travel great distances to the mines. Orwell's time in miners' homes reveals how difficult it is for them to arrange their lives around their work schedule. They barely have more than three or four hours of leisure time. Contradicting the opinion of a Reverend W. R. Pope, who has written that miners are gluttons, Orwell counters that they eat comparatively little. They generally bring their lunch—bread with drippings—to the pit in metal containers called "snap-cans."

Another myth about the lives of miners that Orwell dismisses is the belief that miners are well paid. It is generally held that miners make a respectable wage of 150 pounds per year. Salaries among miners depend on the type of work they do. A "coal getter" receives 150 pounds a year, while a "detailer" (one who attends to the roofing in the pit) receives less. Even the "getters" are paid according to the amount of coal they amass. This, in turn, depends on the quality of the coal seam and whether there are delays due to faulty machinery. It is a misconception that coal miners work strictly six-day shifts all year. Every miner experiences layoffs each year for various reasons. Most estimates of wages do not consider the numerous gaps in work.

Orwell uses the pay stubs from a Yorkshire miner to illustrate the difficulty in estimating miners' wages. The stubs show an average wage in U.S. money of just about $14 per week. The stubs, however, cover the winter months when work is steady. In spring, the work falls off. Orwell cites figures from *The Coal Scuttle* to show that averages can be misleading. In addition, they don't take into consideration various deductions taken out of wages, including insurance, union fees, and even in many cases the hiring of a lamp for use in the pits. The types of deductions vary between districts. When all such costs are figured, Orwell estimates, the average miner earns no more than $10 per week. He then contrasts the wages of miners with the amount of coal they produce, a figure that has risen slowly but steadily over time. The figure for 1934 was 280 tons, though this is an average—those working the coal face produce well over 1,000 tons per year.

The Yorkshire miner's pay stubs are marked with a rubber stamp that reads "death stoppage." Orwell notes the fact that it is rubber-stamped, which shows that such stoppages are common. Accidents in the mine are frequent, and one out of every 900 miners is killed each year, while one in six is injured. Mine owners deduct money from their workers' wages to support the widows of those killed. No other trade is as dangerous or likely to result in some kind of injury. Every veteran miner that Orwell meets has experienced a serious accident or knows someone who has been killed at work.

The most common accident in mines is an explosion caused by gas, which is always present in varying levels in every mine. The miners use a Davy lamp to detect the presence of gas—the flame turns blue to indicate dangerous levels. The gas can ignite by a spark during blasting or from a pickaxe striking stone. Defective lamps or "gob fires"—spontaneous fires that smolder in the coal dust—can also trigger explosions. The most frequent accidents involve cave-ins of the roof. "Potholes appear sometimes in the roof or walls, from which large chunks of rock are shot out by pressure on the surrounding rock. The miners Orwell talks to say—almost to a man—that new machinery has made the pits even more dangerous. With coal being extracted at quicker rates, more sections are left exposed with no bracing. Vibration from the machinery also creates more dangerous conditions. Most miners can sense when the roof is unsafe. They say they can "feel the weight" above them. When injuries do occur, it takes considerable time to get the injured miner to the surface to receive medical attention.

While most miners Orwell meets are healthy, life below ground does make them susceptible to certain health problems. Miners are liable to get rheumatism, and men with weak lungs would not last long in the coal dust. The most characteristic ailment, however, is called nystagmus, which causes the eyeballs to oscillate in bright light. The condition can sometimes lead to blindness. This type of disability—or any other—allows the sufferer to draw a pension from the mining company, which never amounts to more than 29 shillings ($7.25) per week. Disabled miners can qualify for government aid if their pensions fall below 15 shillings ($3.75) per week. Pensions can be drawn weekly or in one lump sum. As the pension fund is not guaranteed, it is preferable to take the lump sum in case the mine goes bankrupt or closes for other reasons.

Orwell stays with a miner suffering from nystagmus. Watching him go to the mine each week to draw his pension reminds Orwell of the effects of "status." The miner has become disabled, doing one of the most useful jobs in England, and he has no say as to how he receives his pension. He is required to line up at the mine—sometimes for hours—to receive his money. For the middle-class person, no such inconvenience exists. Such indignities are indicative of working-class life, in which men and women are pressed down by numerous influences into a "passive role" whereby they do not act but are acted upon. The educated classes live with some anticipation of getting what they want. Orwell suggests that at times of stress, the upper classes distinguish themselves not because they are better educated or more gifted, but because they expect deference, and as a result, they get it.

Chapter 4

The miners in England's industrial districts endure difficult jobs, dangerous working conditions, and meager salaries. In addition, they suffer poor housing options. Most of the houses are the same, except with respect to the number of rooms. None has hot water. Most are also a half-century or more old and are barely habitable. They remain occupied principally because there are no alternatives. People will endure any deprivation for the sake of securing a house. This, in Orwell's view, is one of the worst aggravations of poverty.

In Wigan, there are more than 2,000 houses that have been condemned and are still inhabited. The tenants are caught in a vicious circle. The condemned house cannot be pulled down until the tenants have a new residence, which is next to impossible to find. The landlord will not put any more money than necessary into a condemned house. So the tenant puts up with unsanitary and even dangerous houses. Orwell includes extracts from his notebooks, in which he describes houses he has inspected and notes the various conditions. Some houses have sinking floors, while others have windows that do not open. Walls are routinely in shambles. Many houses leak, most are overcrowded, and all are not fit for inhabiting. However, his words cannot convey the misery of living in such houses, particularly the overcrowding. It is not uncommon to have 10 people living in three rooms. Beds are often shared by as many as four people. The leaks in winter make some rooms uninhabitable, and bugs—once they get in—are impossible to remove. In summer, when the cooking fire burns almost constantly, houses in which the windows do not open become infernos of heat.

Back-to-back houses, Orwell notes, are particularly bad. They are two houses set against each other, where one house enters from the street and the other from the backyard. Those in the front often have to walk 50 yards or more to reach the bathrooms and trash bins. Those in back live in full view of a row of bathrooms. Women in the front houses often throw their garbage into the street gutter rather than walk to the back of the house. Women living under these conditions have more to do than there is time in a day. Daily chores—taking care of the house, cooking meals, and caring for the children—leave little time for cleanliness. Orwell recalls some vividly appalling houses crowded with children and uniformly malnourished people, chamber pots sitting in the middle of the living room. He admits that they don't need to live this way, but the difficulty of their lives and the depth of their poverty do little to improve their self-respect. One determining factor, Orwell notes, is the number of children in a house. Those with no or few children are invariably better kept.

Nothing Orwell sees in the large tract housing compares in squalor to the "caravan dwellings" that are common to most industrial towns. With no hope of getting a house, some 1,200 people in Wigan live in a caravan colony. Orwell claims not to have witnessed such squalor except in Burma. Most of the dwellings are constructed from old single-decker buses. Others are made from wagons with canvas stretched over them. The interiors are small, and Orwell never saw fewer than two people inhabiting single caravans. In one instance, seven people lived in a caravan some 14 feet long. In the winter months, the caravans are never dry, and thin canvas is the only thing between the inhabitants and the freezing cold. Caravan dwellers get their water from a hydrant common to the group, though sometimes people must walk great distances to get it. Residents also construct their own bathrooms by setting up a wooden shack and digging pits for the waste. All the people Orwell sees living in these caravans are filthy. Some residents have lived in such conditions for many years. The housing corporations are trying to eliminate caravans, but without any alternative housing, they still stand. As degraded as their lives have become, residents of the caravans once had their own homes, but as time passes, many have given up hope of a real home. What is still worse, the residents must pay rent for their shabby caravans. Orwell says that he could not find anyone paying less than five shillings $1.25 per week.

Given the housing shortage, Orwell is at a loss to explain why new homes are not being built fast enough or why some towns can borrow more money than others. A corporation house costs between 300 and 400 pounds ($1,500–$2,000), and rent would average about 20 pounds ($100) a year. The reasons given for the delays in building are lack of money and lack of adequate sites. Corporation houses must be built in "estates," not individually. As to money, Orwell wonders why northern towns such as Barnsley spend 150,000 pounds on a new town hall when so many people are in need of decent housing. Despite the slowness, houses are being built. The rows of corporation houses are a common feature on the outskirts of industrial towns. While the quality of these houses is nearly identical from place to place, the reactions of their tenants vary. Some like their new accommodations and can afford the increased expense—fuel costs, furnishings—while others never get comfortable in their new homes, which are invariably better than the slums. They have more room, bathrooms, and a patch of garden. But they are usually well removed from the mines, and some don't have access to bus routes. Shops in these estates are also generally more expensive. Orwell suggests that apartments might be the solution, but the northern working classes dislike apartments and call them tenements. Even the corporation houses are disappointing to many, who never feel quite at home. This, for Orwell, poses the greatest difficulty in solving the housing problem.

In the removal of the slums and the building of corporation houses, Orwell sees "something ruthless and soulless about the whole business." Corporation housing burdens the tenants with numerous restrictions. Inhabitants are not allowed to do what they want with their houses. Some require hedges in every yard to be the same. Poultry and pigeons are not allowed to be kept. Even the number of shops is strictly limited. This poses a threat to the small shopkeeper who makes his living in working-class neighborhoods and is kept out of the new estates. Pubs are almost completely forbidden, except for modern, expensive places. The new housing schemes don't take account of the communal necessities of working-class life. It is not uncommon that new tenants be required to delouse before occupying their new homes, along with all of their possessions. Such indignities make the clearance of the slums rather inhumane. Orwell admits that the new estates are better than the slums, but not by a wide margin.

Orwell concludes his analysis of housing conditions by remarking that in the hundreds of houses he inspected, he was always warmly received by their occupants. He quotes a review of one of his books that suggests that he sees only the bad side of things. He responds that while in Wigan, he enjoyed the place and its people. His only complaint is that the Wigan Pier—which he expressly hoped to see—had been torn down, and that even its location was now uncertain.

Chapter 5

Orwell discovers that unemployment figures in England are deceptive, as they reflect only those on the dole and not their spouses or children. According to a labor exchange official whom Orwell consults, the real figure of people living on unemployment in England can be derived by taking the published figure—about two million—and multiplying by three. This is still an underestimation, of a serious problem, for many people with jobs barely manage to survive on what they earn. Adding these individuals to the mix—along with old-age pensioners and other destitutes—the real number of what Orwell calls the "underfed population" swells to more than 10 million. Some put the figure at twice that number.

In Wigan, a typical industrial and mining district, the number of insured workers is 36,000. The number of unemployed in 1936 was nearly 10,000 in winter, when most mines are working full time. In summer, the number of unemployed would rise to 12,000—out of a population of nearly 87,000. Any unemployed worker—married with three children—receiving insurance stamps earns about 32 shillings per week from the Public Assistance Committee (PAC). When the insurance runs out, unemployed married workers get a transitional benefit of about 38 shillings. A quarter of the worker's benefit is calculated for rent. Rates vary with payment from the PAC after the transition, but the average family of five earns about 32 shillings per week, with a quarter of this figure also calculated for rent. A coal allowance of just over one shilling is included for six weeks prior to and following Christmas. So, the average family on the dole can be said to earn about 30 shillings per week. After rent is considered, each member of the family of five must be fed, clothed, and warmed on just six or seven shillings per week. Orwell calculates that nearly a third of all people living in industrial areas live on this amount.

The Means Test—the rules that determine the eligibility of individuals for government aid—is strictly enforced, and anyone suspected of earning any wage whatever for any type of work is liable to have his aid reduced. Orwell cites an unusual example of a man seen feeding his neighbors' chickens while they were away. He was reported to the authorities as having a job feeding chickens, and he avoided a reduction in aid only with considerable difficulty. The cruelest effect of the Means Test is the way it can break up families. An old-age pensioner would normally live with a family member if he is a widower. Under the rules of the Means Test, he would be counted as a lodger, and his family member would have their aid reduced. So, at an advanced age, he is forced to take cheap lodging in a boardinghouse, turn over his aid to the landlord, and live on a mere pittance.

Despite the shocking numbers of unemployed and those on the dole, extreme poverty seems to be less evident in the industrial districts. While most things are poorer and shabbier, there are fewer who are obviously destitute, and far fewer beggars than are found in London. Moreover, the unemployment regulations do not discourage marriage. A couple who lives on the verge of poverty still has a better life than a single person on the dole, who frequently lives in a common lodging house and must feed and clothe himself on just six shillings per week. Orwell has witnessed unmarried men living in extreme circumstances, but it is not common. For married couples on the dole, unemployment does not alter much their way of life.

Despite these conclusions, Orwell notes that the "deadening, debilitating effect of unemployment" is undeniable. The best intellects could not stand up to it. Orwell has infrequently met unemployed people with justified literary ambitions. They produce so little work—though what is produced is generally better than most—because they have no peace of mind to focus on their writing. Miners suffer a similar debilitation. One cannot look for work every day for years. Programs have been developed to help re-educate or simply occupy the time of miners, like occupational centers, where the unemployed can learn such trades as carpentry, bootmaking, and leather work. They cannot sell the furniture, though, and can only use it in their homes. Socialists generally disparage such programs as merely diversions to keep men occupied. Orwell agrees with this, but suggests that they may offer a better alternative than simply doing nothing.

The best assistance program in Orwell's view is being run by the National Unemployment Workers' Movement—a revolutionary organization intended to keep the unemployed unified and to provide legal counsel to deal with the Means Test. It is an organization formed by the workers themselves, which Orwell admires. The organization runs shelters where men can congregate and hear Communist speakers, though most come simply to get warm and play dominoes. Orwell suggests that a combination of the NUWM and the occupational centers is closer to what is needed, adding that every unemployed man should have a plot of land to tend and tools to work with so that at least he can grow a little extra food for his family.

Orwell claims to have first learned of unemployment in England in 1928, after his return from Burma. What shocked him most is that unemployed men appeared to be ashamed of their situation, particularly because he saw that shrinking job markets and economic forces were to blame, not the individuals themselves. The middle classes at that time perpetuated the myth that the unemployed were simply idlers and could find work if they really wanted to. Orwell's travels among tramps taught him that many of them were respectable working-class men—miners or cotton workers—who could not understand how they lost their jobs. Having been brought up to work hard, they saw that there was little opportunity of working again in the future. In Orwell's opinion, attitudes are changing. The middle classes are slowly accepting that unemployment is more than just laziness, and that the working classes are learning about the economic factors behind unemployment. Orwell credits the *Daily Worker* for helping to change opinion. As more people rely on public assistance to survive, they become less ashamed of their situation.

Orwell is surprised to see that so many people living on the dole have not suffered emotionally or spiritually—something he suggests would not happen with the middle classes. Evidence of this is that so many poor working-class people continue to marry. Orwell suggests that "they realize that losing your job does not mean that you cease to be a human being." Poverty makes many families suffer, but they remain together. Despite their poverty, the working classes still enjoy some luxuries. Orwell thinks that movies and cheap, smart clothing have had a dramatic influence. Since World War I, trade has adjusted, so that luxuries are nearly always cheaper than necessities.

The cheapest of all luxuries, according to Orwell, is gambling, through which the poor manage to buy a little hope. Technology has also offered some compensation. Almost all households have access to radios, and anyone can go to the public library and read the newspapers. This is not the ideal situation, but it seems to have allowed the poor to navigate some kind of meaningful existence. Otherwise, the working classes would descend into despair or attempt insurrections, which would only lead to savage repression. Instead, English workers make the best of their situations, and the possibility of revolution diminishes.

Chapter 6

Having looked at housing costs and the general deprivations consequent to unemployment, Orwell turns to the issue of food. The unemployed generally receive about 32 shillings per week, a quarter of which is allotted for rent. Orwell is surprised by how seldom people consider the importance of food to the health and well-being (not including the future of the family) of the poor. "A man dies and is buried, and his words and actions are forgotten, but the food he has eaten lives after him in the sound or rotten bones of his children."

Orwell analyzes a monthly food budget acquired from an unemployed miner, married with two children, and with an allowance of 32 shillings per week. The list of expenses includes rent, union and insurance dues, clothing subscriptions, meat, vegetables, and miscellaneous items such as sugar, tea, and soup. Orwell notes that the miner's budget leaves out a number of items—spices, razor blades, kindling wood, and repairs to furniture and bedding, to name only a few. There is also no budget for tobacco. If these items were to be purchased, there would be less money for essential items on the list.

The limited funds available through public assistance raises the question of whether it is even possible to live on such a budget. During a national debate over the Means Test, sample budgets appeared in the newspapers claiming that one could live on merely four shillings per week. These lists make no provision for fuel of any kind. Orwell admits—providing that the budget is not a hoax—that it may be theoretically possible to live on four shillings per week. Compared to the unemployed miner's list, the newspaper samples contained notable differences. The miner spends much of his budget on white bread, margarine, and potatoes—all in all, a poor diet. While it would be better if the miner spent less on fuel and more on fruit and brown bread, Orwell suggests that no ordinary human being could be expected to live on such food. The unemployed take comfort in luxuries that are not necessarily healthy or that don't represent the most efficient use of funds. "Unemployment is an endless misery that has got to be constantly palliated."

Orwell suggests that the results of eating a poor diet can be verified by witnessing the physical degeneracy apparent in so many people in England—not just among the working classes. The results of a poor diet are perhaps most dramatically seen in the industrial areas. Despite their well-muscled physiques, the coal miners are physically smaller than men in other parts of the country, and their children are often undernourished. Most people have terrible teeth—a further sign of malnourishment. Few adults in the north have their own teeth. Death rates and infant mortality are almost double that of other regions.

Physical degeneracy can also be seen in other areas of England, from rural villages to the back streets of London. While watching the funeral procession of King George V in Trafalgar Square, Orwell was struck by the shabby, unhealthy appearances of the men and women in the street. Even the guards seemed inferior to those he remembered from his youth. If the physical qualities of the English had declined, Orwell suggests that one reason is that a million young men had died in the First World War without having reproduced. Moreover, in Orwell's opinion, the working classes are generally ignorant and wasteful about food. The habit in the north of baking one's own bread leads to considerable waste. One has time to bake no more than once or twice each week, and a large portion of the quantity produced goes bad before it can be eaten. Almost no one among the working classes eats the more wholesome whole wheat bread, and many opt for tinned goods rather than fresh ones.

Efforts have been made in some districts to educate the working classes about food and managing money, though such programs are controversial. Orwell hears a communist speaker argue heatedly against the practice. It's bad enough to force millions of people to live on almost nothing, but to preach to them about how to spend the little they have is an added insult. Orwell suggests that working-class's inefficiency with money is what keeps their allowance as high as it is. If they were more economical, he doesn't doubt that the PAC would lower the rate of assistance accordingly.

One item that is cheap even for the unemployed is fuel. The price of coal in mining areas is quite low. Despite its cheapness, there is consistent theft of coal, but only in a technical sense. The excess sent up from the mining pits contains usable coal. Many unemployed work diligently to pick it out of the slag heaps. In Wigan, the unemployed compete for the illicit coal in a custom that has come to be called scrambling for coal. Orwell witnesses one such instance. A few hundred men gather at the mountainous dirtpiles near the mine head, each with a sack and a coal hammer. The dirt from the pits is loaded into train carts, which are taken to slag heaps a quarter mile away. The men scramble onto the trucks while the train is moving. The first one to arrive on a truck claims it as his own and proceeds to dig for coal. The train makes multiple runs to the slag heaps, and the driver pays no attention to the men looking for coal.

Women also assist in gathering spare coal. As the men shovel through the dirt, the women and children sift through the dirt that falls to the ground, pulling out lumps of coal the size of an egg or smaller. The trucks don't always contain dirt. Some carry shale, which contains no coal. There is another flammable substance called cannel, which looks like ordinary shale but is slightly darker. It makes tolerable fuel, though it's not good enough to be commercially valuable. In a few hours, the dirt is picked clean and the men and women haul their booty back home.

Robbing the dirt piles takes place every day during the winter, though it can be extremely dangerous. Orwell hears of men who have lost legs and fingers as they tried to board the train. Picking through the slag heaps is technically theft, and occasionally the mining companies prosecute someone for form's sake. When this happens, the coal pickers pool together to pay the fine. The scene of the coal picking remains vivid in Orwell's memory from his travels in Lancashire: women kneeling in the bitter cold in front of the slag heaps, which stretch for miles around, the product of coal mines that could never sell all the coal they are capable of producing.

As one travels north, the most dramatic shift in the landscape occurs after Birmingham. There, one encounters "the real ugliness of industrialism," which compels the visitor to come to terms with it. The landscapes of the north are dominated by interminable stretches of slag heaps, many of them on fire. At night, red and blue flames wind around the great piles. The heaps eventually collapse, and an "evil brown grass" grows over the top. Nonetheless, they are more or less a permanent fixture, even when the years attempt to hide them.

Industrialism—particularly mining—has turned northern villages into alien landscapes full of mud, cinders, and mountains of slag, with little vegetation. Orwell calls Sheffield the ugliest town in the Old World, making Wigan look beautiful by comparison. Sheffield is dominated by gasworks, and he finds the stench of the town almost unbearable. The river flowing through town is yellow, presumably from chemical pollution by the factories. Orwell claims to have counted 33 chimney stacks that could be seen from one street in Sheffield. One particularly vivid memory is of a patch of waste ground littered with newspapers and old saucepans. On one side, the ubiquitous four-room houses sit blackened by smoke; on the other, an interminable vista of factory chimneys stretch into the distance, submerged in a black haze.

At night, Sheffield takes on a certain "sinister magnificence" for Orwell, with the sulfurous chimney smoke tinged with red and flames glowing from the foundries. The pottery towns of the north are just as ugly but in a prettier way. Amid the rows of blackened houses sit the "pot banks"—brick chimneys partially beneath ground and belching smoke. Large clay chasms cut deep into the surrounding landscape where tubs on pulleys carry clay out of the clay pits and workers cling to the steep walls to carve the clay out. Traveling through the north in winter, Orwell notes that even the snow is black. Less than 10 miles away, one leaves the stain of industrialism behind and once again finds undefiled country.

Two questions come to Orwell's mind with regard to the ugly industrial north: Is it all inevitable, and does it matter? Orwell suggests that industrial towns don't have to be ugly. They have become so in the north because they were built in an era when people were more interested in making money. At present, no one seems to care that much about the aesthetics of their towns. In contrast, the industrial villages of the south are built of concrete, glass, and steel, surrounded by manicured lawns and flower beds. Though they are not beautiful in any real sense, they are much nicer than Sheffield. But, then, perhaps it is not advisable for industrialism to disguise itself. He quotes T. H. Huxley as saying that a dark, satanic mill should look like a dark satanic mill, with which Orwell agrees. The horrors of industrial towns are not simply based on their appearances, but rather on the difficulty of their inhabitants' lives. Apart from this, the ugliness can have a certain macabre appeal. As an example, Orwell mentions the Burmese landscapes. They appalled him when he lived in Burma and stayed with him like a nightmare; they continued to haunt him so that he had to write a novel to get rid of them. The horror of industrialism exists much deeper than just the surface ugliness.

When one enters the north of England, one is conscious of entering another country—quite apart from the scenery. There is for Orwell a "cult of northernness" that exists, and it has impressed most people in England with an innate sense of antithesis between the north and south. A Yorkshireman in the South takes pains to claim his superiority—the north is full of "real" people and "real" life, while the south contains nothing but parasites. Northerners are gritty and warmhearted, while southerners are snobbish and effeminate. Orwell characterizes it this way: "Hence, the Southerner goes North, at any rate for the first time, with the vague inferiority complex of a civilized man venturing among savages, while the Yorkshireman, like the Scotchman, comes to London in the spirit of a barbarian out for loot." Such prejudices are often adopted by people who are not native-born northerners. While most intelligent Britons would be horrified by most racial prejudices, they feel the North-South bias keenly.

Orwell speculates that such prejudice derives from historical antecedents. Those in the colder north were considered more energetic and hardy, as many of Orwell's history texts during his student years used to claim. The myth of English superiority in energy has survived for more than 100 years, according to Orwell, and it has been reinforced in the literature of various periods. It was industrialism that gave the North-South antithesis its peculiar character. Only until relatively recently was the North considered the backward part of England. Industry was focused largely in the south, around London. As coal use increased, the North prospered on the image of the boorish, self-made northern businessman—literary examples include Dickens' Mr. Bounderby, whose claims to respectability lie solely in the fact that he knows how to make money. It would be a mistake, however, to think that such obnoxious attitudes extend to the actual working classes. Expecting to be met in the North with rudeness and prejudice, Orwell is treated—at least by the miners—with extraordinary kindness. No one showed any hint of despising him for being from a particular part of the country. This is an important point for Orwell, as English regional snobberies are "nationalism in miniature."

Orwell considers whether it is actually possible to be intimate with the working class. He believes not, but claims that it is easier to attempt it in the North than in the South. Orwell has seen enough of the working classes not to idealize them. The main point for him is that middle-class prejudices are tested by exposure to those who are different, not necessarily better. Working-class attitudes toward honesty and plainspokeness are noteworthy. While impoverished middle classes fall apart, the working classes come together. The working class habit of speaking plainly and honestly can be disconcerting. Many among the working classes have a certain reverence for learning in others but do not aspire to it themselves. Working-class youths want to work more than they want to be educated, as much for themselves as for the money they can bring in for the family. Orwell finds the atmosphere of a working-class home—one in which the father is not unemployed—to be warm, decent, and deeply human. These households are complete and symmetrical to Orwell. Such scenes will not last forever, as the world—and industry—progresses. It is the memories of such interiors, and not the triumphs of the industrial age, that makes Orwell feel that this era has not been entirely bad one in which to live.

Part 2, Chapter 8

Having addressed conditions among the working classes hit hardest by unemployment, Orwell wants to consider possible solutions to the problems presented in part 1, the first seven chapters of the book. The search for a solution inevitably raises the question of whether socialism offers the answer. But before considering socialism, he suggests it is necessary to take up "the terribly difficult issue of class," which is going to involve an autobiographical digression on his part. He describes himself as being born into "the lower-upper-middle" class. The *lower* in that description refers to income, but income, assuming it was a minimum of 300 pounds a year, did not exclude you from membership. If you were a professional in the colonial service, the military, or the church, you still qualified as a member of the upper classes. It was a matter of bearing, clothes, manners, and, of course, accent. In this kind of shabby-genteel family, one is far more conscious of poverty than any working-class family that requires no public assistance. The income of a lower-upper-middle-class family is spent principally on keeping up appearances. The importance of this class of society cannot be overemphasized. They serve, in Orwell's view, as a shock absorber of the bourgeoisie. This cushion is not available to the lower-upper-middle-class, who struggle to keep up the appearance of wealth on what are essentially working-class wages. They are forced into contact, as it were, with the working class, and Orwell suspects that it is from them that the traditional attitudes toward common people derive—an attitude that Orwell describes as "sniggering superiority punctuated by bursts of vicious hatred." Such attitudes have been expressed for decades in newspapers and literary works, where the working classes are portrayed as either figures of fun if they are in difficult straits or as devils if they are too prosperous. To understand how such attitudes took shape, Orwell suggests that one must understand how the working classes appear to those living among them but separated by different habits and traditions.

Orwell claims to have been very young when he became aware of class distinctions. He used to play with the children of a plumber, but he was later prohibited from doing so because they were common. Shabby-genteel families cannot risk having their children grow up with the wrong accents. Early on for Orwell, the working classes became enemies. They hated the shabby-genteel class—indeed the whole of the upper classes. In Orwell's early boyhood, he came to consider the working classes to be subhuman. Before the First World War, there existed in England much more overt class hatred. The upper classes were more likely to be insulted—or even assaulted—on the streets by working-class people. The situation has changed, partly due to unemployment. Now the working classes are more likely to grovel than to cast insults. It is natural to Orwell that the working classes would come to resent being treated unfairly for a century or more. It is also understandable that the children of shabby-genteel families would grow up with a hatred of the working classes.

Orwell now discusses what he considers the secret source of class separation, the almost universal belief that the lower classes smell. This is what the shabby-genteel class—including Orwell—was taught, and nothing is more difficult to overcome than a physical feeling of revulsion. Anyone who has grown up in a home that has a bathroom and at least one servant has been taught to think this way about the lower classes, but Orwell finds it unusual that it is seldom discussed. He can think of only one book—W. Somerset Maugham's *On a Chinese Screen*—in which this idea is expressed honestly. Orwell provides a lengthy excerpt that illustrates the class divide that is based on smell.

But do the lower classes smell? He suggests that, on the whole, they are dirtier than the upper classes because of their living circumstances. But Orwell also suggests that cleanliness is on the rise in England. What he finds detestable is the practice among some of idealizing the working class to such an extent that their uncleanness becomes a virtue. Such attitudes give credence to the myth that the lower classes are dirty by choice rather than circumstance. Those with access to baths generally use them. But the middle classes believe the lower classes are actually dirty—and what is worse, they believe they are inherently dirty. Orwell grew up with such notions, but his experiences among the tramps of England have driven such prejudices from him.

Orwell justifies spending so much time on this subject by saying that you must understand how the classes view each other before you can make progress toward eliminating class distinctions. Orwell grew up before and during World War I, and so attitudes have changed somewhat since then. But in his opinion, the essential feelings still remain. Every middle-class person has a dominant class prejudice that only needs waking. The middle class cannot comprehend that they survive on the exploitation of the classes below them. In fact, they would believe conversely that they are under threat by the working classes, which threaten to obliterate middle-class traditions. Orwell claims that class hatred seems to be diminishing because it does not appear as frequently in print. It can best be studied in personal conversation. Orwell gives an example of one exception. He provides excerpts from the literary critic George Saintsbury, whose writings exhibit severely calloused opinions about the lower class. The only surprising thing about such hatred is that Saintsbury was willing to put it down on paper.

Saintsbury's opinions are rightly seen as reactionary. Orwell considers next the influence of class prejudice in more enlightened groups. The ranks of socialists and communists swell with members of the middle class, whose continued devotion to bourgeois career pursuits is understandable. One has to earn a living. But devotion to the principles of a classless society does little to alter the tastes of these middle-class people. Is there any real change, except that now he votes Labour Party? Such people still associate with their own class. They retain their bourgeois tastes in food and art. They also invariably marry into their own class. Orwell cites Comrade X, the author of *Marxism for Infants.* It so happens that this hypothetical author of this hypothetical book could be an old Etonian. He idealizes the proletariat, but his habits give him away. He would never dream of drinking his tea out of a saucer. Such men, no matter how devoted to their socialist or communist causes, still feel in his heart that "working-class manners" are disgusting.

Chapter 9

Orwell admits that as a teenager he was "an odious little snob," but no more so than other boys at Eton. In fact, he was frequently on the receiving end of the snobbery, since he was a scholarship boy, poorer than the typical student. He felt the best thing was to be a gentleman by birth but to have no money. This is the creed of the lower-upper-middle class. The years he spent at school before and just after the First World War were unusual. England was much closer to revolution than it has been since or than it was a century earlier. The revolutionary spirit was driven by the youth, who died in the millions while the older generation watched from a safe distance. The mood of antimilitarism galvanized the youth of England against orthodoxy and authority. Communism became fashionable. The unorthodox opinions gaining currency—pacifism, feminism, birth-control advocacy—trickled down to schoolboys, who felt that they were enlightened. They continued to enjoy the comforts of their class while also being against the government.

He describes himself "at the age of 18 or 19" as being both a snob and a revolutionary. He resented authority, had read all of Shaw's works, and loosely described himself as a socialist, though he had little idea what a socialist was. He could agonize from a distance over the agony of the working classes, but he still hated them. This was the era of the coal strikes. The working classes were in a fighting mood. Unemployment was not an issue until after the war. Returning soldiers had not accepted the social changes.

Just prior to turning 20, Orwell went to Burma to serve in the Indian Imperial Police. On the surface, the class question in Burma seemed to have been submerged. There was no obvious class friction. The all-important thing in Burma was not what school you attended but whether your skin was technically white. Most of the Englishmen in Burma were not gentlemen, though they tried to live like gentlemen.

Orwell served briefly with a British police regiment that was predominantly made up of lower-class men. Orwell admired the men—most of them had served in the Great War—but they "faintly repelled" him. His class prejudices, formed as a child, prevented him from seeing objectively his fellow officers. What helped him overcome his prejudices was something only indirectly related to the class issue. Orwell's five years in the Indian police instilled in him a hatred of imperialism that one cannot quite feel unless one is stuck in the middle of it. From the outside, imperialism seems necessary, as foreign powers seem to rule the "natives" better than they rule themselves. In the midst of such tyranny, it is impossible to feel like anything other than an intruder, and many more Anglo-Indians felt this way than one would expect. "The truth is that no modern man, in his heart of hearts, believes that it is right to invade a foreign country and hold the population down by force." Thus, every Anglo-Indian is haunted by guilt that must be hidden because of a lack of freedom of speech. Being overheard to criticize the Empire could cause damage to one's career. The only exception is for those who do work that is unconnected to the empire—forest officers, doctors, or engineers. Orwell was in the police, and so he was a member of the machine of despotism. They did the dirty work of empire.

Other foreigners in Burma looked down on such activities. Orwell gives an example of a missionary from America who witnessed the bullying of a Burmese suspect and said that he would hate to have the job of a police officer. Scenes of Burmese squatting in jails, the scars from whippings filled him with loathing. While he was in Burma, Orwell witnessed a hanging that had a profound effect on him. It made him feel like the worst criminal. The result was that Orwell conceived an anarchistic theory that all government was evil, that punishment does more harm than crime, and that people will behave decently if left alone. In later years, he would agree that citizens must be protected from violence, but his objections to punishment arise naturally in one responsible for administering it. The faces of Burmese convicts revealed their disdain for arbitrary justice administered by foreign invaders, and Orwell had not trained himself "to be indifferent to the expression of a human face."

Orwell returned to England on leave in 1927, nearly determined to quit his job. His service in Burma had left him with a bad conscience. He had bullied and snubbed people. He had beaten Burmese with his fists. He felt that he needed to make amends, and he developed the mistaken view that "the oppressed are always right and the oppressors always wrong." Orwell wanted to submerge himself in the lives of the oppressed, to take their side against the oppressor. Failure became a virtue, and any thought of advancing in a career was repugnant. This is the path by which Orwell's attention turned to the working classes. The working classes in England were the equivalent of the Burmese in Burma. Unemployment was on the rise, and he had figured out what caused it. He didn't buy into the rhetoric of the middle classes that such men were merely lazy. At this time, however, he was not interested in socialism or any other political solution. In fact, he thought that economic injustice would end when people decided to end it.

Orwell knew nothing about the reality of working-class life. When he thought of poverty, it had always been in terms of brute starvation, so his attention turned immediately toward tramps and beggars, and all of the lowest sorts in society. Once he was among them and accepted by them, he hoped that some of his guilt would drop away. He decided to disguise himself and enter the world of the down-and-outs. He would learn how to navigate the streets and casual wards, and learn where to meet the social outcasts. His first foray was a common lodging house in Whitechapel. Finally overcoming his fear of the lower classes, he enters, expecting a fight. Instead, he is barely noticed. He was also accepted by the men as one of them. He spent three or four days there, and in coming weeks, he would set out on the road, later documenting his experiences in DOWN AND OUT IN PARIS AND LONDON (1933).

Chapter 10
Orwell admits that one does not overcome class prejudice by making friends with tramps and other social outcasts. These groups are not indicative of all the lower classes or working classes. Orwell found it easy to gain acceptance among the tramps simply on the basis of his appearance and the belief that he was genuinely destitute. Orwell describes the tramp's world as "a small, squalid democracy." One cannot approach the middle classes in the same way. One can approach the working-class intelligentsia through socialism, but they are as untypical of the mass of working classes as the tramps are of the lower classes. Orwell spent some months living in the homes of coal miners. They treated him hospitably and, he hopes, came to like him. But he and they always perceived a subtle difference of social position. Class difference remains, like a glass wall.

It has become fashionable in Orwell's day to think that the glass wall could be penetrated. Everyone recognizes the existence of class prejudices, while also thinking of themselves as exempt. The intelligentsia sneers at social hierarchies that reinforce class difference—the House of Lords, the Royal Family, public schools, etc. Everyone rails against class distinctions, but few people seriously want to abolish them. Orwell uses the work of John Galsworthy to illustrate that he protested against immovable class distinctions, secure in the knowledge that they were immovable. Once he suspected something like real change, he recommended that the working classes be deported to the colonies. Such insincerity, Orwell asserts, runs through all "advanced opinion." He uses imperialism to make the point. Every left-wing intellectual vilifies empire. Even right-wingers look at imperialism with detached amusement. The real question underlying these attitudes is whether such people really want the British Empire to end? In Orwell's opinion, no Englishman can say that he wishes to see the empire crumble. The high quality of life in England depends on holding tight to the colonies. All Englishmen are complicit in the oppressions created by empire. They reinforce that point each time they enjoy the bounty of their home country.

This is where one perceives the unreality surrounding so much of the class question. Most everyone would wish that the lives of coal miners were easier. An elevation in conditions and salary could do much toward eliminating class distinctions. Most people, however, do not appreciate what would be involved. "The fact that has got to be faced is that to abolish class distinctions means abolishing a part of yourself." Orwell is a member of the middle class, and everything he is has been shaped by his upbringing and conditioned by his implicit attitudes toward class. To get outside the "class racket," one would need to change all one's attitudes to such an extent that he or she would be virtually unrecognizable. It's not enough to improve conditions among the working classes or to get over one's snobbishness, but rather a complete abandonment of the upper-class and middle-class attitude toward life.

Many believe, however, that the classless society can be achieved without such abandonment. Middle-class socialists invite members of the proletariat into their worlds in an attitude of brotherhood. Others attempt to raise up the lower classes. Even among the royal family, programs exist that force youth from different class backgrounds together. Orwell believes all such coercive attempts to bring the classes together are mistaken and rather serve to reinforce class distinctions. Most middle-class people come in contact with the proletariat through the intelligentsia, but the intelligentsia comprises two camps: those who remain working class in their employment and habits, and those who succeed in pulling themselves up to a class above. Orwell believes that the first type is among the finest men England has. The second type, however, is less admirable.

Orwell says it is a pity that the proletariat should penetrate the middle class by way of the literary intelligentsia, something not easily accomplished by decent human beings. The highbrow, literary intelligentsia is a "poisonous jungle" in which one succeeds through groveling and sycophancy. The bourgeois class wishing to have contact with the proletariat most often wants such highbrow literary "bum-lickers," for they are the most likely to overcome their class. The result is to drive the bourgeois back into his snobbishness. Not until you meet someone outside your culture do you understand what your own beliefs are. Bourgeois intellectuals soothe their consciences by railing against their traditions—Church of England, patriotism, etc. To one truly outside the bourgeois culture, the similarities between the bourgeois and what they criticize is more evident than the differences.

From the opposite perspective, the proletariat climbs out of his class to a higher one only to find none of the acceptance and equality that he hoped to find. Instead, he finds bourgeois culture dead and hollow. Examples of such conclusions are readily available in leftist journals and among Communist writers. Orwell cites D. H. LAWRENCE as one who often wrote about such things. The gamekeeper in *Lady Chatterley's Lover* is caught between classes. He has no desire to return to the working class, but he is appalled by what he finds among the bourgeoisie. He also cites a Lawrence poem that analogizes the attempt to rise above your class Forced meetings between proletarians and bourgeois only expose real antagonism. The approach must be slow, unforced, and honest. If one feels superior to another class, it is better to say so than to lie about it.

It frequently occurs that a young and ardent socialist becomes, in later life, a snobby conservative. The process of backtracking is understandable to Orwell. A classless society is perhaps not a beautiful state where everyone gets along and snobbishness is snuffed out. Instead, it may be much bleaker and will require the abandonment of all previous codes of behavior and former ideals. The conclusion drawn is that perhaps the elimination of class distinctions is not such an easy business after all. When the bourgeois wishes to greet the proletariat on equal terms and discovers that the proletariat wishes his class dead, he returns just as quickly to his class consciousness, and if the return is quick enough, it may take him all the way to fascism.

Chapter 11

Orwell turns to the issue of socialism. The world, in his view, is a mess. The working classes suffer from poverty or unemployment, and there is little that can be done about it. The middle classes are also feeling the pinch and know neither if they are happy or sad. Many in the bourgeoisie are haunted by the miseries of the lower class. This is just the beginning. England may see something much worse in the coming years. Everyone with a brain knows that global socialism is a way out. Orwell finds that socialism makes so much sense that he cannot understand why it has not been established. The idea that all people must cooperate to do their fair share and receive their fair share is so obvious to Orwell that anyone failing to agree must do so out of a corrupt motive. But socialism is not establishing itself. It is even on the decline. Orwell notes that, as he writes, Madrid is under siege by fascists and will likely fall.

The average thinking person is not simply against socialism but actually hostile to it. There must be something in the way socialism is being presented that puts people off. Orwell proposes to get inside the head of the average objector to socialism. In order to understand socialism, it is necessary to attack it. He plays the devil's advocate on behalf of the people who may feel that socialism is the right course for the world yet shy away from it. If people like this are questioned, they often claim to like socialism but detest socialists. Socialism in England is largely a middle-class movement. Many of these champion socialism in theory but have no intention of abandoning the privileges of their social position. Most middle-class socialists cling desperately to their feelings of superiority. They would flinch at having actual working-class members at their meetings. Even socialist writing suggests this aversion. Socialist and communist pamphlets and books are clearly not written for the working class, since they employ a jargon that is as inexplicable as Latin to a proletarian.

Orwell makes a distinction between the kind of socialism a working-class man practices and that of the book-trained socialist. To the working classes, socialism means better pay, shorter hours, and more rights. To revolutionaries, it is a standard behind which they march toward potential violence. No working-class man, in Orwell's experience, grasps the deeper implications of socialism. Yet he is often a truer socialist than the Marxists, because he remembers that socialism is about "justice and common decency." He does not grasp, however, that such reform as is implicit in socialism would require immense changes in modern civilization and in his own life.

Communists are like recently converted Roman Catholics. Both adhere to the belief that only the "educated" elite are the real thing. This is particularly true of Catholic literary men, whose orthodoxy extends to the minutest details of life, such as what one eats or drinks. Such distinctions mean nothing to working-class people. "It is only the 'educated' man, especially the literary man, who knows how to be a bigot." The same holds true for communism. Orthodoxy is never found in a genuine proletarian. Some might say that middle-class socialists are motivated by a love of the working classes. Orwell cannot say with any conviction what actually motivates the bookish type of socialist. He believes, however, that many are motivated simply by a desire for order. Orwell suggests that Shaw is an example of this kind of socialism. His plays show little insight into genuine working-class people. Rather, Shaw sees the proletariat as contemptible and disgusting. To socialists of this ilk, revolution is not a movement of the masses with which they will associate. It is, rather, a set of reforms imposed by them on the lower classes. While such people cannot show much love for the proletariat, they are capable of showing hatred for the bourgeoisie, the class to which most of these types belong.

Socialism, as Orwell has laid it out, appeals primarily to inhuman types, whether they are denouncers of the bourgeoisie, the weak-blooded types like Shaw, or the literary intelligentsia who are now communist but may one day become fascists. Ordinary, decent people drawn to the essential aims of socialism often feel that there is no room in the movement for them. Besides, the wreck that is modern society was once great—and still retains some of its greatness. The future socialist state, however, is generally something that seems distasteful. Socialist literature is almost uniformly bad, in Orwell's view. The best contemporary writer of socialist literature—W. H. AUDEN—Orwell calls "a gutless Kipling." All the best writers are on the other side. Orwell makes a few exceptions—Ibsen and Zola—both of whom would not exactly correspond to the modern conception of socialism. Orwell claims not to advocate abandoning socialism because of its lack of skilled writers. He states simply that genuinely talented writers are usually indifferent to socialism, or even hostile to it. These are some of the reasons why many sensible men recoil from socialism. They may be superficial, childish, or silly reasons, but they are real.

Chapter 12

Orwell addresses the issue of spiritually recoiling from socialism, a much more serious difficulty in his view than the vocal or temporary recoiling addressed in the previous chapter. Socialism implies in the minds of many a society based on machine production. It is an urban creed and grew up concurrent with industrialism, which prevents individuals from being independent. It leads ultimately to collectivization, and it could just easily lead to a slave state, foreshadowed by fascism. The converse is also true. Machine production suggests socialism. It demands things not compatible with a primitive society. It requires global communication and exchange of goods. It also requires some form of centralized control, an equal standard of living, and uniformity of education.

Socialism is almost always seen as completely mechanized. Mechanical progress becomes a kind of industrial religion or an end in itself. He illustrates this with the propaganda about industrial progress in the Soviet Union. Those who most readily accept socialism view mechanical progress with enthusiasm but have difficulty seeing the other side of the issue. The socialist world will be a well-ordered and efficient world. Everything will be made by machines. Such a future makes many recoil. And such a vision of progress is not an explicit part of socialism, though it has become thought of as being central to socialism. Suspicion of machines and physical science is common among many sensitive people. Anti-industrial attitudes have been propagated through literature. Swift condemned machines because they were nonsensical contraptions that would never work. Dickens condemned industrialism because of its cruelty—especially in its early stages of development. But it is only in the modern age that mechanization loomed as a real threat to living a "fully human life."

People now have come to think that progress (through machines) is a swindle, though they do not understand the steps involved in reaching that conclusion. Orwell proposes to fill in the blanks in reasoning. In considering the function of machines, many think the answer is to save work. This belief can be taken to vulgar extremes by those who raise efficiency to the level of a fetish—that is, to view machines as freeing humans from the drudgery of manual labor, thereby ushering in a utopia where everyone has time to enjoy their leisure. This type of belief rests on the assumption that machines will produce a world in which nothing goes wrong. Such a place would eliminate many cherished human traits. Courage would diminish in value if machines removed any threat of damage, and human beings would become soft if they were never required to use their muscles. So progress becomes perceived as a headlong rush toward a world in which human beings are almost superfluous, where machines are created to do everything for us.

The idea of machines freeing humans from work is misleading. If a workman is freed from digging a ditch by hand, he may nonetheless have private pursuits or hobbies that could rightly be called work that he would pursue with his newfound leisure time. Orwell concludes that the dichotomy between work and play is a false one, made by the worshippers of progress. Human beings need some kind of employment or work to survive. As they approach other pursuits, they will discover that new machines have been created to make those pursuits more efficient—even in the realm of art. Why not enjoy the machines while also avoiding them for creative pursuits? The problem there is that once a machine is available to make the job easier, it is difficult not to use it. No one wants to do anything with more effort than is really necessary. The tendency of mechanical progress, then, is to frustrate the human need for effort and creation. Taken to its absurd end, it is theoretically possible to envision a future where the human being is little more than a brain in a jar. The problem with this is that this notion of progress has become synonymous with socialism. Those who distrust progress distrust socialism.

Sensitive individuals who hate machinery are both unrealistic and wise. The machine is here to stay, but it is wise to be suspicious of it. Machines are useful but addictive. Look, for example, at food production. Canned goods have replaced fresh goods in shops. Many people prefer them to "real" food. The same holds true for other products, made more efficiently but of cheaper quality by machines. There is the tendency for the mechanized society to progress automatically, whether progress is wanted or not. Mechanical invention has become instinctual to a large degree. Any attempt to curb mechanization or invention seems like blasphemy.

These views against the machine are held by the same people who resist socialism, because progress and socialism are linked. More damaging still, socialists don't seem to grasp that this is so. Mention such objections to a real bookish socialist, and he would respond with predictable reasons. It is impossible for society to go back. To do so would return society to the Middle Ages. Such people will not admit that there is any middle ground between progress and the Stone Age. Another response would be that the objections are valid, but nobody really wants to dispense with the comforts provided by machines. Orwell again notes the lack of a middle ground. Perhaps most people don't want to return to the hardships of the past, but they also don't want a future in which human life is reduced to a series of machines.

Orwell returns to thoughtful people, contemplating socialism and its promises for the future. They may think that they ought to be socialists, but they see first the dullness of so many individual socialists, and then the prospects for a mechanized and "soft" future. In the past, such men would retreat to a state of indifference. In modern times, they are increasingly turning to the opposite of socialism, which is fascism. Orwell warns that the socialists can no longer afford to preach to the converted. They must gain new adherents, despite their prejudices against socialism, or risk swelling the ranks of the fascists. Fascism in England is not much of a serious threat. It will likely be a sedate and subtle kind, in Orwell's opinion. But the drive toward fascism and away from socialism is apparent to Orwell in much of the literature of his day. He notes the works of Ezra Pound and T. S. ELIOT, as well as letters published in the *Daily Mail,* in support of the fascist uprising in Spain.

To combat fascism, Orwell maintains that it must be understood, a process that includes recognizing that there is some good to be found in it. Its methods of acquiring and holding power are abhorrent even to many fascists. The feeling that draws people to fascism, however, is more understandable. Many supporters are well-intentioned people with a genuine regard for the underprivileged. Because fascism is spreading, it must be admitted that socialism has failed to make its case in articulating the essential qualities of justice and liberty. Instead, socialists have presented the opposite view: a materialist society heading toward an economic and mechanistic utopia. At the same time, fascism has been able to appeal to patriotism, religion, and military virtues. Orwell's approach is to present its positive side, and then reveal that whatever good it contains is implicit in socialism.

In Orwell's view, the situation is desperate. The conditions he described in the first part of the book show no indication of altering. Fascism is threatening to sweep across Europe. The capitalist countries show no willingness to combat its growth. England's leaders seem more willing to hand over the country to the fascists than to allow socialism to triumph. Fascism has become an international movement that threatens to achieve a global hegemony. While the machine age is pushing the world towards collectivization, it need not be socialist. The fascists are trying to accomplish a similar end, with all power in the hands of a select few. The only solution for Orwell is to make the fundamental element of socialism—justice and liberty—more widely known. Unfortunately, that message has been submerged beneath doctrine, internecine disputes, and "progressivism." Socialism has for a long time called up images of steel and concrete, crank vegetarians, and bolshevism. Socialism in England no longer invokes revolution and the overthrow of tyrants. "It smells of crankishness, machine-worship, and the stupid cult of Russia." If this prejudice is not overcome, fascism may win the battle for the English soul.

Chapter 13

Having addressed in the first part of the book the crisis the modern world faces and in the second part why so many decent people still refuse to embrace socialism, Orwell turns to what might be done to remedy the situation. The most important thing is to capture the decent objectors before fascism does. Many well-meaning people could be mobilized if socialism could be conveyed properly to them. Orwell's next step is to convey a solution to bridge the gap between socialism and its intelligent enemies (whom Orwell defines as against capitalism but queasy about socialism). This kind of objection is based on two things: the inferiority of individual socialists and the impression that socialism is akin to a mechanized, godless conception of progress, "which revolts anyone with a feeling for tradition or the rudiments of an aesthetic sense." As to the second objection, it is not a valid reason for dismissing socialism, because it implies an alternative when there is none. The machines are here to stay, regardless of the form of government. It may be right to hate them, but they are inevitable. The choice is between socialism and fascism. The thinking person's job, then, is to humanize socialism instead of rejecting it outright.

To the first cause, if more decent people would join the socialist cause, they would wrest power from the cranks and doctrinaires, all the individuals who put them off socialism in the first place. Such types are irrelevant, when one considers that the aim of socialism is justice and liberty. With regard to the tract-writing socialist, Orwell warns that the time has come to drop differences and unite. The fear here is that socialists will be drawn into alliances with their enemies for the sake of opposing fascism. Orwell counters that one will never be in danger if one keeps the fundamentals of the movement in the foreground. The real socialist, for Orwell, is one who actively wishes to see tyranny overthrown.

While no compromise is required in essentials of the message, some sacrifice will be required in externals. One will have to put up with the sandal wearers and vegetarians. The "priggishness," as Orwell calls it, of Marxist attitudes toward literature could be eliminated to avoid driving intelligent people away. The jargon of socialism could also be discarded. Even the practice of calling one another "comrade" has driven some people away. It is unnecessary. It must be made clear that there is room in socialism for human beings. This point leads to the question of class difference, which must be faced more realistically than it ever has before.

While the class system in England has outlived its usefulness, it has not died. Marxists often confuse the issue by insisting that social status is determined solely on the basis of income. A larger salary will not remove the traces of one's social upbringing any more than the loss of salary will. The middle class must be told that, while they are ostensibly in a higher social class than the proletariat, their enemies are the same. As it stands, they are conditioned to stand with their oppressors against the proletariat. The middle-class clerk must be recruited to the socialists. To do so, one must remove the myth of the proletariat. The term must be properly defined. It is not just manual laborers. All people with small, insecure incomes are in the same boat. All middle-class workers who have come down in the world are members of the proletariat, and socialism means a fair deal for them.

Orwell admits to implying that different classes must be convinced to act together without, for the moment, being asked to give up their prejudices. There is no cooperation between classes whose interests are opposed. So those of different classes must be convinced that they share common interests. All people who cringe before the boss and fear for their jobs have a common goal. While such people will one day need to drop their prejudices, they need not be asked to do so immediately. To this end, the bourgeois baiting needs to stop. Such rhetoric obscures the essential meaning of socialism. Poverty affects both clerks and dockhands, regardless of the differences in their class. If a member of the bourgeoisie is browbeaten about never having earned a living with his hands, he will only become irritated and hostile toward socialism—making him a target for fascism. This is essentially asking one to deny one's identity and saying that he is useless because he will not reject the habits and traditions of his upbringing—and neither should he want to.

Orwell suggests that class differences are similar to race differences. People can learn to cooperate with foreigners, even if there are feelings of superiority on one side or the other. The middle classes have as yet failed to unite. As there is a danger that the middle class will swing toward the right in the future, it would be well not to drive them more quickly to it by frightening them with bourgeois baiting. Orwell sums up that there is no hope of fixing the mess he documents in the first part of the book and no chance of stopping the spread of fascism unless an effective socialist party can be brought into existence. But it must have genuine revolutionary tendencies. It also must have adequate numbers. This can only be achieved by improving the quality of the propaganda—less about the ideological jingoes and more about justice, liberty, and the plight of the unemployed. The two most important facts must be hammered home: the interests of all exploited people are the same, and socialism is compatible with common decency.

As for class differences, socialists must proceed with caution. Acceptance among different classes will take time and should not be rushed. There is hope, however, that when socialism takes root, the situation will resolve more quickly than expected. If socialism fails to materialize, fascism will come. It may not be the same type as in Germany. Such a development would spark a revolutionary resistance, in Orwell's opinion. And after people from different classes have fought together, they may come to feel differently about each other, and then the misery of class differences will end. Then the sinking middle class will sink further down to the level of the working class, and when they arrive, they will find it not as abhorrent as they feared.

—Philip Bader

COMMENTARY

The book is divided into two parts. The first half is a description of social conditions, with particular emphasis on the unemployed of industrial northern England. The second part is divided into an autobiographically based analysis of the impact of class consciousness on the author's development. The last section of part 2 is devoted to a critique of socialism's failure to attract broad support from the English public. In a letter to his friend JACK COMMON in December 1936, Orwell wrote "It is not a novel this time but a sort of book of essays, but I am afraid I have made rather a mess of parts of it."

The "mess" is in part 2, which is, in many ways, an intemperate and narrow-minded attack on the very people who would be buying the book. This was not what Victor Gollancz had in mind when he commissioned Orwell to visit the industrialized north and report on unemployment in the area. Even part 1, which comes closer to Gollancz's idea, is not exactly a "report," that is, a chronological, objective account of conditions. Orwell, in fact, did keep a casual record of this type, later published as "The Road to Wigan Pier Diary" which contains a number of details that appear in part 1, but the details are transformed in a way that would later lead to the observation that Orwell transformed journalism into literature.

The opening of the first chapter, for example, might be that of a novel. A nameless narrator in a nameless city awakens to the sound of the wooden clogs of the mill girls as they walk to work. He is staying at a cheap lodging house, run by the Brookers, a man and wife who operate a tripe shop on the first floor while renting out rooms on the second. The filth and squalor of the place are so severe that some readers might conclude they are reading a Dickensian fiction and a sensational one at that. After two weeks there, when the narrator notices a "full chamber pot under the breakfast table," he decides to leave, saying, "The place was beginning to depress me." The comedy in the word *beginning* appears to be unintentional.

From the diary we learn that the Brookers' tripe shop was in Wigan. At the end of the first chapter, the narrator is leaving Wigan. But the mine he describes in chapter 2 is also in Wigan, although it is not identified as such in the book, an example of Orwell's disregard for chronology. Chronological or not, chapter 2 is one of Orwell's most powerful and vivid descriptions, brought home to readers all the more forcefully by his use of the second person in describing "traveling," the miners' term for negotiating the mile or more, body bent double, from the mine's elevator to the coal face: "You have got not only to bend double, you have also got to keep your head up . . . so as to see the beams and girders. . . . you have therefore, a constant crick in the neck, but that is nothing to the pain in your knees and thighs. After half a mile it becomes . . . an unbearable agony. You begin to wonder whether you will ever get to the end—still more how on earth you are going to get back." Proof that Orwell was not exaggerating the difficulties of his underground experience comes from Jerry Kennan, the miner who took him down on his first visit:

> "We rigged him out with a helmet and a lamp . . . We hadn't gone 300 yards when Orwell didn't duck his head quick enough. . . . He was flat out . . . Then we revived him, got him around, and we traveled the best part of three-quarters of a mile bent double . . . Well we did get back, but there were three occasions altogether when he was completely out." (Coppard and Crick, 133).

Chapter 3 offers details of the miner's life: the grime and coal dust that cling to every crevice of his body; the foul air that invades his lungs, the length of his working day—officially seven and a half hours—which excludes unpaid "traveling time"; the disruptions of home life created by the shift work; the salary, popularly supposed to be relatively good, but in fact much less, with deductions, such as the rental fee he pays for his lamp, and downtimes, when the mine is closed. Added to these is the danger of the work, made more so by new machinery speeding up the extraction process. The quicker the coal is extracted, the longer the time that the roof is unpropped. Moreover, an experienced miner develops an "ear" that enables him to detect creaks in the wooden props, but the vibration of the new machines creates noise that makes hearing anything very difficult. Another health hazard unique to the miner is nystagmus, an eye disease related to working in semidarkness. Afflicted workers receive a disability pension, but the amount fluctuates according to the dictates of the company and disappears altogether if the company goes bankrupt. To receive the pension, the miner must show up each week at the colliery and stand in the cold until he is paid. This treatment contrasts markedly from the way a middle-class worker in the same situation would react. The latter would insist on his rights, refusing to be completely passive, operating entirely at the convenience of others. The distinction between the reactions of hypothetical middle- and working-class employees is an apt example of what would later be known as "the hidden injuries of class."

In chapter 4, Orwell considers the housing problems of the miners. Here, as in the preceding chapters, the "I" narrator dispenses with any attempt to be an objective observer. Rather, he is an angry middle-class muckraker, determined to have his readers—themselves middle class—see what he saw and share his anger. In regard to the workers' housing, for example, not only are the houses, built in the 19th century, dilapidated, unsanitary, and too small, they are unhealthy, situated near "belching foundries and stinking canals and slag heaps that deluge them with sulfurous smoke." But the final irony of these poor dwellings is that there are not enough of them. Thus, city officials can condemn a house, but they can't pull it down because there's nothing to replace it with.

As bad as these houses are, there is a level below them, the so-called caravans, or groups of old buses that have had their wheels removed and are propped up with struts of wood. Supposedly temporary structures, they have been housing some families for years. Despite the talk about "slum clearance," very little has been done. The efforts that have been made show mixed results.

The housing estates, the European equivalent of the American public-housing projects, are in Orwell's eyes "only marginally better" than the original slums. While they supply significant improvements in material comforts, they represent a spiritual loss insofar as they require the jettisoning of the traditions and values that made the slum dwellers a living community. Orwell perceptively points out some of the problems with public-housing estates, with their elimination of familiar neighborhood and local shops (most importantly, the local pub) with their restrictions, outlawing certain traditions, such as keeping pigeons. The result is that people complain that the new, technically better housing is cold and "unhomelike." Orwell was to make the same judgment of the middle-class movement to the suburbs in his 1939 novel *Coming Up for Air,* in which his protagonist George Bowling depicts his suburban estate as a prison.

The next two chapters—5 and 6—deal with unemployment and the food preferences of working-class people. The two phenomena are not unrelated, as he tries to show in his analysis. First, he deals with the deceptive statistics relating to unemployment. The official figures place it at two million people, but that figure ignores the unemployed person's dependents, which raises the figure conservatively to six million, to which you should add people who are nominally employed but making less than a living wage, about 15 shillings (in 1936, roughly $4 a week for a single person) or old-age pensioners. But beyond the economics of unemployment lies the damage it does to the spirits of people who slowly succumb to the deadening despair that grips a man, in particular, whose very identity is derived from the work he does. Lacking a job for an extended period—in many cases, for years—he loses all sense of himself as a worthy person. But one thing to be said for the depression is that it has alleviated, to some extent, the sense of individual unworthiness that occurs when you lose your job. Now that everyone else is out of work, it is no longer your problem but strong evidence that the system has broken down. Orwell does not conclude from this the workers are primed for revolution. On the contrary, they have adjusted to permanent unemployment by "lowering their standards." An additionally surprising fact is that the lowering of standards has not resulted in cutting out nonessentials but in consuming mass-produced, cheap luxuries "which mitigate the surface of life."

The same principle of "cheap luxuries" obtains in the diet of the unemployed. Rather than spending their limited money on wholesome foods, unemployed people want to dispel the gloom of their condition by food that cheers them up, while it fills them up. Thus, the attraction of the two staples of the working man's diet: fish-and-chips, and sugared tea, the latter "the Englishman's opium." Orwell clearly understands the need of poor people to have something "tasty" rather than wholesome. He was himself a dedicated tea drinker. (See his essay "A NICE CUP OF TEA.") But he deplores the rotten teeth, "puny limbs and sickly faces" that result from this diet. He concludes chapter 5 with a vivid description of the practice of "scrambling" for pieces of coal at the local slag heaps, another reminder of social injustice and human resilience. In the final chapter of part 1, Orwell delivers a discourse on the opposition between the cultures of the North and South of England.

Having reported on the lives of the mostly unemployed working class, Orwell opted to move the book in a new direction. The change was probably dictated by a development that occurred in the time that Orwell was in the north. This was the inauguration of the LEFT BOOK CLUB, the ambitious publishing venture led by Gollancz, the economist Harold Laski, and John Strachey, a prominent communist. Taking the book-of-the month-club format a step further, the Left Book Club not only sold a monthly book choice at a reduced price but also set up centers throughout England to encourage discussion of these works. It is not true that the Left Book Club commissioned Orwell's book; at the time he was in the north (February and March 1936), the Club did not yet exist (Davison *Life,* 67).

However, shortly after his return, Gollancz had been able to start up the club and suggested to Orwell that the as-yet-unwritten book would make a logical club choice. Thus, Orwell had before him a clear sense of his potential audience, not the literary community who read and reviewed *Burmese Days* and *Keep the Aspidistra Flying,* but people who, if anything, tended to look down on novels as escapist fantasies. These were the hardcore, politically committed leftists of all shades, from liberal to communist. It was the announced goal of the club to help create a "people's front," the English version of Spain's popular front—the alignment of all shades of leftists united against fascism.

To Orwell, such an audience represented an irresistible opportunity to catch the conscience of the left, to force them to see themselves as others might see them. The result is a ruthless, scathing picture of some features of socialism and the complacency that underlies it. The problem—and he was well aware of the danger—was that taking on the role of scourge, even under the guise of devil's advocate, would probably disqualify the work as a Left Book Club choice, losing the very audience for which part 2 was written. But as always in cases where self-interest conflicted with the truth as he saw it, he took the risk.

By way of explaining his departure from the format of part 1, he states that his reason for visiting the north was to determine whether "things at present are tolerable or intolerable." Clearly part 1 demonstrates that they are intolerable. Faced with this fact, we have to look for a social system that stands for justice and equality, and that appears to be socialism. But as a first step before we examine socialism, we must grapple with the "terribly difficult" problem of class, and in order to get a handle on this subject, he must examine his own attitude toward it and how that attitude developed. What follows is an abbreviated autobiography/confession. It is the story of a "lower-upper-middle class" child, schoolboy, Etonian, officer in the Burmese police, and down-and-outer, the story of how he acquired and learned to rid himself of many of his class-bred prejudices. The most shocking and eventually controversial of these was the conviction that "the lower classes smell." Whether this was a common opinion of the middle class is one of the controversial points, singled out, for example, by Victor Gollancz in his foreword as a "violent" exaggeration. If in fact it is an exaggeration, it is a pardonable one in Orwell, who was blessed and cursed with an acute sense of smell. In any case, the point that he arrives at is that in order to do away with class consciousness, you must "abolish part of yourself." That is a process that will begin only when you stop pretending you are free from class consciousness.

Seen from the vantage point of the 21st century, the issue of class, as formulated by Orwell, is one that continues to exist in England, but its importance has been diminished, now subsumed under the category of race. The class/race issue continues to play a significant role in a markedly altered pluralistic society—largely the consequence of the convergence of former colonials within England's borders. As for his relations with the working-class men he met in the North, Orwell acknowledges he had at best only partial success in abolishing his own class consciousness. As he describes it:

> I liked them and hoped they liked me; but I went among them as a foreigner, and both of us were aware of it. Which ever way you turn this curse of class-difference confronts you like a wall of stone. Or rather it is not so much like a stone wall as the plate-glass pane of an aquarium; it is so easy to pretend that it isn't there, and so impossible to get through it.

And confirming that opinion, is the comment of Jerry Kennan, one of the miners who befriended Orwell, ". . . he never showed any appreciation of hospitality. He was kind of up in the air and a snob in some ways. . . ." As if to seal the case, Jerry goes on to remark that Orwell failed to send a copy of the book to him or any of the other miners. "Well, I think anyone who showed you around for some weeks . . . would have seen that you at least had an autographed copy, wouldn't you?" (Coppard and Crick, 131) On some unconscious level, Orwell may have felt that the miners would have no interest in a book written for middle-class leftists, which is, of course, as damning an example of unconscious snobbery as is found in the book. The more probable explanation is that he thought Jerry Kennan and others would be offended by some aspects of the book.

In any case, he ended up with a rueful realization of the power of class identity:

> It is easy for me to say that I want to get rid of class distinctions, but nearly everything I think and do is the result of class-distinctions. All my notions—notions of good and evil, of pleasant and unpleasant, of funny and serious, of ugly and beautiful—are essentially middle-class notions. . . .

His pessimism over the persistence of class distinctions is reinforced by the example of "working class intellectuals," scholarship winners, or proletarian writers. "Many of them are very disagreeable people, quite unrepresentative of their class. . . ." Too often, these people resort to "proletarian cant" about the death of the bourgeoisie, etc. Eliminating class distinctions is a complicated, "wild ride into the dark," which, when it loses its way, can lead to fascism. In chapter 10, he returns to the question of socialism, asking why, with capitalism foundering, socialism is unable to seize the opportunity and, in fact, appears to be losing the battle for the minds and hearts of people, in many cases losing them to fascism. The first problem in socialism's presentation of itself are the socialists, too many of whom are middle-class, fruit-juice-drinking, sandal-wearing, vegetarian cranks. The second charge against socialism is to its wholehearted embrace of a mechanized society. Orwell's objections to mechanization and its ramifications are an expanded version of a list first indicated by Gordon Comstock, the protagonist of *Keep the Aspidistra Flying* (chapter 5), when asked what socialism would mean for England:

> Oh! Some kind of Aldous Huxley *Brave New World*; only not so amusing. Four hours a day in a model factory, tightening up bolt number 6003. Rations served out in greaseproof paper at the communal kitchen. Community-hikes from Marx Hostel to Lenin Hostel and back. Free abortion-clinics on all the corners. All very well in its way of course. Only we don't want it.

But all these criticisms notwithstanding, the fact remains that socialism is the only hope "of saving England from fascism." The fascist appeal to working people was strong because it did not reject the past, the national past in particular. It promised a return to mythical heroism, the opportunity for the average person to merge with something greater than himself: membership in a master race. Socialism had its eye exclusively on the future, thereby ignoring the deep roots of patriotism in the interest of an international ideal. Socialists need to learn more respect for the past, for the values, not the dogmas, of Christianity, for example, in order to promote justice and equality.

It is interesting to compare the completed book with the diary notes Orwell kept during his time in the North. (The diary has been reprinted in volume 1 of *CEJL* and volume 10 of *CW*). In some respects, such as his description of the Brookers, the diary is less shocking, which is not to say that he "made up," for example, Mr. Brooker's famous thumbprint, just that it does not appear in the diary. The latter consists primarily of fragments, with notable exceptions, such as the visit to the mine in chapter 2, which is given a careful rendering in both places. One distinction between the book and the diary, as Richard Hoggart points out, is a significant artistic or rhetorical feature of the book, the image of Orwell as the "isolated observer going around and seeing for himself" (Hoggart, 60). What the diary reveals is that Orwell made regular use of political contacts he had been given, with people who were clearly working-class socialists. In the book, working-class socialist was a category he preferred to ignore in making his case that socialism had been captured by the middle class. In the diary, Orwell is less of a lone wolf than in the book. And he carried over that image of the independent, unaffiliated observer in part 1 to part 2, thus adding to his credibility as a critic of socialism.

As for Orwell's use of language in *Wigan Pier,* although the documentary format ordinarily demands an objective, reportorial style, Orwell frequently departs from it in part 1. In part 2, he abandons it altogether. In part 1, he frequently employs a form of "sordid realism to convey his disgust and anger" (Fowler, 84). How effective that approach proved to contemporary readers is evident in a letter from the aristocratic, modernist poet Edith Sitwell: "The horror of the beginning is unsurpassable. He seems to be doing for the modern world what Engels did for the world of 1840–1850. But with this difference. That Orwell is a born writer" (Meyers, 137). Roger Fowler notes that the conclusion to part 1, in which Orwell describes the slag heaps of Wigan and the foundries of Sheffield, is indebted to Charles Dickens's images of "Coketown" in *Hard Times,* evidence that, even in a documentary mode, Orwell was always seeking to marry politics with art (88). As for the language of part 2, it is, at least in the eyes of many, Orwell at his worst: intemperate, offensive, full of generalizations about socialists and socialism. Time, which on so many other occasions has been extraordinarily kind to Orwell, has made him look foolish with his infamous catalog of those attracted to socialism ". . . every fruit-juice drinker, nudist, sandal-wearer, sex-maniac, Quaker, 'nature cure' quack, pacifist and feminist in England." Readers, then and now, have been dismayed by the narrow-mindedness and conventionality of his opinions, even though he claims merely to be playing devil's advocate. A similar flaw lies in his attempt to identify socialism with the march into a mechanized future. Although there is more substance to the latter argument, his case is marred by a failure to recognize a more nuanced position in the socialist theory of the time. This error also speaks to his inadequate knowledge of the intellectual rationale of socialism.

On his return from the North at the end of March 1936, Orwell moved to Wallington, Hertfordshire, where he opened a store and in May of that year began writing *Wigan Pier.* The following month, he and Eileen O'Shaughnessy were married and set up house at the Wallington store. In August he gave a talk at *Adelphi* magazine's summer school, where he no doubt encountered a number of sandal-wearing, socialist vegetarians. By the 15th of December, he sent the completed manuscript of *Wigan Pier* to his agent, Leonard Moore. Gollancz, who had decided to make the book a Left Book Club selection, was understandably worried about the reaction to part 2 by club members. He wanted to publish the full text in a trade edition, but to include only part 1 in the club edition. By this time, Orwell was in Spain, and Eileen, acting on his behalf, refused to accept the idea of an abridged text. As a result, the club edition included both parts, but with a foreword by the publisher. Speaking for his co-committee chairs, John Strachey and Harold Laski, Gollancz thoroughly distanced himself from the insulting picture of socialists and the critique of socialist theory and practice. Among the charges he lays against his author is the fact that ". . . Mr. Orwell does not once define what he *means* by Socialism . . ." However, Gollancz does not fail to bestow lavish praise on part 1. In all, more than 44,000 club copies were sold.

Among Left Book Club readers, the book created a storm of responses from two sides. Those who were more familiar with socialist doctrine objected strongly to the critique in part 2. On the other hand, nonsocialist readers responded to the conditions described in part 1 with passionate appeals, asking how they might help. The numbers responding were powerful enough that Gollancz issued a special edition of the first part only (Stansky and Abraham, 231).

As for the newspaper reviews, they were generally favorable, with the notable exception of the official communist paper, the *Daily Worker,* which lambasted Orwell. Doubtless the *Worker* reviewer did not take kindly to Orwell's occasional references to a mythical "Comrade X, author of *Marxism for Infants.*" Others praised Orwell's compelling portrait of working-class life in the North of England. In the *Tribune* review, novelist and playwright Walter Greenwood noted Orwell's "gift of writing vividly, of creating in the mind's eye a picture of the scene described." In Greenwood's reaction to part 2, however, his enthusiasm is replaced by outrage. Orwell's critique of socialism "has you with him one moment and provoked beyond endurance the next. . . . I cannot remember having been so infuriated by some of the things he says here." Hamish Miles's review for *New Statesman and Nation,* invokes the spirit of the English novelist GEORGE GISSING: "Mr. Orwell has a positively Gissingesque genius for finding the dingiest house in the most sunless street, and he sketches the horribly self-contained, sub-human universe of his landlord and fellow-lodgers with a precision which, at one point or another, pricks each of one's senses in turn into revolt." In a review of a later edition of the book in 1959, Philip Toynbee takes Orwell to task for his intolerance of working-class intellectuals. "They had, in a sense, betrayed him by coming too close, like an adored mistress who suddenly comes down from her pedestal and agrees to go to bed with her lover" (118).

Later critics have run the gamut from calling it "Orwell's worst book" (Hopkinson) to calling it the book that "reveals Orwell as a prophetic social critic of the highest order" (Thiemann, 194). The author of the latter comment is the former dean of the Harvard Divinity School, who brings a spiritual point of view to the much-maligned part 2. He argues that Orwell's critique of socialism is an example of "connected criticism," a term he borrows from Michael Walzer. In Walzer's formulation, a connected critic is one who does not deliver his judgments from an isolated, Olympian distance, but who "stands among the people" even as he "takes stands different from theirs." He speaks as a patriot, loyal to a society's ideals, but critical of a particular regime (Walzer, 238). Thiemann applies the term to Orwell's critique of socialism in part 2. He argues that Orwell saw that in order to achieve socialism's true goals of justice and dignity, it must abandon philosophical materialism and acknowledge "the cultural and spiritual aspects of human life. [Orwell] feared that without a full engagement with the matters that engaged human souls, socialism would lose the battle with fascism" (107). It is not entirely clear that Orwell rejected philosophic materialism, but it is clear that his critique is that of a man who stands with, and speaks for, the people.

Part 2 of the book, in which Orwell examines his personal struggles with class prejudice and his somewhat halting journey toward socialism, was less favorably received by critics, most of whom fell into the category of the socialists Orwell attacks in this section of the work.

PEOPLE

Brooker, Mr. Along with his wife, the owner of a combination tripe shop and lodging house in Wigan. A former miner, Brooker is a small man, "astonishingly dirty," who attends to the tripe, does the cooking and various other duties since his wife is an invalid and does very little. "He moves with incredible slowness from one hated job to another."

Brooker, Mrs. The invalid landlady of the lodging house where Orwell stayed in Wigan until driven out by the dirtiness of the place. One of the irritants was her habit of wiping her face with pieces of newspaper and then tossing them on the floor, where they lay for hours.

Emmie The fiancée of one of the Brooker's absent sons. Although she works all day at one of the mills, she is forced to spend her evenings at the Brookers' doing housework under the watchful eye of Mrs. Brooker.

Hooker A bedridden, old-age pensioner who lives at the Brookers lodging house. Much to the consternation of his landlord, Hooker refuses to die. The Brookers will collect his insurance money when he does die, but in the meantime, they must continue to pay the premiums on his insurance.

Joe An unemployed resident at the Brookers' who is very proud of the fact that he has avoided the "marriage trap."

Old Jack Another old-age pensioner living at the Brookers', Old Jack is a 78-year-old ex-miner, who remembered the old days of mining but was unaware of any modern innovations.

Kennan, Jerry See entry in part 3.

Reilly, Mr. An elderly resident at the Brookers who works aboveground at the coal pits. He leaves for work at 5:00 A.M., which gives Orwell enough room to stretch his legs while sleeping.

WORKS CITED

Coppard, Aubrey, and Bernard Crick, eds. *Orwell Remembered.* New York: Facts On File, 1984.

———. *Collected Essay, Journalism, and Letters of George Orwell.* Edited by Sonia Orwell and Ian Angus. London: Secker & Warburg, 1984.

The Complete Works of George Orwell. Edited by Peter Davison. 20 volumes. London: Secker & Warburg, 1998.

Davison, Peter. *George Orwell: A Literary Life.* New York: St. Martin's, 1996.

Fowler, Roger. *The Language of George Orwell.* New York: St. Martin's, 1995.

Greenwood, Walter. "*The Road to Wigan Pier.*" *Tribune, March 20, 193.* In *George Orwell: The Critical Heritage,* edited by Jeffrey Meyers, 99–100. London: Routledge, 1975.

Hoggart, Richard. "Introduction to *The Road to Wigan Pier.*" In *George Orwell: A Collection of Critical Essays,* edited by Raymond Williams, 34–51. Englewood, N.J.: Publisher, 1974.

Hopkinson, Tom. *George Orwell.* London: Longman, 1953.

Meyers, Jeffrey. *Orwell: Wintry Conscience of a Generation.* New York: Norton, 2000.

Miles, Hamish. "*The Road to Wigan Pier.*" *New Statesman and Nation,* May 1, 1937. In *George Orwell: The Critical Heritage,* edited by Jeffrey Meyers 110–113. London: Routledge, 1975.

Sabin, Marjorie. "Outside/Inside: Searching for Wigan Pier." In *George Orwell: Into the Twenty-First Century,* edited by Thomas Cushman and John Rodden, 243–251. Boulder/London: Paradigm. 2004.

Stansky, Peter and William Abraham. *Orwell: The Transformation.* New York: Knopf, 1979.

Thiemann, Ronald. "The Public Intellectual as Connected Critic." In *George Orwell: Into the Twenty-First Century,* edited by Thomas Cushman and John Rodden, 96–110. Boulder/London: Paradigm, 2004.

Toynbee, Philip. "*The Road to Wigan Pier.*" *Encounter,* August 1959. Reprinted in *George Orwell: The Critical Heritage,* edited by Jeffrey Meyers. London: Routledge, 1975.

Walzer, Michael. *The Company of Critics.* New York: Basic Books, 2002.

"Rudyard Kipling"

Essay first published in *Horizon* (February 1942). The occasion for the essay was the publication of *A Choice of Kipling's Verse* (1941), a volume selected and edited by T. S. ELIOT, who also contributed a substantial introduction to the poems.

During his lifetime (1865–1936), Kipling was celebrated as the popular and powerful celebrant of the British Empire, as well as for his fiction and verse written for children. By the time of his death, he was viewed as an embarrassment by sophisticated literary society, typified by *Horizon,* the journal for which this essay was written.

SYNOPSIS

Orwell begins by lamenting the fact that in his introduction, Eliot should be at pains defending Kipling from the charge that he was a fascist. He agrees that Kipling was not a fascist, but he feels that Eliot overstates the case, in that his exoneration fails to acknowledge the truth about Kipling, that he was a "jingo imperialist . . . morally insensitive and aesthetically disgusting." It is only after acknowledging this fact that one can legitimately move on to considering why he has survived while others have not. One of the reasons for the "fascist" allegation against Kipling arose from quoting him out of context, as in his phrase from "Recessional," "lesser breeds without the law," which is generally thought to refer to natives. In context, however, "the lesser breeds" refers to Germans. The poem, in fact, is a critique of power politics as practiced by Europeans.

In his later, post–World War I phase, Kipling was embittered and confused. He did not understand Britain's decline as a world power after victory in the war. He did not realize the vaunted British Empire was doomed, because he failed to see the economic forces at work in the world. He had the old-fashioned blurred vision of the 19th-century imperialist, which, for all its flaws, maintained a sense of responsibility. In this respect, he differed from left-wing intellectuals who profess to despise imperialism but who would not accept the lower standard of living that would result from the dissolution of the empire. Kipling identified himself with the imperial civil servants, civilian and military. His audience was largely middle class. He was not broadly popular among the working classes. His attitude toward the common soldier was patronizing, seeing him as essentially comic, always speaking in an exaggerated cockney accent. Yet he had considerable empathy for the ordinary soldier, so that, although he tended to glorify war, he dealt realistically with the fear and pain of being under fire. Compare the description of the army in the Kipling poem "The Eathen" with Tennyson's "The Charge of the Light Brigade" to see how much truer to life Kipling is. He has given us the definitive picture of the "old pre-machine-gun-army" life. He was not capable of writing a *War and Peace,* but Tolstoy lived in a great military empire, while the British Empire was and is comparatively demilitarized. Kipling was virtually unique in being able to make a powerful contribution to "colonial literature." He is also the only writer of modern English who has contributed phrases to the general vocabulary, such as "the white man's burden," "somewhere East of Suez," and "the female of the species is deadlier than the male."

In his introduction, Eliot makes a distinction between verse and poetry, adding that Kipling wrote "great verse," while implying that sometimes the line between "great verse" and "poetry" is impossible to determine. Orwell criticizes Eliot for not citing examples of Kipling's "great verse" and, in general, for equivocating on the aesthetic merit of Kipling's poems. He suggests that a better approach to Kipling is through the term *good bad poetry.* A good bad poem "is a general monument to the obvious," a poem that is riddled with sentimentality, but a source of continuing pleasure to large numbers of people because the sentiment that it expresses is largely true. It is "a kind of rhyming proverb."

Kipling was a powerful good bad poet because he absorbed the view of the ruling class, and this warped his political judgment, but it left him with a sense of responsibility, which he expressed largely in platitudes and "since we live in a world of platitudes, much of what he says sticks."

COMMENTARY

This essay displays a characteristic Orwellian strategy, beginning by "facing unpleasant facts" (Kipling as "jingo imperialist") and then moving on to consider what for Orwell was the key test of a writer's value: survival. Kipling has survived to some extent because of his celebration of pre–World War I England and its empire, which by 1942, the date of the essay, was in imminent danger. Burma had fallen into Japanese hands, as had Singapore, while India appeared to be the next to fall, all of which lends an ironic tone to Orwell's view of the empire, now in the first stages of dissolution.

A further irony surrounding the essay lies in the fact that Orwell and T. S. Eliot here share the same goal, the attempt to salvage Kipling's reputation, but Eliot comes in for implicit criticism from Orwell for not acknowledging Kipling's faults and by making a distinction between verse and poetry. In the latter case, Orwell criticizes Eliot's refusal to specify which of Kipling's verse qualifies as poetry. In so doing, Orwell is taking on—and showing up—the most powerful and respected poet and critic in English literature of the time.

As for Kipling, Orwell approaches him as a cultural and political force before moving on to consider his literary achievement. When Orwell singles out Kipling as "the only English writer of our time who has added phrases to the language," a contemporary reader cannot resist amending the line to "except George Orwell."

Six years before this essay, Orwell wrote a short tribute to Kipling on the occasion of his death on January 18, 1936. The eulogy included his autobiographical account of their relationship:

> For my own part I worshipped Kipling at thirteen, loathed him at seventeen, enjoyed him at twenty, despised him at twenty five and now again rather admire him (*CW,* 10, 409).

As for Kipling's imperialist attitude, Orwell suggests that in the imperialism of his day, "it was still possible to be an imperialist and a gentleman, and of Kipling's *personal* decency there can be no doubt."

"Second Thoughts on James Burnham"

Essay first published in *Polemic 3* (May 1946). Later published by the Socialist Book Centre as a pamphlet under the title *James Burnham and the Managerial Revolution* (1946). Orwell had previously reviewed Burnham's *The Machiavellians* (1944) in the *Manchester Evening News* (January 20, 1944) and discussed his *The Managerial Revolution* (1940) in an "As I Please" column in *Tribune* (January 14, 1944). The latter drew a reply from Burnham and a counter reply from Orwell (March 24, 1944).

SYNOPSIS

Orwell begins by offering a summary of James Burnham's *The Managerial Revolution* (1940). Burnham predicts that a new form of society is now emerging, replacing the old capitalist structure not with socialism but with a new model and a new ruling class, the "managers," made up of bureaucrats, business executives, technology specialists, and military figures. These new managerial societies will expand beyond national borders to emerge as a few superstates that will engage in limited wars with each other over those areas of the planet that are still un-colonized. In his next book, *The Machiavellians* (1944), Burnham provides a historical background to his views, maintaining that democracy is an illusion, that hierarchy is an inevitable consequence of human activity and that politics, as Machiavelli pointed out 400 years ago, is inevitably a power struggle. According to Burnham, if these facts were faced, instead of always being obscured, the ruling class would be able to operate more effectively for the general welfare. Also, there would be a certain flexibility occasioned by the recruitment of the "best and the brightest" into the ruling class, what would later to be called a meritocracy. Orwell notes that, although these ideas are not entirely original, they correctly identify a drift towards totalitarianism.

As Burnham sees it, in 1940, "managerialism" is the operative principle in such seemingly diverse countries as Nazi Germany, the Soviet Union, and, in a primitive form, the Roosevelt Administration's New Deal, thus demonstrating that managerialism can exist in a variety of shapes and forms.

Orwell goes on to explain that, within the context of his general theory, Burnham has made a series of short term prophecies: In 1940, he prophesized that Germany would win the war, and in 1942 that they would crush the Soviet Union. In 1944, with allied victory already obvious, he predicted that the Soviet Union would eventually conquer the world, spearheaded by their leader, one of the great men of history, Joseph Stalin, his greatness ratified by his willingness to destroy the lives of millions. In every case, Burnham's pattern has been to bet on the horse that is winning at the time he is writing, and in every case he has been proven wrong.

Returning to Burnham's general theory, Orwell notes the significance of the fact that Burnham is an American. Americans tend to see international relations as power struggles and are essentially indifferent as long as their turf is protected. But aside from that fact, Burnham is basically right about the drift "towards oligarchy" and the growth in power of the managerial class. The problem with Burnham is that he imagines that, because this development is occurring now, its outcome is inevitable. Thus, he assumes that the past determines the future. He fails to recognize that, in the modern age, many people whose working lives in the past involved physical drudgery have been set free by technology, thus allowing them the leisure to think, study, and enter into the political arena, helping to create a more enlightened, democratic society. Burnham doesn't perceive the power and efficiency of a democracy because he doesn't want to. He is always caught up in the obvious manifestations of power, causing him at first to valorize Nazi Germany and later the Soviet Union. What Burnham has failed to incorporate into his "realistic" descriptions of the present and the future is the moral intelligence that recognizes good from evil.

COMMENTARY

This essay represents Orwell's fullest critique of Burnham's ideas. It was supplemented by Orwell's reviews of two of Burnham's books and references to him in other articles. It is possible that Orwell was disturbed by Burnham's views not simply for his stated reasons, but because a part of him—the pessimist, whose despair emerged in writing *Nineteen Eighty-Four*—agreed with Burnham. In *Orwell and the Left,* Alex Zwerdling offers this theory, suggesting that Orwell "appropriates much more from him [Burnham] than he is willing to acknowledge" (103).

Burnham was a former Trotskyist, who, looking at Stalin and Hitler's regimes, saw how they used one plank of the socialist platform—state ownership of industry but with a new ruling class, "the party"—to exercise totalitarian control. Eventually, certain governments would violate national boundaries and expand into superstates. This is, of course, the description of the world of *Nineteen Eighty-Four.* But in the years leading up to his final vision, Orwell was not willing to accept the radical pessimism this view entailed, wrestling with it each time he considered Burnham's prophecies. In the essay, he devotes considerable space to showing the falsity of Burnham's short-range predictions.

When he returns to the general theory, he first sinks to an attack on Burnham as an "American," morally indifferent (perhaps seeing him as he saw another American, HENRY MILLER, as being "inside the whale.") More cogently, he points out that Burnham's mistaken predictions were predicated on the principle that what is happening now (e.g., Germany's early successes in World War II) will determine the future. So, too, with his general theory: the fact that we are drifting toward a managerial totalitarian state does not mean that it is inevitable. In a reply to an earlier critique of Burnham by Orwell ("As I Please," *Tribune,* January 14, 1944), Burnham denied ever saying that totalitarianism was unavoidable. He has maintained that totalitarianism is not unavoidable but *probable.* "Only through absolute clarity about the probability of totalitarianism . . . will we be able precisely to have a chance to overcome or avoid it" (*CW,* 16, 62). Zwerdling also points out that Orwell criticizes Burnham for not exploring why people want power. This is the same objection some readers of *Animal Farm* have raised in connection with the character of Napoleon.

Orwell continued his critique in "Burnham's View of the Contemporary World Struggle," an essay-review of Burnham's book *The Struggle for the World* (1947). Here, Burnham repositions his earlier world view in the light of the atomic bomb. Burnham now agrees that as soon as another nation acquires atomic weapons (this was written before the Soviet Union had done just that), nuclear war will be inevitable. Since Soviet-style communism is a quasi-religious phenomenon, whose followers are fanatical zealots, they will not hesitate to use these weapons. Therefore, it is incumbent for the United States, after forming a partnership with Great Britain, to prepare to wage a preventive war against the Soviets. Burnham is not in favor of the war, but the United States must show its willingness to engage an all-out war in order to prevent it.

Orwell concludes that something like what Burnham suggests appears to be shaping up in a struggle for global dominance between the United States and the USSR. However, Burnham makes the same mistake here that he has made in the past,: assuming that what appears to be happening now must happen in the future. He fails to consider alternative scenarios. One of these is a democratic-socialist United States of Europe, which would cut the ground from under the appeal of communism and provide the undeveloped world with a real choice. Such a development would require 10 or 20 years of "assured peace" to make it a reality. Britain would have to assume a leading role in this federation. What Burnham sees as desirable is a union of the United States and Great Britain, with the latter as the "junior partner" in what would become a worldwide American empire.

Orwell concludes that Burnham is too mesmerized by his "apocalyptic vision" of the future to consider other possibilities. One of these is that "the great powers will simply be too frightened of the effects of atomic weapons ever to make use of them."

For a further discussion of Orwell's view of a "United States of Europe," see "TOWARD EUROPEAN UNITY."

WORKS CITED

The Complete Works of George Orwell, edited by Peter Davison. Vol. 16. London: Secker & Warburg, 1998.

Zwerdling, Alex. *Orwell and the Left*. New Haven, Conn.: Yale University Press, 1974.

"Shooting an Elephant"

Essay first published in *New Writing 2*, 1936. Written some 10 years after the event described, the essay is clearly not a simple recollection but a skillful integration of experience, idea, and artistic employment of language. From that perspective, it has come to be seen as a classic 20th-century example of the art of the essay.

SYNOPSIS

"In Moulmein, in Lower Burma, I was hated by large numbers of people—the only time in my life that I have been important enough for this to happen to me." The essay's striking opening sentence captures the conflict between the rulers and the ruled in imperial Burma, translated into complex and wry personal terms. Orwell is describing his situation as a police officer, dealing with a long-suppressed native population, beginning to express its anger in indirect, infuriating ways. Caught between theoretical and intellectual support for the Burmese cause and a gut level fury over the personal abuse to which he is subjected, he is intensely frustrated. He is convinced that imperialism is "an evil thing." But he does not speak out against it, partly because he thinks of the Raj as an "unbreakable tyranny," destined to rule forever. At the same time, he feels rage against "the evil-spirited, little beasts" with their ability to infuriate him. He did not realize at the time that the British Empire was dying. Nor did the Burmese realize that British rule was a great deal better than the regimes destined to supplant it.

His dilemma takes on a very real form when he is told to respond to a rogue elephant that had broken its chain and is disrupting, even menacing, a certain quarter of town. When he arrives at the quarter, he discovers that the animal has already killed a man, a coolie whom the elephant had caught with its trunk, and with its foot, "ground him into the earth." At that point he dispatches an orderly to bring him an elephant rifle and five bullets. Orwell advances to the area where the elephant now is, a rice paddy. Walking behind him as he advances is virtually the entire population of the quarter, eager to see what will happen. Once he comes within range of the animal, he realizes that the elephant's wildness seems to be passing. It is peacefully eating grass, from all appearances no longer a threat. Moreover, an elephant is a valuable piece of property, as a worker, "comparable to a huge and costly piece of machinery." He decides not to shoot the animal, but as he turns, he discovers that the crowd at his back has now grown to as many as 2,000 people: "And suddenly I realized I would have to shoot the elephant after all." He recognizes that he is trapped in the role of the "superior" white man who has traded in his freedom in order to create a powerful impression on the natives. He has to do what is expected of him. He has to play the role he wrote for himself when he sent for the rifle. To do nothing at this point would make him the object of ridicule and laughter. "And my whole life, every white man's life in the East, was one long struggle not to be laughed at."

Planting himself a safe distance from the elephant, he fires the first shot, bringing the great beast to its knees. With the second shot, the animal rises to his feet, but after a third shot, "his hind legs collapsed behind him . . . and down he came . . . with a crash that seemed to shake the ground." Although the animal can no longer move, it does not die, even when Orwell fires two more shots close-up and a number of shots with a smaller rifle. Still the creature's agony continues. Finally, Orwell walks away, hearing later that it took the elephant a half hour to die while the crowd stripped the body "almost to the bones."

In the aftermath, opinion is divided among the European community as to whether the shooting was necessary. The official inquiry finds the shooting justified because of the death of the coolie. But Orwell knows the real reason he killed the elephant: "to avoid looking like a fool."

COMMENTARY

As in the case of Orwell's other Burma-based essay, "A HANGING," doubts have been cast on the factual basis of "Shooting an Elephant," largely the result of the difficulty in pinning down its time and place. But the statement of George Stuart, an engineer, stationed at Moulmein at the same time as Orwell, recalled a Sunday morning when word reached a local European club that a rogue elephant had broken loose. Stuart saw Orwell, rifle in hand, set off in an old car to investigate the incident. Stuart indicated that the elephant belonged to a large lumber company, not the hapless Indian mentioned in the essay. As a result, Orwell was punished for killing a valuable piece of property. The punishment consisted of a transfer from the relative comfort of Moulmein to the remote outpost of Katha, the close model for the village of Kyauktada in *BURMESE DAYS.* In that novel the hero John Flory tells his beloved Elizabeth Lackersteen that he once shot an elephant.

The celebrated opening sentence of the essay suggests not only the atmosphere that colonialism generates but the perverse satisfaction that such hatred can produce in the one who is hated. To be singled out for jeering and insults is to enjoy a certain celebrity, providing another motive for the decision to give the crowd what it wants. But it is clear that the essay's main purpose is to show that the real "white man's burden" is the recognition that he is the prisoner of his image. He must do what is expected of him rather than the decent, rational thing. As a British policeman, he is the symbol of imperial power. Not to use it—in the mind of the confused, beleaguered young man—is to undermine that power. He has yet to distinguish the show of power from the real thing.

His dilemma is illustrated in the painfully detailed description of the dying elephant. Peacefully munching on grass, his rage now quieted, to kill the elephant now seems a senseless murder, another victim of imperialism. As if to add an additional moral, Orwell tells us that, despite the numerous bullets he pumps into the creature, he is unable to finish it off. He leaves the animal still alive, further indication that the vaunted power of the empire is not omnipotent. There is something in the elephant that predates and transcends that power. Thus, when he fires his first shot, he sees the animal differently: ". . . one could have imagined him thousands of years old." One possibility is clear: The great beast represents traditional Burmese culture reasserting itself, like the Burmese students and Buddhist monks, disturbing the *pax britannica,* and therefore something that must be put down. On the other hand, in *Finding George Orwell in Burma,* Emma Larkin quotes the interpretation of a Burmese professor she met there:

> The Burmese word 'oan' means literally "to swarm," and it was the power of "oan" or collective curiosity, that made the British policeman shoot the elephant (323).

Collective curiosity or the power the oppressed hold over the oppressor—something was at work and was caught by Orwell's artistry.

WORK CITED

Larkin, Emma. *Finding George Orwell in Burma.* London: Penguin, 2004.

"Some Thoughts on the Common Toad"

Brief essay published in *Tribune* on April 12, 1946, reprinted in America in *The New Republic* (May 20,

1946). This essay depicts the coming of spring after the vicious winter of 1945–46.

SYNOPSIS

By way of the emergence of the common English toad from his winter hibernation, Orwell meditates in this essay on the coming of spring to a war-ravaged London, where the winters of past years have seemed all but interminable. The toads arrive early in spring, looking gaunt and pale. After fattening up on insects in the nearest body of water they can find, they urgently seek a mate. A few weeks pass, and the lakes and ponds are full of tadpoles, whose rapid transformation produces a new crop of toads that will carry on the cycle. Orwell's interest in the common toad as a signifier of spring stems from a personal interest, as well as the general disregard shown to them by the poets of the past. As he notes earlier in the essay, the thin and hungry toads emerging from the mud have hollow faces that highlight the extraordinary beauty of their eyes. They are an unusual and unsung element of the British spring. The promise of spring unites all classes and neighborhoods in Britain. Even the most dismal regions of the city register the change of season, while "the policeman's tunic looks positively a pleasant shade of blue" and "the fishmonger greets his customers with a smile."

Having extolled the virtues of spring, Orwell questions whether such ruminations are "politically reprehensible." While England—and the world—suffers under capitalism, an appreciation of the natural world is seen by many as a distraction from more important political realities. "I know by experience that a favorable reference to 'Nature' in one of my articles is liable to bring me abusive letters." Such abuse focuses on two principal objections. First, any pleasure in the "process of life" tends to sidetrack the discontent necessary for political activism. Second, in the age of progress and machines, a love of nature is considered anachronistic. Orwell objects to both claims, in that an appreciation of nature is not antithetical to political activism. Progress—in the age of machines—cannot deny the realities of the natural world without risking a future in which "human beings will have no outlet for their surplus energy except in hatred and leader-worship."

The contemplation of the natural world, in Orwell's view, can be an act of political defiance. Those who think such behavior is politically irresponsible can do nothing to stop the process of the seasons or humanity's appreciation of it. "The atom bombs are piling up in the factories, the police are prowling through the cities, the lies are streaming from the loudspeakers, but the earth is still going round the sun, and neither the dictators nor the bureaucrats . . . are able to prevent it."

COMMENTARY

Like many of Orwell's essays—particularly the entries in his long-running column "As I Please"—this one uses an unconventional topic as a lead-in to a broader and more complex political discussion. On the surface, Orwell's theme in this essay is the beauty and mechanics of spring, seen specifically in the behavior of the oddly compelling common English toad. By the essay's end, however, Orwell has advanced a more profound idea. Orwell's early novels—particularly *Burmese Days,* in which the natural terrain of Burma almost constitutes a character in the novel—reflect his appreciation of the natural world. Even his most political novels, *Animal Farm* and *Nineteen Eighty-Four,* are informed by a great love of nature in general and a love of Britain in particular.

The world of the common English toad stands opposed, in some respects, to the world of political despots, nuclear weapons, and the economic hegemony of Western capitalism. The beauty of nature is free of class prejudice and ideology. It constitutes a necessary retreat from—but not an abandonment of—the complexities of the modern world. Nature also has the added advantage of being impervious to tyranny and propaganda, as long as one is physically free to witness it.

Orwell argues that change cannot be an end in itself. There must be something beyond the "concrete and steel" that he often uses to symbolize modern progress. "I have always suspected that if our economic and political problems are ever really solved, life will become simpler instead of more complex, and that the sort of pleasure one gets from finding the first primrose will loom larger than the sort of pleasure one gets from eating an ice to the tune of a Wurlitzer." The natural world, in other words, balances the desire to improve society. It is part of what makes economic and political justice worth fighting for. "Certainly we ought to be discontented, we ought not simply to find out ways of making the best of a bad job, and yet if we kill all pleasure in the actual process of life, what sort of future are we preparing for ourselves?" Orwell gives this idea its fullest expression in his final novel *Nineteen Eighty-Four,* which envisions a world where fundamental processes of life such as procreation are regulated by the state. The Junior Anti-Sex League strives to remove all pleasure from the process, thereby reducing it to a crude biological mechanism for creating future generations of mindlessly loyal party members. It is no longer an act of love between human beings and has become simply a function of the state. He anticipates another feature of *Nineteen Eighty-Four,* the "Two Minute Hate," when he suggests that the denial of pleasure in nature will leave people with "no outlet for their energy except in hatred and leader worship." "Some Thoughts on the Common Toad" argues for an appreciation of the basic processes of life that are not subject to state control, free to all who take the time to notice them.

"Spike, The"

Article first published in *The Adelphi* (April 1931). Most of this piece is an amalgam of incidents described in chapters 27 and 35 of DOWN AND OUT IN PARIS AND LONDON. *Spike* was the common term for overnight residences for the homeless. Tramps were permitted to stay in a given spike only one night a month (two nights on the weekends) and had to move on to another spike the next day.

SYNOPSIS

Orwell is one of 48 men and one woman waiting for the spike to open at six P.M. The tramps are discussing the tramp major, the person in charge. The major at this spike is regarded as particularly bad, "a tartar, a tyrant, a bawling blasphemous, uncharitable dog." Forbidden to bring any money into the spike, Orwell hides the eight pence he has under a hedge outside the spike. All the men have to hide their tobacco in their socks. When the doors open, the men are herded into the bathroom, where they are stripped and searched. Then, each man has three minutes to wash himself before dinner, which is always the same meal, whatever the time of day: a half pound of bread, some margarine, and a pint of waterish tea. At seven P.M., the men are locked in individual cells with three cotton blankets, which on this early spring evening were inadequate because the heat had been shut off.

The next morning, there is a rush to the bathroom because there is only one tub of water for everyone. In a short time, the water is so black it serves no purpose. Then comes breakfast, only this time the bread was sliced the previous night and "is as hard as a ship's biscuit." But they thank God for their tea. Tea a the tramp's lifeline. This day happens to be a Sunday, so the tramps are not allowed to leave until the next day. They are jammed into the dining room, where with nothing to do and very little room, they spend the next 10 hours. In Orwell's case, the tramp major notices his accent and deduces that he is a "gentleman." Consequently, Orwell is assigned to the adjoining workhouse kitchen, which gives him time to loaf and to share in the workhouse food, which is plentiful. He does the cleaning up after the meal and sees the large amount of extra food that has been thrown out rather than distributed to the tramps. Apparently, it is official policy designed not to "encourage" tramps. As one tramp explains to Orwell, when he returns to the dining room, "They have to do it. . . . If they made these places too pleasant, you'd have all the scum of the country flocking into them." This tramp had managed to separate himself from the others. He has retained a middle-class attitude regardless of his circumstances.

The tramps have their dinner, but by this time, the bread, rock-hard in the morning, is inedible. They are then sent off to their cells, where they remain until the next morning. Finally, the tramps are released. As Orwell heads down the road with his tramping friend Nobby, another tramp catches up with them. It is Scotty, who had had his cigarettes confiscated when he entered the spike on Saturday. Orwell had shared some of his tobacco with him. Scotty explains that the tramp major returned Scotty's cigarette butts as he was leaving. He wants to repay the favor, "and he put four sodden, debauched, loathly cigarette ends into my hand."

COMMENTARY

Orwell wrote "The Spike" in 1929, while he was still in Paris. Seen from that perspective, "The Spike" might be considered the first phase of the Orwellian style: telling details, rendered in terse, crisp language; the opening, as so often in an Orwell narrative, places us in time. "It was late afternoon." The last sentence in this first paragraph offers a metaphor that summarizes what the essay demonstrates: "We defiled the scene, like sardines-tins and paper bags on the seashore." The tramps are society's garbage.

The essay also illustrates Orwell's gift for the unusual observation. Thus he tells us that the real curse of tramping is the boredom of the life, particularly since tramps suffer more from boredom. Better-educated people, for example, have inner resources to combat boredom (Orwell himself once spoke of his reciting the poem "Felix Randal" while on guard duty on the Aragon front.) But the poor tramp is a person for whom standing around waiting is a special torment. It may not be true but insofar as it forces the reader to consider the possibility, it is an example of Orwell's ability to stimulate thought. The incident at the end, in which Scotty attempts to repay a favor by sharing his cigarette butts, summarizes Orwell's thesis: Tramps are not some subhuman species but people with a code of honor and decency at least on par with, if not superior to, that of regular society.

"Spillling the Spanish Beans"

A two-part article published in *New English Weekly*, July 29 and September 2, 1937. This is the essay that was turned down by Kingsley Martin, editor of *The New Statesman and Nation,* a rejection that earned him Orwell's enduring enmity.

SYNOPSIS

Part 1

Although lies and distortions in the English press about the Spanish civil war have been faithfully reported on behalf of both sides, it is the left-wing press that has done the most significant disservice to the basic truth. That truth is this: The republican government "is far more afraid of revolution than of the fascists." Papers such as the *Daily Worker* have covered up the fact that the government has been employing a "reign of terror" against the revolutionary segments of the loyalist forces. In Barcelona, the jails are packed with prisoners, and spying and executions are common. The people responsible for this repression are the Communists.

To explain the current situation, we must briefly review the history of the war. Franco's military insurrection was supported by the aristocracy, business interests, and the church. Arrayed against them were the peasants, workers, and the liberal bourgeoisie who formed the so-called Popular Front government, a fragile alliance at best. Once this war widened into a European conflict, with Germany and Italy supplying Franco with troops and weapons, and the Soviet Union sending arms and advisors to the government, the republican forces eventually came under communist control. As a result, the conduct of the war on the republican side was dictated by the interests of Soviet foreign policy, which was primarily concerned with winning the cooperation of England and France in a coming conflict with Hitler. The implicit government party line became one of counterrevolution.

Part 2

Having suppressed the revolutionary forces fighting on their side, the Communists now maintained that the fight against fascism in Spain was a fight for democracy, disguising the fact that the democracy they spoke of was really a form of bourgeois capitalism. Anyone who pointed out this contradiction was immediately denounced, and in Spain, jailed as a Trotskyist. Communist propaganda portrayed a Trotskyist as a secret fascist, trying to divide the left. The result was a systematic oppression of left-wing parties beginning with the POUM and extending to anarchists and left-wing socialists, in which each group and its leadership have been first marginalized, and then denounced as Trotskyists and "enemies of the people." The goal is the silencing of all dissent, or in effect, fascism.

Meanwhile, what of the war against Franco? It is true that the Communists have created a more disciplined military machine. It is likely that the war will end in a stalemate with the nation divided into two or more zones, with both sides claiming victory.

All this is common knowledge in Spain and France. But in England it comes as news, as a result of a conspiracy of silence about the situation on the grounds that the truth will undermine the fight against Franco. As a result, the British public has been denied the opportunity to see fascism at work under the name of communism.

COMMENTARY

Written in the summer of 1937, when the outcome of the war was still unclear, Orwell takes what turned out to be an optimistic view, assuming that the war would end in a stalemate, resulting in a partitioning of Spain. In his later essay, "LOOKING BACK ON THE SPANISH WAR," written in 1942 or 1943, he traces Franco's victory to the refusal of English and French governments to come to the aid of the republicans. As for the revelations of communist perfidy, they constitute a brief summary of the events detailed so memorably in HOMAGE TO CATALONIA. The refusal of Kingsley Martin to accept this essay for *The New Statesman* underscored its basic message.

"Sporting Spirit, The"

Brief essay first published in *Tribune* (December 1945). In the months following the end of World War II, as a goodwill gesture, the Moscow Dynamos, a Russian soccer team, visited England to play against some British teams. Orwell's essay appeared shortly after the Moscow team left England.

SYNOPSIS

Orwell begins by asserting that with the Russian team gone, the truth can finally be spoken: the notion that international sporting events breed goodwill is manifestly wrong. In fact, these encounters only serve to make enmity between participating countries stronger. Sports frenzy is particularly evident in relatively new countries, where there are no restraining traditions to keep the spectators under control. As it is, international sports can be summed up in a simple phrase: "war minus the shooting." It is clear that the sporting spirit is an offshoot of nationalism, a common cause of war. We have enough problems trying to avoid international conflicts without "encouraging young men to kick each other on the shins amid the roars of infuriated spectators."

This article created a perhaps predictable series of lively letters pro and con. The question as to whether "war minus the shooting" leads to or prevents the other kind of war is not resolved in the exchange. The subsequent history of the World Cup events and other international matches certainly reinforces the principle that nationalism is alive and well among the fans of football.

"Such, Such Were the Joys"

Essay first published in *Partisan Review* in 1952, two years after Orwell's death. The actual composition of the essay is difficult to determine. According to Peter Davison, a first draft was probably written in 1939 or 1940, following the publication of Cyril Connolly's *Enemies of Promise* (1938). Connolly's book included a memoir of his experiences at St Cyprian's, the prep school where he and Orwell were pupils together. From Orwell's perspective, Connolly's recollections had been all too forgiving and tolerant. His essay was designed to correct that error.

SYNOPSIS

Section 1

Orwell recalls that shortly after arriving at St Cyprian's school, he began wetting the bed, a "crime" punishable by a beating. This possibility was first raised for him by the wife of the headmaster, Mrs. Wilkes (nicknamed, Flip), who suggested to him in front of another adult unknown woman that she was going to have the entire sixth form beat him. The other adult vehemently concurred in this decision. As a consequence, the eight-year-old boy assumed that the other woman, whose name he heard as "Mrs. Form," would be the one to beat him. As it turned out, it was the headmaster, Mr. Wilkes (nicknamed Sambo), who delivered the beating. But first the child had to report himself, that is, he was told to "proclaim your offense with your own lips." That first beating—with a riding crop across his bottom—was surprisingly mild. As a result, right after dismissal, he bragged to a group of students in the hall that "it didn't hurt." Unfortunately, Flip overheard this remark and commanded him to "report himself" again. This time, the headmaster broke his riding crop as the boy broke into tears, not from the pain so much as from the sense that he was "imprisoned in a hostile world with rules it was impossible to follow." He saw himself as a sinner, sin being "not necessarily something that you did but something that happened to you." Orwell reports that he took only two impressions from that second beating. One was the sense that he deserved it, since he had in effect bragged about his good fortune, thus eliciting the gods' revenge. The second point was the continuing guilt he felt for the broken riding crop, a sense of guilt he retained for the next 20 or 30 years. The ironic epilogue to the story is that following the beating, he did not, with one exception, ever wet the bed again. He concludes, "So perhaps this barbarous remedy does work, though at a heavy price, I have no doubt."

Section 2

Most of the boys at St Cyprian's came from rich but not aristocratic, families. Some were rich foreigners. Sambo's great ambitions were to attract more aristocratic students—those with titles, particularly—and to train an elite group of students to win scholarships, particularly to Eton. For this purpose, he would accept some students at lower tuition rates. Orwell was one of these students. He was a member of the scholarship class, but even there, students were treated according to the wealth of their parents. Rich boys were never caned, and outside of class, rich children received extras which were denied to those whose parents were, relatively speaking, poor.

Orwell was not aware of his scholarship status until he had spent at least three years at the school. At that time, the pressure to succeed increased and with it the reminders to boys like him that they were ingrates, considering "all we've done for you." He recalls the sense of the seeming omniscience of Flip and Sambo. On a day when he bought some chocolates from a sweet shop in the village, he imagined a stranger looking at him as he left the shop. He was convinced that the man was an agent in the employ of the school.

He believed that Sambo's and Flip's actions were done for his eventual benefit. The canings and threats and humiliations were all designed to save him from the fate of becoming a clerk in an office earning 40 pounds a year. But it left him with a "consciousness of sin" that remained with him for years. That consciousness was rooted in the fact that, although he believed that Sambo and Flip were acting in his best interests, he hated them with a deep passion.

Section 3

There were some happy experiences at St Cyprian's, such as the nature walks or short rail trips to hunt butterflies. The only problem was that participating students drew sneers from Flip, who treated any departure from the classical curriculum as "babyish."

Other features of life at the school that Orwell indicts are the genuine lack of cleanliness in general and in the attention to the boys' personal hygiene in particular; the inadequate, unappetizing food; the bullying by older boys; and, above all, the personality of Flip. She was the reigning queen, whose favor every boy in the school desperately desired, while at the same time, deeply hating her. In response, she exhibited the caprices of a powerful monarch, one day laughing and joking, another fiercely disapproving. The boys were like courtiers, always living under one of her various moods.

Section 4

When Orwell was 12, a sex scandal broke out at the school and although he was not involved his name came to be indirectly connected. In fact, he was even innocent of knowing about sex at this point in his life. At age five or six, Orwell had passed through a brief sexual stage, which consisted of "playing doctor" and falling in love with Elsie, a teenager at the convent school he attended between the ages of six and eight. After that, all sexual feeling effectively disappeared until his own teen years: "Not having desire, I had no curiosity." He found himself among a group of boys being lectured to on the subject of the body as a temple of the Holy Spirit. One boy was expelled, but all the senior boys were made to feel guilty for at least the sin of masturbation and at worst for corrupting the younger students. In Orwell's case, and among many of the other 12-year-olds, they did not even know what they were being accused of.

Section 5

When it came to religious, moral, sexual, and intellectual values, St Cyprian's delivered a series of mixed messages. On the one hand, you were expected to be a good Christian, puritanical in relation to sex, industrious, and an excellent student; on the other hand, you must aim to be a financial and social success. But early on, Orwell recognized that success required a minimum fixed income of 4,000 pounds a year, which would be the interest on a principal of 100,000 pounds. To achieve that goal—as opposed to being born into it—you had to work until you were "fat and old." The alternative for someone of Orwell's class was civil service, which, even at the top rung of the civil service ladder, would take you only so far; you would still be an "underling." The atmosphere at the school reflected the belief that the extravagance and self-indulgence of the wealthy classes would always exist. It was evident whenever upcoming holidays were discussed. At that time, "the cult of Scotland" usually emerged. Anyone who lacked a summer home in Scotland was simply second-rate. Aside from wealth, the social atmosphere at the school celebrated strong, athletic, dominant personalities, even in the choice of sports, where football was preferred to cricket. To young Orwell, football was a variant of fighting, in which the stronger always triumphed over the weaker, younger boys.

While he was at St Cyprian's, he never questioned the dominant values, but he realized that it was impossible for him to conform to them. For example, he was taught to love God and to fear Him, but the idea of loving someone you feared seemed to him a clear contradiction. He was told he must love his father, but his father was a distant and removed elderly grouch whom he barely knew. He wanted to do the right thing but too often the right thing seemed impossible. "The good and the possible never seemed to coincide."

As a result, he emerged from St Cyprian's with a completely negative self-image. He saw himself as ugly, unpopular, smelly, weak, with a chronic cough, destined to be a failure and to die young. These, however, were balanced by one powerful drive: the determination to survive. He recalls one boy, Cliffy Burton, who was prized for his good looks, his strength, and his prowess on the football field. Burton embodied the "law of the stronger" and acted it out in bullying fashion. One day he tormented Orwell, twisting his arm around his back. Determined on revenge, Orwell, without warning, smashed him in the face. Burton challenged him to a fight, but he steadfastly refused, knowing he would be beaten. Burton never picked on him again. He had broken the rules and survived, and for him, survival was all.

Leaving the school for the last time, he shook hands with Flip, reading her facial expression as one of resigned defeat. He had rejected everything the school stood for. From her perspective, the scholarships to Wellington and Eton he had won notwithstanding, he was one of their failures. He left St Cyprian's, happy to be free at last, but knowing that there was no place for him. "In a world where the prime necessities were money, titled-relatives, athleticism, tailor-made clothes, neatly-brushed hair, a charming smile, I was no good."

Section 6

Orwell reminds the reader that these events occurred more than 30 years ago and asks whether things have changed in schools. Clearly, significant changes have been made in religious instruction and in the practice of corporal punishment. The more meaningful question refers to the subjective experiences of children. Children still conceal their real feelings from adults. Their reactions to adults are mixed with elements of fear, admiration, ridicule, and physical distaste. Thus, we cannot be certain that boarding school, at least, "is not still for many children as dreadful an experience as it used to be." Take away God, Latin, the cane, class distinctions, sexual taboos, and the fear, the hatred, the snobbery and the misunderstanding might still all be there."

One thing seems certain, "that boarding schools are worse than day schools." In fact, it may be the case that the problems of the English upper classes are in part the result of sending young children of seven or eight years away from the sanctuary of home to a boarding school.

Orwell concludes by asserting that he has never returned to St Cyprian's, his anger pretty well dissipated, replaced by indifference. He didn't even care to inquire about the rumor that the place had burned down.

COMMENTARY

The title of this essay is taken from a line in a poem by William Blake, "The Echoing Green":

> Such, such were the joys
> When we all, girls and boys
> In our youth time were seen
> On the echoing green

Orwell's title sets up a strong, ironic contrast with his message. What immediately follows is one of his celebrated, attention-getting opening sentences: "Soon after arriving at St Cyprian's . . . I began wetting my bed." Persistent bed-wetting can provoke a sense of shame and frustration for any child, but in a boarding school where it soon becomes public knowledge, it transforms the shame into humiliation. In Orwell's case, it raised a fundamental moral dilemma, the realization that "sin was not something you did, it might be something that happened to you," something you had no control over. Orwell biographer Bernard Crick maintains that such a perception would have been too sophisticated for an eight-year-old boy. Crick suggests that the comment reflects Orwell's mature analysis (29). However, young Eric Blair may have already come to grips with this idea, either from the Ursuline nuns at the convent school he attended or from the pulpit of his parish church, in the doctrine of Original Sin. In any case, the seed of Orwell's subsequent silent rebellion at the school seems to be rooted in this dilemma. As Connolly pointed out, "I was the stage rebel; Orwell a true one."

In part 2 of the essay, Orwell takes on the subject of wealth in the school. Wealthy students were granted privileges denied to students less well off, a policy that contributed to a general tone of snobbery on the part of the wealthy and shame on the part of the poorer students. Orwell recounts this experience not only here but also in his description of the school experience of Gordon Comstock, the protagonist of *Keep the Aspidistra Flying*. In part 3, he zeroes in on Mrs. Wilkes, a reigning queen right out of Lewis Carroll, whose capricious moods left her student courtiers in a constant state of anxiety as to whether, on any given day, they might be "in" or "out." As Connolly attested, Eric refused to play the game and was therefore permanently *out*, even while he won prizes and scholarships. "Simplifying the relationship to its irreduciable element, . . . he wanted her approval and never got it, she wanted his affection and never got it" (Stansky and Abraham, 62).

In many respects, some of the charges he makes about the school's values, the emphasis on success, athleticism, and "character" might with equal justice be leveled against society itself. With the exception of the distinctive personalities of Flip and Sambo, St Cyprian's seems not all that different from most of the prep schools in existence at the time. However, it is clear that he felt damaged by the school and needed to give voice to the rage he felt but was obliged to suppress as a child. Having done just that, he was able to summarize it objectively by declaring that "boarding schools are worse than day schools."

The idea that the experience at St Cyprian's left permanent damage on Orwell was first advanced by the critic Anthony West in an article in the *New Yorker* (January 26, 1956).

West argued that the terrors Orwell described in *Nineteen Eighty-Four* were unconscious projections of the childhood fears he experienced at St Cyprian's. Thus Room 101 is the headmaster's office transformed with Flip, undergoing a sexual change, as Big Brother. In 1956, psychoanalytical interpretations tended to be given more credence than they received in later years, so that the West article enjoyed a wide readership. West, perhaps indulging in a spot of revenge for Orwell's rude treatment of his father H. G. WELLS, uses his analysis to reduce *Nineteen Eighty-Four* to the expression of childhood hysteria. A more balanced view is advanced by George Woodcock. He suggests that looking back at his school days, Orwell saw the resemblance between a child, subject to the arbitrary rules of a boarding school, and an adult "locked in the equally arbitrary system of a totalitarian society" (164).

WORKS CITED

Connolly, Cyril. *Enemies of Promise.* London: Routledge and Regan Paul, 1938.

Crick, Bernardo. *George Orwell: A Life.* Boston: Little, Brown, 1980.

Stansky, Peter and William Abrahams. *The Unknown Orwell.* New York: Knoff, 1972.

West, Anthony. "Hidden Damage." *New Yorker.* January 28, 1956, 98–104.

Woodcock, George. *The Crystal Spirit.* London: Jonathan Cape, 1967.

Talking to India (1943)

A collection of talks given on the BBC Eastern Service, edited with an introduction by Orwell. He also included one of his own talks, "THE REDISCOVERY OF EUROPE," in the collection. Other contributors included E. M. Forster, Reginald Reynolds, Cyril Connolly, and Mulk Raj Anand. Another contributor was Sudhas Chandra Bose (1898–1945), an outspoken anti-English Indian who broadcast anti-English propaganda from Berlin during the war. A selection from a Bose broadcast was included by way of comparison as an example of Axis propaganda. As Orwell explains in his introduction, Bose avoids mentioning "major issues of the war," such as the Japanese invasion of China and the German invasion of the Soviet Union. In Bose's view, the English and Americans are the only real enemies of India.

To point up the contrast between "honest and dishonest" propaganda, Orwell includes excerpts from his *BBC* newsletters.

Orwell's introduction indicates that the BBC's Eastern Service provided daily broadcasts in Hindustani and weekly broadcasts in other Indian languages. In addition, there were daily broadcasts in English for the five million Indians who were English speakers. These include the hundreds of thousands of Indians with degrees in English literature and many more studying for such degrees. This explains the heavy cultural emphasis in these programs, although there are political broadcasts as well.

THEATER REVIEWS

The onset of World War II found Orwell desperately trying to participate in some meaningful way. His attempts to enlist failed because of his frail health. He was also judged physically unfit to serve as a war correspondent. Blacklisted from many positions in journalism because of his strong anti-Soviet stance, he accepted a position with *Time and Tide* magazine as a theater critic, to which he later added FILM REVIEWS.

His first review (May 1940) was of the Shaw play "In Good King Charles's Golden Days." In viewing it he was perhaps reminded of *CHARLES II*, the school play he had written, and the costumes he had slaved over while teaching at the Hawthorns in 1932. In any case, he had a better time with the Shaw play, applauding it except for "the hideousness of the costumes." In August of that year, he reviewed another play of Shaw, *The Devil's Disciple,* which he described as "perhaps the best play Shaw ever wrote." Although enthusiastic about the play, he could not resist a gibe at its author, "Mr. Shaw . . . the seeming rebel was actually an apostle of the authoritarian state." As for Shakespeare, he reviewed *King John* (July 1941), noting that the trickery, betrayal, and cynicism that are rife in the play gave it a strong contemporary feeling. He was considerably less pleased with an Old Vic production of *The Tempest* (June 1940), which used high jinks and slapstick to amuse an audience that clearly didn't know the text of the play. The only exception was John Gielgud's Prospero, "a performance that was a long way ahead of the rest of the company." Among contemporary plays that met with his approval was Robert Ardrey's *Thunder Rock* (June 1940). The play, which was first produced by New York's Group Theater, focuses on a man who, in his disgust with the world, has retreated to an isolated lighthouse, which 90 years earlier had been the scene of a shipwreck, resulting in the deaths of seven people. The man soon finds himself conversing with the ghosts of these seven victims. He discovers that some of the goals these people strove for in life have been achieved, forcing the man to recognize that life is not in fact as futile as he had imagined. Something like human progress does occur. Orwell singles out Michael Redgrave's performance in the lead role. Another play that he enjoyed was Winifred Holtby's *Take Back Your Freedom* (August 24, 1940). On July 12, 1941, he reviewed Noel Coward's *Blithe Spirit,* which he praised for its ability to send up spiritualism by presenting life after death as boring. He takes particular delight in Margaret Rutherford's Madame Arcati, a medium who is "bluff and hearty, an outdoor woman and keen bicyclist who . . . goes in and out of trances as resiliently as a jack-in-the-box."

Orwell's final review, which appeared on August 9, 1941, was of W. O. Somin's *Close Quarters,* a two-character melodrama with political overtones. Orwell ended his his stint as a theater and film reviewer when he joined the BBC Eastern Service. See BBC WRITINGS.

"Toward European Unity"

An essay that appeared in *Partisan Review* (July–August 1947) as part of the series "The Future of Socialism."

SYNOPSIS

Orwell begins by describing socialism as a patient that is almost certainly going to die, but if it is to live, certain possibilities must *not* become real. One is that the United States wage a preventive war against the Soviet Union, using nuclear weapons, an event that is not likely but possible. The second is that the cold war will continue with an atomic build-up on both sides, resulting in a nuclear war in which civilization will be destroyed and mankind will be back in the equivalent of the stone age. Possible and more likely. The third is that there will be a nuclear build-up, but that, out of fear, no one will dare use these weapons. However, each state will become increasingly tyrannical within its own borders, an event that is probable.

The only way to avoid one of these three outcomes is to establish democratic socialism, and the only place where that might be possible is Western Europe. In other words, at this time, a socialist United States of Europe is the only viable alternative to one type of catastrophe or another. The major obstacle to such a development is the inability for the mass of people to accept something really new, even when their own survival is at stake. In addition, there are four other barriers to such a union:

1. Russian hostility: The Russians will resist and undermine any socialist state that they do not control.
2. American hostility: The Americans, unhappy with any form of socialism, will exert economic power in England in order to draw it away from the union.
3. Imperialism: For the union to work, its members must divest themselves of the colonies. What is not recognized in England, at least, is that such a move will result in a reduction of the standard of living of the English working class.
4. The Catholic Church: The Church is perfectly capable of coming to terms with socialism, but it will always strive against "any form of society tending to promote earthly happiness."

Considering these obstacles and the enormous changes in people's thinking that would be needed to make such a federation work, it seems that it will never occur. Of course, there is always the possibility of the unexpected: The United States may turn socialist, or a new generation in Russia may come to power, "eager for more freedom and more friendly to the West." Another is that the world will become dominated by three "super-states," with the Anglo-American segment maintaining its liberal tradition, keeping life tolerable with occasional glimmers of progress. But this is wishful thinking. Realistically, the outlook ". . . is very dark and any serious thought should start from there."

COMMENTARY

Looking back on Orwell's views in 1947, today's reader is struck by his mixed performance as a prophet. First, and most striking, is his prediction of what is now the European Union, although he was not the only person to foresee that development. The negative side of this genuinely prescient possibility was his belief that such a union could only be achieved through socialism. In 1941, in *The Lion and the Unicorn,* he made a similar mistake in insisting that the war could only be won with a socialist government. His error in both cases came from underestimating the flexibility of the capitalist system on the one hand, and the flexibility of many European democratic socialists who transformed themselves into social democrats on the other. In the process, the compromise known as the modern welfare state was born, usually oscillating between left- and right-wing regimes. Far from being a socialist ideal, it is still a world, which Orwell described in the 1920s, in terms of a popular song, "The rich get richer/And the poor get children. . . ," but he never believed in a socialist utopia any more than in a Christian heaven. He only asked for improvement, and from that point of view, the lives of the people of Western Europe have improved. But now the problem has arisen on a global scale. Not even Orwell could predict that outcome.

"W. B. Yeats"

Review/essay first published in *Horizon* (January 1943). The book under review was *The Development of William Butler Yeats* (1942) by V. K. Narayana Menon.

SYNOPSIS

Orwell begins by inquiring as to whether there is a connection between a writer's style and his political "tendency." Yeats's "tendency" was fascist, and one might locate a strain of fascism in the "artificiality" of Yeats's language, revealed in his occasional straining for stylistic effect. One example is his use of the word "loveliness," which Orwell considers "a vulgar word." These occasional false notes are always overcome by the power of the rest of his verse.

The book under discussion is less concerned with Yeats's language than with his philosophical system, as that is constructed in Yeats's *A Vision.* The system consists of historical cycles, reincarnation, spiritualism, and aspects of astrology, which Orwell sees as leading to fascist ideology. As "a great hater of democracy," Yeats was attracted to the strong leader, as exemplified by the Italian dictator Benito Mussolini. Yeats's political ideal imagines a ruling aristocracy, but his old-fashioned ruling class has long since vanished. In the modern world it has been replaced by bureaucrats and murdering gangsters. "Had he lived long enough, he might have changed his opinion of modern fascism, but it is impossible to know."

The connection of this fascist tendency with occult philosophy can also be seen in Yeats's cyclical view of history. If we exist in an endless series of cycles, the whole idea of human progress is an illusion. Another is the sense in occultism of the truth as being available "only to a small circle of initiates," comparable to the "secret cult" that characterizes the origins of fascism.

It is still a problem of great concern, that "the best writers of our time have been reactionary in tendency." Orwell concludes by hoping that Menon will write another book, in which, using Yeats as his example, he explores the relationship between fascism and the great modernist writers.

A few months after this review appeared, Orwell reviewed the same book for *Time and Tide* in April 1943. In deference to a broader, less "literary" audience, in *Time and Tide* Orwell begins the review with a short summary on Yeats's biography, explaining that his career covered three distinct phases. The earliest was the aesthetic, "art for art's sake" phase of the 1890s. This was followed by the "Celtic twilight" phase, in which he celebrated and helped to revive ancient Irish mythology as well as the Gaelic language. In his last phase, his modernist period, he adopted a new poetic vocabulary, "the astonishing final phase in which he produced his best work . . . when he was more than sixty years of age."

The one consistent strain throughout these phases is his hatred of the modern western world, an emotion that drove him to a political posture that bordered on fascism, based on a mixture of occult beliefs in astrology, spiritualism, and reincarnation, along with a cyclical view of history. But despite his odd beliefs, he exhibited a rigorous "artistic integrity," as his poetic achievement attests.

COMMENTARY

Orwell more than once raised the question of the conservative/reactionary tendencies of some of the great modernist writers of the early 20th century, such as Yeats, D. H. Lawrence, T. S. Eliot, Ezra Pound, James Joyce, and among Orwell's contemporaries, Anthony Powell and Evelyn Waugh. In his essay "THE REDISCOVERY OF EUROPE," he suggests that the great modernists, ironically, were repelled by the modern world, industrialization, democratization, the loss of tradition, myth, and the tragic sense of life.

On a less serious note, when Orwell's first review appeared in *Horizon,* it was commented on in *The Times Literary Supplement (TLS).* The anonymous author accused Orwell of what we now call "political correctness" in relation to Yeats, but more egregious, from the *TLS* author's point of view, was Orwell's rejection of the word *loveliness* as "squashy and vulgar." Orwell replied, defending himself in speaking of Yeats's politics and for professing a dislike of the word *loveliness.* In the *TLS* author's brief reply, he comments on Orwell's rejection of *loveliness* as "insolent censorship." As the letter exchange continued, the Victorian scholar Lord David Cecil joined in and, having been challenged by Orwell to find an appropriate example of the word *lovenest* did so. The controversy ended with a conciliatory letter from Cecil, who had won the point. This correspondence is reprinted in the *Complete Works,* as an appendix to the first review.

WORK CITES

The Complete Works of George Orwell. Edited by Peter Davison. Vols. 14: 279–289; 15: 69–71. London: Secker & Warburg, 1998.

"Wells, Hitler and the World State"

Review/essay first published in *Horizon,* August 1941. The book under review was H. G. Wells's *A Guide to the New World* (1941), a collection of newspaper articles Wells had recently written.

SYNOPSIS

The essay opens with a series of quotations by the novelist H. G. WELLS on the war as of January 1941. They testify to Wells's conviction that the German army's victorious days were over. Hitler, whom Wells calls "that screaming little defective," has exhausted his supplies, his air power, and his overrated troops. Orwell mocks Wells's overconfidence, pointing out the successes of the German army in the months following Wells's remarks. He then turns to Wells's endorsement of a World State and his specific proposal for international control of air power, outlawing bombing of nonmilitary targets. Orwell remarks that all reasonable people desire such a thing but none of the major governments will go along with it. This unrealistic idealism is typical of Wells. For the past two decades, he has persisted in promoting ideas that fail to consider the forces that really motivate people, particularly the role of patriotism. In his mind, Wells inhabits a world in which all that is good is represented by science and all that is bad by nationalism. His habits of mind, developed over his entire life, render him incapable of understanding Hitler and the power he wields. He cannot even face the obvious fact that Nazi Germany is more scientific than England. Germany's scientific achievements, however, are all in the service of ideas that belong to the Stone Age, which leads Orwell to conclude, "So much for the inherent goodness of science."

Orwell backs up to describe the importance of Wells to Orwell's generation, people born around 1900: ". . . it was an illuminating experience for a boy to discover H. G. Wells. . . . Here was this wonderful man who could tell you about the inhabitants of the planets . . . and who knew that the future was not going to be what respectable people imagined." However, because Wells was and is a 19th-century liberal, he underrates the power of "nationalism, religious bigotry and feudal loyalty." As a result, he is too sane to understand the modern world, and he dismisses Hitler as an "unimportant lunatic." "The people who best understand fascism are those who have suffered under it or those who have a fascist streak in themselves." Wells's rationalism precludes his grasping the evil inherent in a Hitler or Stalin. Among his contemporaries, you might pick Kipling as a man who would be better equipped to deal with fascism and the mind of a Hitler. Orwell concludes on a conciliatory note: For the last 20 years, Wells has "squandered his talents"; still it is something to have had those talents to begin with.

COMMENTARY

As he acknowledges in this essay, H. G. Wells exerted a powerful influence on the young Orwell. Born in 1866, Wells straddled the 19th and 20th centuries. His early writings, those for which he is still best known, were in the new field of science fiction: *The Time Machine* (1895), *The Invisible Man* (189?), and *The War of the Worlds* (1898) celebrated a future in which scientific progress would help create a utopian society. But Wells was also politically progressive, becoming an early leader in the Fabian socialist movement. As a result, he turned from science fiction to realistic depictions of the lower middle classes in novels such as *The History of Mr. Polly* (1910), one of the sources of Orwell's *Coming up for Air.* Among other Wells works that influenced Orwell was *The Island of Dr. Moreau* (1896), a source for NINETEEN EIGHTY-FOUR. In 1941, Orwell adapted a short story by Wells, "A Slip under the Microscope," for BBC radio.

All of which suggests that Orwell was not exaggerating when he posed the rhetorical question in the review, "But is it not a kind of parricide for a person of my age . . . to find fault with H. G. Wells. . . . The minds of all of us . . . would be perceptively different if Wells had never existed." However Orwell renewed his attack on a BBC broadcast "The Rediscovery of Europe," in which he compared the short stories of Wells with those of D. H. Lawrence, by way of demonstrating the greater depth of Lawrence's work. He then went on to compare Aldous Huxley's *Brave New World* (1932) with Wells's *A Modern Utopia* (1904), stressing the latter's "naive" faith in science as the final answer to life's basic questions. In effect, Orwell was simply reinforcing the critique he delivered in this essay.

"Why I Write"

Essay first published in *Gangrel* (1946) and written in response to the question implied in the title. It may be the most quoted and alluded to of all of Orwell's essays.

SYNOPSIS

Orwell explains that from an early age he knew he would become a writer although there was a period in his twenties when he tried to evade his vocation. He had a lonely childhood and as a result made up stories. Early on, he exhibited two important skills, "a facility with words and the power of facing unpleasant facts." In 1914, at the age of 11, he published a poem at the outbreak of World War I and another, two years later, on the death of General Kitchener, both of which were published in the local newspaper. At 16, he discovered the joy of language in a passage from *Paradise Lost.* When he began seriously to write, he wanted to produce large, serious novels "with unhappy endings, full of detailed descriptions and arresting similes." His first published novel, *Burmese Days,* conformed somewhat to that model.

He has provided these biographical details because he believes that while a writer's subject matter emerges from the outer world he lives in, his emotional approach to his subject derives from his formative years. He should strive to recognize and control those psychological ties but not sever them altogether. To do so would be to cut off his creative roots.

Aside from the desire to earn a living, there are four distinct motives that propel a writer: sheer egoism, the wish to be seen as someone special, along with the desire for revenge. But on the whole it is the selfish determination to live one's own life. A second motive is aesthetic enthusiasm, the appeal of beauty either in the natural world or in the order of words. Even writers of nonliterary prose exhibit faint examples of this gratification. The third spur for a writer is the historical impulse, the wish to report what one sees as the truth about one's time and to pass it on to future generations. The fourth motive is political purpose, the desire to help bring about a better society. No writer is exempt from politics. "Art for art's sake" is itself a political statement. Obviously, these four impulses frequently conflict with each other. Speaking for himself, Orwell asserts that in a different historical period he would have been primarily a non-political writer. His experiences, first in Burma, later as a down-and-outer and among the working-class miners, while clearly important, were not enough to transform him into a political writer until his experiences in the Spanish civil war in 1936 and 1937. "Every line of serious work since 1936 has been written *against* totalitarianism and *for* democratic Socialism. . . . What I have wanted to do throughout the past ten years is to make political writing into an art."

He begins a piece of writing not with the purpose of producing a work of art but with a political goal, exposing a lie or calling attention to a particular fact, but the act of writing has to be an aesthetic experience, which in his case means never abandoning "the world-view I acquired in childhood." Among these elemental touchstones are the love of good prose, "the surface of the earth," and delight in "solid objects and scraps of useless information."

He now sees himself as a committed political writer, capable of writing, when necessary, pure propaganda, but never without a powerful belief in the beauty of language. One example of this is his *Homage to Catalonia,* which he strove mightily to make a beautiful book. But when it came to the question of including information and data, he had to include that particular chapter even though it detracted from the book's aesthetic integrity. Had he not done so, he would have betrayed innocent men. In terms of the use of language, Orwell declares that he has of late tried to write with a more precise understanding of what he was attempting, that is, to fuse the political and the aesthetic into a meaningful whole. To date, *Animal Farm* is his most successful example of that attempt.

Finally, let it be said that, although writers are "vain, selfish and lazy," they find that good writing occurs only when their own personality is not evident in the work. "Good prose is like a window pane." In any case, it is clear that for him, of the four impulses listed above, the strongest is clearly the political.

COMMENTARY

"Why I Write" not only answers the title's implicit question, but it also exemplifies the answer in itself. Orwell takes us back to his childhood not simply because he was conscious of his desire to be a writer at an early age but because he believes that one cannot determine "a writer's motives without knowing something of his early development." He then goes on to make the surprising judgment that the writer will never completely escape the emotional structure of that experience, and even more surprising, that he never *should* escape, ". . . if he escapes from his early influences altogether, he will have killed his impulse to write." Lurking in that statement is the qualifier "for better or for worse." Orwell's writing exhibits "better" and "worse" recreations of those early influences. The depiction of George Bowling's childhood in *Coming Up for Air* is that of a lost paradise perhaps connected to the passage from *Paradise Lost* in the essay. As for the "worse" and its inescapability, there is the emotional power of "Such, Such Were the Joys", the two influences combining in the formation of the "Tory radical," "the "revolutionary in love with 1910." This paradox defined his work until *Homage to Catalonia,* his first attempt "to make political writing an art." Thus of the four basic motives of the writer—egoism, aesthetic impulse, historical recorder, and the political—the "desire to push the world in a certain direction," it is the last that is the most important for him. In achieving that goal, he writes of his belief that the writer must "efface his personality" in order to achieve prose "like a window pane." This famous comment has been repeated countless times by students of Orwell but there are those admirers of Orwell who argue that the real distinction of his writing is that it so clearly expresses its author. That is, with Orwell, the style is the man. Some, however, would counter that "the Orwell personality" is the "implied author" of the work, a character created by the actual author, a temporary identity who exists only for the duration of the work he is creating. In this respect, Orwell might be correct in asserting that the author must "efface his personality."

"Writers and Leviathan"

Short essay first published in *Politics and Letters* (1948), treating the role of the writer in his relation to the state.

SYNOPSIS

Orwell's subject is the problem the writer faces in adopting a political position. Since we live in an intensely political age, we cannot help being conscious of the political implications, if not outright assertions, of any piece of writing, whether ours or someone else's. But this is a particular problem in relation to creative literature. The dominant literary/political attitude of the past fifteen years has been left, democratic, and antifascist—in one word, progressive. Certainly this orthodoxy of the left is an improvement over the old conservative orthodoxy, but it, too, has its taboos and self-censorship of subjects and issues, about which one tends not to speak the truth, thereby cutting off serious discussion.

Chief among these is the tacit acceptance of the Soviet Union as a socialist state, knowing full well that it is a tyrannical dictatorship. Another grows out of the fact that we now have a Labour government in power, confronting a problem that the left had not faced up to in the past: an economic crisis brought on by the impending dissolution of the British Empire. The orthodox leftist position that imperialism was an evil failed to acknowledge it was an evil that enabled the English working man to earn a living wage. Liberals and left-wingers have never been really forthcoming about this easily foreseeable outcome of disbanding the empire. Still another is fear and loathing of industrialism on the one hand and the recognition that "the conquest of poverty and the emancipation of the working class demand, not less industrialism, but more and more." To speak out honestly in these circumstances is to be "disloyal" to the party of whatever group one belongs to.

It seems that any type of *-ism*—left, right, or center—is poisonous to literature. This is not to suggest that a writer should avoid politics. Writers, like every other citizen, should participate in the political process, but as a person, not as a writer. This means that you can write about politics as an individual, an outsider, but not as a socialist or a conservative. This splitting of the self into two compartments may seem foolish or impossible, but it seems to be the only solution for the writer's dilemma. When writing fiction or poetry, the writer must free himself of his political loyalties and seek the truth, even when it leaves him outside his party's orthodoxy. The artist should engage in an election campaign, in his capacity as a citizen, but he should never tailor his art to fit a particular ideology.

COMMENTARY

This short piece embraces a subject Orwell addressed from a variety of points of view, particularly in "Inside the Whale" and "Why I Write." What immediately strikes a reader of this essay is how to reconcile its message with that of his famous statement in "Why I Write": "Everything I have written since 1936 has been in support of democratic Socialism." His answer might be that democratic socialism can be his goal, his end, but for the writer, the means must never be subordinated to his end. Corruption of the means inevitably results in corruption of the end. If a poet or novelist distorts or evades the artistic truth as he knows it to be, in order to make a case for a specific cause, he betrays himself as a writer and he betrays his cause. If, in *Homage to Catalonia,* Orwell had portrayed the members of his POUM unit as heroic and pure of heart, he would have fatally weakened his book. His description of their military ineptitude, their lack of discipline, their reluctance to work hard brings them to life as fallible, credible human beings. As a result, even readers who disagree with Orwell's view of the Spanish civil war, acknowledge that *Homage to Catalonia* is a classic, authentic account of that struggle. Still another example is the complaint registered over the "despairing conclusion" to *Nineteen Eighty-Four.* Were Orwell to supply a more tolerable ending to that novel—the ending, for example that the producers of the 1956 film version supplied (Winston and Julia defiantly shouting "Down with Big Brother" as they die with their arms around each other)—he would be tailoring his work to project a more optimistic view of the future than he envisioned. Presumably everyone would have been happier except Orwell, who would have felt that he had sold out.

"You and the Atom Bomb"

Essay first published in *Tribune* (1945).

SYNOPSIS

The question of immediate importance about the atomic bomb relates to the difficulty of making one. The news that it is an enormously expensive and complex process is reassuring in that it reduces the possibility of the proliferation of these deadly weapons. However, the certainty that nuclear weapons will be produced by powerful nations in the near future is not a good sign for democracy. History has shown that when weapons are complex and expensive, the power of the state increases and the move toward tyranny becomes greater. The simplicity and relative ease of producing the musket were significant factors in the success of the American and French revolutions, but the present age of tanks, battleships, and bombers has greatly increased the power of the state over the people.

The fact is that the Russians will probably have the bomb within five years. But as James Burnham pointed out in his *The Managerial Revolution,* it is probable that the two superstates (the U.S. and the USSR), with China eventually becoming a third, will engage in limited wars, but not risk all-out destruction. What seems likely is that these superstates will engage in a permanent cold war, with unimaginable consequences for the social structure and worldview of such states.

COMMENTARY

In a letter to *Tribune* the week after this article appeared, Alex Comfort suggested that the atomic bomb would be of no use to a government against its own people. The rulers' weapons would have to be what they always have been: "Terrorism, secret police, wholesale execution, and propaganda." It is striking that the combination of Orwell's references to the three oligarchical superstates, predicted by James Burnham, and Alex Comfort's comment clearly foreshadow the conditions in *Nineteen Eighty-Four.* This essay is also notable for its use of the term *cold war.* Although there is some question as to whether Orwell was the first to use the term, his usage predates Bernard Baruch's better-known employment in April 1947 and in the *Oxford English Dictionary,* Orwell is given credit for the term's first use.

PART III

Related People, Places, and Topics

Adelphi, The Socialist publication edited by RICHARD REES and Max Plowman, to which Orwell submitted numerous early essays, poems and reviews. Among the notable essays he wrote for this journal were "A HANGING" (1931) and "THE SPIKE" (1931); poems included "On a Ruined Farm near the His Master's Voice Gramophone Factory" (1934) and "St. Andrew's Day" (1935); and many book reviews. Orwell used *The Adelphi* as the model for the journal *The Antichrist* in *Keep the Aspidistra Flying*.

America See UNITED STATES

Anand, Mulk Raj (1905–2004) Indian novelist and critic. Anand is best known as the author of two protest novels in the 1930s, *Untouchable* (1935), dealing with the problem of caste in India, and *Coolie* (1936), focusing on poverty in that country.

In 1942, Orwell reviewed Anand's novel *The Sword and the Sickle* (1942) in *Horizon*, hailing the book as an important contribution to the new genre, a novel by an Indian novelist writing in English. In his review, although he expected that the coming independence of India would hamper the growth of English there, Orwell expressed the hope that its continued use would contribute to the development of international socialism in India's post-colonial future. During World War II, Anand became a colleague of Orwell in the Indian Section of the BBC. As an Indian nationalist, he had serious qualms about broadcasting for the British at a time when Indian leaders like Gandhi and Nehru were being jailed for subversive activities. Orwell was able to convince him that English colonialism was far preferable to what the country would face if conquered by Japan. Anand played an important role in the development of Orwell's VOICE project for the BBC. In a letter written in 1983, Anand recalled one impression of Orwell: ". . . his voice was restrained. He talked in furtive whispers. . . . And I seldom saw him show anger on his face, though the two deep lines in his cheeks and his furrowed brow signified permanent despair" (*CW*, 13, 100).

anarchism As a political theory rejecting governmental authority, anarchism has assumed a variety of forms ranging from nonviolent pacifist groups to those who advocate change by terrorism or other violent means. Thus, there has always existed an "anarchism of the good kind" as well as that of the once-popular image of the bomb-throwing assassin.

When he came back from Burma in 1927, Orwell left the ship in Marseille and traveled through France, witnessing demonstrations of protest against the executions in the United States of the anarchists Sacco and Vanzetti, whose trial and conviction had attracted worldwide attention. In the early 1930s, he referred to himself as a "Tory anarchist," calling attention to two abiding features of his character: his dislike of modern culture, and particularly its twin worship of money and the machine, and on the anarchist side, his profound distrust of government control of people's lives. Here he was using *anarchist* in the loose sense of the word. When he joined the POUM in Spain, he encountered the real thing—men ready to die for formal anarchist principles. Although he disagreed with those principles, he was strongly drawn to their style and approach to life. As his friend Julian Symons put it, he was more interested in "the personalities of unpractical anarchists than in the slide rule of journalists who made up the bulk of the British Parliamentary Labour party." With the outbreak of World War II, however, he attacked the anarchists for their pacifist position, an example of his tendency to conflate anarchism with PACIFISM. As the war wound down, his criticism became less severe.

One interesting example of Orwell's ambivalence is the attack on anarchism that forms a coda to his essay "Lear, Tolstoy and the Fool." Here he renders the harsh judgment that "creeds like pacifism and anarchism" try to control others more insidiously than by the obvious external use of force. Although appearing to renounce power, they try to control from within. The fact that these creeds shun the dirty world of politics indicates their moral superiority, and since they are superior, "the more natural that everyone else should be bullied into thinking likewise." In his study of Orwell, his anarchist friend George Woodcock argues that Orwell is attacking Tolstoy and the Christian anarchism he embraced for the same reason he attributes to Tolstoy's criticism of *King Lear*: He sees in Tolstoy's failure to achieve satisfaction from his renunciation of wealth and power the image of his own failure to cross "the great gulf of caste" (243).

Work Cited

Woodcock, George. *The Crystal Spirit.* London: Jonathan Cape, 1967, 243.

Astor, David (1912–1993) Friend of Orwell. Astor was the longtime publisher and editor of *The Observer,* the Sunday paper, which, under his leadership, assumed a prominent role in English politics and culture. Scion of a well-known aristocratic family, Astor was a lifelong man of the left. He and Orwell met during the war when the latter was working at the BBC, and the two men became close friends. To Astor, Orwell was the ideal man to help him regenerate *The Observer,* at that time a stodgy, rather boring publication. In 1945, Orwell became a regular contributor to the paper, serving, as the war was coming to an end, as foreign correspondent for it and the *Manchester Evening News.*

Orwell first became aware of the island of JURA because Astor's family had a summer place there. When Orwell was seriously ill and needed to have the drug streptomycin imported from the United States, he turned to Astor, who arranged and paid for the shipment. Astor also made the arrangements for Orwell's burial in the churchyard of All Saints, Sutton Courtney, Berkshire.

Auden, W. H. (1907–1973) English poet who in the 1930s became the most prominent poet of the left, particularly in his support of the Republican government in the Spanish civil war. But by the end of the decade, Auden returned to the Anglican Church of his birth, moved to New York and, in his famous poem "September 1, 1939," dismissed the 1930s as a "low, dishonest decade." In his essay "Inside the Whale," Orwell attacked Auden as a representative of the "pansy left," whose radicalism was superficial. He was particularly critical of the phrase "the necessary murder" in Auden's poem "Spain," taking it as the typically facile remark of someone who is miles away "when the trigger is being pulled." Auden was sufficiently struck by the comment that he changed the wording in a later edition of the poem. In the course of his critical remarks, Orwell also pointed out that "Spain" was the best poem that had been written about the Spanish civil war.

Aung Maung Htin Burmese scholar, onetime vice chancellor of Rangoon University. In a memoir, Aung recounted an incident in November 1924 between the English policeman Eric Blair and a group of university students, including Aung. At a railway station, the students were fooling around with the result that one of them bumped into Blair, knocking him down some stairs. Furious, Blair raised his baton to strike the boy on the head but changed his mind and struck him on his back. The other boys surrounded the "tall, gaunt Englishman" and angrily protested, following Blair into his compartment until the argument finally wore down. The incident seems to be the basis for a fight in *Burmese Days* between the racist Englishman Ellis and a group of boys, one of whom he strikes across the eyes, blinding the boy. The incident leads to a near-riot tat is quelled by the quick thinking of the novel's protagonist John Flory.

Work Cited

Aung Maung Htin. "George Orwell in Burma." In *The World of George Orwell.* Edited by Miriam Gross. New York: Simon and Schuster, 1971. 19–30.

B

Barcelona Principal city and capital of the province of Catalonia in northeastern Spain. When Orwell arrived there in December 1936, the city was still largely controlled by the anarchists and independent working-class groups that had successfully defended it from the incursions of Franco's troops in the early months of the Spanish civil war. The openly egalitarian spirit of the city, in which, as Orwell saw it, "the working class was in the driver's seat," made a profound impression on him. However, when he returned from the front five months later, he was uneasy at the changes that had taken place. This was followed by the police and regular army's attack on the local telephone office and on members of the POUM. He returned to the front was wounded, and when he came back to Barcelona, he was warned by his wife not to enter the hotel where he and she had been staying. He had to hide out, sleeping in parks, before getting a visa from the British consulate. He finally fled the city, but he never lost the memory of that first encounter.

It might be said that the city returned the favor when in 1998 it renamed a square in the older section of the city Placa Orwell. Later, with a final Orwellian touch, the city authorities "chose Placa Orwell—of all the squares in Barcelona—to install some inconspicuous cameras in a pilot scheme for surveillance of public thoroughfares" (Berga, 293).

Work Cited

Berga, Miquel. "May Days in Barcelona: Orwell, Langdon-Davies, and the Cultural Memory of War." In *George Orwell: Into the Twentieth-First Century*, edited by Thomas Cushman and John Rodden, 286–294. Boulder, Colo.: Paradigm, 2004.

Barnhill See JURA, SCOTLAND

BBC (British Broadcasting Company) From August 18, 1941, to November 24, 1943, Orwell served first as Talks assistant, then as Talks producer in the Eastern Service, India section of the BBC. During that period, he produced an enormous amount of work: more than 200 news-related reports, many of which he also read on the air. He also wrote commentaries, designed to be translated into various vernacular Southeast Asian languages. Beyond this basic work, he designed and produced a series of courses corresponding to courses given at Indian Universities, not only in literature but also in areas such as science, agriculture, and medicine. No small part of his efforts was attracting leading figures from these fields to appear on these programs. Among innovative programs devoted to the great books and discussions of contemporary topics of interest, he was particularly proud of VOICE, a series of six programs focusing on poetry, for which he corraled T. S. ELIOT, HERBERT READ, and STEPHEN SPENDER to appear as guests. He also adapted a number of short stories and a commentary on and extracts from his favorite Shakespearean play, *Macbeth*.

After leaving the BBC, he did several assignments for the company, most notably an adaptation of ANIMAL FARM in 1947. Still another Orwell contribution to the BBC was his sensitive explication of Gerard Manley Hopkins's "Felix Randal." See "THE MEANING OF A POEM."

Although Orwell considered his wartime work at the BBC "wasted years," his various experiments had also taught him to work under the pressure of almost daily deadlines. It may not be an accident that, after leaving there in 1943, he produced in quality as well as quantity the best work of his life. See BBC WRITINGS in PART 2.

Bevan, Aneurin (1897–1960) Leader of the left wing of the British Labour Party and Minister of Health in Clement Atlee's postwar Labour government. In 1946, Bevan established the controversial National Health Service, which substantially still exists in Britain. Bevan, the son of a Welsh coal miner, was characterized by Orwell as "someone who thinks and feels like a working man." In 1943, after leaving the BBC, Orwell became the literary editor and contributor to *The Tribune,* of which Bevan was the editor. In 1948, Bevan, then Minister of Health, approved the import from the United States of the then-experimental drug streptomycin for the treatment of Orwell's tuberculosis.

Blair, Avril (1908–78) Orwell's younger sister. Like the sister of Gordon Comstock, the protagonist of *Keep the Aspidistra Flying,* she worked in a tea shop for a time. After the death of his wife Eileen, Orwell asked Avril to act as housekeeper and guardian of his adopted son, Richard, on the island of Jura. After Orwell's death, she married William Dunn, a neighbor on Jura, and the two became the acting parents of Richard, eventually moving to Wales. Her recollections of her brother were broadcast on the BBC and later recorded in *Orwell Remembered.* Among the observations she made about her brother was to insist that he did not have an unhappy childhood.

Work Cited

Coppard, Audrey and Bernard Crick, eds. *Orwell Remembered.* New York: Facts On File, 1984, 25–32.

Blair, Eileen See O'SHAUGHNESSY, EILEEN.

Blair, Ida Mabel (1875–1943) Orwell's mother, born in England but raised in Burma, where her father's family—the Limouzins—were engaged in the teak trade. She married Richard Blair, who was 18 years older than she, in 1896 and endured living in a remote outpost in Bengal, India, where she gave birth to two children, Marjorie in 1898 and Eric in 1903. In 1905, she and the children moved back to England, perhaps in response to continuing outbreaks of plague in India during those years, although it also seems very likely that she preferred the social life and climate of the town of Henley-on-Thames in Oxfordshire to a dank outpost in India. In 1908, following a home leave of her husband the previous year, she gave birth to her last child, Avril. Her husband retired in 1912 and she moved to London during World War I, working there while he was serving in the army. After the war, the family moved to Southwold, a resort town on the Suffolk coast. Among the people they knew there was RUTH PITTER, who offered this description of her:

> Mrs. Blair was not a conciliating person . . . very kind to anyone poorer than herself. But if you had tuppence more, God help you. . . . She had a very penetrating wit. There's no doubt any satirical, any attacking moods in her son must have come from her (Coppard and Crick, 71).

After the death of her husband and the outbreak of war in 1939, she moved to London. She died of a heart attack in 1943. All the evidence suggests that Orwell's relationship with his mother was a good one, although his behavior must at times have left her puzzled. Evidence of that is provided by Orwell's wife, Eileen. She recorded that prior to their wedding, Ida Blair took her aside to warn her about what she was getting into.

Work Cited

Coppard, Audrey and Bernard Crick, eds. *Orwell Remembered.* New York: Facts On File, 1984.

Blair, Marjorie [Dakin] (1898–1946) The first child of Richard and Ida Blair, Marjorie was born in Bengal, India, in 1898. She attended a convent school run by French Ursuline nuns, remaining with them to finish her education when the Ursulines returned to France around 1912. In 1917, she moved with her mother to London, where she joined the Women's Legion. In 1920, she married her childhood sweetheart, HUMPHREY DAKIN. The couple set up in London, where Orwell stayed with them in 1922 before departing for Burma. This was the first of a number of visits he would make to the Dakins' homes. During his trip to the industrial north that formed the basis of *THE ROAD TO WIGAN PIER*, he stayed with the Dakins, who were then living in Leeds, updating his notes while recovering from the rigors of the trip. Although her brother and her husband did not get on well—their enmity dating back to their childhood years in Henley—Marjorie herself was a warm and receptive older sister. After her death from kidney failure, Marjorie's three children, Henry, Jane, and Lucy, visited Orwell at his home in Jura in 1947. Henry and Lucy were involved in a near-calamitous boating incident when Orwell misread the tides off the island of Jura (see HENRY DAKIN).

Blair, Richard Horatio (1944–) Son of Orwell and his wife, Eileen, adopted by them three weeks after his birth. Eileen gave up her job at the ministry of food to stay with the baby. Despite her misgivings about her maternal skills, she proved to be a devoted mother.

Ten months after the adoption, Eileen died. Now a single parent, Orwell became more acutely aware of his responsibilities. He hired SUSAN WATSON to take care of Richard, but with the move to JURA, Susan was displaced by Orwell's sister AVRIL BLAIR. With Orwell's death, Avril, who in 1951 married Bill Dunn, a neighboring farmer on Jura, became Richard's guardian. Richard was educated in Scotland with Avril and Bill Dunn and later became a salesman of farm equipment. He is married with two sons, and has only fleeting memories of his famous father.

Blair, Richard Walmsley (1857–1939) Orwell's father. The second of ten children of an Anglican vicar and his wife, he had limited career opportunites, when his father died while Richard was still a child. At the age of 18, he entered the colonial service, joining the Opium Department in India as an assistant sub-deputy agent, fifth grade. When he retired thiry-two years later, his rank was sub-deputy opium agent, first grade, an indication that his advancement was less than mercurial. In 1896, at the age of 39, he married Ida Limouzin. The couple's first child, Marjorie, was born in 1898 in Theta, India; the second child; Eric, came along in 1903. The following year, Ida and the two children moved to Henley-on-Thames, in Oxfordshire. Richard took a leave of absence to accompany the family, returning to India until 1907, when he returned home again on leave. During his stay, the couple conceived their third child, Avril, born in 1908. In 1912, Richard retired from the colonial service and joined the family in Henley. In 1916, in response to the desperate need for officers to serve in World War I, he joined the army at the advanced age of 59. Commissioned as a second lieutenant, he was assigned to a mule depot near Marseilles.

He was a shadowy, distant figure in his son's early years. JACINTHA BUDDICOM remembered him as a kind of cranky old man who didn't like children. She also maintained that Eric did not go on to a university because of his father's unwillingness to pay the tuition, but all the evidence suggests that he did not try to do well scholastically at Eton and was very ambivalent about going on to university. Clearly, Eric's decision to resign from the Burmese police in order to pursue a career as a writer did not sit well with Richard. It also put a financial strain on the family, since his son spent periods of time convalescing at home and occasionally in hospitals. But as the years wore on, Richard came to accept, doubtless grudgingly, the unorthodox, unpredictable man who was his son. He cannot have been pleased with the depiction of English colonists in *Burmese Days*. When Richard was on his deathbed, his daughter read to him a complimentary review of *Coming Up for Air* in the *London Times* and the old man seemed pleased.

Blair, Thomas Richard (1802–67) Orwell's paternal grandfather, an Anglican priest who served as the Vicar of Milborne Saint Andrew in

Dorset. He married Frances Hare, and the couple had 10 children. (Hare is the last name of the clergyman and his daughter in Orwell's novel of that name.) Their second son, Richard Walmsley Blair, Orwell's father, was born on January 7, 1857. Orwell may have been thinking of his grandfather's apparently pleasant life when, he wrote the poem "A Happy Vicar I Might Have Been" in 1935.

Booklovers' Corner Bookstore near Hampstead Heath in North London, where Orwell worked from October 1934 to January 1936. The store was owned by Francis and Myfanwy Westrope, members of the ILP (Independent Labour Party) and friends of MABEL FIERZ, who recommended Orwell for the job.

Borkenau, Franz (1900–57) Austrian scholar and author, whom Orwell admired for his views on the Spanish civil war. Borkenau joined the Communist Party as a young man, but became disillusioned while working for the Party in Moscow. He visited Spain in August 1936 and again in January 1937, where he observed the struggle between the revolutionary faction (chiefly anarchists) and the antirevolutionary (communist-controlled) republican government. His book revealing the communist suppression of the revolutionary faction was published as *The Spanish Cockpit* (1937). Orwell was asked to review this book by Kingsley Martin, editor of *The New Statesman and Nation,* but when Martin read Orwell's review praising Borkenau, he refused to publish it, just as he had earlier declined to publish Orwell's essay on the war. The review was then published in *Time and Tide.*

Orwell demonstrated his continued admiration of Borkenau in two reviews of his later books *The Communist International* (1938) and *The Totalitarian Enemy* (1940). After reading *Nineteen Eighty-Four,* Borkenau wrote Orwell a letter of congratulations: "Yours is the only book which seems to convey fully what a totalitarian regime means in terms of the individuals living under it."

British class system See CLASS.

British Empire See IMPERIALISM.

Brockway, Fenner (1888–1988) English activist, member of Parliament, and pacifist. Brockway was born in India and educated in England. After his schooling, he became active in pacifist causes, suffering imprisonment during World War I for his refusal to be recruited into the army. In the 1930s, he became a leader in the Independent Labour Party.

In 1936, he wrote a letter of introduction to JOHN MCNAIR, which Orwell took with him when he left for Spain in December of that year. When Orwell and Eileen escaped across the French border during the suppression of the POUM, Brockway was on his way to Barcelona, hoping to secure the release of imprisoned ILP and POUM members. They had a long conversation at the border town before moving on their opposite directions. Brockway recalled the meeting, "I only saw him for a few hours, but I liked and respected him at once" (Coppard and Crick, 157).

Work Cited

Coppard, Audrey and Bernard Crick, eds. *Orwell Remembered.* New York: Facts On File, 1984, 156–157.

Brownell [Orwell], Sonia (1918–80) Orwell's second wife. Like the man who became her first husband, Sonia was born in India, and later attended a convent school, from which she emerged with a passionate dislike of the Catholic Church. As a young, attractive woman, she became an artist's model, where she developed a reputation as a hard-driving, sexually liberated, modern woman. Beneath this surface she also carried a burden of guilt over the death of a friend in a boating accident. She became an editorial assistant at *Horizon,* where she gradually assumed increasingly important duties.

She and Orwell had a brief sexual encounter in 1945, which led to his proposing marriage, in which she showed no interest. She then spent some time in France, where she had an intense affair with the French philosopher Maurice Merleau Ponty. The affair ended when he refused to leave his wife. Back in England in 1949, she visited Orwell in the sanatorium at Cranham a few weeks after the publication of *Ninety Eighty-Four.* He proposed again, and after consulting with his publisher at the time,

Fredric Warburg, she accepted. The wedding took place on October 13, 1949, at University College Hospital in London.

The assumption underlying the marriage was that it might strengthen Orwell's will to live. After his death in January 1950, she became a controversial figure, on the one hand committed to doing justice to the legacy of her late husband, and on the other a volatile, difficult, increasingly hard-drinking person. She had an unsuccessful second marriage to an openly gay man and was cheated by an unscrupulous accountant of a significant amount of the money that Orwell had earned posthumously. To her credit, she participated in the editing of *The Collected Essays, Journalism and Letters,* a four-volume work that confirmed Orwell's outstanding achievement as a journalist. She also chose Bernard Crick as his first biographer. She was not pleased with his work, but the biography *George Orwell: A Life* has been celebrated by later readers. The one feature of her life that everyone agrees on is that she was, to a significant extent, the model for Julia in *Nineteen Eighty-Four,* a fact reflected in the title of Hilary Spurling's biography of her, *The Girl from the Fiction Department.*

Jacintha Buddicom, a bridesmaid at a family wedding, September 1918

Buddicom, Jacintha (1901–93) Neighbor and close friend of Eric Blair during his adolescent years. The two met in 1914 when Eric befriended Jacintha, her brother, Prosper, and her younger sister, Guinever. Jacintha, who was two years older than her friend, shared with him a love of reading. Their friendship ripened when Eric and his sister spent the Christmas holidays of 1917 and 1918 at the Buddicoms. It was during the 1918 holiday that Eric wrote a love sonnet to Jacintha, an early indication that for him, now 15, the friendship had been transformed into something more.

The Pagan
So here are you and here am I,
Where we may thank our gods to be;
Above the earth, beneath the sky,
Naked souls alive and free.

Dione Venables suggests that "The Pagan" celebrates their first kiss and that for the next three years, "Jacintha was pleasantly attracted to Eric."

But that all changed in September 1921, when Jacintha wrote to Eric, relating her shock at being held down by him in an attempt to force her to have sex. She described how he persisted, tearing her skirt and bruising her shoulder and hip. She screamed at him to stop, and he finally desisted. She saw him briefly after that, but he did not spend the summer holidays of the following year with the Buddicoms. Shortly afterward, he left for Burma. He wrote her three letters from Burma, full of distress and what she felt was self-pity. She answered the first but not the last two. When he returned in 1927, he visited the Buddicoms, but Jacintha was not there. The reason, however, had nothing to do with him. The year before, she had fallen in love and become pregnant, and was later deserted by her lover. The baby was born a few months before Orwell's return. She gave up the baby to her aunt. The baby grew up thinking of her mother as a cousin. Jacintha never married but lived for 30 years as the mistress of "a peer of the realm."

In 1949, when she learned the true identity of the famous writer George Orwell, she wrote to him. He wrote back lovingly and telephoned a number of times. It seemed to her that, as his health worsened, he wanted her to be his son's guardian. In 1949, Jacintha was very involved with the care of her dying mother and was tormented by the prospect of renewing her relationship with Eric. She attended his funeral in London, sitting alone, unknown to everyone there. In 1974, she published a memoir, *Eric & Us*, which depicts their relationship as essentially platonic. Her memoir includes a chapter titled "Eric and Sex," which proclaims in effect that the subject never came up. The revelation of his forcing himself on her surfaced after her death when her sister, Guinever, discovered a copy of the letter written in September 1921. Guinever told the story to their second cousin Dione Venables, who recounted it in a postscript to a new edition of *Eric & Us*, published in 2006.

Work Cited

Buddicom, Jacintha. *Eric & Us*: including a postscript by Dione Venables. Chichester: Finlay, 2006.

Burgess, Anthony (1917–93) English novelist, whose best-known novel, *A Clockwork Orange* (1963) invited comparisons with *Nineteen Eighty-Four* as a dark satire set in a near-future England in which a new language is introduced. Another Burgess novel, *1985* (1978) is an explicitly anti–Labour Party satire, in which the "Big Brother" poster of Orwell's novel shows the face of "Bill, the Symbolic Worker."

Burnham, James (1905–87) American political theorist. Educated at Princeton and Oxford, he helped found the Socialist Workers Party, a Trotskyist, anti-Stalinist group. He left the party in 1940, eventually abandoning communism in any form. In 1941, he published *The Managerial Revolution,* which created a stir on both sides of the Atlantic. Burnham speculated that the future would see the rise of a new class, following the collapse of capitalism. The new class would be the managers—not the owners, but the executives, technical experts, bureaucrats, and military segments of society. This government would be, as it was in Germany and Russia in 1940, socialist in name only. Real power would lie with "the Party." Burnham followed up *The Managerial Revolution* with *The Machiavellians* (1943), which established the historical roots of the definition of politics associated with the Renaissance political theorist Niccolo Machiavelli (1469–1527). Machiavelli maintained that politics is essentially a struggle for power, that the emergence of a ruling class is inevitable and that the ruling class holds power by "force and fraud."

During the war, Burnham served with the OSS (Office of Strategic Services), the forerunner of the CIA. After the war, he returned to the faculty of New York University as a professor of philosophy. In 1947, Burnham published *The Struggle for the World,* which criticized the American policy of containment of the Soviet Union as defensive and ultimately ineffective. Burnham called for an active rollback of communist power in eastern Europe and China, a position supported by the right wing in America and Britain. He became increasingly conservative, joining William Buckley in founding *The National Review.*

Orwell wrote several reviews and essays on Burnham, some of whose ideas emerge in *Nineteen Eighty-Four.* See PART 2: "SECOND THOUGHTS ON JAMES BURNHAM."

C

capitalism The principle of private ownership of the means of production. In traditional Marxist theory, capitalism is viewed as a transitional phase in human history, an intermediary between feudalism and the ultimate triumph of the proletariat that would usher in a classless utopia. Like many observers in the 1930s, Orwell was convinced that capitalism had entered its last days, the result of its inability to contend with the problem of unemployment, which in the Great Depression had assumed a central place in the world economic picture. The two powerful political forces that emerged at that time, fascism and communism, represented themselves as new alternatives to the capitalist system. So, too, did the various forms of socialism that had surfaced earlier at the turn of the 20th century. All three offered control of the economy by a centralized government, but for the fascist and communist nations, that control extended to include totalitarian features along with aggressive military incursions into other nations. Thus, for Orwell and many others, socialism seemed the only viable and just choice. He did not foresee or had little faith in the alternative of an active government intervening in the economic system to stimulate the economy in times of recession or high unemployment, or in the threat represented by inflation. Therefore, while still upholding the system of private ownership, governments assumed an active role in the economy, taking the form of the welfare state. Orwell remained a staunch socialist, but faced with the choices of Soviet communism and American capitalism, he acknowledged the greater freedom that existed under the latter system, particularly for writers. In his essay "Riding Down to Bangor," he suggested that late 19th-century America as depicted in books like Louisa May Alcott's *Little Women* (1868–69) represented "capitalism at its best."

Catholicism Anti-Catholicism appears to have been a lifelong preoccupation of Orwell's. His friend Brenda Salkeld described how in the early 1930s, ". . . he would rail against Roman Catholicism," a view supported by Orwell himself, apologizing to her in a letter for her "having to listen to my obsession with R.C.'s." Jon Kimche, who worked with him at the Booklovers' Corner 1934 and 1935, recalled that most "conversations" with Orwell featured his attacks on Roman Catholics. Perhaps the origins of his anti-Catholicism can be traced to the Ursuline nuns who, according to biographer Gordon Bowker, ran a convent school attended by Eric Blair from the ages of five to eight, but it seems odd that Orwell should leave no indication that he had been taught by Catholic nuns, for example as a prelude to "Such, Such Were the Joys," his prosecutorial indictment of his prep school, St Cyprian's. In *COMING UP FOR AIR*, his fictional recounting of his early childhood, he has nothing but praise for "church," his experience of Anglican ritual, but his case against Catholicism lay not on liturgical but political grounds. He saw the Church as a proto-totalitarian institution, offering in the 1930s a conveniently safe haven from the emptiness of modern secularism. As a result, he distrusted intellectuals who took the "cowardly" route and chose faith, belief in immortality, and the promise of salvation over the grim reality faced by his heroine, Dorothy Hare, in *A Clergyman's Daughter*.

He also deplored what he called "political Catholics," those who injected their religion into every subject they discussed. His chief example of this attitude was the political Catholic *par excellence* G. K. Chesterton, yet Orwell admired Chesterton, particularly his love of paradoxes. In *The Road to Wigan Pier,* Orwell compared the recent Catholic convert to a new recruit to communism in terms of their obsessive zeal.

As for contemporary Catholic writers, he was friendly with Graham Greene, but he wrote a negative review in the *New Yorker* of Greene's *The Heart of the Matter,* identifying as the novel's chief theme the idea that "it is better, spiritually higher, to be an erring Catholic than a virtuous pagan" (66). The other contemporary Catholic writer he admired was Evelyn Waugh, an ultraconservative but one with a beautiful prose style. He also envied Waugh for an entirely nonreligious reason: Waugh had served with the commandos during World War II.

It may have crossed his mind that a belief system that could embrace a leftist such as Greene and an old-fashioned upholder of aristocracy such as Waugh could not be as resolutely totalitarian as he assumed, unless, of course, both writers were guilty of doublethink. One of the unfinished items on his writing agenda was an essay on Waugh. Perhaps he would have dealt with this possibility there.

Work Cited

Orwell, George. "The Sanctified Sinner." *New Yorker,* July 17, 1948: 66–71.

Chesterton, G[ilbert] K[eith] (1874–1936) English essayist, novelist, critic and religious polemicist. Best known for his clerical detective Father Brown and his allegorical thriller *The Man Who Was Thursday* (1909), Chesterton was also a conspicuous defender of CATHOLICISM, to which he had been converted from Anglicanism. In 1928, Orwell published his first article in an English publication, "A Farthing Newspaper" in Chesterton's *G. K.'s Weekly*. In his essay on CHARLES DICKENS, Orwell quoted approvingly Chesterton's comment that for Dickens there was "one fact, the tyranny of man over man and he struck at it when he saw it." Orwell also borrowed a term from Chesterton—*good/bad books*—for an essay on that topic.

In "Notes on Nationalism," Orwell singles out Chesterton as the supreme exemplar of the form of "nationalism" he calls "political Catholicism." Everything Chesterton wrote after his conversion, according to Orwell, had but one goal: to demonstrate the superiority of Catholicism to other religions. So carried away by this belief was he that he became a total Francophile, extolling its supposed Catholic virtues to an obsessive degree. Nevertheless, KAY EKEVAL, a former girlfriend of Orwell, recalled in an interview that Orwell's anti-Catholic remarks always exempted Chesterton.

Echoes of Chesterton's work appear in *Nineteen Eighty-Four* in the form of "the intellectual police" in *The Man Who Was Thursday,* and in Chesterton's futuristic novel *The Napoleon of Notting Hill* (1904), which opens in the year 1984 and depicts a tyrannical government.

Works Cited

Burkhardt, Louis. "G. K. Chesterton and *Nineteen Eighty-Four.*" In *George Orwell,* edited by Courtney Weymyss and Alexj Ugrinsky. Westport, Conn.: Greenwood Press, 1987.

Churchill, Winston (1874–1965) As a leader of the Conservative Party, Churchill was the natural enemy of Orwell for many years. When Churchill replaced Neville Chamberlain as Prime Minister in 1940, Orwell noted in his diary (June 8, 1940), "Who would have thought seven years ago that Winston Churchill had any kind of political future before him?" However, as the great wartime leader he proved to be, he won over Orwell's skepticism. In a spirited exchange of ad hominem verse with Alex Comfort over PACIFISM in wartime, he stated his preference for Churchill's rhetoric rather than that of the pacifist: "What will sound better in the days to come / "Blood, toil and sweat" or "Kiss the Nazi's bum?" One of the last reviews Orwell wrote was of Churchill's *Their Finest Hour,* in which he salutes Churchill's courage and geniality in the darkest of times: "Whether or not 1940 was anyone else's finest hour, it was certainly Churchill's."

His final tribute to Churchill may lie in the choice of his name for the hero of *Nineteen-Eighty Four,* Winston Smith.

class Orwell saw the British class system as the most deeply ingrained and pervasive characteristic of English society. For proof of that claim, he had only to look at his own class-dictated attitudes and prejudices, which is precisely what he did in the second section of *The Road to Wigan Pier.* There he explores the history of his own class consciousness. He was the product of a "lower-upper-middle class" family, a group with the values, habits and manners of the upper middle class but not the income. As a scholarship boy at exclusive schools he developed an acute sense of inferiority, which he compensated for by adopting an air of intellectual superiority. By the time he graduated from Eton, he had adopted fashionable, advanced socialist ideas while privately living in fear and dread of working-class people. As a policeman in Burma, he participated in the "dirty work of empire," oppressing the native population. When he returned to England, looking to atone for the guilt he felt, he explored the lower depths of society, although the tramps were an atypical, classless group. However, in Wigan and the other industrial sites he visited, he had the opportunity to stay with real working-class families, with whom he got along well, but always found that there was "a glass wall" separating him from them. He draws a melancholy conclusion:

> . . . to abolish class distinctions means abolishing a part of yourself. . . . I have got to alter myself so completely that at the end I should hardly be recognizable as the same person.

The experience of Barcelona and the Aragon front in the following year, 1937, dispelled any doubts about the possibility of a classless society. The first few months in Spain he experienced himself breaking through that glass wall. Despite the communist perfidy that brought that experience to a tragic end, Spain left an indelible mark on George Orwell. He had witnessed and participated in something that was as close to a classless society as he ever expected to see.

In *The Lion and the Unicorn,* written in 1940, he again takes up the subject for which "England is famous: class consciousness." But beneath that consciousness is a deeper one, that of patriotism, which at this time of crisis (1941) is overcoming the former. In any case, he argues that the ruling class has been in a state of decay for the past two decades, as evidenced by the management of the governments in this period. The other development is the rise of the managerial middle class, people with technical and professional skills. They frequently draw large salaries and move into positions of power, and their success is open to some members of the working class. He predicts that the war will play a strong role in diminishing the importance of class consciousness in England's future.

This sanguine view of class structure is of course not reflected in *Nineteen Eighty-Four,* where the gap between the inner party members, who maintain absolute power, and outer party members, who lead a zombielike existence, is vast. As for the proles, they are more free than the outer party people, but thanks to prolefeed, hate week, and other distractions, they pose no threat to the ruling group even though they constitute 85 percent of the population.

colonialism See IMPERIALISM.

Common, Jack (1903–68) Proletarian author of *The Freedom of the Streets* (1958) and friend of Orwell and his wife. In the 1930s, Common worked as a staff member for the *Adelphi,* where he first met Orwell and was initially put off by his Etonian accent and "cool air of superiority." The two became friends, and Common occupied their house in Wallington, when the Orwells were staying in Marrakech in the fall and winter of 1938 and 1939. He recalled visiting a pub in the country, in which the landlord, on hearing Orwell speak, called him "sir," doubtless reminding Orwell, once again, of the pervasiveness of class consciousness.

Work Cited

Coppard, Audrey and Bernard Crick, eds. *Orwell Remembered.* New York: Facts On File, 1984.

communism Although as an Eton scholar, Orwell was probably among those "fashionably radical" students who designated Lenin as one of the great heroes in world history, there is little evidence of any early interest on his part in communism. He may have, for argument's sake, adopted a procommunist line in Paris when visiting Eugene Adam, his aunt's consort, since Adam was a Russian refugee. Certainly his references to it, for example his mention of Comrade X, author of *Marxism for Infants,* in *The Road to Wigan Pier* were wholly negative. His first recorded experience with a communist was his interview with Harry Pollit, cofounder and longtime leader of the British Communist Party. Orwell needed credentials to cover the International Brigades fighting in Spain. After a brief exchange, Pollitt refused him. According to Orwell, "Pollitt, after questioning me, evidently decided I was politically unreachable, and . . . tried to frighten me out of going by talking a lot about anarchist terrorism." That rejection was the first of many that communists would make in dealing with Orwell. Had he gone to Madrid, he might have met the same fate as other independent observers: imprisonment or death. In any event, he would not have gone to Barcelona and witnessed the fact that the communists were serving the interests of Russian foreign policy rather than those of the loyalist forces in Spain. Even before this, he had been aware of Stalin's purge trials but was not really familiar with the reality of life inside the Soviet Union. His Spanish experience opened his eyes to the methods of the totalitarian state Russia had become.

When he arrived back in England, he experienced his second great shock, the extent of the collusion between the majority of the intellectual left and the party line. The willful blindness of men who should know better seemed to him as great a crime as the suppression of the POUM. But something else had happened to him in Spain. The perfidy of Stalinism notwithstanding, he had become committed to socialism. His first 10 weeks in Barcelona, followed by his life with the POUM and the ILP brigade, had bought home to him the real possibilities of the ideal that Stalin had betrayed. Thus, his attack on communism was never from the right but from the position of a democratic socialist.

In the years immediately following, his audience became more attentive, enormously helped by the Hitler-Stalin pact in force from 1939 to June 1941, until Hitler made the momentous mistake of invading the Soviet Union. At that point, the Russians became an ally and Stalin was seen as Uncle Joe, a tough old bird, if not exactly lovable certainly "one of us." The British Communist party, which during the period of the pact was preaching a pacifist line, suddenly became proponents of all-out war.

Along with everyone else, Orwell recognized the indomitable spirit of the Russian people and its army, but he never lost his view of Hitler and Stalin as twin evils. By 1943, with the war having clearly shifted to the allied side, he recognized that it was time for a reminder, a history lesson in the form of beast fable.

To Orwell's keen eye, the need for a wake-up call in the West was signaled by the Teheran Conference in November of that year. Such was the prestige of the Soviet Union at the time that it took a year to find a publisher. The result was that *Animal Farm* was not published until August 1945, the month that the war with Japan ended.

Before *Animal Farm,* Orwell's audience had been a small influential group of mostly left-wing intellectuals. In a few years' time, his book would become not merely an enormous bestseller in England and America but a universal publishing phenomenon, translated into 17 languages in 10 years, and a potent weapon in the cold war, its power exceeded only by *Nineteen Eighty-Four.*

Connolly, Cyril (1903–74) English author, critic, and editor of HORIZON and Orwell's oldest friend. The two met as young students at ST CYPRIAN'S school, where they regularly finished one/two in literary contests. Their friendship grew even stronger at ETON. It was in reference to those years that Connolly made his famous comment about Orwell: "I was a stage rebel. He was the real thing." Their friendship was renewed in the 1930s, and in 1940, when Connolly and STEPHEN SPENDER started up the monthly literary journal *Horizon,* Orwell became a regular contributor. In 1938, Connolly published *Enemies of Promise (1938),* which contained memories of St Cyprian's and Eton. Among his recollections of Orwell, he recalled a conversation during World War I, in which the young Eric Blair prophesied "... whoever wins this war, we shall emerge a second-rate nation." When *Enemies of Promise* first appeared, Orwell wrote to him, saying "I wonder you can write about St Cyprian's. It's like an awful nightmare to me." Eventually, however, he did write his memorable attack, "Such, Such, Were the Joys."

The two men regularly reviewed each others books. Connolly's mixed review of *Keep the Aspidistra Flying* is reflected in the observation that the hero's obsessively bitter ruminating about money makes "the reader feel he is sitting in the dentist's chair with the drill whirring." His review of *Animal Farm* opens with the memorable "Mr. Orwell is a revolutionary in love with 1910." He goes on to praise the novel, comparing Orwell to his "master, Swift." In 1938, Connolly published a very brief (five-page) short story, "Year Nine," which anticipates many of the features of *Nineteen Eighty-Four,* including a totalitarian state with a hero who keeps a diary and whose affair with a woman violates the state's laws. His final forced confession precedes his execution.

It was through Connolly that Orwell met his second wife, Sonia Brownell, who worked at *Horizon* as an editorial assistant, gradually assuming more editorial duties until she became an important member of the staff.

Works Cited

Connolly, Cyril. *Enemies of Promise.* London: Routledge and Kegan Paul, 1938.

———. "Year Nine." Nineteen Eighty-Four: *Text, Sources and Criticism.* Edited by Irving Howe. New York: Harcourt Brace, 1982, 232–237.

Conrad, Joseph (1857–1924) Polish-born English novelist and short-story writer. Despite acquiring English as a second language, Conrad developed into a major English novelist. For Orwell, he represented the exemplar of an ideal, a writer capable of turning political writing into an art, as in such novels as *The Secret Agent* (1907) and *Under Western Eyes* (1911). Orwell was impressed with Conrad's knowledge of European politics. Although his was the view of an aristocrat, he was also a member of an oppressed group (he was Polish) and "had a remarkable understanding of conspiratorial politics ... he understood just why people throw bombs, even if he disapproved of such activities" (*CW,* 17, 196). One of Orwell's incomplete projects at his death was a long essay on Conrad's work.

Work Cited

The Complete Works of George Orwell, edited by Peter Davison, Vol. 3, London: Secker & Warburg, 1998.

Cooper, Lettice (1897–1994) Novelist, biographer, and friend of Orwell's wife Eileen. The two women worked together at the Ministry of Food during World War II and often lunched together. Eileen was very interested in food and was a good if tardy cook, but Cooper confirmed the story that George and she often gave their rations away. "She and George were always hard up, always bombed out, always in difficulties, but always helping somebody else, and never really ruffled by their difficulties" (Coppard and Crick, 161–66). Cooper portrayed Eileen as a sympathetic wife with a "brilliant, erratic husband" in her novel *Black Bethlehem* (1947).

Work Cited

Coppard, Audrey, and Bernard Crick, eds. *Orwell Remembered.* New York: Facts On File, 1984.

Cottman, Stafford (1918–1999) A young ILP soldier who fought alongside Orwell in the Spanish civil war. Like Orwell, he chafed at the idea of being confined to the relatively inactive Aragon front, hoping to be transferred to the International Brigades fighting near Madrid. Again like Orwell, he had a change of heart once the communist suppression of the POUM began in May 1937. Interviewed about his recollections of Orwell as a soldier, Cottman described him as a man with "an air of authority," always willing to help others, who insisted that men take proper care of their weapons. He was among the most popular soldiers of the group. Cottman accompanied Orwell and Eileen, along with John McNair, in their escape from Spain (Coppard and Crick, 148–155).

During World War II, Cottman served in the Royal Air Force (RAF). Orwell wrote him a letter, informing him of Eileen's death.

Work Cited

Coppard, Audrey, and Bernard Crick, eds. *Orwell Remembered.* New York: Facts On File, 1984.

Crook, David (1910–2000) Communist spy who infiltrated the Barcelona offices of the ILP, copying documents that were later filed in the KGB archives in Moscow. Crook was born in London but left to attend Columbia University, returning to England in 1936, by which time he had become an underground member of the Communist Party. He joined the International Brigade and was wounded in action in the battle of Jarama. While recuperating, he was recruited to spy on the POUM and their ILP affilates in Barcelona. He arrived in Barcelona the day after Orwell and his colleagues had arrived there on leave from the front. Crook stayed at the same hotel as Eileen, now joined by George. He befriended them and as a result gained access to the ILP offices. When everyone else on the staff would go to lunch, he would remove files from the office to have them photographed at the Russian embassy, quickly returning them before the staff came back from lunch. After the arrest of Orwell's friend and superior officer GEORGES KOPP, Crook was placed in the same cell in order to glean more information from him. When Crook was released, Kopp gave him a letter to be sent to Eileen via her brother Laurence O'Shaughnessy. That letter never arrived, but another copy that Kopp made did. Crook probably turned over the original to his communist control. After Spain, Crook worked for the party in China, returning to England during the war, but he was back in China after Mao's victory in 1948.

Work Cited

Bowker, Gordon. *Inside George Orwell.* New York: Palgrave Macmillan, 2003.

cultural studies See POPULAR CULTURE.

Dakin, Henry (1927–) Orwell's nephew, son of Humphrey Dakin and Orwell's elder sister, Marjorie. In 1947, Henry, on leave from the army, accompanied his two sisters, Jane and Lucy visited "Uncle Eric" at JURA. During the visit, they went on a camping trip to the other side of the island, negotiating around a formidable whirlpool. On the way back, Orwell misread the tide schedule, causing the boat to be caught in a minor whirlpool. They were able to scramble ashore to a tiny island from which they were later rescued. Throughout the entire experience, Dakin recalled, Orwell never lost his normal "Uncle Eric face."

Work Cited

Coppard, Audrey and Bernard Crick, eds. *Orwell Remembered.* New York: Facts On File, 1984.

Dakin, Humphrey (1896–1970) Orwell's brother-in-law, the husband of Orwell's older sister, Marjorie. Dakin was a native of Henley-on-Thames, to which the Blair family moved in 1905. The son of a local doctor, he was, as a teenager, the leader of a gang of boys in which Orwell was the youngest member. According to Dakin, Orwell "was a little fat boy and he was always whining." Dakin's critical view of his future brother-in-law continued into adulthood, probably exacerbated by Orwell's sometimes extended visits to the Dakins. He believed Orwell "disliked his fellow man. He had a contempt for his fellow man . . . What changed Eric completely was the Spanish war. He came back a changed man" (Coppard and Crick, 130). Dakin was also impressed by Orwell's work ethic: "I've never known anyone that worked as hard as Eric did." Dakin, a "pub man," as he described himself, may have been a partial model for the gregarious, pubgoing salesman Flaxman in *Keep the Aspidistra Flying.*

Work Cited

Coppard, Audrey, and Bernard Crick, eds. *Orwell Remembered.* New York: Facts On File, 1984.

Davison, Peter (1926–) Distinguished English scholar and editor. Davison edited the 20-volume *Complete Works of George Orwell* (1998), a monumental definitive edition, including all the known books, essays, plays, letters, journalism, broadcasts, and diaries. Edited with the assistance of Ian Angus and Sheila Davison, this edition is a model of textual scholarship and a fitting tribute to its subject. Davison is also the author of *George Orwell: A Literary Life* (1996), an account of Orwell's writing life, outlining the professional and publishing context of his career, and the editor of *The Lost Orwell* (2006), which constitutes a supplementary volume of the *Complete Works.*

Dickens, Charles See CHARLES DICKENS in section 2.

dystopian fiction Term for novels and stories that project a future society in which people live lives noticeably worse than those of the present time. Dystopia represents a reversal and a rejection of utopian literature, with its depiction of an idealized community, such as in Thomas Moore's 16th century *Utopia* (1516) or William Morris's *News from Nowhere* (1890), in which an idealized socialist community is imagined. In the sadder but wiser 20th century, utopias were eclipsed by dystopian fiction, a growing recognition of the growth of totalitarianism and the dehumanizing implications suggested by some scientific progress. Among the most significant of these for readers of Orwell are Eugene Zamyatin's *We* (1927), Aldous Huxley's *Brave New World* (1932), Jack London's *The Iron Heel* (1909) and H. G. Wells's *The Sleeper Awakes* (1910). See also NINETY EIGHTY-FOUR: SOURCES.

Edwards, Robert "Bob" (1906–1990) Leader of the Independent Labour Party group to which Orwell belonged during the Spanish civil war. Included among Orwell's idiosyncracies recalled by Edwards was his phobic reaction to rats. On one occasion, he shot a rat, causing the whole front to begin firing on both sides.

When Edwards was called back to England from the front, Orwell was elected by the men to replace him as leader. Edwards wrote an introduction to a special edition of HOMAGE TO CATALONIA, in which he asserted that Orwell came to Spain in order to write a book on the war. As Michael Shelden points out in his biography, Orwell "was there to fight fascism and he did it bravely, as Edwards was well aware. He did not show up, write a few things and then leave after six weeks. But that is what Edwards did. . . . It is unfortunate that he should have chosen, after leaving Spain, to exaggerate his part in the war and to cast doubt—without justification—on Orwell's motives" (265).

Later in his career, Edwards was a Labour Party member of Parliament.

Work Cited

Shelden, Michael. *Orwell: The Authorized Biography.* New York: HarperCollins, 1991.

Ekeval, Kay (1911–) A girlfriend of Orwell's, whom he met while working in Booklovers' Corner near the end of 1934. Ekeval ran a typing bureau, and she frequented the book shop in the neighborhood. She recalled that Orwell at one time was working on an "epic poem" on English history from the time of Chaucer to the present day, but after completing part 1, he abandoned it. In connection with *Keep the Aspidistra Flying,* she recalled that "he had a phobia about money. Especially with women. He hated you to offer to go dutch with him" (101). She disliked *The Road to Wigan Pier,* because she felt he was unfair to socialists. It was one of his weaknesses that "he imposed his prejudices on people without finding out what they really were" (103).

Work Cited

Coppard, Audrey, and Bernard Crick, eds. *Orwell Remembered.* New York: Facts On File, 1984, 98–106.

Eliot, T. S. (Thomas Stearns Eliot) (1888–1969) American-born, English poet, critic and dramatist, who was an extraordinarily powerful literary figure in his lifetime. His importance as a poet, beginning with the publication of *The Waste Land* in 1922 was matched by his influence as a literary critic. A staunch conservative and a devout Anglican, he was a penetrating observer and severe critic of 20th-century life.

Even Orwell, clearly on the opposite side of the political/social fence, revered Eliot's early poetry, viewing him as one of the great modernists, along with W. B. YEATS, D. H. LAWRENCE, and JAMES JOYCE, one of those whose artistic achievements, in Orwell's eyes, rose, if not above politics, at least independent of it.

But on a more pragmatic level, the relationship of the two men emerged from Eliot's position as an editor at the publishing house of Faber and Faber. In 1931, Orwell submitted an early version of *Down and Out in Paris and London* to Eliot, who rejected it on the grounds of its loose structure: "The French and English episodes fall into two parts with very little to connect them." In 1943, Eliot, after describing it as "a distinguished piece of writing . . . something very few authors have achieved since *Gulliver*," rejected *Animal Farm* on the grounds of its negativity, its "Trotskyite" position. But these rejections did not do any great damage to their personal relationship, limited as it was to a few lunches and Eliot's participation in at least one of the BBC broadcasts produced by Orwell. A notable example occurred when, at Orwell's invitation, Eliot read the "What the Thunder Said" portion of *The Waste Land* on the BBC Eastern Service.

The critic Graham Good argues for a deeper interaction between the two men on the question of the past and future of Western culture. He maintains that although the two shared a common distaste for the modern world, Eliot's principles were rooted in a collectivist, Catholic, medieval vision as opposed to Orwell's individualist, Protestant, Enlightenment conception. Another striking and provocative view of the Eliot/Orwell relationship is Patricia Rae's thesis that Eliot and his literary principles are satirized in the antique shop of Mr. Charrington in *Nineteen Eighty-Four*.

Works Cited

Good, Graham. "Orwell and Eliot: Politics, Poetry and Prose." In *George Orwell: A Reassessment*, edited by Peter Buitenhuis and Ira Nadel, 139–156. New York: St. Martin's Press, 1988.

Rae, Patricia. "Mr. Charrington's Junk Shop: T. S. Eliot and Modernist Poetics in *Nineteen Eighty-Four*." *Twentieth Century Literature* 43, 2 (Summer 1997): 196–220.

Empson, William (1906–84) Distinguished English poet and critic, author of *Seven Types of Ambiguity* (1934), a highly influential text in the development of modern literary criticism. Empson worked with Orwell at the BBC during World War II. They shared adjoining cubicles in the Eastern Services section, broadcasting in Orwell's case to India, while Empson focused on China. They developed a warm friendship, recalled by Empson in his essay "Orwell at the BBC."

Orwell's friendship with Empson also extended to Empson's attractive, spirited, sharp-witted wife, Hetta. Orwell developed a strong crush on Hetta despite the fact that she was an active member of the Communist Party, and the two regularly engaged in arguments. As Hetta recalled it, "I was a Marxist, he was a Trot" (Haffenden, 46). While rejecting any amorous advances of his, she saw Orwell as "enchanting, very imaginative and very sweet, child-like in a way" (Haffenden, 47).

At one point, Empson tried to act as a referee in a battle between Orwell and H. G. WELLS. Empson's biographer, John Haffenden, considers the question of why Orwell did not include William or Hetta in Orwell's List, his list of "Crypto-Communists," since Orwell was not a man to let personal feelings dictate his duty as a citizen. He concludes that at the time (1949), the Empsons were in Communist China, where Hetta's Western communism would not be useful, while William's deeply rooted English patriotism would preclude any possibility of their being a security threat (Haffenden, 55–56).

When Orwell sent him a copy of *Animal Farm*, Empson wrote back, applauding "the beautifully limpid prose style" but warning him that "you must expect to be 'misunderstood' on a large scale about this book." He was speaking from personal experience, citing the reaction of his "teen age Tory" son, who read it as a right-wing text. Empson's critcal study *The Structure of Complex Words* (1952) contains an article on *King Lear*, in which he praises Orwell's essay "LEAR, TOLSTOY AND THE FOOL," as being the first to recognize the centrality of the theme of renunciation in Shakespeare's play.

Works Cited

Empson, William. "Orwell at the BBC." In *The World of George Orwell*. Edited by Miriam Gross. New York: Simon and Schuster, 1973.

Haffenden, John. *William Empson: Against the Christians*. Oxford: Oxford University Press, 2005.

England With the outbreak of World War II, Orwell discovered he was "a patriot after all," but much earlier, he had seen himself as a "Tory radical" and part of the Tory element was his deep love affair with pre–World War I England. In COMING UP FOR AIR, his nostalgia for the England of his childhood forms the backdrop of his satirical critique of the 1930s England. He deplored its growing suburbanization, fast food, advertising, and the consumer culture it generated. The other shock he had to endure was the discovery of another England in THE ROAD TO WIGAN PIER. To a southern Englander, like himself, the industrial north seemed another country of slagheaps, smoke, and a people he admired but had difficulty getting close to. In Spain, he could feel a mystical bond with an anonymous Italian soldier, but he never sent a copy of *Wigan Pier* to JERRY (JOE) KENNAN or any of the other miners who helped and sheltered him during his trip north.

After his conversion to Socialism in Spain, he confronted the question of the Socialist creed's commitment to internationalism and his deeply rooted feelings for his country by drawing a distinction between patriotism and Nationalism. In THE LION AND THE UNICORN he establishes his argument of the inherent compatibility of patriotism and socialism, despite the tendency of left-wing English intellectuals to disparage the former. His basic argument in *Lion* asserts that the combination of patriotism and socialism would offer the best possible means of defeating Hitler. He saw the HOME GUARD as the nucleus of a movement that could bring about a distinctive English Socialism, one that preserved the customs and traditions (for example, the pubs and the monarchy) while centralizing industry and the economy. Another distinctive feature of his projected English socialist state would be the establishment of the twin virtues of equality and justice as its fundamental priorities. But the soil in which these two seeds should be planted was the customs and values of the English people. He elaborated on this theme in THE ENGLISH PEOPLE, which was published in 1947 but written earlier during the war years. He offers a picture of the national character, which attempts to balance its virtues and its flaws, summarized in his statement that "a profound, almost unconscious patriotism and an inability to think logically are the abiding features of the English character." Some of his critics might cite those words as a more apt description of George Orwell than of the nation as a whole. Thus the final section of *The English People*. "The Future of the English People," in which he proposes a whole range of proposals, some of which have a dictatorial ring: The English people "must breed faster, work harder, live more simply, think more deeply, get rid of their snobbishness and their anachronistic class distinctions, and pay more attention to the world and less to their own backyards."

Eton College Founded in 1440 by King Henry VI, the school boasts among its graduates many of the most influential people in English history, among whom are 18 British prime ministers. Orwell attended Eton as a Kings Scholar (KS) from 1917 to 1921. Unlike his experience at St Cyprian's School, which he pilloried in his autobiographical essay "Such, Such Were the Joys," he seemed to enjoy his years at Eton, although he described himself at that age as an "odious young snob." Subjects he studied at Eton included Latin, Greek, French, English, Mathematics, and Science and Divinity. He also contributed to a number of school publications.

fascism Although it has roots in old dictatorships, fascism was a 20th-century phenomenon, an offshoot of the First World War. The term was first used by Benito Mussolini to designate the movement that brought him to power in Italy in 1922. It makes its appeal on the basis of race, glorifying the race of the particular nation in which it operates, viewing minorities such as Jews or foreign-born citizens as contaminants that threaten the purity of the race. Another common feature is the strong man leader, exemplified in Mussolini and ADOLF HITLER. Closer to home, from Orwell's point of view, was the British Union of Fascists, led by Sir Oswald Moseley (1896–1980). Founded in 1932, the group, who were known by their uniforms as the Blackshirts, attracted many working-class people who were disillusioned and alienated by high unemployment. But after a particularly rowdy demonstration in 1936, the British government passed a Public Order Act, which prohibited the wearing of uniforms in public demonstrations. The order had the effect of nipping the English fascist movement in the bud. In 1940, Moseley was interned by British authorities. Orwell declared himself in favor of the internment in 1940, when a clear and present danger of a Nazi invasion existed, but he deplored the continuance of the practice into 1943, when the danger of invasion had passed.

Fierz, Mabel (1890–1990) Friend and benefactor of Orwell, who provided important encouragement during his early years as a writer. It was Mabel Fierz who, after Orwell had given up hope of finding a publisher for *Down and Out in London and Paris,* brought it to the agent LEONARD MOORE, who in turn sold it to the publisher VICTOR GOLLANCZ. She also introduced Orwell to her neighbor Max Plowman, coeditor with RICHARD REES, of *The Adelphi,* the journal to which he became a regular contributor. Mabel and her husband, Francis, frequently put him up as their houseguest, where he sometimes stored his tramping clothes between outings. In 1935, while he was still working at the Booklovers' Corner, Mabel found a room for Orwell to sublet in a flat near Hampton Heath. It was at a party here that he met his first wife, Eileen. Mabel Fierz's recollections of Orwell include this observation on his and Eileen's married relationship: "He thought a lot of her and she thought a lot of him. But they weren't idyllically happy. But they made the grade" (Coppard and Crick, 97).

Work Cited

Coppard, Audrey, and Bernard Crick, eds. *Orwell Remembered.* New York: Facts On File, 1984, 94–98.

film adaptations See *FILM AND TELEVISION ADAPTATIONS* in *KEEP THE ASPIDISTRA FLYING, ANIMAL FARM,* and *NINETEEN EIGHTY-FOUR.*

Forster, E. M. (1879–1970) English novelist and essayist. Forster was the author of four significant novels: *Where Angels Fear to Tread* (1905), *A Room with a View* (1908), *Howard's End* (1910), and *A*

Passage to India (1924). He also wrote *Aspects of the Novel* (1927), a highly influential critical study of fiction, which considered, for example, the need in a novel for both "round" and "flat" figures. During the war, when Orwell was a producer in the Indian section of the BBC, he asked Forster to broadcast. Forster accepted and became a regular contributor to a series known as "Some Books."

In 1946, Forster joined Orwell and others in protesting the trial and imprisonment of the editors of an anarchist magazine, *Now*. Forster also joined the Freedom Defense Committee, of which Orwell served as vice-chairman. In a brief reference to *Passage to India,* Orwell described it as "not the perfect novel about India but it is the best we have ever had and the best we are likely to get." For his part, Forster gave a snapshot portrait of Orwell that rings true, speaking of his "peculiar mixture of gaiety and grimness" (Crick, 333).

Work Cited

Crick, Bernard. *George Orwell: A Life*. Boston: Little Brown, 1980.

Frankford, Frank (1913–) Colleague of Orwell in the ILP unit in Spain. During the war, he was imprisoned in Barcelona for possession of paintings taken from churches. A report attributed to him in the *Daily Worker* (September 14, 1937), claimed that nighttime ILP sentries had heard carts passing over into nationalist front lines, suggesting that the POUM militias were secretly supplying aid to fascist forces. This and other charges were roundly refuted by Orwell in a detailed letter to *The New Leader*. He surmised that Frankford allowed the communist press to use his name for these slanderous accusations in order to "save his skin," that is, to get released from prison. Orwell's letter was cosigned by 14 of his comrades from the ILP unit. Later, Frankford denied that he had ever written or signed the statement, but he retained a professional animus against Orwell. He told biographer Bernard Crick that Orwell was a right-winger who had contempt for the working class and that he was disliked by his comrades. The fact that Orwell was elected leader of his group after Bob Edwards was called away suggests that this charge was also false.

Almost 20 years after Frankford's conversation with Crick, Jeffrey Meyers interviewed him for his Orwell biography. Well into his eighties and partially deaf, Frankford explained that he had been released from prison through the intervention of Sam Lesser, then the Barcelona correspondent for the *Daily Worker*. Although Lesser, also interviewed by Meyers, denied any recollection of having written the *Worker* article, it seemed obvious that Frankford, who in 1937 appeared in the ILP London office in tears and begging forgiveness, was not the author of the slander and that Sam Lesser was.

Works Cited

Crick, Bernard. *Orwell: George Orwell: A Life*. Boston: Little, Brown. 1980.

Meyers, Jeffrey. *Orwell: Wintry Conscience of a Generation*. New York: Norton, 2000.

Freedom Defense Committee A British civil rights group formed in 1945 in response to the arrest and subsequent imprisonment of the editors of *War Commentary*, an anarchist/pacifist paper, for its antimilitarist positions. The committee, which operated from 1945 to 1949, boasted a significant number of distinguished people from literature and the arts, including E. M. Forster, Bertrand Russell, Benjamin Britten, Augustus John, Henry Moore, and Cyril Connolly. Orwell's friend George Woodcock was a member of the committee. Herbert Read was named chairman and Orwell reluctantly—he was desperately overworked—agreed to be vice chairman. According to Woodcock, Orwell not only contributed his time but also a considerable amount of money, since in this period he was beginning to receive royalties from *Animal Farm*.

Work Cited

Woodcock, George. *The Crystal Spirit*. London: Jonathan Cape, 1967.

Fyvel, T. R. (1907–1985) Close friend with whom Orwell collaborated on the SEARCHLIGHT BOOKS project. Fyvel succeeded Orwell as literary editor of *Tribune*. He was the son of a prominent Viennese associate of Chaim Herzog, the founder of the Zionist movement. Fyvel himself lived in Jerusalem in the 1930s. As he describes it in his memoir of Orwell, the two became friends, despite the fact that they disagreed about Zionism, Orwell holding the opinion that the British government's position was unfair to Palestinians. On the subject of Orwell's alleged anti-Semitism, Fyvel made a judicious comment. He recalled a conversation about Orwell's essay "REVENGE IS SOUR," in which he describes a Viennese-born Jewish officer in the U.S. Army kicking a captured SS officer:

> I said that here in Hitler's so-called "Final Solution to the Jewish Question," one had the greatest deliberate crime committed in man's history, and yet all Orwell did was mention it in one brief, dismissive sentence. Moreover what was Orwell's point in referring to this particular man throughout the article simply as 'the Jew' . . . I can remember that his reaction was one of sheer astonishment . . . he obviously thought I was hypersensitive and overreacting . . . but I think he took my point about language. He never again referred to anyone simply as 'the Jew' (180).

Work Cited

Fyvel, T. R. *George Orwell: A Personal Memoir.* New York: Macmillan, 1982.

Gissing, George (1857–1903) English novelist, one of Orwell's favorite writers. In his essay "GEORGE GISSING," Orwell identifies him as a true novelist, defining a "true novel" as one in which, "at least two characters, probably more . . . are described from the inside," with credible motives that bring them into conflict, exemplified in Gissing's *New Grub Street* (1891), which focuses on the tragic collision between a serious writer and a wife whose sole interest is in social advancement. The novel also deals with the commercialization of literature, in which serious writers cannot make a living while hacks succeed. This theme surfaces in *Keep the Aspidistra Flying,* in which the novel's protagonist Gordon Comstock rails against certain popular novelists of the 1930s. Orwell's interest in Gissing was also fueled by the latter's powerful depiction of vulgarity, squalor, and failure. In that respect, Gissing's influence on Orwell's first three novels is clear.

Gollancz, Victor (1893–1967) Orwell's publisher of his early books and novels. Gollancz published *Down and Out in Paris and London, Burmese Days, A Clergyman's Daughter, Keep the Aspidistra Flying, The Road to Wigan Pier,* and *Coming Up for Air.* His objection to Orwell's critique of socialism and socialists in part 2 of *Wigan Pier* led him to write a foreword to the book, outlining his differences with his author. His refusal to publish *Homage to Catalonia* and *Animal Farm* for political reasons led to a parting of the two men by mutual consent. He and Orwell had a somewhat stormy relationship; neither one really liked the other. Gollancz's rejection of *Animal Farm* was the great mistake of his professional career, but otherwise he was a successful publisher.

Gorer, Geoffrey (1905–1985) Distinguished English social anthropologist and longtime friend and correspondent of Orwell. Among his professional works are *The American People: A Study in National Character* (1964) and *Grief and Mourning in Contemporary Britain* (1965). His relationship with Orwell began when he wrote him a letter in praise of *Burmese Days.* In subsequent correspondence, Orwell expressed an interest in approaching contemporary English society from an anthropological point of view, which he later realized in his essays on POPULAR CULTURE. Gorer visited Orwell and Eileen in their cottage in Wallington, coming away with the impression that he had never seen Orwell happier.

In 1938, Gorer reviewed *Homage to Catalonia,* characterizing it as ". . . a work of first-class literature and a political document of the greatest importance" (121), praising both the political and "the magnificent literary qualities of the book." Gorer goes on to indict the USSR for its betrayal of the revolutionary cause. Gorer considered Orwell "one of the most interesting people I've ever known."

Work Cited

Gorer, Geoffrey. In *George Orwell: The Critical Heritage.* Edited by Jeffrey Meyers, 121–123. London: Routledge, 1973.

Gow, Andrew (1886–1978) Orwell's tutor and classics teacher at Eton. Gow later held a fellowship at Cambridge. Although he considered Orwell an interesting student, Gow did not recommend that he should go on to a university after Eton. When Orwell returned to England from Burma in 1927, he visited Gow in Cambridge and found that ". . . although he was very kind, it seemed to me that I had moved out of his orbit and he out of mine." Although they corresponded now and then, the sense of two different worlds pervaded their relationship. The gap is explicitly demonstrated in the characterization of the classicist Porteous in *Coming Up for Air,* who regards anything occurring in the modern world as essentially insignificant. Orwell's fellow classmate at Eton DENYS KING-FARLOW, for whom Gow also acted as tutor, gives him more credit for Orwell's later development than has been generally recognized.

> . . . Gow recognized in the stubborn, willfully unattractive, embryo-Orwell, qualities for which the other masters had no time. . . . He set out to encourage and make Blair compose, not the weekly essays exacted by most tutors, but fables, short stories, accounts of things liked and detested (Coppard and Crick, 57).

Work Cited

Coppard, Audrey, and Bernard Crick, eds. *Orwell Remembered.* New York: Facts On File, 1984.

H

Halliley, Thérèse (Limouzin) (1843–1925) Orwell's maternal grandmother. English by birth, she married Frank Limouzin, and the couple had eight children. After the death of her husband, she remarried in Moulmein. Orwell met his grandmother when he came to Burma in 1922. By that time she had adopted native dress and was apparently something of an outcast in European circles, but much to Orwell's dismay she had never taken the trouble to learn to speak Burmese.

Henley and South Oxfordshire Standard Local newspaper that published two of Orwell's youthful POEMS.

Henley-on-Thames A town in south Oxfordshire, best known for its Henley Royal Regatta and other rowing races. The Blair family moved here in 1904. In 1912, they moved to nearby Shiplake, returning to Henley in 1915 where they remained until 1917, when Orwell's father entered the army and his mother moved to London to work in the Ministry of Pensions. Henley served as the source for Lower Binfield in *Coming Up for Air,* which suggests that the town (as opposed to the school where he boarded, St Cyprian's) provided Orwell with a host of happy memories.

Heppenstall, Rayner (1911–1981) Literary critic and author who shared a flat with Orwell and Michael Sayers in 1935. The share ended one night when Heppenstall arrived home drunk and got into an argument with Orwell, who then threatened Heppenstall with a shooting stick (that is, a stick with a sharp metal point). The next morning, Orwell informed Heppenstall that he must move out. A few months later, the two made up and remained cautious friends. During the war, Heppenstall worked with Orwell at the BBC. In 1947, he produced a radio adaptation of *Animal Farm,* written by Orwell. He produced and wrote a second version of the fable in 1952. In 1960, he published his recollections of Orwell, which form part of his book *Four Absentees* (1960).

Hitler, Adolf (1889–1945) German dictator, born in Austria, the son of a housemaid and a customs official. He left school early and moved to Vienna, where he failed to gain acceptance to the Vienna Art School. He moved to Munich, and at the outbreak of World War I he joined the army. After the war, he joined the fledging Nazi Party, becoming its leader in 1921. Following the failure of his Munich Putsch, he spent nine months in prison, where he wrote his manifesto, *Mein Kampf,* in which he articulated his racial and political theories. In the economic crisis that engulfed Germany in the late 1920s, he rose to power rapidly. By 1933, he was appointed chancellor by a reluctant President Von Hindenburg. After the latter's death the following year, Hitler became the führer, whereupon he began a massive militarization program and proceeded to annex adjacent territories, meeting with little or no resistance, but with the invasion of Poland, Britain and France declared war on Germany. His success in the first two years of the war was enormously impressive, and he seemed unstoppable. His major mistake was the invasion of the Soviet Union in June 1941, violating a nonaggression pact between the two nations. That and his declaration of war on the United States, in addition to his failure to subdue England in an air war assured his defeat and marked the beginning of the end, which occurred with his suicide in 1945, with Russian troops virtually at the door of his bunker.

Orwell reviewed *Mein Kampf* in 1940, describing its paradoxical appeal to the German people, offering "struggle, danger and death" as opposed to the "good time" offered by capitalism and socialism. Orwell maintained that the source of Hitler early success was that he struck a deeper psychological chord than that of shallow hedonism, and that it would be folly to fail to recognize its appeal.

Holden, Inez (1904–1974) English novelist and journalist, a friend and lover of Orwell. During the war, Holden worked in an airplane factory, an experience that formed the basis of her novel *Night Shift* (1941). In 1941, she and Orwell began meeting for lunch. On one occasion, he brought her back to his flat and "pounced" on her, that presumably being the beginning of a sexual relationship, which he claimed his wife was aware of. The two remained friends and presumably sexual partners throughout the 1940s. In her diary, Holden noted the developing reputation of her friend at least among other writers. She describes a 1941 PEN lunch, at which Arthur Koestler bet five bottles of burgundy that Orwell would write a bestseller within five years. During the Blitz, Holden's flat was destroyed, and H. G. WELLS let her stay in the carriage house behind his large place. She arranged a dinner party for the two men to meet, resulting in a fierce exchange of words between them. At the BBC, Orwell called on Holden to participate in some programs. He included a short story of hers, though read by someone else, in the first VOICE program he produced. She was also one of the contributing authors to his serialized story that ran on BBC for a few weeks. She visited his summer place, Barnhill, on Jura in the Hebrides, complaining in her diary about the length and difficulty of the trip. She also visited him at Cranham sanatorium, where they discussed Evelyn Waugh's new novel *Brideshead Revisited.* She confided to a friend that she hoped Orwell would ask her to marry him, but she was no match for the glamorous SONIA BROWNELL.

Hollis, Christopher (1902–1977) Conservative Catholic and friend of Orwell. Hollis was a fellow Etonian, a year ahead of Orwell. A few years later, Hollis was traveling through Burma and had dinner with his former schoolmate, now a Burmese police officer, leaving Hollis with the impression that the former left-leaning fellow student was now a solid upholder of the colonialist point of view. Hollis's *A Study of George Orwell: The Man and His Work* (1956) is an early critical study of Orwell, notable in its emphasis on what Hollis sees as Orwell's unconscious attraction to Catholicism.

Home Guard In 1940, a community-based militia in England formed to combat what was thought to be an imminent German invasion. It was originally known as the Local Defense Volunteers, later renamed the Home Guard. Orwell joined the group early on, and was appointed a sergeant, because of his prior military experience in Spain, in what became the St. John's Wood Company of the London battalion. The rank and file consisted largely of men between 35 and 50, hence their nickname "Dad's Army." In June 1940, Orwell wrote a letter to *Time and Tide* which began, "It is almost certain that England will be invaded within the next few days or weeks . . . At such time our slogan should be 'Arm the People.'" Specifically, he recommended that shotguns be distributed to members of the guard. Once the immediate threat of invasion faded, Orwell clung to the view that the Home Guard could become the nucleus of a "people's army." Orwell served in the Home Guard for three years in the rank of sergeant. (His corporal was his publisher FREDRIC WARBURG.)

For his American readers of *Partisan Review,* Orwell described the Home Guard as "the most antifascist body existing in England at this moment, and at the same time, an astonishing phenomenon, a sort of People's Army officered by Blimps" (*CW,* 12, 474). The Blimps reference is to the fact that the officer corps of the Guard was made up of high-ranking military retirees from World War I. Orwell regularly exhorted socialists to join in the hope of the Guard's becoming a factor in a possible socialist revolution (Crick, 268–271).

Works Cited

The Complete Works of George Orwell. Edited by Peter Davison, Vol. 12. London: Secker & Warburg, 1998.

Crick, Bernard. *George Orwell: A Life.* Boston: Little, Brown, 1980.

Hopkins, Gerard Manley (1844–1889) An English poet and Jesuit priest who never attempted to publish his work in his lifetime. His *Collected Poems* were first published in 1918, thanks to the efforts of his friend, the poet Robert Bridges. Orwell credited Hopkins with writing the best short poem in the English language, "Felix Randal." Earlier he had referred to it as "a lovely poem, in which the rhythm seems to eddy out of the name like smoke out of an ember . . ." When, during his stint in Spain, he was stationed on the Aragon hills in freezing January weather, Orwell later told the poet Stephen Spender, "I remember on sentry-go in the trenches near Alcubierre I used to do Hopkins' poem 'Felix Randal,' I expect you know it, over and over to myself to pass the time away in that bloody cold" (Shelden, 255). In a BBC talk titled "THE MEANING OF A POEM," Orwell used "Felix Randal" to illustrate his points.

Work Cited

Shelden, Michael. *Orwell: The Authorized Biography.* New York: HarperCollins, 1991.

Horizon Literary journal founded by Cyril Connolly and Stephen Spender, who published its first issue in January 1940. For the next 10 years, it occupied an important position in English literature. Ian McEwan's *Atonement* (2006) contains a marvelous fictional rejection letter from Connolly that is a tribute to the high quality the journal maintained. Orwell published many essays and book reviews in *Horizon,* including "Wells, Hitler and the World State," "Boys' Weeklies," "The Art of Donald McGill," and "Politics and the English Language." The editorial assistant for most of the existence of the journal was SONIA BROWNELL, who in 1949 became Orwell's second wife.

Work Cited

McEwan, Ian. *Atonement.* London: Jonathan Cape, 2001.

Howe, Irving (1920–1993) Prominent American literary and social critic, author of *Politics and the Novel* (1957), which contains a seminal discussion of *Nineteen Eighty-Four,* "History as Nightmare." Howe was associated with the group of New York intellectuals who were contributors to *Partisan Review.* Later, when that publication took on a neoconservative tone, Howe became coeditor of *Dissent,* committed to the principles of democratic socialism. Howe also edited a special edition of *Nineteen Eighty-Four* that contains, in addition to the text, excerpts from sources such as Aldous Huxley's *Brave New World* and Eugene Zamyatin's *We,* essays by Orwell and from a variety of critics and theorists, such as Hannah Arendt, Richard Lowenthal, and Michael Harrington. In 1983, he edited another collection, *1984 Revisited: Totalitarianism in Our Century,* which includes, in addition to essays on the book, others devoted to an examination of TOTALITARIANISM.

Works Cited

1984 Revisited: Totalitarianism in Our Century. Edited by Irving Howe. New York: Harper & Row, 1983.

Orwell's Nineteeen Eighty-Four: *Text, Sources and Criticism.* 2nd edition. Edited by Irving Howe. New York: Harcourt Brace, 1982.

Huxley, Aldous (1894–1963) English satirical novelist, who, before he devoted all his time to his writing, taught at ETON, where Eric Blair was one of his pupils. Huxley's early novels *Crome Yellow* (1921), *Antic Hay* (1923), and *Point Counterpoint* (1928) combined wit with malice in a depiction of English literary culture of the 1920s. In 1932, he published his best-known work, *Brave New World,* a novel of the future that has often been linked to *Nineteen Eighty-Four.* The two books share a similar skepticism about scientific and technological progress, and the mind-numbing conformity that the future might create. *Brave New World* projects a dystopian future in which hedonism rules and people feast on feel-good drugs, in a pleasantly dehumanized existence. In the debate over who was the more accurate prophet, Huxley or Orwell, the jury is still out.

I

immortality Orwell lived his life as a secular humanist, but he never lost sight of what he considered the central crisis of modern man: the loss of belief in individual immortality. He equates the importance of the disappearance of immortality, at least as formulated in Christianity, with the "rise of machine civilization." Whether he sees the latter as instrumental in the decay of the former is a point he leaves unexamined, possibly, taking the connection for granted. In his second novel, *A Clergyman's Daughter,* he employs this loss as the novel's central theme. Unfortunately, in the view of most readers, he fails to imbue his main character with enough vitality to raise her experience to a significant level. Of course, Orwell might have replied that the exposure of a "lie" is not tragic but liberating. However, there is no sense of liberation in the mind of Dorothy Hare, the protagonist of the novel:

> Life, if the grave really ends it, is monstrous and dreadful. No use trying to argue it away. Think of life as it really is, think of the *details* of life; and then think that there is no meaning in it, no purpose, no goal except the grave . . . Either life on earth is a preparation for something greater and more lasting, or it is meaningless, dark and dreadful.

For Orwell, however, although Christianity may be founded on an illusion, it managed to carve out a core set of values that in some mysterious fashion enhance life. Dorothy grapples with that sense as she vows to continue living as a Christian despite her loss of faith:

> What she would have said was that though her faith had left her, she had not changed, could not change, did not want to change, the spiritual background of her mind; that her cosmos, though now it seemed to her empty and meaningless, was still in a sense the Christian cosmos; that the Christian way of life was still the way that must come naturally to her.

Thus, as with most things Orwellian, we see the subject forcefully confronted ("facing unpleasant facts") with an acceptance qualified by something like hope.

Independent Labour Party (ILP) Political party founded by a group of left-wing members of the Labour Party who broke away from the parent group in 1932. In 1936, when Orwell was seeking credentials to cover the Spanish civil war, he was rejected by the British Communist Party. He applied to the ILP, which provided him with an introduction to its agent in Barcelona, JOHN MCNAIR. In Spain, the ILP was affiliated with the POUM. After one day in Barcelona, Orwell was so impressed that he signed up with the POUM, not as a journalist, but as a regular soldier. After a short time, he was transferred to an ILP English unit, serving with the POUM. When he returned to England in 1937, he attended the ILP summer conference and joined the ILP. As a member, he adopted the party's antiwar position, leading

Independent Labour Party summer school, Letchworth in Hertfordshire, England, August 1937. Left to right: John McNair, Douglas Moyle, Stafford Cottman, George Orwell, and Jock Branthwaite *(Orwell Archive, UCL Library Services, Special Collections)*

him to greet the Munich Pact of 1938 with guarded optimism. The Hitler-Stalin Pact, followed shortly after by the delaration of war in 1939, caused him to abandon the pacifist position of the ILP. However, he never lost touch with his ILP comrades with whom he had served in Spain.

imperialism The feature of English life about which Orwell was most critical was what he saw as the prevailing hypocrisy regarding imperialism. His anti-imperialist convictions were derived from his experiences as a police officer in Burma from 1922 to 1927. Once there, doing "the dirty work of empire," he became increasingly aware of the great evil in which he was participating. "Not only were we hanging people and putting them in jail . . . we were doing it in the capacity of unwanted foreign invaders." Even worse for Orwell was the code of silence that smothered any attempt to speak out against the system. That prohibition constitutes a large element in the despair of John Flory, the protagonist of *BURMESE DAYS*, who thinks of himself as trapped in "a world in which every word and every thought is censored." Looking back on that time, Orwell recalled, in *THE ROAD TO WIGAN PIER*, a single exception to the code. Sitting up all night on a train with another Englishman, the two, after feeling each other out to ensure that it was "safe" to talk, "damned the British empire . . . it did us both good. But we had been speaking forbidden things, and . . . when the train crawled into Mandalay, we parted as guiltily as any adulterous couple." Another form of oppression experienced by the oppressor constitutes the theme of *SHOOTING AN ELEPHANT*. In this brilliant essay, Orwell focuses on the plight of the English police officer, trapped by his need to uphold the image of the powerful, forceful sahib. He therefore sees imperialism as a double curse, landing on the oppressor as well as the oppressed.

Throughout the 1930s, he was an outspoken critic of imperialism, calling particularly for Indian and Burmese independence. But when war broke out, he assumed a more ambivalent stance. He had always maintained that for all its injustices, British imperialists were the best of a bad lot. Compared with the fascists of Germany and Italy and the ruthless militarists of Japan, the British colonial system seemed like more of an enlightened despotism, clearly the lesser of two evils. After experiencing Japanese occupation in World War II, many Burmese came to a similar conclusion. In its postwar history, Burma, now Myanmar, has become a police state.

Orwell lived to see the first stages of the dissolution of the British Empire. In 1946, when the possibility of dissolving the empire loomed on the horizon, Orwell maintained his position regarding independence; however, he stressed the importance of the government's informing the British public that the loss of colonies would probably adversely affect the economy. As it turned out, he was unnecessarily pessimistic. Independence was achieved, and the English economy eventually prospered. But the legacy of British imperialism continued to haunt the modern world in ways unimagined by Orwell, notably in the Middle East.

Information Research Department (IRD) Intelligence agency to which Orwell submitted a list of suspected "crypto-communists" in 1949. See ORWELL'S LIST.

J

Jackson, Lydia (1899–1993) Russian-born novelist (under the pen name Elisaveta Fen), psychologist and friend of EILEEN O'SHAUGHNESSY, Orwell's first wife. In Russia, she met and married Meredith Jackson, a member of the law faculty at Cambridge, and moved to England. In 1935, the two divorced and she pursued graduate study in psychology at the University of London, where she met Eileen O'Shaughnessy. The two became close friends. Lydia had a mixed reaction to Eileen's impending marriage. She felt that it would mean the end of Eileen's research and of the possibility of her having a career of her own. In her autobiography, *A Russian's Life in England,* written under her pseudonym, Elisaveta Fen, she describes a pre-marital visit to Wallington by Eileen's family, her brother, Laurence, his wife Gwen, and her mother, Mrs. O'Shaughnessy. All of them were out for a walk when suddenly Eileen broke loose from the group and began running ahead on her own. She later explained her behavior to Lydia, "I just couldn't bear it any longer . . . I had to run" (348). She visited Eileen a number of times at Wallington while Orwell was in Spain.

When Orwell was confined to a sanitorium after his return from Spain in 1938, Jackson visited him. During a walk, he tried to kiss her and, although she had no desire for him, she felt sorry for him and allowed him to do so. Later he wrote to her from Marrakech, hoping to set up a meeting when he returned, a letter in which she rightly detected "masculine conceit," not to mention masculine deceit, in relation to Eileen. Nevertheless, despite her initial rejection, the two continued a friendship before and after Eileen's death, but according to her account, the relationship remained platonic.

Work Cited

Fen, Elisaveta *A Russian's Life in England.* Warick: Paul Gordon, 1976.

Joyce, James (1889–1940) Irish writer, whose *Ulysses* (1922) is generally regarded as the finest English-language novel of the 20th century. Orwell read *Ulysses* in 1933, which proved to be an overwhelming experience: "I rather wish I had never read it. It gives me an inferiority complex. When I read a book like that and come back to my own work, I feel like a eunuch." Joyce's influence is evident in the Trafalgar Square episode of *A Clergyman's Daughter,* where Orwell attempts a surrealistic rendering of a group of homeless people, desperately trying to stay warm, modeled on the Circe episode (the Nighttown scene) in *Ulysses.* Although generally regarded as a failure, Orwell's effort is, at least, an ambitious and even courageous attempt to explore a new mode of narration.

Jura, Scotland A secluded island in the Hebrides where Orwell spent much of his time during the last years of his life. There, in 1947, Orwell rented Barnhill, a country house in a remote spot on an already remote island.

K

Kennan, Joseph ("Jerry") A former Wigan miner and a member of the Independent Labour Party whom Orwell contacted when he first arrived in Wigan in 1936. Kennan arranged and accompanied Orwell's first visit to a mine, an experience from which it took him a week to recover. Kennan also supplied him with notes and showed him around. He found Orwell "very cynical" and was disappointed that he never sent him or any other miner a copy of *The Road to Wigan Pier* even when he was reminded to do so.

Work Cited

Coppard, Audrey, and Bernard Crick, eds. *Orwell Remembered.* New York: Facts On File, 1984, 130–33.

Kimche, Jon (1909–1994) Friend and colleague of Orwell at *Tribune.* Born in Switzerland of Jewish parents, he emigrated to England at the age of 12. Orwell and he met in 1934, when the two men were working in BOOKLOVERS' CORNER, a book store in Hampstead. They renewed their acquaintance in Barcelona in 1937, when Kimche visited the city as a representative of the Independent Labour Party (ILP). In 1942, he was hired as assistant editor at *Tribune* a year before Orwell joined the staff. Eventually, Kimche became managing editor of *Tribune.* In the postwar years, Kimche became increasingly involved, both as a writer and participant, in the establishment of the Israeli state.

King-Farlow, Denys (1903–1982) Successful businessman, who was in the same election (class) as Orwell at Eton and served as his coeditor of the student paper *College Days.* On June 9, 1936, Orwell responded to a letter from King-Farlow, inviting him to a reunion by informing him that "I am getting married on this very morning." A few weeks later, King-Farlow visited his old classmate and his "pretty, dark haired wife." King-Farlow made several more visits, in which the chief topic was the outbreak of civil war in Spain. Months later, having heard from Eileen of their adventures in Spain, his bullet wound and his recent illness and confinement in Aylesford Sanitarium, King-Farlow visited Orwell there. With the declaration of war in 1939, Orwell called on him, hoping that he had some influence that would enable him to do some useful war work. King Farlow's recollections of teenaged Eric Blair were of a boy "obsessed with smells . . . [who] loved to go fishing . . . a good shot with the service rifle, [who] always enjoyed playing the lone wolf" (Coppard and Crick, 56–7).

Work Cited

Coppard, Audrey, and Bernard Crick, eds. *Orwell Remembered.* New York: Facts On File, 1984, 54–60.

Kipling, Rudyard (1865–1936) Popular English novelist, short-story writer and poet. Kipling's appeal extended from adult fiction, in which he celebrated the British imperial presence in India,

Burma, and South Africa, to children's literature, such as the *Just So Stories* (1902) and *Jungle Book* (1894). Orwell devoured his books as a child. In his 1942 essay "RUDYARD KIPLING," Orwell considered Kipling's importance as a poet, novelist, short-story writer, and chronicler of British imperialism.

Kirwan, Celia (Goodman) (1918–1999) Friend, onetime love interest of Orwell's, and the employee of the Foreign Office's Information Research Department (IRD) to whom Orwell gave his list of suspected communists and fellow travelers. Celia was an extremely attractive young woman, the twin sister of Arthur Koestler's wife. She and Orwell got to know each other during a Christmas 1945 visit to the Koestlers' home in Wales. Orwell had brought along his adopted infant son, Richard, to whom Celia was very attentive. Sometime later, Orwell proposed marriage to her, and she turned him down, much to the dismay of Koestler, who was very fond of Orwell. In 1949, she visited Orwell while he was a patient at the Cotswold Sanitarium in Cranham, Goucestershire. During the visit, he agreed to send her a list of people who he thought should *not* be asked to contribute to the IRD's anticommunist campaign. He subsequently sent her a list of 38 names. See ORWELL'S LIST.

Koestler, Arthur (1905–1983) Hungarian-born novelist, journalist, and close friend of Orwell's. Koestler went to Spain in 1936, ostensibly as a journalist to cover the civil war, but since 1932, he had been a member of the Communist Party, and been sent to Spain by the party as a propagandist. His book *Spanish Testament* (1937) was a product of his propagandist efforts. He was captured by Franco's troops and imprisoned in Seville for three months, where he spent many nights listening to the shots from the firing squads, expecting any day to be one of the victims. He recorded that experience in his *Dialogue with Death* (1940).

After his release he left the party, disillusioned by Stalinism, particularly the purge trials in the Soviet Union, which were to become the subject of his best-known novel *Darkness at Noon* (1940), favorably reviewed by Orwell. At the beginning of World War II, Koestler was in France, narrowly escaping to England after France's fall. He and Orwell became friends. Not long after arriving in London, Koestler offered a group of friends a wager that Orwell would write a best-seller within five years time. After Eileen's death, Koestler tried to talk his wife's twin sister, CELIA KIRWAN, into accepting Orwell's proposal of marriage. When Orwell had to give up his London Letter to *Partisan Review* for health reasons, he arranged for Koestler to replace him. In the latter phase of his career, Koestler became interested in scientific and quasiscientific subjects, such as parapsychology.

Orwell once criticized Koestler for his "hedonism." Koestler responded, saying of Orwell, "He was unkind to himself, and he was unkind to his friends . . . The closer somebody was to him, the more he felt he was entitled to treat that friend like he treated himself. . . ." (Coppard and Crick, 169).

In her interesting comparative study of the two men, Jenni Calder argues that a major difference lay in their conception of language. Koestler's early exposure to the orthodox language of communism, what he himself called "the dialectical tom-tom," had a lasting effect on his writing. The result, according to Calder, was that his style is removed from experience—always clever, but sometimes glib. In his defense, as she points out, English was Koestler's third language. Orwell, on the other hand, "chose to communicate political belief via his own experience, but it was the experience that was important, not himself" (266).

In 1944, Orwell wrote a full-length essay titled "Arthur Koestler," in which he describes Koestler as one of a handful of European writers who has viewed "totalitarianism from the inside . . . the special world created by secret police forces, censorship of opinion, torture and frame-up trials . . ." As a consequence, he has come to look upon revolutions as inherently corrupting, forcing him back to "a position not far removed from pessimistic conservatism." In DARKNESS AT NOON, the main character who had been a Bolshevik leader in the revolution confesses, out of despair, to crimes he never committed. He sees that the revolution itself has been a corrupting process.

Works Cited

Calder, Jenni. *Chronicles of Conscience: A Study of George Orwell and Arthur Koestler.* London: Secker & Warburg, 1968.

Coppard, Audrey, and Bernard Crick, eds. *Orwell Remembered.* New York: Facts On File, 1984.

Kopp, Georges (1902–1951) Born in Russia, and while he was still a child, his family moved to Belgium. Trained as an engineer, he became involved with shipping weapons and ammunition illegally to the Republican forces in Spain. Eventually he went to Spain and signed on with POUM; Kopp was Orwell's battalion commander when he was serving with the POUM and ILP unit in Spain. Arrested in the communist suppression of the POUM in 1937, he was visited in prison by Orwell and his wife Eileen shortly before they escaped into France. At considerable danger to himself, Orwell appealed to the local authorities to recognize that at the time of his arrest Kopp was on his way to deliver an important message. Orwell was able to secure the letter, but not the release of Kopp. More than a year later he was released and eventually made his way to England, where he renewed his friendship with Orwell and Eileen, eventually marrying Doreen Hunton, the sister of Eileen's sister-in-law, Gwen O'Shaughnessy. The Kopps lived at Canonbury Square London at the same time as Orwell and Eileen.

In 1947, when Kopp was living in Scotland and Orwell was staying at his summer place on the island of Jura, Kopp sold him an old car, which fell apart as soon as it was delivered by boat to Jura. The incident was apparently typical of Kopp, who was by all accounts an unreliable character. He was a very brave soldier but also something of a confidence man. Recent revelations in letters, written by Eileen to a friend and published in *The Lost Orwell,* indicate that she and Kopp had had a romance while they were in Spain, but that it apparently meant more to Kopp than to Eileen.

Work Cited

Davison, Peter. *The Lost Orwell.* Chichester, England: Timewell Press, 2007.

L

Lawrence, D. H. (1885–1930) English novelist, short-story writer, and poet. Lawrence was a controversial figure during his life. His novel *The Rainbow* (1915) was banned on the grounds that it was obscene. His pacifism and his wife's German nationality caused him great difficulties with the authorities during World War I. After the war, he moved to Italy, and then to Australia, and then to Taos, New Mexico, before returning to Italy and France. He died in 1930 of tuberculosis. He was attended by Dr. Andrew Morland, the same physician who was treating Orwell at the time of his death.

Orwell regarded Lawrence very highly. He drew on Lawrence's short story "Daughters of the Vicar" in his characterization of Dorothy Hare, the protagonist of *A* CLERGYMAN'S *DAUGHTER.*

Lee, Jenny (1904–1988) Daughter of a miner, she was a member of the Independent Labour Party (ILP). In 1942, she left the ILP in protest over its pacifist stand as Orwell had done earlier. She served in parliament from 1945 to 1970 and was the first minister of the arts. In 1934, she married ANEURIN BEVAN. She took over the "AS I PLEASE" column from Orwell when he went abroad as a foreign correspondent in February 1945.

Left Book Club A book club founded by the publisher Victor Gollancz as a vehicle for the spread of socialist ideas. Its coeditors were two prominent socialists, John Strachey and Harold Laski. In 1937, the club enjoyed surprisingly wide popularity very early on, acquiring 50,000 members. In addition to the monthly book selections, the club set up over 300 centers for discussion of the books' ideas. Gollancz, who had previously published *Down and Out in Paris and London,* commissioned Orwell to write a book on the conditions of the unemployed in northern England, which became *The Road to Wigan Pier.* On the strength of the first part of the book, the editors agreed to choose it as a club selection, even though part 2 contained a virulent attack on the attitudes and beliefs of English socialists, the very audience the club wished to attract. To offset the effects of part 2, Gollancz wrote a preface to the club edition, critiquing and disagreeing with Orwell's remarks.

In *Coming Up for Air,* George Bowling attends a lecture on "The Menace of Fascism," sponsored by the club. Orwell uses the occasion to satirize the Left Book Club membership and its speaker.

Lenin, Vladimir (1870–1924) Leader of the Bolshevik Party and founding father of the Soviet Union. His leadership was cut short in the last year of his life by a series of strokes that left him powerless to prevent JOSEPH STALIN from becoming his successor. Lenin was not only a political leader but an influential theorist who, as early as 1902, introduced a crucial revision of traditional Marxist theory. He argued for a revolution, not of the working class per se, but one spearheaded and directed by a core of professionals. This innovation in traditional

Marxism came to be the distinguishing characteristic of the Bolshevik Party. As Orwell illustrated through the example of the pigs in *Animal Farm,* it proved to be the seed that led to the corruption of the Russian Revolution.

A further example of that corruption, from Orwell's perspective, lay in Lenin's view that art and literature must become instruments of the party's ideology, and therefore that artistic expression must be controlled by the state. Lenin set up a top-down system in which the rulers of the party dictated what would be acceptable or desirable and passed these principles to the Commissariat of Education, which in turn informed organizations such as the Soviet Writers Union on what came to be known the "party line." In Stalin's time, this control became more severely repressive, but the process originated with Lenin, who saw the writer's chief role to be that of propagandist for the revolution.

One intriguing Orwellian question in relation to Lenin is the latter's omission from *Animal Farm.* In his historical allegory, Orwell clearly indicates that Major is Karl Marx; Napoleon, Joseph Stalin; Snowball, LEON TROTSKY. In omitting Lenin, Orwell departs from the strict historical record. The critic Alex Zwerdling suggests that, taking the long view of the history of the revolution, Lenin's "brief period of power may have seemed like an irrelevant interlude in the stark drama that was unfolding" (91). Perhaps Orwell saw Lenin's reign not so much irrelevant as foundational, with Stalinism as a logical, if not inevitable, development. In any case, Orwell was convinced that Lenin's short reign exhibited many of the tyrannical features that achieved malignant fruition under Stalin.

Work Cited

Zwerdling, Alex. *Orwell and the Left.* New Haven, Conn.: Yale University Press, 1974.

Limouzin, Charles (1868–) Orwell's maternal uncle. Like his sister Ida, Orwell's mother, Charles chose to live in England. Charles was secretary of a golf club, where Orwell and his sister Avril spent a few days of their summer vacation. As a teenager, Orwell admired his uncle because "he treated him like a grown-up and had adult conversations with him." (Bowker, 46).

Work Cited

Bowker, Gordon. *Inside George Orwell.* New York: Palgrave, 2003.

Limouzin, Frank [Frank Matthew] (1833–1915) Orwell's maternal grandfather. Born in Limoges, France, he moved to Moulmein, Burma, in the 1850s. After the death of his first wife, he married Thérèse Halliley, who bore him eight children, of whom Orwell's mother, Ida, was the sixth. Frank entered the timber business, where he was very successful. In later years, his business fell on hard times and most of his children returned to England. He died in 1915.

Limouzin, Helene ("Nellie") (1870–1950) Orwell's aunt, an older sister of Orwell's mother. Nellie moved to England as a young woman, becoming involved with suffragette and Fabian socialist causes there. She lived in the Notting Hill section of London while Orwell was at Eton, and he may have acquired his taste for music halls during visits with her (Bowker, 60).

After his return from Burma, he visited Nellie, still living in London with Eugene Adam, a leading figure in the Esperanto movement. She moved to Paris with Adam to work and live at the Esperanto headquarters there in 1928. When Orwell came to Paris, he was a frequent visitor to their apartment, where he met some prominent radicals, among other visitors. Here, Orwell received an introduction into European politics. Nellie also connected him to L. T. Bailey, an agent for a newspaper syndicate, to whom Orwell submitted some stories with no success. Orwell's visits did not go unremarked by Britain's MI5, which opened up a secret file on him at the time.

Nellie also helped him out financially during his down-and-out days in Paris and, later, after his return to England. In a letter to him dated June 3, 1933, she included some franc notes along with information about disarmament matters in the face of Hitler's rise. Three years later, having been abandoned by Adam, she returned to England, living for two months with the newly married George and Eileen in their ancient cottage in Wallington. When Eileen joined Orwell in Spain in February 1937, she left Nellie in charge of the cottage and store. When they returned some months later, they found the place in disarray. After Eileen's death in 1945, Nellie wrote to Orwell's sister Marjorie, indicating that Orwell wrote her a letter "at some length" discussing Eileen's death. She attended Orwell's funeral in January 1950 and died five months later, at the age of 79.

Limouzin, Thérèse See HALLILEY, THÉRÈSE.

London, Jack (1876–1916) American novelist, journalist, and adventurer. Early in his career, London went on the road, tramping across the continent, joining the Socialist Party and traveling to Alaska, the scene of some of his best-known works, *The Call of the Wild* (1903) and *White Fang* (1906). While visiting England in 1903, he disguised himself as a tramp, an experience that formed the basis of *The People of the Abyss* (1903). Orwell read this book while still at Eton, and he used it as a guide 10 years later when he began his first descent into the London slums in 1927. According to his biographer, Gordon Bowker, he followed directly in Jack London's footsteps, "seemingly taking *The People of the Abyss* as his guide book" (103).

London's novel *The Iron Heel* (1908), a description of a future fascist takeover of the United States, served as one of the sources for *Nineteen Eighty-Four.* In 1945, Orwell wrote an introduction to a collection of London's short stories called *Love of Life and Other Stories.* In the same year, he gave a BBC talk called "Jack London," in which he described chapter 21 of *The Iron Heel* as containing "one of the best statements of the outlook of the ruling class . . . that has ever been written."

Works Cited

Bowker, Gordon. *Inside George Orwell.* New York: Palgrave, 2003.

Tambling, Victor. "Jack London and George Orwell: A Literary Kinship." In *George Orwell.* Edited by Courtney Wemyss and Alexej Ugrinsky. Westport, Conn.: Greenwood Press, 1987.

M

Macdonald, Dwight (1906–1981) Controversial essayist, editor, film critic, political activist, and theorist, sometimes referred to as the "American George Orwell." The friendship of the two men began in 1941, when Orwell started writing his London Letter for the *PARTISAN REVIEW*. The Letter was a regular contribution to the journal, reflecting Orwell's observations on the political and social issues surfacing in post-blitz London during the war. Macdonald was an editor at *Partisan Review*. Among his tasks was the editing of Orwell's contributions. Although the two men disagreed on a number of large issues—Macdonald characterized his own position as an "Anti-Stalinist Marxist pacifist"—arguing that supporting the war should come only after a successful socialist government came to power in England. Orwell, more pragmatic, argued that the Socialist Party had failed to produce the strong leadership needed to match that of Churchill and the conservatives. In 1944, Macdonald broke with the other chief editors of *Partisan*, Phillip Rahv and William Phillips, to start a new journal, *Politics*. Orwell took the position that he would contribute to both journals. Thus, while he continued to write his London Letter for *Partisan*, he sent *Politics* an essay, "The Ethics of the Detective Story," which Macdonald published in 1944.

After the war, the two, while still disagreeing on the level of ideology, had formed a genuine liking for and reliance on each other, as evidenced in Orwell's request that Macdonald send him a pair of shoes, since his size (12) was impossible to find in the "austerity era" of postwar Britain. Macdonald agreed and followed Orwell's instructions to send the two shoes in separate packages, ". . . then it's not worth anyone's while to pinch them."

In 1958, when *THE ROAD TO WIGAN PIER* was published for the first time in the United States, Macdonald reviewed it for the *New Yorker*, describing it as "the best sociological reporting I know. . . . [He] lived the life of the people he wrote about."

Works Cited

Costello, David R., "My Kind of Guy: George Orwell and Dwight Macdonald," *Journal of Contemporary History* 40 (2002), 79–94.

Williams, Orville, "Dwight Macdonald, Another Orwell," *America* (June 21, 1958): 224–226.

Marx, Karl (1818–1883) Political theorist who along with his collaborator Friedrich Engels (1820–1895) developed COMMUNISM as a political philosophy. Their fundamental conception was based upon a belief in "dialectical materialism" as a governing law of history. Marx maintained that the rule of the proletariat, the mass of workers who had been disinherited by capitalism, would be accomplished through a workers' revolution. As related to Orwell, John Rodden makes a useful distinction between Marx and the marxism that existed in Orwell's lifetime (181). Orwell's quarrel with Marx rested on communism's exclusive focus and insistence on the importance of the economic motive, to the exclusion of such powerful forces as religion, morality, and patriotism. He also rejected the utopian ideal of a classless society as being essentially unachievable. Old Major, the prize boar, who preaches the doctrine of "animalism" in the opening chapter of *Animal Farm* is modeled on Marx.

Work Cited

Rodden, John. *Scenes from an Afterlife: The Legacy of George Orwell.* Wilmington, Del.: ISI Books, 2003.

Maugham, W[illiam] Somerset (1874–1965) Popular English novelist, playwright, and short-story writer. Among his best-known works are *Of Human Bondage* (1915), *The Moon and Sixpence* (1919), and *The Razor's Edge* (1944). Orwell held a very high opinion of Maugham as a novelist. Among a list of "best books" he recommended to BRENDA SALKELD was *Ashenden* (1928), a superior spy thriller by Maugham. In an autobiographical sketch he submitted to an American reference work in 1940, he noted, ". . . I believe the modern writer who has influenced me the most is Somerset Maugham for his power of telling a story straightforwardly and without frills" (1058). Maugham's influence can be seen in Orwell's first novel, *Burmese Days.*

Work Cited

Kunitz, Stanley and Howard Haycraft. *Twentieth-Century Authors.* New York: H. W. Wilson, 1942, pp. 1,058–1,059.

McNair, John (1887–1968) Official and, from 1939 to 1955, the general secretary of the Independent Labour Party (ILP). In 1936 and 1937, McNair was in charge of the ILP office in Barcelona. Years later, McNair described his first meeting with Orwell, who said he was "looking for a chap named McNair." The Etonian diction put McNair off at first, but when he discovered that this was George Orwell, two of whose books he had read, things warmed up. But Orwell made it clear that he was there to fight first and write later. McNair set him up with a POUM unit, and when he checked him out three days later, he found Orwell in charge of the group. Shortly after, in mid-February, McNair received a bonus from the Orwell presence. Eileen, Orwell's wife, joined the ILP office as a secretary, and a very skilled one. She had written to her friend that she liked McNair as a person, despite his "calamitous prose style." When the suppression of the POUM reached a dangerous level, McNair and a young recruit, Stafford Cottman, accompanied the Orwells in their narrow escape into France. McNair later wrote a favorable review of *Homage to Catalonia.*

Miller, Henry See INSIDE THE WHALE.

Milton, Harry (fl. 1937) American volunteer in Orwell's unit, the 3rd regiment, in Spain. A former union organizer and Trotskyite, Milton was a politically savvy New Yorker who distrusted the communists and tried to talk Orwell out of transferring to the Communist-dominated International Brigades. Appalled at Orwell's political naiveté, Milton warned him that given his fiercely independent spirit, the Communists would liquidate him sooner or later. It was while he was talking to Milton that Orwell was shot through the neck. Milton administered first aid, successfully stopping the bleeding. In a letter to a friend, Milton described the crackdown on the POUM. "Every foreigner not a Stalinist is suspect and scores have been arrested. . . . All prisoners are held incommunicado, gigantic frame-up is being concocted." Soon after Milton was arrested, writing "The conditions here in jail beggar description, a long damp stone room, about 100 persons in it." Milton was later released through the intervention of the American consulate.

Works Cited

Jacobs, David. "The Man Who Saved Orwell."

Hoover Digest Archives. Available online. URL: Hoover.org/publications/digest/3475881.html. 2001. Accessed December 3, 2008.

Moore, Leonard (d. 1959) Orwell's literary agent and friend. Moore's agency was named Christy and Moore, with offices in the Strand. Moore became Orwell's agent through the intercession of MABEL FIERZ, who brought the manuscript of *Down and*

Out in Paris and London to him in 1933. Moore submitted it to the publisher VICTOR GOLLANCZ, who published it the same year. From that point on, Moore became Orwell's sole agent.

Morris, William (1834–1896) English poet, designer and pioneer socialist. A man of diverse and impressive talents, Morris was a member of the pre-Raphaelite movement both as a poet and a fine-arts designer. Later, he took up the production of beautifully designed books, such as *The Complete Works of Geoffrey Chaucer,* the crowning achievement of the Kelmscott Press, which he founded. He brought that same creativity to his espousal of socialism. His *News From Nowhere* (1890), set in England in 2090, is "a utopian romance," in which, as a result of the triumph of socialism, poverty and money have been abolished and honest work is deemed the greatest virtue. Orwell dismissed *News From Nowhere* as a "Goody-Goody" view of the future.

Muggeridge, Malcolm (1903–1990) Author, radio personality, and Christian apologist who became a friend late in Orwell's life. In the early 1930s, Muggeridge served as a part-time correspondent for the *Manchester Guardian* in Russia, coming to recognize that the truth about Stalin's regime was unwelcome news in progressive circles. In this respect, he anticipated Orwell's experience in seeking to publish *Homage to Catalonia* and *Animal Farm.* In 1940, Orwell reviewed his book *The Thirties,* a pessimistic account of the era, which Orwell largely endorsed, although he suggested that Muggeridge's seeming negativism was belied by his military service. (Muggeridge had joined the army at the beginning of the war and served with distinction, if not without controversy, throughout World War II.) In his review, Orwell saw Muggeridge as he saw himself: someone who, confronted with the crisis of the war, discovered he was "a patriot after all."

In 1945 and 1946, Muggeridge and the novelists ANTHONY POWELL and JULIAN SYMONS regularly lunched together with Orwell. In his recollective essay "The Knight of the Woeful Countenance"—a reference to Orwell's Don Quixote–like appearance, his "cadaverous" face and "sad eyes"—Muggeridge noted Orwell's "obsessive sense of being physically unattractive." Muggeridge asserts that such a self-image was "quite absurd. He was decidedly attractive to both men and women" (Gross, 169). As for Orwell's unconventional "uniform," a worn tweed sports jacket and baggy corduroy trousers, he reminds his readers that the Orwell dress became the popular style for future generations of university students and faculty. Consistent with his Christian orthodoxy, Muggeridge maintained that Orwell, although a consistent atheist, saw the question of a religious view of life as fundamental problem for modern times.

In the fall of 1949, Muggeridge and Anthony Powell were frequent visitors to Orwell's bedside at University Hospital in London. During one visit, Orwell jokingly referred to his forthcoming "deathbed marriage" to Sonia Brownell. Two controversial remarks in Muggeridge's diary have tended to have a boomerang effect, suggesting that they tell us more about Muggeridge than Orwell: The first refers to the presence of a large number of Jews at Orwell's funeral, since in his view, "George . . . was at heart strongly anti-Semitic." The second is a reference to Orwell's obituaries. He asserts that they were inherently false, since they stressed that Orwell was "not given to self-pity, whereas it was of course his dominant emotion" (Coppard and Crick, 271). The line is typical of Muggerridge's fondness for aphorisms that turn accepted beliefs on its head, even when there is no factual substance to them.

Works Cited

Muggeridge, Malcolm. "The Knight of the Woeful Countenance." In *The World of George Orwell,* edited by Miriam Gross, 165–175. New York: Simon and Schuster, 1971.

Coppard, Audrey, and Bernard Crick, eds. *Orwell Remembered.* New York: Facts On File, 1984, 266–271.

Myers, L. H. (1881–1944) English novelist best known for his tetralogy *The Root and the Flower* (1929–1940). He was an admirer of Orwell's work and met him on one or two occasions. He was a man of independent means, and when he heard that Orwell had been advised to go to a warmer climate during the winter of 1938 and 1939, he became the anonymous donor of a loan of 300 pounds. Orwell never learned who his benefactor was, but he repaid the loan in 1945 after the success of *Animal Farm.* Unfortunately, Myers had committed suicide the previous year.

N

Nin, Andreas (1892–1937) Spanish leader of the POUM, the anti-Stalinist anarchist group who fought in Catalonia. Nin was not only a political figure but a literary one, the translator of Dostoevsky's *Crime and Punishment* and Tolstoy's *Anna Karenina* into the Catalan language. When the Moscow-directed suppression of the POUM began in 1937, Nin was kidnapped, tortured and died without making the false confession that his torturers insisted on. Thus, he short-circuited the plan to stage a series of show trials in Spain, modeled on those conducted in the Soviet Union at the time. As a result, he probably saved the lives of many of his imprisoned men, including the Orwells' friend GEORGES KOPP. Christopher Hitchens comments on the traits that Nin and Orwell shared:

> Both were willing to risk calumny and anathema rather than acquiesce in a lie. Both witnessed to a dramatic and almost unbelievable truth—that the Spanish Revolution was not safeguarded or aided by Moscow, but actually strangled by it (4).

Work Cited

Hitchens, Christopher. "George Orwell and Raymond Williams." *Critical Quarterly,* 41, no. 3 (2001): 3–20.

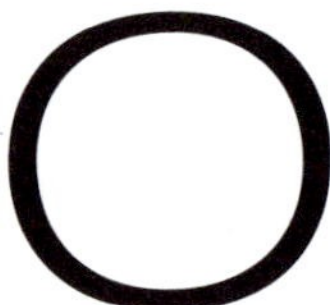

Orwell's List One of the notebooks kept by Orwell included a list of names of "crypto-communists and fellow travelers," which he and his friend RICHARD REES compiled, according to Rees, in the spirit of a kind of private game. When Orwell's friend CELIA KIRWAN visited him at the Cotswold Sanatorium in 1949, she indicated that she had a new job working for the Information Research Department (IRD) in the British Foreign Office. The IRD was set up by the Labour Government to counteract Soviet propaganda against Britain, already well under way by 1948. Kirwan asked Orwell if he would be willing to write some articles for the department, but he replied that he was too ill to take on this work. He did agree to send her the names of writers whom he recommended to be recruited. He also sent her a list of 38 names of people who he felt should *not* be asked to write for the department. This list was selected from the original 135 names in his notebook. He did not, as was later alleged, turn in the notebook itself to the IRD. When Orwell sent Kirwan his list on May 2, 1949, the Soviet blockade of Berlin was still in full force, a powerful example of the threat of Stalinism in Europe at that time.

The revelation in 1996 that Orwell had submitted a list of names of "crypto-communists and fellow travelers" to the IRD set off a firestorm in the press. A representative headline was *The Daily Telegraph*'s "Orwell is revealed in role of state informer." Orwell's critics, some of them settling old scores, lost no time in rushing to judgment. Christopher Hill, a Marxist historian whose book *The English Revolution* had been roundly trashed by Orwell in a 1940 book review, put his ad hominem attack bluntly, "I always knew he was two-faced." Among Orwell's defenders were his biographer Bernard Crick, editor Peter Davison, and the political analysts Timothy Garton Ash and Christopher Hitchens. Davison put it succinctly: "All he was doing, in effect, was to say: 'Don't use these people for anti-communist propaganda because they are probably communists or communist sympathizers'" (*CW*, 20). Davison did acknowledge that it was "disquieting" to read some of the comments Orwell attached to some of the names, identifying them as "Jew," "Negro," or "homosexual." The reference to STEPHEN SPENDER as "Sentimental sympathizer . . . tendency towards homosexuality" is particularly egregious, since Spender was by this time a personal friend.

Orwell's List included at least two people who turned out to be KGB agents, Tom Driberg and Peter Smollett, the latter likely to have been the government official who advised Jonathan Cape not to publish *Animal Farm*. It is interesting that Guy Burgess, the famous "Mole," who was working at the Home Service Department, a job in the BBC comparable to Orwell's, escaped Orwell's watchful eye. Along with everyone else, Orwell appears to have been taken in by Burgess's frivolous, playboy persona.

Christopher Hitchens summarizes the Orwell defense, putting it in the context of the cold war:

> The Cold War involved many things, including a vertiginously dangerous arms race, an attempt to keep colonialism on a life-support system, and an unguessed-at level of suborning (or persecuting and intimidating) of public intellectuals, and even some overt collusion with former pro-Nazi elements in Eastern and Central Europe. But it also involved a confrontation with the poisonous illusion that the Soviet system had a claim on the democratic Left. In this essential confrontation, Orwell kept his little corner of the Cold War fairly clean (169).

In his supplementary volume to the *Complete Works of George Orwell*, titled *The Lost Orwell*, Peter Davison includes the complete list of those names that Orwell submitted.

Works Cited

Davison, Peter. *The Lost Orwell*. London: Timewell Press, 2006.

Hitchens, Christopher. *Why Orwell Matters*. New York: Basic Books, 2002.

O'Shaughnessy, Eileen (1905–1945) Orwell's first wife, whose appearance and personal charm were vividly captured by her friend, the writer LETTICE COOPER: "Small with blue eyes and nearly black hair; pretty with pretty hands and feet, and a body beautifully poised on her legs . . . She generally walked as if she wasn't thinking where she was going, as indeed she seldom was" (Coppard and Crick 163). Born in South Shields, Eileen attended a 10th-anniversary reunion of her high school class in 1934. She wrote a satiric poem for the occasion, set 50 years into the future: 1984. She went on to Oxford, no easy feat for a woman at that time, graduating with a degree in English. From there, she tried a variety of jobs, including teaching, serving as a companion, and running a typing agency. Finally, she entered the graduate psychology program at the University of London. In all these efforts, she may have been spurred on by the example of her brilliant brother Laurence, a distinguished thoracic surgeon, for whom she sometimes acted as a secretary.

At a party given by Rosalind Obermeyer, one of her fellow students at the University of London, she met Rosalind's subtenant, Eric Blair. Later that evening, he told Rosalind that he had met the girl he would like to marry. Not long after, he proposed, but she wanted to wait until the following June, when she would be receiving her degree. They were married in June 1936, moving to an ancient, amenity-deprived cottage in Wallington, Hertfordshire. One of the recently discovered letters to her friend Norah Myles reveals that a honeymoon with Orwell was no picnic at the beach. Eric "complained bitterly when we had been married a week that he mustn't have his work interrupted that he'd only done two good days' work out of seven. . . . I forgot to mention that he had his 'bronchitis' for three weeks in July & that it rained every day for six weeks during the whole of which the kitchen was flooded & all the food went mouldy . . . " (Davison, 64).

On December 23, 1936, not even waiting to celebrate their first Christmas together, he left for Spain. Six weeks later, Eileen followed him, having landed a position in the Barcelona offices of the Independent Labour Party (ILP). There she encountered GEORGES KOPP, Orwell's commanding officer with whom she had an affair of an indeterminate nature. More important, she found herself identified by communist spies working in the ILP office as a "Trotskyite" traitor in league with her husband (See DAVID CROOK). The two narrowly escaped imprisonment and death as they successfully crossed the border into France. Among those left behind was Georges Kopp, destined to be confined under inhuman conditions while being periodically tortured until his release in December 1938. In a letter to Myles written on New Year's Day 1938, she confessed that she was not in love with Kopp, but was so moved by his courage and the sense that he was going to be killed in action that she entered into a presumably sexual relationship with him. Before escaping into France, she and Orwell had visited

Kopp in jail, and she didn't have the heart to tell him "that he could never be a rival to George" (Davison 71).

Almost a year later, in December 1938, Eileen wrote to Myles from Marrakech, where they had gone to escape the English winter so that George might convalesce from the incipient tuberculosis he had recently been hospitalized for. They returned to England six months before the declaration of war in September 1939. Eileen began work at the censorship bureau, later switching to the Ministry of Food. In June 1940, she received a crushing blow, the news of the death of her beloved brother Laurence, who was killed while attending to the wounded at Dunkirk. A measure of their devotion to each other is reflected in a comment she made to a friend, "If we were at opposite ends of the earth and I sent him a telegram saying, 'Come at once,' he would come. George would not do that. For him, work comes before everything."

The death of her brother caused a deep depression, in which she neglected her appearance and her health. As Lydia Jackson saw it, "Her brother's death left her with a half-assumed, half-sincere indifference towards her own life, towards herself" (Wadhams, 68).

When in 1944 they succeeded in adopting a child, she quit work and devoted herself to mothering their son, Richard, an experience that brought her back to her old self. However, less than a year later, she developed distressing physical symptoms that led to her undergoing an operation. She died of a heart attack suffered during the administering of anesthesia.

Works Cited

Coppard, Audrey, and Bernard Crick. *Orwell Remembered.* New York: Facts On File, 1984.

Davison, Peter, ed. *The Lost Orwell.* London: Timewell Press, 2006.

Wadhams, Stephen. *Remembering Orwell.* Ontario, Can.: Penguin, 1984.

P

pacifism For a brief period in 1938 and 1939, Orwell adopted an antiwar position, reflected in *Coming Up for Air* (1939) when George Bowling attends a Left Book Club lecture against fascism and hears in the speaker's voice the same murderous attitude as the fascists. In June 1938, he became a member of the Independent Labour Party (ILP), the only political party he ever formally joined. The ILP's position at the time was antiwar rather than strictly pacifist, reserving the right to employ violent means in some future revolutionary activity. He also wrote an antiwar pamphlet at this time but it was apparently never published and no trace of it has been found. As late as February 1939, he wrote to the mother of his friend RICHARD REES, "The idea of a war is a nightmare to me."

The Hitler-Stalin pact in August 1939, followed the next month by the outbreak of war, brought him to a 180-degree change. His change of heart in regard to pacifism turned into an overreaction, as he abused pacifists, at one time calling them "objectively fascist" in the pages of *Partisan Review*. The controversy that ensued was developed further in *Tribune*, where he and Alex Comfort traded satirical verses. Earlier, he had reviewed Comfort's pacifist novel *No Such Liberty* (1941), in which he asserted that "the notion that you can defeat violence by submitting to it is simply a flight from fact."

As the war moved to a conclusion he became more tolerant of pacifism, but not completely so. In "LEAR, TOLSTOY AND THE FOOL," written in 1945, he concluded his excellent literary analysis by taking a swipe at anarchists and pacifists for playing on a moral level the same power game as the politicians. In "Notes on Nationalism," Orwell indicts pacifism as a form of "transferred nationalism." He proceeds to argue that a certain minority of pacifists are motivated by a "hatred of western democracy and admiration for totalitarianism." He goes on, supplying virtually no evidence, to assert that "pacifism, as it appears among a section of the intelligentsia, is secretly inspired by an admiration for power and successful cruelty." His critique of pacifism extended to the figure of Gandhi, for many pacifists the "saint" of the movement. Nevertheless, in "REFLECTIONS ON GANDHI," his last essay, he acknowledged that, in the light of the awful reality of the nuclear age, pacifism might emerge as a viable possibility.

Partisan Review A monthly American journal of culture and politics, founded in the 1930s by a group of Anti-Stalinist, left-wing writers, including Phillip Rahv, Harold Rosenberg, Mary McCarthy, LIONEL TRILLING and DWIGHT MACDONALD. In 1940, one of the editors, Clement Greenberg, wrote Orwell, asking him to contribute a regular "Letter from London" feature, in which he would be free to comment on politics, the conduct of the war, and any other observations on life in war-torn London.

Among the controversial opinions Orwell aired in his letters was his 1942 argument that pacifism was "objectively pro-fascist," referring to one pacifist group as "fascifist." In 1946, he reported without any evidence that the right-wing novelist Wyndham Lewis had become a communist. Among other, somewhat fanciful ideas he floated in his letters was the notion that the Home Guard (the civilian army in which Orwell served as a sergeant) could, after the war, constitute the armed wing of a social revolution. Despite these and other excesses, Orwell's Letters—he wrote 15 in all from 1941 to 1946—were very popular with the *Review*'s readers and editors, attracted by Orwell's lively, distinctive style and unorthodox opinions. Characteristically, his last letter was devoted to a consideration of the predictions he had made that turned out to be wrong. When, for health reasons, Orwell discontinued writing the "Letters," he arranged for his friend ARTHUR KOESTLER to succeed him.

In addition to the Letters, Orwell also published articles in *Partisan Review,* notably his devastating memoir of his prep school, St Cyprian's, "SUCH, SUCH WERE THE JOYS," and his last completed essay, "REFLECTIONS ON GANDHI."

Pitter, Ruth (1897–1992) English poet, friend of the Blair family and of Orwell in his early years as a writer. Pitter became a friend of Orwell's sister Marjorie, while Marjorie and her mother were living and working in London during World War I. It was the recommendation of a friend of Pitter that induced the Blairs to move to Southwold after the war. She first met Orwell at his sister's flat when he was 17, still a student at Eton. When he returned from Burma, he wrote to her, requesting help finding a room in London. She found him a place nearby in the Portobello Road, which was also close to the flat of his aunt, Nellie Limouzin. Here he lived from autumn 1927 to spring 1928, before moving to Paris. He showed Pitter and her roommate his early attempts in verse and fiction, and they laughed at his efforts, saying that, as a writer, "He was like a cow with a musket."

Some years later in 1942, when she dined at the Orwells', Pitter was shocked to see his emaciated, pale face and thought that "he must be dying: she had brought a bunch of grapes and a rose, very hard to come by in wartime London and she recalled his "holding up the grapes with a smile of admiration and cupping the rose in his wasted hands, breathing in the scent with a kind of reverent joy" (Coppard and Crick, 75).

Work Cited

Coppard, Audrey, and Bernard Crick, eds. *Orwell Remembered.* New York: Facts On File, 1984, 68–75.

Polemic Journal launched in 1945, edited by Humphrey Slater and bankrolled by Rodney Phillips, a wealthy Australian. Among its distinguished contributors were Bertrand Russell and ARTHUR KOESTLER. Orwell contributed his essay "NOTES ON NATIONALISM" to the first issue, in October 1945. Among other essays first appearing in *Polemic* were "THE PREVENTION OF LITERATURE," "SECOND THOUGHTS ON JAMES BURNHAM," "POLITICS AND LITERATURE," and "LEAR, TOLSTOY AND THE FOOL."

Pollitt, Harry (1890–1960) Longtime General Secretary of the British Communist Party. Born into a working-class, socialist family, he became a communist in the 1920s and was named General Secretary of the party in 1929. He followed the Moscow-dictated party line faithfully until 1939, when he supported the war against Hitler, despite the Hitler-Stalin pact, which required party members to adopt an antiwar position. As a result he had to resign his position in the party. However, he was reinstated in 1941 after the German invasion of the Soviet Union.

In 1936, when Orwell wished to go to Spain, he applied to Pollitt for credentials to be admitted at the border. Pollitt refused to help but suggested that Orwell join the International Brigade. Orwell replied that he would not join any group until he could see what was happening. Pollitt also advised him to try to get a safe-conduct pass at the Spanish Embassy. At that point Orwell turned to the ILP for assistance. In March 1937, while Orwell was in Spain, Pollitt reviewed *The Road to Wigan Pier,* denouncing its author in a fierce review. Pollitt's denunciation set the tone for a series of attacks on Orwell by communists and fellow travelers in the years that followed.

popular culture Orwell wrote three major essays on popular culture: "BOYS' WEEKLIES," "THE ART OF DONALD MCGILL," and "RAFFLES AND MISS BLANDISH," but his interest in the subject is evident in other reviews and essays aimed at exploring the thoughts, emotions, and tastes of the English people. As early as 1936, he wrote to the social anthropologist Geoffrey Gorer:

> What you say about trying to study our own customs from an anthropological point of view opens up a lot of fields of thought, but one thing to notice about ourselves is that people's habits etc. are formed not only by their upbringing and such but also very largely by books. I have often thought it would be very interesting to study the conventions etc. of *books* from an anthropological point of view. I don't know if you ever read Elmer Rice's "A Voyage to Purilia." It contains a most interesting analysis of certain conventions—taken for granted and never even mentioned—existing in the ordinary film. It would be interesting & I believe valuable to work out the underlying belief & general imaginative background of a writer like Edgar Wallace. [Wallace was a very popular author of detective and suspense stories during the first three decades of the 20th century.]

Four years later, he reminds Gorer of the earlier letter:

> You remember perhaps my saying to you some years back that very popular fiction ought to be looked into and instancing Edgar Wallace.

He goes on to suggest that Gorer would be interested in "Boys' Weeklies," his recently published essay, "as it rather overlaps with your own interests." In addition to "Boys' Weeklies," he also refers to another essay in the collection "CHARLES DICKENS."

> I find this kind of semi-sociological literary criticism very interesting & I'd like to do a lot of other writers, but unfortunately there's no money in it.

The essay on Charles Dickens is a brilliant form of writing within the parameters of traditional literary criticism, but "Boys' Weeklies" stakes out another territory, magazines for teenage boys, popular in England in the first half of the 20th century. Orwell looks at their underlying assumptions and themes to locate a consistent pattern of class consciousness, best described as "snob appeal." In "The Art of Donald McGill," he examines the rules governing humorous postcards, arguing that they speak to and for the "Sancho Panza" in all of us. In "Raffles and Miss Blandish," he contrasts the turn-of-the-century gentleman thief Raffles with a particularly gruesome example of the modern crime story as an index of the coarsening of contemporary culture.

POUM (Partido Obrero de Unificación Marxista) Small, independent Marxist party, in whose militia Orwell signed up when he arrived in Barcelona. POUM had played an important role in the successful defense of Barcelona in the early months of the war. The POUM faction was led by ANDREAS NIN, who had been a Communist, later a follower of Leon Trotsky, and still later, an anarchist. Orwell found the spirit and comradeship of the POUM troops extremely congenial, although their lack of adequate training, arms and equipment left him skeptical of any future military success. His *centuria* (group of 100 men) was commanded by GEORGES KOPP, an engineer by profession, noted for his bravery. The POUM was pathetically short of guns and ammunition. Fortunately, the Aragon front, where they were operating, was relatively quiet. What really inspired Orwell about the group was the social equality that existed between officers and regular soldiers, with everyone receiving the same pay, no one addressed as "sir" or saluted. The result was not anarchy as he might have imagined but a group of self-motivated men acting responsibly.

The POUM's insistence on a policy of pursuing revolutionary goals at the same time as the war brought them into direct conflict with the Communist-controlled Republican government, which argued for military victory first, revolution later. Orwell saw this as a reasonable disagreement, but what was not reasonable was the systematic Soviet policy that set out to crush the POUM, by killing or imprisoning its members. As was later revealed with opening of the Soviet archives, the decision to crush the POUM was made in Moscow, without any regard for the good of the Loyalist cause but simply to further the interests of Soviet foreign policy.

Powell, Anthony (1905–2000) English novelist and friend to Orwell in his final years. Powell is best known for his 12-volume series of novels *Dance to the Music of Time* (1951–1975), In the 1940s, his acquaintance with Orwell ripened into a true friendship, despite their different politics. Powell, like another friend of both men, MALCOLM MUGGERIDGE, was a conservative. In 1936, Powell wrote Orwell, congratulating him on *Keep the Aspidistra Flying,* which Powell had enjoyed and felt the reviewers of the book had not understood. Although they had been at Eton, Powell was two years younger and they did not meet until the war years—a meeting in which Powell, on leave from the army, felt he was looking at the original Don Quixote.

He and Muggeridge visited Orwell regularly in the last months of his life. The two men also organized the funeral service at Christ Church in London. Powell chose the selections from the bible that were read as well as the hymns that were sung. Nonetheless, he described it as "one of the most harrowing [funerals] I have ever attended" (Bowker, 415). Powell's recollections of Orwell are included in his memoir, *Infants of the Spring.*

Work Cited

Bowker, Gordon. *Inside George Orwell.* New York: Palgrave, Macmillan, 2003.

Pritchett, V. S. (1900–1997) English short-story writer and critic who came to know Orwell in London during the war. He described Orwell as having "rather liked the war for he saw it as a fight against the governing class as well as a fight against the Nazis." He served as the literary editor of the *New Statesman and Nation.* His obituary on Orwell in that journal, later reprinted in the *New York Times Book Review,* proved to be a major first step in securing Orwell's posthumous reputation. First published on January 28, 1950, a week after Orwell's death, the obituary celebrated his fierce individualism, calling attention to his honesty ("the wintry conscience of his generation"), and his sojourns among down-and-outers and coal miners ("a man who went native in his own country"). Pritchett earlier had reviewed *Nineteen Eighty-Four,* characterizing it as "a book that goes through the reader like an east wind, cracking the skin, opening the sores. . . . I do not think I have ever read a novel more frightening and depressing; and yet, such are the originality, the suspense, the speed of writing and withering indignation that it is impossible to put the book down" (291).

Pritchett was knighted for his service to literature in 1975.

Work Cited

Pritchett, V. S. "Review of *1984.*" In Nineteeen Eighty-Four: *Text, Sources and Criticism.* 2nd edition. Edited by Irving Howe, 291–292. New York: Harcourt Brace, 1982.

R

Read, Herbert (1893–1968) English poet, critic of art and literature, and a politically active figure. Among his political/literary works was *Poetry and Anarchism* (1938), leading the critic GEORGE WOODCOCK to refer to him as "a kind of godfather of anarchism in Britain." Orwell invited Read to participate in "The Voice," programs that he produced on the BBC, on which he read both his own and other poets' work. When Orwell sent him a copy of *Animal Farm*, Read wrote to him, noting that his young son, to whom he read a chapter a night, took great delight in the story. "He delighted in it innocently as much as I did maliciously." With the formation of the FREEDOM DEFENCE LEAGUE in 1946, Read became chairman and Orwell vice-chairman of the organization.

Rees, Sir Richard (1900–1970) Close friend, benefactor, and editor of ADELPHI magazine, to which Orwell submitted articles, reviews, and poems in the 1930s. As an editor, Rees was quick to recognize Orwell's talent as an essayist and reviewer. Thus *Adelphi* was the first journal to give Orwell a regular venue for his work. At the same time, the two men developed a friendship that lasted until Orwell's death.

Rees was in Spain at the same time as Orwell. While the latter was on active duty on the Aragon front, Rees visited Eileen, who was working in Barcelona in April 1937, just when the communists were undertaking the suppression of the POUM. He found that she seemed wary and frightened, as she warned him not to be seen in public with her. Rees later realized that he was witnessing in her the "first victim of terror." Later, he served as an ambulance driver on the Madrid front.

Richard Rees, Orwell's good friend and benefactor during the lean years of the depression *(Orwell Archive, UCL Library Services, Special Collections)*

Rees was the model for the character of the socialist editor, Ravelston, in *Keep the Aspidistra Flying,* who demonstrates extraordinary tolerance and support of Gordon Comstock. As such, he is the target of some good-natured satire. Rees's memoir, George *Orwell: Fugitive from the Camp of Victory* (1961), contains valuable insights into the character of his friend.

religion As with any subject he considered seriously, Orwell's thoughts about religion were neither simple nor static. As a committed humanist, he saw religion—particularly Christianity, with its belief in the immortality of the soul—as intellectually untenable. However, he saw that belief in the hereafter, however delusional, formed a solid foundation underpinning the principles of ethics and social justice. The loss of belief in immortality created the central crisis of modern life. The widespread loss of that belief has played a major role in the barbarism of the 20th century. This was particularly relevant to the rise of fascism and Soviet communism, two forces that offered their followers substitute religions, or "something to believe in." His most decisively negative view of religion appears in *Animal Farm* in the portrait of Moses the raven, who preaches the belief in Sugarcandy Mountain.

Orwell treats the decline of religious faith in two others of his novels, *A Clergyman's Daughter* and *Coming Up for Air.* In the former, he satirizes such features of Anglicanism as communion and arcane liturgical quarrels. In *Coming Up for Air,* however, his narrator, George Bowling, evokes a powerful sense of "Church," which plays a central role in Bowling's Proustian recollection of his childhood. The one religion that Orwell was particularly disposed against was CATHOLICISM.

Orwell's deathbed instructions, that he be buried according to the ritual of the Church of England, reflects his enduring respect for the Anglican liturgy.

Reynolds, Reginald (1905–1958) English pacifist, friend, and sometime literary collaborator with Orwell. Reynolds was a Quaker who respectfully disagreed with Orwell on a number of issues. One of these is reflected in the dedication to Orwell by Reynolds's wife, Ethel Mannin (1900–1984), in her novel *Rolling in the Dew:*

> To George Orwell, who so abominates the bearded, fruit-juice-drinking, sandal—wearers of the roll-in-the-dew-before-breakfast school.

Mannin's reference is to Orwell's celebrated attacks on middle-class socialists in *The Road to Wigan Pier* and *Coming Up for Air.* Reynolds collaborated with Orwell in editing *BRITISH PAMPHLETEERS.* Reynolds did the actual editing, while Orwell wrote the introduction to volume one of the two-volume work. His recollection of Orwell appears in his memoir, *My Life and Crimes* (1956). Like Orwell, Reynolds was also a severe critic of British imperialism. His best-known work is *The White Sahibs in India* (1937).

Work Cited

Reynolds, Reginald. *My Life and Crimes.* London: Jarrolds, 1956.

Roman Catholic Church *See* CATHOLICISM.

S

St Cyprian's A preparatory school in Eastbourne, Sussex, about 60 miles from London. The school was founded in 1899 and quickly developed a reputation for academic rigor. In September 1911, at the age of eight, Eric Blair began his first year there. He remained at the school until December 1916. The school had an excellent reputation for its students' record of winning scholarships to prominent public schools, but it also prided itself on building character and achieving academic excellence. In 1939, the school was destroyed in a fire. Orwell's powerful, if somewhat exaggeratd, indictment of the school and of its headmaster and headmistress LESLIE AND CELIA WILKES is the subject of his essay "SUCH, SUCH WERE THE JOYS."

Salkeld, Brenda (1903–) Longtime romantic interest of Orwell. He met her in Southwold in 1928, when he had returned from Burma, and she was a gym teacher at a local school. Many of his early letters to her include recommendations of books to read or to ignore. In this respect, he seems to be playing the expert passing on his wisdom. In other ways, however, she held her own. Take, for example, the matter of his tramping experiences: As she reported in a BBC interview, her opinion that "putting on tramp's clothes and walking does not make you a tramp because you always know you can go back again" (Coppard and Crick, 68). Their relationship apparently did not become sexual, but it was not for lack of trying on Orwell's part. When Orwell returned to Southwold for his father's funeral, he made contact with Brenda, suggesting an affair, but she nipped such talk in the bud. Later, while Eileen was working in London, he met Brenda in Wallington, which sparked gossip in the village that eventually got back to Eileen. She confessed her distress to LYDIA JACKSON, who was feeling guilty herself about conducting a secret correspondence with Orwell (Bowker, 252–254).

Brenda, the daughter of a clergyman, is the probable model for Dorothy Hare, the "frigid" heroine of *A Clergyman's Daughter*.

Works Cited

Coppard, Audrey, and Bernard Crick, eds. *Orwell Remembered.* New York: Facts On File, 1984.

Bowker, Gordon. *Inside George Orwell.* New York: Palgrave, 2003.

Sayers, Michael (1912–) Irish poet and writer who shared a flat with Orwell and RAYNER HEPPENSTALL in 1935. In August 1935, he reviewed *Burmese Days* and *A Clergyman's Daughter* in the *Adelphi.* He later moved to the United States, where he cowrote two books defending the Stalin regime, one of which, *The Great Conspiracy against Soviet Russia* (1946), indicates how far apart the two former roommates found themselves.

Searchlight Books A series of pamphlets edited by Orwell and T. R. FYVEL, published by Secker & Warburg. The aim of the pamphlets was to build the morale needed to withstand the terrifying threat of a Nazi invasion. In addition to serving as coeditor, Orwell inaugurated the series by writing the first pamphlet, THE LION AND THE UNICORN, which was published in February 1941. Additional pamphlets followed Orwell's, but they did not have the success of *The Lion,* which sold 12,000 copies, and the series was eventually canceled.

Shakespeare, William (1564–1616) English poet and playwright. Orwell's favorite Shakespeare play appears to have been *Macbeth.* In October 1943, he adapted and produced a 30-minute version of the play as part of a Great Dramatists series for the BBC Eastern Services. The Shakespearean lines were read by members of the BBC repertory company, interspersed with commentary read by Orwell. He calls *Macbeth* the most perfect of Shakespeare's plays ". . . full of poetry of the highest order, but it is also a perfectly constructed play . . ." The full text of the program is reprinted in Volume XV of *CW,* 278–287.

Macbeth also plays an important role in Chapter IV of *A Clergyman's Daughter,* when the protagonist Dorothy Hare, employed as a schoolteacher, invites the wrath of the school's parents for explaining to her class the meaning of the phrase. ". . . from his mother's womb/Untimely ripped."

In his essay "Lear, Tolstoy and the Fool," Orwell brilliantly defended *King Lear* from an attack on the play leveled by Leo Tolstoy. In the process, Orwell pinpoints *renunciation* as a major theme of *King Lear.* During his brief tenure as a theatre reviewer for *Time and Tide,* Orwell reviewed productions of *The Taming of the Shrew, King John, The Merry Wives of Windsor,* and *The Tempest.*

Shaw, George Bernard (1856–1950) Irish playwright and critic. Shaw began his career as a music and drama critic. His best-known plays (but not his best, from Orwell's point of view) are *Man and Superman* (1903), *Major Barbara* (1907), *Heartbreak House* (1919), and *Saint Joan* (1924), for which he was awarded the Nobel Prize.

Politically, Shaw was an advocate of Fabian socialism, an influential voice in that movement and an outspoken antiwar polemicist during World War I. As a teenager, Orwell read and admired Shaw's plays and criticism, but as he did with Rudyard Kipling and H. G. Wells, he eventually outgrew—or he might say saw through—him.

Orwell's most sustained look at Shaw appears in a talk on the BBC in January 1943, which was later published as a BBC pamphlet, part of the BBC's *Books and Authors* series. In the talk he focuses on Shaw's *Arms and the Man* (1894), including the enactment of a scene from the play. After briefly summarizing the plot, Orwell indicates that the author's purpose is to de-romanticize the image of war as a heroic, glorious, even glamorous, experience. Shaw is not saying that wars are not necessary, only that "killing and being killed" are not romantic experiences, a truth that World War I infamously illustrated.

Orwell goes on to say that many of Shaw's other satiric plays have not stood the test of time as well as *Arms and the Man* because the issues they address have diminished or changed so that their shock value is no longer powerful. Shaw was writing for a Victorian audience, who were much more self-satisfied and confident than we are today: To a significant degree, Shaw has helped bring about the more enlightened audience of our time. He concludes that he does not do Shaw justice by treating him entirely in terms of his message. He is also a brilliant stage craftsman, exemplified in his best plays—*Arms and the Man* and *The Devil's Disciple*—which exhibit a "most perfect mastery of character, dialogue and situation."

During his stint as a theater reviewer for *Time and Tide,* Orwell reviewed two Shaw plays, *In Good King Charles' Golden Days* and *The Devil's Disciple.* He gave both productions positive reviews. See THEATER REVIEWS.

Silone, Ignazio (1900–1978) Italian novelist and one of the founders of the Italian Communist Party, although he left the party after the revelations of Stalin's crimes, an experience he describes in his best-known novel, *Bread and Wine* (1934). An earlier novel, *Fontamara* (1930), explored the plight of peasants exploited by large landowners and Mussolini's Fascist government. During the Mussolini era, he fled to Switzerland, returning to Italy immediately after the war. As the editor of *Advanti,* a widely read newspaper, he became a leading figure in the Italian Socialist Party. At that time, he was quoted as advocating a fusion of the communist and socialist parties. When Silone and his wife visited London in 1946, Orwell took them to lunch, where he assured Orwell that he was completely against a union of the socialist and communist parties in Italy. In 1943, Orwell adapted a Silone short story, "The Fox," for BBC radio. "The Fox" was set on a pig farm, which may have served as a warm-up for *Animal Farm,* soon to follow.

Smillie, Bob (1917?–1937) Smillie was the grandson of a noted Scottish labor leader. In 1936, he left Glasgow University to fight in Spain with Orwell's Independent Labour Party (ILP) unit. When the battalion went on leave in April, Smillie intended to go home. He was arrested at the border for carrying a bomb, which was in fact a dud that he was bringing back as a souvenir. Shortly before they were to leave Spain, the Orwells heard the news that Smillie had died while in prison. The official cause was listed as appendicitis. In *Homage to Catalonia,* Orwell recorded his intense feelings upon hearing the news.

> Smillie's death is not a thing I can easily forgive. Here was this brave and gifted boy, who had thrown up his career at Glasgow University in order to come and fight against fascism and who, as I saw for myself, had done his job with flawless courage and willingness, and all they could find to do with him was to fling him into jail and let him die like a neglected animal . . .

The attempt to determine circumstances of Smillie's death generated considerable debate within the ILP in the late 1930s.

Work Cited

Buchanan, Tom. "The Death of Bob Smillie, the Spanish Civil War and the Eclipse of the Independent Labour Party." *The Historical Journal.* 40, no. 2 (June 1997): 435–461.

Smith, Stevie (1902–1971) English poet novelist, and friend of Orwell during his BBC years. She was introduced to Orwell by a mutual friend, Inez Holden. Orwell included one of Smith's poems ("It was a Cynical Babe") to be read on one of his *Voice* programs. She may have used him for a satiric portrait in her novel *The Holiday* (1949), where, according to biographer Gordon Bowker, ". . . he appears as two characters, representing what she sees as two halves of the schizophrenic Orwell" (284).

Work Cited

Bowker, Gordon. *Inside George Orwell.* New Yotk: Palgrave, 2003.

socialism For Orwell, the road to socialism was neither straight nor narrow. As a student at Eton, he read *GEORGE BERNARD SHAW* and *H. G. WELLS,* presumably absorbing their brands of Fabian Socialism. But as he indicated in *The Road to Wigan Pier,* he "was against all authority . . . I loosely described myself as a Socialist . . . with not much grasp of what socialism meant." When he returned from Burma in 1927, he asserted, "I had at the time no interest in Socialism or any other economic theory." In 1930, he referred to himself as a Tory anarchist. He adhered to that self-definition for several years. As late as 1936, the publication date of *Keep the Aspidistra Flying,* he offers in that novel the first version of his critique of socialism. Asked by his socialist friend Ravelston what a socialist state would be like, Gordon Comstock replies, "Four hours a day in a model factory, tightening bolt number 6003. Rations served out in greaseproof paper at the communal kitchen. Community hikes from Marx Hostel to Lenin Hostel and back. Free abortion clinics on all the corners. All very well in its way, of course. Only we don't want it."

In the infamous part 2 of *The Road to Wigan Pier,* he attacks not so much socialism as socialists, caricaturing them as middle-class, sandal-wearing, bearded vegetarians "who have no intention of giving up their class privileges and merging with the working class." A more important critique involved his argument that the class system was deeply inbred in the British people, suggesting that any attempt to create a classless society in England would require enormous effort. However, despite the onslaught against socialism for being too removed from the working class, too much a middle-class movement that is encased in a narcissistic illusion, the reader begins to develop the idea that the gentleman doth protest too much. The tone and intensity of his argument provide clear evidence that the author is no longer standing at a distance but is poised on the socialist steps, half consciously ready to be dragged kicking and screaming through the front door.

It took only one or two days in Barcelona to bring about that crossover. From a hospital bed there, while recovering from a bullet wound in his neck, he wrote to his old classmate CYRIL CONNOLLY: "I have seen wonderful things and at last really believe in Socialism, which I never did before." The subsequent communist-inspired treachery that crushed these "wonderful things" turned Orwell into a militant anti-Stalinist and strengthened his commitment to socialism.

On his return from Spain, he joined the Independent Labor Party, adopting for a while the party's pacifist position in connection with the oncoming war. However, the Hitler-Stalin pact in August 1939 proved to be a critical turning point, forcing him into a realization that the two totalitarian states posed too great a threat for pacifist idealism. He left the ILP, realizing that with the invasion of Britain an almost certain prospect, he was "a patriot after all." But again, the movement away from the ILP did not lessen his commitment to what he came to call democratic socialism.

In that context, he considered closely the question of revolution and its relevance to socialism. On the one hand, he speaks glibly of the revolutionary possibilities created by the war, the notion for example that the HOME GUARD might constitute a future citizen's army. On the other hand, he acknowledges that the English people would never engage in a class war with each other. His ambivalence about the role of revolution in the formation of a socialist state is evident in *Animal Farm,* which continues to excite debate as to whether its critique applies only to the Russian Revolution or to revolution in general.

In his journalism, particularly for the left-wing readers of *TRIBUNE* and *PARTISAN REVIEW,* he operated as an independent democratic socialist, functioning as "the Left's loyal opposition" (Zwerdling, 3). He also tried to make the socialist case to the average citizen, for example, in his popular pamphlet *THE LION AND THE UNICORN* (1941), in which he argued for the necessity of having a socialist government as a precondition for winning the war. Four years later, in an article entitled "What Is Socialism" for the *Manchester Evening News,* he spelled out the socialist dilemma that had arisen from the example of the Soviet Union. There, the first modern socialist state had been transformed into a monstrous dictatorship, which had provoked an intellectual and moral crisis for socialists everywhere. But much has been learned from that crisis, and the possibility of a truly democratic socialism remained a viable possibility for the postwar world. He concluded his article with recommended reading of important anti-Stalinist socialist writers, such as Arthur Koestler, Ignazio Silone, and Andre Malraux.

As he moved into his last years, the years of writing *Nineteen Eighty-Four,* he complicated his life (and those of his readers) by choosing INGSOC as the name of the ruling party of the novel's totalitarian state, a decision that continues to raise questions, hovering like a cloud over the meaning of the novel. Is it a warning that oligarchical collectivism is more likely to emerge on the left than the right? Or is it a challenge to fellow socialists to "face unpleasant facts" and hammer out non-utopian goals for a socialist society, which must always be in the process of moving, however slowly, toward justice and equality, without deluding oneself that one has ever reached those goals. Or is it the case, as Mary McCarthy suggested, that he never really examined socialism in a rigorous intellectual fashion, that he was a sentimental socialist after all?

Works Cited

McCarthy, Mary. "The Handwriting on the Wall." *New York Review of Books,* January 30, 1969, 3–6.

Zwerdling, Alex. *Orwell and the Left.* New Haven, Conn.: Yale University Press, 1974.

Southwold A summer resort town on the Suffolk coast. It was the home of the Blair family from 1921 to 1942.

Spanish civil war (1936–1939) In July 1936, Spanish army troops in Morocco, led by General Francisco Franco, staged an insurrection against the recently elected left-wing Popular Front government. (*Popular Front* was a term for an international Communist policy advocating Communist participation in coalition governments threatened by the rising tide of fascism in Europe.) The Nationalists, or Falangists, as Franco's supporters were also known, were backed by large landowners, the clergy, and, eventually, by increasing numbers of the middle class. The Loyalists, defenders of the elected Republican government, drew their support from urban areas and the peasant class. Both sides looked to foreign governments for external support. Franco received military aid from the two existing fascist governments, Italy and Germany, while the Loyalists, or Republicans, were supplied with arms by the Soviet Union. In addition, more than 40,000 men and women from around the world formed Loyalist "International Brigades" to fight "the good fight," as the war was known in leftist circles.

Initially, Franco's forces made rapid advances, reaching the suburbs of Madrid in early November, but the Republicans held the city, despite continued aerial attacks, and followed it up with a victory at the battle of Guadalajara. Similarly, in Catalonia, a coalition of left-wing forces dominated by anarchists and socialist militias successfully defended Barcelona. However, in 1937, republican forces failed to capture the Alcázar in the city of Toledo, and German bombers delivered a devastating air attack on the city of Guernica. In 1938, the failure of the Loyalist attempt to capture and hold the city of Teruel in the Aragon province left them in a desperate position. They attempted a last-ditch counterattack at the battle of the Ebro River in November 1938 but were beaten back. Shortly after, in January 1939, Barcelona was captured, and in March of that year, Madrid fell to the Nationalists. On April 1, 1939, General Franco declared victory. His dictatorial regime would rule Spain until his death in 1975.

The retrospective significance of the Spanish civil war is that it proved to be a prelude to World War II. At the beginning of the war, all of the other European nations agreed not to intervene in this internal struggle, but within a very short time, Germany, Italy, the Soviet Union, and Mexico became active participants. The Italians supplied as many as 50,000 troops, and German bomber pilots fought on the Nationalist side. The Soviets contributed to the Republican cause arms and iniquity—the latter in the form of their treacherous attempt to eliminate anarchist and other left-wing factions on the Republican side. In Orwell's modest account of his experiences in *Homage to Catalonia,* he did not lay claim to seeing the big picture as far as the conduct of the war was concerned. In fact, he tended to agree in principle that the war should be the first priority, with the revolution to follow, but the reign of terror unleashed against the POUM, the murders of Andreas Nin, Bob Smillie and countless others, convinced him that the Communists were at least the equal of the fascists as enemies of justice and freedom. He was never to lose that conviction.

Spender, Stephen (1909–1995) English poet, critic, and friend of Orwell. Along with W. H. AUDEN, C. Day Lewis, and Louis Macneice, Spender was one of the young poets who adopted a strong leftist political position in their work. This was the group Orwell regularly attacked as "nancy boy poets." In an angry 1938 letter to Nancy Cunard in relation to the Spanish civil war, he adds, "Tell your pansy friend Spender that I am preserving specimens of his war heroics . . ." Four months later, he wrote to Cyril Connolly, expressing a desire to meet Spender, noting that he had "often said rude things about him . . . but I dare say he won't know or mind." The two men eventually did meet and become friends, Spender sending him a copy of his verse play *The Trial of a Judge* (1938). Orwell replied, explaining that in attacking him, he had been attacking a type, but that once he met and liked someone, he found it impossible to abuse them. Orwell was writing from the Preston Hall Sanitorium, where he was hospitalized in 1938. Spender visited him there. Their friendship grew when Spender joined Cyril Connolly as coeditors of *HORIZON,* a journal to which Orwell was to contribute some of his best essays. Spender appeared as a guest on one of Orwell's VOICE programs on the BBC, where he read his poem "An Elementary School Class in a Slum." Orwell also enlisted Spender to give a BBC talk on E. M. Forster's novel *Howard's End.*

Despite their friendship, Orwell included Spender's name in list of crypto-communists and fellow travelers, but did not include his name in the final list he submitted to the IRD. Ironically, in 1953, Spender was one of the founders and coeditors of the Anglo/American journal *Encounter,* from which he resigned in 1967 when he discovered that the journal was being funded by the CIA.

Stalin, Joseph (1879–1953) Soviet leader from 1924 until his death in 1953. His 39-year reign was marked by terror and cruelty second only to ADOLF HITLER's. He was responsible for a ruthless policy of collectivization of agriculture and a subsequent famine in which millions died as well as for the purge of members of the Communist Party, high-ranking officers of the Russian army, and large numbers of the professional classes. Perhaps most heinous of all was his creation of the GULAG, the bureau that administered the hundreds of prisons and camps, in which an estimated 15 million people died during his reign. These camps held in effect a vast slave labor population that boosted the Soviet economy. Three years after his death, Nikita Khruschev exposed Stalin's crimes at the 20th Communist Party Conference.

Orwell's first direct encounter with Stalinism occurred in May 1937, while on leave in Barcelona, where Soviet spies and secret police began their campaign to crush the anarchist movement, presumably to appease England and France, with whom Stalin was at that time seeking to negotiate better relations. The Hitler-Stalin pact of 1939 only confirmed Orwell's worst suspicions.

In his portrait of Stalin as the ruthless pig Napoleon in *Animal Farm,* Orwell made one last change to the text after meeting a survivor of Stalin's GULAG in Paris in 1945, who nevertheless described Stalin as a great man who had stayed in Moscow when the invading German army was at the gates, inspiring the nation. As a result, Orwell wrote his publisher asking for a prepublication change in chapter 8 of the fable. In a line reading "all the animals including Napoleon falling to the ground" should read "except Napoleon," an example of Orwell's willingness to give the devil his due.

Struve, Gleb (1898–1985) Russian-born scholar, later a Soviet émigré, who taught at the University of London and the University of California at Berkeley. He was the author of *Soviet Literature 1917–95* and *Soviet Literature in Exile.* In 1944, Orwell wrote Struve thanking him for sending him one of his books. Orwell pointed out that he was particularly interested in Struve's description of Eugene Zamyatin's *We,* a book that Orwell was to use as a source for *Nineteen Eighty-Four.* Struve wrote Orwell again to call his attention to some recent examples of the official Soviet publications in which historical events, such as the Hitler-Stalin Pact, were deleted from the official Soviet historical record.

Having received a copy of *Animal Farm* from Orwell, he wrote asking if Orwell would be interested in his translating it into Russian for Russians living abroad, which he later did.

Swift, Jonathan (1667–1745) Famous English satirist who profoundly influenced Orwell both as a child reader and an adult writer. According to the critic Patrick Reilly, "The key to understanding Orwell is his understanding of Swift" (197). Swift was a writer heavily involved with the politics of his age. An Anglican priest, he began his political life as a Whig, later switching to the Tories. Many of his satires contained strong contemporary political allusions, including his masterpiece, *Gulliver's Travels.* Orwell's fascination with *Gullliver's Travels,* a copy of which he received as a present on his eighth birthday, remained with him throughout his life. Orwell's deep attachment to Swift and *Gulliver* makes all the more puzzling his treatment of the book and its author in his essay "POLITICS VS. LITERATURE: AN EXAMINATION OF *GULLIVER'S TRAVELS.*" Instead of fulsome praise, he adopts a decidedly negative tone, describing *Gulliver* as "a rancorous and pessimistic book" and its author as a dissident, "driven by a perverse Toryism"in the face of Whig mendacity. He argues that Swift's vision of human nature—and specifically of the English nation—is the product of a profound despair regarding the human race, a despair that ultimately led to madness. In his conclusion, Orwell attempts to set a balance, asserting that the greatness of *Gulliver* and all of Swift's work lies in a terrifying partial truth, a partial truth that Swift mistook for the whole. But all we have is a world of partial truths, and Swift's is a powerful and important one.

Orwell's friend and critic George Woodcock observes that Orwell's criticism of Swift's "despair" anticipates the view of many critics that *Nineteen Eighty-Four* represents Orwell's despairing vision (See: *NINETEEN EIGHTY-FOUR:* CRITICISM). He points out that Orwell's critique of Swift belies a semiconscious awareness of their fundamental similarity (244).

In a much lighter vein, in 1942, Orwell conducted on the BBC "An Imaginary Interview" with Swift, in which he declares that "*Gulliver's Travels* has meant more to me than any book ever written." Much of the interview consists of Swift, played by journalist and editor Henry Wickham Steed, employing many of Swift's most memorable quotes, set up by questions from Orwell, playing the perfect straight man (*CW,* 14, 156–163).

Works Cited

Reilly, Patrick. *George Orwell: The Age's Adversary.* New York: Macmillan, 1986.

Woodcock, George. *The Crystal Spirit* London: Jonathan Cape, 1967.

Symons, Julian (1912–1994) Novelist, critic, and friend of Orwell, whom he first met at the *Horizon* office in 1944. Symons was one of a group that included MALCOLM MUGGERIDGE, ANTHONY POWELL, and Orwell that met regularly for lunch. In 1946, when Orwell stopped writing for the *Manchester Evening New,* he recommended Symons as his replacement. Symons became well known as a writer and a critic of detective novels. He was the brother of A. J. A. Symons (1900–1941), the author of *The Quest for Baron Corvo,* a classic of modern biography.

Symons wrote the first review of *Nineteen Eighty-Four,* in which he places it in the context of Orwell's earlier novels, particularly his first, *Burmese Days.* Unlike most of the early reviews of the novel, Symons records some serious reservations, including what he describes as the "schoolboyish sensationalism" of the torture scenes. Shortly after the review appeared, Orwell wrote Symons, "I must thank you for such a brilliant as well as generous review . . . You are of course right about the vulgarity of the 'Room 101' business. I was aware of this while writing it, but I didn't know another way of getting somewhere near the effect I wanted."

T

Tolstoy, Leo (1828–1910) Russian novelist, by common consent one of the world's greatest. His monumental achievement *War and Peace* (1865–1869) along with his extraordinary tragic novel *Anna Karenina* (1875–1877) form milestones of modern literature. In the last phase of his life, Tolstoy adopted a religious view, characterized by a rejection of the world and total submission to the will of God.

In 1944, Orwell reviewed a biography of Tolstoy, in which he describes Tolstoy's religious faith as a kind of Christian anarchism. Orwell sees in its extremism a form of egoism, which in Tolstoy's case took the form of intellectual bullying, a notable example of which is Tolstoy's essay on Shakespeare. Three years later, Orwell took this theme up in one of his greatest essays, "LEAR, TOLSTOY AND THE FOOL." Orwell describes Tolstoy's essay on Shakespeare's *King Lear* as remarkable in its wrongheadedness. Tolstoy had argued that Shakespeare is the world's most overrated writer and that *King Lear* in not only a flawed play but inferior to its anonymous, primitive source play, *The Troublesome Reign of King Leir.* After considering Tolstoy's critique in detail, Orwell then pinpoints the reason for Tolstoy's extraordinary reaction, and in so doing, zeroes in a key theme of the play that no critic had ever sufficiently recognized, the theme of renunciation. Near the end of his life, Tolstoy had, like Lear, given up his worldly power, his wealth, and his title in the expectation that he would be rewarded by the happiness that would come from submitting himself to the will of God. In short, Orwell maintains, Tolstoy's renunciation was, at bottom, again like Lear's, a form of egoism, which brought him not peace but a sword.

The critic George Woodcock looks at Orwell's essays on Tolstoy and on JONATHAN SWIFT and sees that in both cases, Orwell recognized a significant part of himself in the two writers he both admired yet severely criticized.

Work Cited

Woodcock, George. *The Crystal Spirit.* London: Jonathan Cape, 1967.

totalitarianism The term was first used in 1923 by Benito Mussolini, proudly proclaiming the broad scope of the fascist state under his leadership. He used it to refer to an all-powerful state, expressing the collective will of the people. In effect, totalitarianism opposed itself to liberalism with its emphasis on individual freedom as opposed to the collective liberty of a state that controls the economy, social institutions, the press and other media, and the "education" (read indoctrination) of its citizens. Although Mussolini used it in a positive sense, it later acquired a negative connotation when applied to Nazi Germany and Stalinist Russia, as well as to Italy.

After his narrow escape from Spain in 1937, Orwell had time to absorb what he had seen there: the realization that fascism and communism, as implemented by Hitler and Stalin, were aspects of the same phenomenon—the totalitarian lust for power. What terrified him was the capacity of modern dictators to control the minds of their subjects through radio and press propaganda and the use of secret police. These were just the beginning. In *Coming Up for Air,* Orwell has his protagonist George Bowling describe what lies ahead:

> The barbed wire. The rubber truncheons. The secret cells where the electric light burns night and day, and the detective watching you while you sleep. And the processions and the posters with enormous faces, and the crowds of a million people all cheering for the leader till they deafen themselves that they really worship him, and all the time, underneath, they hate him . . . it's all going to happen. Or isn't it?

Bowling's vision would be fully realized in two features of *Nineteen Eighty-Four*'s Oceania: the basement of the Ministry of Truth, and Hate Week.

For Orwell, the Hitler-Stalin pact of 1939 cleared away any doubts that the two governments were sisters under the skin. Hitler's invasion of Russia two years later cast Stalin and his regime into the role of the brave ally. By the end of the war, Stalin was more powerful than ever. One of the most disturbing features of the new totalitarianism was that, unlike past dictatorships, power was not hereditary. The Soviet system, Orwell believed, was less likely to become weakened or ineffective since the people who seek power must be, as Stalin was, adept at the power game. Nor does it seem likely that a totalitarian state could be overthrown by a revolution since the state's capacity to indoctrinate its people has reached historically unprecedented technological and terroristic means of sustaining and increasing that power.

Orwell explored these problems in a number of essays, particularly in relation to the theories of JAMES BURNHAM. Burnham maintained that the new form of totalitarianism he called managerialism, a disguised and corrupted form of socialism, was an inevitable future development in a world dominated by three superstates. In his essay "SECOND THOUGHTS ON JAMES BURNHAM," Orwell argues that the slave societies Burnham envisions, although partly realized in Stalin's Russia, will not survive. Modern people will not tolerate slavery in any form or for very long. Nevertheless, he recognized a tendency toward the all-powerful state, and he set about issuing warnings of the totalitarian threat.

The great proving grounds of his ideas were *Animal Farm* and *Nineteen Eighty-Four.* The first, using the history of the Soviet Union from the revolution to 1943, illustrated how an elite corps of insiders, led by a power-mad despot, could assume total control of a society through terror and manipulative language. *Animal Farm* ends when the process of transformation is complete. The pigs are indistinguishable from the humans, and the communists are no different than the fascists or capitalists. *Nineteen Eighty-Four* describes in detail what an advanced totalitarian state might look like. At the base of his thinking lies the conviction that totalitarianism is not inevitable but constitutes a formidable threat. *Animal Farm* suggests how it might have been nipped in the bud, if the animals had been alert to the first sign when the pigs acquired privileges for themselves. But *Nineteen Eighty-Four* offers a much darker picture of a totalitarian regime already in existence. This possibility of reforming such a powerful evil presence seems much more remote, but not impossible. The apparently negative conclusion of the novel is designed to alert the reader to its early warning signs. Little did he realize how effectively he achieved that goal. Sixty years later, the watchword among a vast array of people, faced with some governmental or corporate incursion on individual rights, is simply *Big Brother.*

Tribune Leftist political biweekly review founded by Stafford Cripps in 1937. When Orwell resigned from the BBC, he became *Tribune*'s literary editor. The general editor at this time was ANEURIN BEVAN. As literary editor, Orwell was notoriously too tender-hearted, finding it hard to turn down any submission. When he gave up the position, he was replaced by his friend T. R. FYVEL.

A more important connection to the journal was the essays he contributed to the review, particularly gems like "SOME THOUGHTS ON THE COMMON

TOAD," "RIDING DOWN FROM BANGOR," and "A GOOD WORD FOR THE VICAR OF BRAY."

Equally memorable were the regular columns he wrote under the title "AS I PLEASE," many of which exhibit his lighter side. The key word in most of these pieces was *provocative.* And provoked readers responded in kind, leading to speculation by the *Tribune* editorial board as to whether he was alienating too many readers, but Bevan consistently defended him. In all, he wrote 80 of these columns before leaving the paper in 1947.

Trilling, Lionel (1905–1975) American literary critic and novelist. A distinguished professor at Columbia University, Trilling was a leading figure of the New York intellectuals and a contributor to the *Partisan Review.* He wrote one novel called *The Middle of the Journey* (1947), in which he attempted to "draw out some of the moral and intellectual implications of the powerful attraction to communism felt by a considerable part of the American intellectual class during the Thirties and Forties" (7). This is a subject very close to Orwell's, but Trilling approached it not in a satiric vein but as a novel of ideas with a sharp psychological focus.

Trilling reviewed *Nineteen Eighty-Four* in the *New Yorker,* calling it "a profound, terrifying, and wholly fascinating book" (78). In 1952, he wrote an introduction to the first American edition of *Homage to Catalonia,* in which he focused on the man as much as on the book. In it, he used a phrase that was to project an image of Orwell which struck a powerful chord with sophisticated readers, coming as it did from a highly sophisticated literary lion. He said that Orwell was not a genius but something even rarer: "a virtuous man" (*Introduction,* VIII).

Works Cited

Trilling, Lionel. "Orwell on the Future." *New Yorker.* June 18, 1949, 78–83.

———. Introduction. *Homage to Catalonia.* New York: Harcourt, Brace, 1952.

Trotsky, Leon (1879–1940) Russian revolutionary leader, allegorized as "Snowball" in *Animal Farm.* Trotsky, who did not join the Bolshevik party until 1917, emerged as a powerful force, playing a critical role in the revolution and later in the Russian civil war, in which he served as commander of the Red Army. After the death of VLADIMIR LENIN in 1924, Trotsky was widely expected to succeed him, but he was outmaneuvered by JOSEPH STALIN. The two men disagreed on fundamental issues, such as whether the economic emphasis should be on industrialization (Trotsky) or agriculture (Stalin), and in foreign affairs, whether the revolution should be exported to other nations (Trotsky) or confined to the Soviet Union (Stalin). Eventually Trotsky was expelled from the Party and, in 1929, sent into exile. He continued his crusade in exile until 1940, when he was murdered at his home in Mexico by a Stalinist agent.

Although Orwell was never a follower of Trotsky, he was frequently saddled with that charge. He and his wife Eileen were identified as such by the Spanish tribunal that condemned them as traitors and Trotskyites in 1937. As part of Orwell's ongoing quarrel with H. G. WELLS, Wells referred to him as "A Trotskyite with big feet." Another disputant of his, Hetta Empson, the wife of WILLIAM EMPSON, recalled spirited exchanges in which "I was a Marxist and he was a Trot." But despite the relatively positive treatment "Snowball" received in *Animal Farm,* Orwell was no Trotskyist. Witness his comment:

> "Trotsky, in exile, denounces the Russian dictatorship, but he is probably as much responsible for it as any man now living, and there is no certainty that as a dictator he would be preferable to Stalin, though undoubtedly he has a much more interesting mind" (Meyers, 249).

Work Cited

Meyers, Jeffrey. *Orwell: Wintry Conscience of a Generation.* New York: Norton, 2000.

U

United States In writing about Orwell, the word *ambivalent* occurs so often as to be predictable. But it is an inevitable choice in describing his reaction to the American presence on the world scene. It begins with his estimate, recorded in one of his London Letters to the *Partisan Review:* "Until about 1930 nearly all 'cultivated' people loathed the U.S.A., which was regarded as the vulgariser of England and Europe." Whether he shared that view is not clear, but his essays reveal frequent references to the effect that American music, films, and popular culture had and continued to have a negative impact on English life. Essays such as "RAFFLES AND MISS BLANDISH" and "THE DECLINE OF THE ENGLISH MURDER" are unsparing in their denunciation of the violence and sadism associated with the big-shouldered bully across the Atlantic. Another American vice, from Orwell's perspective, was the specter of advertising. Near the end of *Keep the Aspidistra Flying,* the protagonist, Gordon Comstock, weighing the prospect of returning to his job at an advertising agency, peruses an American magazine, profusely illustrated with ads:

> A panorama of ignorance, greed, vulgarity, snobbishness, whoredom and disease . . . But of course it was an American paper. The Americans always go one better on any kind of beastliness, whether it is ice-cream soda, racketeering or theosophy.

He was also not happy with presence of rude and boisterous American soldiers in London during the war. He criticized not only Yanks but "Yank mags," popular pulp fiction filled with heavy doses of violence and blood. Nor, in his stint as a film critic, was he happy with Hollywood films, for the most part.

In addition to its cultural sins, America was also a supremely capitalist and, with the development of the atomic bomb, dangerous state. In *Nineteen Eighty-Four,* it serves as the superpower Oceania, in which England has been reduced to Airstrip One.

On the other hand, there is his idyllic description of 19th-century America, as depicted in popular novels such as Louisa May Allcott's *Little Women* and John Harberton's *Helen's Babies.* What emerged from these descriptions was a sense of individual opportunity and freedom, "capitalist civilization at its best." He realized that world had long ago disappeared, but the sense of it as a basic element of the American heritage, as was its wilder, cruder frontier tradition, was seen by him as an essential part of America's strength.

Another experience that deepened his view of America were his London Letters, written for *PARTISAN REVIEW* during the war years. Here, he found not only compatible minds in its editors, including Philip Rahv and Dwight MacDonald, but a wide audience of readers who, like their English equivalents, the readers of *TRIBUNE,* frequently and volubly disagreed with him but always looked forward to the experience of reading him.

As the cold war began to take shape, he deplored the tendency of the intellectual left to view Anglo-American capitalism and Soviet communism as equally evil. From Orwell's socialist perspective, capitalism was the lesser of two evils. Faced with an either/or, Orwell chose the third path of a socialist European Union:

> In the end, the European people may have to accept American domination as a way of avoiding domination by Russia, but they ought to realize, while there is yet time, that there are other possibilitiities.

The other possibility he had in mind, as he described it in his essay "TOWARD EUROPEAN UNITY" was a "socialist United States of Europe." The emergence of the European Union, while not socialist, suggests that his prophetic powers were as usual not far from the eventual outcome.

Orwell was, however, disturbed by a major development that accompanied the broad success of *Animal Farm* and *Nineteen Eighty-Four* in America. This was the tendency of some major newspapers and magazines to read both books as satires not only on communism but on socialism as well. The corrections that Orwell issued did little to dispel the common impression, promoted by the *New York Daily News,* the paper with the largest circulation in the country, and *Life,* the widely read picture magazine, that *Nineteen Eighty-Four* in particular depicted a nightmarish socialist world, ruled by Ingsoc.

V

Voice A literary "Magazine of the Air," created by Orwell while a talks producer at the BBC's Eastern Services Department. The first program was aired in August 1942. At this time, the American navy in the Pacific had scored a crucial victory at the Battle of Midwood, but the two other "turning points" of the war, the British victory at El Alamein and the Russian annihilation of the German 6th Army at Stalingrad, had not yet occurred. Thus, Orwell was being accurate when, in his introduction to the program, he called it "the worst possible moment to be starting a magazine . . . concerned primarily with poetry." The first program consisted of a poem ("The Contrary Experience") read by its author, Herbert Read; a short prose monologue by Inez Holden ("Poor Relation"), read by Vida Hope; a poem by Dylan Thomas ("In Memory of Ann Jones"), read by William Empson; followed by a brief exchange on the poem by Orwell, Empson, and Mulk Raj Anand; three poems by Henry Treece, read by John Atkins; followed by a discussion of all the participants of Treece's poems, and, in closing, a Wordsworth sonnet ("The World Is Too Much with Us ") read by Herbert Read.

The selection of poems by Henry Treece and Dylan Thomas underscores Orwell's intention to have the program showcase young poets. The ironic fact about the discussions was that they had to be scripted beforehand, to meet the requirements of the censor. Empson, who worked in the cubicle next to Orwell, may have assisted Orwell here, since the best lines in the discussion are assigned to him.

The second program in the series had "war poetry" as its theme. It began with a reading of W. H. Auden's "September, 1939" (misidentified by Orwell as "September, 1941"), read by Herbert Read. This was followed by William Empson reading the last half of a poem by G. S. Frazer, "Letter to Ann Ridler," and then a prose selection from T. E. Lawrence's "Revolt in the Desert." The poet Edmund Blunden was a guest on the program and read two of his poems, "Rural Economy 1917" and "Report on Experience." The program concluded with Godfrey Kenton's reading of Byron's "The Isles of Greece."

The theme of the third episode was "childhood." The first selection was William Blake's "Holy Thursday," read by Herbert Read; followed by Rabindranath Tagore's "First Jasmines," read by Mulk Raj Anand; D. H. Lawrence's "The Piano," read by Empson; and a prose extract from Herbert Read's "The Innocent Eye," read by Read. To illustrate the pathos and fear of childhood, there were excerpts from Stevie Smith's "It was a cynical babe" and W. H. Davies's "The Two Children," and finally a passage from *David Copperfield* (the influence of the Murdstones on David's lessons). The program concluded with Stephen Spender reading his poem "An Elementary School in a Slum."

The fourth episode (aired in November 1942) was devoted to American literature. The first selection: Archibad MacLeish's "The Burying Ground by the Ties," read by William Empson. As an example of "expatriate American poetry," Herbert Read read

T. S. Eliot's "The Love Song of J. Alfred Prufrock." As an example of black poetry, Una Marson, a West Indian poet, read her poem "The Banjo Boy." For a sample of 19th century American writers, a passage from Herman Melville's *White Jacket* and Bret Harte's tribute to Charles Dickens, "Dickens in Camp," was read by Empson. The program concluded with Walt Whitman's "O Captain! My Captain!" and "Ann Rutledge" by Edgar Lee Masters.

The theme of the fifth episode (December, 1942) was "Oriental influence on English literature." Unfortunately, the script of this broadcast has been lost. This was the program that included T. S. Eliot reading "What the Thunder Said" from *The Waste Land.*

The sixth and last episode of *Voice* (December 29, 1942) had a Christmas theme, geared for an audience not necessarily familiar with the holiday. The program opened with a recording of *Adeste Fideles,* the Christmas carol "See Amid the Winter Snow," and the Robert Bridges poem "London Snow," read by Christopher Pemberton. Two more recorded carols were followed by the scriptural account of the birth of Jesus, as given in the Gospel According to St. Matthew. This was followed by John Milton's "Nativity Ode," read by Herbert Read, and followed by another carol. The highlight of the broadcast was a recording of T. S. Eliot's "The Journey of the Magi," read by the poet himself.

The episode concluded with the announcement that the next program would be broadcast on March 19, 1943, but the Christmas program turned out to be the last of the series.

W

Wain, John (1925–1994) English poet, novelist, and critic. Of the writers who came of age in the 1950s, Wain was the one who most consistently adhered to Orwell as a role model, both intellectually and ethically. Wain was associated with the group of young 1950s poets known as the Movement, who rejected the florid and romantic poetic style of the 1940s as represented by Dylan Thomas. Orwell's celebrated plain style and his unpretentious and down-to-earth empiricism represented the perfect prose equivalent of the poetry they wished to champion. Wain was prominent among this group, which included Philip Larkin and Robert Conquest, all of whom looked to Orwell as a model. However, as a group, the Movement remained remote from everyday politics. Wain's early novel, *Hurry On Down* (1953), came to be seen as one of the harbingers of the politically conscious "angry young men" of the late 1950s, but the radical student movement of the sixties forced many of the Movement and the Angries into a more conservative posture. Wain found Orwell easily adaptable to a Tory anticommunist as opposed to a socialist anticommunist position. In his 1983 "Dear George Orwell," he suggested that if Orwell were alive he would deplore the leaders of the National Union Mine Workers who have become a "new aristocracy," able "to bring an economy to a standstill . . . unanswerable to the moral authority of a democratic state" (quoted in Rodden, 251). The striking feature of Wain's attitude toward Orwell is that, however he shifted his political and social views, he never lost confidence that Orwell was there with him.

Work Cited

Rodden, John. "'The Rope that Connects Me Directly with You': John Wain and the Movement Writers' Orwell." In *The Revised Orwell,* edited by Jonathan Rose, 235–256. East Lansing: Michigan University Press, 1992.

Wallington Rural village in Hertsfordshire, where Orwell and his wife Eileen lived from 1936 to 1940.

Warburg, Fredric (1898–1981) The son of Jewish parents, Warburg served as an artillery officer in the First World War. In 1935, he and his partner took over a bankrupt publishing firm, Martin Secker, and renamed it Secker & Warburg. When, in 1938, Warburg learned that Orwell's publisher Victor Gollancz had turned down *Homage to Catalonia* for political reasons, he contacted Orwell and agreed to publish the book. In the midst of the war and a serious paper shortage, Warburg also published *Animal Farm,* which turned out to be a young publisher's dream. Four years later, he published *Nineteen Eighty-Four,* knowing immediately that he had another great success on his hands. In the meantime, he and Orwell had formed a real friendship, cemented during the war years, in which he served as a corporal in the same unit of the HOME GUARD, in which Orwell was his sergeant. He followed Orwell's illness attentively, visiting him frequently and recommending a specialist who became Orwell's physician.

Waugh, Evelyn (1903–1966) English novelist, noted for his satirical works, although best known as the author of *Brideshead Revisited* (1945), a story of an aristocratic Roman Catholic English family, whose members experience complex relationships to their faith. Though at opposite poles politically and ideologically, Waugh and Orwell respected each other's work and were united in their contempt for many features of modern life. In his review of Orwell's *Collected Essays* in 1946, Waugh wrote, "He frequently brings his argument to the point when, having with great acuteness, seen the falsity and contradiction of the humanist view of life, there seems no alternative but the acceptance of a revealed religion, and then stops short" (214). For his part, in 1949, Orwell began writing an essay on Waugh that he never completed before his death in January 1950. There he applauds Waugh's independence, "In our own day, the English novelist who has most conspicuously defied his contemporaries is Evelyn Waugh . . . Waugh is the latest, perhaps the last, of a long list of English writers whose real driving force is a romantic belief in aristocracy" (*CW*, 20, 75). In his notes for the article, Orwell concluded, "Waugh is as good a novelist as one can be . . . while holding untenable opinions" (*CW*, 20, 77).

Waugh lived in the area near the Cranham sanitorium where Orwell was a patient, and he visited him there. 2008 saw the appearance of an overly simplified but highly readable study of the two writers by David Lebedoff.

Work Cited

The Complete Works of George Orwell. Edited by Peter Davison, Vol. 2. London: Secker & Warburg, 1998.

Lebedoff, David. *The Same Man: George Orwell and Evelyn Waugh in Love and War.* New York: Random House, 2008.

Waugh, Evelyn. Review of *Collected Essays. George Orwell: The Critical Heritage.* London: Routledge, 1975.

Wells, H. G. (Herbert George Wells) (1866–1946) English novelist, historian, and journalist. Wells is best known for his science-fiction novels, such as *The Invisible Man* (1897) and *The War of the Worlds* (1898), but young Eric Blair grew up familiar with his entire work. Wells was a Fabian socialist, a believer in the evolutionary, as opposed to revolutionary, establishment of a socialist government. As a result, he turned from science fiction to realistic depictions of the lower middle classes in novels such as *The History of Mr. Polly* (1910), one of the sources of Orwell's *Coming Up for Air.* Among other Wells works that influenced Orwell was *The Island of Dr. Moreau* (1896), a minor source for *Nineteen Eighty-Four.*

In 1941, Orwell adapted a short story by Wells, "A Slip Under the Microscope" for BBC radio. Given his debt to Wells, he was quite right to convict himself of parricide in his treatment of Wells in his essay "WELLS, HITLER AND THE WORLD STATE." He characterizes Wells as a "nineteenth-century liberal," too rational a man to understand the modern phenomenon of totalitarianism and the mind of a man like Hitler. Orwell argues that Wells sees Hitler as insane and therefore not a person to be taken seriously. Wells's belief in scientific rationalism leaves him incapable of understanding radical evil.

Inez Holden, a friend of Orwell and of Wells, arranged a dinner in which the two might form a friendship. Wells had not read this review before. He obtained a copy just prior to the dinner. Wells brought the articles with him to the dinner, and they argued at length but parted amicably. But Orwell dismissed Wells as out of date in a subsequent radio talk "The Rediscovery of Europe," prompting a letter from Wells referring to Orwell as "you shit." Orwell made amends in an obituary notice he wrote in 1946, published in Peter Davison's *The Lost Orwell* (pp. 136–140).

West, Anthony (1914–1987) Biographer, critic, and novelist. West was the illegitimate son of Rebecca West and H. G. WELLS, of whom he wrote a biography: *H. G. Wells: Aspects of a Life* (1984). In relation to Orwell, he is best known for his "hidden wound" theory, first published in the *New Yorker* and reprinted in his essay collection *Principles and Persuasions* (1984). His theory holds that in *Nineteen Eighty-Four,* Orwell unconsciously projected his experience at St Cyprian's, as he recorded it in "SUCH, SUCH WERE THE JOYS," into the world of Oceania. West maintained that the novel is "a fantasy of universal ruin . . . not a rational attempt to imagine a probable future." The whole pattern of society shapes up along the lines of fear laid down in "Such, Such Were in the Joys," until the final point of the dread summons to the headmaster's study for the inevitable beating. "In *1984,* the study becomes Room 101 in the Ministry of Love and the torturers correspond closely to the schoolmasters . . ." (102). It is worth noting that West speaks of the "torturers" and the "headmasters" in the plural because he is unable to find an adequate equivalent for O'Brien. In West's scheme, CECILY WILKES, the obvious candidate, has been assigned the role of Big Brother.

Work Cited

West, Anthony. "Hidden Damage." *New Yorker,* January 28, 1956, 98–104.

Wilkes, Cecily Vaughan (1875–1967) Headmistress and wife of the headmaster LEWIS VAUGHN WILKES of St Cyprian's school, which Orwell attended from 1911 to 1916. Of the two, she appears to have been the more dominant, particularly in the experience of the boys at the school. She cultivated favorites, treating those in favor particularly well, but she was capricious and given to mood swings. One might fall out of her favor without knowing why and, in equally mysterious fashion, be restored to favor. Orwell distinguished himself by remaining consistently out of favor. From the beginning, she saw him as a boy who lacked "warmth." Nevertheless, when he achieved some distinction, such as when he had two poems published in his local newspaper, she made a point of celebrating his achievements. The picture of her that emerges in "Such, Such Were the Joys," his ferocious attack on the school, is umremittingly negative. The majority of "St Cyp's" graduates who have commented on Orwell's essay have felt that he exaggerated her flaws and overlooked her positive virtues, although a few have expressed agreement with him. Of course, few of the boys had the sensitive awareness and self-consciousness of Eric Blair, just as few had his verbal skills. One who did was CYRIL CONNOLLY, whose bittersweet recollection of Flip, as she was known by the students, provoked Orwell into writing his version of the story. Stansky and Abrahams summarize the relationship succinctly, ". . . he wanted her approval and never got it, she wanted his affection and never got it" (62). St Cyprian's was destroyed by a fire in 1939, but Wilkes spent her retirement years living in a lodge at the entrance to the old school. She died at the age of 91.

Works Cited

Connolly, Cyril. *Enemies of Promise.* London: Routledge, 1938.

Stansky, Peter and William Abrahams. *The Unknown Orwell.* New York: Knopf, 1972.

Wilkes, Lewis Vaughan (1869–1947) Headmaster of Orwell's prep school, St Cyprian's. Although overshadowed by his wife, Cecily, he was important to the boys since it was he who administered corporal punishment, both formally in his office and informally in class where he had a habit of hitting students on the head with a silver pencil. Nevertheless, even Orwell conceded that he was not particularly heavy-handed when caning a boy's bottom. In fact, it was not the physical punishment that Orwell objected to most strongly in his memoir but the headmaster's reminder of the boy's lack of gratitude for the reduced fees his parents were paying. (See "SUCH, SUCH WERE THE JOYS.")

Williams, Raymond (1921–1988) Distinguished social theorist, novelist, critic, and pioneer in the field of cultural studies, Williams was the product of a working-class Welsh family. While still in his teens, he joined the Communist Party but parted company when he joined the army in 1940, in defiance of the party rules. For the rest of his life, he remained a committed marxian socialist. In 1948, Williams was one of three editors of a new journal, *Politics and Letters,* to which Orwell contributed his essay "WRITERS AND LEVIATHAN." In his notes for that essay, Orwell reminds himself to make a point "against R.W.," an indication of differences of opinion that were to become clear in Williams's later writings on Orwell.

One of Williams's best-known works is *Culture and Society* (1958), a history of the idea of culture as traced through writers from the 18th to the 20th centuries. Orwell is included as one of these writers. During the next two decades, Williams wrote about Orwell on a number of occasions, including *George Orwell* (1971), a slim volume in the Modern Masters series; as the editor of *George Orwell: A Collection of Critical Essays* (1974); and finally a chapter in *Politics and Letters,* which consists of an interview with Williams by three young radicals on the subject of Orwell and his influence. Over this period, Williams developed an increasingly critical view, moving from a respectful difference to a rejection of Orwell as an unintentionally malignant influence in the history of English socialism. In an impressive analysis of Williams's shifting views of Orwell, Christopher Hitchens argues that Williams's animus was rooted, to a significant extent, in professional envy.

Work Cited

Hitchens, Christopher. "George Orwell and Raymond Williams." *Critical Quarterly* 4, 2000, 3, 3–20.

Wilson, Edmund (1895–1972) American literary critic and man of letters. Among Wilson's most important works are *Axel's Castle* (1931), a study of symbolist poetry; *To the Finland Station* (1940), a history of the intellectual background of the Russian Revolution; and *The Wound and the Bow* (1941), a collection of his essays, which Orwell reviewed for *The Observer* in 1942. In his review Orwell concentrated exclusively on two essays dealing with Charles Dickens and Rudyard Kipling, choosing to ignore the title essay, which is one of Wilson's most famous. For a number of years, Wilson was the chief reviewer of the *New Yorker,* in which he reviewed *Animal Farm,* calling it "absolutely first-rate,' adding that he thought *Burmese Days* had been unjustly neglected: "It is illuminating as a picture of Burma and distinguished as a work of literature." In 1951, Wilson reviewed *Shooting an Elephant and Other Essays,* singling out as particularly noteworthy "SECOND THOUGHTS ON JAMES BURNHAM" as "the best job of destructive criticism that I have seen in recent years." Wilson ended his review with a chilling farewell to Orwell: "When he died . . . he had written in the nightmare prophecy of *Nineteen Eighty-Four* the sentence of death for everything he had trusted and loved" (311).

Work Cited

Wilson, Edmond. "Shooting an Elephant and Orwell Essays." In *George Orwell: The Critical Heritage,* edited by Jeffrey Meyers, 309–311. London: Routledge, 1975.

Wodehouse, P. G. (Percival Grenville Wodehouse) (1881–1975) English novelist, playwright, lyricist, and screenwriter. An extraordinarily prolific and successful writer, Wodehouse is best known for his fictional farces, novels, and short stories, featuring the not-too-bright socialite Bertie Wooster and his perfect valet, Jeeves. In 1940, while living in France, Wodehouse was captured by the Germans. In 1941, he made several broadcasts to the then-neutral United States from Radio Berlin. They were amusing and politically insignificant, but the charge of collaboration was raised against him after the war. In his essay "IN DEFENSE OF WODEHOUSE" (1946), Orwell argues that the author was a creature of an earlier age, a political innocent who had in fact not said anything defamatory about England. Wodehouse later wrote to Orwell, thanking him for his defense.

women "He didn't really like women." This was the judgment of BRENDA SALKELD, longtime friend and correspondent of Orwell. By way of expanding her statement, Salkeld added "he was a sadist and that was why he had this feeling about women" (Coppard and Crick, 68). It is possible that she derived this idea from a letter Orwell had written her, in which he described a conversation with a man who is "a bit of a feminist. . . . He tells me that my antifeminist views are probably due to sadism." If a tendency to pounce on women is evidence of sadism, then perhaps the connection between the two is valid, evident in the recent revelation of his attempt to force JACINTHA BUDDICOM to have sex. His motivation becomes a little clearer in the light of a comment in his last literary notebook. There he recalls, using the third person, overhearing as a child his mother and her friends discussing men. He learned from them that "women did not like men" and that sexual intercourse gives pleasure to the man, not to the woman. He knew that sexual intercourse had something to do with the man getting on top of the woman ". . . forcing her down and jumping on top of her, as he had often seen a cock do to a hen" (*CW*, 20, 206). It does not excuse his behavior with Jacintha or other women, but it does identify the appalling lack of sexual knowledge that an educated young man of his time possessed.

In his overall celebration of Orwell, *Why Orwell Matters* (2002), Christopher Hitchens meets some of the challenges raised by feminist critics against Orwell, but he overlooks, or chooses to overlook, the most formidable feminist critique, Daphne Patai's *The Orwell Mystique: A Study of Male Ideology* (1984). Patai employs the term *androcentrism* to zero in on what she sees as the particular type of misogyny Orwell exhibited in his works. She elevates androcentrism into a key element in Orwell's thought, connecting it even to his anti-communism and other issues on which he took controversial stands. She argues that underlying all these radical positions was the implicit message that Orwell was "one of the boys" and therefore ultimately "safe" as far as upholding male hegemony was concerned. In her detailed explication of Orwell's work, she makes a clear case that in him we have a male-centered man of his time. As in the case of ANTI-SEMITISM, Orwell was not only *not* ahead of his time, but he was actually lagging behind. He had many women friends, most of whom did not share Brenda Salkeld's view. Patai's argument that this flaw infected and weakened everything he stood for appears to be an example of critical overkill in an argument that is otherwise not without merit.

Works Cited

Coppard, Audrey, and Bernard Crick, eds. *Orwell Remembered.* New York: Facts On File, 1984.

Hitchens, Christopher. *Why Orwell Matters.* New York: Basic Books, 2002.

Patai, Daphne. *The Orwell Mystique: A Study of Male Ideology.* Albany, NY: SUNY Press, 1984.

Woodcock, George (1912–1995) Canadian man of letters who lived and worked in England in the 1940s. From 1940 to 1947, he edited the anarchist/pacifist journal *Now.* He came to know Orwell when the two of them engaged in a controversy, sparked by Orwell's negative characterization of pacifists and anarchists in a London Letter to the *Partisan Review* (March–April 1942). Despite their sharp differences over pacifism and anarchism, two subjects about which Woodcock was clearly more knowledgeable, the two men became close friends and in 1946, Orwell contributed an article to *Now.* Woodcock persuaded Orwell to accept the title of vice chairman of the FREEDOM DEFENSE COMMITTEE on which Woodcock served as secretary. In the 1950s, Woodcock returned to Canada, where in 1966 he published his study of Orwell, *The Crystal Spirit,* regarded by many as the finest full-length critical analysis of Orwell's work, and *Orwell's Message: 1984 and the Present* (1984). The distinctive feature of *The Crystal Spirit* is that it is a critical study in the full sense of the term. Woodcock's treatment of Orwell's work acknowledges both the surface inconsistencies and the deeper emotional conflicts that resist any attempt to smooth out and simplify his thought. In addition, in his final chapter, Woodcock examines Orwell's prose style, demonstrating its inextricable relation to his ultimate theme of justice and equality.

Works Cited

Woodcock, George. *The Crystal Spirit* London: Jonathan Cape, 1967.

———. *Orwell: Message: 1984 and the Present.* Madira Park, B.C.: Harbour Publishers, 1984.

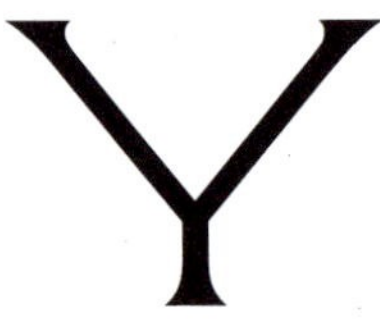

Yeats, W. B. (1865–1939) Irish poet considered the greatest English-language poet of the 20th century. Yeats was the subject of a 1943 book review by Orwell in which he describes the poet as a great hater of democracy. He sees Yeats as the outstanding example of a troubling phenomenon: "the relationship between fascism and the literary intelligentsia of the modern world. . . ." The book he reviewed was a biography of Yeats by V. K. Narayana Menon, and Orwell agrees with Menon that Yeats's great hatred of the modern world had driven him to the illusion that fascism would in some way bring about the return of a heroic past, one in which greatness and glory will once again dominate men's goals. (See part 2: W. B. YEATS.)

Work Cited

Menon, V. K. Narayana. *The Development of William Butler Yeats* 1943.

Z

Zamyatin, Yevgeny (1884–1937) Russian satirical novelist. He joined the Bolshevik Party at the time of the Russian Revolution of 1905, was arrested, and eventually was forced into exile. He returned with the Bolshevik victory in 1917. His satiric pen got him into trouble with the Soviet authorities, and he was exiled to Paris in 1931, where he worked with Jean Renoir on the director's film adaptation of Maxim Gorky's play *The Lower Depths*. He died of a heart attack in 1937.

Zamyatin's best-known work is *We* (1921), a dystopian satire many centuries in the future following the Two Hundred Years War, a conflict involving superweapons that have wiped out most of the world's population.

In a 1946 *Tribune* review of Zamyatin's satire, Orwell gives a brief account of the publishing history of *We*. Its publication was not permitted in the Soviet Union, but translated versions in French, Czech, and English have appeared. The English version was published in America, and Orwell declares that he has had no success acquiring a copy. However, he has been able to secure a copy of the French translation. He summarizes the book's theme as the opposition of freedom and happiness. In this future state ruled by the Benefactor, the basic principle is that freedom and happiness are incompatible. As a result, the state has removed freedom from the lives of its citizens and substituted a synthetic happiness. The cities of the state are walled, keeping out nature and its unruly character. The state rules by mathematical logic, in which people's names have given way to numbers. Machines do the work. Even teachers are robots. Individuality, particularly the individual imagination, is the enemy.

Orwell indicates that the Soviet regime was not the principal target of this satire. The target is rather the specter of the industrialized machine, "the genie that man has thoughtlessly let out of the bottle and cannot put back again." Orwell clearly acknowledged his debt to *We* in writing *Nineteen Eighty-Four*.

PART IV

Appendices

George Orwell Chronology

1857
January 7 Birth of father, Richard Walmesley Blair

1875
Richard Blair joins the Opium Department of the Indian Civil Service
May 19 Birth of mother, Ida Mabel Limouzin

1897
June 15 Marriage of Richard Blair and Ida Limouzin

1898
April 21 Sister Marjorie Blair is born

1899–1903
Boer War (discussed in *Coming Up for Air*)

1901
January 22 Death of Queen Victoria; accession of King Edward VII

1903
June 25 Birth of Eric Arthur Blair at Motihari, Bengal, India

1904
Brought to England. Mother, sister, and Eric settle in Henley-on-Thames, Oxfordshire. Father returns to India

1905
February 25 Birth of Eileen Maud O'Shaughnessy, Orwell's first wife
September 27 Blairs move to Ermadale, Vicarage Road, Henley

1907
Summer Richard Blair returns to England on leave for three months

1908–1911
Eric and his sisters educated at convent school run by Ursuline nuns

1908
April Blairs move to the Nutshell, Western Road, Henley
April 6 Sister Avril Nora Blair is born

1910
May 6 Death of King Edward VII; accession of King George V

1911–16
Student (until 1916) at St Cyprian's in Eastbourne, Sussex

1912
January Father retires from Indian Civil Service and returns to England
Autumn Family moves to Shiplake, a village two miles south of Henley

1914
August 4 Beginning of World War I
Summer Makes friends with Jacintha Buddicom, her brother Prosper; and her sister Guinever

October 2 First published poem, "Awake Young Men of England," in *Henley and South Oxfordshire Standard*

1915

September Blair family moves back to Henley

1916

July 21 His poem "Kitchener" is published in *Henley and South Oxfordshire Standard*

1917

Enters Wellington College on scholarship

March 8 Outbreak of first phase of Russian Revolution ("February Revolution")

March 15 Czar Nicholas II abdicates, and chaos reigns in Russia

April 6 United States declares war on Germany

May Transfers as a King's Scholar to Eton College, where he counts Cyril Connolly, Stephen Runciman, and Dennis King-Farlow among his friends

September 13 Despite advanced age, Richard Walmesley Blair enlists in the army and is posted to Marseille. Ida Blair moves to London (Earl's Court) to work at the Ministry of Pensions

November 7 Led by Vladimir Lenin and Leon Trotsky, Bolsheviks seize power in Russia's October Revolution

1918

June 3 Publishes four pieces of writing in the *Election Times,* a handwritten student journal

July 16 Czar Nicholas II and his family are executed by Bolsheviks

August 25 Birth of Sonia Brownell, Orwell's second wife

September Writes poem "The Pagan" for Jacintha Buddicom

November 11 Armstice Day; World War I ends

1919

April 13 Amritsar Massacre; British troops open fire on unarmed Indian protesters, killing 379 and wounding more than 1,200 (discussed in *Burmese Days*)

December 9 Father is discharged from the army and joins his wife in London

1920

January 10 League of Nations is formed

April 7 Spends Easter holidays (April 7–30) with the Buddicoms in Shiplake

July Sister Marjorie Blair marries Humphrey Dakin

August Spends August with the Buddicom family

1921

August The Blair family and the Buddicoms share a summer house at Glencroft, Rickmansworth

August Eric and Jacintha exchange poems, his suggesting frustrated passion, hers counseling caution

September 4 Jacintha Buddicom writes a letter expressing her fury at his attempt to force her to have sex with him

December Blairs move to Southwold on the Suffolk coast

December 20 Finishes his last term at Eton and returns to Southwold

1922

January At Southwold, prepares to take India Office examinations

July 4 Completes his examination for Indian Imperial Police at the Civil Service Commission

October 27 Leaves England and sails to Burma

November 29 Attends Mandalay Police Training School

1924

January 21 Death of Vladimir Lenin, leader of the USSR

January 25 Completes training at Mandalay Police Training School

1926

April 19 Posted to Moulmein, third-largest city in Burma, home of mother's family, the Limouzins. Shoots a rogue elephant

May 4–12 General strike in England in support of the mine workers who went on strike on May 1 brings country to a standstill. Government declares a state of emergency. Strike is called off on May 12

December 23 Transferred to Katha, a remote area of northern Burma, 200 miles north of Mandalay

1927

Leon Trotsky is ousted from Soviet leadership by Joseph Stalin

Blair contracts dengue fever while in Katha

June Applies for leave on medical grounds and is granted eight months starting on July 1, 1927

July 14 Leaves Burma

August 22 Execution of the anarchists Nicola Sacco and Bartolomeo Vanzetti in Massachusetts. Arrives in Marseille amid demonstrations protesting executions

September Arrives home and announces his intention to resign from the Burmese police

Autumn Spends two weeks at Ticklerton with Prosper and Guinever Buddicom, but Jacintha is absent

Autumn Moves to London at Portobello Road, Notting Hill. Visits East End of London on the first of his tramping expeditions

Autumn Trotsky expelled from the Communist Party

November 26 Writes official letter of resignation to Imperial Police in Burma

1928

April Moves to Paris, staying at 6, rue du Pot de Fer, on Left Bank

April Works on short stories and novel, which he destroys

October 6 Publishes "La Censure en Angleterre" (Censorship in England) in *Le Monde,* his first professionally published writing

December 29 Publishes "A Farthing Newspaper" in *G. K.'s Weekly,* his first professionally published writing in English

1929

MI 5 opens a secret file on Eric Blair, partly based on his unexplained resignation from the Burmese police

March 7 Admitted to Hôpital Cochin in Paris with a case of influenza. Released after two weeks. Experience forms the basis of his essay "How the Poor Die"

October–December Works as a dishwasher at an unnamed hotel from October to early December

October 29 Crash of U.S. stock market helps launch worldwide depression

December Returns to England before Christmas and joins parents in Southwold

1930

March Visits sister Marjorie and her husband, Humphrey Dakin, at Bramley, Yorkshire, where he works on draft of *Down and Out in Paris and London*

June Takes on job as tutor-companion for sons of Mr and Mrs C. R. Peters

October Finishes draft of *Down and Out in Paris and London* and sends to the publisher Jonathan Cape

1931

April Publishes "The Spike" in *Adelphi*

August Publishes "A Hanging" in *Adelphi*

August Types a new draft of *Down and Out in Paris and London* at the home of Mabel Fierz

August 28 Engages in hop-picking in Kent

October Manuscript of *Down and Out in Paris and London* rejected by Jonathan Cape

October 17 Publishes "Hop Picking" article in *New Statesman & Nation*

December 14 Sends manuscript of *Down and Out in Paris and London* (under the title "A Scullion's Diary") to T. S. Eliot at Faber & Faber. Eliot rejects it

1932

Gives manuscript of *Down and Out in Paris and London* to Mabel Fierz with instructions to destroy it. She brings it to literary agent Leonard Moore, who submits it to Victor Gollancz. Gollancz agrees to publish it after minor changes

April Begins teaching at a private school for boys, the Hawthornes, in Hayes, Middlesex

November 19 Offers Leonard Moore four possible pseudonyms for *Down and Out in Paris and London* authorship: P. S. Burton, Kenneth Miles, George Orwell, and H. Lewis Allways. Blair writes, "I rather favour George Orwell"

December Writes, directs, and does the costumes for *Charles II,* a school play at Hawthornes

December 23 Joins his family in Southwold for Christmas

1933

January 9 *Down and Out in Paris and London* is published by Victor Gollancz

January 18 Returns to teaching at the Hawthornes

March Publishes poem "Sometimes in the Middle Autumn Days" in *Adelphi*

May Publishes poem "Summer-Like" in *Adelphi*

June 30 American edition of *Down and Out in Paris and London* is published by Harper in New York

August In Southwold for holiday

September Teaches at Frays College, Uxbridge, Middlesex

October Publishes poem "A Dressed Man and a Naked Man" in *Adelphi*

December Hospitalized with pneumonia in Uxbridge for two weeks

1934

January *Burmese Days* is rejected by Victor Gollancz but American publisher Harper agrees to publish it

January 8 Discharged from hospital, returns to parents' home in Southwold, where he recuperates. Writes first draft of *A Clergyman's Daughter*

April Publishes poem "On a Ruined Farm near the His Master's Voice Gramophone Factory" in *Adelphi*

October 15 Returns to London from Southwold and accepts a position at Booklovers' Corner, Hampstead, and lives in a flat above the shop

October 25 Harper in New York publishes the American edition of *Burmese Days*

October 30 Sends the typescript of the completed manuscript of *A Clergyman's Daughter* to Leonard Moore

1935

January 22 Victor Gollancz agrees to publish *A Clergyman's Daughter*

February 1 Victor Gollancz expresses renewed interest in *Burmese Days* and asks to read it again

March Moves early in March to 77 Parliament Hill, Hampstead, where he meets Eileen O'Shaughnessy at a party

March 11 *A Clergyman's Daughter* is published by Victor Gollancz

May French edition of *Down and Out in Paris and London* is published under the title *La Vache Enragée,* with a preface written by Orwell

June 24 Revised edition of *Burmese Days* is published by Victor Gollancz

August Moves to a flat at 50 Lawford Road, Kentish Town, where he shares rooms with Rayner Heppenstall and Michael Sayers

October Proposes marriage to Eileen O'Shaughnessy, who refuses to consider it until she has completed her degree

November Publishes poem "St. Andrew's Day, 1935" in *Adelphi*

November 14 Reviews *Tropic of Cancer* by Henry Miller for *New English Weekly*

1936

January 15 Sends the typescript of *Keep the Aspidistra Flying* to Victor Gollancz

January 20 Death of King George V; accession of King Edward VIII

January 23 Publishes "On Kipling's Death" in *New English Weekly,* on the occasion of Kipling's death

January 30–March 30 Visits industrial north of England, studying effects of unemployment there. Results will later be published as *The Road to Wigan Pier*

April 2 Rents a village shop at the Stores, Wallington, Hertfordshire, a cottage with no electricity or indoor plumbing

April 20 *Keep the Aspidistra Flying* published by Victor Gollancz

May Begins work on *The Road to Wigan Pier*

May Victor Gollancz founds the Left Book Club

June 9 Marries Eileen O'Shaughnessy at village church in Wallington

July Attends Independent Labour Party (ILP) summer school in Letchworth, Hertfordshire

July 18 Fighting between Republican and Nationalist forces in Spain marks the beginning of the Spanish civil war

August Stalin's purge trials, focusing on those communist leaders who disagree with his policies, begin in Moscow, with each defendant pleading guilty as charged

August 17 Harper in New York publishes the American edition of *A Clergyman's Daughter*

September Essay "Shooting an Elephant" published in *New Writing*

October Finishes first draft of *The Road to Wigan Pier*

November Essay "Bookshop Memories" published in *Fortnightly*

November 12 Essay "In Defence of the Novel" published in *New English Weekly*

December Publishes poem "A Happy Vicar" in *Adelphi*

December 11 King Edward VIII announces his abdication and is succeeded by his brother George VI

December 15 Submits manuscript of *The Road to Wigan Pier* to Leonard Moore

December 23 Leaves England for Spain

December 24 Stops in Paris to obtain Spanish travel documents and visits Henry Miller

December 26 Arrives in Barcelona, Spain

December 30 Joins the POUM (Workers' Party of Marxist Unification) militia

1937

January With POUM unit in Barcelona during first week of January

January 7 At front lines in Alcubierre, where he stays until early February

February 2 Transfers to a contingent of the ILP, affiliated with POUM

February 15 Eileen Blair arrives in Barcelona to work with John McNair in the offices of the ILP

March 8 *The Road to Wigan Pier* published by Victor Gollancz as a regular trade book and as a Left Book Club selection, the latter with a preface by the publisher

March 13 Eileen Blair visits Orwell at the front

April 28 Gets leave at the end of April and applies for his discharge, intending to join the International Brigade

May 3–7 Fighting erupts in Barcelona between POUM and Republican forces, the latter under Communist control. Orwell helps guard the POUM headquarters

May 10 Returns to the Aragon Front, having given up the idea of joining the International Brigade

May 20 Shot in the throat by sniper and taken to field hospital at Monflorite, then transferred to Siétamo

May 29 Recuperates in sanatorium at Mount Tibidabo, near Barcelona

June 15 Returns to the front to receive his medical discharge papers

June 16 POUM is outlawed by Spanish government, and its members are arrested and tortured

June 20 Hides out in Barcelona while waiting for papers from British Consulate

June 23 Leaves Spain with wife, Eileen, passing over the border at Banyuls-sur-Mer on the French Mediterranean coast, where he and Eileen rest until their return to London

July Returns writing *Homage to Catalonia*

July 13 Eric and Eileen Blair are charged with "rabid Trotskyism" and being agents of POUM, in a deposition presented to the Tribunal for Espionage and High Treason, Valencia, Spain

July 29 Publishes Part I of "Spilling the Spanish Beans" in *New English Weekly*. Part II appears in September

July 31 Reviews *The Spanish Cockpit* by Franz Borkenau for *Time and Tide*

August Publishes "Eye-Witness in Barcelona" in *Controversy*

1938

January Completes final draft of *Homage to Catalonia*

February 5 Reviews *Spanish Testament* by Arthur Koestler for *Time and Tide*

March 8 Suffers a lung hemorrhage while living at Wallington

March 12–14 Anschluss: annexation of Austria by Germany

March 15 Hospitalized at Preston Hall Sanatorium in Aylesford, Kent

April 25 *Homage to Catalonia* is published by Secker & Warburg

June Joins the ILP

June 9 Reviews *Assignment in Utopia* by Eugene Lyons for *New English Weekly*

June 16 Reviews *The Freedom of the Streets* by Jack Common for *New English Weekly*

June 24 Publishes "Why I Joined the Independent Labour Party" in *New Leader*

September Begins work on new novel *Coming Up for Air*

September 1–2 Leaves Preston Hall Sanatorium to spend the winter in Morocco for health reasons

September 11 Orwells arrive in Morocco and arrange to lease a villa right outside of Marrakech

September 29 Munich Conference, in which Britain and France agree to Germany's annexation of the Sudetenland in exchange for a promise of peace. British prime minister Neville Chamberlain returns, proclaiming the achievement of "peace in our time"

1939

January 29 Fall of Barcelona to General Franco's troops

March 28 Madrid surrenders to General Franco, ending the Spanish civil war

March 30 Blair returns to England and delivers manuscript of *Coming Up for Air* to Victor Gollancz before traveling to visit his ailing father in Southwold

June 12 *Coming Up for Air* is published by Victor Gollancz

June 28 Death of Richard Walmesley Blair

August 23 Non-aggression Pact (Nazi-Soviet Pact) signed by Germany and Russia

August 24 Dreams war has broken out. Abandons pacifist position

September 1–3 German army invades Poland. Britain and France declare war on Germany

September Eileen moves in with her brother's wife at Crooms Hill, Greenwich, to be closer to the Ministry of Information's Censorship Department, where she has secured a position. She visits Wallington on weekends

September 3 Resigns from the ILP over its opposition to the war with Germany

December Completes *Inside the Whale*

December Essay "Marrakech" published in *New Writing*

1940

February Essay "The Lessons of War" published in *Horizon*

March Essay "Boys' Weeklies" published in *Horizon*

March 11 Victor Gollancz publishes *Inside the Whale*, a collection of essays

March 21 Reviews *Mein Kampf* by Adolf Hitler for *New English Weekly*

April 6 Essay "Notes on the Way" published in *Time and Tide*

April 17 Writes "Autobiographical Note" for *Twentieth Century Authors*, published in New York, 1942

May Moves from Wallington to London, 18 Dorset Chambers, Chagford Street, near Regent's Park.

May 4 Reviews *The Totalitarian Enemy* by Franz Borkenau for *Time and Tide*

May 29 Evacuation of Dunkirk

June 3 Eileen's brother Dr. Laurence O'Shaughnessy is killed tending to the wounded at Dunkirk

August 3 Reviews *The Devil's Disciple* by George Bernard Shaw for *Time and Tide*

August 17 Publishes the essay "Charles Reade" in *New Statesman*

August 20 Leon Trotsky is assassinated

August–October Battle of Britain

September Essay "My Country Right or Left" published in *Folios of New Writing*

December Essay "The Ruling Class" published in *Horizon*

December 19 A transcript of the BBC Home Service's broadcast of "The Proletarian Writer," a dialogue between Desmond Hawkins and Orwell, is published in the *Listener*

December 21 Favorably reviews film *The Great Dictator* by Charlie Chaplin for *Time and Tide*

1941

February 19 Publication of booklet *The Lion and the Unicorn,* first in a series called "Searchlight Books," edited by Orwell and T. R. Fyvel

March First of 15 "London Letters" published in the American journal *Partisan Review*

March 3 Publication of Victor Gollancz's *The Betrayal of the Left,* containing reprints of two of Orwell's essays

April Orwells move to a flat at 111 Langford Court, Abbey Road, St. John's Wood

May BBC talk "Tolstoy and Shakespeare," later reprinted in *The Listener*

May BBC talk "The Meaning of a Poem," later reprinted in *The Listener*

May 23 Delivers lecture at the Oxford University English Club titled "Literature and Totalitarianism," reprinted in the *Listener*

June 22 Hitler launches a surprise attack against the Soviet Union (which then enters the war on the side of the Allies)

August Essay "Wells, Hitler, and the World State" published in *Horizon*

August 17 Accepts a position at BBC in the Indian Section of the Eastern Service, broadcasting to India and Southeast Asia

October Publishes "Why Not War Writers? A Manifesto" in *Horizon*

December 20–March 1943 BBC Eastern Service broadcasts 200 newsletters on the war written by Orwell

1942

February Essay "The Art of Donald McGill" published in *Horizon*

February Essay "Rudyard Kipling" published in *Horizon*

March BBC talk "The Rediscovery of Europe" published in *The Listener*

March 8 First of seven anonymous columns, titled "Mood of the Moment," is published in the *Observer.* The first and last columns are identified by David Astor as the work of Orwell

March 10 BBC talk titled "The Rediscovery of Europe" is published in the *Listener*

April Eileen Blair starts a new job at the Ministry of Food

May 10 Reviews *The Wound and the Bow* by Edmund Wilson for the *Observer*

Summer Orwells move to 10a Mortimer Crescent, Maida Vale

July Reviews *The Sword and the Sickle* by Mulk Raj Anand for *Horizon*

August 11 First "Voice" program, a poetry magazine for BBC Eastern Services

October 9 Presents first part of "Story by Five Authors" on BBC Eastern Service

November 2 Broadcasts "Jonathan Swift, an Imaginary Interview"

1943

January Essay "W. B. Yeats" published in *Horizon*

January 8 BBC talk "Edmund Blunden"

January 9 Essay "Pamphlet Literature" published in *New Statesman*

January 22 BBC talk "Bernard Shaw"

March "Looking Back on the Spanish Civil War" published in *New Road*

March 5 BBC talk "Jack London"

March 19 Mother, Ida Mabel Blair, dies

April 2 Publishes "Not Enough Money: A Sketch of George Gissing" in *Tribune*

May 9 Publishes "Three Years of the Home Guard: A Unique Symbol of Stability" in the *Observer*

June 4 Publishes the essay "Literature and the Left" in *Tribune*

June 13 BBC talk "English Poetry since 1900"

June 18 Publishes satiric verse "As One Non-Combatant to Another: A Letter to 'Obiadiah Hornbrooke'" in *Tribune*

September Review of *Gandhi in Mayfair* in *Horizon*

September 9 Radio adaptation of "The Fox" by Ignazio Silone

September 24 Submits letter of resignation to BBC, which takes effect on November 24, 1943

October 6 BBC adaptation of "A Slip under the Microscope" by H. G. Wells

October 17 BBC talk on *Macbeth*

November Begins work on a new book, "a kind of parable," in which animals take over a farm

November 18 *Talking to India,* edited and with an introduction by Orwell, is published

November 18 BBC adaptation by Orwell of "The Emperor's New Clothes" by Hans Christian Andersen

November 23 Resigns from the Home Guard

November 24 Leaves the BBC to become literary editor and columnist for *Tribune*

November 26 Essay "Mark Twain—the Licensed Jester" published in *Tribune*

November 28–December 1 Teheran Conference. Meeting of the leaders of the United States, Great Britain, and the Soviet Union to discuss the conduct of the war and postwar problems. Satirized by Orwell in the conclusion of *Animal Farm*

December Begins submitting regular reviews for the *Observer*

December 3 Publishes his first "As I Please" column in *Tribune*. The column runs regularly from February 1945 to August 1946 and again in April 1947

December 24 Publishes the essay "Can Socialists Be Happy?" in *Tribune*, using the pseudonym John Freeman

1944

January 21 Publishes poem "Memories of the Blitz" in *Tribune*

April 4 *Animal Farm* is rejected by Victor Gollancz

May Finishes the manuscript of *The English People*

June The Orwells adopt a baby boy, Richard Horatio Blair, born May 14

June 19 The publisher Jonathan Cape rejects the manuscript of *Animal Farm*

June 28 Sends manuscript of *Animal Farm* to T. S. Eliot at Faber and Faber

June 28 Orwells' flat destroyed at 10a Mortimer Crescent

July 13 T. S. Eliot at Faber and Faber rejects *Animal Farm* while praising its style

August 29 Fredric Warburg decides to publish *Animal Farm* when paper, rationed during the war, is made available

September Orwell makes his first visit to Jura

September 3 Publishes the essay "Back to the Land" in the *Observer*

September 22 Publishes "Tobias Smollett: Scotland's Best Novelist" in *Tribune*

October The Orwells move to a new flat at 27b Canonbury Square, Islington

October Publishes "Raffles and Miss Blandish" in *Horizon*

October 15 Publishes "Home Guard: Lessons for the Future" in the *Observer*

December 22 Publishes "Oysters and Brown Stout" in *Tribune*

1945

January 14 Reviews *The Unquiet Grave* by Cyril Connolly for the *Observer*

February Resigns his position as literary editor for *Tribune*. Succeeded by T. R. Fyvel

March Serves as war correspondent for the *Observer* and the *Manchester Evening News* in Germany, France, and Austria

March Hospitalized, with lung disease while in Cologne, Germany

March "Poetry and the Microphone" published in *New Saxon Pamphlet*

March 29 Eileen Blair dies in hospital while under anesthesia in preparation for a hysterectomy

March 30 News of Eileen's death reaches Orwell in Cologne, Germany, and he leaves immediately for England

April "Antisemitism in Britain" published in *Contemporary Jewish Record*

April 8 Returns to the continent as a war correspondent

April 8 Publishes the article "The Future of a Ruined Germany" in the *Observer*

April 12 Death of Franklin Delano Roosevelt

April 30 Suicide of Adolf Hitler

May 4 Publishes the article "Now Germany Faces Hunger" in the *Manchester Evening News*

May 8 VE Day; World War II in Europe ends

May 24 Returns to London

May 27 Publishes the article "Obstacles to Joint Rule in Germany" in the *Observer*

June–July In "London Letter" in *Partisan Review* predicts a Conservative victory by a "small minority" in upcoming general election

July "In Defence of P. G. Wodehouse" published in *Windmill*

July 3 Writes to Leonard Moore that he has started a new novel

July 3 Contracts to write four essays for *Polemic*

July 26 British Labour Party wins landslide victory in general election. Clement Atlee replaces Churchill as prime minister

August Agrees to serve as vice chairman of the Freedom Defence Committee

August 6 United States drops atomic bomb on Hiroshima, Japan

August 9 United States drops atomic bomb on Nagasaki, Japan

August 14 Japan announces cease-fire with the United States to end World War II

August 17 *Animal Farm* is published by Secker & Warburg

September 10 Visits the island of Jura in the Scottish Hebrides for two weeks

October "Notes on Nationalism" for *Polemic*

October 8 BBC talk "Jack London"

October 14 Principal author of "Profile of Aneurin Bevan" in the *Observer*

October 19 "You and the Atom Bomb" published in *Tribune*

November "Catastrophic Gradualism" published in *Common Wealth Review*

November 2 "Good Bad Books" published in *Tribune*

November 9 "Revenge Is Sour" published in *Tribune*

December 7 "Freedom of the Park" published in *Tribune*

December 14 "The Sporting Spirit" published in *Tribune*

December 15 "In Defence of English Cooking" published in *Evening Standard*

December 21 "Nonsense Poetry" published in *Tribune*

December 25 Orwell and son Richard enjoy Christmas visit with Arthur Koestler at Koestler's home in North Wales. There he meets and proposes marriage to Celia Kirwan, Koestler's sister-in-law. She turns him down but the two remain friends

1946

January "The Prevention of Literature" published in *Polemic*

January 4 "Freedom v. Happiness" published in *Tribune*

January 12 "A Nice Cup of Tea" published in *Evening Standard*

January 18 "The Politics of Starvation" published in *Tribune*

January 19 "Songs We Used to Sing" published in *Evening Standard*

January 31 "What Is Socialism?" published in the *Manchester Evening News*

February Suffers another lung hemorrhage while at Canonbury Square in mid-February. Refuses to notify a doctor and spends two weeks in bed

February 8 "Books versus Cigarettes" published in *Tribune*

February 9 "The Moon under Water" published in *Evening Standard*

February 14 "Pacifism and Progress" published in the *Manchester Evening News*

February 14 Publication of Orwell's *Critical Essays*, published later in the United States as *Dickens, Dali, and Others*. In the English edition, essay on Dali called "Benefit of Clergy" is cut out, although listed in the table of contents

February 15 "Decline of the English Murder" published in *Tribune*

March Writes pamphlet "British Cookery" for the British Council, which remains unpublished until 2000

March 22 Publishes the essay "In Front of Your Nose" in *Tribune*

March 29 Talk on "The Voyage of the *Beagle*" for BBC's Third Programme

April "Politics and the English Language" published in *Horizon*

April 12 "Some Thoughts on the Common Toad" published in *Tribune*

April 26 "A Good Word for the Vicar of Bray" published in *Tribune*

April 29 Reynal & Hitchcock of New York publish the U.S. edition of *Critical Essays* under the title *Dickens, Dali, and Others*

May Publishes the essay "James Burnham and the Managerial Revolution" in *Polemic*

May 3 Marjorie Dakin, née Blair, Orwell's older sister, dies

May 3 "Confessions of a Book Reviewer" published in *Tribune*

May 4 Sends a copy of *Life of Stalin* by Leon Trotsky to Fredric Warburg; travels to Nottingham to attend his sister's funeral

May 23 Arrives at Barnhill, the house he has rented on Jura in Scotland

May 31 Avril Blair, Orwell's younger sister, arrives on Jura to serve as housekeeper

June "Why I Write" published in *Gangrel*

July 9 Adaptation of *Little Red Riding Hood* for BBC Children's Hour

August Begins *Nineteen Eighty-Four* with the working title of "The Last Man in Europe"

August 26 Harcourt Brace in New York publishes the U.S. edition of *Animal Farm*

September "Politics versus Literature: An Examination of *Gulliver's Travels*" published in *Polemic*

October 13 Returns to London residence at Canonbery Square, Islington

November "How the Poor Die" published in *Now*

November Publication of Jack London's *Love of Life and Other Stories,* with an introduction by Orwell

November 8 Resumes his column "As I Please" in *Tribune* after a nearly two-year hiatus

November 22 "Riding Down from Bangor" published in *Tribune*

1947

January "Arthur Koestler" published in *Focus*

January 14 Adapts *Animal Farm* for a radio broadcast by BBC's Third Programme

March "Lear, Tolstoy and the Fool" published in *Polemic*

March 29 "Burnham's View of the Contemporary World Struggle" published in New York's *New Leader*

April Victor Gollancz agrees to release Orwell from his publishing contract

April 4 Publishes his final "As I Please" column in *Tribune*

April 11 Returns to Jura with sister Avril and son Richard, where he remains until December 20, 1947

May 31 Writes to Fredric Warburg that he has completed a third of the manuscript of *Nineteen Eighty-Four*

July Richard Rees arrives on Jura for a two-month visit

July–August "Toward European Unity" published in *Partisan Review*

August Publication of *The English People*

August 15 India and Pakistan become independent

August 17 While in a boat off the coast of Jura, Orwell, his son, his niece, and his nephew almost drown when their small boat is caught in a whirlpool

September–October Health declines during September and October

October Edits *Coming Up for Air,* the first volume in Secker & Warburg's uniform edition of his works, Glasgow

November 7 Completes first draft of *Nineteen Eighty-Four*

December Diagnosed with tuberculosis

December 24 Begins a seven-month cycle of treatment (December 1947 to July 1948) with streptomycin at Hairmyres Hospital in East Kilbride, Glasgow. Treatment provides only temporary improvement

1948

January 4 Burma is declared an independent republic

January 30 Assassination of Gandhi

February 1 Seeks David Astor's assistance in obtaining streptomycin for his tuberculosis

May 9 Reviews *The Soul of Man under Socialism* by Oscar Wilde for the *Observer*

May 13 Publication of first volume of Secker & Warburg's uniform edition of Orwell's works, *Coming Up for Air*

June 19 "Writers and Leviathan" published in New York's *New Leader*

July 17 "The Sanctified Sinner," an unfavorable review of *The Heart of the Matter* by Graham Greene, published in the *New Yorker*

July 28 Discharged from hospital and returns to Jura

September Suffers relapse of tuberculosis and is again bedridden

October "Britain's Struggle for Survival" published in *Commentary*

October "The Labour Government after Three Years" in *Commentary*

November 7 Reviews unfavorably *Portrait of an Antisemite* by Jean-Paul Sartre for the *Observer*

November 15 First volume of *British Pamphleteers* is published, with introduction by Orwell

December 4 Completes final draft of *Nineteen Eighty-Four* and sends copies to Leonard Moore and Fredric Warburg. Suffers severe relapse

1949

January Publishes "Reflections on Gandhi" for *Partisan Review*. Chooses *Nineteen Eighty-Four* as the title of new novel

January 2 Leaves Jura for Cotswold Sanatorium, Cranham, Gloucestershire

February 9 Receives a letter from first love, Jacintha Buddicom, and writes a warm response

March Reads proofs of *Nineteen Eighty-Four*

March 17 Writes to Leonard Moore that he refuses to make any alterations to *Nineteen Eighty-Four* for the American Book of the Month Club edition

April 10 "Conrad's Place and Rank in English Letters" published in the Polish literary journal *Wiadomości*

May "The Question of the Pound Award" published in *Partisan Review*

May 14 Reviews *Their Finest Hour* by Winston Churchill for New York's *New Leader*

May 18 Receives a letter from Jacintha Buddicom; writes to Jacintha Buddicom "I've been most horribly ill and am not very grand now"

June 8 *Nineteen Eighty-Four* published by Secker & Warburg

June 13 Harcourt Brace in New York publishes the American edition of *Nineteen Eighty-Four*

June 15 Fredric Warburg visits Orwell at Cotswold. Takes notes on Orwell's reply to those who think the novel is an attack on English socialism

July *Nineteen Eighty-Four* is selected by the American Book of the Month Club

July Sonia Brownell accepts Orwell's proposal of marriage

August Prepares a new collection of essays to be titled *Shooting an Elephant*

September Revelation that the Soviet Union had successfully tested an atomic bomb

September 3 Transferred from Cotswold Sanatorium to University College Hospital in London

October 13 Marries Sonia Brownell in a ceremony at University College Hospital, with David Astor serving as best man and Sonia's friend Janetta Key as bridesmaid

1950

Secker & Warburg publishes a collection of Orwell's essays under the title *Shooting an Elephant*

January Plans a trip to a Swiss sanatorium and prepares to leave on January 25, 1950

January 18 Names Sonia and Richard Rees as literary executors and stipulates that no biography be written of him

January 21 Orwell dies at University College Hospital in London from a hemorrhaged lung resulting from tuberculosis

January 26 In accordance with his last wish that he be buried with the rites of the Anglican Church, a funeral service is held at Christ Church, Albany Street, London. He is buried in the parish churchyard of All Saints, Sutton Courtenay, Oxfordshire. The name on the tombstone reads simply "Eric Arthur Blair"

Sources

Bowker, Gordon. *Inside George Orwell.* New York: Palgrave, 2003.

Davison, Peter. *George Orwell: A Literary Life*. New York: St. Martin's Press, 1996.

Hammond, J. R. *A George Orwell Chronology*. Houndmills, Basingstoke, Hampshire, England: Palgrave Macmillan, 2000.

Palmowski, Jan. *A Dictionary of Twentieth Century World History*. Oxford: Oxford University Press, 1997.

A Newspeak Glossary

Newspeak is the official language of the totalitarian state Oceania in Orwell's *Nineteen Eighty-Four*.

Note: The term doublespeak does not appear in *Nineteen Eighty-Four.*

Bellyfeel—Intuitive absorption of party doctrine.

Blackwhite—"The ability to assert that black is white, when required by party discipline."

Crimestop—"The ability to abort any thought that might be dissident."

Crimethink—Synonym of Thoughtcrime.

Doublepus—Superlative prefix.

Doublethink—"The power of holding two contradictory beliefs in one's mind and accepting both of them."

Duckspeak—To spray forth correct opinions without thinking. Literally, to quack like a duck. A word with two opposing meanings. "Applied to an opponent it is abuse, applied to someone you agree with, it is praise."

Ficdep—The fiction department of the ministry of truth; where Julia works as a mechanic maintaining the fiction writing machine.

-ful—Suffix indicating an adjective.

Goodsex—Intercourse between a man and wife solely to beget children and without physical pleasure for the woman.

Goodthink—As a noun, orthodoxy, as a verb, "to think in an orthodox manner."

Hate Week—An annual event in which the population undergoes a mass frenzy of hatred accompanied by displays of military might, tanks, planes and marching troops, banners, posters and seemingly endless speeches by members of the Inner Party.

Miniluv—The ministry of love, "which maintained law and order."

Minipax—The ministry of peace—"which was responsible for economic affairs."

Miniplenty—Ministry dealing with the economy

Minitrue—Ministry of truth "which concerned itself with news, entertainment, education and the fine arts."

Newspeak—Official language of Oceania.

Oldspeak—Standard English.

Oldthink—A word connoting wickedness or decadence.

Ownlife—The heresy of individualism, reflected, for example, in taking a walk alone.

Plus—Comparative prefix

Pornosec—A subsection of the fiction department (ficdep), devoted to providing "the lowest kinds of pornography for distribution to the proles. Pornosec is sent out in sealed packages, which no party member . . . was permitted to look at." All the workers in Pornosec are women.

Prolefeed—Lowest forms of popular entertainment, books, films and music, designed to distract the proles.

Recdep—The records department in the Ministry of Truth (where Winston works).

Sexcrime—Any sexual activity engaged in for pleasure.

Speakwrite—A mechanism that types the spoken messages it receives.

Thinkpol—Thought police.

Thoughtcrime—"The essential crime that contained all the others in itself."

versificator—A machine that automatically produces popular songs for the prole public.

-wise—Suffix indicating an adverb.

Bibliography of Orwell's Works

(Works are listed in chronological order by date of publication.)

Down and Out in Paris and London. London: Victor Gollancz, 1933. Reprint, New York: Harper and Brothers, 1933.

Burmese Days. New York: Harper and Brothers, 1934. Reprint, London: Victor Gollancz, 1935.

A Clergyman's Daughter. London: Victor Gollancz, 1935. Reprint, New York: Harper and Brothers, 1936.

Keep the Aspidistra Flying. London: Victor Gollancz, 1936. Reprint, New York: Harcourt, Brace, 1955.

The Road to Wigan Pier. London: Victor Gollancz, 1937. Reprint, New York: Harcourt, Brace, 1958.

Homage to Catalonia. London: Secker & Warburg, 1938. Reprint, New York: Harcourt, Brace, 1950.

Coming Up for Air. London: Victor Gollancz. 1939. Reprint, New York: Harcourt, Brace, 1950.

Inside the Whale and Other Essays. London: Victor Gollancz, 1940.

The Lion and the Unicorn. London: Secker & Warburg, 1941.

Animal Farm. London: Secker & Warburg, 1945. Reprint, New York: Harcourt, Brace, 1945. (Selection of Book of the Month Club; 540,000 copies.)

Critical Essays. London: Secker & Warburg, 1946. (American title: *Dickens, Dali and Others.* New York: Reynal & Hitchcock, 1946).

The English People (one of the series *Britain in Pictures*). London: Collins, 1947.

Nineteen Eighty-Four. London: Secker & Warburg, 1949. Reprint, New York: Harcourt, Brace, 1949. (Selection of the Book of the Month Club, 190,000 copies.)

Collected Essays, Journalism and Letters. 4 vols. Edited by Sonia Orwell and Ian Angus. New York: Harcourt, Brace, 1968; London: Secker & Warburg, 1969.

The Complete Works of George Orwell. 20 vols. Edited by Peter Davison. London: Secker & Warburg, 1998.

The Lost Orwell. Edited by Peter Davison. London: Timewell Press, 2006.

Bibliography of Secondary Sources

Biographies, Memoirs, Reminiscences

Collections of Essays

Coppard, Audrey, and Bernard Crick, eds. *Orwell Remembered.* New York: Facts On File, 1984.

Gross, Miriam, ed. *The World of George Orwell.* London: Weidenfeld & Nicholson, 1971.

Wadhams, Stephen, ed. *Remembering Orwell.* New York: Penguin, 1984.

Individual Studies

Averill, Roger. "Empathy, Externality, and Character in Biography: A Consideration of the Authorized Versions of George Orwell," *CLIO* 31, no. 1 (Fall 2001): 1–31.

Bowker, Gordon. *Inside George Orwell.* New York: Palgrave Macmillan, 2003.

Buddicom, Jacintha. *Eric & Us.* Chichester, England: Finlay, 2006.

Common, Jack. "Recollections." In *Orwell Remembered,* edited by Audrey Coppard and Bernard Crick, 139–143. New York: Facts On File, 1984.

Connolly, Cyril. *Enemies of Promise.* London: Routledge and Kegan Paul, 1938.

Cooper, Lettice. "Eileen Blair." In *Orwell Remembered,* edited by Audrey Coppard and Bernard Crick, 161–166. New York: Facts On File, 1984.

Crick, Bernard. *George Orwell: A Life.* Boston: Little, Brown, 1980.

Davison, Peter. *George Orwell: A Literary Life.* New York: St. Martin's Press, 1996.

———, ed. *The Lost Orwell.* London: Timewell Press, 2006.

Dunn, Avril. "My Brother, George Orwell," *Twentieth Century* 169 (March 1961): 255–261.

Fen, Elisaveta. [Lydia Jackson] "George Orwell's First Wife." *Twentieth Century* 167 (August 1960): 115–126.

———. *A Russian's Life in England.* Warwick: Paul Gordon, 1976.

Fyvel, T. R. "George Orwell and Eric Blair: Glimpses of a Dual Life," *Encounter* 13 (July 1959): 60–65.

———. *George Orwell: A Personal Memoir.* New York: Macmillan, 1982.

Heppenstall, Rayner. *Four Absentees.* London: Barrie and Rockliff, 1960.

Hollis, Christopher. "On Orwell at Eton." In *Orwell Remembered,* edited by Audrey Coppard and Bernard Crick, 37–50. New York: Facts On File, 1984.

Kazin, Alfred. "Not One of Us." *New York Review of Books,* June 14, 2004, 13–18.

Koestler, Arthur. "On His Friend." In *Orwell Remembered,* edited by Audrey Coppard and Bernard Crick, 167–170. New York: Facts On File, 1984.

Kopp, Georges. "Bullet in the Neck." In *Orwell Remembered,* edited by Audrey Coppard and Bernard Crick, 158–161. New York: Facts On File, 1984.

Lewis, Peter. *George Orwell: The Road to* 1984. New York: Harcourt Brace, 1981.

Lucas, Scott. *Orwell.* London: Haus Publishing, 2003.

Meyers, Jeffrey. *Orwell: Wintry Conscience of a Generation.* New York: W. W. Norton, 2000.

Muggeridge, Malcolm. "A Knight of the Woeful Countenance." In Nineteen Eighty-Four *to 1984,* edited by C. J. Kuppig, 271–287. New York: Carroll & Graf, 1984.

Potts, Paul. "Quixote on a Bicycle." In *Orwell Remembered,* edited by Audrey Coppard and Bernard Crick, 248–260. New York: Facts On File, 1984.

Powell, Anthony. "George Orwell: A Memoir." *The Atlantic,* October 1967, 62–68.

Pritchett, V. S. "The *New Statesman & Nation*'s Obituary." In *Orwell Remembered,* edited by Audrey Coppard and Bernard Crick, 275–277. New York: Facts On File, 1984.

Rees, Sir Richard. *George Orwell: Fugitive from the Camp of Victory.* Carbondale: Southern Illinois University Press, 1961.

Rose, Jonathan. "Eric Blair's School Days." In *The Revised Orwell,* edited by Jonathan Rose, 75–95. East Lansing: Michigan State University Press, 1992.

Laskowski Jr., William E. "George Orwell and the Tory-Radical Tradition" In *The Revised Orwell,* edited by Jonathan Rose, 149–190. East Lansing: Michigan State University Press, 1992.

Salkeld, Brenda. "He Didn't Really Like Women." In *Orwell Remembered,* edited by Audrey Coppard and Bernard Crick, 67–68. New York: Facts On File, 1984.

Shelden, Michael. *Orwell: The Authorized Biography.* New York: Harper Perennial, 1992.

Spurling, Hilary. *The Girl from the Fiction Department.* London: Hamish Hamilton, 2002.

Stansky, Peter and William Abrahams. *The Unknown Orwell.* New York: Knopf, 1972.

———. *Orwell: The Transformation.* New York: Knopf, 1980.

Symons, Julian. "Orwell, a Reminiscence." *London Magazine 3* (September 1963): 33–49.

———. "*Tribune*'s Obituary." In *Orwell Remembered,* edited by Audrey Coppard and Bernard Crick, 271–275. New York: Facts On File, 1984.

Taylor, D. J. *Orwell: The Life.* New York: Henry Holt & Co., 2003.

Thompson, John. *Orwell's London.* New York: Schocken, 1984.

Venables, Dione. Postcript to *Eric & Us* by Jacintha Buddicom. Chichester, England: Finlay, 2006.

Warburg, Fredric. *All Authors Are Equal.* New York: St. Martin's Press, 1973.

———. An *Occupation for Gentleman.* Boston: Houghton, Mifflin, 1960.

General Critical Studies

Collections of Essays

Bloom, Harold, ed. *George Orwell.* Bloom's Modern Critical Views. New York: Chelsea House, 1987.

———, ed. *George Orwell.* Updated Edition. Bloom's Modern Critical Interpretations. New York, Chelsea House, 2007.

Buitenhuis, Peter and Ira B. Nadel, eds. *George Orwell: A Reassessment.* New York: St. Martin's Press, 1988.

Cushman, Thomas and John Rodden, eds. *George Orwell: Into the Twenty-First Century.* Boulder, Colo.: Paradigm Publishers, 2004.

Holderness, Graham, Bryan Loughrey, and Nahem Yousaf, eds. *George Orwell.* New York: St. Martin's Press, 1998.

Hynes, Samuel, ed. *20th Century Interpretations of George Orwell.* Englewood Cliffs, N.J.: Prentice-Hall, 1971.

Jensen, Ejner, ed. *The Future of 1984.* Ann Arbor: University of Michigan Press, 1984.

Kuppig, C. J., ed. *Nineteen Eighty-Four to 1984.* New York: Carroll & Graf, 1984.

Lazaro, Alberto, ed. *The Road from George Orwell: His Achievement and Legacy.* Bern, Switzerland: Peter Lang, 2001.

Meyers, Jeffrey, ed. *George Orwell: The Critical Heritage.* London; New York: Routledge, 1975.

Norris, Christopher, ed. *Inside the Myth: Orwell, Views from the Left.* London: Lawrence and Wishart, 1984.

Oldsey, Bernard, and Joseph Browne, eds. *Critical Essays on George Orwell.* Boston: G. K. Hall, 1986.

Richardson, J. M., ed. *Orwell x 8: A Symposium.* Winnipeg, Manitoba: Frye, 1986.

Rodden, John, ed. *The Cambridge Companion to George Orwell.* Cambridge: Cambridge University Press, 2007.

Rose, Jonathan, ed. *The Revised Orwell.* East Lansing: Michigan State University Press, 1992.

Savage, Robert, et al. eds. *The Orwellian Moment.* Fayetteville: University of Arkansas Press, 1989.

Wemyss, Courtney, and Alexej Ugrinsky, eds. *George Orwell.* Westport, Conn.: Greenwood Press, 1987.

Williams, Keith, and Steven Matthews, eds. *Rewriting the Thirties: Modernism and After.* London: Longman, 1997.

Williams, Raymond, ed. *George Orwell: A Collection of Critical Essays.* Englewood Cliffs, N.J.: Prentice-Hall, 1974.

Individual Studies

Alldritt, Keith. *The Making of George Orwell: An Essay in Literary History.* New York: St. Martin's Press, 1961.

Atkins, John. *George Orwell: A Literary Study.* London: Calder and Boyars, 1954.

Auden, W. H. "George Orwell." *Spectator,* January 16, 1971, 86–87.

Beadle, Gordon. "George Orwell and the Death of God," *Colorado Quarterly* 23 (1974).

Berman, Ronald. *Modernity and Progress: Fitzgerald, Hemingway, Orwell.* Tuscaloosa: University of Alabama Press, 2005.

Bhat, Yashoda. *Aldous Huxley and George Orwell: A Comparative Study of Satire in Their Novels.* New Delhi: Sterling Publishers; New York: Distributed by Apt Books, 1991.

Birrell, T. A. "Is Integrity Enough? A Study of George Orwell," *Dublin Review* 224 (Autumn 1950): 49–65.

Bluemel, Kristin. *George Orwell and the Radical Eccentrics: Intermodernism in Literary London.* New York: Palgrave Macmillan, 2004.

Brander, Laurence. *George Orwell.* London: Longmans, 1954.

Brannigan, John. *Orwell to the Present: Literature in England, 1945–2000.* Houndmills, Basingstoke, Hampshire; New York: Palgrave Macmillan, 2003.

Breton, Rob. *Gospels and Grit: Work and Labour in Carlyle, Conrad and Orwell.* Toronto, Ontario; Buffalo, N.Y.: University of Toronto Press, 2005.

———. "Crisis? Whose Crisis? George Orwell and Liberal Guilt," *College Literature* 29, no. 4 (Fall 2002): 47–66.

Broderick, John. *George Orwell and 'Nineteen Eighty-Four.'* Washington, D.C: Library of Congress, 1985.

Brunsdale, Mitzi. *Student Companion to George Orwell.* Westport, Conn.: Greenwood Press, 2000.

Caine, William E. "Orwell's Perversity: An Approach to the Collected Essays." In *George Orwell: Into the Twenty-First Century,* edited by Thomas Cushman and John Rodden, 215–228. Boulder, Colo.: Paradigm Publishers, 2004.

Calder, Jenni. *Chronicles of Conscience: A Study of George Orwell and Arthur Koestler.* London: Secker & Warburg, 1968.

Carter, Michael. *George Orwell and the Problem of Authentic Existence.* Totowa, New Jersey: Barnes & Noble, 1985.

Carter, Steven. "The Rites of Memory: Orwell, Pynchon, DeLillo, and the American Millennium," *Prospero* 6 (1999): 5–21.

Coles, Robert. "George Orwell's Sensibility." In *Reflections on America, 1984,* edited by Robert Mulhivill, 46–57. Athens: University of Georgia Press, 1986.

Comfort, Alex. "1939 and 1984: George Orwell and the Vision of Judgement." In *On* Nineteen Eighty-Four, edited by Peter Stansky, New York: W. H. Freeman, 1983.

Connelly, Mark. *Orwell and Gissing.* New York: Peter Land, 1997.

Crick, Bernard. "Orwell and English Socialiam." In *George Orwell: A Reassessment,* edited by Peter Buitenhuis and Ira B. Nadel, 3–19. New York: St. Martin's Press, 1988.

De Lange, Adriaan M. *The Influence of Political Bias in Selected Essays of George Orwell.* Lewiston, N.Y.: Edwin Mellen Press, 1992.

Donoghue, Denis. "Plain English," *London Review of Books,* 6, no. 24 (December 20, 1984–January 24, 1985): 7–8.

Eagleton, Terry. "George Orwell and the Lower Middle-Class Novel." In *Exiles and Emigrés: Studies in Modern Literature,* 78–108. London: Chatto and Windus, 1970.

Eckstein, Arthur M. "George Orwell's Second Thoughts on Capitalism." In *The Revised Orwell,* edited by Jonathan Rose, 191–204. East Lansing: Michigan State University Press, 1992.

Engholm, G. F. "Orwell's Socialism." In *Orwell x 8: A Symposium,* edited by J. M. Richardson, 1–16. Winnipeg, Manitoba: Frye, 1986.

Fotheringham, John. "George Orwell and Ernst Toller: The Dilemma of the Politically Committed Writer," *Neophilologus* 84, no. 1 (January 2000): 1–18.

Fowler, Roger. *The Language of George Orwell.* New York: St. Martin's Press, 1995.

Fussell, Paul. *Thank God for the Atom Bomb.* New York: Summit Books, 1988.

Futhey, J. F. "For the Love of Language: Orwell and Swift." In *Orwell x 8: A Symposium,* edited by J. M. Richardson, 27–36. Winnipeg, Manitoba: Frye, 1986.

Gardner, Averil. *George Orwell.* Boston: Twayne, 1987.

Gitlin, Todd. "Varieties of Patriotic Experience." In *George Orwell: Into the Twenty-First Century,* edited by Thomas Cushman and John Rodden, 126–144. Boulder, Colo.: Paradigm Publishers, 2004.

Glicksberg, Charles I. *The Literature of Commitment.* Lewisburg, Pa.: Bucknell University Press, 1976.

Good, Graham. "Orwell and Eliot: Politics, Poetry, and Prose." In *George Orwell: A Reassessment,* edited by Peter Buitenhuis and Ira B. Nadel, New York: St. Martin's Press, 1988.

Goodheart, Eugene. "Orwell and the Bad Writing Controversy," *CLIO* 28, no. 4 (Summer 1999): 439–443.

Greenblatt, Stephen. *Three Modern Satirists: Waugh, Orwell and Huxley.* New Haven, Conn.: Yale University Press, 1965.

Hammond, J. R. *A George Orwell Companion.* New York: St. Martin's Press, 1982.

———. *A George Orwell Chronology.* Houndshire, Basingstoke, England: Palgrave Macmillan, 2000.

Heppenstall, Geoffrey. "Orwell and Bohemia," *Contemporary Review* 264, no. 1539 (April 1994): 211–214.

Hitchens, Christopher. *Why Orwell Matters.* New York: Basic Books, 2002.

Hopkinson, Tom. *George Orwell.* London: Longmans, 1956.

Howe, Irving. *Politics and the Novel,* 235–251. New York: Horizon Press, 1957.

———. *Decline of the New.* New York: Horizon Press, 1970.

Hunter, Lynette. *George Orwell: The Search for a Voice.* Milton Keynes, England: Open University Press, 1984.

———. "Blood and Marmalade: Negotiations between the State and the Domestic in George Orwell's Early Novels." In *Rewriting the Thirties: Modernism and After,* edited by Keith Williams and Steven Matthews, 202–216. London: Longman, 1997.

———. "Prescience and Resilience in George Orwell's Political Aesthetics." In *George Orwell: Into the Twenty-First Century,* edited by Thomas Cushman and John Rodden, 229–242. Boulder, Colo.: Paradigm Publishers, 2004.

Imber, Jonathan B. "Orwell in an Age of Celebrity." In *George Orwell: Into the Twenty-First Century,* edited by Thomas Cushman and John Rodden, 178–186. Boulder, Colo.: Paradigm Publishers, 2004.

Ingle, Stephen. *George Orwell: A Political Life.* Manchester: Manchester University Press, 1993.

Kalechofsky, Roberta. *George Orwell.* New York: Frederick Ungar, 1973.

Karl, Frederick R. *A Reader's Guide to the Contemporary English Novel.* New York: Farrar Straus & Cudahy, 1962, 148–166.

Katz, Wendy. "Imperialism and Patriotism: Orwell's Dilemma in 1940," *Modernist Studies: Literature and Culture* 3 (1979): 99–105.

Kenner, Hugh. "The Politics of the Plain Style." In *Reflections on America, 1984,* edited by Robert Mulvihill, 58–65. Athens: University of Georgia Press, 1986.

Kerr, Douglas. "Colonial Habits: Orwell and Woolf in the Jungle," *English Studies* 78, no. 12 (March 1997): 149–161.

———. *George Orwell.* Tavistock, Devon, England: Northcote House in association with the British Council, 2003.

———. "In the Picture: Orwell, India and the BBC," *Literature and History.* 13, no. 1 (Spring 2004): 43–57.

Kingsbury, Melinda Spencer. "Orwell's Ideology of Style: From 'Politics and the English Language' to *1984,*" *Journal of Kentucky Studies* 19 (September 2002): 108–113.

Klawitter, Uwe. *The Theme of Totalitarianism in "English" Fiction: Koestler, Orwell, Vonnegut, Kosinski, Burgess, Atwood, Amis.* Frankfurt am Main, Germany; New York: Peter Lang, 1997.

Kubal, David. *Outside the Whale: George Orwell's Art and Politics.* Notre Dame, Ind.: University of Notre Dame Press, 1972.

———. "Freud, Orwell, and the Bourgeois Interior." *Yale Review* 67, no. 3 (March 1978), 389–403.

Labedz, Leopold. "Will George Orwell Survive 1984? Of Doublethink and Doubletalk, Body-Snatching and Other Silly Pranks." *Encounter* 63 (July/August 1984).

Lazaro, Alberto. "George Orwell's *Homage to Catalonia*: A Politically Incorrect Story." In *The Road from George Orwell: His Achievement and Legacy,* edited by Alberto Lazaro, 71–92. Bern: Peter Lang, 2001.

Leavis, Q. D. "The Literary Life Respectable," *Scrutiny* (September 1940): 173–176.

Lee, Robert. *Orwell's Fiction.* Notre Dame, Ind.: University of Notre Dame Press, 1969.

Lief, Ruth. *Homage to Oceania: The Prophetic Vision of George Orwell.* Columbus: Ohio State University Press, 1969.

Lewis, Wyndham. *The Writer and the Absolute.* London: Methuen, 1952.

Lodge, David. *The Modes of Modern Writing.* Ithaca, N.Y.: Cornell University Press; London: Edward Arnold, 1977.

Lutman, Stephen. "Orwell's Patriotism." *Journal of Contemporary History* 2, no. 2 (1967): 149–158.

MacDonald, Dwight. "Varieties of Political Experience." *New Yorker,* March 28, 1959, 132–147.

Martin, J. D. "Indeed It Is 1984: Repression Today." In *Orwell x 8: A Symposium,* edited by J. M. Richardson, 59–66. Winnipeg, Manitoba: Frye, 1986.

McCarthy, Mary. "The Writing on the Wall." *New York Review of Books,* January 30, 1969, 3–6.

Menand, Louis. "Honest, Decent, Wrong: The Invention of George Orwell." *New Yorker,* January 29, 2003.

Meyers, Jeffrey. *A Reader's Guide to George Orwell.* Totowa, New Jersey: Littlefield Adams, 1977; London: Thames & Hudson, 1975.

———. "George Orwell and the Art of Writing," *Kenyon Review* 27, no. 4 (Fall 2005): 92–114.

Meyers, Jeffrey, and Valerie Meyers. *George Orwell: An Annotated Bibliography of Criticism.* New York: Garland, 1977.

Meyers, Valerie. *George Orwell.* New York: St. Martin's Press, 1991.

Miller, Henry. "The Art of Fiction," *Paris Review* (1962): 146–147.

Miller, T. B. "Little Sister: The Place of Poverty in Orwell's Fiction." In *Orwell x 8: A Symposium,* edited by J. M. Richardson, 17–26. Winnipeg, Manitoba: Frye, 1986.

Moya, Ana. "George Orwell's Exploration of Discourses of Power in *Burmese Days.*" In *The Road from George Orwell: His Achievement and Legacy,* edited by Alberto Lazaro, 93–104. Bern: Peter Lang, 2001.

New, M. "Orwell and Antisemitism: Toward 1984." *Modern Fiction* 21, no. 1 (1975).

Newsinger, John. *Orwell's Politics.* New York; London: St. Martin's Press, Macmillan Press, 1999.

Nock, D. A. "George Orwell: Sociologist Manque." In *Orwell x 8: Symposium,* edited by J. M. Richardson, 111. Winnipeg, Manitoba: Frye, 1986.

Orwell, Sonia, and Ian Angus, eds. *The Collected Essays, Journalism, and Letters of George Orwell.* London: Secker & Warburg, 1968.

Oxley, B. T. *George Orwell.* London: Evans Brothers, 1967.

Patai, Daphne. *The Orwell Mystique: A Study in Male Ideology.* Amherst: University of Massachusetts Press, 1984.

———. "Third Thoughts about Orwell?" In *George Orwell: Into the Twenty-First Century,* edited by Thomas Cushman and John Rodden, 200–214. Boulder, Colo.: Paradigm Publishers, 2004.

Plank, Robert. *George Orwell's Guide Through Hell: A Psychological Study of 1984.* San Bernardino, Calif.: Borgo Press, 1994.

Posner, Richard A. *Public Intellectuals: A Study of Decline.* Cambridge, Mass.: Harvard University Press, 2001.

Rai, Alok. *Orwell and the Politics of Despair.* Cambridge: Cambridge University Press, 1988.

Rees, Richard. *George Orwell: Fugitive from the Camp of Victory.* Carbondale: Southern Illinois University Press, 1962.

Reilly, Patrick. *George Orwell: The Age's Adversary.* New York: St. Martin's Press, 1986.

Resch, Robert Paul. "Utopia, Dystopia, and the Middle Class in George Orwell's *Nineteen Eighty-Four,*" *Boundary 2* 23, no. 1 (Spring 1997): 137–176.

Roazan, Paul. "Orwell, Freud and *1984,*" *Virginia Quarterly Review* 54 (1978): 675–695.

Robinson, J. M. "Complexity, Symmetry and Security." In *Orwell x 8: A Symposium,* edited by J. M. Richardson, 49–58. Winnipeg, Manitoba: Frye, 1986.

Rorty, Richard. *Contingency, Irony, and Solidarity.* Cambridge: Cambridge University Press, 1989.

Rosenbaum, Ron. "The Man Who Would Be Orwell," *New York Observer,* 23 (March 2002).

Rosenfeld, Aaron S. "The 'Scanty Plot': Orwell, Pynchon, and the Poetics of Paranoia," *Twentieth Century Literature: A Scholarly and Critical Journal* 50, no. 4 (Winter 2004): 337–367.

Rosenwald, Lawrence. "Orwell, Pacifism, Pacifists." In *George Orwell: Into the Twenty-First Century*, edited by Thomas Cushman and John Rodden, 111–125. Boulder, Colo.: Paradigm Publishers, 2004.

Rossi, John. "Orwell and Patriotism," *Contemporary Review* (August 1992): 95–98.

Sandison, Alan. *The Last Man in Europe: An Essay on George Orwell.* New York, N.Y.: Barnes & Noble, 1974.

Schmidt, Mark Ray. "Rebellion, Freedom, and Other Philosophical Issues in Orwell's *1984*," *Publications of the Arkansas Philological Association* 22, no. 1 (Spring 1996): 79–85.

Schweizer, Bernard. *Radicals on the Road: The Politics of English Travel Writing in the 1930s.* Charlottesville: University Press of Virginia, 2001.

Shlapentokh, Vladimir. "Russia's Tocqueville." In *George Orwell: Into the Twenty-First Century*, edited by Thomas Cushman and John Rodden, 267–285. Boulder, Colo.: Paradigm Publishers, 2004.

Slater, Ian. *Orwell: The Road to Airstrip One.* New York and London: W. W. Norton & Co., 1985.

Sleeper, Jim. "Orwell's 'Smelly Little Orthodoxies'—and Ours." In *George Orwell: Into the Twenty-First Century*, edited by Thomas Cushman and John Rodden, 160–177. Boulder, Colo.: Paradigm Publishers, 2004.

Small, Christopher. *The Road to Miniluv: George Orwell, the State, and God.* Pittsburgh, Pa.: University of Pittsburgh Press, 1975.

Smith, Alan E. "Orwell's Writing Degree Zero: Language and Ideology in *Homage to Catalonia*," *Letras Peninsulares* 11, no. 1 (Spring 1998): 295–307.

Smith, Jimmy Dean. "'A Stench in Genteel Nostrils': The Filth Motif in George Orwell's Cultural Travels," *Kentucky Philological Review* 19 (2005): 43–49.

Smyer, Richard I. *Primal Dream and Primal Crime: Orwell's Development as a Psychological Novelist.* Columbia and London: University of Missouri Press, 1979.

Stansky, Peter. *From William Morris to Sergeant Pepper: Studies in the Radical Domestic.* Palo Alto, Calif.: Society for the Promotion of Science and Scholarship, 1999.

Spiller, Leroy. "George Orwell's Anti-Catholicism," *Logos* (Fall 2003): 158–163.

Spurling, Hilary. *The Girl from the Fiction Department.* London: Hamish Hamilton, 2002.

Steiner, George. "True to Life." *New Yorker*, March 29, 1969, 139–151.

Sterny, Vincent. "George Orwell and T. S. Eliot: The Sense of the Past," *College Literature* 14 (Spring 1987): 85–100.

Stewart, Anthony. *George Orwell, Doubleness, and the Value of Decency.* New York: Routledge, 2003.

———. "Vulgar Nationalism and Insulting Nicknames: George Orwell's Progressive Reflections on Race." In *George Orwell: Into the Twenty-First Century*, edited by Thomas Cushman and John Rodden, 145–159. Boulder, Colo.: Paradigm Publishers, 2004.

Thomas, Edward M. *Orwell.* Edinburgh, Scotland: Oliver & Boyd, 1965.

Thompson, E. P., ed. *Out of Apathy.* London: New Left Books, 1960.

Todorov, Tzvetan. "Politics, Morality, and the Writer's Life: Notes on George Orwell," *Stanford French Review* 16, no. 1 (1992): 136–142.

Toynbee, Philip. "Orwell's Passion," *Encounter* (August 1950).

Trilling, Lionel. *The Opposing Self.* New York: Viking, 1955, 151–172.

———. "Orwell on the Future." *New Yorker*, June 18, 1949, 78–83.

Varricchio, Mario. "Power of Images/Images of Power in *Brave New World* and *Nineteen Eighty-Four*," *Utopian Studies* 10, no. 1 (1999): 98–114.

Voorhees, Richard. *The Paradox of George Orwell.* Lafayette, Ind.: Purdue University Press, 1961.

Wain, John. *A House for the Truth.* New York: Viking Press, 1972, 43–66.

———. "Dear George Orwell: A Personal Letter." *American Scholar* (February 1983): 30–37.

———. "Orwell and the Intelligensia," *Encounter* 21 (December 1968): 74–80.

Walton, D. "George Orwell and Antisemitism," *Patterns of Prejudice* 16, no. 1 (1982).

West, Anthony. "Hidden Damage." *New Yorker*, January 28, 1956, 98–104.

West, W. J. *The Larger Evils:* Nineteen Eighty-Four: *The Truth behind the Satire.* Edinburgh, Scotland: Canongate Press, 1992.

Williams, Raymond. *George Orwell.* New York: Viking Press, 1971.

Wilson, Brendan. "Satire and Subversion: Orwell and the Uses of Anti-Climax," *Connotations: A Journal for Critical Debate* 4, no. 3 (1994–1995): 207–224.

Wilson, Edmund. "George Orwell's Cricketing Burglar." *New Yorker,* May 25, 1946, 86–90.

Wood, Neil. *Communism and British Intellectuals.* New York: Columbia University Press, 1959.

Woodcock, George. *The Crystal Spirit: A Study of George Orwell.* Boston: Little Brown, 1966.

Wykes, David. *A Preface to George Orwell.* New York: Longman, 1987.

Young, John Wesley. *Totalitarian Language.* Charlottesville: University of Virginia Press, 1991.

Zabel, Morton. *Craft and Character in Modern Fiction.* New York: Viking Press, 1957.

Zwerdling, Alex. *Orwell and the Left.* New Haven, Conn.: Yale University Press, 1974.

Studies of Animal Farm

Collections of Essays

Bloom, Harold, ed. *George Orwell's* Animal Farm. New York: Chelsea House, 1999.

———. *George Orwell's* Animal Farm: *Updated Edition.* New York: Chelsea House, 2006.

Meyers, Jeffrey, ed. *George Orwell: The Critical Heritage.* London: Routledge, 1975.

O'Neill, Terry. *Readings on* Animal Farm. San Diego, Calif.: Greenhaven Press, 1998.

Rodden, John, ed. *Understanding* Animal Farm. Westport, Conn.: Greenwood, 1999.

Individual Studies

Cook, Timothy. "Upton Sinclair's *The Jungle* and Orwell's *Animal Farm:* A Relationship Explored," *Modern Fiction Studies* 30 (1984): 696–703.

Davis, Robert Murray. "Politics in the Pig-Pen," *Journal of Popular Culture* 2 (1968): 314–320.

Fergenson, Laraine. "Language As Theme in *Animal Farm,*" *International Fiction Review* (1992): 31–38.

Frye, Northrop. "*Animal Farm.*" In *George Orwell: The Critical Heritage,* edited by Jeffrey Meyers, 206–208. London: Routledge, 1975.

Greene, Graham. "*Animal Farm.*" In *George Orwell: The Critical Heritage,* edited by Jeffrey Meyers, 195–196. London: Routledge, 1975.

Gottlieb, Erica. "George Orwell's Dystopias: *Animal Farm* and *Nineteen Eighty-Four.*" In *A Companion to British and Irish Novels, 1945–2000,* edited by Brian Shaffer, 241–253. Malden, Mass.: Blackwell, 2005.

———. "Orwell's Satirical Vision on the Screen." In *George Orwell: Into the Twenty-First Century,* edited by Thomas Cushman and John Rodden, 252–266. Boulder, Colo.: Paradigm Publishers, 2004.

Hodgart, Matthew. "From *Animal Farm* to *Nineteen Eighty-Four.*" In *The World of George Orwell,* edited by Miriam Gross. New York: Simon and Schuster, 1971.

Hunter, Lynette. "*Animal Farm:* Satire into Allegory." In *George Orwell,* edited by Graham Holderness, Bryan Loughrey, and Nahem Yonsaf, 15–30. New York: St. Martin's Press, 1998.

———. *George Orwell: The Search for a Voice.* Milton Keynes, England: Open University Press, 1984.

Kerr, Douglas. "Orwell, Animals, and the East," *Essays in Criticism* 49, no. 3 (July 1999): 234–255.

Kirschner, Paul. "The Dual Purpose of *Animal Farm.*" In *George Orwell.* Updated Edition, edited by Harold Bloom, 145–180. New York: Chelsea House, 2007.

Letermendia, V. C. "Revolution on *Animal Farm:* Orwell's Neglected Commentary." In *George Orwell,* edited by Graham Holderness, Bryan Loughrey, and Nahem Yousaf, 15–30, New York, St. Martin's Press, 1998.

Lewis, Anthony. "T. S. Eliot and Animal Farm." *New York Times Book Review,* January 26, 1969.

Martin, Kingsley. "*Animal Farm.*" In *George Orwell: The Critical Heritage,* edited by Jeffrey Meyers, 197–199. London; New York: Routledge, 1975.

Meyers, Jeffrey. "Orwell's Bestiary: The Political Allegory of *Animal Farm,*" *Studies in the Twentieth Century* (1971): 65–84.

Paden, Frances Freeman. "Narrative Dynamics in *Animal Farm.*" *Literature in Performance* 5 (April 1985): 49–55.

Pearce, Robert. "Orwell, Tolstoy, and *Animal Farm,*" *Review of English Studies* 49, no. 193 (February 1998): 64–69.

Smyer, Richard I. Animal Farm: *Pastoralism and Politics*. Boston, Mass.: Twayne, 1988.

Solomon, Robert. "Ant Farm: An Orwellian Allegory." In *Reflections on America, 1984,* edited by Robert Mulvihill, 114–129. Athens: University of Georgia Press, 1986.

Symons, Julian. Introduction to *Animal Farm* by George Orwell. New York: Knopf, 1993.

Tolkien, J. R. R. *Tree and Leaf*. London: Unwin Books, 1964.

Davison, Peter. *George Orwell: A Literary Life*. New York: St. Martin's Press, 1996.

Wilson, Edmund. "*Animal Farm*." In *George Orwell: The Critical Heritage,* edited by Jeffrey Meyers, 204–205. London; New York, N.Y.: Routledge, 1975.

Studies of Nineteen Eighty-Four

Collections of Essays

Bloom, Harold, ed. *George Orwell's* 1984. New York: Chelsea, 1987.

———, ed. *George Orwell's* 1984. Updated Edition. New York: Chelsea, 2007.

Cushman, Thomas, and John Rodden. *George Orwell: Into the Twenty-First Century*. Boulder: Paradigm Publishers, 2004.

Gleason, Abbott, Jack Goldsmith, and Martha C. Nussbaum. *On* Nineteen Eighty-Four: *Orwell and Our Future*. Princeton, N.J.: Princeton University Press, 2005.

Howe, Irving, ed. *1984 Revisited: Totalitarianism in Our Century*. New York: Harper and Row, 1983.

———. *Orwell's* 1984: *Text, Sources, Criticism*. New York: Harcourt Brace, 1982.

Hynes, Samuel, ed. *Twentieth Century Interpretations of* 1984. Englewood Cliffs, N.J.: Prentice-Hall, 1971.

Stansky, Peter. *On Nineteen Eighty-Four*. New York: W. H. Freeman, 1983.

Individual Studies

Arrow, Kenneth. "The Economics of *Nineteen Eighty-Four*." In *On* Nineteen Eighty-Four, edited by Peter Stansky 43–49. New York: W. H. Freeman, 1983.

Agathocleous, Tanya. *George Orwell: Battling Big Brother*. New York: Oxford University Press, 2000.

Brown, Edward J. "Zamyatin's *We* and *Nineteen Eighty-Four*." In On *Nineteen Eighty-Four,* edited by Peter Stansky, 159–169. New York: W. H. Freeman, 1983.

Burgess, Anthony. "Ingsoc Considered." In *George Orwell's* 1984. Bloom's Modern Critical Views, edited by Harold Bloom. New York: Chelsea House, 1987.

Casement, William. "*Nineteen Eighty-Four* and Philosophical Realism," *Midwest Quarterly* 30, no. 2 (Winter 1989): 215–228.

Crick, Bernard. "Reading Nineteen *Eighty-Four* as Satire." In *Reflections on America, 1984,* edited by Robert Mulvihill, 15–45. Athens: University of Georgia Press, 1986.

———. "Critical Introduction and Annotations to George Orwell's *Nineteen Eighty-Four*." In *Nineteen Eighty-Four*. Oxford: Clarendon Press, 1984.

Decker, James. "George Orwell's *1984* and Political Ideology." In *George Orwell*. Updated Edition. Bloom's Modern Critical Views, edited by Harold Bloom, 133–144. New York: Chelsea House, 2007.

Deutscher, Isaac. "*1984*—The Mysticism of Cruelty." 332–343. New York: Horizon Press, 1959.

Dickstein, Morris. "Hope Against Hope: Orwell's Posthumous Novel." In *George Orwell: Into the Twenty-First Century,* edited by Thomas Cushman and John Rodden, 63–76. Boulder, Colo.: Paradigm Publishers, 2004.

Eckstein, Arthur M. "The Classical Heritage of Airstrip One." In *The Revised Orwell,* edited by Jonathan Rose, 97–116. East Lansing: Michigan State University Press, 1992.

Elliott, Robert. *The Shape of Utopia: Studies in a Literary Genre*. Chicago: University of Chicago Press, 1970.

Fiedler, Leslie. Keynote address. *1984* Forum. Seneca College, Toronto, February 27, 1984.

Fink, Howard. "Orwell versus Koestler: *Nineteen Eighty-Four* as Optimistic Satire." In *George Orwell,* edited by Courtney Wemyss and Alexej Ugrinsky. Contributions to Study of World Literature #23. Westport, Conn.: Greenwood Press, 1987.

Fortunati, Vita. "It Makes No Difference: A Utopia of Simulation and Transparency." In *George Orwell's* 1984, edited by Harold Bloom, 109–120. New York: Chelsea House, 1987.

Gorfman, Bernard, and Jonathan Pool. "Language as Political Control: Newspeak Revisited." *Delivered* at *George Orwell: A Reassessment.* Vancouver, B.C., November 23–24, 1984.

Gottlieb, Erika. *The Orwell Conundrum: A Cry of Despair or Faith in the Spirit of Man?* Ottawa, Ontario: Carleton University Press, 1992.

Gray, W. Russel. "'That Frightful Torrent of Trash': Crime/Detective Fiction and *Nineteen Eighty-Four.*" In *The Revised Orwell,* edited by Jonathan Rose, 117–130. East Lansing: Michigan State University Press, 1992.

Hamburger, Philip. "Television: *Nineteen Eighty-Four.*" *New Yorker,* October 3, 1953, 84–85.

Harrington, Michael. "*1984* Revisited." In *Orwell's* 1984: *Text, Sources and Criticism,* edited by Irving Howe, 429–439. New York: Harcourt, 1982.

Harris, Roy. "The Misunderstanding of Newspeak." In *George Orwell's* 1984, edited by Harold Bloom, 87–93. New York: Chelsea House, 1987.

Howe, Irving. "*1984*: History as Nightmare." In *Orwell's* 1984: *Text, Sources and Criticism,* edited by Irving Howe, 320–332. New York: Harcourt Brace, 1982.

———. "Enigmas of Power." In 1984, *Revisited: Totalitarianism in Our Century,* edited by Irving Howe, 3–18. New York: Harper and Row, 1983.

Huber, Peter W. *Orwell's Revenge: The* 1984 *Palimpsest.* New York: Free Press; Toronto: Maxwell Macmillan Canada; New York: Maxwell Macmillan International, 1994.

Ingersoll, Earl G. "The Decentering of Tragic Narrative in George Orwell's *Nineteen Eighty-Four,*" *Studies in the Humanities* 16, no. 2 (December 1989): 69–83.

Kennedy, Alan. "The Inversion of Form: Deconstructing *1984.*" In *George Orwell,* edited by Graham Holderness, Bryan Loughrey, and Nahem Yousaf, 76–95. New York, N.Y.: St. Martin's Press, 1998.

Kies, Daniel. "Fourteen Types of Passivity: Suppressing Agency in *Nineteen Eighty-Four.*" In *The Revised Orwell,* edited by Jonathan Rose, 47–60. East Lansing: Michigan State University Press, 1992.

Lonoff, Sue. "Composing *Nineteen Eighty-Four*: The Art of Nightmare." In *The Revised Orwell,* edited by Jonathan Rose, 25–46. East Lansing: Michigan State University Press, 1992.

Matthew, Kenneth. "'Guardian of the Human Spirit': The Moral Foundation of *Nineteen Eighty-Four,*" *Christianity and Literature* 40, no. 2 (Winter 1991): 157–167.

Mellor, Anne K. "You're Only a Rebel from the Waist Downwards." In *On Nineteen Eighty-Four,* edited by Peter Stansky, 115–125. New York: W. H. Freeman, 1983.

Newsinger, John. "*Nineteen Eighty-Four* since the Collapse of Communism." *Foundation: The Review of Science Fiction* 56 (Autumn 1992): 75–84.

Phelan, James. "Charcter, Progression, and Thematism in *1984.*" In *George Orwell,* edited by Graham Holderness, Bryan Loughrey, and Nahem Yousaf, 97–115. New York: St. Martin's Press, 1998.

Porter, Laurence M. "Psychomachia versus Socialism in *Nineteen Eighty-Four*: A Psychoanalytical View." In *The Revised Orwell,* edited by Jonathan Rose, 61–74. East Lansing: Michigan State University Press, 1992.

Rahv, Philip. "The Unfuture of Utopia." In *Orwell's* 1984: *Text, Sources and Criticism,* edited by Irving Howe, 310–316. New York: Harcourt Brace, 1982.

Reilly, Patrick. "*Nineteen Eighty-Four:* The Insufficient Self." In *George Orwell,* edited by Graham Holderness, Bryan Loughrey, and Nahem Yousaf, 116–138. New York: St. Martin's Press, 1998.

Rorty, Richard. *Contingency, Irony, and Solidarity.* Cambridge: Cambridge University Press, 1989.

Rose, Jonathan. "The Invisible Sources of *Nineteen Eighty-Four.*" In *The Revised Orwell,* edited by Jonathan Rose, 131–148. East Lansing: Michigan State University Press, 1992.

Rosenfeld, Isaac. "Decency and Death." In *Orwell's* 1984: *Text, Sources and Criticism,* edited by Irving Howe, 316–320. New York: Harcourt Brace, 1982.

Schorer, Mark. "An Indignant and Prophetic Novel." In *Orwell's* 1984: *Text, Sources and Criticism,* edited by Irving Howe, 294–295. New York: Harcourt Brace, 1982.

Sillen, Samuel. "Maggot-of-the-Month." In *Orwell's* 1984: *Text, Sources and Criticism,* edited by Irving Howe, 297–299. New York: Harcourt Brace, 1982.

Steinhoff, William. *George Orwell and the Literary Origins of 1984.* Ann Arbor: University of Michigan Press, 1975.

Symons, Julian. "George Orwell's Utopia." In *Orwell's* 1984: *Text, Sources and Criticism,* edited by Irving Howe, 293–294. New York: Harcourt Brace, 1982.

Tirohl, Blu. "'We Are the Dead . . . You Are the Dead': An Examination of Sexuality as a Weapon of Revolt in Orwell's *Nineteen Eighty-Four,*" *Journal of Gender Studies* 9, no. 1 (March 2000): 55–61.

Young, John Wesley. *Totalitarian Language: Orwell's Newspeak and its Nazi and Communist Antecedents.* Charlottesville: University Press of Virginia, 1991.

Studies of Orwell's Reputation and Influence

Collections of Essays

Cushman, Thomas and John Rodden. *George Orwell: Into the Twenty-First Century.* Boulder, Colo.: Paradigm Publishers, 2004.

Gleason, Abbott, Jack Goldsmith, and Martha C. Nussbaum. *On* Nineteen Eighty-Four: *Orwell and Our Future.* Princeton, N.J.: Princeton University Press, 2005.

Jensen, Ejner, ed. *The Future of* 1984. Ann Arbor:University of Michigan Press, 1984.

Lazaro, Alberto, ed. *The Road from George Orwell: His Achievement and Legacy.* Bern, Switzerland: Peter Lang, 2001.

Mulvihill, Robert, ed. *Reflections on America, 1984.* Athens: University of Georgia Press, 1986.

Norris, Christopher, ed. *Inside the Myth: Orwell, Views from the Left.* London: Lawrence and Wishart, 1984.

Richardson, J. M., ed. *Orwell x 8: A Symposium.* Winnipeg, Manitoba: Frye, 1986.

Stansky, Peter, ed. *On* Nineteen Eighty-Four. New York: W. H. Freeman, 1983.

Individual Studies

Bellow, Saul. Mr. *Sammler's Planet.* New York: Viking Press, 1970.

Berga, Miguel. "Orwell's Catalonia Revisited: Textual Strategies and the Eyewitness Account." In *The Road from George Orwell: His Achievement and Legacy,* edited by Alberto Lazaro, 53–70. Bern, Switzerland; Peter Lang, 2001.

Brown, Alex. "Examining Orwell: Political and Literary Values in Education." In *The Orwell Myth, Orwell, Views from the Left,* edited by Christopher Norris, 39–61. London: Lawrence and Wishart, 1984.

Campbell, Beatrix. "Orwell—Paterfamilias or Big Brother?" In *George Orwell,* edited by Graham Holderness, Bryan Loughrey, and Nahem Yousaf, 64–75. New York: St. Martin's Press, 1998.

Chalikova, Victoria. "A Russian Preface to George Orwell." In *The Revised Orwell,* edited by Jonathan Rose, 5–12. East Lansing: Michigan State University Press, 1992.

Clarke, Ben. "Orwell and the Evolution of Utopian Writing." In *The Road from George Orwell: His Achievement and Legacy,* edited by Alberto Lazaro, 225–240. Bern, Switzerland: Peter Lang, 2001.

Clayton, Raymond B. "The Biomedical Revolution and Totalitarian Control." In *On* Nineteen Eighty-Four, edited by Peter Stansky, 76–85. New York: W. H. Freeman, 1983.

Conant, James. "Rorty and Orwell On Truth." In *On* Nineteen Eighty-Four: *Orwell and Our Future,* edited by Abbott Gleason, Jack Goldsmith, and Martha C. Nussbaum, 86–111. Princeton, N.J.: Princeton University Press, 2005.

Conquest, Robert. "In Celia's Office: Orwell and the Cold War," *TLS* (August 21, 1998): 4–5.

Elices, Juan Francisco. "The Satiric and Dystopic Legacy of George Orwell in Robert Harris's *Fatherland.*" In *The Road from George Orwell: His Achievement and Legacy,* edited by Alberto Lazaro, 199–224. Bern: Peter Lang, 2001.

Fairbairns, Zoe. "1984 Came and Went." In *The Road from George Orwell: His Achievement and Legacy,* edited by Alberto Lazaro, 123–138. Bern: Peter Lang, 2001.

Gleason, Abbott. "Puritanism and Power Politics During the Cold War: George Orwell and Historical Objectivity." In *On* Nineteen Eighty-Four: *Orwell and Our Future,* edited by Abbott Gleason, Jack Goldsmith, and Martha C. Nussbaum, 73–85. Princeton, N.J.: Princeton University Press, 2005.

Haldane, John. "*Nineteen Eighty-Four,* Catholicism, and the Meaning of Human Sexuality." In *On* Nineteen Eighty-Four: *Orwell and Our Future,* edited by Abbott Gleason, Jack Goldsmith, and

Martha C. Nussbaum, 261–276. Princeton, N.J.: Princeton University Press, 2005.

Herman, Edward. "From *Ingsoc* and *Newspeak* to *Amcap Amerigood* and *Marketspeak*." In *On* Nineteen Eighty-Four: *Orwell and Our Future,* edited by Abbott Gleason, Jack Goldsmith, and Martha C. Nussbaum, 112–124. Princeton, N.J.: Princeton University Press, 2005.

Hitchens, Christopher. *Why Orwell Matters.* New York: Basic Books, 2002.

Leab, Daniel. *Orwell Subverted: The CIA, and the Filming of Animal Farm.* University Park, Pa.: Penn State University Press, 2007.

Lessig, Lawrence. "On the Internet and the Benign Invasions of *Nineteen Eighty-Four.*" In *On* Nineteen Eighty-Four: *Orwell and Our Future,* edited by Abbott Gleason, Jack Goldsmith, and Martha C. Nussbaum, 212–221. Princeton, N.J.: Princeton University Press, 2005.

Macklin, Ruth. "Modifying Behavior, Thought, and Feeling: Can Big Brother Control from Within?" In *Reflections on America, 1984,* edited by Robert Mulvihill, 159–178. Athens: University of Georgia Press, 1986.

McGinn, Robert. "The Politics of Technology and the Technology of Politics." In *On* Nineteen Eighty-Four, edited by Peter Stansky, 67–75. New York: W. H. Freeman, 1983.

Miller, Mark Crispin. "Big Brother is You, Watching." In *Reflections on America, 1984,* edited by Robert Mulvihill, 179–201. Athens: University of Georgia Press, 1986.

Norris, Christopher. "Language, Truth and Ideology: Orwell and the Post-War Left." In *Inside the Myth: Orwell, Views from the Left,* edited by Christopher Norris, 242–262. London: Lawrence and Wishart, 1984.

Nussbaum, Martha C. "The Death of Pity: Orwell in American Political Life." In *On* Nineteen Eighty-Four: *Orwell and Our Future,* edited by Abbott Gleason, Jack Goldsmith, and Martha C. Nussbaum, 279–299. Princeton, N.J.: Princeton University Press, 2005.

Podhortez, Norman. "If Orwell Were Alive Today." *Harpers,* January 1983, 30–37.

Posner, Richard. "Orwell versus Huxley: Economics, Technology, Privacy, and Satire." In *On* Nineteen Eighty-Four: *Orwell and Our Future,* edited by Abbott Gleason, Jack Goldsmith, and Martha C. Nussbaum, 183–211. Princeton, N.J.: Princeton University Press, 2005.

Rodden, John. "On the Political Sociology of Intellectuals: George Orwell and the London Left Intelligentsia." In *George Orwell,* edited by Graham Holderness, Bryan Loughrey, and Nahem Yousaf, 161–181. New York: St. Martin's Press, 1998.

———. *The Politics of Literary Reputation.* New York: Oxford University Press, 1989.

———. *Scenes from an Afterlife: The Legacy of George Orwell.* Wilmington, Del.: ISI Books, 2003.

———. *Every Intellectuals' Big Brother: George Orwell's Literary Siblings.* Austin: University of Texas Press, 2006.

Rothbard, Murray N. "George Orwell and the Cold War: A Reconsideration." In *Reflections on America, 1984,* edited by Robert Mulvihill, 5–14. Athens: University of Georgia Press, 1986.

Russell, Elizabeth. "Looking Backwards and Forwards from *Nineteen Eighty-Four*: Women Writing Men's Worlds." In *The Road from George Orwell: His Achievement and Legacy,* edited by Alberto Lazaro, 157–178. Bern: Peter Lang, 2001.

Sabin, Marjorie. "Outside/Inside: Searching for Wigan Pier." In *George Orwell: Into the Twenty-First Century,* edited by Thomas Cushman and John Rodden, 243–251. Boulder, Colo.: Paradigm Publishers, 2004.

Shlapentokh, Vladimir. "George Orwell: Russia's Tocqueville." In *George Orwell: Into the Twenty-First Century,* edited by Thomas Cushman and John Rodden, 267–285. Boulder, Colo.: Paradigm Publishers, 2004.

Shulevitz, Judith. "What Would Orwell Do?" *New York Times Book Review,* September 8, 2002.

Thiemann, Ronald F. "The Public Intellectual as Connected Critic: George Orwell and Religion." In *George Orwell: Into the Twenty-First Century,* edited by Thomas Cushman and John Rodden, 96–110. Boulder, Colo.: Paradigm Publishers, 2004.

Wain, John. "Dear George Orwell: A Personal Letter," *American Scholar* (February, 1983).

Weizenbaum, Joseph. "The Computer in the Orwellian Year." In *Reflections on America, 1984,* edited by Robert Mulvihill, 130–135. Athens: University of Georgia Press, 1986.

Zimbardo, Philip G. "Mind Control in Orwell's *Nineteen Eighty-Four:* Fictional Concepts Become Operational Realities in Jim Jones' Jungle Experiment." In *On* Nineteen Eighty-Four: *Orwell and Our Future,* edited by Abbott Gleason, Jack Goldsmith, and Martha C. Nussbaum, 127–154. Princeton, N.J.: Princeton University Press, 2005.

———. "Mind Control, Political Fiction and Psychological Reality." In *On* Nineteen Eighty-Four, edited by Peter Stansky, 197–215. New York: W. H. Freeman, 1983.

Zwerdling, Alex. "Rethinking the Modernist Legacy in *Nineteen Eighty-Four.*" In *The Revised Orwell,* edited by Jonathan Rose, 13–24. East Lansing: Michigan State University Press, 1992.

INDEX

Note: Page numbers in **boldface** refer to main articles. Page numbers in *italic* refer to illustrations.

B

C

G

M

O

Y

Z